The Third Wave of Democratization in Latin America
Advances and Setbacks

The late twentieth century witnessed the birth of an impressive number of new democracies in Latin America. This wave of democratization since 1978 has been by far the broadest and most durable in the history of Latin America, but many of the resulting democratic regimes also suffer from profound deficiencies. What caused democratic regimes to emerge and survive? What are their main achievements and shortcomings? This volume offers an ambitious and comprehensive overview of the unprecedented advances as well as the setbacks in the post-1978 wave of democratization. It seeks to explain the sea change from a region dominated by authoritarian regimes to one in which openly authoritarian regimes are the rare exception, and it analyzes why some countries have achieved striking gains in democratization while others have experienced erosions. The book presents general theoretical arguments about what causes and sustains democracy and analyses of nine theoretically compelling country cases.

Frances Hagopian is the Michael P. Grace II Associate Professor of Latin American Studies in the Department of Political Science and former Director of the Kellogg Institute for International Studies at the University of Notre Dame. She is the author of *Traditional Politics and Regime Change in Brazil* (Cambridge University Press, 1996), which was named a Choice Outstanding Book in Comparative Politics, and several articles on democratization that have appeared in *World Politics*, *Comparative Political Studies*, and several other publications. Her current research focuses on economic liberalization and political representation in Brazil, Argentina, Chile, and Mexico. Hagopian previously taught at Harvard, Tufts, and MIT.

Scott P. Mainwaring is Eugene Conley Professor of Political Science and Director of the Kellogg Institute for International Studies at the University of Notre Dame. Among his books are *Democratic Accountability in Latin America* (2003), *Christian Democracy in Latin America* (2003), *Rethinking Party Systems in the Third Wave of Democratization: The Case of Brazil* (1999), *Presidentialism and Democracy in Latin America* (Cambridge University Press, 1997), and *Building Democratic Institutions: Party Systems in Latin America* (1995). He received a John Simon Guggenheim Memorial Foundation fellowship in 2000 for work on a project on authoritarianism and democracy in Latin America from 1945 to 2000.

The Third Wave of Democratization in Latin America

Advances and Setbacks

Edited by

FRANCES HAGOPIAN
University of Notre Dame

SCOTT P. MAINWARING
University of Notre Dame

CAMBRIDGE UNIVERSITY PRESS
Cambridge, New York, Melbourne, Madrid, Cape Town, Singapore, São Paulo

Cambridge University Press
40 West 20th Street, New York, NY 10011-4211, USA

www.cambridge.org
Information on this title: www.cambridge.org/9780521824613

First published 2005

Printed in the United States of America

A catalog record for this publication is available from the British Library.

Library of Congress Cataloging in Publication Data

The third wave of democratization in Latin America : advances and setbacks / edited by
Frances Hagopian, Scott P. Mainwaring.
　　p.　cm.
Originated in a conference held Apr. 23–24, 2001, University of Notre Dame.
Includes bibliographical references and index.
ISBN-13: 978-0-521-82461-3 (HB)
ISBN-10: 0-521-82461-3 (HB)
ISBN-13: 978-0-521-61320-0 (PB)
ISBN-10: 0-521-61320-5 (PB)
1. Democratization – Latin America.　2. Democratization – Latin America – History –
20th century.　3. Latin America – Politics and government – 1980–　I. Hagopian, Frances.
II. Mainwaring, Scott, 1954–
JL966.T47　2005
320.98 – dc22　　　　　　　　　　　　　　　　　　　　　　　　2004062942

ISBN-13　978-0-521-82461-3 hardback
ISBN-10　0-521-82461-3 hardback

ISBN-13　978-0-521-61320-0 paperback
ISBN-10　0-521-61320-5 paperback

For our children,
Michael Messina and
Benjamin Mainwaring and Grace Mainwaring
With our love

Contents

List of Figures

List of Tables

List of Contributors

Ana María Bejarano is Assistant Professor of Political Science at the University of Toronto. She holds a Ph.D. in Political Science from Columbia University. She previously was professor of Political Science at the Universidad de Los Andes in Bogotá, where she also served as Director of the Center for Social and Legal Research (CIJUS). She co-edited *Elecciones y Democracia en Colombia, 1997–1998* (Bogotá, 1998). Recent publications include articles in *Constellations* and the *Canadian Journal of Latin American and Caribbean Studies*. She is finishing a book on the historical origins and divergent trajectories of democracy in Colombia and Venezuela. Her current research deals with regime change, institution building, and constitution making in the Andes.

Michael Coppedge is Associate Professor in the Department of Political Science and a Fellow of the Kellogg Institute for International Studies at the University of Notre Dame. He previously taught at Yale, Princeton, Georgetown, Johns Hopkins, and the Universities of Belgrano and Salamanca. He has published *Strong Parties and Lame Ducks: Presidential Partyarchy and Factionalism in Venezuela*, as well as book chapters and articles in journals including *Comparative Politics, Comparative Political Studies*, and *Journal of Democracy*. Coppedge has received World Society Foundation, Fulbright-Hays, and Tinker grants. His current research focuses on approaches to democratization, democratic diffusion, and the causes and consequences of party-system characteristics in Latin America.

Frances Hagopian is the Michael P. Grace II Associate Professor of Latin American Studies in the Department of Political Science and former Director of the Kellogg Institute for International Studies at the University of Notre Dame. She is the author of *Traditional Politics and Regime Change in Brazil* (Cambridge University Press, 1996), which was named a Choice Outstanding Book in Comparative Politics, and articles on democratization that have appeared in *World Politics, Comparative Political Studies*, and several other publications. Her current research focuses on economic liberalization and political representation in Brazil, Argentina, Chile, and Mexico. Hagopian previously taught at Harvard, Tufts, and MIT, and she has held fellowships from the Center for Latin American Studies and The Howard Heinz Endowment of the University of Pittsburgh, the Social Science Research Council, the American Council of Learned Societies, and the U.S. Department of Education (Fulbright-Hays program). She is a former member of the Executive Council of the American Political Science Association.

Steven Levitsky is John L. Loeb Associate Professor of the Social Sciences at Harvard University. He specializes in comparative and Latin American politics. His areas of research include political parties and party change, informal institutions, and political regimes and regime change. He is author of *Transforming Labor-Based Parties in Latin America: Argentine Peronism in Comparative Perspective* (Cambridge University Press, 2003). He has published articles on Argentine politics in *Comparative Politics, World Politics, Comparative Political Studies, Latin American Research Review, Journal of Latin American Studies*, and *Journal of Democracy*. He is currently writing a book on the emergence and dynamics of hybrid political regimes in the post–Cold War era.

Beatriz Magaloni is Assistant Professor of Political Science at Stanford University. She is currently finishing a book on the politics of party hegemony and its demise. Her research interests also include the politics of clientelism and vote buying, the rule of law and the courts, democratization and market-oriented reforms in Latin America, and voting behavior. She has been a Visiting Fellow in the Political Science Department at Harvard University and a Visiting Professor at the Political Science Department at UCLA. Before arriving at Stanford, Magaloni was the Director of Political Science at ITAM (Instituto Tecnológico Autónomo de México) from 1997 to 1999. Some of her articles have appeared in the *Journal of Theoretical Politics* and *Política y Gobierno*. She also has published various chapters in edited volumes on Mexican and Latin American politics.

Scott Mainwaring is Eugene Conley Professor of Political Science and Director of the Kellogg Institute for International Studies at the University of Notre Dame. His books include *Democratic Accountability in Latin America* (Oxford University Press, coedited, 2003), *Christian Democracy in Latin America* (Stanford University Press, coedited, 2003), *Rethinking Party Systems in the Third Wave of Democratization: The Case of Brazil* (Stanford University Press, 1999), *Presidentialism and Democracy in Latin America* (Cambridge University Press, coedited, 1997), and *Building Democratic Institutions: Party Systems in Latin America* (Stanford University Press, coedited, 1995). He received a John Simon Guggenheim Memorial Foundation fellowship in 2000 for work on a project on authoritarianism and democracy in Latin America from 1945 to 2000.

René Antonio Mayorga is a Senior Researcher at the Centro Boliviano de Estudios Multidisciplinarios (CEBEM). He is also Professor of Political Science at the Facultad Latinoamericana de Ciencias Sociales (FLACSO) in Ecuador, and in the Joint Master's Program of CEBEM, FLACSO, and the Universidad Complutense of Madrid. He has been a visiting professor at the universities of Salamanca, Berlin, and Notre Dame, among others. His books include *De la Anomia Política al Orden Democrático?* (La Paz, CEBEM, 1991), *Antipolítica y Neopopulismo* (La Paz, CEBEM, 1995), and *La cuestión militar en cuestión: Democracia y Fuerzas Armadas* (La Paz, CEBEM, 1994). He is editor of *Democracia y Gobernabilidad en América Latina* (Carácas, Nueva Sociedad, 1992). He also contributed to *Transitional Justice and the Rule of Law in New Democracies* (Notre Dame, 1997) and to *Mixed-Member Electoral Systems: The Best of Both Worlds?* (Oxford University Press, 2001).

Aníbal Pérez-Liñán is Assistant Professor of Political Science and a member of the Center for Latin American Studies at the University of Pittsburgh. His research focuses on democratic institutions and governability. He has published articles in *Electoral Studies, Latin American Research Review,* and *Legislative Studies Quarterly,* among other journals. He is currently completing a book on presidential impeachment in Latin America.

Eduardo Pizarro is Professor at the Universidad Nacional de Colombia in Bogotá and served as Director of its Instituto de Estudios Políticos y Relaciones Internacionales (IEPRI). He was a Visiting Fellow at the Kellogg Institute for International Studies in 2000–01. He has published several scholarly analyses of the conflict in Colombia, including *Una Democracia Asediada. Balance y perspectivas del conflicto armado en Colombia* (Editorial Norma, 2004), and he is a weekly contributor to the national newspaper *El Tiempo.*

Mitchell A. Seligson is Centennial Professor of Political Science at Vanderbilt University and Director of the Latin American Public Opinion Project. He previously held the Daniel H. Wallace Chair of Political Science at the University of Pittsburgh, where he also served as Director of the Center for Latin American Studies. His current work involves survey research projects in Mexico, Guatemala, El Salvador, Honduras, Nicaragua, Costa Rica, Panama, Colombia, Ecuador, and Bolivia. Seligson has held grants and fellowships from the Rockefeller Foundation, the Ford Foundation, the National Science Foundation, Fulbright, USAID, and others; he has published more than eighty articles and more than a dozen books and monographs. His recent published books include *Elections and Democracy in Central America, Revisited* (University of North Carolina Press) and *Development and Underdevelopment: The Political Economy of Global Inequality* (Lynne Rienner).

Martín Tanaka holds a Ph.D. in Political Science from the Facultad Latinoamericana de Ciencias Sociales (FLACSO) in Mexico City. Currently he is Senior

Researcher and Research Director at the Instituto de Estudios Peruanos in Lima. Tanaka has written about Peruvian politics, Latin American politics, and social movements and participation in Peru. He is author of *Los espejis- mos de la democracia. El colapso del sistema de partidos en el Perú, 1980–1995, en perspectiva comparada* (Instituto de Estudios Peruanos, 1998) and "The Po- litical Constraints on Market Reform in Peru," in Carol Wise, Riordan Roett, and Guadalupe Paz, eds., *Post-Stabilization Politics in Latin America* (Brookings Institution Press, 2003).

Kurt Weyland is Professor of Government at the University of Texas at Austin. He is the author of *Democracy without Equity: Failures of Reform in Brazil* (University of Pittsburgh Press, 1996); *The Politics of Market Reform in Fragile Democracies: Argentina, Brazil, Peru, and Venezuela* (Princeton University Press, 2002); and numerous refereed journal articles on democratization, market re- form, social policy, and populist politics in Latin America. His current book project focuses on the diffusion of innovations in Latin American social sector reform; an edited volume on this topic, *Learning from Foreign Models in Latin American Policy Reform*, was published by Woodrow Wilson Center Press in 2004.

Elisabeth Jean Wood teaches comparative politics at Yale University. Her re- search interests include social movements, democratization, political violence, civil wars, and development in Latin America and in Africa. She is the author of *Forging Democracy from Below: Insurgent Transitions in South Africa and El Sal- vador* (Cambridge University Press, 2000) and *Insurgent Collective Action and Civil War in El Salvador* (Cambridge University Press, 2003).

Acknowledgments

Many people have supported our efforts in producing *The Third Wave of Democratization in Latin America*. This project had its origins in a conference held at the University of Notre Dame on April 23–24, 2001. Our first debt is to the Coca-Cola Corporation for its financial support for this conference and to the Kellogg Institute for International Studies, which hosted it. The staff of the Kellogg Institute spent long hours arranging the travel of participants, designing posters, and making sure that everyone was fed and watered. Several discussants – Diego Abente Brun, Michael Coppedge, Gretchen Helmke, Guillermo O'Donnell, Luis Tonelli, Francisco Weffort, and Rubén Zamora – provided stimulating comments during the conference. Our greatest gratitude is owed to the contributing authors, who walked the fine line between doing justice to the countries they know better than anyone else and at the same time conforming to the broader questions we asked them to address.

This volume is of course a product of the editors and authors. It is also a Kellogg Institute product. Since its inception in 1982, the Kellogg Institute has attempted to promote outstanding research on some of the most important normative issues that confront humanity, including democracy. Our scholarly interests and perspectives have been shaped by the rich intellectual debate at the Kellogg Institute on this theme. Seven of the authors in this volume are former Visiting Fellows of the Institute, three contributors are current Kellogg Faculty Fellows, and one is a former graduate student of the University of Notre Dame. Six of seven discussants who enriched our conference have been either Visiting or Faculty Fellows. We especially thank our colleague, Guillermo O'Donnell, who since the 1970s has set the agenda on debates about democratization.

We also wish to acknowledge the steadfast support of Lew Bateman and the insightful comments of two anonymous reviewers for Cambridge University Press. Scott Mainwaring acknowledges the financial support of the John Simon Guggenheim Foundation. Elizabeth Rankin provided invaluable help with copyediting and preparing the volume for publication.

Working with each other has been a pleasure. We began our conversations about democracy in Latin America with each other 17 years ago. In that time, we have benefited from formal collaboration as well as from informal collegiality. However, if the secret should be revealed, what we talk about much of the time with each other is not the latest theories of democratization, but rather the love of our families. For that, and for their patience with us, we are deeply grateful. Only Tony and Sue know just how much we have to thank them for. We dedicate this book to our children – Michael Messina, Benjamin Mainwaring, and Grace Mainwaring – in recognition of our love for them, and with the profound hope that they may live in a world in which governments are democratic and just and provide decent lives for all their citizens.

Introduction

The Third Wave of Democratization in Latin America

Scott Mainwaring and Frances Hagopian

A sea change has occurred in Latin American politics. In most of the region, until the wave of democratization that began in 1978, authoritarian regimes were pervasive. Many democracies were short-lived, and many countries had experienced literally no taste whatsoever of democratic political regimes.

The situation has changed profoundly in the past quarter century. By 1990 virtually every government in the region had competitively elected regimes, and since 1978 democracy has been far more extensive and also more durable than ever before. In many countries democratic and semidemocratic regimes[1] have survived despite poor social and economic performances and despite lengthy authoritarian traditions. In Argentina, Bolivia, and Brazil, democratic governments withstood annual inflation rates that went far into quadruple digits. In El Salvador and Guatemala, countries with histories of ruthless dictatorships, consistent repression of the indigenous populations, and horrendous civil wars, warring factions signed peace treaties and established competitively elected regimes in the 1990s.

The capacity of elected governments to survive in the face of daunting challenges and poor social and economic performance confounds most observers' expectations – and considerable comparative and theoretical literature on democratization as well. Today, the scholarly community takes for granted that competitive political regimes have survived, but when the transitions to elected governments took place, few observers expected that these regimes would be able to withstand relentless economic crises such as those experienced in the 1980s, widespread poverty, egregious income inequalities, and other nettlesome challenges.

Not only has democracy lasted longer in the region than ever before, but it is also broader and more comprehensive. Never before have as many people

[1] Mainwaring and Pérez-Liñán define democratic and semidemocratic regimes in Chapter 1.

We are grateful to Michael Coppedge, Steve Levitsky, Aníbal Pérez-Liñán, and Kurt Weyland for helpful comments.

I

exercised the franchise, and mass publics have held local and national governments more accountable than at any time in the past. Latin America's achievements are all the more impressive when one considers that *mass* democracies have taken root where earlier, narrower, elitist democracies failed routinely.

Yet the post-1978 wave of democratization has been far from an unqualified success. Notwithstanding some democratic advances in the 1990s in several countries – most notably Mexico – democratization experienced setbacks across the Andean region and continued to be truncated in other countries. These setbacks are attributable in part to dismal government performance. In most countries, democratic regimes have failed to promote growth, reduce poverty, ameliorate inequalities, and address rampant crime. In the context of two decades of meager economic growth, soaring crime rates in many countries, and the poor performance of most regimes in addressing citizen needs, satisfaction with democracy declined, opening the door to more antiestablishment populists with equivocal attitudes toward democracy. In recent years, the situation has worsened in many countries. The banking system in Argentina collapsed in 2000, and along with it, much of the confidence of the Argentine electorate in established political parties and politicians. Popular uprisings, military actions, or legislative deposals have ousted presidents in Ecuador (1997 and 2000), Argentina (2001), and Bolivia (2003). Most of the recent scholarship on the post-1978 wave of democratization has focused on these and other deficiencies of democratic and semidemocratic regimes. We focus on the deficiencies but also emphasize the democratic transformation of the region. Both are important.

This volume, which offers an ambitious and comprehensive overview of the post-1978 wave of democratization in Latin America, has three objectives. The first is to chart these unprecedented and unanticipated advances as well as the setbacks in what Huntington (1991) called on a global scale the "third wave" of democratization. In early 1978, among the twenty countries listed in Table I.1, only Colombia, Costa Rica, and Venezuela were democracies. The other seventeen had patently authoritarian regimes. By the beginning of 1992, fifteen of these seventeen authoritarian regimes had given rise to semidemocracies or democracies. During this protracted burst of democratization, there was not a single breakdown of a democratic or semidemocratic regime. The pattern since 1992 has been mixed, with some advances and setbacks, but as of mid-2004 the region had only two openly authoritarian regimes, Cuba and Haiti. Given its breadth and durability, the trend that it ushered in can no longer be considered a mere swing of a pendulum, as seemed possible not so long ago (Pastor 1989a).

Second, the book seeks to explain both the post-1978 sea change from a region dominated by authoritarian regimes to one in which openly authoritarian regimes are the rare exception, and why some countries have achieved advances in democratization while others (including four of the Andean countries) have experienced setbacks. The analysis highlights the poor regime performance of

TABLE I.I. *Classification of Latin American Political Regimes, 1945–2003*

Country	Year	Regime	Country	Year	Regime
Argentina	1945	A	Guatemala	1945–1953	S
	1946–1950	S		1954–1985	A
	1951–1957	A		1986–2003	S
	1958–1961	S	Haiti	1945–2003	A
	1962	A	Honduras	1945–1956	A
	1963–1965	S		1957–1962	S
	1966–1972	A		1963–1981	A
	1973–1974	D		1982–2003	S
	1975	S	Mexico	1945–1987	A
	1976–1982	A		1988–1999	S
	1983–2003	D		2000–2003	D
Bolivia	1945–1955	A	Nicaragua	1945–1983	A
	1956–1963	S		1984–2003	S
	1964–1981	A	Panama	1945–1947	S
	1982–2003	D		1948–1955	A
Brazil	1945	A		1956–1967	S
	1946–1963	D		1968–1989	A
	1964–1984	A		1990–1993	S
	1985–2003	D		1994–2003	D
Chile	1945–1972	D	Paraguay	1945–1988	A
	1973–1989	A		1989–2003	S
	1990–2003	D	Peru	1945–1947	S
Colombia	1945–1948	S		1948–1955	A
	1949–1957	A		1956–1961	S
	1958–1973	S		1962	A
	1974–1989	D		1963–1967	D
	1990–2003	S		1968–1979	A
Costa Rica	1945–1948	S		1980–1982	D
	1949–2003	D		1983–1984	S
Cuba	1945–1951	S		1985–1987	D
	1952–2003	A		1988–1991	S
Dominican Republic	1945–1965	A		1992–1994	A
	1966–1973	S		1995–2000	S
	1974–1977	A		2001–2003	D
	1978–1993	D	Uruguay	1945–1972	D
	1994–1995	S		1973–1984	A
	1996–2003	D		1985–2003	D
Ecuador	1945–1947	A	Venezuela	1945	A
	1948–1962	S		1946	S
	1963–1967	A		1947	D
	1968–1969	S		1948–1957	A
	1970–1978	A		1958–1998	D
	1979–1999	D		1999	S
	2000	S		2000–2001	D
	2001–2003	D		2002–2003	S
El Salvador	1945–1983	A			
	1984–1991	S			
	1992–2003	D			

Key: D, democratic; S, semidemocratic; A, authoritarian.
Note: The year of a regime transition is coded as belonging to the new regime.
Source: Mainwaring et al. (2001), updated.

most post-1978 democracies and semidemocracies and the growing disillusionment with democracy. Third, the book aspires to contribute to the broader comparative literature on what makes democracy thrive, survive without thriving, or fail.

In an attempt to achieve these three goals, the first and concluding chapters present arguments about general trends and causes of democratization, while the nine chapters on countries, which were selected on the basis of their theoretical interest, pay attention to country-level specificities. Chapter 1 provides an overview of regime change in Latin America since the beginning of the Third Wave of democratization in 1978. Scott Mainwaring and Aníbal Pérez-Liñán address two main questions: What explains the dramatic and historically unprecedented burst of democratization between 1978 and 1992, and what explains the difficulties of achieving further advances in democratization since 1992? To the best of our knowledge, this chapter is the first quantitative analysis of democratic breakdowns, transitions, and erosions in Latin America. While building on the broader literature in comparative politics and political sociology about regime change, the authors underscore that Latin America has distinctive regional dynamics, such that many findings in the larger literature do not hold up for Latin America. They highlight as auspicious for the region the embrace of democracy by the left (which in turn has diminished the fear of the right of a democratic order), and the new international, and especially U.S. and Organization of American States (OAS), support for democracy in the hemisphere. They attribute the democratic erosions of recent years above all to poor government performance.

The nine country chapters are not primarily intended to be historical overviews, informative descriptions, or accounts of current events. Rather, they analyze political regimes focusing on two central questions. First, how should advances and limits in democratization in each country be characterized over an extended period of time? Second, what explains democracy's achievements and shortcomings, advances, and regressions?

Three chapters examine the building of democracy in large countries with mainly authoritarian political heritages until their recent transitions: Argentina since 1983, Brazil since 1985, and Mexico since it began its transition to democracy in the 1980s. Three chapters examine the emergence of democracy or semidemocracy in countries with deeply authoritarian pasts and unfavorable social and economic conditions: Bolivia since 1982, El Salvador since 1985, and Guatemala since 1986. The other three country chapters study democratic erosions (Colombia and Venezuela since the early 1990s) or breakdown (Peru in 1992). Each country chapter takes as a beginning point the inauguration of a new competitive or semicompetitive regime where this transition occurred after 1978. For example, the chapter on Argentina addresses the twenty-one years of democracy since 1983. The chapters on Colombia and Venezuela trace patterns primarily since 1978. Taken together, these chapters offer a composite portrait of the region as a whole; taken separately, they preserve what is analytically distinctive about each case.

In the conclusion, Frances Hagopian analyzes why faltering economies destabilize some democracies, while in other countries public tolerance for economic stagnation and declining public services is higher. On the basis of the country studies presented in this volume, she argues that democracy is possible in inauspicious circumstances where civil society is connected to political parties and institutions. Such connections permit public tolerance for economic crisis and even personal insecurity. Her analysis suggests that the survival of democratic regimes depends not only on government performance in issue areas of high public salience but also on the quality of political representation.

DEMOCRACY IN HARD TIMES AND INAUSPICIOUS PLACES

Beyond charting the course of the Third Wave, we also aspire to contribute theoretically to the understanding of why democracies emerge, become stable or not, break down or not, and become solid or remain vulnerable and erode. Although there are minor theoretical divergences among the authors, this volume collectively offers some clear theoretical arguments.

The foremost theoretical contribution of this volume revolves around the hitherto unprecedented phenomenon of competitively elected regimes that survive despite widespread poverty, terrible inequalities, and (in most countries) bad economic performance. During the post-1978 period, democracy has survived in poor countries (Bolivia, Nicaragua), in countries with the worst income distributions in the world (Brazil, Guatemala), in countries with profound ethnic divides (Bolivia, Brazil, Ecuador, Guatemala, Peru), and in countries that have performed very poorly economically.[2] Democracy can and has lasted in hard times and inauspicious places. At the same time, this volume shows that the combination of inhospitable structural variables (poverty and inequality) and poor regime performance easily has corrosive effects on regime solidity and quality. By regime solidity we mean the extent to which competitively elected regimes are reasonably full democracies (as opposed to semidemocracies) and appear to be relatively immune to breakdown or erosion. This concept cannot be understood in a static way; a regime that is solid today may yet erode somewhere down the line, as the deterioration of Venezuela's democracy since 1989 underscores.

Bolivia's stability in the 1985–2000 period epitomizes the ability of democracy to endure in unlikely places and under adverse conditions. Prior to 1982, Bolivia had been plagued by a long history of instability and chronic military coups. The country had little and restricted experience with democracy prior to 1982. Between July 1978 and October 1982, the country had nine different presidents – two democratic civilians who were quickly overthrown and seven

---

[2] India is the quintessential example of democracy surviving, albeit with a short-lived and partial breakdown from 1975 to 1977, despite seemingly long odds: terrible poverty when democracy was born in 1947, great linguistic diversity, and occasionally intractable religious conflict. On the survival of democracy in India under these conditions, see Varshney (1998).

different *golpista* military officers. Hernán Siles Suazo, the new democratic president (1982–85), inherited disastrous economic conditions and proceeded to make them worse. Inflation soared to an annual rate of 8,171 percent in 1985, and per capita income experienced a downward slide throughout most of the first decade of democracy. This economic decline exacerbated poverty in what was already one of the poorest countries in Latin America. Bolivia also has one of the most ethnically divided societies in Latin America, with an indigenous majority that for centuries has been exploited by a *ladino* (of white origin) minority. All these conditions augured poorly for democracy.

Observers writing in the early 1980s were understandably skeptical about the prospects for democracy in Bolivia (e.g., Whitehead 1986). Although the new regime tottered during its first years, by the mid-1990s, democracy had become stable, as René Mayorga's contribution to this volume attests. Until things began to unravel around 2000, the Bolivian case was a remarkable example of a democracy surviving despite formidable structural and economic circumstances and an authoritarian past. But events since 2000 have once again demonstrated the difficulty of building a solid democracy in a country with widespread poverty, egregious inequalities, and a weakened state.

Bolivia is not the only case of an elected government surviving in the face of imposing challenges. El Salvador and Guatemala also fit this description, as the chapters by Elisabeth Jean Wood and Mitchell Seligson show. The capacity of democratic and semidemocratic regimes to survive in hard times and inauspicious places has consequences for the theoretical understanding of what makes democracies endure. It supports some theoretical approaches to that question, and it works against other theoretical understandings.

Let us begin with the latter. One of the most influential theoretical approaches to studying democracy is modernization theory, which was originally formulated by Lipset (1959) and subsequently supported empirically by a large number of other scholars. Modernization theorists argued with ample empirical evidence that democracy was more likely to emerge in more developed countries. They did not postulate that democracy was impossible in countries with a low level of development, but they did contend that building democracy in poor countries was a difficult enterprise. Przeworski et al.'s (2000) path-breaking work similarly argued that democracies were less likely to endure in less developed countries.

The Third Wave of Democratization poses empirical and theoretical challenges to modernization arguments as applied to Latin America. Poor countries initiated the Third Wave in Latin America, and notwithstanding many daunting challenges, only one of them – Peru – has experienced a full democratic breakdown in the post-1978 period. The book shows that the relationship between the level of development and democracy has been surprisingly indeterminate throughout Latin America for a lengthy historical period. Of course, we are not dismissing the solid research that has shown that more economically developed countries are more likely to be democratic. The question is one of emphasis. The level of development generally affects the likelihood of the emergence of democracies and the likelihood of their durability, but in a Latin American subsample, as Mainwaring and Pérez-Liñán (this volume) show, this effect is very weak (see also Mainwaring and Pérez-Liñán 2003). Indeed, more economically developed countries actually had a slightly higher rate of breakdowns of elected regimes between 1945 and 1999.

Our collective emphasis on the possibility of democracy or semidemocracy in hard times and difficult circumstances also runs against the central argument of class approaches that claim that democracy requires either a strong bourgeoisie (Moore 1966) or a strong working class (Rueschemeyer, Stephens, and Stephens 1992). In Latin America, competitive regimes have emerged and endured in places where the class structure is not favorable to it, including the three countries analyzed in Part II (Bolivia, El Salvador, Guatemala). It has failed in countries where the class structure was (according to Rueschemeyer et al.'s theory) favorable, including most prominently Argentina in 1963, 1966, and 1976, as well as in Chile and Uruguay in 1973.

Finally, our emphasis on the possibilities of democratic or semidemocratic survival despite poor economic performance is at odds with work that has seen democracy in developing countries as resting significantly on economic growth. Performance-based arguments about the survival of new democracies are old (Lipset 1959) and intuitively sensible. The Latin American experience since 1978 suggests, however, that the impact of economic performance on regime survival is mediated by political factors. Almost surely democracy in most of Latin America would be in better shape if economic performance had been better. Nevertheless, although poor economic performance and poor results in other salient policy issues such as public security have weakened many regimes, they have not yet doomed them.

At a theoretical level, this book shows that attitudes toward democracy and a favorable international political environment – for this region, more than the structural variables tapped by modernization theory – have made a decisive difference in whether competitive regimes survive or break down. If the main actors are committed to democracy and if the international political environment is favorable, democracy can survive – at least for an extended time – despite widespread poverty, glaring inequalities, and bad performance. If key actors are not committed to democracy and the international political environment is not favorable, democracy may falter even if economic performance is credible and per capita income is moderately high. Of course, there are limits to the explanatory power of international variables. They usually explain change over time better than variance across countries at a given point in time, and in Latin America they have rarely been the main cause of a regime change. Moreover, international support does little or nothing to enhance the quality of democracy in contexts where it can be perilously low. The international community has devised mechanisms to deal with overt attempts to impose authoritarian rule, but it is ill equipped to deal with more subtle or gradual authoritarian regressions.

The flip side of our argument that democracy can survive in hard times and inauspicious places is that it need not endure even in seemingly favorable conditions. Our cases show that even at moderately high levels of per capita income, democracy in Latin America has been, and again can be, vulnerable. This vulnerability may grow if the United States becomes less concerned with supporting democracy; its initial support for the April 2002 coup in Venezuela suggests that this is a realistic possibility, in the aftermath of September 11, 2001.

In downplaying the independent effect of structural factors and emphasizing the central role of political factors (especially the importance of actors' commitment to democracy) in explaining the common thread of regime durability and the weak regime solidity in Latin America in the past quarter century, this book resonates theoretically with earlier works by Robert Dahl (1971: 124–88), Daniel Levine (1973), Arend Lijphart (1977), Juan Linz (1978), Guillermo O'Donnell and Philippe Schmitter (1986), Adam Przeworski (1991: 51–99), Alfred Stepan (1978), and Arturo Valenzuela (1978). These scholars emphasized that attitudes toward democracy (Dahl, Levine, Lijphart, Linz), capable leadership or the lack thereof (Linz, Stepan), the effective functioning of political institutions (Valenzuela), and the strategic behavior of political leaders (O'Donnell and Schmitter, Przeworski) are critical factors in understanding regime change and stability. Several chapters in this volume build on this tradition, including Mayorga's view of the salutary effect of Bolivia's posttransition institutional reform in the 1985–97 period, and Beatriz Magaloni's contribution to understanding Mexico's democratization through the prism of the strategic bargains among elite actors that led to the creation of a key institution, the Federal Election Institute.

A key theme of this book is that what allows a democracy to emerge and survive does not guarantee that democracy will be good or immune from antisystem challenges and citizen disaffection. Mainwaring and Pérez-Liñán advance the argument that regime durability and regime solidity may have sharply divergent causes. Whereas elite attitudes toward democracy and a favorable international political environment have been key factors in understanding regime durability, regime solidity is better explained by the interplay of structural factors, regime performance, and mass political attitudes.

A fundamental argument of this volume is that regime performance does not predict the ability of democratic and semidemocratic governments to endure. Political factors are key in understanding when regimes can survive despite poor performance. While accepting the primacy of political variables in understanding the viability of democracy, this volume pushes this tradition farther by considering not merely elite but also mass attitudes toward democracy and citizen connections to political parties. Whether democracy can survive withering economic crises and poor performance in other policy arenas depends not only on elites but also on the behavior and attitudes of the mass citizenry and the linkages between citizens and elites. In the countries examined here, public tolerance for economic crisis, unemployment, corruption, crime, and flawed justice systems has varied. In their chapters, Michael Coppedge and Mitchell Seligson argue that poor government performance in Venezuela and Guatemala in areas of high public salience has jeopardized public support for faltering governments and weakened regime solidity. But elsewhere, mass support for democracy has allowed governments to stay afloat in turbulent economic waters. Mass support, in turn, may be abetted by the connections of civil society to political parties and political institutions. Steven Levitsky's chapter suggests that the dense networks of the Peronist party cushioned a faltering regime in Argentina from public rejection. In Bolivia, according to Mayorga's analysis, deteriorating networks of representation could not do the same. In the conclusion, Hagopian highlights the importance of quality political representation for understanding why some democratic regimes remain solid in hard times, while others, given the same or even better economic circumstances, are more fragile and vulnerable to antisystem political agents.

THE CASES

The nine country cases included in this volume represent a wide range in the post-1978 evolution of political regimes. This case selection is consistent with the objective of maximizing variance on the dependent variable – in this case, regime outcomes. Because the post-1978 wave ran counter to the expectations of some previous social science findings, and because it could not have been expected on the basis of Latin America's past, it was important to include some cases of unexpected though partial advances in democracy under especially adverse conditions. It was also important to include some cases of democratic erosion or breakdown. Finally, we included the countries with the three largest economies, which previously had largely unsuccessful experiences with democracy but have now built some of the fuller democracies in contemporary Latin America.

We eschewed a strategy of including chapters on every major country in the region, opting instead for a more thorough analysis of a set of cases carefully selected for their theoretical import for understanding advances and setback in democratization. We were especially interested in cases whose outcomes were not overdetermined. For this reason, this volume does not include country chapters on Costa Rica, Uruguay, and Chile, the most likely cases of democratic endurance. Though Uruguay and Chile experienced authoritarian regimes in the 1970s and 1980s, before 1973 they had the strongest democratic heritages in Latin America. Costa Rica has had uninterrupted democracy since 1949. That democracy has survived in Costa Rica, Uruguay, and Chile is therefore not surprising.

Part I: Advances in Democratization Despite Authoritarian Heritages

Argentina, Brazil, and Mexico have long been less than stable, exemplary democracies. The difficulty of establishing and maintaining democracy in Latin America's three largest economies not only has been disappointing but has also confounded social science theory. Democracies are supposed to flourish where certain minimal socioeconomic preconditions are met, and these are middle-income countries with highly urbanized societies, strong industrial sectors, and reasonably well-educated work forces. Yet the political histories of these countries are troubled. Despite its wealth and high level of adult literacy, Argentina experienced a half-century of failed presidencies and authoritarian closures of political space punctuated by very few years of democracy between 1930 and 1983. Levitsky aptly tags Argentina as "one of the world's leading democratic under-achievers for much of the twentieth century." If Argentina appears to be an "easy" case of building democracy in retrospect, it certainly did not appear so in 1983, when the new democratic regime was inaugurated. Brazil had a longer period of political democracy in the post World War II period (1946–64) than either Mexico or Argentina, but it also had a stable and well-entrenched military dictatorship for more than two decades (1964–85), which poignantly illustrates the difficulty of establishing an inclusive mass democracy in a country with gross inequality. Mexico experienced seven decades of one-party, authoritarian rule and never enjoyed democracy before 2000.

Seen from the expectations that existed when the Third Wave began in Latin America and from the vantage point of regime economic performance, Argentina, Brazil, and Mexico are cases of surprising success in democratization. Argentina may be the most intriguing of these three cases. Since 1983 it has enjoyed its longest period ever of democracy despite experiencing a profound economic crisis in the late 1980s and again in 2001–03, what Levitsky aptly calls "the most serious depression in the country's history." In 2002, as Argentina was experiencing a crisis of the presidency, the banking system lay in shambles, and public confidence in government had plummeted to all time lows, some wondered whether Argentine democracy might collapse. We offered Steve Levitsky an opportunity to revise his fine chapter, and asked him specifically if he wished to abandon ship. With either the optimism of a naïve Pollyanna or the prescience of a Greek oracle, Levitsky stayed on board and on course. We agree with Levitsky that Argentina's democratic prospects are solid. The fact that the political system did not outright collapse amid such an economic catastrophe is as remarkable as any positive development in Latin America's democratization of the past quarter century. Democracy in Argentina has weathered economic disaster to a far greater extent than one would have imagined given the country's history, and also more than other countries on the continent with democratic pasts.

Brazil has sustained a democratic regime since 1985, and democracy has become more stable in recent years. In his chapter, Kurt Weyland classifies the Brazilian democratic regime since 1995 as "immune to challenges." Although he calls Brazil's democracy "low quality," Brazilian democracy is more robust today than it has ever been. The steady transfer of presidential power in January 2003 from Fernando Henrique Cardoso to Luiz Inácio Lula da Silva, a man whom in 1989 many actors regarded as a threat to democratic and economic stability, attests to the maturing of Brazilian democracy.

Whether one counts the election of an opposition majority in the national Congress (in 1997) or the election of a president from a party other than the

Institutionalized Revolutionary Party (in 2000) as the inaugural point, Mexico has finally unambiguously achieved a democratic regime. No longer is the Mexican Congress a rubber stamp for an all-powerful presidency. If Mexican democracy was late in coming, it is maturing rapidly.

Part II: Surprising but Weak Competitive Regimes

Bolivia, El Salvador, and Guatemala are among the region's most surprising examples of democratic and semidemocratic regimes taking root on infertile soils, yet they also highlight the severe shortcomings of many competitively elected regimes in contemporary Latin America. In 1980 had someone said that Bolivia, El Salvador, and Guatemala would be democracies two decades hence, and that Venezuelan democracy would be falling apart, one might have suspected delirium. Bolivia had experienced grave instability for most of its life as an independent republic, and it demonstrated difficulty in exiting from the Banzer dictatorship (1971–78). A civil war that pitted leftist guerrillas against a repressive military regime backed by the United States was heating up in El Salvador; that war lasted for over a decade and eventually claimed 70,000 lives. And in Guatemala, brutal regimes had ruled since 1954 and unleashed horrific violence against Indian villages. Estimated deaths over the decades of repression and war range as high as 180,000 persons. Both countries faced daunting odds in constructing stable semidemocratic or democratic regimes. Their recent histories had been plagued not only by enormous political violence but also by sharp polarization and seemingly intractable intransigence on the part of both the political left and right, grafted onto a far longer history of high levels of poverty, social and political exclusion, deep ethnic cleavages, and sharp inequalities.

Since 1982 (Bolivia), 1985 (El Salvador), and 1986 (Guatemala), all three countries have maintained democratic or semidemocratic regimes. In comparison with their pasts, the progress toward democracy is, as Wood describes it, "breathtaking." But democracy in these countries, as Wood, Mayorga, and Seligson make apparent in this volume, is also gravely flawed. The rates of electoral abstention in El Salvador are now the highest of any of the nine countries in this volume, surpassing Guatemala and Colombia, long the two countries with the region's lowest rates of electoral participation. Guatemala has obvious potential for further regime erosion or even breakdown. Indeed, without international pressure, President Jorge Serrano's attempted palace coup in 1993, when he tried to close congress and assume dictatorial powers, probably would have succeeded. The party system has been characterized by extreme volatility, and human rights violations are still common. Bolivia suffers from high levels of perceived corruption (its scores were the worst of our nine cases recorded by Transparency International over the years). The 2003 uprising that led to the resignation of President Gonzalo Sánchez de Lozada signals the end of a period of successful regime building (circa 1985 to circa 1997), followed by gradual erosion.

Part III: Democracies That Erode or Break Down

Advances in democratization are neither linear nor impregnable. For this reason, our volume also includes two cases of democratic erosion in the period since 1978, Colombia and Venezuela, as well as the sole case of an outright democratic breakdown, Peru. Colombia and Venezuela boasted a tradition of democratic stability beginning in 1958 that persisted even as so many of their neighbors faltered in the 1970s. In 1978, at the start of Third Wave democratization in Latin America, they were, along with Costa Rica, the only democracies in Latin America.

The most disheartening political development of the past decade in Latin America has been the unraveling of Venezuela's once stable democracy, which Levine (1973) and Kornblith and Levine (1995) depicted as vibrant, participatory, and well supported by its own citizens. Venezuela's once well-institutionalized party system collapsed, and the country is polarized between supporters of Hugo Chávez and his opponents. The April 2002 coup attempt underscored the vulnerability and erosion of democracy in a country where it was formerly robust.

For many years, Colombia has experienced, as Ana María Bejarano and Eduardo Pizarro persuasively argue, a crisis not merely or especially of the regime but of the state itself in major parts of the territory. Violence has been rampant, the party system has fractionalized, and Colombian citizens have been subject to high levels of personal insecurity. If, as Linz and Stepan (1996) and O'Donnell (1993b, 2003) have argued, democracy cannot flourish without state order, then it follows that democracy has been besieged for some time. Since the election of President Alvaro Úribe in 2002, public assessments of democracy's future in Colombia have turned decidedly more optimistic, in no small part because of his aggressive efforts to reestablish state authority.

Peru fits into this volume in a unique way. Among all the countries of Latin America, in the post-1978 period it occupies a distinctive place as the clearest example of a democratic breakdown (in 1992). Given Peru's history of lengthy dictatorships for much of the twentieth century, the economic decline of 1980–90, and the brutal internal military conflict that claimed 69,000 lives, this democratic breakdown was hardly surprising. Indeed, much of the literature sees the breakdown as an almost inevitable outcome of a powerful and violent guerrilla movement and a severe economic crisis highlighted by hyperinflation and declining standards of living. In contrast to this dominant perspective on the Peruvian breakdown, Martín Tanaka argues in his chapter that a regime breakdown could have been avoided. Following the lines of argument developed by Linz (1978) and Stepan (1978), he asserts that the actions of specific historical figures were decisive in the breakdown.

When we invited Martín Tanaka to write a chapter on Peru in early 2000, Peru was a clear case of a regression in democratization after 1992. What we could not have anticipated at that time was that the pendulum would swing back toward democracy in Peru only a few months later. In 2001 a new democratic government was inaugurated, and perceived corruption levels began to decline. Thus, Peru, which once exemplified democratic regression in the post-1978 wave of democratization, has also come to exemplify the regime vicissitudes that long characterized much of the region before 1978 and could do so again in the future.

Such a dramatic change in Latin American politics as the wave of democratization that has endured for the past quarter century deserves to be brought to the fore, described, analyzed, and explained. Each chapter in this volume contributes to our understanding of the expansion of political competition and inclusion; the distribution of political power, economic resources, and social advantage; and the hopes and dissatisfaction of ordinary people with democracy in the late twentieth and early twenty-first century. In some cases included in this volume, democracy has survived against great odds. In others, democratic and semidemocratic regimes are vulnerable especially because they have failed to resolve pressing citizen needs, and they have not developed mechanisms of inclusion and representation to compensate for their performance failures. The past quarter century of Latin American democracy has been the broadest, deepest, and most inclusive ever. If this volume is not to serve as Latin American democracy's epithet, governments must generate jobs, provide public services, and create public security, and democratic regimes must strengthen the ties that bind citizens to their institutions of representative democracy. The future of democracy depends on no less.

I

Latin American Democratization since 1978

Democratic Transitions, Breakdowns, and Erosions

Scott Mainwaring and Aníbal Pérez-Liñán

What explains the remarkable burst of democratization that Latin America experienced between 1978 and 1992? And what explains the stagnation of democratization since 1992? These are the fundamental questions of this chapter.

Many of our answers to these questions run contrary to conventional wisdom based on worldwide analyses. For example, many authors have argued that more economically developed countries are more likely to be democratic. In contrast, for Latin America during the fifty-five years covered in our analysis, in particular from 1946 to 1977, economically more developed democracies were actually slightly more vulnerable to regime breakdowns. Theories of democracy based on modernization, class structure, and economic performance are poor explanations of the post-1978 democratic transformation.

Our analysis underscores the importance of the regional political environment – a factor that was downplayed until the 1990s in writings on democratization. Decreasing polarization and stronger commitment of political elites to democracy also help explain the post-1978 democratization.

Our second major objective is to examine and interpret the impasse that the wave of democratization encountered after 1992. A number of nonconstitutional depositions of democratically elected presidents occurred; some democratic regimes eroded and became semidemocratic; more antiparty presidents have been elected, with potentially negative consequences for democracy; and the legitimacy of democracy as measured in public opinion surveys declined. Three factors help explain the impasse of democratization. First, although international actors have developed effective means of combating coups and egregious electoral fraud, international actors are almost powerless to improve the quality of democracy and to avoid erosions in the quality of democracy. Second,

We are grateful to Kathleen Collins, Mark Gasiorowski, Fran Hagopian, Steve Levitsky, René Mayorga, Covadonga Meseguer, Guillermo O'Donnell, Iván Orozco, Mitch Sanders, Rich Snyder, Mariano Torcal, Kurt Weyland, and an anonymous reviewer for helpful comments. Mainwaring acknowledges the support of the John Simon Guggenheim Memorial Foundation.

poor economic growth has limited structural transformations that would have been favorable to democracy. Finally, the economic, social, and security performance of most democratic and semidemocratic governments in Latin America has been poor, reinforcing problems of democratic legitimacy and paving the way to antiparty presidents.

This chapter focuses on broad regional trends and on questions of regime change and durability. We deal only in passing with what might be broadly (if vaguely) called the quality of democracy – a key theme that the country chapters examine in detail. In terms of the regionwide scope, this chapter and Hagopian's conclusion are different from the country-specific analyses that follow. These different approaches complement one another. In this chapter, we show that there are powerful regionwide trends and influences that the country-specific chapters do not address. At the same time, the regional trends leave a great deal of regime change and durability unexplained; country-specific factors are very important. Methodologically, the combination of some analysis of region-wide trends and some of country-specific dynamics is ideal for understanding the post-1978 wave of democratization in Latin America.

I. TRENDS IN DEMOCRATIZATION IN LATIN AMERICA

The post-1978 wave of democratization has been far more extensive, involving far more countries, and has lasted for longer than any previous wave of democracy in Latin America. But what is a "wave," anyway? And how can we assess the magnitude of this change?

To assess trends in democratization in Latin America, we developed a trichotomous scale of democracy (Mainwaring, Brinks, and Pérez-Liñán 2001). This measure classifies governments as democratic, semidemocratic, or authoritarian for the period from 1945 until 2003. We defined as democratic every regime that during a particular year met four characteristics: (1) the government was elected in free and fair elections; (2) there were good protections for civil liberties; (3) the electorate included most of the adult population; and (4) there was no encroachment of the military or other nonelected actors in the domain of elected powers. If one or more attributes are only partially compromised (e.g., circumscribed episodes of electoral fraud are reported, gross human rights violations take place in certain regions of the country but do not disrupt the operation of the regime at the national level), we classify the regime as semidemocratic. If any of those attributes is missing, the regime is coded as authoritarian (or more precisely, nondemocratic). We sometimes refer to the combined set of democracies and semidemocracies as competitive regimes.

Table 1.1 in the Introduction showed the Mainwaring/Brinks/Pérez-Liñán coding of twenty Latin American countries for 1945–2003. Any summary classification of a political competitive regime compresses a tremendous amount of information and hence fails to provide the rich, more detailed portrait of political regimes found in the country studies in this volume. On the plus side,

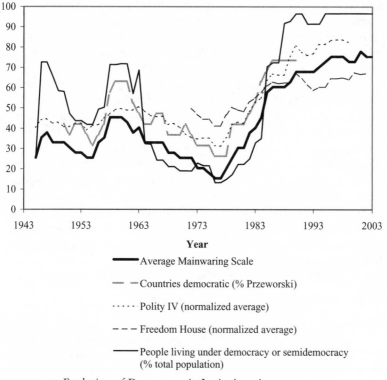

FIGURE 1.1. Evolution of Democracy in Latin America, 1945–2003.

our measure makes it possible to assess the level of democracy in the region and to analyze regime changes partially through quantitative data – two virtues.

Throughout the rest of this chapter, we use this classification for assessing regime change to and from democracy (and semidemocracy).[1] For analyzing democratic transitions and breakdowns, our categorical measure of democracy has advantages over continuous or interval measures such as those used by Freedom House and Polity. For these continuous or interval measures, one would need to impose artificial cut-points to determine when a transition or breakdown had occurred.

To trace the evolution of regime patterns over time, Figure 1.1 compares this scale with three other measures of democracy commonly employed in comparative politics: the dichotomous classification by Przeworski et al. (2000),

---

[1] In most cases, assessing when a regime has changed from authoritarian to (semi)democratic or vice-versa is straightforward. For example, a dictatorship may sponsor elections and lose, giving rise to a semidemocracy or a democracy. Conversely, a military coup may topple an elected civilian government, beginning a period of patently authoritarian rule. In a few cases, transitions are less abrupt and therefore harder to date. For example, we code Argentina as moving from a semidemocracy to an authoritarian regime in 1951 (when Juan Perón won reelection), but 1949, when the Radical Party opposition abandoned the constituent assembly in protest, could have been an alternative date.

Freedom House scores for the post-1972 period (Gastil 1991), and the Polity scale (Gurr, Jaggers, and Moore 1990; Jaggers and Gurr 1995; Polity IV Project 2000). Figure 1.1 depicts the evolution of democracy in twenty Latin American countries according to these four indicators. In Figure 1.1, for purposes of comparability, we normalized all four indicators to range from zero to one hundred.[2]

All four indicators depict a similar trend for 1945–2003, suggesting a high level of reliability in the overall picture.[3] Democracy expanded somewhat in the late 1950s and early 1960s and then hit a nadir in the 1970s followed by an unprecedented surge during the 1980s. Figure 1.1 thus confirms the occurrence of two waves of democratization during the second half of the twentieth century and illustrates the unprecedented strength of the change during 1978–92. The increase in the number of democracies and semidemocracies in Latin America between 1978 and 1992 was dramatic. At the beginning of this period, Latin America had only three democracies: Colombia, Costa Rica, and Venezuela. By 1990, every government in the region with the exceptions of Cuba and Haiti was democratic or semidemocratic. Moreover, in contrast to what occurred in earlier waves of democratization in Latin America, this wave has lasted much longer and has been broader in scope.

Figure 1.1 also shows the percentage of the total Latin American population living under democratic rule according to our trichotomous classification. This final measure of democracy is consistent with the other four. In 1969 only 21 percent of Latin Americans lived under democracy or semidemocracy; in 1999, however, 59 percent lived under democracy, and another 37 percent under semidemocratic conditions.

Figure 1.2 shows Polity scores, the only of these five indicators that is available for the pre-1945 period, to assess levels of democracy from 1903 (when Panama became independent) to 1945. The evolution of the normalized mean Polity value for these nineteen countries was flat during these decades, ranging from a high of 47.1 in 1918 to a low of 35.3 in 1936, with a long-term (1903–45)

[2] The formulas used to rescale the different measures of democracy to range between 0 and 100 were (1) for Polity: (Polity score + 10)*5; (2) for Freedom House: (14 − [Political rights + Civil liberties])*100/12; (3) Przeworski's classification: (democracy dummy)*100; and (4) Mainwaring et al.'s trichotomous scale: Score*50 (where Score equals 0 for authoritarian regimes, 1 for semidemocracies, and 2 for democracies). In Figure 1.1, though not elsewhere in this chapter, we treat our trichotomous indicator as a continuous scale ranging from 0 for authoritarian regimes to 50 for semidemocracies to 100 for democracies to make possible the comparison with the other measures.

[3] These four measures of democracy are strongly correlated. Taking each regime-year (one regime in one year) as a single case, the Mainwaring scale correlates (Pearson correlation) at .82 with the Alvarez, Cheibub, Limongi, and Przeworski (ACLP) dummy, at .82 with Freedom House scores, and at .85 with the Polity variable. The ACLP dummy correlates at .79 with Polity and .80 with Freedom House scores, and Polity classifications correlate at .85 with Freedom House. The four series (i.e., the annual averages for nineteen countries) are even more strongly correlated. The proportion of democracies and semidemocracies according to the Mainwaring et al. three-point scale correlates at .956 with the Przeworski series, at .959 with Freedom House scores, and at .957 with the Polity index.

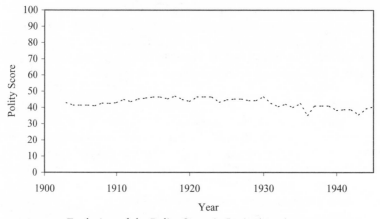

FIGURE 1.2. Evolution of the Polity Score in Latin America, 1903–1945.

average annual rate of change of just −0.1 points on a scale between 0 and 100. Thus, the wave of democratization that began in 1978 is unique in Latin American history, both in duration and in breadth.

Figure 1.1 suggests two important questions. First, why has democracy and semidemocracy been much more widespread since the 1980s than ever before? Second, why has democratization not advanced more since 1992? Only by posing both questions is it possible to appreciate both the achievements in the face of daunting challenges and the serious shortcomings of democracy.

"Waves" of Democracy?

How useful is the notion of "waves" to describe the historical vicissitudes of democratic rule in Latin America? According to Huntington's classic book (1991: 15), "a wave of democratization is a group of transitions from non-democratic to democratic regimes that occur within a specified period of time and that significantly outnumber transitions in the opposite direction." Because Huntington did not provide any concrete operational rules, the number and duration of such "specified periods" of democratic expansion requires further clarification (Doorenspleet 2000). Huntington identified three global waves of democratization: 1828–1926, 1943–62, and 1974–91 (when his book was published). We adopt Huntington's periodization as an initial heuristic and provide a more operational definition of wavelike historical change. Because, as is reflected in Figure 1.2, Huntington's first wave had little influence in Latin America (it involved only Argentina, Chile, Uruguay, and to some extent Costa Rica), we focus on the evolution and the magnitude of the second and the third waves.

To compare the impact and magnitude of the "second" and "third" waves of democratization, in Latin America, we need an operational definition of "wave." We label as a wave of democratization a continuous time spell during which there is a sustained decline in the number of authoritarian regimes. A wave is considered to be terminated if the number of authoritarian regimes increases during any one year or remains constant for more than three years in a row. It is possible to evaluate the impact of a wave in terms of its *magnitude* (the difference between the number of democracies and semidemocracies in the initial and in the final year) and its *duration* (the length of the time-spell as determined by the termination rule above).

According to this definition, two waves of democratization took place in Latin America between 1946 and 2003: from 1956 until 1962 and from 1978 until 1992. We use Huntington's denomination of "third wave" to refer to the post-1978 period. In Latin America, the magnitude of this wave was significantly greater than the one of 1956–62. The earlier wave lasted for six years and expanded the number of democracies and semidemocracies by seven (from five in 1955 to twelve in 1961). The wave that started in 1978 lasted fourteen years and enlarged the democratic and semidemocratic camp from three cases in 1977 to eighteen in 1991. In contrast to what occurred in earlier waves of democratization in Latin America, this wave has lasted much longer and has been broader in scope. A region that throughout its history was overwhelmingly authoritarian became mostly democratic and semidemocratic.

Even more striking, the 1956–62 wave was followed by fifteen continuous years of democratic regression or stagnation, while the 1978–92 wave was followed (after the Peruvian palace coup in 1992 terminated the expansive cycle) by eight years of democratic stability or growth between 1993 and 2000. This aftermath, however, is not free of complications, which we address later.

The 1978 wave was not only unique in Latin America's history but also one of the most dramatic waves of democratization ever accomplished in the world. Greece, Portugal, and Spain began the Third Wave of democratization, but Latin America turned it into a wave rather than what might have been a mere ripple.

Two Puzzles

The post-1978 historical transformation could result from one or both of two different processes. One is that transitions to democracy became more frequent after 1977 than in previous decades; the other is that semidemocratic and democratic regimes have endured for more time (Przeworski et al. 2000). If transitions to democracy were more frequent after 1977, the absolute number of democracies and semidemocracies would increase even if the breakdown rate did not change because new democracies would emerge at a faster pace than the older ones collapsed. In a similar vein, even if the rate of transitions from authoritarianism remained constant, their absolute number would increase if the breakdown rate of elected governments decreased because democracies would survive once established.

Table 1.1 shows that both possibilities account for the post-1978 upsurge.[4] The incidence of transitions to semidemocratic or democratic regimes from

---

[4] In the rest of this paper, we exclude Cuba from the analysis because of the difficulty in finding reliable socioeconomic data that are directly comparable to the data we have for other countries.

TABLE 1.1. *Rate of Transitions and Democratic Breakdowns, 1945–1999*

Period	Breakdowns			Transitions to Democracy or Semidemocracy		
	N	Total	Breakdown Rate (%)	N	Total	Transition Rate (%)
1945–1977	20	242	8.3	16	368	4.3
1978–1999	1	283	0.4	16	135	11.9
1945–1999	21	525	4.0	32	503	6.4

N: Number of breakdowns of democracy or semidemocracy, or transitions from authoritarianism.
Total: number of regime-years of authoritarianism or democracy/semidemocracy.
Breakdown (or transition) rate: number of breakdowns over total number of regime-years of democracy.
Source: Based on the Latin American Democracy Dataset (LADD), electronic dataset compiled by Aníbal Pérez-Liñán, Scott Mainwaring, and Daniel Brinks.

authoritarianism nearly tripled between 1978 and 1999 compared to that in 1945–77. The likelihood that any randomly chosen authoritarian regime would undergo a transition to democracy in a particular year increased from 4.3 to 11.9 percent. The incidence of breakdowns of democratic and semidemocratic regimes fell much more dramatically. Breakdowns were *twenty* times more likely for a given competitive regime in a given year before 1978 than they have been since then. Democratic breakdowns before 1978 were very common (twenty in number); between 1978 and 1999, they virtually ceased to occur. The only breakdown after 1978 was Peru in 1992, and it took tremendously adverse conditions for democracy to break down that year: a devastating and prolonged economic recession (a mean growth rate of −2.36 percent per capita per year from 1980 to 1991) coupled with hyperinflation (a mean inflation rate of 1,060 percent from 1980 to 1991), one of the most virulent and powerful terrorist groups (Sendero Luminoso) in the history of Latin America, and intense conflict between the president and the executive (Kenney 2004; Tanaka, this volume). This increased survival rate of democratic and semidemocratic regimes is the more important key to explaining the far greater proportion of democracies in Latin America since 1978.

Table 1.1 suggests two puzzles that provide the key to understanding the sea change in Latin American politics after 1978. First, what explains the increase in the likelihood of transitions to democracy in Latin America? Second, what explains the increase in the durability of democratic and semidemocratic regimes in the region?[5]

Most standard sources, such as the Economic Commission for Latin America and the Caribbean, published little data on Cuba during much of the post-1959 period.

[5] To keep the terminology short and consistent, in this chapter the terms "regime breakdown," "breakdown," and "breakdown rate" refer exclusively to changes from democracy and semidemocracy to authoritarianism. We use other terminology for the breakdown of authoritarian regimes.

2. DEPENDENT AND INDEPENDENT VARIABLES

When it is possible to measure theoretically important independent and dependent variables in a reasonably efficient and valid manner, quantitative analysis allows for a more rigorous assessment of the causal impact of the independent variables. We therefore begin our exploration of regime changes with a quantitative analysis. Each political regime in each year counts as one case for our analysis; we hereafter call this unit a regime-year. The dependent variable for all authoritarian regimes is whether the regime changes to a democracy or semidemocracy in a given year. The dependent variable for all democratic and semidemocratic regimes is whether it breaks down into authoritarianism in a given year.

According to our definition, a new regime is inaugurated every time authoritarian rule becomes democratic or semidemocratic, or a democracy or semidemocracy breaks down into authoritarianism.[6] The probability of a regime change is exactly opposite to the probability of regime durability because a regime either changes or it does not. Thus, if the probability of regime breakdown for any given year is p, the probability of survival is $1 - p$. We model regime change using rare event logistic regression (RELogit), a statistical technique designed for dependent variables in which the distribution of the dichotomous outcome is very uneven. This is the situation with regime changes. In our dataset with 1,026 regime-years, there are 53 regime changes (32 transitions to democracy or semidemocracy and 21 breakdowns). The quantitative analysis enables us to systematically test for the first time the impact of some important theoretical approaches to regime change in Latin America.

Quantitative analysis should be grounded in a theoretical understanding of politics. For this reason, in the remainder of this section, we explore some leading empirical theories of democracy and their capacity to provide insights into the two puzzles introduced in the previous section. We discuss six quantifiable theoretical approaches that have been presented as explanations of either the emergence or the survival of democracies: the level of economic development as a proxy for modernization, class structure, economic performance, the regional political environment in Latin America, party system fragmentation, and party system polarization.

---

[6] Several "regimes" may emerge and break down during an otherwise continuous period of authoritarianism. For instance, the age of Colorado hegemony in Paraguay following the civil war (1947–54) was eventually replaced by the *Stronato* (1954–89) without any improvement in democratization. Since we are concerned with democratic transition and breakdown, we focus on the inauguration of regime *types* (democracy, semidemocracy, and dictatorship) and their survival rather than on the replacement of the ruling cliques. With our operationalization of regime types, the beginning of a new regime does not always coincide with the beginning of a new government. The MNR (Movimiento Nacionalista Revolucionario or National Revolutionary Movement) government in Bolivia took power in 1952, but it did not hold elections until 1956. For this reason, the 1952–55 period is a continuation of authoritarian rule, while 1956 marks the beginning of a semidemocracy. For operational reasons, our measure of long-term performance does not go back beyond 1945.

Level of Development

One of the most consistent findings in the democratization literature has been that the level of modernization has a major impact on the likelihood of democracy (Bollen 1980; Bollen and Jackman 1985; Burkhart and Lewis-Beck 1994; Coppedge 1997; Dahl 1971: 62–80; Diamond 1992; Huntington 1984, 1991; Jackman 1973; Lipset 1959; Lipset, Seong, and Torres 1993; Londregan and Poole 1996; Przeworski et al. 2000; Rueschemeyer, Stephens, and Stephens 1992).[7] We measure the level of development using per capita income (GDP) in 1995 U.S. dollars, following the World Development Indicators (World Bank 2001b).[8]

Class Structure

Diamond (1992), Lipset (1959), Moore (1966), and Rueschemeyer et al. (1992), among others, see the prospects for democracy as resting significantly on the nature of the class structure. Rueschemeyer et al. argued that "capitalist development is associated with democracy because it transforms the class structure, strengthening the working and middle classes and weakening the landed upper class" (p. 7). According to them, "[t]he working class was the most consistently pro-democratic force. The class had a strong interest in effecting its political inclusion..." (p. 8). They also argued that a powerful landed aristocracy is inimical to democracy (pp. 60–61).

We use the percentage of labor force in manufacturing as a gross indicator of the numerical leverage of the working class. The size of different classes should be relevant to testing Rueschemeyer et al.'s arguments; indeed, they explicitly argued that class size is an important determinant of democracy (p. 59). Per capita GDP is correlated at .682 with the percentage of the labor force working in manufacturing ($p < .001$).

[7] This finding has been challenged in the Latin American context. O'Donnell (1973) argued that bottlenecks of development in the most industrialized Latin American countries triggered the emergence of military regimes in the 1960s and 1970s. Domínguez (1993) and Valenzuela and Valenzuela (1983) argued that democracy in some Latin American countries has thrived at low per capita income levels. Muller (1988, 1995) claimed that for countries with intermediate income levels, the likelihood of democracy would diminish when per capita income increases. Przeworski and his collaborators found the relationship between development and democratic survival to be statistically insignificant among presidential regimes and concluded that "the chances of survival for presidential democracies are independent of per capita income" (Przeworski et al. 2000: 132). Mainwaring and Pérez-Liñán (2003) documented a weak and nonlinear relationship between levels of development and democracy in Latin America. See also Landman (1999).

[8] In principle, a positive correlation between per capita income and the likelihood of democracy could occur because democracies promoted more rapid economic growth than nondemocracies. If this were the case, even if the two kinds of regimes started out at the same per capita level, the democracies would end up with a higher per capita income, accounting for the positive correlation. This type of bicausality is not a problem with our sample because democracies did not grow at a faster pace than nondemocracies. The average annual per capita growth rate for democracies was 1.60 percent; for semidemocracies it was 1.04 percent, and for authoritarian regimes it was 1.59 percent. For semidemocratic and democratic regimes together, the average annual per capita growth rate was 1.49 percent.

Regime Economic Performance

Several scholars (Diamond 1999: 77–93; Diamond and Linz 1989: 44–4ᴏ Gasiorowski 1995; Geddes 1999b; Haggard and Kaufman 1995; Lipset et al. 1993; Przeworski et al. 2000) have argued that competitively elected and/or authoritarian regimes are more likely to break down if their economic performance is poor. We used two variables to measure a regime's economic performance: change in per capita income (i.e., the rate of economic growth) and the consumer price index (CPI) (i.e., inflation).[9] For both growth and inflation, we use a short-term measure (the previous year) and a medium-term measure (average growth or inflation of a given regime since its inception, for up to ten years).[10]

Regional Political Environment

Until the 1990s research on political regimes focused heavily on domestic factors (for an exception, see Whitehead 1986). Since the 1990s, however, scholars have paid more attention to international factors in regime change and stability (Brown 2000; Gleditsch 2002; Lowenthal 1991; Pevehouse 2002; Pridham 1991; Starr 1991; Whitehead 1996). A favorable international environment might enhance chances for democracy, while an unpropitious environment might work against democracy. To explore this possibility, we included a variable ("region") to assess the impact of Latin America's regional political context on the likelihood of regime durability and change. We measured the regional political environment through the number of strictly democratic countries in the region every year, excluding the country in question if it was democratic. The coding for this independent variable was based on our trichotomous measure of democracy. The value of this variable can theoretically range from zero, if none of the other nineteen countries in the region were democratic in a given year, to nineteen if all twenty countries were democratic in that year. We exclude the country in question to avoid problems of endogeneity. We expected a more democratic regional environment to encourage democracy (Gleditsch 2002; Starr 1991; Whitehead 1986, 1991, 1996).

---

[9] Growth was estimated based on our per capita GDP figures. Inflation was obtained from the World Development Indicators (World Bank 2001b) database for 1961–99 and from the Global Financial Database and ECLAC (the Economic Commission for Latin America and the Caribbean) reports for 1945–60 (ECLAC 2001).

[10] The impact of inflation on regime changes should be nonlinear, given the existence of many episodes of three- and four-digit inflation rates in our Latin American sample (Gasiorowski 1995, 1998). Presumably, an increase in inflation from 0 to 100 percent should have a greater impact on regime stability than an increase from 900 to 1,000 percent. To many actors, an increase in inflation from 0 to 100 percent would have profound negative repercussions; an increase from 900 to 1,000 percent would not. For this reason, we used the natural logarithm of the inflation rate. The actual formula employed was $\ln[1 + i(t-1)]$ for any case of $i \geq 0$ and $-\ln[1 + |i(t-1)|]$ for $i < 0$ (i.e., deflation), where i is the annual percent change in the CPI (Gasiorowski 2000: 326).

U.S. Foreign Policy

As a hegemonic power in the Americas, the United States can affect the likelihood of transitions to competitive regimes and of regime breakdowns. We code a 0 for years in which U.S. foreign policy subordinated democracy to other issues (1945–76, 1981–84) and 1 for years in which democracy was an important item on the agenda (1977–80, 1984–99).

Party System Fragmentation

An extensive literature has emphasized the role of institutional design in creating stable conditions for democracy. One such argument has centered on the nature of presidential regimes. Linz (1994), Mainwaring (1993), and Stepan and Skach (1994) argued that presidential regimes with fragmented party systems are more prone to breakdown. They claimed that when presidents had minority support in congress, impasses between the president and congress were more common, sometimes leading to democratic breakdown (see also Kenney 2004). Cheibub (2002) challenged this analysis, arguing that there is no linear relationship between party system fragmentation and democratic survival in presidential systems. The debate about the impact of party system fragmentation on democratic stability in presidential regimes is not relevant for explaining transitions from authoritarianism, but it might help explain the *stability* of democratic and semidemocratic regimes.

To assess the role of this factor, we created a dichotomous variable coded as 1 if the effective number of parties in the lower (or only) chamber was equal or greater than 3.0 in a given year. The effective number of parties (ENP) is a mathematical calculation that weights parties according to their size and indicates the level of party system fragmentation; an effective number of 3.0 or more parties clearly indicates multipartism.[11] We employ a dichotomous indicator for theoretical reasons and because of missing information on the precise number of parties for Ecuador in the 1950s and Peru in the mid-1940s.[12]

Party System Polarization

In his classic work, Sartori (1976: 140) argued that polarized party systems are more vulnerable to paralysis and less able to deal with crises (see also Sani and

---

[11] The formula for the effective number of parties is $1/[\text{Sum}\,(p^2)]$, where p is the proportion of seats (or votes) obtained by each party (Laakso and Taagepera 1979). The effective number of parties can be calculated in votes or in seats. Because our interest here is the relationship between the president and congress, we use the ENP in seats.

[12] A threshold of 3.0 is a stronger indicator of multipartism than a lower number, but a 2.5 threshold did not alter the overall results. The use of exact ENP figures in our statistical analysis, excluding Ecuador from 1950 to 1959 and Peru from 1945 to 1948, did not alter any of the major conclusions presented here. The ENP variable consistently had the expected sign in all models, but it failed to achieve conventional levels of significance. This is not surprising since we do not expect a monotonic increase in breakdown rates with changes in the effective number of parties (e.g., a system with 2.3 parties is not expected to be less stable than a party system with 1.8 parties). Rather, we hypothesize that breakdown rates behave as a step function of ENP, with a significant increase after the system moves into multipartism.

Sartori 1983; Valenzuela 1978). As is the case with multipartism, this issue is relevant for understanding democratic breakdowns, but not for understanding transitions to democracy.

For democratic and semidemocratic regimes, we used Coppedge's (1998: 556–57) index of party systems in eleven countries (Argentina, Bolivia, Brazil, Chile, Colombia, Costa Rica, Ecuador, Mexico, Peru, Uruguay, and Venezuela) during democratic and semidemocratic periods (1946–99). Coppedge's index adopts values between 0 (when all votes in an election are located at the center of the political spectrum) and 100 (when all the votes are equally split between extreme left and extreme right parties). Unfortunately, scores for the remaining eight countries in our sample are not available.[13]

Our dataset covers a total of 19 countries over 54 years (1946–99), providing data for 1,026 country-years. Six hundred and eight cases correspond to 1946–77 and the remaining 418 to the Third Wave period.

3. STATISTICAL ANALYSIS

In this section, we employ rare event logistic regression (RELogit) to analyze how the probability of regime change during any given year is shaped by the independent variables discussed in the previous section (King and Zeng 2001a, 2001b). We use logistic regression because our two dependent variables – transition from authoritarian rule and democratic breakdown – are dichotomous (1 = change of a regime; 0 = no change of the regime).[14]

Transitions to Democracy and Semidemocracy

The fundamental question in this section is what caused the post-1978 increase in the rate of transitions to competitive regimes, from 4.3 percent in 1945–77 to 11.9 percent in 1978–99. The strongest finding of the quantitative analysis is that a regional environment that was more favorable to democracy was a key factor.

Between 1946 and 1999, thirty-two transitions from authoritarianism took place in the region (sixteen before 1978 and the remaining sixteen afterward). Table 1.2 presents mean values for seven independent variables for the regime-years in which a transition to democracy occurred and those when it did not,

---

[13] See Coppedge (1998: 556–57) for the formula for this index. For operational reasons, we assumed that ideological polarization could change at each election but remained constant between elections.

[14] Because the behavior of observations in our dataset (specific regime-years) is presumably independent across countries but not within countries, we used Huber-White (sandwich) standard errors adjusted for clustering by country. Huber-White standard errors relax the ordinary least squares assumption of independence across units. The limited number of transitions and breakdowns complicated the use of fixed-effect models.

TABLE 1.2. *Mean Values of Independent Variables for Years of Dictatorship in Latin America, 1946–1977 and 1978–1999*

	Mean Per Capita GDP ($t-1$)	Mean Labor Force in Industry (%)	Mean Growth ($t-1$)	Mean Annual Growth (last 10 years)	Mean Inflation ($t-1$)	Mean Annual Inflation (last 10 years)	Mean # of Democracies in Latin America	N (Regime-years)
1946–77								
All Dictatorships	1,457	16.7	2.2	2.3	17	15	4.42	368
Years of Transitions	2,485	20.4	1.3	2.0	15	16	4.44	16
Years without Transition	1,410	16.5	2.2	2.3	17	15	4.42	352
1978–99								
All Dictatorships	2,258	19.9	0.0	1.4	33	35	7.11	135
Years of Transitions	2,352	21.7	1.4	0.9	50	38	7.44	16
Years without Transition	2,246	19.7	−0.2	1.4	31	35	7.07	119

Notes: Year 1945 is missing because the behavior of structural predictors during one year is expected to affect regime survival the following year (i.e., 1946). Cuba is excluded owing to the lack of data.

Mean per capita GDP is in capita U.S. 1995 dollars in the year before the given year of dictatorship.

Mean Growth ($t-1$) is mean per capita growth in the year before the given year of dictatorship.

Mean Annual Growth for the last 10 years is for that particular regime only. If a dictatorship has been in existence for under 10 years, then the growth figure for a given regime-year is the average annual figure for the lifetime of the regime.

Mean inflation ($t-1$) is mean inflation in the year before the given year of dictatorship.

Mean Annual Inflation for the last 10 years is for that particular regime only. If a dictatorship has been in existence for under 10 years, then the inflation figure for a given regime-year is the average annual figure for the lifetime of the regime.

Source: Based on the Latin American Democracy Dataset (LADD), electronic dataset compiled by Aníbal Pérez-Liñán, Scott Mainwaring, and Daniel Brinks.

dividing the sample into 1945–77 and 1978–99.[15] Based on the expectations of some previous scholarship, the changes that took place in all seven quantitative variables between 1945–77 and 1978–99 were favorable to the increased likelihood of democratic transitions in the latter period. The per capita income in the average dictatorship increased substantially (from $1,457 to $2,258); the share of the labor force in industry increased (from 16.7 to 19.9 percent of the labor force); the mean economic performance of dictatorships worsened for both inflation (17 to 33 percent) and growth (2.2 to 0.0 percent), making more likely the demise of these dictatorships if economic performance affected their regime durability; and the mean number of democracies in the region, excluding the country in question, rose considerably (4.42 to 7.11), creating a less favorable regional environment for authoritarian regimes' survival.

Table 1.3 presents three statistical models based on RELogit of transitions from authoritarian rule into democracy or semidemocracy for the entire 1946–99 period. Years are coded 1 if a transition took place, 0 otherwise. The first model includes structural and macroeconomic predictors of democracy and the regional political variable (region). The level of development and the size of the labor force in industry were not significantly related to the probability of a democratic transition between 1946 and 1999 in Latin America. This is consistent with Przeworski et al.'s (2000) claim that the level of development does not explain the emergence of democracies and with the earlier arguments of Di Palma (1990), O'Donnell and Schmitter (1986), and Przeworski (1991) that transitions to democracy depend fundamentally on strategic bargaining and not centrally on the level of development. Among the performance indicators, only medium-term growth (i.e., up to ten years) was related to democratic transitions; the lower the performance of an authoritarian regime, the greater the likelihood of a democratic transition. The region variable is highly significant and has the expected positive coefficient; a larger number of democracies in the region in a given year enhanced the likelihood that any particular authoritarian regime would undergo a transition.

Model 3.2 includes a "Third Wave" dummy variable coded 0 for 1946–1977 and 1 for 1978–99. This control variable captures many changes in the region after 1977 that we cannot measure easily. This variable was not statistically significant in Model 3.2 because of a strong correlation with the region variable ($r = .788$). Because the number of democracies in the region grew substantially after 1977, the inclusion of the Third Wave variable erodes the statistical significance of the region term. A joint likelihood ratio test, however, showed that these two variables together did have, as expected, a highly significant impact on the likelihood of democratic transitions; each variable alone does not because of

---

[15] Tables 1.3 and 1.6 are intended to provide basic information in an easy-to-read format rather than a formal test of causal relationships. Although the comparison of means typically implies that the categories (not the interval variables) are the predictors, presenting the data as we do provides a better format than the alternative cross-tabulations with arbitrary cutoffs for the interval variables.

TABLE 1.3. *Predictors of Democratic Transitions, 1946–1999*

Model Variable	3.1	3.2	3.3
Per Capita GDP ($t-1$)	−0.052	−0.069	−0.047
	(0.214)	(0.205)	(0.216)
Labor Force in Industry (%)	0.104	0.107	0.104
	(0.068)	(0.066)	(0.068)
Growth ($t-1$)	0.052	0.058	0.049
	(0.057)	(0.056)	(0.057)
Inflation (ln, $t-1$)	0.025	0.007	0.010
	(0.206)	(0.223)	(0.211)
Growth (last 10 years)	−0.169	−0.190**	−0.177
	(0.097)	(0.095)	(0.097)
Inflation (ln, last 10 years)	−0.075	−0.134	−0.096
	(0.277)	(0.284)	(0.289)
Region	0.255***	0.164	0.198**
	(0.079)	(0.115)	(0.098)
Third Wave (1978–99)		0.642	
		(0.416)	
U.S. Policy			0.438
			(0.503)
Constant	−5.603***	−5.150***	−5.314**
	(1.080)	(1.150)	(1.124)
N	452	452	452
Pseudo-R²	0.0913	0.0967	0.0944

Entries are RELogit coefficients (robust standard errors adjusted for clustering by country). Pseudo-R² corresponds to standard logistic model with equivalent specification.
* Significant at .1 level; ** Significant at .05 level; *** Significant at .01 level.
Source: Based on the Latin American Democracy Dataset (LADD), electronic dataset compiled by Aníbal Pérez-Liñán, Scott Mainwaring, and Daniel Brinks.

the substantial overlap between them ($\Delta G^2 = 8.68, d.f. = 2, p < .02$).[16] This suggests that some of what we see with the region variable alone (i.e., without the Third Wave dummy variable) is not strictly an effect of having more democracies in the region (which is what the variable directly measures) but rather of other changes in the international political environment. Model 3.3 treats U.S. foreign policy separately from other regional environmental effects.

If it were possible to measure all relevant independent variables, the greater likelihood of transitions to democracy after 1978 compared to 1946–77 would result from two causal conditions or their combination. One possibility is that the values of some causal factors changed in a direction favorable to more transitions. For example, a higher level of development among authoritarian regimes might have been more favorable to transitions. The other possibility is

[16] RELogit does not provide the log-likelihood, so this calculation is based on standard logistic regression.

TABLE 1.4. *Predicted Impact of Selected Variables on the Probability of Transition*

Variable	1946–77 Predicted Transition Rate (%)	1978–99 Predicted Transition Rate (%)
Growth (10 years)	4.9	5.7
Region	4.3	8.1
All 7 Variables	4.0	9.8
Actual Transition Rate	4.3	11.9

Note: Based on Model 3.1. The selected independent variable in a given row is set at its mean for 1946–77 and 1978–99, respectively. All other variables are set at their historical means (1946–99).

Source: Based on the Latin American Democracy Dataset (LADD), electronic dataset compiled by Aníbal Pérez-Liñán, Scott Mainwaring, and Daniel Brinks.

that some variables had a historically contingent impact on regime transitions; that is, they had one kind of impact in the earlier period and a different one in the later. For instance, in the context of high ideological polarization in the 1960s, some actors might have been less tolerant of bad economic performance under democracy. Or they might have been more willing to stand bad economic performance under authoritarianism if they feared that a democratic regime would threaten their economic interests. In the absence of high ideological polarization, those reactions might have changed after 1977. The quantitative literature in political science has not been very attuned to such period effects,[17] but they are theoretically possible.

We first assess whether the changes in the levels of the seven independent variables contributed to the greater likelihood of democratic transitions after 1978. Although all seven independent variables in Table 1.2 changed in a direction that some previous studies found favorable to democracy, for Latin America, as Model 3.1 showed, only two of them were statistically significant. Table 1.4 shows the predicted impact of these two independent variables from Model 3.1 and of the joint effect of all seven variables on the probability of a transition. The combined effect of the change in all seven independent variables (from Model 3.1) accounts for most of the change in the increase in the transition rate after 1977. By far, the change in the mean level of the region variable accounts for the biggest part of this increase. If we keep constant all other independent variables (holding them at their means for 1946–99) but allow the region variable to shift from its actual mean of 4.44 democracies for 1946–77 to 7.11 democracies in 1978–99, the predicted probability of a transition would nearly double, from 4.3 percent per regime-year in 1946–77 to 8.1 percent in 1978–99. This increase of 3.8 percent represents half of the actual observed increase of 7.6 percent in the transition rate, from 4.3 to 11.9 percent.

[17] Gasiorowski (1995) and Gasiorowski and Power (1998) are exceptions.

Thus a change in the regional political environment is an important part of the explanation for the increase in the transition rate.

We explored two different ways of statistically assessing whether changes in the impact of the independent variables (without a change in the level of the variables) help account for the increased likelihood of transitions to democracy after 1978. One test, a comparison of Models 5.1 and 5.2, runs the same regression for the two different temporal samples. From 1946 to 1977, the previous year growth record of authoritarian regimes did not affect the likelihood of a transition to a competitively elected regime, but from 1978–99, authoritarian regimes with a higher growth performance – contrary to expectations – actually were more vulnerable to a regime change (Table 1.5). Previous year growth changed from a negative but insignificant coefficient from 1946–77 to a positive and significant one from 1978–99; thus, it seems that its impact changed between the two periods.

The other alternative is to run the entire 1946–99 period with a dummy variable for the Third Wave and to use interaction terms to test for historically contingent effects of the independent variables on the likelihood of a regime transition (Model 5.3). If an independent variable had a markedly different impact on the likelihood of a transition to democracy or semidemocracy in 1978–99 compared to 1945–77, the interaction terms should be statistically significant. None of the interaction terms achieves conventional levels of significance, and only one independent variable, the regional political environment, achieves (and barely) conventional levels of statistical significance. Given the large number of independent variables in the model and the small number (thirty-two) of transitions to competitive regimes, it is difficult to reach a definitive statistical conclusion on this issue.

In sum, more than any other variable we quantified, a more favorable regional political environment helped boost the rate of transitions to competitive regimes after 1977. International factors only occasionally are the driving force behind a transition to democracy; in our large dataset, Panama in 1990, with the U.S. invasion that deposed an authoritarian regime and installed a democratically elected president, was the only unequivocal example. But international factors can significantly alter the odds for or against transitions. Except for Whitehead (1986), little of the pioneering work on transitions was attuned to this interplay between domestic actors and the international political environment.

Having said this, the predictive capacity of these models is low. As a reference, Tables 1.3 and 1.5 include the pseudo-R^2 corresponding to standard logistic regression models following the same specification of the rare event logits (rare events logistic regression in Stata does not generate a default pseudo-R^2 value). The pseudo-R^2 is only 12 percent in Model 5.2 and 14 percent in Model 5.3. The limited performance of these models suggests that scholars seeking to understand transitions to democracy (Di Palma 1990; Levine 1973; Linz and Stepan 1996; O'Donnell and Schmitter 1986; Przeworski 1986, 1991) were right to emphasize the role of contingency and agency rather than structural

TABLE 1.5. *Transitions Models with Changing Effects in Two Historical Periods*

Model Variable	5.1 (1946–77)	5.2 (1978–99)	5.3 (1946–99)
Per capita GDP ($t-1$)	0.492	−0.309	0.492
	(0.545)	(0.209)	(0.540)
Labor Force in Industry (%)	−0.033	0.163	−0.033
	(0.151)	(0.103)	(0.150)
Growth ($t-1$)	−0.034	0.120*	−0.034
	(0.095)	(0.065)	(0.094)
Inflation (ln, $t-1$)	−0.151	0.505	−0.151
	(0.239)	(0.481)	(0.237)
Growth (last 10 years)	−0.063	−0.320	−0.063
	(0.087)	(0.202)	(0.086)
Inflation (ln, last 10 years)	0.244	−0.534	0.244
	(0.348)	(0.639)	(0.345)
Region	0.554	0.101	0.554*
	(0.338)	(0.133)	(0.334)
Third Wave (1978–99)			1.032
			(2.241)
GDP ($t-1$)* Third Wave			−0.801
			(0.542)
Labor Force* Third Wave			0.196
			(0.196)
Growth ($t-1$)* Third Wave			0.153
			(0.108)
Inflation (ln, $t-1$)* Third Wave			0.656
			(0.560)
Growth (10 years)* Third Wave			−0.257
			(0.193)
Inflation (10 years)* Third Wave			−0.778
			(0.735)
Region* Third Wave			−0.453
			(0.307)
Constant	−5.790***	−4.757**	−5.790***
	(1.691)	(1.990)	(1.674)
N	317	135	452
Pseudo-R^2	0.0893	0.1219	0.1406

RELogit coefficients (standard errors adjusted for clustering by country). Pseudo-R^2 corresponds to standard logistic model with equivalent specification.
* Significant at .1 level; ** at .05 level; *** at .01 level.
Source: Based on the Latin American Democracy Dataset (LADD), electronic dataset compiled by Aníbal Pérez-Liñán, Scott Mainwaring, and Daniel Brinks.

factors. The most influential work on transitions to democracy, O'Donnell and Schmitter (1986), argued that transitions were marked by a high degree of indeterminacy. Our results support the claim that transitions in Latin America were not very much determined by structural and regime performance factors. For example, per capita income had no effect on the likelihood of a transition for the entire period or for the periods before or after 1978.

Democratic Breakdowns and Durability

The main question in this section is what accounts for the dramatic decrease in the breakdown rate after 1977, which is the most important factor behind the post-1978 increase in the number of democracies. Our dataset contains 525 regime-years of democracy and semidemocracy between 1946 and 1999. We have information covering all the independent variables discussed previously for 517 cases (344 cases if we include the index of party system polarization, which is available for only eleven countries). During these 517 regime-years of democracy and semidemocracy, there were twenty-one regime breakdowns.

Table 1.6 lists the mean values of the independent variables for the regime years of breakdowns and nonbreakdowns for 1946–77 and 1978–99. Even information presented in this simple manner poses serious doubts about some of the conventional wisdom regarding the causes of the greater durability of democracy and semidemocracy. For Latin America, it is implausible that higher levels of development, changes in the class structure, or better economic performance could account for the vastly greater durability of democracy after 1977.

A modernization argument based on the idea that democracy is less vulnerable at higher levels of development does not hold face value plausibility. The mean per capita income of the regime-years of democracy and semidemocracy was only 18 percent higher for 1978–99 than for 1945–77. Similarly, it is implausible that the small increase in industrial workers (from a mean of 20.8% of the labor force from 1945–77 to 23.7% in 1978–99) would dramatically strengthen democracy. A political economy argument based on regime performance is even less promising for explaining the greater durability of democratic and semidemocratic governments after 1977. The mean performance in terms of both inflation and growth, as measured by both a very short term (one year) and a longer term (up to the last ten years of the regime), was vastly worse in 1978–99 than in 1945–77. The only variable that showed a major positive transformation over time is the region variable.

Table 1.7 shows the results of a RELogit predicting a change from democracy or semidemocracy to authoritarianism in any particular regime-year for the entire 1946–99 period. In Model 7.1 (structural and regime performance variables) only one predictor achieves conventional levels of significance. Against received theoretical expectations, the coefficient for per capita income is significant but *positive* (the greater the level of development, the greater the probability of breakdown). The pseudo-R^2 in Model 7.1 is very low (.03), indicating

TABLE 1.6. *Mean Values of Independent Variables for Years of Democracies and Semidemocracies in Latin America, 1946–1977 and 1978–1999*

	Mean Per Capita GDP $(t-1)$	Mean Labor Force in Industry (%)	Mean Growth $(t-1)$	Mean Annual Growth (last 10 years)	Mean Inflation $(t-1)$	Mean Annual Inflation (last 10 years)	Mean # of Democracies in Latin America	Mean Party* System Polarization	% of Multipartism	N
1946–77										
All Years of Democracies/										
Semidemocracies	2190	20.8	2.2	2.1	18	15	4.17	39.5	44.4	242
Years of Breakdown	2516	21.0	2.0	1.5	32	30	4.45	35.7	55.0	20
All Other Years of Democracies and										
Semidemocracies	2161	20.8	2.2	2.2	16	13	4.14	39.8	43.4	222
1978–99										
All Years of Democracies/										
Semidemocracies	2586	23.7	0.9	0.8	275	318	9.20	40.2	37.1	283
Years of Breakdown	1909	20.8	0.3	−3.0	410	1,258	10.00	20.6	100.0	1
All Other Years of Democracies and										
Semidemocracies	2588	23.7	0.9	0.8	274	315	9.20	40.4	36.9	282

* Data for Party System Polarization available for only eleven countries.

Mean per capita GDP is in capita U.S. 1995 dollars in the year before the given year of democracy.

Mean Growth $(t-1)$ is mean per capita growth in the year before the given year of democracy.

Mean Annual Growth for the last 10 years is for that particular regime only. If a democracy has been in existence for under 10 years, then the growth figure for a given regime-year is the average annual figure for the lifetime of the regime.

Mean inflation $(t-1)$ is mean inflation in the year before the given year of democracy.

Mean Annual Inflation for the last 10 years is for that particular regime only. If a democracy has been in existence for under 10 years, then the inflation figure for a given regime-year is the average annual figure for the lifetime of the regime.

Mean Party System Polarization is based on Coppedge (1998).

Source: Based on the Latin American Democracy Dataset (LADD), electronic dataset compiled by Aníbal Pérez-Liñán, Scott Mainwaring, and Daniel Brinks.

TABLE 1.7. *Predictors of Democratic Breakdown, 1946–1999*

Model Variable	7.1	7.2	7.3	7.4	7.5
Per Capita GDP $(t-1)$	0.283*	0.317**	0.283*	0.388***	0.298*
	(0.146)	(0.136)	(0.148)	(0.136)	(0.142)
Labor Force in	−0.118	−0.075	−0.091*	−0.135***	−0.087*
Industry (%)	(0.079)	(0.051)	(0.052)	(0.043)	(0.050)
Growth $(t-1)$	0.052	0.051	0.042	−0.047	0.045
	(0.042)	(0.043)	(0.043)	(0.054)	(0.042)
Inflation (ln, $t-1$)	0.209	0.118	0.222	−0.229	0.209
	(0.163)	(0.212)	(0.285)	(0.284)	(0.291)
Growth (last 10 years)	−0.130	−0.121**	−0.090*	−0.115	−0.091*
	(0.094)	(0.055)	(0.052)	(0.098)	(0.052)
Inflation (ln, last	−0.158	0.349	0.508	0.956**	0.466*
10 years)	(0.173)	(0.229)	(0.315)	(0.393)	(0.278)
Region		−0.601***	−0.114	−0.023	−0.233
		(0.109)	(0.253)	(0.377)	(0.220)
Multipartism		1.210**	1.027**	1.693**	1.082*
		(0.434)	(0.451)	(0.715)	(0.439)
Semidemocracy		2.546***	1.974***	2.578***	2.161***
		(0.382)	(0.438)	(0.594)	(0.374)
Third Wave (1978–99)			−3.706**	−4.911**	
			(1.599)	(2.194)	
IP (Polarization Index)				0.022**	
				(0.011)	
U.S. Policy					−2.861**
					(1.449)
Constant	−1.164	−1.884***	−3.676***	−4.368**	−3.312***
	(1.328)	(0.723)	(0.992)	(1.726)	(0.933)
N	517	517	517	344	517
Pseudo-R²	0.0313	0.3028	0.3356	0.3912	0.3277

RELogit coefficients (standard errors adjusted for clustering by country). Pseudo-R² corresponds to standard logistic model with equivalent specification.

* Significant at .1 level; ** at .05 level; *** at .01 level.

Source: Based on the Latin American Democracy Dataset (LADD), electronic dataset compiled by Aníbal Pérez-Liñán, Scott Mainwaring, and Daniel Brinks.

the very weak explanatory capacity of the structural and regime performance variables.

O'Donnell and Schmitter (1986) and Przeworski et al. (2000) argued that there is an asymmetry between transitions and breakdowns. They claimed that transitions did not depend on structural factors, but that structural factors were a better predictor of democratic breakdowns. For Latin America between 1946 and 1999, the evidence does not support this asymmetry argument. The structural and regime performance variables were weak predictors of both transitions and breakdowns.

These results improve dramatically after we add political variables to the equation (Model 7.2). Political factors provide a much better explanation of democratic survival; the pseudo-R^2 jumped from 3 percent in Model 7.1 to 30 percent in Model 7.2. As anticipated, a more democratic regional environment reduces the chances of breakdown ($p < .001$). Multiparty systems and semidemocratic regimes were more prone to breakdown than democracies with fewer than 3.0 effective parties and than full-fledged democracies. Per capita income retains its significance; more developed countries were slightly more vulnerable to breakdown. This finding is consistent with O'Donnell's well-known argument (1973) that the more developed countries of South America were especially prone to bureaucratic authoritarianism in the 1960s and 1970s and also with an earlier finding that in a wide income band, Latin American countries with a higher level of development were less likely to be democratic (Mainwaring and Pérez-Liñán 2003; also Landman 1999). One of the performance indicators also becomes significant: Democracies with a better medium-term growth performance were less likely to break down.

As in Table 1.5, the significance of the region variable declined after we incorporated a Third Wave dummy to account for other changes after 1977 (Model 7.3). With the minor exception that the variable for the percentage of the labor force in industrial activities became significant, other findings are consistent with Model 7.2. Model 7.5 distinguishes U.S. foreign policy from other effects of the regional political environment. Whereas the region variable was significant for explaining transitions even when U.S. foreign policy is treated separately, the U.S. policy variable is more important for breakdowns. Finally, Model 7.4 includes Coppedge's (1998) indicator of party system polarization for eleven countries. Consistent with theoretical expectations, greater polarization significantly increased the probability of a democratic breakdown.

Consistent with the arguments of Levine (1973), Linz (1978), and Stepan (1978), the findings in Table 1.7 emphasize the critical role of political factors in explaining the survival of democracies and semidemocracies. Semidemocracies tended to survive for shorter periods than fully democratic regimes, and sharp party system polarization promoted the demise of democratic rule. Regimes with 3.0 or more effective parties in the legislature were more likely to experience breakdowns. This finding is consistent with an earlier literature that emphasized the difficulties of multipartism under presidentialism (Linz 1994; Mainwaring 1993; Stepan and Skach 1994).[18]

Some of the most interesting findings in Table 1.7 are negative. Whereas previous literature had emphasized the impact of economic crises (Haggard and Kaufman 1995; O'Donnell 1973) or inflation (Skidmore 1977) on democratic breakdowns, we find weak or no effect. Counterintuitively, poor economic performance did not have a direct negative impact on democratic durability. The impact of poor economic performance on democracy was rather mediated

---

[18] We ran Model 7.4 using ENP instead of the multipartism dummy. The results were similar, but the p value for ENP was .17.

by the expectations and perceptions of citizens (Powers 2001; Stokes 1996) and by the ways in which elites politicized economic failures.

Przeworski et al. (2000) showed that at a global level, democratic governments are more likely to endure at a higher per capita income level. Their finding was consistent with a much larger literature that argued that more developed countries were more likely to be democracies. A higher level of development, however, had no immunizing impact for democracy in Latin America (see also Landman 1999; Mainwaring and Pérez-Liñán 2003; O'Donnell 1973). Democratic and semidemocratic regimes were vulnerable to breakdown at even fairly high levels of development. Argentina, which during this fifty-four-year period consistently had one of the highest per capita incomes in Latin America, nevertheless suffered frequent breakdowns of semidemocratic or democratic regimes: 1951 (an erosion of an existing semidemocratic regime into authoritarianism), 1962, 1966, and 1976. Conversely, the only country that experienced democracy or semidemocracy without a breakdown during the 1945–77 period was Costa Rica. Costa Rica's per capita income was a meager $1,310 (in 1995 U.S. dollars) in 1949, when the current democratic regime came into being.

Do changes in the values of the independent variables individually or jointly help explain the vastly greater stability of democratic and semidemocratic regimes after 1978? Table 1.8 addresses this possibility. The mean change in the region variable from 4.17 for 1946–77 to 9.20 for 1978–99 (see Table 1.6) made a large difference in the likelihood of a democratic breakdown. If all other variables had remained at the 1946–99 mean while the region variable shifted from 4.17 to 9.20, the predicted probability that a given democracy or semidemocracy would break down in a particular year would have plummeted from 7.0 to 0.4 percent. A more favorable regional political environment is

TABLE 1.8. *Predicted Impact of Selected Variables on the Probability of Regime Breakdown*

Variable	Predicted Breakdown Rate, 1946–77 (%)	Predicted Breakdown Rate, 1978–99 (%)
Per Capita GDP $(t-1)$	1.4	1.5
Growth (10 years)	1.3	1.6
Region	7.0	0.4
Multipartism	1.5	1.4
Semidemocracy	1.6	1.3
All 9 Variables	5.5	0.5
Actual Breakdown Rate	8.3	0.4

Note: Based on Model 7.2. The selected independent variable in a given row is set at its mean for 1946–77 and 1978–99, respectively. All other variables are set at their historical means (1946–99). Values for multipartism and semidemocracy rows are the predicted probabilities of a regime breakdown if all other variables are set at the 1946–99 mean and this particular variable has the actual probability for 1946–77 and 1978–99, respectively.

Source: Based on the Latin American Democracy Dataset (LADD), electronic dataset compiled by Aníbal Pérez-Liñán, Scott Mainwaring, and Daniel Brinks.

TABLE 1.9. *Predictors of Democratic Breakdown, 1946–77*

Model Variables	9.1	9.2
Per capita GDP $(t-1)$	0.283	0.458**
	(0.174)	(0.206)
Labor Force in Industry (%)	−0.083	−0.147***
	(0.055)	(0.043)
Growth $(t-1)$	0.030	−0.078*
	(0.042)	(0.046)
Inflation (ln, $t-1$)	0.402	−0.161
	(0.367)	(0.601)
Growth (last 10 years)	−0.098*	−0.111
	(0.052)	(0.093)
Inflation (ln, last 10 years)	0.269	0.853
	(0.336)	(0.752)
Region	−0.153	−0.068
	(0.279)	(0.409)
Multipartism	0.942**	1.579**
	(0.467)	(0.660)
Semidemocracy	1.922***	2.577***
	(0.491)	(0.616)
IP (Polarization Index)		0.029**
		(0.014)
Constant	−3.360***	−4.080**
	(1.119)	(1.738)
N	234	186
Pseudo-R²	0.1977	0.3077

RELogit coefficients (standard errors adjusted for clustering by country). Pseudo-R^2 corresponds to standard logistic model with equivalent specification.
* Significant at .1 level; ** at .05 level; *** at .01 level.

therefore a key to understanding the sharp post-1978 reduction in the breakdown rate. Changes in the levels of the other independent variables did not have much effect on the predicted probability of a democratic breakdown.

Another possibility is that the impact of some independent variables (such as inflation) on the probability of regime breakdown changed after 1977. In the case of democratic breakdowns, it proved difficult to test statistically for this possibility through interaction terms.[19] As a result, we turned to a more intuitive test.

Table 1.9 presents two additional models for the 1946–77 period based on Models 7.3 and 7.4. The overall results are consistent with the previous findings, although some variables (per capita income and industry in Model 9.1, and medium-term inflation in Model 9.2) lose statistical significance. For

[19] The calculation of interaction terms with all the independent variables in the same model was impossible in Stata. The combination of only one breakdown after 1977 and a large number of independent variables because of the interaction terms prevented tests of statistical significance.

1945–77 semidemocracies and democracies with a higher per capita income (against theoretical expectations), multiparty systems, regimes with greater party system polarization, and (in Model 9.1 but not 9.2) a poor medium-term growth rate were more vulnerable to regime breakdowns. Semidemocracies were more susceptible than democracies to breakdowns.

There was only one breakdown after 1978 (Peru's coup in 1992). No model estimation was feasible for the post–Third Wave part of the sample because of the lack of variance in the dependent variable. Hence it was not possible to test statistically whether the impact of some independent variables had changed over time, in the sense of having one kind of impact in 1945–77 and a different one in 1978–99. Nevertheless, it is obvious that in the Third Wave some independent variables had a changing impact on the likelihood of survival of democratic and semidemocratic regimes. Democracies were more able to withstand polarized party systems after 1978. They were more likely to survive with multipartism. Finally, and above all, they were better able to survive despite a vastly worse economic record after 1978. Many of the conditions for democratic survival were less favorable after 1978 than they were between 1945 and 1977, yet democracies and semidemocracies were far less prone to breakdown. Adverse economic conditions that would have significantly increased the odds of a democratic breakdown before 1978 had little impact on those odds after 1978. Competitive regimes became far less vulnerable under stressful conditions.

In sum, two kinds of change help account for the dramatic decrease in the breakdown rate of competitive regimes after 1978. A more favorable regional political environment helped reduce the breakdown rate after 1978 (a favorable change in the *level* of the region variable). In addition, democracies after 1978 were able to withstand some factors (multipartism, party system polarization, a poor medium-term growth record, and semidemocracy) that made them vulnerable to breakdown between 1945 and 1977 (a favorable change in the *impact* of these variables).

4. REGIONAL POLITICAL EFFECTS

The quantitative analysis showed that a more favorable regional political environment was a major factor in accounting for both the increased transition rate and the sharp drop in the breakdown rate after 1977. Regional political trends and influences have been important in the waves of regime transformations. The regional variable taps the effects of several interrelated changes in the international system; problems of overparametrization and measurement make it impossible to disentangle the effects of these interrelated changes in a dataset with a limited number of regime changes.[20] In this section, we provide a qualitative interpretation of the quantitative finding that a more favorable regional political environment is a key to understanding the increase in the

---

[20] An additional statistical complication is that the Third Wave dummy variable that is needed to test for interactive effects is almost perfectly collinear with important changes in U.S. foreign policy and in the role of the Organization of American States in supporting democracy.

transition rate to democracy and semidemocracy and in the sharp reduction in the breakdown rate of democracies and semidemocracies after 1978. We briefly address what actors and processes create regional political effects.

The International Ideological Context

Domestic political actors do not operate in a vacuum, sealed in by national borders. They act in a world of permeable borders and freely flowing information. Books and journals, television and radio, electronic communication, international conferences, international political organizations such as the Christian Democratic and Socialist Internationals, and international travel and exchanges of ideas and communication by scholars, politicians, policy makers, and activists (Htun 2003; Keck and Sikkink 1998) act as means of disseminating information. Cross-country dissemination of information and norms has become especially intense in recent years with the advent of a much more powerful internationalized media (e.g., CNN) and the internet.

Rather than constituting independent developments in Latin American countries, changing attitudes had powerful demonstration effects across borders – what Starr (1991) calls diffusion effects. Leftist groups in one country witnessed the futility of trying to win power through revolutionary means in neighboring countries. Intellectuals met at international conferences and exchanged ideas. Parties that were members of the Socialist International observed parallel transformations in Western Europe and Latin America.

These channels of communication are particularly significant for actors of proximate ideological persuasion. On the left of the political spectrum, growing acceptance and valuing of democracy in Latin America was fueled by developments in Western Europe in the 1970s and by the withering of socialism in the 1980s. Many Latin American intellectuals and politicians who spearheaded the left's reevaluation of democracy lived in exile in Western or Eastern Europe. In Western Europe, they were influenced by growing criticisms of extant socialist regimes and by progressive challenges from new social movements and green parties to the old authoritarian left. Those on the left who did not go into exile were also influenced by the changing international climate.

In the Third Wave of democratization, with the partial exception of President Reagan's first four years in office, the international ideological context has been relatively favorable to democracy in Latin America. This favorable ideological context does not guarantee that specific countries will become or remain democratic, but it enhances the likelihood of democracy. International factors only exceptionally *determine* regime transitions and processes, but they significantly alter the odds for or against democracy.

International Actors: The Catholic Church

Changes in the Catholic Church also affected the regional political environment. The Church has traditionally been an actor of political import in most Latin American countries, and until the 1960s, it frequently sided with authoritarians.

It was a protagonist in several coups against democratic or semidemocratic governments across the region. The revolutions in Mexico and Cuba were trenchantly anticlerical, and the Church consistently opposed leftist movements and governments. The Church applauded coups in Venezuela in 1948 (Levine 1973), Colombia in 1949, Brazil in 1964, and Argentina in 1976.

Since the 1970s, the Catholic Church has usually supported democratization (Huntington 1991: 74–85). Under the sway of the Second Vatican Council, the Church came to accept and promote democracy in most of the region. In Brazil, the Church spearheaded the opposition to military rule in the 1970s and strongly advocated a return to democracy (Mainwaring 1986). Elsewhere, the Church reached a peaceful *modus vivendi* with democratic governments (Levine 1981), notwithstanding conflict over issues such as abortion. In a few cases, such as Argentina and Guatemala, the Church supported authoritarian rule in the 1970s and early 1980s, but even those churches have not attempted to undermine democracy since its inception. In Chile, El Salvador, Nicaragua, and Peru, the Church criticized authoritarian regimes and promoted transitions to democracy.

The U.S. Government and Governmental Agencies

Democratic transitions and breakdowns can be thought of as "tipping games," in which different actors bet on a regime change, continue to support the existing regime, or remain on the sidelines. External actors such as the United States can affect the likelihood of coups and democratic transitions in a range of ways: (1) moral suasion that changes the attitudes and behavior of domestic actors; (2) symbolic statements that embolden some actors, strengthen their position, and weaken other actors; (3) sanctions against governments; (4) conspiracies against governments; and (5) military actions that overthrow the regime and install a new one. In the first three kinds of influence, external actors shape regime change by influencing domestic actors; in the final one, external actors directly determine regime change. This final possibility has been the rare exception in Latin America, but external actors, especially the U.S. government and since 1990, the Organization of American States (OAS), have frequently shaped the logic, costs, and benefits of domestic actors through the first three kinds of influence. By doing so, the United States and OAS have significantly affected the regional political environment.

During most of the post-1977 period, the United States supported transitions to competitive regimes and opposed breakdowns of such regimes. Its positions have raised the costs of coups to potential coup players. Under such circumstances, some players that would otherwise have probably supported coups have not done so. The threat of sanctions by the United States and the OAS makes the expected benefit–cost ratio of supporting a coup unfavorable.

Historically, the United States several times supported coups against democratic governments (Brazil in 1964, Chile in 1973). Occasionally it was a leading protagonist in coups (Guatemala in 1954), and only rarely did it vigorously promote democracy in Latin America. From the early twentieth century until Jimmy Carter's administration (1977–81), cozying up to friendly dictators was commonplace.

This practice started to change under President Carter, who publicly criticized human rights violations committed by authoritarian governments friendly to the United States (Argentina, Brazil, Chile, and Uruguay). Carter also supported democratic transitions in the Dominican Republic, Ecuador, and Peru. In the Dominican Republic in 1978, his initiative blocked electoral fraud that would have extended authoritarian rule. By promoting an honest vote count, Carter helped pave the road for the first democratic transition of Latin America's Third Wave. His policy started to change the public discourse in the United States regarding foreign policy.

Early indications after President Ronald Reagan's inauguration in 1981 were that the new president would abandon the Carter administration's concern with democracy and human rights. Surprisingly, the Reagan administration's foreign policy efforts began to emphasize democracy during the president's second term (Carothers 1991). The 1982 war in the South Atlantic between Britain and Argentina contributed to the administration's reorientation by unveiling the potential bellicosity and erratic behavior of authoritarian regimes. The administration supported Britain in the conflagration and thereafter never again coddled Argentina's generals.

To bolster the credibility of its much criticized military offensive against the Sandinistas, the administration used prodemocracy rhetoric and ultimately criticized authoritarianism of the right (Arnson 1993; Whitehead 1991). Without a minimal effort to promote democracy elsewhere in Latin America, the crusade against the Sandinistas and support for the regimes in El Salvador and Guatemala would have encountered more congressional and public resistance than it already did. The Reagan administration declared its opposition to military uprisings in Argentina in 1987 and 1988, and it pressured for democratic change in Chile, Paraguay, Panama, and Haiti.

Under the first President Bush (1989–93), the United States generally supported democratic initiatives in Latin America. Supporting democratic governments was made easier by the collapse of the Soviet Union and the Sandinistas' setback at the polls in 1990. Anticommunism receded, and the United States no longer had the communist threat to contend with. The first Bush and Clinton administrations promoted democratization in Haiti, criticized authoritarian involutions in Peru (1992) and Guatemala (1993), and applied pressure against coup mongers in Peru (1989), Venezuela (1992), and Paraguay (1996). The 1989 invasion of Panama ousted dictator Manuel Noriega and led to the installation of a government that had been denied office through electoral fraud. The United States has used diplomatic pressure, public pronouncements, and economic sanctions to bolster democracy and hinder authoritarian regimes (Pastor 1989b). Several U.S. governmental agencies including the Agency for International Development have also attempted to foster democracy in Latin America.

The United States could have done more to bolster democracy in the hemisphere. But the contrast to the pre-1977 pattern of supporting coups and dictators helps account for greater democratic survivability in the Third Wave.

The OAS and Other Multilateral Organizations

In the early 1990s, an important change occurred in international mechanisms for supporting democracy. Previously, in its efforts to support democracy in Latin America, the U.S. government had relied mainly on moral suasion, public support for democracy, and public criticisms of authoritarianism. The efficacy of such measures did not rest exclusively on their capacity to change the thinking of actors in Latin America. U.S. support can embolden the democratic opposition to authoritarian regimes and delegitimize regimes, thus tipping the strategic calculations of critical domestic actors. But the impact of such ideological support for democracy is enhanced if authoritarian incumbents and potential coup players face direct sanctions. The likelihood of direct sanctions arose in 1991–92, when the OAS approved new measures for the multilateral defense of democracy. In 1991 the OAS passed Resolution 1080, which called for a meeting of the foreign ministers of the Western Hemisphere countries within the first few days of a democratic breakdown and legitimated OAS intervention in such cases. Resolution 1080 prompted OAS interventions in Haiti (1991), Peru (1992), Guatemala (1993), and Paraguay (1996). In the aftermath of approving Resolution 1080, in December 1992, the OAS approved the Washington Protocol, which enables the OAS General Assembly to approve suspending the membership of any member country that experiences a coup (Burrell and Shifter 2000; Perina 2000). Resolution 1080 significantly raised the costs of a coup and in several crisis moments altered the calculations and behavior of domestic political actors. In Latin America the threat of international sanctions against coup players was clear when coup mongers in Paraguay (1996) and Guatemala (1993) backed off when confronted with the likelihood of sanctions, and when Fujimori (Peru, 1992) responded to international pressures by restoring elections.

Democratic governments in Latin America have supported efforts to encourage democracy and to impose sanctions against authoritarian regimes. Collectively, non-governmental organizations, multilateral agencies, and the governments of Latin America, Western Europe, and North America have created a norm of disapproval of authoritarianism and support – ideological, if not material – for democracy.

Groups that monitor elections have enhanced the integrity of the electoral process. Such monitoring was important in Chile in the 1988 plebiscite and in Nicaragua in 1990. In both cases, massive foreign intervention promoted citizen expectations of fair elections and encouraged the incumbents to respect unfavorable results at the polls.

Other institutional mechanisms to enforce democratic norms have emerged. In July 1996 the presidents of the Mercosur countries – Brazil, Argentina, Uruguay, Paraguay, Bolivia, and Chile – signed an agreement stating that any member nation would be expelled if democracy broke down. Pressure from neighboring Mercosur nations helped avert a coup in Paraguay in April 1996. In an age of growing international economic integration, authoritarian governments now faced the possibility of economic sanctions such as those that crippled the economies of Panama under Noriega and Haiti after the military deposed Aristide. The United States, UN, and OAS have applied sanctions against patently authoritarian governments.

Never before in the Americas has there existed anything like the near universal ideological elite support for democracy that has been present since President Reagan's second term. Even in this context, democratic breakdowns can occur, as happened in Peru in 1992. But they have been vastly less common. At almost any other time in the history of Latin America before 1978, regimes such as those in Venezuela (2002), Guatemala (1993), Paraguay (1996, 2000), and Ecuador (2000) would probably have suffered breakdowns.

Decreasing Polarization in the Third Wave

The quantitative analysis showed that party system polarization has an important impact on the rate of democratic and semidemocratic breakdowns in Latin America. Party system polarization is related to but not coterminous with other forms of political polarization.

The proximate cause of most breakdowns of democratic and semidemocratic regimes in Latin America has been intense political polarization, and a proximate cause of the greater durability of democracy after 1978 has been diminished political polarization. This effect is suggested by but not fully captured by Coppedge's index of party system of polarization employed earlier. Some forms of polarization take place outside the party system. Moreover, Coppedge's index measures party system polarization at elections and cannot capture short bursts of intense polarization that may trigger a coup a year or more after the election. Finally, although Coppedge's index is very useful, it does not fully capture changes in the meaning of left and right. The chasm that divided the left and right in Latin America during the apex of the Cold War has narrowed as the positions of the left and right have evolved.

Before 1978, in most Latin American countries, democracy allowed for the articulation of interests of political actors with intensely different and seemingly irreconcilable objectives. The Cuban revolution (1959) brought about intensified conflict and inspired young leftists to fight for their dreams of revolutionary socialism. It prompted conservatives and reactionaries to view leftists and reformists with heightened fear and suspicion. The 1960s and 1970s marked the zenith of polarized politics if we assess regionwide tendencies. Democracy could not blossom in this breeding ground of intense polarization. For political actors on both the left and the right, politics often approached the logic of war: The objective was complete victory. This logic made democracy "an impossible game," to use the term that O'Donnell (1973, 1978a) aptly coined to describe Argentine politics from 1955 to 1973 (see also Cavarozzi 1983). But it was not only in Argentina that democracy was an impossible game for protracted periods of time. The same was true of many other countries in the region. High levels of political polarization and intense political conflict in the 1960s and 1970s triggered most democratic breakdowns during this period.

The shift from zero-sum polarized politics to the politics of compromise and moderation occurred at different times in different countries. In Venezuela, following the intense conflict of 1945–48 and the regime breakdown in 1948, political leaders in 1958 began to forge a new democracy based on moderation, with centralization of power in disciplined political parties and state office holders (Levine 1973, 1978). In Colombia, after the violent rampages of the 1948–57 period, political elites forged a stable albeit exclusionary democracy whose pillars remained largely intact until the 1991 constitution (Bejarano and Pizarro, this volume; Hartlyn 1988). But these two countries were outliers.

Polarization began to recede in Argentina, Brazil, Chile, and Uruguay in the late 1970s. In all four countries, the revolutionary left was vanquished by military dictatorships (though somewhat later in Chile). The majority of what remained of the left in Argentina, Brazil, and Uruguay renounced violence and embraced democracy. In Argentina, the intense polarization between Peronists and anti-Peronists that had characterized the 1945–73 period abated greatly (Cavarozzi 1983). Polarization receded in Bolivia in the mid- to late 1980s and in Peru, El Salvador, Guatemala, and Nicaragua in the early 1990s. Diminishing polarization made managing conflict within the bounds of democracy easier.

Attitudes toward Democracy

The effects of polarization on democratic stability and of regional factors on the stability of both authoritarian and competitively elected regimes were indicated by the quantitative analysis. For these two explanatory variables, the qualitative analysis extended the quantitative analysis. Changing attitudes toward democracy also made possible the dramatic post-1978 transformation in Latin America. We do not have a reasonably efficient and valid way to measure attitudes toward democracy for nineteen countries over an extended period of time, so we build this argument exclusively on the basis of qualitative data (see also Diamond 1996; Weffort 1986).

The greatest change in attitudes toward democracy in Latin America came on the left. Never a numerically large force, the revolutionary left nonetheless had a major impact in many Latin American countries in the 1960s and 1970s. It was authoritarian in its practices and in its preferred political system, and it resorted to violence to accomplish its objectives (Gillespie 1982; Ollier 1998). It regarded liberal democracy as a bourgeois formalism, believed that violence was needed to "liberate" the working class, and advocated revolutionary socialism, which is incompatible with democracy.

By the mid-1980s, the revolutionary left had become a nonactor in most countries (Castañeda 1993), though Peru, El Salvador, Guatemala, and Nicaragua were still exceptions. In most countries, it was physically annihilated. It had become obvious that its biggest effect was not to free "the people," but to spur the armed forces toward ruthless repression. In Brazil and the southern cone, most of the revolutionary left reassessed and rejected its earlier political convictions and practices (Ollier 1998). Having experienced life under brutal dictatorships, most survivors concluded that democracy was necessary and desirable. The Soviet Union and China increasingly appeared to the Latin American left as authoritarian models and were rejected. The crisis of real socialism, culminating in the collapse of the Soviet Union, further diminished the appeal of authoritarian leftist ideologies.

By 1990 the left in most of South America had substantially changed its political views, but the Central American left (particularly in Nicaragua, El Salvador, and Guatemala) had not. The withering of the Sandinista regime in Nicaragua and its eventual defeat at the polls in 1990 initiated a process of critical reflection among Central American revolutionaries. The crushing defeat of Sendero Luminoso in Peru and the decision of the revolutionary left to give up arms in El Salvador and Guatemala moved the tide further away from revolution. By the mid-1990s, the revolutionary fervor was even weaker than it had been a decade before, and the civil wars in Central America came to a gradual halt.

Intellectuals have historically had more political influence in Latin America than in the United States, and this remains the case to this day. In the 1960s and 1970s, most politically influential Latin American intellectuals were on the left, hostile to capitalism and ambivalent (or worse) about liberal democracy. Dependency theory was in its heyday. Most intellectuals considered radical social change a more urgent priority than liberal democracy. Many doubted that "bourgeois" democracy was possible under conditions of dependent development.

In the post-1978 period, progressive intellectuals became more convinced of the importance of democracy (Lamounier 1979; Packenham 1986; Weffort 1986). By the late 1980s, dependency theory had lost much of its credibility (Packenham 1992), and the fascination with revolution had subsided. These changes occurred as part of an international trend; intellectuals in Europe, too, increasingly questioned the authoritarian left, renounced Marxism, and embraced liberal democracy.

Change on the left extended to electorally significant parties. Committed to Leninist ideals and rhetorically favorable to a revolutionary uprising in the 1960s and 1970s, the Chilean Socialist Party became a stalwart of liberal democracy in the 1980s (Walker 1990). In 1972 the Central Committee of the Socialist Party criticized Salvador Allende's socialist government for respecting "bourgeois mechanisms that are precisely what impede us from accomplishing the changes that we need" and called for a dictatorship of the proletariat (Walker 1990: 159). By 1982, a mere decade later, the wing of the party that had most vigorously denounced bourgeois institutionality explicitly rejected real socialism, affirming that it had failed to "create mechanisms of democratic governance capable of resolving the conflicts that emerge in a modern society. For this reason, it does not constitute an inspiring model for Chilean socialism" (Walker 1990: 188; see also Roberts 1998). Having previously been

ambivalent about liberal democracy, the Bolivian MNR (National Revolutionary Movement, Movimiento Nacionalista Revolucianario) embraced it in the
1980s. Notorious for its authoritarian past, the Peronist party in Argentina, of
a predominantly center–left orientation until the 1980s, also largely accepted
democracy by the 1980s. Before the 1973 breakdown, the Frente Amplio in
Uruguay was dominated by semiloyal and disloyal elements, in Linz's (1978)
terms. By the early 1990s, most party leaders fully accepted democracy.

Change on the right was equally important. Historically, the right was the
greatest obstacle to democracy in Latin America. In most of Latin America,
traditional elites maintained virtually unfettered power until some time (varying
by country) in the twentieth century (Hagopian 1996a, 1996b), and they refused
to accept democracy when doing so could threaten their core interests. As
the revolutionary left became more significant in the aftermath of the Cuban
revolution, the right became more disposed to undermine democracy (where it
existed) to protect its interests and less willing to contemplate democracy where
it did not. Conservative political elites frequently conspired against democracy
in Brazil between 1946 and 1964 (Benevides 1981) and in Argentina between
1930 and 1966 (Gibson 1996).

As the specter of communism faded, much of the right became willing to
abide by democratic rules of the game, and the other sectors became less prone
to support coups. The left's transformation in a more democratic direction fostered a similar trajectory on the right. One of the most dramatic transformations
occurred with the right wing party in El Salvador, Arena. Known for its close
linkages to death squads and the oligarchy in the early 1980s, by the mid-1990s
Arena had helped engineer the peace treaty that ended El Salvador's civil war
and incorporated the former guerrillas into the political process (Wood 2000b
and her chapter in this volume).

Less can be said about the military's shifting attitudes because little research
has been done on this subject (for an exception, see Fitch 1998). Past research
has suggested that few coups are successful without the support of powerful
civilian allies (Stepan 1971). Therefore, even if the armed forces have not undergone a significant change in values, the changing attitudes of other actors
have prompted different military behavior in the political arena.

The changing attitudes toward democracy in Latin America created a virtuous cycle. Change in one actor fostered change in others. The conversion of
leftist groups to democratic politics, for example, reduced the fears of rightist
actors that democracy could lead to their destruction. Similarly, the growing
willingness of rightist groups and governments to abide by electoral politics
signaled to the left that some positive change – minimally, the end to massive
human rights violations – could occur through democracy.

These changes had profound implications. By the 1990s politics was less
polemical and less threatening. Gone was the sense that politics is an all
important, zero-sum game, a low-intensity warfare. Under these conditions,
sustaining democracy is easier. Actors became willing to accept minor losses
under democracy; earlier, they were not willing to play a game that might

TABLE 1.10. *Changes in Polarization, International Environment, and Attitudes toward Democracy, 1946–1977 versus 1978–1999*

	1945–1977	1978–1999
Political polarization	High in most of the region	Lower, especially in Argentina after 1978, Bolivia after 1985, Brazil after 1989, Chile after late 1970s, El Salvador after 1992, Guatemala after 1995, Peru after 1992, and Uruguay after late 1970s
Catholic Church support for democracy	Inconsistent across countries; supported some coups	Solid by the 1980s
U.S. government support for democracy	Inconsistent; supported some coups	Solid 1977–81 and after mid-1980s
OAS support for democracy	Not an important actor	Solid by 1980s; major actor by 1990s
Leftist attitudes toward democracy	Instrumental	Support (change came late El Salvador, Guatemala, Nicaragua, and Peru)
Rightist attitudes toward democracy	Opposition at moments of intense polarization	Acceptance

entail catastrophic losses. These changing attitudes about democracy and politics have insulated democracy from poor economic and social performance by governments.

This argument about changing attitudes toward democracy is consistent with the quantitative results presented earlier. These changing attitudes are reasonably closely correlated with decreasing party system polarization. Changes in the regional political environment facilitated and also reflected the changes in attitudes of domestic actors toward democracy. We summarize the qualitative arguments of the last three sections in Table 1.10.

5. THE IMPASSE OF LATIN AMERICAN DEMOCRATIZATION: 1992–2003

One theme of this book is that by the end of the twentieth century, the process of democratization had stagnated. Figure 1.1, which provides a highly aggregated picture of trends in democracy, shows that between 1992 and 2003, regime change in a democratic direction stabilized. In keeping with our emphasis on the unprecedented nature of the post-1978 wave of democratization, this stagnation occurred at a level of democracy that Latin America had never experienced before. Further advances were more difficult because most countries were already democratic or semidemocratic.

This highly aggregated picture reflects a few cases of democratic advances, a few of erosion, several countries that had remained stuck with semidemocratic regimes, and two cases (Cuba and Haiti) of persistent authoritarianism. The "impasse" of democratization refers to the combination of several democratic erosions (changes from democracy to semidemocracy), several cases of stagnation of semidemocracy, and the two persistent authoritarian regimes. Jointly, these phenomena allow for considerably more democratization than has been achieved.

Democracy advanced in Mexico, the region's second most populous country (see Magaloni's chapter), but it eroded in Colombia in the early 1990s (Bejarano and Pizarro's chapter) and in Venezuela (Coppedge's chapter) late in the decade. As of early 2005, the region had several robust democracies including Brazil, Chile, Costa Rica, Mexico, Uruguay despite its economic crisis, and even Argentina (as Levitsky skillfully and counterintuitively argues in his chapter) despite its precipitous economic decline of 2001–02.[21] A democratic breakdown in these countries seemed highly improbable. Several other regimes, however, were far more fragile, including those of El Salvador (see Wood's chapter) and Guatemala (Seligson's chapter), as well as Ecuador, Paraguay, and Venezuela (Coppedge's chapter). After nearly fifteen years of unexpected democratic stability (1985–2000), Bolivia's democracy became more fragile in the new millennium, leading up to President Sánchez de Lozada's forced ouster in 2003 (Mayorga's chapter).

Several countries in the region have experienced near-breakdowns since the Peruvian breakdown of 1992. In Venezuela in 1992, a faction of the military led by Colonel Hugo Chávez attempted to overthrow President Carlos Andrés Pérez. At that time, Venezuela had Latin America's second oldest democracy (next to Costa Rica's); once it had served as an exemplar of how to build democracy in a country with an authoritarian past (Levine 1973). In Guatemala in 1993, President Jorge Serrano attempted a palace coup along the lines of what Peruvian President Alberto Fujimori had done the previous year. Thanks to international pressures and domestic mobilization, Serrano was defeated and was forced to resign. In Paraguay factional disputes within the ruling Colorado Party have created several episodes of political instability in recent years. In 1996 General Lino Oviedo attempted a coup, which was defeated in good measure because of international pressure (Mora 2000). The assassination of Paraguayan Vice-President Luis M. Argaña in 1999 triggered several days of political turmoil that led to the collapse of the Raúl Cubas Grau administration (Abente Brun 1999). In May 2000 a new military coup attempt took place, but it was rapidly defeated.

---

[21] The Brazilian and Mexican regimes and to a lesser extent the Argentine regime are less than fully democratic at the subnational level in some regions of the country. For general discussions of this problem, see O'Donnell (1993b); Samuels and Snyder (2001); Snyder (2000).

In Ecuador the Congress deposed President Abdalá Bucaram in 1997, claiming that he was mentally impaired – a procedure of dubious constitutionality. Three years later, popular mobilization and a military coup led to the ouster of President Jamil Mahuad. Much of Ecuador's political elite supported the coup; some prominent political leaders had even called for it, making manifest their tenuous commitment to democracy. The military almost immediately turned power over to the vice president, but widespread public support for the coup underscored the growing public willingness to tolerate nondemocratic processes. In December 2001 an armed group attempted without success to take over the presidential palace in Haiti. A few days later, mass protests in Argentina forced the resignation of President Fernando de la Rúa. In the context of high levels of unemployment and an unpopular bank account freeze, food riots and middle-class protests triggered an institutional debacle that led to the congressional appointment of two caretaker presidents within just ten days. Fortunately, the military publicly declared that it would not intervene. In contrast, in April 2002 a military coup toppled Venezuela's President Hugo Chávez, though he returned to power two days later when the coup collapsed.

In some countries, impeachments (Brazil 1992, Venezuela 1993) and pseudo-constitutional forms of deposing presidents (Ecuador 1997) have become substitutes for military coups (Pérez-Liñán 2003). In the new inter-American system, the costs of overtly authoritarian rule have been prohibitively high. In contrast, the costs of alternative, even nondemocratic means of deposing presidents are low, provided that the leaders of the effort to depose the president turn over power to someone else. In the last decade Latin America has witnessed a new pattern of political instability, characterized by (1) the fragility (and in some cases the collapse) of many elected governments; (2) the unwillingness or inability of military officers to take over even when they are able to depose a president; (3) popular protest as a key driving force behind the demise of elected presidents; and (4) the growing role of legislatures as the institutional arena to provide a short-term resolution for political crises.

In the late 1990s and first years of the new millennium, several individuals with dubious attitudes toward democracy made successful or nearly successful runs at the presidency. In 1998 Hugo Chávez, who led the 1992 coup attempt, was elected president of Venezuela. Michael Coppedge's chapter underscores the erosion of democratic practice during Chávez's presidency. In 2002 Lucio Gutiérrez, the leader of the military coup that deposed President Mahuad two years earlier, won the presidency in Ecuador. Both Chávez and Gutiérrez ran as antiparty politicians. The rise of antiparty politicians – especially former coup leaders – often spells troubles for democracy; whatever the flaws of particular parties and the shortcomings of particular party systems, parties remain an indispensable mechanism of representation in democratic politics. Earlier in 2002, another antiparty candidate with questionable attitudes toward democracy, Evo Morales, made it to the presidential runoff in Bolivia. In 2001 a populist with no ties to established parties, Alejandro Toledo, won the presidency in Peru, succeeding another populist with no ties to established parties (Fujimori, 1990–2000) after a one-year interregnum (2000–01).

Notwithstanding some potential for breakdowns in a few countries, the main problem confronting democracy in most countries is not sheer durability but rather a panoply of problems such as poor economic and social performance, weak states, high crime rates, and citizen disgruntlement. Remarkably, competitively elected regimes have survived in the face of all this.

Public opinion surveys register disaffection with democracy and in most countries a moderate citizen commitment to it. Table 1.11 shows the results of Latinobarómetro surveys about citizen support for democracy in the region in 1996, 2000, 2001, 2002, and 2003. Between 1996 and 2003, in fourteen of seventeen countries there was a decrease in the share of citizens who agreed that "Democracy is always preferable to any other kind of government." The question also provided two other options: "In some circumstances, an authoritarian government can be preferable to a democracy," and "For someone like me, it does not matter whether the regime is democratic or not." In only two countries, Costa Rica and Uruguay, was the percentage of those who said democracy is always the best political regime above 60 percent in all five surveys. In several countries, this percentage is alarmingly low. Latin American citizens gave considerable latitude to democratic and semidemocratic governments for poor

TABLE 1.11. *Support for Democracy, 1996–2003*

Country	1996	2000	2001	2002	2003	Change 1996–2003
Uruguay	80	84	79	78	78	−2
Costa Rica	80	83	71	77	77	−3
Argentina	71	71	58	65	68	−3
Venezuela	62	61	57	75	67	5
Honduras	42	64	57	57	55	13
Mexico	53	45	46	63	53	0
Peru	63	64	62	57	52	−11
Nicaragua	59	64	43	63	51	−8
Panama	75	62	34	55	51	−24
Chile	54	57	45	50	50	−4
Bolivia	64	62	54	56	50	−14
Ecuador	52	54	40	49	46	−6
Colombia	60	50	36	39	46	−14
El Salvador	56	63	25	40	45	−11
Paraguay	59	48	35	45	40	−19
Brazil	50	39	30	37	35	−15
Guatemala	51	45	33	45	33	−18

Cells show percentage of respondents who agreed that "Democracy is preferable to any other kind of government."
Source: The Economist (2003), based on Latinobarómetro surveys.

performance in the short and middle term, but it seems that in the late 1990s they valued concrete results at the expense of democracy.[22]

In earlier sections, we argued that decreasing polarization, a deeper commitment to democracy among key actors, and a favorable international political context have been supportive of democracy in Latin America in the post-1978 period. Since the late 1990s, there have been hints of change in the opposite direction in these three trends in a few countries. Venezuelan politics has become dramatically polarized, not so much along the traditional left–right axis (although conflict along this axis is significant) as between pro- and anti-Chávez supporters. Polarization escalated in Colombia as drug lords, guerrillas, the paramilitary, and the armed forces struggled to control the country's territory. In Bolivia, the outbreak of social mobilization in 2000, the nearly successful presidential candidacy of Evo Morales in 2002, and renewed anti-system mobilization in 2003 that led to Sánchez de Lozada's forced resignation indicated rising polarization (see Mayorga's chapter). Several factors suggest a minor dip in the commitment to democracy: the successful presidential bids of ex-*golpistas* Hugo Chávez in Venezuela and Lucio Gutiérrez in Ecuador; the initial popularity of Fujimori's coup in 1992 and his ability to win presidential elections in 1995 and 2000 despite leading a coup; the willingness of political leaders to use nondemocratic means to oust presidents in Ecuador in 2000 and Venezuela in 2002; the already cited Latinobarómetro data on citizen attitudes toward democracy; and the political turmoil that has roiled Paraguay. The U.S. government had an equivocal attitude toward the April 2002 coup against Chávez, initially appearing to support the coup. In the aftermath of September 11, the George W. Bush administration has focused more on terrorism and less on democracy building than any U.S. administration since Nixon and Ford (1969–77).

The Impasse of Democratization: Three Contributing Factors

In this section, we briefly discuss three factors that have contributed to the stagnation of democratization in Latin America. The first and third are related to both the cases of stagnation at semidemocratic regimes (Guatemala, Honduras, Nicaragua, Paraguay) and to the cases of erosion from democracy to semidemocracy. The second focuses on the failure of several semidemocracies to become full democracies.

First, there is an asymmetry in the effects of the OAS and other international actors such as Mercosur. The OAS and Mercosur have greatly increased the price of overtly authoritarian regimes, but they are powerless to prod semidemocratic regimes into further democratization. Even in the face of openly

---

[22] Surprisingly, public opinion about regime preference is not a good measure of the solidity of democracy in Latin America. Support for democracy was low in some democracies (Chile and Brazil) that were quite robust. Support for democracy was high in some countries (Venezuela) where the regime was tottering.

authoritarian regimes, the OAS faces a delicate balance: At what point is it going too far in intervening in the internal affairs of another country? When a regime sponsors reasonably free and fair elections but falls short of other criteria of democracy, this dilemma has been insurmountable for the OAS. The OAS has also been powerless against erosions of democratic regimes. In a similar vein, multilateral actors have had almost no capacity to nudge semidemocracies into becoming more democratic. They are often key in encouraging transitions from authoritarianism to semidemocracy or democracy and in discouraging democratic breakdowns, but developing a more robust democracy hinges overwhelmingly on domestic politics.

Second, the difficulties of democratic deepening have been greater in the poorer countries of the region. It is especially among these countries that semidemocratic governments have taken root in the post-1978 period. While 56 percent of the cases of democracy corresponded to regime-years above the average per capita GDP in this period ($2,480), only 17 percent of the cases of semidemocracy fell in this group. Between 1978 and 1999, the average per capita income (one-year lag) for democracies was $3,033, as opposed to $1,669 for semidemocracies. Notwithstanding the exceptions of Venezuela and Colombia, the wealthier countries have been more able to sustain fuller democracies.[23] A low level of development has not impeded transitions to competitive regimes or induced more democratic breakdowns, but it has been strongly associated with semidemocracy as opposed to fuller democracy. In the poor countries, nondemocratic traditional elites are more powerful than in the middle-income countries. In this respect, poor economic growth has limited structural transformations that would have been auspicious for democracy.

A third factor that has contributed to the impasse of democratization is that, since the early 1980s, most democratic and semidemocratic governments have governed poorly. Notwithstanding a few success stories, the mean performance in such domains as economic growth, job generation, income inequalities, poverty reduction, corruption, and citizen security has been deficient. Table 1.12 provides information on the performance in economic growth (1992–2001), inflation (1997–2001), and unemployment (2001), as well as Transparency International's subjective evaluations of corruption, which has also been at the forefront of voters' concerns. Economic growth was better in the 1990s than during the dismal 1980s, but the region's aggregate performance was still worse than analysts hoped for and far worse than it was between 1945 and 1980. From 1998 through 2002, taking the region as a whole, per capita income was stagnant. The Dominican Republic and Chile had strong growth performances during the decade from 1993 to 2002, but only one other country, Peru, came close to them. Per capita income declined in five countries (Argentina,

---

[23] This observation is consistent with the expectations of modernization theory, which posited that wealthy countries were more likely to be democratic. Because Latin America has frequently confounded this expectation (Landman 1999; Mainwaring and Pérez-Liñán 2003; O'Donnell 1973), this development is notable.

TABLE 1.12. *Economic Performance Indicators and Transparency International Rating of Corruption, 1993–2002*

	Percentage Change in Per Capita Income, 1993–2002	Mean Inflation, 1998–2002 (%)	Urban Unemployment, 2002/03 (%)	TI Corruption Perceptions Index, 2002
Argentina	−7	8	16	2.8
Bolivia	11	3	9	2.2
Brazil	15	7	12	4.0
Chile	36	3	9	7.5
Colombia	5	10	18	3.6
Costa Rica	18	11	7	4.5
Dominican Republic	45	7	16	3.5
Ecuador	2	39	10	2.2
El Salvador	18	2	6	3.4
Guatemala	11	6	4	2.5
Haiti	−14	12	–	2.2
Honduras	1	11	6	2.7
Mexico	11	10	3	3.6
Nicaragua	13	9	12	2.5
Panama	10	1	16	3.0
Paraguay	−12	10	15	1.7
Peru	30	3	10	4.0
Uruguay	−6	9	18	5.1
Venezuela	−18	21	20	2.5

Source for economic data: ECLAC (2002, 2003). All 2002 and 2003 (unemployment) figures are preliminary. Figures for urban unemployment employ different methodologies in different countries. Figures for urban employment for Argentina, Brazil, Chile, Colombia, Ecuador, Mexico, Peru, Uruguay, and Venezuela are for 2003. See ECLAC (2001) for details.

The Transparency International corruption score is a subjective ranking that ranges from 1 (most corrupt) to 10 (least corrupt). Source: Transparency International (2003).

Haiti, Paraguay, Uruguay, and Venezuela) during this period. As of 2003, unemployment was high in virtually the entire region. Employment generation is important for alleviating poverty and income inequality, so the dismal mean performance in creating new jobs has taken a heavy social toll.

The performance deficiencies extend beyond the economy and perceptions of corruption. Most Latin American governments have done a poor job of addressing crime and citizen security. El Salvador, Guatemala, and Colombia have among the highest murder rates in the world today, and crime is a serious problem in virtually every major Latin American city. In most countries, state performance in health, education, and infrastructure has been deficient.

The generally mediocre regime performances have had deleterious effects on democracy. The regimes with the worst performance have been weaker regimes, and they have been more vulnerable to coup attempts. A coup attempt is a simple yet powerful indicator of regime vulnerability. Since 1998 there have been coup attempts in Ecuador, Haiti, Paraguay, and Venezuela among the nineteen countries covered in this chapter. The mean per capita growth performance of these four countries over the 1993–2002 decade was −11%. In 2002, the mean Transparency Index for these four countries was a dismal 2.15, compared to a poor but markedly better mean index of 3.7 for the other fifteen countries.

Poor regime performance has also bred citizen disaffection and paved the way to populist politicians with dubious democratic credentials. In contexts of considerable poverty and sharper inequalities than are found in any other region of the world, citizens became frustrated with democratic and semidemocratic regimes that failed to deliver.

Before the 1990s most analysts expected that democracy's fate in Latin America would hinge on its performance – especially its economic performance. This expectation has not been borne out in terms of regime durability, but it has affected the solidity of competitively elected regimes. Some Latin American democracies of the post-1978 period have been among the worst democracies in world history in economic performance, yet they have endured. If we restrict the analysis to regime survival, the Latin American experience since 1978 strongly supports the views of Linz and Stepan (1989: 42–48), who argued that democracy can be relatively impervious to performance failures. Yet the cases of Ecuador, Haiti, Paraguay, Peru from 1980 to 1992, and Venezuela suggest, not surprisingly, that bad performance over an extended period of time makes competitively elected regimes more vulnerable. These regimes with particularly bad performances have not broken down, partly because international sanctions have made overt breakdowns costly, but the quality of democracy has suffered.

To provide a systematic test of this idea, we looked at four dichotomous indicators of democratic erosion in Latin America between 1980 and 2001. First, we created a dichotomous variable to capture "democratic erosions" when, according to our coding of political regimes, democracies turned into semidemocracies (Model 13.1). Only seven such erosions affected the 204 democratic regime-years between 1980 and 2001. Second, we used a dummy to document the occurrence of military rebellions against democratic or semidemocratic governments. Thirteen military rebellions threatened a total of 312 democratic or semidemocratic country-years during this period. Although these rebellions were generally unsuccessful, they typically signaled an underlying weakness of competitive regimes (Model 13.2). Third, based on a systematic coding of the newsletter *Latin American Weekly Report* (all issues between 1980 and 2001), we documented all instances in which mass demonstrations called for the resignation of the president (Model 13.3). Of the 312 regime-years of democracy or semidemocracy, 22 presented mass protests against the elected president. The fourth dichotomous variable captured the presence of "presidential crises," instances in which an elected president threatened to close an elected congress or the legislators attempted to remove the president from office (Model 13.4).

TABLE 1.13. *Predictors of Democratic Erosion, 1980–2001*

Model Variable	13.1 Regime Erosion	13.2 Military Rebellions	13.3 Mass Protests	13.4 Presidential Crisis
Per Capita GDP $(t-1)$	0.180	0.188	−0.055	−0.313
	(0.660)	(0.251)	(0.186)	(0.195)
Growth $(t-1)$	−0.253	0.033	−0.076	−0.034
	(0.434)	(0.071)	(0.113)	(0.070)
Inflation (ln, $t-1$)	−1.785	0.263	0.181	0.148
	(2.215)	(0.275)	(0.335)	(0.174)
Growth (last 10 years)	−0.260	−0.141**	−0.106	−0.233*
	(0.753)	(0.057)	(0.158)	(0.133)
Inflation (ln, last 10 years)	1.389	−0.170	−0.355	−0.315
	(1.498)	(0.263)	(0.423)	(0.216)
Multipartism	−1.182	−0.329	−0.053	0.797
	(3.000)	(0.852)	(0.463)	(0.563)
Scandals (last 5 years)	−1.383	0.010	0.176***	0.196*
	(4.065)	(0.078)	(0.060)	(0.108)
Constant	0.691	−3.502***	−2.293***	−2.342***
	(2.414)	(0.998)	(0.736)	(0.869)
N	204	311	311	311
Pseudo-R^2	.665****	.044	.090	.150

RELogit coefficients (standard errors adjusted for clustering by country). Pseudo-R^2 corresponds to standard logistic model with equivalent specification.

* Significant at .1 level; ** at .05 level; *** at .01 level; **** Coefficients for Growth (10 years), Inflation (10 years), Multipartism, and Scandals are significant at the .1 level in the standard logit model.

Source: Based on the Latin American Democracy Dataset (LADD), *World Development Indicators* (2003), and *Latin American Weekly Report* (1980–2001).

According to *The Latin American Weekly Report*, 20 presidential crises occurred during the 312 regime-years under study.

The results of the four RELogits are presented in Table 1.13. The independent variables reflect the level of development, growth, and inflation, as well as the presence of a multiparty system. An additional variable captured the number of scandals of corruption or abuse of power involving the elected governments over a period of five years (or since the installation of the competitive regime) as reported by *The Latin American Weekly Report*. In spite of the small number of events under observation, the evidence suggests that poor medium-term growth and poor government performance reflected in media scandals may significantly hurt democratic solidity over time.[24]

---

[24] Unfortunately, systematic data on unemployment were not available for most countries until the 1990s. When we ran the models with the available information on unemployment (from World Development Indicators), this variable was a significant predictor of mass protests calling for the president's ouster.

In the post-1978 period, there has been an asymmetry in the causal impact of three variables on regime solidity as opposed to regime durability in Latin America. The structural and regime performance variables were not important for understanding regime transitions or breakdowns, but they are key for understanding regime quality (democracy versus semidemocracy) and solidity after 1978. This is the mirror image of the international political environment and U.S. foreign policy, which were important for understanding the emergence and durability of competitive regimes, but which have little or no impact in preventing democratic erosions, in enhancing the character of low quality, competitively elected regimes, or in distinguishing between democratic and semidemocratic regimes.

As Mainwaring and Hagopian argue in the introduction, both structural and regime performance variables and political variables (U.S. policy, diffusion, multipartism, polarization) are important in explaining different kinds of regime outcomes. The former help identify vulnerable regimes and low quality (semidemocratic) competitive regimes; the latter help explain transitions and breakdowns. As noted earlier, there is an underlying reason for this asymmetry: International actors can impose costly sanctions on patently authoritarian regimes, thus allowing vulnerable competitive regimes to survive, but they cannot enhance the quality or performance of such regimes.

6. CONCLUSIONS

What have we learned about the post-1978 wave of democratization in Latin America on the basis of this chapter? First, this wave of democratization is by far the longest lasting and the broadest that Latin America has ever experienced. A region that had previously usually been dominated by openly authoritarian regimes in most countries was transformed into one where openly authoritarian regimes were the rare exception. Nobody expected such a transformation (Domínguez 1998: 1–12; Mainwaring 1999c). Indeed, even by the mid-1980s, when the stunning period of democratization from 1978–92 was half over temporally and had already made most of its advances in terms of number of countries, many analysts still emphasized the difficulties of achieving and sustaining democracy.

A second important theme in this chapter is that this burst of democratization defied many expectations in the broader literature. Previous large-N studies (e.g., Przeworski et al. 2000) argued that democratic regimes are more likely to survive at higher levels of development. In Latin America, in contrast, for 1946–77, democratic and semidemocratic regimes were slightly more vulnerable to breakdown at a higher level of development. Democracy has endured in Latin America at fairly low levels of development, especially but not only in the post-1978 period. Countries with low GDPs such as Bolivia, Ecuador, and El Salvador have remained semidemocratic or democratic in the post-1978 period, during which there has been only one clear regime breakdown (Peru in 1992). Moreover, some moderately poor countries (the Dominican Republic in 1978,

Ecuador in 1979, and Peru in 1980) initiated the post-1978 democratization while most of the region's wealthier countries (e.g., Argentina, Brazil, Chile, and Mexico) were mired in authoritarian rule.

In a similar vein, some literature indicated that democratic and authoritarian regimes are more likely to survive if their economic performance is better. In Latin America, inflation and growth has had little or no impact on the survival of democratic and semidemocratic regimes or of authoritarian ones. Democracy has survived with a much greater likelihood since 1978 compared to 1945–77, even though median regime economic performance fell from solid in the earlier period to poor.

When patterns in a major region of the world fly in the face of wisdom that has been sustained by careful social science research (e.g., Przeworski et al. 2000), observers must take stock of this fact. Latin American exceptionalism suggests the need to reexamine some of the conventional wisdom. Many scholars have argued that higher levels of development were causally associated with a greater likelihood of democracy (Coppedge 1997; Diamond 1992; Lipset 1959; Przeworski et al. 2000). Most implied that this finding was generalizable across time and regions. The evidence here shows that this seemingly robust finding, while not precisely regionally specific, nevertheless does not hold for an intra-Latin American analysis for the lengthy period under examination here.

Restated in a different way, Latin America has important regional and temporal specificities. While the search for generalizable findings in the social sciences is laudable – indeed essential – it should not blind us to regional and temporal specificities (Bunce 2000). Modernization theory has considerable deductive power, and its results have held up across many different kinds of empirical tests. Yet it does not hold for Latin America during this lengthy time period.

Third, structural variables such as per capita income and the share of the labor force in manufacturing and regime performance variables are not important factors in explaining the increase in the durability of competitive regimes or the increased vulnerability of authoritarian regimes after 1978. In contrast, political variables have been powerful contributing factors to the Third Wave of democratization.

In Latin America, regime survival has depended far more on political factors than on economic performance and the level of development. Decreased polarization, a greater appreciation of democracy, and a changed international environment including tough sanctions against openly authoritarian regimes contributed significantly to the sea change in Latin American politics. After 1978 democracy became more sustainable because the stakes were perceived as being lower, and the actors were more tolerant of conflict given these lower stakes. Open authoritarianism became less viable because of international pressures. Throughout Latin America, the Cold War had a pernicious impact on prospects for democracy. It fueled polarization on the left and right, elevated the stakes of politics, and made the United States suspicious of reformist and leftist democratic governments and willing to support authoritarian rightist governments. In Brazil and the southern cone, the Cold War ended in the late 1970s, as the left was vanquished and relinquished the former ideal of revolutionary socialism.

Fourth, most quantitative approaches to understanding democracy – and some qualitative ones as well – have assumed temporal causal homogeneity, that is, that independent variables have a similar effect at all moments in time. Some attention to causal temporal heterogeneity is wise. In Latin America several independent variables had different effects before and after 1978, especially on regime breakdowns. Democratic and semidemocratic regimes were much more able to survive in the face of poor regime performance after 1978 than in the earlier period. This finding supports the view (Ragin 1987) that sometimes important causal processes in the social sciences are combinatorial rather than linear and additive (i.e., specific and historically contingent combinations produce an outcome, and absent some of these conditions, the outcome will not obtain, even if other important causal factors are present).

Fifth, our analysis underscores the importance of regional political effects and trends. It is impossible to understand the post-1978 transformation of Latin American politics exclusively in terms of the cumulative effect of isolated political processes in individual countries. What happens in one country affects others. Moreover, developments among transnational and internationalized actors that affect and/or act in many countries (the United States, the OAS, international movements and organizations, the media) affect political regimes in multiple countries. Of course, it is also impossible to understand this transformation and other waves of regime changes in Latin America mainly as a result of regional effects; country-specific processes are very important.

The importance of regional political trends and influences has been neglected in political science (for exceptions, see Bunce 2000; Gleditsch 2002; Meseguer 2002). Regions of the world are contiguous countries that experience some common political trends and mutual influences that explain those common trends. Although our analysis underscores the importance of regional trends and influences, we reject regional analyses predicated on gross generalizations for the entire region.[25] Our analysis, which assigns a different value for all independent variables (except U.S. foreign policy) for each country in a given year, takes into account each country's specificities while also considering regional trends and influences. We believe that this is the way that regions of the world should be studied. This region has important common trends and influences, but it also has huge cross-country differences. By treating each country as different while simultaneously analyzing regional influences, we have taken into account both the diversity and the common effects within Latin America. In a similar vein, through a combination of regional overviews and single-country chapters, this volume as a whole combines analysis of the broader pattern with attention to country specificities.

---

[25] These gross generalizations about Latin America as a whole are common in works that emphasize Iberian political culture.

Finally, after stunning and unprecedented progress, this wave of democratization ground to a halt in the 1990s. Because of the favorable international environment for democracy, among other factors, there has been only one democratic breakdown in the period since 1992 – Peru. But democracy has eroded in several countries including Venezuela and Colombia; unconstitutional means of deposing presidents (but not through traditional coups leading to military regimes) have become more common; and more citizens now than in 1996 question that democracy is always the best form of political regime. As the chapters that follow argue, democratic governments face daunting problems in most of the region. Nevertheless, it is remarkable how resilient competitive regimes have been in the face of these problems and poor regime performance.

PART I

THREE DEMOCRATIC GIANTS WITH AUTHORITARIAN PASTS

Argentina, Brazil, and Mexico

2

Argentina

Democratic Survival amidst Economic Failure

Steven Levitsky

Latin American regimes followed diverging paths during the Third Wave of democratization. Although a few democracies consolidated (Chile, Uruguay), many others (Dominican Republic, Ecuador, Guatemala, Peru, Venezuela) suffered repeated and often severe institutional crises. Most accounts place Argentina's post-1983 democracy in this latter, "crisis-ridden" category. During the 1980s, the country suffered three military rebellions, severe distributive conflict, and an eventual descent into hyperinflation. Although the economy stabilized during the 1990s, the government of Carlos Menem concentrated and abused power to such a degree that Argentina was viewed as a leading case of what Guillermo O'Donnell (1994) called "delegative democracy." Finally, the political–economic crisis of 2001–02, during which massive protests led to the resignation of two presidents within two weeks, again brought Argentina's democratic institutions to the brink of collapse.

Yet Argentine democracy differed in important ways from other crisis-ridden regimes in Latin America. First, Argentina was one of only a handful of Latin American countries that remained fully democratic during the 1990s.[1] The fairness of elections was unquestioned, basic civil liberties were broadly protected, and unlike many other countries in the region (including Chile), the military played virtually no role in politics. Second, the country's core democratic institutions proved remarkably robust. Argentine democracy survived a series of extraordinary tests, including the 1989–90 hyperinflationary crisis, the Menem government's radical economic reforms, and, most recently, the most severe depression in the country's history. Few Latin American democracies have survived such economic shocks.

---

[1] According to Mainwaring et al. (2001: 49), 8 of 19 Latin American countries remained fully democratic throughout the 1990s: Argentina, Bolivia, Brazil, Chile, Costa Rica, Ecuador, Uruguay, and Venezuela. Of these, Chile was arguably less than fully democratic in the early 1990s, and both Ecuador and Venezuela suffered serious democratic crises at the end of the decade.

This chapter seeks to explain the surprising resilience of Argentina's post-1983 democracy, as well as its persistent difficulties. It argues that democratic stability was partly a product of a broad societal consensus against military rule, but that it was also critically reinforced by relatively strong political parties and a robust civil society. Party strength – particularly that of the (Peronist) Justicialist Party (PJ; Partido Justicialista) – ensured relatively smooth executive-legislative relations, limited the space for antisystem outsider appeals, and facilitated the (democratic) implementation of far-reaching economic reforms. The country's powerful media and substantial infrastructure of civic organizations helped to ensure that state abuses would be routinely exposed and denounced, which raised the political cost of those abuses. At the same time, however, Argentine democracy suffered from persistent and widespread institutional weakness. For much of the twentieth century, the rules and procedures governing the country's political and economic life were weakly institutionalized (Spiller and Tommasi 2000). In the absence of stable rules of the game, politics was characterized by high uncertainty, short time horizons, and low levels of trust and cooperation. The result was frequent cycles of praetorian conflict, economic failure, and regime breakdown. Although democracy was relatively well established after 1983, the rules governing executive–legislative relations, the judiciary, and other aspects of democratic politics remained fluid. Consequently, even though the regime survived, it suffered a series of debilitating institutional crises that eroded its quality and eventually its stability.

THE CENTRALITY OF INSTITUTIONAL AND ORGANIZATIONAL STRENGTH

Efforts to explain variation in the stability and performance of contemporary Latin American democracies have had mixed results, at best. The relative success of democracy in countries like Bolivia and El Salvador points to the limits of structural approaches that focus on variables such as class structure, political culture, or level of economic development. Yet the contingency or leadership-centered approaches that dominated the earlier literature on regime change (Di Palma 1990; Linz and Stepan 1978; O'Donnell and Schmitter 1986) also lack explanatory power. In many countries, including Argentina and Brazil, democracy survived despite ineffective, irresponsible, and at times abusive leadership.[2] Given the limitations of both structural and agency-oriented explanations, many scholars have turned to a meso-level of analysis, highlighting the centrality of institutional and organizational structures. Although meso-level variables cannot explain either long-term patterns of regime change or the specific "when" and "how" of regime change in particular cases, they are useful in

---

[2] Although these outcomes may be attributed in part to the highly favorable post–Cold War international environment, continued variation in Latin American regime trajectories – fewer than half of the countries in Latin America remained fully democratic throughout the 1990s (Mainwaring et al. 2001: 49) – suggests that domestic factors continued to play a central role.

explaining variation across cases that are embedded in a common international historical–structural context (Mahoney and Snyder 1999).

Meso-level analyses of Latin American regimes during the 1990s tended to focus on issues of institutional design (Carey and Shugart 1998b; Crisp 2000; Jones 1995; Linz and Valenzuela 1994; Mainwaring and Shugart 1997; Shugart and Carey 1992), paying less attention to questions of institutional *strength*.[3] Yet the institutionalization of political rules, in the sense that they are widely known, accepted, practiced, and even "taken for granted," is at least as important to regime stability as their design. Strong institutions reduce uncertainty, facilitate cooperation, and lengthen actors' time horizons (O'Donnell 1994). Where institutions are weak, politics becomes a Hobbesian world of uncertainty, short time horizons, and low levels of mutual trust and cooperation. There is "a sense that 'everything is possible'" (Chalmers 1977: 26), and social and political actors routinely pursue objectives through extrainstitutional means. Such praetorian conflict may seriously threaten democratic regimes (Huntington 1968: 196; O'Donnell 1994).

Another crucial institutional dimension is that of the strength of political organizations, particularly parties and civic organizations. Strong parties and civil societies are critical to democratic stability. Parties structure voters' electoral choices, organize the legislative process, and provide governments with stable linkages to society. When they fail and party systems fragment or decompose, democratic governance becomes difficult and democratic regimes often become vulnerable. Party system decomposition may weaken democracies in two ways. First, it undermines governability. Inchoate or fragmented party systems have been associated with legislative gridlock, executive–legislative conflict, policy ineffectiveness, and failed economic reform (Mainwaring 1999b; Mainwaring and Scully 1995). In the 1990s, these problems generated severe governability crises in Brazil, Ecuador, Guatemala, Nicaragua, and Peru. Second, party system decomposition may give rise to outsider or "neopopulist" politicians with weak commitments to democratic institutions (Roberts 1995; Weyland 1999). In Peru and Venezuela, the collapse of established parties paved the way for the rise of Alberto Fujimori and Hugo Chavez, both of whom appealed to unattached voters and ultimately mobilized them on behalf of authoritarian projects.

The relationship between civil society and democracy has been theorized in different ways.[4] One approach emphasizes the role of civil society in transforming political attitudes or values (Putnam 1993; Diamond 1999). According to this approach, participation in civic organizations fosters trust and social capital, teaches "skills of democratic citizenship," and helps to inculcate "deeper values of democratic culture, such as tolerance, moderation, a willingness to

---

[3] Exceptions include Mainwaring and Scully (1995), Mainwaring (1999b), and O'Donnell (1994).

[4] Following Linz and Stepan, civil society may be defined as the "arena of the polity where self-organizing groups, movements, and individuals, relatively autonomously from the state, attempt to articulate values, create associations and solidarities, and advance their interests" (1996: 7).

compromise, and a respect for opposing viewpoints" (Diamond 1999: 242). A second approach focuses on civil society as a "counterweight to state power" (Diamond 1999: 239–42; Rueschemeyer et al. 1992: 6). According to this approach, civil society plays a critical checking and balancing function, providing society with the financial, organizational, and human resources to defend itself against authoritarian encroachments. The present chapter employs this latter approach. To serve as a buffer against authoritarianism, civil society must be democratic. Civic organizations may be democratic in two senses. They may be *internally* democratic, and thus serve as Tocquevillean "free schools for democracy" (Diamond 1999: 228), or they may simply be committed to achieving or defending a democratic regime, without necessarily being internally democratic.[5] Given this chapter's focus on civil society as a counterweight to state power, it is in this latter sense that democracy matters most.

THE ROOTS OF REGIME INSTABILITY IN PRE-1983 ARGENTINA

For much of the twentieth century, Argentina was one of the world's leading democratic underachievers. The country possessed many of the structural conditions that are said to favor democracy, including high levels of wealth and education, a large middle class, and the absence of labor-repressive agriculture. It also possessed a strong civil society and, after 1945, the foundation for a stable party system. Nevertheless, civilian regimes repeatedly broke down between 1930 and 1976. Beginning with the second government of Hipólito Yrigoyen (1928–30), every government that came to power through elections – including those of Juan Perón (1946–55), Arturo Frondizi (1958–62), Arturo Illia (1963–66), and Juan and María Estela (Isabel) Martínez de Perón (1973–76) – ended in a military coup. In 1976, Argentina was the wealthiest country in history to suffer a democratic breakdown (Przeworski and Limongi 1997: 170).

Whereas earlier explanations of democratic failure in Argentina focused largely on economic causes, primarily those related to the country's pattern of development (Corradi 1985; O'Donnell 1973, 1978b; Waisman 1987), recent studies have highlighted the centrality of institutional factors, particularly the party system (Cavarozzi 1986; Collier and Collier 1991; Gibson 1996; McGuire 1997). For much of the twentieth century, Argentine parties failed to integrate powerful socioeconomic actors into the electoral arena effectively. First, as scholars such as Gibson (1996) and Di Tella (1968) have argued, the system lacked a strong conservative party. The absence of a substantial peasantry (which provided the bases for conservative parties in countries like Brazil, Chile, and Colombia), together with deep regional divisions among conservative elites, led to the demise of the Argentine right soon after the establishment of universal male suffrage in 1912. Unable to defend their interests in the electoral arena, economic elites never developed a stake in electoral politics. Consequently, they were frequently tempted to "kick over the chess board" whenever

---

[5] This is the case, for example, with many trade unions.

their interests were perceived to be threatened (Boron 1992: 76; Gibson 1996: 23–28).

The party system also failed to integrate organized labor (Collier and Collier 1991; McGuire 1997). The Argentine labor movement, organized into the General Labor Confederation (Confederacíon General de Trabajo; CGT), was the most powerful in Latin America throughout most of the twentieth century. Although powerful labor movements do not necessarily pose a threat to democracy,[6] regime stability in such cases often requires that labor be integrated into the party system in a way that does not threaten elite interests (Collier and Collier 1991). Thus, in Mexico after the 1930s and Venezuela after 1958, labor movements were integrated into moderate multiclass populist parties that had reached a basic accommodation with economic elites (Collier and Collier 1991). Although the CGT was aligned with Peronism throughout the post-1945 period, such an integrative dynamic never took hold in Argentina, for at least two reasons. First, the polarization surrounding Perón's initial mobilization of labor (1943–45) and the first Peronist government (1946–55) generated such a profound cleavage between Peronism and its opponents that economic and military elites resorted to proscribing Peronism from the electoral arena. Second, as James McGuire (1997) has argued, the Peronist party's lack of institutionalization prevented unions from developing a strong stake in electoral politics. Tied to a weakly institutionalized party that was banned throughout most of the 1955–83 period, unions had little disincentive to flex their considerable muscle in ways that threatened civilian regimes.

Argentine politics was thus deadlocked between 1955 and 1973.[7] On the one hand, lifting the ban on Peronism would almost certainly result in a Peronist victory, which was unacceptable to key elite sectors. On the other hand, Peronism's exclusion from the electoral arena proved equally destabilizing. Lacking representation in the party system, trade unions opted for praetorian tactics – such as general strikes, factory occupations, and mass protests – that undermined governability and destabilized regimes (Cavarozzi 1986; McGuire 1997). As a result, non-Peronist governments tended to be politically weak. Without broad electoral bases or ties to labor, both civilian and military governments found their economic programs repeatedly blocked by the Peronist unions (Collier and Collier 1991: 490–92; 738).

The party system's failure to integrate powerful organized interests thus lay at the heart of Argentina's post-1930 regime instability. Inadequately represented in the party system, key economic and political actors never developed a strong commitment to democratic institutions and frequently pursued power through nonelectoral means (McGuire 1997). In this context, strong parties and organized interests contributed not to democratic stability, but to praetorianism.

---

[6] Indeed, as scholars such as Collier (1999) and Rueschemeyer et al. (1992) have shown, labor movements often play a major role in bringing about democracy.

[7] The classic discussion of this period remains O'Donnell's (1973: 166–97) analysis of the "impossible game." Also see Collier and Collier (1991: 721–42).

Intense sociopolitical conflict among agrarian elites, industrialists, unions, and leftist youths undermined governability, threatened established elites, and created a generalized atmosphere of violence and disorder, which left civilian governments vulnerable to military intervention (O'Donnell 1988).

STRENGTHS AND WEAKNESSES OF ARGENTINA'S POST-1983 DEMOCRACY

Argentina's post-1983 democracy differed in important ways from earlier civilian regimes. First of all, it was a full democracy, in that it met "procedural minimum" standards for democracy throughout the 1983–2003 period. The fairness of elections was never questioned, and despite severe institutional crises in 1989 and 2001, there were no interruptions of the democratic order. Moreover, civil liberties were broadly protected. Government opponents of all ideological stripes enjoyed substantial freedom, and press freedom was among the most extensive in Latin America. When state abuses did occur, as in the violent police repression of protesters in December 2001 and June 2002, they triggered large-scale civic mobilizations that imposed severe political costs on governments.

Finally, post-1983 governments established substantial civilian control over the military. Unlike posttransition Brazil and Chile, key areas of military decision making, including the budget, procurement, and national defense strategy, were placed under a civilian-led defense ministry. The 1988 Defense Law prohibited the armed forces from intervening in matters of internal security and denied them any role in the policy-making process. Although civil–military relations remained volatile in the 1980s (with four military uprisings between 1987 and 1990) (Norden 1996), after 1990, when the Menem government crushed a military rebellion and issued a controversial pardon of military officers convicted of human rights violations, the armed forces virtually disappeared from the political arena. During the 1990s, the military had no role in the cabinet, military officers did not issue independent proclamations, and there were no military shows of force in the streets of the capital. Indeed, the armed forces were remarkably quiet as the Menem government slashed the military's budget and size, abolished the draft, and privatized military-owned enterprises. By the latter part of the decade, military spending was under the exclusive control of the economic ministry, responsibility for determining the missions and deployment of the armed forces was in the hands of the foreign ministry, and the "bulk of serious military effort" was being devoted to external peacekeeping missions (Trinkunas 2000: 100). The transformation of civil–military relations was made strikingly manifest during the December 2001 economic collapse, when, despite a severe institutional crisis and widespread perceptions of social chaos, the military refused either to repress protesters or to intervene in the political process.

Argentine democracy also proved remarkably robust. Between 1983 and 2003, Argentina experienced a series of profound socioeconomic crises, including the 1989 hyperinflation, which was accompanied by a wave of mass looting and forced the early resignation of President Raúl Alfonsín, and the 2001–02 financial collapse, which triggered two successive presidential resignations and threw the country into the deepest depression in its history. Few democracies anywhere have survived crises this deep. In addition, the Menem government's economic reforms during the 1990s were among the most rapid and far-reaching economic reform programs in the world. Yet in contrast to other cases of radical reform, such as Chile, Mexico, and Peru, the Argentine reforms were undertaken in a fully democratic context.

Sources of Democratic Strength: Civil Society and Party Strength

The relative strength of Argentina's post-1983 democracy was rooted in several important changes. One was the emergence of an unprecedented societal consensus around democratic rules of the game. During the 1960s and 1970s, paramilitary groups on both the right and the left had systematically flaunted democratic rules of the game, and at various times, business and conservative leaders, Peronists, and union bosses had all backed nondemocratic alternatives. This changed considerably after the 1976–83 dictatorship. The brutality and dramatic failures of the military regime discredited the armed forces among all sectors of society, and as a result, military intervention was not considered a serious option after 1983. At the same time, key societal actors converged around democratic rules of the game. Antidemocratic forces on the left and right disappeared, and conservative and business elites began to invest seriously in electoral politics for the first time in decades (Gibson 1996).[8] Peronism and the unions were also transformed. By the 1990s, the PJ was no longer led by a charismatic leader or by corporatist unions, but rather by territorial politicians with a clear stake in electoral politics. At the mass level, the traumatic experience of the Dirty War led to a "profound metamorphosis of Argentine political culture" (Peruzzotti 2001: 140). Issues of human rights and democracy gained unprecedented salience among the electorate (Catterberg 1991: 82–84), and surveys found a high level of commitment to democracy throughout the 1990s.

Yet the robustness of Argentina's post-1983 democracy also had structural roots, particularly the relative strength of its civil society and political parties. Argentine civil society contained several important components. One was organized labor. Though weakened by military rule, unions played a major role in the 1982–83 democratic transition (Munck 1998: 134–61). During the 1980s, organized labor was complemented by a burgeoning human rights movement, which engendered a "permanent associative network for the supervision of

---

[8] The right's democratic commitment was reinforced by a change in the balance of class power. Deindustrialization, economic crisis, and the expansion of the informal sector weakened organized labor, which reduced the threat that working class mobilization posed to elite economic interests.

state authorities" (Peruzzotti 2001: 142). Although the movement weakened over the course of the decade, it gave rise to a "second wave" of civic and rights-oriented organizations that ranged from the broadly oriented *Conciencia* and *Poder Ciudadano* to scores of associations that were created in response to individual abuse cases (Peruzzotti 2001: 142; 2002). These civic groups were complemented by a powerful media. The Argentine print and electronic media were among the most vigorous, independent, and sophisticated in Latin America in the 1980s and 1990s. Daily newspapers and television news programs played an important watchdog role, routinely challenging governments from both the right and the left (Waisbord 2000).

Civic and media organizations were at times critical in defending democracy in the post-1983 period. For example, the April 1987 military uprising triggered a massive civic countermobilization that – in contrast to the failed coup attempts in Venezuela in 1992 – contributed to the political isolation of the rebels and helped to discourage other social, political, and military actors from engaging in semiloyal behavior. In December 2001, when the government of President Fernando De la Rua declared a state of siege and brutally repressed protesters, a series of massive public demonstrations not only derailed the state of siege but forced De la Rua's resignation. Smaller scale threats to democratic rights also triggered vigorous civic responses. For example, government efforts to limit press freedom, such as the 1992 "Truth in Press" bill and President Menem's 1997 proposal for a "law of the stick" (which encouraged citizens to take matters into their own hands when offended by the media), were met with such immense public opposition that they were quickly abandoned.

Civic and media organizations also played a critical role in exposing and denouncing state abuses, effectively serving as agents of "societal accountability" (Smulovitz and Peruzzotti 2000, 2003; Peruzzotti 2002). For example, in 1990, when the provincial government in Catamarca attempted to cover up the murder of teenager María Soledad Morales (in which members of the governing Saadi clan were implicated), local Church, student, and civic groups organized eighty-two "marches of silence" – some of which mobilized as many as 30,000 people, or 10 percent of Catamarca's population – as part of a campaign for justice (Smulovitz and Peruzzotti 2003). The campaign drew national media attention to the case and forced a federal takeover of the provincial judiciary, which paved the way for a nationally televised trial and the eventual conviction of the accused attackers. Similarly, in 1997, when news photographer José Luis Cabezas was murdered by a mafia boss (Alfredo Yabran) with close ties to the government, the journalists' union, media outlets, and human rights organizations organized a massive campaign to bring the perpetrators to justice. Throughout 1997, Buenos Aires was flooded with "Who killed Cabezas?" posters, fliers, and television, radio, and newspaper announcements. The campaign transformed the Cabezas case into a central issue in the 1997 midterm elections, forcing Buenos Aires governor – and presidential hopeful – Eduardo Duhalde to push the investigation forward.[9]

---

[9] The crime was eventually traced to Yabran, who committed suicide in the face of imminent arrest.

Democratic governance was also facilitated by the relative strength of Argentina's political parties, particularly the PJ. Compared to many other countries in Latin America, the Argentine party system was fairly well institutionalized during much of the 1980s and 1990s (Mainwaring and Scully 1995). Throughout most of this period, the country maintained a predominantly two-party system, with Peronism representing the working and lower classes and the centrist Radical Civic Union (Un_ion Cívica Radical; UCR) – together with small left-of-center, conservative, and provincial parties – representing the middle and upper middle classes.[10] Both the PJ and the UCR possessed national organizations and relatively stable core electorates, but Peronism was particularly strong. The party maintained powerful grassroots organization and a large-scale activist base with deep roots in working- and lower-class society (Auyero 2000; Levitsky 2001, 2003; Ostiguy 1998). Surveys carried out during the mid-1990s found that between 25 and 30 percent of voters identified themselves as Peronist,[11] and the PJ never fell below 33 percent of the vote in the twelve national elections held between 1983 and 2003. The PJ also maintained close ties to organized labor. According to one survey, more than 80 percent of national unions and more than 90 percent of local unions participated in PJ activities in the late 1990s (Levitsky 2003: 137–39).

Although Peronism's strength was a source of regime instability between 1945 and 1976, the PJ's post-1983 renovation transformed it into an asset for democratic governance. In addition to committing themselves to democratic rules of the game, PJ leaders built a strong territorial organization and reduced trade union influence in the party. By the late 1980s, the PJ had transformed into a moderate and predominantly patronage-based party that posed little threat to elite interests. As a result, what had been a stalemated party system took on features of what Collier and Collier (1991) call an integrative party system, in which the PJ's working-class and union ties enhanced, rather than undermined, democratic governance.

The PJ's (and to a lesser extent, the UCR's) electoral strength helped Argentina avoid the kinds of governability crises that are frequently associated with weak parties and party system fragmentation (Mainwaring and Scully 1995). Particularly during Peronist administrations, the strength of the major parties helped ensure the relatively smooth passage of the bulk of the executive's most important legislative initiatives, thereby preventing the kind of executive-legislative deadlock that undermined governability – and created incentives for executive power grabs – in countries like in Brazil, Ecuador, Guatemala, and Peru. At the same time, the PJ's continued strength among the working and lower classes also limited the space for antiestablishment or "neopopulist"

---

[10] In 1983, the PJ and UCR accounted for 92 percent of the presidential vote, and in 1989, they accounted for 86 percent of the presidential vote. Although these figures fell slightly in midterm elections, analysts generally described Argentina as having a predominantly two-party system (Catterberg 1991: 50; Jones 1997: 264–69; McGuire 1995: 224–26).

[11] Surveys were carried out in Greater Buenos Aires by Hugo Haime and Associates in October 1993 and April 1994, and a national survey was carried out by Hugo Haime and Associates in April 1995. Data were provided to the author by Hugo Haime and Associates.

outsiders similar to Alberto Fujimori in Peru or Hugo Chavez in Venezuela. Political outsiders failed repeatedly to gain a foothold among the electorate, even after the massive antigovernment protests of 2001–02. Indeed, the most successful antiestablishment outsider, former military rebel Aldo Rico, peaked at just 9.2 percent of the vote in the 1994 constituent assembly election and joined the PJ soon thereafter.

Sources of Democratic Weakness: Institutional Instability

If an elite democratic consensus and relatively strong parties and civic organizations provided a foundation for democratic stability after 1983, the persistent weakness of Argentina's political institutions posed a constant challenge to that stability. Institutional instability was a major feature of Argentine politics throughout most of the twentieth century (Spiller and Tommasi 2000). At the regime level, successive military coups – 14 military presidents governed the country between 1930 and 1983 – repeatedly led to the removal of presidents, legislators, and Supreme Court justices before the end of their mandates. For example, notwithstanding the fixed presidential terms mandated by the Constitution, only two elected presidents – Juan Perón and Carlos Menem – completed their full terms in office between 1928 and 2003. Similarly, despite a formal guarantee of lifetime tenure security for Supreme Court justices, virtually every change of government or regime after 1946 was accompanied by court stacking (Helmke 2005). As a result, the average tenure of Supreme Court Justices between 1960 and 1999 was less than four years, compared to nine years in Chile and thirteen years in the United States (Spiller and Tommasi 2000: 22–23). Similar patterns of institutional instability could be found in executive–legislative relations, in the federal system, in the tax and financial systems, and within the Peronist party. Indeed, institutional weakness became a dominant feature of twentieth-century Argentine politics: Whenever the political or economic rules of the game were perceived to harm the short-term interests of those in power, they were circumvented, manipulated, or changed.

The political and economic consequences of this institutional instability were often devastating. In the absence of stable rules of the game, politics became a Hobbesian world of high uncertainty, narrow time horizons, and low trust and cooperation. The result was repeated economic failure, political instability, and at times – most notably, the 1970s – descents into praetorian conflict and violent chaos. Indeed, persistent institutional instability is a major reason why Argentine democracy has consistently underperformed – relative to the country's class structure and levels of development and education – since 1930.

This pattern of institutional instability did not change fundamentally after 1983. Although the core elements of democracy (elections, civil liberties, civilian control over the military) were relatively institutionalized, the rules of the game *within* the democratic regime remained fluid and contested and were frequently manipulated or ignored. The Supreme Court continued to be purged and stacked by elected presidents. Two of the first three elected presidents (Raúl

Alfonsín and Fernando De la Rua) failed to complete their mandates, while the third (Carlos Menem) modified the Constitution to obtain a second term. The rules of the game governing areas as important as executive–legislative relations, the federal system, the role of the Central Bank, and the prosecution of military officers implicated in human rights abuses were also repeatedly challenged, violated, manipulated, or changed. This institutional weakness exacerbated political and economic crises, at times transforming hard economic times into periods of regime-threatening institutional meltdown. Such patterns may be contrasted to neighboring Uruguay, where political institutions remained largely intact despite several severe economic crises during the 1985–2003 period.

In sum, the political foundations of Argentina's post-1983 democracy were somewhat contradictory. On the one hand, a broad democratic consensus and the existence of relatively strong parties and a robust civil society provided the bases for a fairly stable democratic regime. On the other hand, many of the rules of the game *within* the democratic regime remained highly unstable, and as a result, the Argentine polity and economy remained vulnerable to crisis.

DEMOCRATIC STABILITY IN HARD TIMES: CRISIS AND REGIME SURVIVAL FROM ALFONSÍN TO KIRCHNER

Argentina's post-1983 democracy was both robust *and* crisis-prone. As the following sections show, the regime survived two severe socioeconomic crises, radical economic reforms, and the antiinstitutional behavior of the Menem government. Yet the persistent weakness of the subregime-level institutions exacerbated the country's periodic crises, preventing the consolidation of a more stable and effective democracy.

The Alfonsín Government: From Democratization to Hyperinflation

The presidency of Raúl Alfonsín (1983–89) strengthened democratic institutions on several fronts. First, the Radical government oversaw the forging of an unprecedented democratic consensus. The PJ, led by the Renovation faction after 1987, abandoned its previously ambiguous stance toward liberal democracy. This reorientation was made manifest during the April 1987 *carapintada* military rebellion, when PJ leaders rushed to join Alfonsín on the balcony of the presidential palace in a joint defense of democracy. At the same time, conservatives who had turned previously to the military for protection invested in electoral politics, creating the center–right Center Democratic Union (Union del Centro Democrático; UCEDE) in 1983 (Gibson 1996).

The Alfonsín government also set important precedents in its encouragement of independent civic organization and its respect for civil liberties, press freedom, and – albeit less systematically – legislative and judicial independence. It took significant steps toward institutionalizing the protection of human rights, including the prosecution of military officers involved in human rights violations during the 1976–83 dictatorship. Although the government ultimately limited the scope of the trials,[12] and although the convicted officers were later pardoned,[13] the political–cultural impact of the trials was nevertheless substantial. Finally, the Radical government also made progress toward establishing civilian control over the military. It cut military spending, brought key areas of military decision making under civilian control, and – through the 1988 Defense Law – prohibited the armed forces from intervening in domestic affairs.

Yet the Alfonsín administration – and very nearly democracy itself – was ultimately overcome by political and economic crisis. In April 1987, the government's human rights offensive triggered the first in a series of military rebellions. Subsequent concessions to the rebels, particularly the 1987 Due Obedience Law (which protected junior officers from prosecution), raised questions about the government's capacity to maintain civilian supremacy. Even more devastating was the economic challenge posed by the debt crisis and the mounting crisis of Argentina's import-substituting industrialization model. The Alfonsín government's heterodox stabilization policies, embodied in the 1985 Austral Plan, fell victim to severe distributional conflict (Smith 1990). Efforts to negotiate a social pact with Peronist unions failed, and the CGT led an astounding thirteen general strikes between 1984 and 1988 (McGuire 1997: 185–207). The resurgence of inflation, together with the UCR's crushing defeat in the 1987 midterm elections, badly weakened the government and pushed the economy into a spiral of recession and inflation. As the specter of a Peronist victory in 1989 elections grew, capital flight and financial speculation soared, culminating in a hyperinflationary burst that brought the economy to the brink of collapse.

In this context, Argentina's political institutional structure began to unravel. Actors on both the right and the left began to deviate from democratic rules of the game. Military rebellions erupted in January (Monte Caseros) and December (Villa Martelli) of 1988, and in January 1989, a long-dormant leftist guerrilla group attacked the La Tablada army barracks,[14] provoking a gun battle that left dozens dead. In May 1989, the hyperinflationary crisis triggered a wave of mass looting in several cities across the country. In this context of social and economic chaos, President Alfonsín was unable to complete his mandate: Arrangements were hastily made for an early transfer of power, and six months before the end of his presidency, Alfonsín resigned.

Yet the 1989 crisis was also noteworthy for what did not occur. Most centrally, the democratic regime did not break down. Notwithstanding a

[12] The December 1986 *Punto Final* law set a deadline for all charges against military officials, and the 1987 Due Obedience Law limited the scope of charges to those above the rank of colonel.
[13] President Carlos Menem pardoned and released top military and guerrilla leaders in December 1990.
[14] The Everyone for the Fatherland Movement (Movimiento Todos por la Patria; MTP) was mainly composed of ex-members of the People's Revolutionary Army (Ejercito Revolucionario del Pueblo; ERP), a left-wing guerrilla group that had been active in the 1970s.

socioeconomic crisis far worse than those that preceded earlier democratic breakdowns, there was no coup or state of emergency, and there were no serious violations of civil liberties. Elections were free of violence or fraud, and unlike crisis-ridden elections held in Brazil, Peru, and Venezuela during the early 1990s, they did not result in party system collapse or the rise of a political outsider. The PJ and UCR remained dominant, garnering 80 percent of the 1989 presidential vote. Notwithstanding his outsider image, president-elect Menem was a longtime PJ politician, and unlike Fujimori in Peru and Collor in Brazil, his partisan allies gained a majority in the Senate and a near-majority in the Chamber of Deputies. The 1989 transition marked the first time in Argentine history that power was handed from one democratically elected president to another from a different party. Hence, although the 1989 hyperinflation produced a serious institutional crisis and a frenzied revision of the presidential transition schedule, the democratic regime survived intact.

The Menem Government: Combining Democracy and Radical Economic Reform

During its first term in office (1989–95), the Menem government stabilized and reactivated the Argentine economy through a set of radical market-oriented reforms. These reforms have been characterized as the most extensive in Latin America – and among the most far-reaching in the world – during the 1990s (Gwartney, Lawson, and Block 1996: 113; IDB 1997: 96). Yet what is particularly striking about the Argentine case is that it combined radical market-oriented reform and democracy in a way that was unparalleled in Latin America. Virtually none of the most radical economic reforms in post-1973 Latin America were undertaken in a context of full-fledged democracy. In Chile and Mexico, reforms were carried out under authoritarian regimes. In Peru, they were accompanied by an *autogolpe* in which the congress and the judiciary were dissolved and the leading opponent of neoliberalism was forced into exile. Even in Bolivia, which is generally viewed as having maintained a democratic regime in the 1980s, orthodox stabilization was implemented via distinctly authoritarian mechanisms, including states of siege and harsh labor repression. By contrast, in democracies such as Costa Rica, Uruguay, Venezuela, and Brazil, economic reform was slower and less extensive. Placed in comparative perspective, then, Argentina's capacity to reconcile radical reform and democracy was striking: Among fully democratic cases, Argentina carried out the most rapid and far-reaching economic reforms; among cases of deep crisis and radical reform, Argentina was the most democratic.

The Menem government's capacity to combine democracy and radical economic reform was rooted, in large part, in the strength of the Peronist party. The PJ's strong linkages to working- and lower-class society allowed it to deliver the acquiescence of many of the expected losers under neoliberal reform, which limited the availability of those sectors for antireform appeals. This integrative dynamic allowed the Menem government to carry out radical neoliberal reforms, and thus put an end to a regime-threatening hyperinflationary crisis, within the context of a democratic regime.

The PJ's integrative capacity was clearly seen with respect to organized labor. Though weakened by economic crisis, the Argentine labor movement remained among the most powerful in Latin America. Indeed, labor mobilization had contributed to the failure of the Alfonsín government's heterodox stabilization policies in the 1980s. Yet the Menem government gained a remarkable degree of labor acquiescence to – and even cooperation with – much more radical reforms (McGuire 1997: 226–41; Levitsky and Way 1998; Murillo 2001). The CGT did not lead a single general strike during Menem's first three and a half years in office and led only one general strike during Menem's entire first term. Although dissident labor organizations such as the Argentine Workers Congress (Central de Trabajadores Argentinos; CTA) and Argentine Workers Movement (Movimiento de Trabajadores Argentinos; MTA) mobilized repeatedly against the Menem reforms during the 1990s, most large unions refused to join them. As a result, these labor protests failed to mobilize large numbers of workers.

There are several reasons why labor acquiesced to the Menem reforms, including pragmatism in the face of hyperinflation, memories of the 1973–76 period (when labor mobilization contributed to the collapse of a Peronist government), rank-and-file support for the reforms, and the fact that unions extracted important organizational benefits in exchange for their support (Murillo 1997, 2001).[15] Perhaps the most decisive factor, however, was the unions' longstanding ties to Peronism. The vast majority of union leaders were Peronist, and most of them remained active in PJ politics in the 1990s. More than two-dozen unionists held posts in the PJ leadership and congressional bloc when Menem took office, and many others gained positions in the Menem government.[16] Indeed, twenty-four of thirty-nine national unions surveyed in 1997 reported having placed one of its members in the PJ leadership or the government during the 1990s (Levitsky 2003: 138–39). These ties gave union leaders a stake in the government's success and an incentive to limit public opposition to Menem. Union bosses also maintained longstanding personal ties to PJ leaders, many of which were forged during periods of shared adversity and struggle against military rule. By enhancing trust and communication between government and union officials, these ties lengthened the unionists' time horizons and facilitated the negotiation of a variety of deals – including both programmatic accords and individual side payments – that were critical to keeping many unions in the progovernment camp (Levitsky and Way 1998: 176–78).

The PJ's territorial linkages to working- and lower-class society also helped to limit antireform mobilization. The PJ's vast infrastructure of neighborhood

---

[15] For example, unions such as the oil workers, light and power workers, telephone workers, and railway workers gained shares of newly privatized companies in exchange for their support for privatization. Similarly, in exchange for supporting the privatization of the pension system, major unions gained the right to participate in the newly privatized pension fund market.

[16] For example, cabinet or subcabinet positions were awarded to Luis Barrionuevo (food service workers), Roberto Digón (tobacco employees), and Jorge Triaca (plastic workers).

branches, soup kitchens, clubs, and informal social networks played a critical role in limiting working- and lower-class opposition to the reforms. During the 1989–90 hyperinflationary crisis, for example, tens of thousands of PJ activists worked to dampen popular protest in working- and lower-class zones. This was achieved through a variety of means, including persuasion, the physical expulsion of leftist activists from working- and lower-class neighborhoods, and a multitude of neighborhood-based emergency social welfare programs. A 1997 study of local PJ branches found that 96 percent engaged in some form of social assistance (Levitsky 2001: 53). Local PJ organizations also provided residents of lower-class neighborhoods with access to the state. Neighborhood-level Peronist "problem solving networks" (Auyero 2000) obtained wheelchairs, disability pensions, scholarships, funeral expenses, and odd jobs – as well as collective goods such as street lights or road pavement – for working- and lower-class residents who lacked alternative sources of social assistance.

The PJ's powerful organized presence in working- and lower-class society facilitated the economic reform process in at least three ways. First, it helped to prevent the kind of mass urban looting and protest that shook both the Alfonsín government and the second Pérez government in Venezuela. Second, it helped the PJ retain the bulk of its traditional working- and lower-class electorate in the 1990s, which limited the prospects for antireform appeals. In the early 1990s, several political forces, including the dissident Peronist Group of Eight, CGT leader Saúl Ubaldini, and the ultranationalist Movement for Dignity and Independence (Movimiento por la Dignidad y la Andependenim; MODIN), targeted traditional Peronist voters with antineoliberal appeals. Yet the PJ's continued hegemony among the working and lower classes limited the effectiveness of these appeals. For example, in the critical 1991 midterm elections, Ubaldini won just 2 percent of the vote in his bid to be governor of Buenos Aires, and the Group of Eight failed to elect a single member to Congress.[17] The stability of the PJ vote, together with the government's successful stabilization of the economy, helped the PJ score easy victories in the 1991 and 1993 midterm elections and the 1995 presidential election. Third, Peronism's electoral success provided the Menem government with a virtual legislative majority that ensured – with the help of small conservative and provincial parties – the relatively smooth passage of its most important reform measures (Llanos 2001; Corrales 2002). The PJ's legislative strength thus prevented the kind of executive-legislative deadlock that undermined reform efforts in Brazil, Ecuador, and Peru. It also reduced the incentive for President Menem to bypass Congress or – as occurred in Guatemala and Peru – attempt to shut it down.

The PJ's electoral strength also helped to stabilize the party system during the early and mid-1990s. In the aftermath of the 1989 hyperinflationary crisis, traditional party identities had begun to erode, and the country's predominantly two-party system began to crumble. Whereas the PJ and the UCR had accounted

---

[17] Although MODIN made modest inroads into the Peronist electorate between 1991 and 1994, these gains were largely confined to the province of Buenos Aires. They also proved short-lived, as MODIN disappeared from the political map after 1995.

for 86.6 percent of the vote in the 1983 legislative elections, by 1991, this figure had fallen to just 69.5 percent (Fraga 1995: 34).[18] Surveys found that confidence in and attachment to established parties was eroding, leading scholars to raise concerns about a "crisis of representation" (Novaro 1994). The political space created by the decline of traditional party identities began to be filled by a variety of antiparty "outsiders" (Novaro 1994). Some of these outsiders were athletes (such as auto racer Carlos Reutemann) or other popular cultural figures (such as pop singer Palito Ortega). Several others, however, were former military officers (such as retired general Antonio Bussi and ex-military-rebel Aldo Rico) with clear authoritarian profiles.

Yet Argentina did not follow the Peruvian or Venezuelan path toward party system decomposition. This outcome can be attributed, in large part, to the continued electoral strength of Peronism. The PJ's continued electoral hegemony among the working- and lower-class electorate reduced the space for outsider appeals. Indeed, the only new political force to establish itself during the Menem period, the Front for a Country in Solidarity (Frente por un País Solidario; FREPASO), drew the bulk of its support from the middle classes. After the UCR and FREPASO formed the Alliance for Jobs, Justice, and Education in 1997, the party system again took on a two-party dynamic. The PJ and the Alliance accounted for 81.9 percent of the vote in the 1997 midterm elections and 86.8 percent of the vote in the 1999 presidential elections. The stabilization of the party system limited the prospects for outsider or antisystem politicians. Indeed, the success of outsider candidates diminished considerably over the course of the 1990s. Aldo Rico's MODIN, which peaked at 9 percent of the vote in the 1994 constituent assembly elections, collapsed in 1995, and no major antisystem candidates emerged in the second half of the decade.

Menemism and the Limits of Delegative Democracy

Although the stabilization and reactivation of the economy enhanced democratic governance during the 1990s, the Menem government generated a new set of political and institutional crises. Menem's concentration and occasional abuse of power weakened the country's already fragile system of checks and balances, or what O'Donnell (1994) has called "horizontal accountability." During his first years in office, President Menem governed in a unilateral – and at times marginally constitutional – manner, and as a result, Argentina came to be viewed as a leading case of "delegative democracy" (Diamond 1999: 34–35; Larkins 1998; Linz and Stepan 1996: 203; O'Donnell 1994). For example, in an effort to circumvent the legislative process, Menem made repeated use of his ambiguously constitutional authority to issue Decrees of Necessity and Urgency (NUDs) (Ferreira Rubio and Goretti 1998). Whereas constitutional presidents issued fewer than 20 NUDs between 1853 and 1983 and President Alfonsín

---

[18] Much of this decline was caused by the crisis of the UCR, which saw its share of the electorate fall from 52 percent in 1983 to 17 percent in 1995.

issued just 10 NUDs between 1983 and 1989, Menem issued 545 NUDs over the course of his presidency (Ferreira Rubio and Goretti 2000: 1, 4).

Menem also assaulted judicial independence. In 1990, the government pushed through legislation – over the objections of the UCR and with a contested quorum – expanding the size of the Supreme Court from five to nine (Larkins 1998: 427–29). It then stacked the court with loyalists, creating what came to be known as the "automatic majority." The new Supreme Court rarely ruled against Menem on issues of importance, and many of its decisions – such as its controversial 1990 ruling upholding the constitutionality of executive decrees – were critical to the success of Menem's political and economic project. Although the judiciary was never fully subordinated to the executive branch, the creation of an "automatic majority" and the government's cozy relationship with many federal judges seriously eroded its legitimacy.[19] It also permitted a substantial amount of corruption. A substantial number of top government officials were implicated in illicit activities during the 1990s. Virtually none were brought to justice during the Menem administration.

Finally, Menem's repeated efforts to reform the constitution to gain his own reelection twice brought the country to the brink of an institutional crisis. In 1994, Menem used his popular support to bully a majority faction of the UCR into accepting a constitutional reform permitting reelection by threatening to hold a plebiscite on the issue (surveys suggested that Menem would easily win such a vote). Four years later, despite the clear unconstitutionality of running for a third term, Menem publicly toyed with the idea, allowing his allies to explore the possibility of a referendum on the issue and even seeking a court ruling permitting his candidacy.

Yet in many ways, Argentine democracy proved remarkably robust under Menem. Unlike many other nominally democratic regimes in Latin America, Argentina's core democratic institutions were never seriously violated during the 1990s. There were no states of emergency, civil liberties were broadly protected, and press freedom remained substantial.[20] And notwithstanding Menem's much-criticized pardon of top military officers convicted of human rights violations, military influence during the 1990s was virtually nil.

Even on the dimension of horizontal accountability, the Menem government's abuses were comparatively limited. To the extent that the delegative democracy label fits the Argentine case, it does so only for the 1989–90 period. President Menem did not routinely bypass parties or the legislature after 1990. The bulk of the government's post-1990 reform measures were approved by Congress, and most of these involved arduous negotiations with (and important concessions to) legislative leaders, governors, and business and labor leaders (Etchemendy and Palermo 1998; Corrales 2002; Llanos 2001). Many reform

---

[19] Surveys found that as many as 80 percent of Argentines neither trusted the judicial branch nor believed it to be independent (Helmke 2003: 218).

[20] Although Menem government officials launched a handful of libel suits against journalists and media outlets, they lost the most important of these cases.

bills, including those to privatize social security, natural gas, and petroleum, were modified heavily by the legislature (Llanos 2001: 85–96). Others, such as labor law reform, were blocked entirely.

Menem's capacity to dominate other branches of government diminished considerably during his second term. Beginning in 1996, a group of approximately forty Peronist legislators aligned with Buenos Aires governor Eduardo Duhalde routinely joined the opposition in blocking legislation pushed by the president. As a result, legislation to liberalize labor markets and privatize the airports and the postal system was stalled for years (Llanos 2001: 92–95). Although Menem frequently threatened to impose key reforms by decree, these threats were generally not carried out. Indeed, the number of NUDs issued by the executive branch declined significantly over the course of the 1990s.[21] Judicial rulings against the government also increased during Menem's second term. In 1999, for example, the Supreme Court voted, for the first time, to limit executive discretion in issuing NUDs (Helmke 2003: 222–23).

The resilience of Argentina's democratic institutions was made particularly manifest in 1998, when President Menem engaged in a reckless, if half-hearted, attempt to run for a third term. In contrast to 1994, Menem's "re-reelection" bid was opposed by a strong and united opposition, as well as by roughly half of his own Peronist party. Although Menem supporters sought to obtain a favorable ruling from the Menemist-dominated Supreme Court, the justices quickly made it clear that they would take no such action (Helmke 2003: 222–23). As a result, Menem was left with no alternative but to hand over the presidency, as scheduled, in December 1999.

The Post-Menemist Crisis

When Carlos Menem left the presidency, Argentine democracy was more stable than at any time in the country's history. The 1999 presidential election, in which Fernando De la Rua of the opposition Alliance defeated PJ candidate Eduardo Duhalde, was a highly routinized affair. Whereas in 1989 the hyperinflationary crisis had forced Alfonsín to abandon the presidency six months before the end of his mandate, the 1999 transition took place virtually without a hitch.

Yet the De la Rua government inherited a set of difficult economic and political problems, many of which were legacies of the Menem presidency. On the political front, the Menem government had done little to strengthen – and in many respects had weakened – democratic institutions. It continued the established pattern of circumventing or changing inconvenient political rules of the game for its own short-term benefit. For example, Menem made widespread use of executive decree authority between 1989 and 1994, despite the ambiguously

---

[21] Whereas Menem issued an average of sixty-eight NUDs a year between 1989 and 1993, he issued only thirty-six NUDs a year between 1994 and 1998 (Ferreira Rubio and Goretti 2000: 8).

constitutional status of such authority. Although the 1994 Constitution permitted decrees in cases of "public emergency," Menem used them liberally, setting a precedent that his successors would continue. In the judicial arena, Menem's stacking of the Supreme Court and repeated efforts to exert political control over federal judges reinforced a long pattern of judicial tenure insecurity (Helmke 2005). Finally, Menem's effort to reform (in 1994) and later violate (in 1998) the Constitution in order to gain reelection twice brought the country to the brink of an institutional crisis. These abuses, together with widespread perceptions of corruption, eroded public trust in the country's politicians and political institutions.

The Menem government also left problematic economic legacies. One was the 1991 Convertibility Law, which pegged the peso to the dollar at a one-to-one rate, essentially converting the Central Bank into a currency board. Though widely credited with ending hyperinflation, the Convertibility Law took monetary and exchange-rate policy out of the hands of governments, leaving them without the policy tools to respond to economic shocks and downturns. Such a downturn began in 1998 in the aftermath of the Asian financial crisis. Another legacy of the Menem period was widespread social exclusion. The unemployment rate, which had traditionally been negligible in Argentina, soared to a record 18.6 percent in 1995 and remained in double digits for the rest of the decade. These economic legacies left Menem's successors in a difficult bind: Future governments would face growing demands to address long unmet social needs, but a rigid monetary and exchange-rate system would seriously limit their capacity to meet those demands.

Though elected on a platform of combating corruption and addressing the social costs of neoliberalism, the De la Rua government failed on both the political and economic fronts. Within a year of taking office, the Alliance began to unravel. In August 2000, allegations surfaced that government officials had bribed a handful of senators in an effort to pass labor reform legislation. Vice President (and FREPASO leader) Carlos "Chacho" Alvarez, whose party had made anticorruption its central plank, called publicly for a serious investigation into the scandal. When De la Rua balked, Alvarez resigned. The scandal destroyed the Alliance and shattered its claim to represent a "new way" of doing politics, which convinced many of its (predominantly middle-class) supporters that none of the major parties effectively represented them.

The Alliance's greatest failure, however, lay in the economic realm. After averaging 6.2 percent annual growth since 1991, the Argentine economy – battered by external shocks such as the 1997 Asian financial crisis, a strengthening U.S. dollar, and Brazil's 1999 devaluation – slumped beginning in 1998. Yet the Convertibility system prevented the De la Rua government from using the exchange rate or monetary policy to reactivate the economy, and a heavy debt burden, jittery bond markets, and pressure from the International Monetary Fund (IMF) discouraged countercyclical deficit spending. Unwilling to abandon Convertibility, De la Rua opted for a series of procyclical austerity measures that prolonged and deepened the economic downturn. In late 2001, as the recession entered its fourth consecutive year and the unemployment rate approached 20 percent, public frustration reached a boiling point.

The first manifestation of public anger was seen in the October 2001 midterm legislative elections. Not only was the Alliance's share of the legislative vote cut nearly in half relative to 1999, but the percentage of voters who cast blank and spoiled ballots – a protest against the entire political elite – soared to an unprecedented 22 percent of the overall vote. The blank and spoiled vote exceeded that of the governing Alliance, and in two of the country's largest districts (the Federal Capital and Santa Fe), it exceeded those of all parties.

De la Rua never recovered from the October 2001 election. Within weeks, mounting fear of debt default or currency devaluation triggered a severe financial crisis. The U.S. government, which had acted swiftly to help Mexico recover from its 1994–95 financial crisis, remained on the sidelines. In November, in an effort to stave off financial collapse, Economic Minister Domingo Cavallo imposed strict limits on currency movements and bank deposit withdrawals. The so-called *corralito* (playpen) deprived the middle classes of their savings and starved the cash-dependent informal economy that sustained much of the poor. The political consequences were devastating. On December 18 and 19, Argentina exploded in a wave of rioting and protest. Widespread looting erupted in Greater Buenos Aires, and in various parts of the country, unemployed protesters (*piqueteros*) blocked major roads and highways. In the capital, protesters took to the streets banging pots and pans in protests known as *cacerolazos*. The government declared a state of siege and ordered a police repression that resulted in more than two-dozen deaths. The killings eroded the last vestiges of De la Rua's authority, and on December 20, he resigned. With the vice presidency vacant, Congress selected Peronist governor Adolfo Rodriguez Saá to serve as interim president. Rodriguez Saá immediately declared a default on Argentina's $132 million debt – the largest default in history. He did little else. After another round of rioting and amid severe conflict within his own party, Rodriguez Saá resigned on December 30.

On January 1, 2002, when Congress selected PJ senator Eduardo Duhalde as Argentina's third president in less than two weeks, Argentina stood on the brink of anarchy. What had begun as anti-De la Rua protests had now grown into a massive rebellion against the entire political elite. Protesters surrounded each branch of government, banging pots and pans and demanding the resignation of all of the members of Congress and the Supreme Court. The public mood was crystallized in an extraordinary slogan: *que se vayan todos* ("throw everyone out"). Citizen anger reached such heights that Argentines began to attack politicians physically on the street, in restaurants, and in other public places.

Duhalde's initial move was to end the Convertibility system. In a context of international isolation and widespread institutional collapse, the move plunged the economy further into chaos. Within weeks, the value of the peso had deteriorated by more than 70 percent, triggering fears of hyperinflation. The economy, in recession since 1998, now fell into a full-scale depression. With the banking system paralyzed and no immediate prospect of international assistance, economy activity ground to a halt. The consequences were devastating. Argentina's GDP contracted by 16 percent in the first quarter of 2002, and the unemployment rate climbed to nearly 25 percent. More than five million people fell into poverty between October 2001 and June 2002, and by mid-2002 more than half the population was living in poverty (compared to just 22 percent in 1994).

The 2001–02 crisis triggered yet another round of institutional collapse. Institutions governing everything from property rights and currency emission to judicial independence, presidential mandates, and the electoral cycle were dismantled, violated, or seriously threatened. Core economic institutions such as central bank autonomy and the Convertibility system were overturned – in a matter of hours – virtually without legislative debate. In the political realm, protesters called for the resignation of all elected officials and the entire Supreme Court. Presidential elections were rescheduled four times, and throughout much of 2002, there was little certainty as to when elections would be held, which offices would be up for election, or how candidates would be selected. Conflict between branches of government reached near-praetorian levels. In early 2002, for example, Congress initiated impeachment proceedings against the entire Supreme Court, and in an extraordinarily irresponsible act of self-defense, a majority of justices threatened rulings that were likely to trigger a financial collapse.

The crisis also decimated the party system. A striking number of Argentines began to reject all established parties – and politicians – in 2001, raising the specter of a Peru- or Venezuela-like party system collapse. Although the PJ survived the crisis, the parties of the Alliance suffered an extraordinary meltdown. FREPASO ceased to exist, and the UCR, which had been one of Argentina's leading parties for more than a century, barely registered in opinion polls. As the UCR collapsed, key party leaders abandoned it. Thus, Elisa Carrió, a legislative backbencher who had emerged as a popular anticorruption crusader, left the UCR to form the left-of-center Alternative for a Republic of Equals (Alternative por una República de Iguales; ARI), and Ricardo López Murphy, who had served as defense minister and minister of the economy under De la Rua, launched the conservative Federal Recreate Movement (Moviemiénto Federal Recrear; MFR). As the established parties weakened, antiestablishment challengers emerged. For example, Luis Zamora, a previously marginal left-wing politician who gained popularity during the December 2001 protests, led calls for the immediate resignation of all public office holders and then called on voters to cast blank ballots in an effort to "throw everyone out."

Remarkably, the 2001–02 crisis did not lead to an interruption of democratic rule. Despite several months of mass protest and widespread perception of chaos, the armed forces remained on the political sidelines. The military refused to intervene to repress protesters, made no independent proclamations or shows of force, and did not seek to exert behind-the-scenes influence over political events. Nor was serious thought given to a Fujimori- or Yeltsin-style presidential coup. Moreover, civil liberties remained largely intact. Although the

December 2001 state of siege and violent repression of protesters constituted a serious blow against civil liberties, the massive civic mobilization triggered by the repression not only derailed the state of siege but also forced De la Rua's resignation. Finally, it is noteworthy that no antisystem outsider gained broad public support during this period. Given the depth of the crisis and Argentina's history of regime instability, the survival of its core democratic institutions was a remarkable achievement. Indeed, few democracies in the world have survived economic crises as deep as that which hit Argentina in 2001–02.

Conventional accounts of the 2001–02 crisis locate its causes in the political arena. According to these analyses, the roots of the crisis lay in pervasive corruption and clientelism, runaway political spending, and a cartel-like party system, or "partyarchy."[22] Yet relative to other middle-income countries, the levels of corruption, clientelism, and fiscal profligacy in Argentina were moderate.[23] There is little evidence that corruption and clientelism were more pervasive than in countries like Brazil or Mexico, and although provincial spending was a source of fiscal strain, Argentina's fiscal deficits never surpassed the level required for entry into the European Maastrict Treaty. Moreover, the Argentine party system was far from closed. Although the PJ and the UCR remained the country's leading parties, low legal requirements for party formation and a low-threshold proportional representation system allowed a variety of parties to gain election to Congress. Indeed, voters confronted a broad array of electoral alternatives throughout the post-1983 period, including the center–left Intransigent Party (PI), FREPASO, and ARI, the conservative UCEDE and Action for the Republic, and the nationalist MODIN.

What distinguished Argentina from other Latin American countries was the depth of the economic crisis. Eroding competitiveness and a series of external shocks threw the Argentine economy into a recession from which successive governments, shackled by Convertibility, were unable to dig out. The economic crisis was exacerbated by the international community's refusal to help stave off a financial collapse. Had international actors intervened in late 2001 or early 2002, allowing the government to end the *corralito* and salvage the financial system, Argentine economic and political history might have taken a markedly different path.

Yet if the roots of the 2001–02 crisis were primarily economic, institutional weakness clearly exacerbated it. As in past crises, the political rules of the game quickly unraveled in 2001 and early 2002. The absence of clear and stable rules generated extreme uncertainty, which narrowed actors' time horizons and made cooperation extremely difficult. In this context, politicians, business leaders, *piqueteros*, and even Supreme Court justices turned to praetorian tactics. Here

---

[22] See, for example, Mariano Grondona in *La Nación*, 31 March 2002.

[23] Between 1995 and 2000, Argentina was consistently located in the middle of the pack on Transparency International's annual Corruption Perception Index: more or less on par with Brazil and Mexico, only a notch below the Czech Republic, Greece, Italy, and South Korea, and substantially better than China, India, and Thailand.

the contrast with Uruguay is striking. Although Uruguay also suffered a severe economic downturn in 2001–02, its political institutional structure was stronger. As a result, political and social actors responded to the crisis by working through institutional channels, and no significant anti-political-establishment movement emerged.

Back to the Ballot Box: Democratic Survival in 2002–2003

Argentine politics stabilized under the Duhalde government during the second half of 2002. Social protest slowly subsided, and both political and economic activity returned to more institutional channels. Although Duhalde was forced to advance the presidential elections from September 2003 to April 2003, his administration managed to restore a minimum of governability, complete its (now shortened) mandate, and transfer power to a new elected government.

The 2003 election was characterized by substantial uncertainty. The party system was in disarray. With FREPASO defunct and the UCR barely register-ing in opinion polls, personalistic candidates – such as former Radicals Elisa Carrió and Ricardo López Murphy and leftist leader Luis Zamora – ascended in the polls. Although the PJ remained strong in electoral terms, it was deeply divided between Menem, who sought to return to the presidency, and Duhalde, who sought desperately to block him. Unable to choose a candidate, the PJ was forced to allow three Peronists – Menem, ex-interim President Adolfo Rodriguez Saá, and Santa Cruz governor Nestor Kirchner – to run. The sever-ity of the PJ's internal conflict and the general atmosphere of institutional in-stability led many observers to fear that, for the first time since the return to democracy, the April 2003 election would be marred by violence or fraud.

Yet the election went remarkably smoothly. Despite a highly competitive race in which five candidates – Menem, Rodriguez Saá, Kirchner, Carrió, and López Murphy – had a legitimate chance to qualify for the second-round runoff, the first-round voting proceeded without incident, and the results of the election were uncontested. Turnout – 78 percent – was relatively high. And notwith-standing widespread anger at the political elite, establishment candidates car-ried the day. The top two finishers were both Peronists: Menem, a former two-term president, and Kirchner, a three-term governor who was backed by the Duhalde government. Among the major candidates, the one who most closely approximated an antiestablishment outsider, Carrió, finished fifth with just 14 percent of the vote. No other antiestablishment candidate received even 2 percent of the vote, and the blank and spoiled vote, which had surpassed 20 percent in 2001, fell to just 2.5 percent. When Menem – trailing badly in opinion polls – abandoned the race in the second round, Kirchner, the candidate of the incumbent Peronist government, became president.

President Kirchner brought a new generation of politicians, Peronists and progressive non-Peronists, into power and immediately embarked on a series of bold reforms. He restructured the military and police hierarchies, shook up state agencies long linked to corruption; launched an effort to reform the judiciary, pushed for the reversal of existing immunity laws so as to permit the prosecution of military officers responsible for past human rights violations, and distanced himself from the neoliberal economic policies of the Menem and De la Rua governments. Public opinion surveys showed broad support for the new government and a striking degree of optimism about Argentina's future. Although the political and economic prospects for the Kirchner government remained uncertain at the time of this writing, there is little doubt that the 2003 election restored a minimum of public credibility to Argentina's democratic institutions.

The reequilibration of Argentine democracy was rooted in several factors. One was the economic recovery that began in mid-2002. After four years of recession, the Argentine economy experienced rapid growth in 2003. Another important factor was the Duhalde government's capacity to restore a minimum of social peace. This was achieved, in part, through a set of relatively effective emergency social policies, including the large-scale distribution of low-cost medicine and the allocation of monthly subsidies to more than two million unemployed heads of households. Yet political stabilization was also rooted in the continued strength of the Peronist party. Duhalde's capacity to restore governability was greatly enhanced by the PJ's extensive roots in working- and lower-class society. Local Peronist machines and activist networks helped to dampen social protest in a variety of ways, ranging from distributing food and subsidies in poor neighborhoods and dissuading local residents from looting supermarkets to co-opting *piquetero* leaders and physically "clearing the streets" of left-wing activists. These – sometimes unsavory – means of achieving governability simply would not have been available to a non-Peronist president.

The PJ's persistent strength also helped Argentina avoid a full-scale meltdown of the party system. In Peru and Venezuela, the success of outsider candidates was rooted in the collapse of established populist parties, which left a large number of low-income voters available for antiestablishment or "neopopulist" appeals (Roberts 1995; Weyland 1999). In Argentina, by contrast, Peronism proved highly resilient in 2003. Rather than collapsing in the wake of the *que se vayan todos* protests, the PJ scored a series of impressive electoral victories: It easily retained the presidency (its three candidates won a total of 61 percent of the first round vote), won a solid majority in the legislature, and captured all but a handful of the country's governorships. Peronism's survival meant that Argentina's party system collapse was only partial. The throw-everyone-out vote was largely confined to the non-Peronist electorate: middle-class voters who had previously backed the UCR, FREPASO, and small conservative Peronist and progressive non-Peronist parties.[24] This limited the space for anti-establishment outsiders.

---

[24] Studies have shown that the blank and spoiled ballots of 2001 were drawn primarily from 1999 Alliance voters (Escolar and Calvo 2003).

ISSUES AND PROSPECTS FOR THE FUTURE

The performance of Argentina's post-1983 democracy is not easy to evaluate. Although the regime suffered a series of extraordinary political and economic crises, it also proved remarkably robust, surviving the 1989 hyperinflation, radical economic reform, the Menem government's abuses, and the 2001–02 economic collapse. Argentina's regime trajectory suggests a few general conclusions. First, leadership does *not* appear to have played a decisive role in Argentina's post-1983 regime outcomes. Democracy survived despite being governed by both ineffective (Alfonsín, De la Rua) and irresponsible (Menem) leaders. The Argentine case also points to the limits of regime analyses that focus on institutional design. Argentine governments experimented with a variety of political and economic institutional arrangements – many of which were widely praised by international observers – over the course of the twentieth century. Yet what is most striking about most of these institutions is their failure to take root. Arguably, then, the principal problem with Argentina's political institutions has been not their design but their *weakness*.

Issues of institutional strength are likely to be central to the future of Argentine democracy. One key area of concern is the party system. This chapter has argued that party strength was critical to democratic governance during the 1990s. In 2001, however, the party system suffered a partial collapse. The successive failures of the (Radical) Alfonsín and (UCR–FREPASO) De la Rua governments left much of the predominantly middle-class non-Peronist electorate without effective partisan representation, which alienated it politically and generated widespread hostility toward the political elite. It was largely this sector that cast blank and spoiled ballots in October 2001 (Escolar and Calvo 2003) and joined the throw-everyone-out protests in 2001 and 2002.

Although the collapse of FREPASO and the UCR could trigger the emergence of a more representative and effective party system, developments in Peru and Venezuela during the 1990s suggest an alternative, less optimistic scenario: The collapse of established parties may result in full-scale party-system decomposition and the rise of anti-political-establishment outsiders, with highly negative consequences for the quality and stability of democracy. Because the spread of mass media technologies has reduced politicians' incentives to invest in party building, new parties and party systems have proven extremely difficult to rebuild in the contemporary period (Levitsky and Cameron 2003). In post-1983 Argentina, only the Radicals and the Peronists have succeeded in penetrating the entire national territory. All new and alternative political forces – from the center-left PI and FREPASO to the center-right UCEDE and Action for the Republic – were weakly organized, Buenos Aires-based parties. All of them disappeared within a decade. The center–right ARI and center–right MFR, which emerged as potential leaders of the anti-Peronist opposition in 2003, similarly lack national organizations and support bases outside the metropolitan centers. If they fail to extend into the peripheral provinces, they will likely suffer the same fate as their predecessors.

If the UCR does not recover from its post-2001 collapse, the Argentine party system could be transformed into a fragmented universe of provincial parties, middle-class, Buenos Aires-centered parties, and outsiders. Such fragmentation would pose a significant threat to democratic governance, particularly in the realm of executive–legislative relations. It would also encourage the rise of anti-political-establishment outsiders. Finally, a collapse of the party system could bring about a return to the problems of sociopolitical representation that plagued Argentine democracy between 1930 and 1976. If key social and economic actors lack effective representation in the party system, they will be more likely to pursue their goals outside the electoral arena.

A second issue has to do with institutional change. The broad discrediting of Argentina's political institutions after 2001 generated widespread demands for institutional restructuring. Argentines from across the political spectrum demanded that the slate (again) be wiped clean. There were calls for the mass resignation of all elected officials, the replacement of the entire Supreme Court, a new constitution, and an overhaul of the electoral and campaign finance systems. For many, the crisis constituted an opportunity to throw out a failed political elite and rewrite the political rules so as to do away with entrenched problems – such as clientelism, corruption, and fiscal profligacy – that had undermined the quality of democracy. Responding to these public demands, the Kirchner government embarked on a series of bold reform initiatives in 2003, including a shake-up of the military and police hierarchies, the annulment of amnesty laws protecting military officers from prosecution for human rights violations, and the encouragement of impeachment proceedings against Menemist Supreme Court justices. Not surprisingly, these measures generated broad public support.[25]

Yet as Argentine history makes clear, there are costs to repeated institutional change. Another round of large-scale reform, even if done with the best of intentions, would reinforce the country's long-term pattern of institutional weakness. A clear example of this dilemma is the Supreme Court. During the 2001–02 crisis, many Argentines simultaneously complained about the absence of judicial independence and called for the impeachment of the Supreme Court. Whatever the benefits of Kirchner's partial purge of the Supreme Court, it comes at the cost of another blow to the institution of judicial tenure security, which may reinforce long-established patterns of judicial weakness.

The issue of institutional reform thus presents a difficult dilemma. On the one hand, it may be essential to restoring public confidence in representative institutions. On the other hand, it would reinforce a pattern that has predominated since 1930: When the going gets tough, the players and the rules get changed. Building stable institutions is a difficult process. It often requires that institutions weather a few major storms – and that political and economic actors adhere to them even when they expect the rules to yield short-term inefficiencies or losses. As long as Argentina lacks political institutions strong enough to

---

[25] *Página/*12, 1 June 2003.

weather crises (or in some cases, changes of government), short-sighted, non-cooperative, and socially irresponsible behavior will continue to be the rule.

In the decades to come, Argentine democracy will likely continue to benefit from several favorable structural conditions, including relatively high levels of wealth and education and a strong civil society. Yet these conditions are clearly insufficient to ensure long-term democratic stability, much less a high-quality democracy. For democracy to function well over the long haul, politicians must do more than get the institutions right. Rather, they must also undertake the slower, more arduous, and less politically rewarding task of sustaining and strengthening those institutions.

3

The Growing Sustainability of Brazil's Low-Quality Democracy

Kurt Weyland

THE COMPLEX ISSUE OF DEMOCRATIC SUSTAINABILITY

During the last two decades, liberal, representative democracy in Latin America has been surprisingly stable. Whereas the Second Wave of democratization (1940s–1950s) was followed by a strong rip tide that undermined many new civilian regimes in the 1960s and 1970s, the Third Wave has spawned few reversals, especially outside the Andean region. One of the most striking cases of relative success is Brazil, whose first "experiment in democracy" after 1946 (Skidmore 1967) was rocked by military rebellions, threatened by serious succession crises, and finally derailed by sociopolitical polarization that triggered the military coup of 1964. By contrast, the "New Republic" installed in 1985 has faced fewer and less serious challenges, and the crises that did occur have been resolved inside the democratic institutional framework. Besides having a better record on sustainability, the new democracy also features higher quality on some important dimensions, such as popular participation, the vibrancy of civil society, the accountability of top political and government leaders, and the independence of civilian politics from military interference.

These accomplishments are noteworthy given that Brazil continues to suffer from serious structural problems, such as large-scale poverty and egregious social inequality, which are often regarded as obstacles to stable democracy. And economic growth, which could provide resources for buying off discontented sectors, has not been higher and steadier after 1985 than before 1964. Also, the new democracy suffered two important "accidents," namely the untimely death of President-elect Tancredo Neves in 1985 and the impeachment of President Fernando Collor de Mello in 1992, which catapulted Vice Presidents José Sarney

I am grateful to Rachel Meneguello and Simone Aranha (CESOP/UNICAMP) and to Andrew Stein for unearthing crucial opinion poll data on Brazil's first democracy; to Timothy Power for using his amazing knowledge of Brazil to answer numerous queries; and to Frances Hagopian, Wendy Hunter, Scott Mainwaring, Francisco Weffort, an anonymous reviewer, and the participants of the Notre Dame conference for excellent comments.

and Itamar Franco to power. As a result, for seven out of the first ten years of the postauthoritarian regime, the president had low legitimacy and was politically weak – not a good precondition for governability and democratic stability.

What, then, accounts for the surprising sustainability and improved quality of Brazilian democracy? Political science has not advanced a unified, coherent theory of democratic stability. Instead, scholars have made disparate efforts at explanation that invoke a wide range of causal factors. One important reason for this heterogeneity is methodological. Like "health" in the field of medicine, "democratic stability" is often defined or operationalized via the absence of its opposite, namely democratic breakdown. And as people can fall ill from many different causes, so democracy can stumble over a variety of obstacles, such as severe economic downturns, growing ideological polarization, or defeat in external war. Also, as medicine considers both immediate triggers – such as a new virus – and underlying weaknesses that exacerbate a person's susceptibility to these triggers – such as a weakening of the immune system – so political science needs to assess the relative importance of different types of causes. For instance, a presidential system of government may increase the risk of democratic breakdown (Linz 1994), but not destroy democracy on its own; a collapse will only occur if problems such as deep social inequality trigger serious conflict in such an unpropitious institutional setting. An explanation of the surprising stability of democracy in contemporary Brazil is therefore inevitably complex; it needs to discuss a variety of causal factors.

The literature on democratic stability has indeed advanced variegated arguments that reflect divergent theoretical perspectives. Such explanations are mostly derived from theories about the emergence of democracy, which are themselves diverse. For instance, authors who depict democracy as the product of socioeconomic modernization assume that advanced urbanization, mass education, participation, and so forth also sustain democracy. Scholars who claim that transformations of the class structure bring forth democracy argue that a breakdown of democracy results from class conflict.

Thus, an assessment of democratic stability in Brazil needs to examine a variety of arguments[1] that emphasize socioeconomic development, changes in the class structure, institutional reforms, and the evolution of ideas and values. Furthermore, some authors locate the principal operative causes inside Brazil, whereas others stress international factors. For instance, value change can result from domestic socioeconomic modernization or learning from prior experiences (such as the dictatorship's horrors), but it can also emanate from the international diffusion of ideas.

The following analysis classifies these different arguments in four groupings. First, authors inspired by revised versions of modernization theory or neo-Marxist ideas à la Barrington Moore (1966) emphasize socioeconomic structures and transformations, such as urbanization, mass education, and spreading

---

[1] Recent analyses of democratic sustainability have indeed been mostly *tests* of hypotheses (Przeworski et al. 1996; Remmer 1996; Mainwaring 1999a; Mainwaring and Pérez-Liñán 2003).

participation or the rise and decline of certain social classes, respectively. Second, scholars who are influenced more and more by rational-choice assumptions stress political–institutional factors, such as the much-discussed problems of presidentialism. Third, "culturalists" – broadly defined – point to value change, such as the advance of participatory norms and growing commitment to democracy. Finally, scholars of globalization locate the crucial factors at the world system – not the national – level. They therefore point to secular trends, especially the growing international integration in the economy, communications, and transportation, or to monumental specific changes, such as the fall of communism and the wave of neoliberalism that has swept across the world in the last two decades.

While based on competing theories and rival paradigms, these divergent arguments are not necessarily incompatible. In fact, the different elements they stress can be combined into a coherent explanation. Social–structuralists essentially analyze the interests and power capabilities of (differently defined) sociopolitical forces, elucidating the balance of influence among supporters versus opponents of democracy. Political institutionalists analyze the (often-unintended) consequences of strategic interaction among different political actors, explaining the actual outcomes of competition among supporters and opponents of democracy. Culturalists examine normative constraints that shape how actors define and push their interests and how they pursue certain political strategies; culturalists can thus explain why in unfavorable social–structural or political–institutional settings, democracy may nevertheless survive. Finally, "globalists" investigate external sources of the changes that the other three groups of authors analyze. Thus, elements of these divergent arguments can be combined to unravel the puzzle of democratic sustainability in contemporary Latin America.

Adopting such a "catholic" approach, my analysis shows that domestically based social–structural changes, political–institutional innovations, and ideational developments have in fact made some contribution to the stability of Brazil's new democracy. But their effect has been limited; by themselves, they do not guarantee democracy's survival. By contrast, two international transformations – the collapse of "real socialism" and the wave of market reform – have been more consequential, confounding the left worldwide, narrowing the ideological spectrum inside Brazil, putting political and socioeconomic elites at ease, and thus stimulating greater acceptance of the uncertainty created by democracy. These international changes ensure the stability of Brazilian democracy for the foreseeable future. Thus, whereas social–structural developments, political–institutional reforms, and value change diminished the probability of an interruption of democracy in Brazil, the fall of communism and the spread of "neoliberalism" have precluded this possibility for the time being.

In fact, Brazilian democracy became much more stable after the early 1990s, when the two global transformations – especially market reform – took full effect. During its first decade, the postauthoritarian regime still faced some potential roadblocks, especially advancing left radicalism, reactionary countermobilization on the right, and pronounced military tutelage. Despite their stability-enhancing effects, social–structural changes, political–institutional innovations, and ideational developments did not preclude crisis episodes, such as the panic caused among the right by the possibility of a socialist victory in the 1989 presidential election; the political uncertainty surrounding the unprecedented impeachment of President Collor in 1992; and the worrisome machinations provoked by the power vacuum under President Franco in 1993–94. After 1995, by contrast, the new democracy has been virtually secure as a result of the ideological convergence brought about by the fall of communism and the spread of market reform, which finally took hold in Brazil under President Fernando Henrique Cardoso (1995–2002).

Looking beyond Brazil, the two momentous changes emphasized in this chapter are crucial for explaining the surprising sustainability of democracy in Latin America as a whole (see Mainwaring 1999a). For instance, the end of the Cold War greatly facilitated the negotiated resolution of civil wars in Central America; the adoption of market reform by Argentina's President Carlos Menem overcame the gulf between the Peronist party and its enemies that had precluded stable democracy since the 1940s; and the adoption of the North American Free Trade Agreement (NAFTA) – a crucial step in Mexico's neoliberal program – tied the hands of Mexico's incumbent Partido Revolucionario Institucional (PRI; Institutional Revolutionary Party) and contributed significantly to its electoral defeats in 1997 and 2000, which ushered in full democracy. Thus, a comparative perspective confirms the crucial importance of the international transformations stressed in this essay.

To flesh out these arguments, the next section documents the significant advances of Brazil's postauthoritarian regime, while acknowledging the many persistent obstacles to a high-quality democracy. The third section analyzes the impact of social–structural developments – especially socioeconomic modernization and the transformation of Brazil's class structure – on democratic sustainability. The fourth section focuses on political–institutional factors, examining changes in the rules governing the civilian political game and in the organization of the military. The fifth section assesses the extent and effect of value change at the elite and mass level. The sixth section emphasizes the stability-enhancing repercussions of two international transformations, namely the fall of communism and the advance of "neoliberalism." The conclusion stresses the importance of advancing such a complex argument.

BRAZIL'S NEW DEMOCRACY: SIGNIFICANT ADVANCES DESPITE PERSISTENT PROBLEMS

Is Brazil's new democracy more stable and of higher quality than the civilian regime aborted by the 1964 coup? Given this volume's interest in advances and setbacks of democracy, the present assessment focuses on change over time. It applies a relative, historical standard, not an absolute, ideal standard. Accordingly, the postauthoritarian regime has progressed significantly in sustainability and quality, although it continues to face considerable problems and challenges. In brief, democracy in Brazil is doing better – although it is not always doing well – and it has become better but is far from being good. Brazil shares these improvements with a number of other Latin American countries, where democracy has shown surprising sustainability and higher quality than in earlier time periods, as this volume shows. In the Brazilian case, there has also been a continuing advance toward greater stability (i.e., a slow process of "consolidation"). Whereas during its first decade the postauthoritarian regime still was vulnerable, it has become immune to challenges thereafter.

The New Republic has clearly been less unstable than the Second Wave democracy, which confronted several military rebellions and dangerous succession crises. From 1946 to 1964, factions in the armed forces with close ties to civilian sectors frequently interfered in politics and showed little hesitation to use force. On several occasions, civilian political groupings and important "powers-that-be," especially the armed forces, also challenged constitutional rules for presidential succession. This disloyal opposition contested the election of Juscelino Kubitschek in 1955–56 and the assumption of power by Vice President João Goulart after the unexpected resignation of President Jânio Quadros in 1961. The latter conflict, which severely strained democracy, triggered intense bargaining that forced an ad hoc transformation of Brazil's presidential system into a semipresidential regime (Mainwaring 1997: 90–91; Skidmore 1967: 205–15). Thus, important political actors did not respect the established institutional rules, sought to overturn the results of elections, and applied their special power capabilities in ways that violated the democratic principle of political equality. As a result, the 1946–64 regime never achieved consolidation but remained fragile and contested.

By contrast, the Third Wave democracy has seen no military uprising, and the armed forces have operated inside the democratic institutional parameters, especially after the resumption of direct presidential elections in 1989. In fact, Presidents Collor and Cardoso subordinated the military to civilian direction (Hunter 2000: 111–16). Problems of presidential succession have not endangered democracy either. Collor's impeachment in 1992 proceeded entirely according to legal and constitutional rules, although the successor, Vice President Franco, encountered distrust from important sociopolitical forces, especially business; attempts by a military leader to organize pressure on Collor to resign foundered at resistance inside the armed forces.[2] And when newly installed President Franco quickly proved his utter ineptitude, (self-)coup rumors and military saber-rattling (see Brener, Suassuna, and Contreiras 1993; Dimenstein and de Souza 1994: 14, 110–11, 138–43) never led to an effort to interrupt democracy; instead, the rules of the game pointed to an easy solution – namely the democratic election of a successor in the upcoming 1994 contest. Thus, while not enjoying unchallengeable stability, Brazil's postauthoritarian regime

---

[2] Confidential author interview with a leading member of the Collor government, Rio de Janeiro, 1995.

has never come to the brink of breakdown, as the second-wave democracy did in 1954–55, 1961, and 1963–64.

Only one leadership succession after 1985 could have jeopardized democracy's survival. If Luiz Inácio Lula da Silva from the socialist Partido dos Trabalhadores (PT; Workers' Party) had won the 1989 presidential election, which stimulated serious left–right polarization, conservative politicians, businesspeople, and the military may have perceived a level of threat that could have triggered antidemocratic maneuvers. Even though the PT leadership was aware of this risk and therefore planned to chart a moderate course, it may not have managed to control its radical party militants (as Chilean President Salvador Allende failed to do in 1970–73). The panic gripping the right before the 1989 runoff, when Lula seemed to pull ahead in the polls,[3] suggests that conservative forces would have used any means to block leftist threats to their core interests. If this polarization had triggered social turmoil and political unrest, the military may eventually have dislodged a PT government. But, of course, Collor won in 1989, putting the right at ease and averting this breakdown scenario.

In sum, Brazil's postauthoritarian regime has been significantly more stable than the Second Wave democracy and has become more stable over time. While it passed through some danger zones in its first decade, it has not confronted any risk since then. For instance, the traumatic currency devaluation of January 1999, which jeopardized hard-won economic stability and weakened President Cardoso's leadership, did not trigger the slightest threat to democracy. Neither did the 2002 presidential victory of the PT's Lula, who despite his significant ideological moderation continued to instill concerns among domestic and foreign investors. Thus, the New Republic has by now acquired the sustainability to survive crises – though perhaps not catastrophes – without any challenge.

Just as the postauthoritarian regime has never faced the risk of "violent death," it has also not undergone an involution and atrophy that could cause its "slow death," as happened in Peru in the late 1990s. Certainly, policy making is elitist, and many decisions are predetermined by technical experts inside the executive branch, rather than being thoroughly deliberated in Congress. Also, presidents have extensive decree powers, which allow them to usurp Congressional prerogatives, at least in agenda setting (Shugart and Mainwaring 1997: 49).

But the tendencies toward presidential autocracy and rule by experts are limited in Brazil, in clear contrast to Fujimori's Peru. For instance, presidential decrees have only temporary legal validity. To become permanent statutes, they need Congressional approval. Over the years, the legislature has indeed rejected or thoroughly amended a number of important presidential decrees. Also, experts in the Brazilian state lack monopolistic control over policy making. Even though they define the parameters for many decisions and have tremendous

---

[3] Confidential author interviews with businesspeople in São Paulo, November–December 1989. In 1992, FIESP president Mário Amato vividly recalled these fears in an interview (São Paulo, 9 June).

control in economic policy, they face considerable questioning and opposition from Congress and public opinion on social and political issues, as the long-standing, highly controversial debates about social security and administrative reform under the Cardoso government demonstrate. Also, Brazilian experts are not unified. Pluralism and competition keep "technocracy" in check and give democratic politicians "the last word." Thus, public decision making is not dominated by an unaccountable, uncontrollable power center.

This absence of presidential autocracy and technocratic domination is note-worthy because Brazil has long had a particularly strong, active state. The new civilian regime has tamed this Leviathan, which was especially powerful under the dictatorship. Congress acts as an important counterweight to the executive. While the government retains the upper hand in many policy arenas, Congress exercises considerable influence and oversight. Thus, the new civilian regime is not headed toward a "slow death" by presidential strangulation or technocratic suffocation.

Furthermore, citizens have important avenues for participation and broad choice in selecting their representatives. Brazil's loose electoral system, while permitting problematic levels of party fragmentation, keeps political entry barriers low. This openness allows new political forces to rise, including parties that seek to represent popular interests, such as the PT. These groupings can compete under rules that – while frequently changed in manipulative ways – are upheld with reasonable consistency. In particular, there has been no serious electoral manipulation or harassment of the opposition, as occurred in Peru's 2000 presidential contest and in Venezuelan gubernatorial races in 2000. Thus, voters enjoy wide freedom of choice. Also, many Brazilians actually exercise their democratic rights. With 77.1 percent of citizens casting a ballot in the 1998 presidential contest (IBGE 1999: 187), electoral participation has remained reasonably high, contrary to the large-scale abstention prevailing in troubled democracies, such as Venezuela. Furthermore, like Argentina (see Levitsky's chapter), Brazil has a vibrant civil society and an independent press, which provide citizens with ample information about politics and try to organize them for collective action. Indeed, trade union density and participation in voluntary associations seem to be higher in Brazil than in other countries of the region. In 1993, 66 percent of Brazilian survey respondents reported membership in voluntary associations, a comparatively high percentage (McDonough, Shin, and Moisés 1998: 920). In sum, Brazil's postauthoritarian regime is not at risk of losing its democratic character, as in Peru during the late 1990s.

In fact, by comparison to the Second Wave regime, the quality of Brazilian democracy has improved on several dimensions, especially individual and collective participation; the accessibility, accountability, and responsiveness of the government; and political competitiveness.[4] As regards individual participation, the enfranchisement of illiterates in 1985 eliminated the last barrier to universal suffrage; as a result, 55 percent of the population voted in the 1989

---

[4] On these components of democratic quality, see Schmitter (1983: 888–90).

election, compared to only 22 percent in 1960 (Lamounier 1996: 176). Certainly, this inclusionary measure had a cost by strengthening clientelism and thus allowing elitist, oligarchical politicians to perpetuate their power (cf. Hagopian 1996a). But with continuing urbanization, the routinization of democratic competition, deliberate organizational efforts by "popular," left-wing forces, and anticlientelist government programs, clientelist domination is slowly diminishing in force, permitting lower-status people to enhance their bargaining power by playing rival patrons off against each other. In a similar vein, corporatism has eroded considerably, allowing for greater competition among interest groups, such as ideologically diverse trade union confederations. In particular, state control over associations, which was pronounced during most of the Second Wave democracy, has virtually disappeared after the guaranteeing of associational autonomy in the 1988 constitution. Thus, Brazil joins other Latin American countries in which clientelism and corporatism are slowly decaying, most prominently Mexico. As a result of these trends, political participation is nowadays more widespread, independent, and active than it has ever been in Brazil.

As regards collective participation, civil society is more active and energetic than under the Second Wave democracy. Corporatism's decay and clientelism's slow erosion have facilitated the proliferation of independent interest associations, social movements, and non-governmental organizations. With socioeconomic modernization, Brazil has acquired a rich array of groups, some of which vigorously push for their interests and advance their ideas (Dos Santos 1992; Hochstetler 2000; Power and Roberts 2000: 254–57). While the very multiplication of groupings has problematic aspects by causing pronounced fragmentation, it gives Brazil's new democracy an extensive organizational infrastructure, prevents individualistic atomization, and – potentially – instills participatory norms in sectors of the population. Also, with pronounced rural unionization, civil society is less confined to urban centers and has a broader scope and more balanced density than in earlier decades.

Moreover, citizens nowadays have better access to the policy-making process. Whereas under the previous democracy, only interest associations of businesspeople, professionals, and formal-sector workers advanced their interests and "lobbied" successfully, nowadays rural unions and an array of social movements also have some political voice. For instance, the Movement of Landless Rural Workers had considerable indirect influence on governmental decisions concerning land reform under the Cardoso administration (Ondetti 2002) and has obtained many positions inside the state apparatus under the Lula government. This broader access has resulted from organizational advances in civil society and from some institutional innovations. For instance, the Constituent Assembly of 1987/88 allowed for "popular amendments," which gave groups without direct representation in Congress the opportunity to advance proposals. Moreover, many state agencies have created advisory councils that include organized civil society. These new channels of access have led to the initiation of reforms – for instance, in health policy – that would otherwise be unimaginable.

The accountability of political leaders and government officials has also begin to improve, though very slowly. As in Argentina, independent media and an active civil society have started to crack the traditional pact of immunity among the "political class." For instance, whereas in the 1946–64 period, the prevailing attitude toward corruption was *"rouba mas faz"* (he steals, but he gets things done), contemporary politicians and state officials run serious risks to their political survival by engaging in malfeasance. Corruption scandals have irreparably damaged important political careers, especially those of President Collor and former São Paulo governor Orestes Quércia, a powerful party boss. In a country with endemic graft, the frequent scandals erupting under the postauthoritarian regime are actually signs of progress. They show that standards of evaluation have risen: important sectors of the citizenry no longer resign themselves to graft as an unavoidable vice of their leaders. The outcome of these scandals – especially President Collor's impeachment and the expulsion of several powerful Congressmen for budgetary malfeasance in early 1994 – have communicated to politicians and public servants that cleaner government pays politically. Therefore, governmental corruption seems to have diminished from the early 1990s onward.

Less clearly, the responsiveness of politicians and policy makers now seems somewhat higher than under the 1946–64 regime. Although many serious problems and important needs remain unaddressed, the executive and legislative branches do attend to some of the citizenry's most pressing demands or expectations. For instance, the widespread yearning for an end to explosive inflation eventually induced all civilian governments to decree economic stabilization plans. Also, some social sector reforms, such as the institution of universal health care coverage, the improvement of rural social security benefits, and the reform of basic education, were triggered partly by popular demands or, more frequently, by professionals who claimed to speak for poorer sectors (Weyland 1996a). Thus, the new democratic governments have been somewhat responsive to lower-class people – though much more generous to the privileged, whose benefits continue to be subsidized by the poor.

Finally, Brazilian politics has become significantly more competitive. For most of the 1946–64 period, an alliance of two parties founded by outgoing dictator Getúlio Vargas, the Partido Social Democrático (PSD; Social Democratic Party) and the Partido Trabalhista Brasileiro (PTB; Brazilian Labor Party), had predominant influence, marginalizing the opposition União Democrática Nacional (UDN; National Democratic Union). Until the early 1960s, the civilian regime was led by a well-entrenched elite cartel that could not be easily dislodged via elections. After 1985, by contrast, electoral outcomes and the composition and policy direction of the government have been much more uncertain. Although still socially quite skewed, Brazil's political elite is nowadays more heterogeneous and fragmented in organizational and ideological terms. The broad opposition front under the military regime, organized in the Partido do Movimento Democrático Brasileiro (PMDB; Party of the Brazilian Democratic Movement), seemed to attain hegemony with a landslide victory in the

1986 legislative and gubernatorial elections, but it soon splintered and lost support, becoming just one among several major parties. And even though the Partido da Frente Liberal (PFL; Party of the Liberal Front), whose founders broke with the military regime in 1984 and allied with the ascendant PMDB, has almost always been in the government, it has never had exclusive control over the executive branch. Instead, there has been considerable turnover. Thus, democratic politics in contemporary Brazil is more competitive than between 1946 and 1964.

Furthermore, a crucial unelected actor – the military – nowadays commands less power to constrain elected authorities. Military interference in civilian politics, which reached high levels under the Second Wave democracy, has been low since the resumption of direct presidential elections in 1989. Whereas under the transitional government of José Sarney tutelage by the armed forces was still pronounced, it virtually disappeared in the 1990s, except during the power vacuum created by President Franco's ineptitude in 1993–94 (Hunter 1997). In present-day Brazil, active-duty officers rarely make public pronouncements about general political issues and do not use pressure to influence any decisions outside their specific sphere of competence. As civilian politicians enjoy unrestrained latitude, political competitiveness has increased in the Third Wave democracy.

In sum, the postauthoritarian regime boasts a higher quality than the 1946–64 democracy. In a historical perspective, there has been progress. Obviously, however, democracy in Brazil continues to suffer from innumerable problems. The New Republic falls short of reasonable absolute standards of meaningful participation, accessibility, accountability, responsiveness, and competitiveness (Ames 2001; Hagopian 1996a; Mainwaring 1999b; Power 2000; Weyland 1996a). Thus, the quality of democracy continues to be deficient.

Political participation remains distorted by persistent – though slowly eroding – clientelism, especially in poor urban neighborhoods and rural regions. Pressing socioeconomic needs continue to induce many Brazilians to seek help and protection from higher-status people, in return for supporting the patrons' political goals. Therefore, they effectively cannot exercise their political rights autonomously, which is crucial for full citizenship. Political participation in Brazil is also marred by violent repression against rural unionists (Pereira 1997: ch. 6). Thus, the weak rule of law has negative political repercussions in ample regions.

Moreover, political access in contemporary Brazil is highly unequal across social strata. This skews the responsiveness of political authorities. While better-off sectors get priority treatment, common citizens receive little attention. They clearly lack "unimpaired opportunities . . . to have their preferences weighed *equally* in the conduct of the government" (Dahl 1971: 2; emphasis added). As is common in Latin America (Transparency International 2000), widespread corruption further distorts responsiveness as Brazilians with ample means can literally buy favorable decisions, whereas lower-class people are subject to draconian rules. This discrimination, poignantly captured in the maxim "*para os amigos, tudo; para os enemigos, a lei*" (for our friends, anything; for our enemies, the law), certainly weakens the quality of democracy. For these reasons, pressing problems that affect the majority – such as basic needs for decent nutrition, housing, education, and health care – often remain unresolved. Responding to Brazil's deep social inequality, most politicians spout "progressive" rhetoric; for instance, right-wing parties claim to be "social-democratic" and "reformist" – but they clearly act in inegalitarian and regressive ways. Thus, political responsiveness is often more fiction than reality.

While political accountability has begun to improve, Brazil's new democracy still has a long way to go. Malfeasance continues to be widespread among politicians and public officials. Brazil therefore ranks far below First World countries as well as Chile and Costa Rica in Transparency International's corruption index. With a score of 3.9 out of ten, it occupied the forty-ninth rank among ninety countries in 2000 (Transparency International 2000). More acts of malfeasance are nowadays investigated, and some guilty office holders have been removed or forced to resign; however, barely any perpetrator has ever gone to jail. Furthermore, Brazil's odd system of open-list proportional representation makes it difficult for voters to punish electorally those politicians who neglect their duties. Because one leading vote-getter can guarantee additional legislative seats for her party (cf. Mainwaring 1999b: 249), even politicians who individually receive few votes may "by accident" end up in Congress. Therefore, citizens cannot reliably hold politicians accountable.

Even though competitiveness has improved over the Second Wave democracy, Brazil's political elite continues to be predominantly narrow in social terms. In several poorer, backward states (such as Bahia, Maranhão, and Rio Grande do Norte), but also in developed, modern Santa Catarina, family dynasties still hold sway. At the local level, many politicians try to control certain areas (*redutos*) and exclude competitors. And although voters nowadays enjoy a wide range of ideological choice, many politicians are disturbingly similar in political style. Specifically, many former opponents to the military regime, who pressed for clean government and faithful political representation when resisting the dictatorship, adopted long-established shady practices during the transition to democracy. In order not to lose out against well-entrenched conservatives, they also came to use patronage to buy support and established clientelist networks to gain a captive electoral base. As these practices spread, political options became more similar, limiting competitiveness.

In sum, the quality of Brazilian democracy is clearly deficient. While the postauthoritarian regime shares many of these problems with other Latin American countries, the deficits in participation, accountability, and responsiveness seem significantly more severe than in Chile, Costa Rica, and Uruguay. Nevertheless, Brazil's new democracy has achieved clear advances, both in stability and quality. What accounts for this noticeable – though painfully slow and woefully incomplete – improvement? Through comparisons with the troubled democracy of 1946–64, the following sections assess the role of social–structural, political–institutional, and cultural factors and then focus on the fall of communism and the advance of neoliberalism.

THE IMPACT OF SOCIOECONOMIC DEVELOPMENT AND CHANGES IN CLASS STRUCTURE

Based on robust statistical findings that socioeconomic modernization correlates with democracy and enhances the stability of competitive civilian regimes, numerous authors have argued that various aspects of development have a causal effect on democratic transition and consolidation. Economic growth alleviates scarcity and may thus reduce social conflict and forestall political polarization. Improvements in education allow citizens to engage in more autonomous and meaningful political participation and hold their representatives accountable. Urbanization and industrialization diminish the number and clout of landowners, peasants, and rural workers, who are more likely to support antidemocratic movements, and reinforce urban middle and working classes, who are more committed to democracy.

Between the Second and Third Waves of democratization, Brazil certainly experienced tremendous change in all those dimensions (overview in Power and Roberts 2000). The positive effect of these changes on democratic stability has, however, remained limited. For instance, even though economic growth has benefited all sectors of the population, it has by no means eliminated scarcity. Large-scale material deprivation has persisted. In 1990, 27 percent of the population classified as poor, living on less than one quarter of the minimum wage (Oliveira 1993: 34). In 1998, 50.8 percent of the economically active population earned less than two times the minimum wage, which at about US$73.30 was truly minimal. Only 8 percent of the economically active population (EAP) received more than ten times the minimum wage, thus enjoying a comfortable lifestyle (IBGE 1998: 14). Furthermore, Brazil continues to suffer from tremendous social inequality. In 1990, the top 10 percent of the EAP received 48.1 percent of all income, while the bottom 40 percent had to make do with a meager 7.9 percent (Oliveira 1993: 32). Brazil's Gini index of inequality, which regularly hovers around 0.6, ranks among the highest in the world. Thus, socioeconomic development has not abolished the material preconditions that could, in principle, trigger severe political conflict.

Improvements in education are also unlikely to account for the postauthoritarian regime's stability. The main reason is that under the Second Wave democracy, the uneducated did not participate much in politics because illiterates lacked the vote. Since the new democracy lifted this barrier, the average educational level of the voting population is probably not much higher nowadays than before 1964. In fact, the enfranchisement of illiterates – advocated by the left in the name of political equality – has ironically furthered the political survival of conservative rural elites, who held about 30 percent of Congressional seats in the late 1990s.[5] Thus, the elimination of literacy requirements – a progressive measure – has cushioned conservative forces against the political repercussions of socioeconomic modernization.

While the direct effects of socioeconomic change have remained limited, transformations of Brazil's class structure have enhanced democratic stability in significant – though far from decisive – ways. In particular, rapid urbanization and industrialization have reduced the socioeconomic and political importance of the agricultural sector. Therefore, conflicts over the highly unequal distribution of land, which helped derail Brazilian democracy in the 1960s, are nowadays much less consequential. As a result of "the end of the peasantry" (Pereira 1997), the push for land reform no longer involves a major proportion of the population. Even if successful, it would not usher in a fundamental transformation of economy or society – not to speak of a social revolution. Whereas agrarian reform was ranked as the second or third most important "problem confronting Brazil" in the early 1960s ("Tendências" 1996: 5), it did not appear at all among the fifteen most frequently mentioned problems in 2000 (IBOPE 2000a: question 6), despite the continued agitation of the Movement of Landless Rural Workers, which grew tremendously in the mid-1990s (Ondetti 2002). Because this issue is not nearly as important and explosive as in 1961–64, landowners cannot count on much support for their counterviolence, as the widespread rejection of the reactionary União Democrática Ruralista (Democratic Rural Union) suggests. In particular, they clearly could not incite any effort to derail democracy.[6]

Urban society has also gained greater complexity, which dissipates conflict. With the proliferation of different branches of industry and the tremendous growth of the service sector, Brazil's socioeconomic structure has become highly heterogeneous. This diversity has perpetuated and exacerbated organizational fragmentation (see following discussion), which in turn prevents lower-class people from advancing their demands in a powerful united front. Instead, specific sectors or groupings press their own, narrow interests, which aim at inclusion, not radical transformation. They want a piece of the pie, not a turnover of the whole cake or a replacement of the baker. In fact, their focus on specific interests makes these fragmented groups susceptible to divide-and-rule tactics and cooptation (Mainwaring 1987).

This fragmentation is obvious among trade unions, which constitute one of the best instruments for forceful collective action by lower-class individuals. In contemporary Brazil, however, ideological disunity prevails in the labor movement, weakening its overall power. For instance, while the metal workers' union in the city of São Paulo is affiliated with the ideologically moderate, politically

---

[5] Landed elites are operationalized here as the landowners' caucus (*bancada ruralista*). Given the imprecision and unreliability of deputies' professional self-classification, membership in this informal interest group is a better indicator.

[6] Mainwaring and Pérez-Liñán (2003: 1048–50) show that the diminishing weight of the rural sector favors democracy in Latin America.

conservative Força Sindical (Union Force), its counterpart in the industrial suburbs militates in the radical, socialist Central Única dos Trabalhadores (CUT; Unified Workers' Central). These confederations often pull in different directions. Such disagreements limit labor's influence and, above all, prevent any serious threat to the established socioeconomic order.[7]

Class conflict is also mitigated because CUT is strongest and most militant among public sector workers, whereas many private sector unions have joined more moderate confederations; even CUT unions in the private sector often prefer cooperation over confrontation, as is evident in their participation in meso-corporatist arrangements, such as the Câmara Setorial (Sectoral Chamber) of the auto industry. Thus, radicalism does not pit workers against capitalists, but public employees against the state – which usually makes concessions. As a result, private business does not directly face union militancy that threatens its core interests. Entrepreneurs, therefore, see little need for governmental repression or military intervention.

Brazil's urbanization and industrialization have also changed the balance of entrepreneurial assets, rendering fixed agricultural property less important while enhancing the weight of movable capital, especially highly mobile financial assets. In the 1946–64 period, a larger share of wealth was embodied in land, which obviously cannot "exit" to escape expropriation, taxation, or onerous regulation. To protect their property, owners therefore had to rely on voice – ultimately, calls for military intervention. Nowadays, a substantial share of wealth is held in liquid assets that can easily be transferred out of Brazil. Businesspeople, therefore, have greater exit options, as indicated by the threat of Mario Amato, president of Brazil's most powerful business association, FIESP (Federação das Indústrias do Estado de São Paulo or Federation of Industries of the State of São Paulo), that a victory of socialist Lula (PT) in the 1989 presidential election would induce 800,000 entrepreneurs to abandon their country. In this way, capitalists could perhaps strangle a radical-left experiment economically and may not see the need to oust it – and thus overthrow democracy – by appealing to the military.

In sum, Brazil's increasingly modern, pluralistic, and organizationally fragmented society dissipates the potential for fierce, broad-based social conflict. While sectoral or local challenges to elite interests do occur, an overall assault on the established order has become less likely than in the 1946–64 period. Social–structural change has thus diminished the reasons for fear among privileged sectors, especially private business and conservative politicians. Even before the fall of communism and the dramatic advance of neoliberalism, which have sealed the defeat of the left and put the right at ease (see the section entitled "The Importance of Communism's Fall and 'Neoliberalism's' Rise" in this

---

[7] On the crucial impact that threat perceptions by business, conservative politicians, and the military have on democratic stability, see the classic treatment in O'Donnell (1978b: 7; 1979: 68–70) and more recently in Bellin (2000: 181–82, 186–96). For evidence of such fears in Brazil, see Mettenheim (1990: 28); Payne (1994: chs. 2, 5); and Reis and Cheibub (1995: 42, 49).

chapter), Brazilian democracy was not very likely to fall as a result of escalating class conflict.

Thus, sociostructural change helped to stabilize the postauthoritarian regime. But the political impact of this socioeconomic transformation was limited. First of all, these developments did not prevent the gradual advance of the socialist Workers' Party (PT) during the 1980s. Through diligent base-level organization, this new party overcame the cleavages dividing the popular sectors and forged a broad-based coalition behind a radical reform program. Even though the PT drew firm support from only a narrow slice of the electorate,[8] it received enough diffuse backing to come close to capturing the presidency in 1989. Had it won, many of its militant cadres would probably have pushed for profound socioeconomic change. Since the more moderate party leadership would have had difficulty controlling these radicals, turmoil and polarization would have resulted. Thus, social–structural transformations did not completely preclude fierce conflict in Brazil's New Republic. Those changes alone cannot account for the postauthoritarian regime's sustainability.

In general, the Brazilian case proves that socioeconomic structures by no means determine democracy's fate. After all, the New Republic has remained fairly stable despite large-scale poverty and egregious social inequality, which many social–structural arguments depict as likely triggers of serious conflict and threats to democratic survival. In fact, Brazilian elites worry that the tremendous inequity could cause severe turmoil. Sixty-three percent of respondents in an elite survey regarded it as likely or even certain that Brazil's social problems would produce "a chronic state of social convulsion" (De Souza and Lamounier 1992: 12).

This socioeconomic dynamite is unlikely to precipitate a political explosion even though it contributes to widespread crime and other social problems. What is striking about Brazil are not the few instances of mass mobilization and resulting political turmoil but the infrequency of these occurrences. Clearly, important filters prevent the translation of potential grievances into actual contention. In the 1946–64 period cultural factors – such as widespread deference and acceptance of hierarchy – may have played a major role, but nowadays political–organizational mechanisms are crucial. These obstacles block the negative repercussions that Brazil's egregious inequalities could, in principle, have for democratic stability. In fact, the previously mentioned deficiencies in the quality of Brazilian democracy – especially weak representation and low accountability – help prevent the translation of socioeconomic problems into open political conflict, which could endanger democratic sustainability. Thus, as a result of deep socioeconomic inequity, democratic quality and stability stand in an inverse relationship in Brazil. Tragically, a more faithful representation of popular interests could diminish democratic stability by prompting a fierce defensive response from established elites. In a situation of open class

---

[8] Lula won only 16.1 percent of the vote in the first round of the 1989 presidential contest.

conflict, privileged sectors would probably see a high-quality democracy as a threat to their core interests.

What are the filters that prevent open social conflict from erupting in Brazil? Above all, the non-elite, "popular sectors" are divided and weakened by pronounced organizational fragmentation (Weyland 1996a). Many of the poor living in the countryside or the urban periphery use clientelistic connections to higher-status patrons to obtain minimal protection and particularistic benefits. While slowly eroding, these vertical linkages hinder horizontal collective action and allow elites to "divide and rule," thus forestalling challenges from below. Where social movements and other "contentious" organizations have emerged among the poor, their membership has remained fairly limited (Dos Santos 1992: 65, 76). Also, many of these associations focus more on specific local problems than on structural reform at the national level. Therefore, they are also susceptible to clientelism and cooptation (Mainwaring 1987).

Interest groups formed by formal-sector workers or middle sectors have greater leverage, and many of them are affiliated with national-level peak associations that advance overarching ideas or programs. But in their actual demand making, these groupings often focus on much narrower concerns, including interests that are at odds with their confederation's overall orientation. For instance, public employee unions affiliated with the socialist CUT have steadfastly defended their members' privileges in Brazil's inequitable social security system, although CUT's poor constituents have had to shoulder part of the burden through their indirect tax payments. Interest groups' narrow focus has resulted not only from the sectoral differentiation of Brazil's increasingly complex society but also from the legacies of state corporatism, which deliberately confined interest groups to sectoral and local constituencies. While democratization has undermined state corporatism, the resulting segmentation of associations has mostly persisted, inducing these groupings to push circumscribed interests.

As a result, Brazil's civil society speaks with innumerable voices and has great difficulty advancing overarching goals, such as redistributive reforms. Because of the organizational indiscipline and programmatic weakness of most political parties (Mainwaring 1999b; Ames 2001), interest aggregation is underdeveloped. Most parties lack firm links with societal groupings and do not serve as their representatives. Thus, the inchoate nature of Brazilian parties disables the main institutional mechanism that could, in principle, advance bottom-up pressure for a systemic transformation. Politics in Brazil has a disaggregative – rather than aggregative – impact, corroding collective demand making and dissipating socioeconomic conflict. For these reasons, most of the time severe structural problems – especially mass poverty and egregious social inequality – do not translate into open political contention and ideological polarization.[9]

---

[9] In a fundamentally similar vein, Remmer (1996: 617–19, 630–31) argues that economic problems do not necessarily weaken democratic sustainability because open political competition generates regime support that allows democracies to withstand hard times. By contrast, Przeworski et al. (1996: 42, 49–50) find that economic trouble endangers democratic survival.

The deficient quality of Brazilian democracy actually bolsters the stability of the postauthoritarian regime.

These conclusions suggest that even though socioeconomic structures are undeniably important, they are clearly not decisive for democratic stability in Brazil; instead, the organizational configuration of the polity also plays an important role.[10] The discussion therefore turns to political–institutional factors.

THE EFFECT OF POLITICAL–INSTITUTIONAL INNOVATION

In Brazil's institutional framework, continuities with the 1946–64 period prevail over change. Both the Second and Third Wave democracies have had presidential systems of government, open-list proportional representation, and mostly inchoate, programmatically incoherent, and organizationally fluid parties. Important elements of this institutional configuration have continued to bolster democratic sustainability. As just mentioned, for instance, the weakness of most parties has hindered the eruption of severe social conflict. Paradoxically, the deficits that Brazil's rather unrepresentative, unaccountable parties create for democratic quality (Mainwaring 1999b; Ames 2001; Hagopian 1996a; Weyland 1996a) enhance democratic stability.

The breadth of Brazil's party system also furthers the sustainability of democracy. Above all, powerful, predominantly conservative elite sectors such as landowners, big business, and rightist political leaders continue to have substantial representation inside a range of parties and an influential voice in Congress (Power 2000, Kingstone 1999).[11] Therefore, these elites have a strong incentive to advance their demands through formal institutional channels, rather than knocking at the barracks' door, as the politically weak Argentine right did for most of the twentieth century (Gibson 1996). In the postauthoritarian regime, conservative elites have indeed used this political influence to forestall threats to their interests, for instance by ensuring that the 1988 Constitution exempts "productive" land from expropriation.

Different from the Second Wave democracy, the far left is nowadays represented in the party system as well. After 1947, the Brazilian Communist Party (Partido Comunista Brasileiro; PCB) was officially banned. In reaction to this prohibition, "the PCB returned to...extremist voluntarism" (French 1992: 266). Barred from open electoral participation, it infiltrated the union movement to stimulate class conflict. This communist "subversion" in turn triggered concern among the right, helping to fuel the polarization of the early 1960s, which eventually derailed democracy (Skidmore 1967: 225–26, 279, 283; Goldenberg 1971: 427–33).

By contrast, the postauthoritarian regime immediately lifted the ban on communist parties. Even the outgoing military regime had allowed the radical,

---

[10] See for Latin America in general, Mainwaring and Pérez-Liñán (2003: 1033, 1060).

[11] As Power (1997: 199–205) shows, the political right strengthened its (initially weak) commitment to political parties during the 1990s.

socialist PT to form and run in elections. While the PT initially shunned compromise and alliances (Keck 1992: ch. 6), the quest for electoral success induced it over time to reach out to other political forces and to appeal to broader sectors of the population, beyond its original working-class constituency (Marques 1993; Nylen 2000). Its gradually increasing representation in Congress and victories in municipal and gubernatorial elections also motivated party leaders to seek agreements with other groupings to get some of its proposals enacted. For these reasons, the PT gradually turned less radical in its programmatic orientation and political tactics (Nylen 2000: 127–28, 132, 138–40). Rather than promoting conflict and polarization, as in the Second Wave democracy, the left has contributed to centripetal competition under the postauthoritarian regime. As a result of this political dynamic – and of the global ideological transformation discussed in the section entitled "The Importance of Communism's Fall and 'Neoliberalism's' Rise" – the right has perceived the left less and less as a threat.

According to important institutionalist arguments (especially Mainwaring 1993), however, the political inclusion of the left could have exacerbated instability by making Brazil's presidentialist system even less manageable. By extending the party system's ideological spectrum and introducing an organizationally unified and programmatically oriented contender, the PT's rise increased party system fragmentation, which could make it even more difficult for chief executives to garner parliamentary support. Therefore, stalemate and gridlock – important risks in presidential systems – could have worsened.

Until they took over the government in early 2003, the PT and other leftist parties indeed offered obstreperous resistance to many presidential initiatives and successfully practiced obstruction, helping, for instance, to derail the constitutional revision of 1993–94. But the left's limited size restricted its veto power, confining it mostly to constitutional changes, which require supermajorities. Whenever centrist and rightist parties allied and deterred defection among their members, they defeated the left, even on constitutional amendments, as the numerous modifications of the 1988 charter engineered by the Cardoso government show. Thus, the left did not immobilize decision making.

In fact, the threat of leftist victories, especially in presidential elections, induced center and right-wing parties to act in greater unison. The broad coalition sustaining the Cardoso government was formed in the election year of 1994, when socialist Lula initially seemed well placed to win the presidency. Thus, the gradual advance of the left for years gave the government leverage for holding its own political base together, easing gridlock in Brazil's presidential system.

When such strategic considerations do not guarantee sufficient Congressional backing, presidents retain ample patronage resources to "buy" support. Because many Brazilian politicians garner votes by doling out particularistic benefits, they are susceptible to presidential courting. Thus, the very indiscipline and fickle programmatic commitments of Brazilian parties allow chief executives to build coalitions (see in general Tsebelis 1995: 311–13). Admittedly, however, these efforts at cobbling together support are by no means uniformly successful. In fact, the government's supporters have an incentive to threaten resistance to extract even more patronage. Despite these difficulties, patronage provides crucial oil for greasing the squeaky wheels of Brazilian presidentialism (Pereira and Mueller 2004).

Furthermore, the 1988 Constitution gives presidents an important institutional instrument for pursuing their initiatives in Congress that did not exist under the 1946–64 regime, namely ample legislative decree powers (Power 1998; Shugart and Mainwaring 1997: 49). While these "provisional measures" (MP) eventually need Congressional approval to become law, their temporary validity often creates faits accomplis that are difficult to reverse. For instance, if Congress had rejected the temporary confiscation of financial assets that President Collor decreed in March 1990, hyperinflation would have exploded; Congress, therefore, had to approve Collor's edict. Thus, presidents can sometimes force Congress to approve their projects. Also, until 2002, they successfully claimed the right to reissue indefinitely the MPs that Congress had not dispatched, thus extending their temporary validity far beyond the constitutionally stipulated thirty days. Crucial economic programs, especially the antiinflationary Real Plan of 1994, were enacted and fine-tuned via a succession of MPs (Figueiredo and Limongi 1997: 142–52; Power 1998: 212–13). By allowing presidents to legislate temporarily in a flexible fashion, this new institution thus constitutes a highly useful instrument for combating crises. The chief executive also sets the agenda for parliamentary deliberations by emitting MPs, which Congress must give priority attention. Finally, these decree powers allow legislators to delegate the resolution of complicated, controversial, or highly technical issues to the executive (Carey and Shugart 1998a). In all these ways, these proactive prerogatives, which did not exist in Brazil's first experiment with democracy, strengthen the president vis-à-vis parliament. They thus further ease the danger of deadlock created by pronounced party fragmentation in Brazil's presidential system.

Certainly, the MP itself has turned into a bone of contention in executive–legislative relations. Because the 1988 Constitution did not clarify important aspects – for instance, whether presidents could reissue MPs – chief executives claimed greater prerogatives than intended by the framers; Congress on several occasions sought to contain this further expansion of presidential powers and eventually restricted the reissuing of MPs in 2002. On the other hand, the MPs have arguably enhanced governability and the substantive performance of the new democracy. The Real Plan, which finally restored economic stability, was enacted via MPs, which give presidents a flexible instrument for fine-tuning reforms and making rapid adjustments to changing circumstances. Thus, while the MP can tempt weak presidents to make futile efforts to impose their will, inflaming executive–legislative relations, it also allows strong presidents to enact decisive changes efficiently without having to engage in constant deal making with patronage-obsessed parliamentarians. Over time, Congressional efforts to rein in the misuse of MPs have deterred unrealistic efforts at imposition (Power 1998: 211–12); consequently, the governability-enhancing effects of this institution have come to the fore. On balance, then, this decree authority has enhanced the postauthoritarian regime's sustainability.

Yet even though the MP has diminished the danger of gridlock in Brazil's presidential system, it cannot reliably preclude such a stalemate. Eventually, MPs require Congressional approval to gain permanent validity. Since the MP does not abridge Congress's role as the ultimate legislator, it does not give the president free rein. Therefore, interbranch clashes remain possible. But they are less likely than under the constitutional regime of 1946–64. In general, governing remains difficult in Brazil's postauthoritarian regime, which disperses power to a pronounced extent (Ames 2001; Mainwaring 1997, 1999b; Weyland 1996a; contra Figueiredo and Limongi 2000). But the New Republic has not been nearly as polarized and stalemated as the Second Wave democracy during its last few years (cf. Dos Santos 1986). Thus, the potential dangers of presidentialism are not about to undermine the new democracy's sustainability, as in 1964.

Ironically, again, deficits in the quality of Brazilian democracy – the inchoate party system and extensive presidential decree powers – heighten its stability. Most parties' lack of organizational cohesion and many politicians' hunger for patronage provide the necessary flexibility for constructing legislative backing for governmental projects. And the president's attribution to legislate "provisionally" reshapes Brazil's system of checks and balances, strengthening executive leadership. While limiting the responsiveness and accountability of Brazil's "political class" to the citizenry, these features help to make presidentialism work.

Finally, Brazil's imaginative political class has found an innovative way of ousting a president who is politically isolated and has insufficient support in Congress. President Collor's impeachment on corruption charges has set a precedent for removing deeply unpopular chief executives. While Collor and his entourage certainly were corrupt and while the accusations raised by his own brother were difficult to ignore, many other Brazilian politicians have probably engaged in wrongdoing. Indeed, the left opposition considered proposing President Cardoso's impeachment on much less striking evidence of malfeasance. Other Latin American presidents have, in fact, been ousted based on questionable accusations of violations of budget rules (Venezuela's Carlos Andrés Pérez in 1993) or "mental incapacity" (Ecuador's Abdalá Bucaram in 1997) (Weyland 1998: 117–20). The possibility of impeaching the chief executive opens up an escape from lengthy stalemates in presidential systems, which could undermine democracy.

All these political changes and institutional innovations, which affect primarily civilian politics, have thus made the postauthoritarian regime more stable than the Second Wave democracy. In addition, the military's capacity and willingness to intervene in politics and undermine or overthrow democracy have diminished greatly. The 1946–64 regime often faced strong military pressure and confronted several rebellions. This political interference was driven by pronounced factionalism inside the armed forces (Hunter 1992: 72–106). Lack of institutional unity and discipline allowed military groupings to get involved in fights among different power contenders (see, e.g., Skidmore 1967: 103–08, 127–29, 140–41, 149–56, 207–11, 221, 249, 261–66). Civilian politicians often appealed to their allies in uniform for support (Stepan 1971: 64, 67, 80). Discontented military sectors also advanced their interests on their own, via saber rattling or uprisings.

Concerned about this lack of unity and intent upon limiting the armed forces' corrosive politicization, the authoritarian regime of 1964–85 enacted a series of institutional reforms to turn the military more cohesive and accentuate its boundary to civilian politics (Hunter 1992: 106–18). Dissident officers were purged, and challenges to hierarchical authority were discouraged by sanctions. Furthermore, new rules of promotion gave the top leadership more discretion over officers' careers, which it used systematically to ensure internal cohesion. Finally, active military personnel were barred from exercising civilian office; all officers who assumed governmental positions had to step down from the armed forces. In these ways, the dictatorship successfully combated factionalism and created a much more unified and professional military.

In the New Republic, divisions and politicization inside the armed forces have therefore been much less pronounced than before 1964. Greater institutional unity and discipline allow the top brass – and indirectly the president, as commander in chief – to keep renegade officers under control. Therefore, military groupings have not been drawn into struggles among civilian political forces nor started rebellions on their own. Organizational unification has also induced the upper ranks to advance the institutional goals of the military as a whole, not specific sectoral interests. In particular, generals are more aware of the damage that excessive interventionism – especially taking sides in fights among civilian politicians – creates for the military institution. More unified organization leads the military leadership to internalize the costs of their actions for the reputation, political standing, and budget of the armed forces.[12] In fact, the overbearing guardianship that some generals exercised over the weak transition government of José Sarney created a backlash that motivated the first democratically elected president, Fernando Collor, to make deliberate, ostentatious, and successful efforts to reduce military influence substantially. Top officers quickly learned that attempts at tutelage carry heavy costs under the new democracy and modified their behavior accordingly. In situations of limited political polarization and low threat to the armed forces' basic interests – as under the New Republic – prudence and caution have, therefore, come to predominate. For these reasons, the military has been much more reluctant to intervene in politics than during the first experiment in democracy, and not a single military rebellion has erupted (Hunter 2000: 109–16).

Certainly, however, the military's institutional unification does not absolutely preclude political intervention, including the ouster of an elected government. In fact, reduced factionalism gives the armed forces greater *capability* to act if

---

[12] For the general logic of this argument, see Olson (1986).

the top leadership considers it necessary. Given their self-ascribed mission as ultimate guarantors of law and order, which the 1988 Constitution confirmed (article 142), the military could interfere in politics under some scenarios. Specifically, if the armed forces perceived a serious threat to their central institutional interests or a fundamental challenge to social order and political stability, they would be prepared to interrupt democracy (cf. Hunter 1997: 143–46). Thus, the military's reorganization alone does not guarantee democratic stability. It has this effect only in a setting of sociopolitical tranquility, which prevails in contemporary Brazil as a result of the structural and institutional changes discussed previously and, especially, the international transformations, which are analyzed in the section entitled "The Importance of Communism's Fall and 'Neoliberalism's' Rise."

In conclusion, political changes and institutional reforms have helped to stabilize Brazil's new democracy. In particular, the inclusion of socialists and communists into the party system has moderated the left while inducing the center and right to become somewhat more cohesive. Furthermore, the 1988 Constitution increased presidential prerogatives, especially decree powers. For both reasons, Brazil's presidential system nowadays faces a lower risk of deadlock than in the early 1960s (cf. Dos Santos 1986). Finally, the military's reorganization has diminished its propensity to intervene in politics.

THE REPERCUSSIONS OF VALUE CHANGE

Cultural developments have also contributed to the relative stability of the postauthoritarian regime. Specifically, the traumatic downfall of Brazil's first experiment with democracy and the horrors of prolonged dictatorship have induced political elites to attribute greater importance to the preservation of liberal, competitive rule. To what extent this new appreciation of democracy would drive actual political behavior, especially in crisis situations, is unclear, however. Also, value change at the mass level has remained limited and unsteady, providing a weak foundation for democratic sustainability. Therefore, while bolstering stability to some extent (which is difficult to ascertain more precisely), ideational and cultural changes do not seem to guarantee the survival of Brazilian democracy.

The available evidence suggests that among political and societal elites, commitment to democracy is somewhat stronger under the postauthoritarian regime than under the Second Wave democracy. The experience of prolonged, harsh authoritarian rule – with hundreds of political murders and thousands of torture victims – led important actors to value democracy more. The very duration of the dictatorship showed civilian politicians that the armed forces could not be used to oust a government they opposed, hold new elections, and restart the democratic process immediately. By staying in power for twenty-one years, the military broke with this traditional pattern of acting simply as a "moderator" (*poder moderador*) among civilian power contenders. Instead, by monopolizing positions of top authority, the generals stunted politicians' ambitions. Even though Congress continued to operate, it had minimal influence until the early 1980s. Thus, civilian politicians learned that knocking at the barracks' door was risky, imposing great costs on the political class.

The revaluation of democracy has been particularly pronounced among the left. In the 1960s, the radicalizing influence of the Cuban revolution made sectors of the left denounce liberal democracy as a bourgeois formality and assign priority to socioeconomic transformation over political liberty. The tremendous suffering inflicted especially on leftists in the dictatorship's torture chambers caused a profound change of mind. The left came to see democracy with its protection of civil liberties as indispensable (Packenham 1986; Weffort 1986: 59–62, 94–95, 118–33). This rethinking of crucial value trade-offs clearly had a deradicalizing impact, discouraging efforts to smash the existing system. Attempts at structural change became acceptable only if they did not endanger democracy (Weffort 1986: 101–33).

The renovation of the left, in turn, has eased fears on the right, which has not faced any serious efforts at full-scale revolution. The right has, therefore, seen less need to call for repression. The undisturbed operation of democracy, which allows the left to proselytize, no longer constitutes a threat to the right's core interests. Compared to the early 1960s, political polarization has diminished; the forces on opposite ends of the ideological spectrum have found more common ground. Basic elite convergence, a precondition for democracy, has increased.

As a result, 64 percent of elite respondents surveyed in 1989–90 saw a high likelihood that Brazilian democracy would achieve consolidation during the 1990s (De Souza and Lamounier 1992: 11; Lamounier and Marques 1992: 148). This prediction can function as a self-fulfilling prophecy, inducing major power contenders to play by the new rules of the game and causing a habituation of behavior. Evaluative attitudes have also betrayed widespread commitment to democracy. For instance, 80 percent of elites surveyed in 1993–94 felt that Congress – the democratic institution par excellence – should have "decisive influence" (Soares de Lima and Boschi 1995: 14).

Even under the postauthoritarian regime, however, elite attitudes have by no means been uniformly democratic. Instead, support for democratic institutions has coexisted with pronounced elitist, hierarchical tendencies (Soares de Lima and Boschi 1995: 20–23). Also, 48 percent of elite respondents in 1989–90 strongly agreed that "the armed forces must maintain internal law and order if they were convoked for this purpose" [by one of the three constitutional powers – an ambiguous provision of the 1988 Constitution], and 55 percent saw some chance (33 percent) or a high likelihood (22 percent) that the military would return to power (De Souza and Lamounier 1992: 12–13).[13] Thus, while having clear prodemocratic currents, elite political culture also retained worrisome authoritarian components.

---

[13] By contrast, not a single elite respondent surveyed in 1993–94 mentioned "the possibility of military intervention" as a "principal obstacle to democracy in Brazil" (Soares de Lima and Cheibub 1994: 11; Reis and Cheibub 1995: 40).

Given these contradictory tendencies, it remains unclear how strongly and reliably prodemocratic attitudes drive elite behavior, especially in potential crises. If radicalism reemerged and conflict escalated, the new appreciation for democracy might fade, and civilian power contenders might again be tempted to call the military to the rescue. Polarization would put rival political forces into a prisoners' dilemma, which might push them "inevitably" toward the destruction of democracy, as during the early 1960s (Cohen 1994: chs. 5–6).

Two incidents under the postauthoritarian regime provide evidence for these dangers. First, Lula's advance before the 1989 runoff instilled panic among right-wing forces, elicited threats of capital flight, and triggered preparations for problematic constitutional manipulation, such as proposals to introduce a "parliamentary" system (designed, as in 1961, to limit drastically the powers of a leftist president). If the socialist candidate had actually won, conflict could well have escalated, eventually destroying the new democracy. Second, the power vacuum created in 1993–94 by the dismal performance of mercurial President Franco triggered coup rumors and significant military saber rattling. These episodes show that democratic values among the elite are not strong enough to immunize Brazilian democracy against all challenges.

In fact, even when concern for democratic stability drives politicians, the outcome is not necessarily favorable. Shortly after the regime transition, for instance, the leader of the PMDB, Ulysses Guimarães, who had been marked by the horrors of the dictatorship and was therefore determined to ensure democratic sustainability, supported the weak Sarney government for years – much longer than important sectors in his own party wanted. But this persistence discredited Guimarães and his party, which garnered a dismal 4.4 percent of the vote in the 1989 presidential election. This virtual collapse allowed for the rise of outsider Collor, whose imperious style, obsession with autonomy, and large-scale graft exposed Brazil's new democracy to particular tests. Thus, in the medium run, Guimarães' effort to stabilize democracy had the opposite effect.

In sum, value change at the elite level has probably made some contribution to democratic stability, but it is not a decisive factor. More important than a genuine rethinking of democracy may be the increased international protection of democracy, which imposes an external constraint on Brazilian elites. Because major foreign powers, especially the United States, nowadays consider authoritarian rule illegitimate, Brazilian decision makers, who have long sought to enhance their country's prestige, are probably reluctant to defy a worldwide trend and help install an authoritarian regime, which Brazil's economic partners and political friends would treat as an outcast. Therefore, the suggestions in late 1993 that President Franco should execute a self-coup à la Fujimori did not find many followers. As an external check on antidemocratic machinations – more than as an internal impetus to democratic behavior – international value change therefore contributed to democratic sustainability.

At the mass level, value change is even weaker than at the elite level. The scarcity and low quality of the opinion surveys conducted before 1964 complicates comparisons; nevertheless, the available evidence suggests that un-conditional commitment to democracy has not significantly increased from the Second to the Third Wave democracy. When asked in 1952 whether "Brazil would bear an enlightened dictatorship or whether it was quite mature for democracy" – certainly, odd question wording – 44.4 percent of respondents in Rio and São Paulo chose the democratic option, whereas 21.4 percent sided with the "enlightened dictatorship" and 34.2 percent "did not know" (UNICAMP-AEL, IBOPE 1952: 669). In September 1989, 43 percent of a national sample preferred democracy under all circumstances, whereas 18 percent regarded dic-tatorship as sometimes better, another 22 percent saw no difference, and 15 per-cent did not know (Moisés 1995: 127). And in 2000, 39 percent of Brazilians opted for democracy; 24 percent considered an authoritarian government as sometimes preferable (Lagos 2001: 139). While differences in sample and ques-tion wording hinder a comparison, these data certainly do not show a sea change toward greater democratic commitment.

As regards specific elements of democracy, there has also been little evolution. While 41 percent of Cariocas looked "favorably upon the participation of the military in the country's political life" in 1955 ("Tendências" 1994: 11),[14] 42–46 percent of two national samples approved of military intervention in politics in 1989, and 36 percent approved of it in 1990 and 1993 (Moisés 1995: 117). Moreover, popular support for the legalization of communist parties (often in-terpreted as an indicator of political tolerance) grew significantly higher than under the Second Wave democracy only after this liberalizing measure was actu-ally taken – and after it became obvious that the repercussions were negligible. Thirty percent of respondents in Rio approved of this step in 1955, and a mi-nuscule 13 percent of Paulistanos expressed approval in March 1964 (Lavareda 1991: 159; "Tendências" 1994: 11, 15); a similarly low 15 percent did so in 1982, at the very end of the military regime (Muszynski and Mendes 1990: 63). Approval rose to 47 percent in 1986 and 57 percent in 1988 (Muszynski and Mendes 1990: 63) – only *after* communist parties became legal in 1985 (i.e., after the question's meaning changed).

Furthermore, commitment to democracy has remained at disturbingly low absolute levels under the postauthoritarian regime. "Preference for democracy under all circumstances" fluctuated between 42 and 59 percent of respondents in the late 1980s and early 1990s, while 14–23 percent continued to favor dic-tatorship in certain situations, and 14–26 percent indicated indifference (Linz and Stepan 1996: 171–75; Moisés 1995: 126–27; Muszynski and Mendes 1990: 68–73). Surprisingly, despite the recuperation of governability under President Cardoso, support for democracy declined from 50 percent in 1996 to a wor-risome 39 percent in 2000 and 37 percent in 2002 – the lowest score among the seventeen countries in the *Latinobarómetro* survey in 2000 and 2002 (Lagos 2001: 139; Latinobarómetro 2002: 6). Thus, mass commitment to democracy is very limited in Brazil.

---

[14] In 1962, 61 percent of respondents stated that "military influence should be excluded from government and politics whenever possible" (Lamounier and de Souza 1991: 315).

Popular assessments of democratic stability are also not particularly strong. In a 2000 survey, 46 percent of respondents thought that "Brazilian democracy is consolidated because elections are held regularly," but 36 percent disagreed (IBOPE 2000b: question 7C). Thus, many citizens continue to question democracy's sustainability. And whereas the perception of democratic consolidation can induce people to respect the rules of the game, the divided views prevailing in Brazil may encourage some discontented sectors to undermine democracy.

Finally, it is difficult to ascertain what survey respondents exactly mean by "democracy." Even if they identify as unconditional democrats, they may not embrace the principles that scholars associate with this term in defining it in procedural and institutional terms. For instance, 78–82 percent of Peruvians approved of President Fujimori's self-coup in April and May 1992, yet 73 percent simultaneously professed commitment to democracy (Carrión 1994: 2–4; Conaghan 1995: 236). In fact, "54 percent of those polled after April 5 characterized the [Fujimori] government as 'democratic' rather than 'dictatorial'" (Conaghan 1995: 241), probably feeling that the *autogolpe* had removed an "oligarchical" partyarchy led by an unaccountable political class. Many Peruvians thus applied a notion of democracy that does not exclude violent infringements on democratic procedures.

Similarly, a majority of Brazilians holds conflicting values. In a 1989 survey, only 10 percent qualified as consistent democrats, and another 29 percent were fairly consistent. By contrast, 51 percent mixed pro- and antidemocratic orientations (Muszynski and Mendes 1990: 65–67). Which tendency would prevail and guide political behavior is unclear. Thus, the cultural foundation of Brazilian democracy is not particularly firm.

In sum, it does not appear that increased elite or mass commitment to democracy has made a major contribution to stabilizing Brazil's postauthoritarian regime. Evidence of value change is weak. On a number of important dimensions, the available data suggest continuity rather than profound transformation. Also, Brazilians remain divided in their regime preferences; at the mass level, support for democracy is strikingly low. And insofar as elites and masses are committed to democracy, it is unclear to what extent such principles would govern their actions, especially in crisis situations. Thus, value change does not seem to account for the relative stability of Brazil's Third Wave democracy.

THE IMPORTANCE OF COMMUNISM'S FALL AND "NEOLIBERALISM'S" RISE

As shown so far, structural, political–institutional, and ideational developments have furthered democratic sustainability in Brazil to some extent, but their effect has been limited. In fact, these developments did not immunize the postauthoritarian regime against all challenges. Collor's impeachment and Franco's incompetence exposed the civilian regime to some threats in the early 1990s, and a Lula victory in 1989 could have unleashed lethal polarization and escalation, as in the early 1960s. Thus, during its first decade, Brazil's new democracy remained vulnerable.

Two international changes in the early and mid-1990s greatly enhanced the stability of Brazil's postauthoritarian regime, reinforcing the conflict-dissipating effects of social–structural and political transformations and easing the goal trade-offs that could induce political actors to sacrifice democracy. First, the collapse of communism confounded and further moderated the left, which the right therefore saw no longer as a fundamental threat. Second, the worldwide diffusion of neoliberal ideas and the adoption of market reform in Brazil precluded any effort at radical systemic transformation and provided additional protection for the core interests of conservative sectors, especially business. Brazil's ideological spectrum has therefore narrowed, greatly diminishing the danger of polarization. Because the left nowadays lacks a fundamental alternative to the established order, it has little reason to jeopardize democracy. And because the right – big business, large landowners, conservative politicians, and the military – no longer faces a basic threat to its vital concerns, it sees no need to sacrifice democracy either. For these reasons, the uncertain results of democratic decision making are unlikely to provoke all-out opposition from any major sociopolitical force. Democracy has turned into an "equilibrium solution" (Przeworski 1991: 26–34) from which no relevant actor has an interest to deviate.

These two international transformations had a profound effect on Latin America, helping to advance and stabilize democracy from the Rio Grande to Tierra del Fuego. For instance, the end of the Cold War was decisive for ending the Central American civil wars and ushering in democratization. Market reform in general and NAFTA in particular limited the PRI regime's room to maneuver, facilitating Mexico's long-awaited transition to full democracy. And the adoption of neoliberalism by a Peronist president overcame a deep cleavage that had for decades jeopardized democracy in Argentina. Although the two global changes have affected many Latin American countries, they have had a particularly important impact on Brazil, for two reasons. First, Brazilian elites have long sought to turn their country into a well-respected great power and have, therefore, been especially attentive to international trends. As the self-proclaimed "country of the future," Brazil does not want to miss the train of history. Second, because the particularly stark social inequality prevailing in Brazil could potentially trigger fierce conflict, the weakening and further deradicalization of the left prompted by the fall of communism and the advance of neoliberalism were crucial for calming fears among the right, which no longer sees the need to knock at the barracks' door. Thus, the collapse of "real socialism" and the wave of market reform, which have favored the installation and consolidation of democracy throughout Latin America, have had an especially salutary effect on Brazil.

With communism's demise and the end of the Cold War, ideological conflict inside Brazil lost its dangerous edge, and the international protection of democracy became much firmer. Although by the late 1980s, few Brazilian leftists saw the USSR as a model, the collapse of 'real socialism' deprived socialist parties all over the world of a minimally feasible alternative to a market economy (Lemke and Marks 1992: 3–7). Capitalism won; even reform-socialist proposals and other compromises between capitalism and communism came to be seen as unviable. Whereas history generally seemed to move towards the left during the preceding decades – with growing state interventionism and expanding welfare states in most countries – now political and economic liberalism appeared as the final stage of history (cf. Fukuyama 1989). The left, which had claimed the mantle of progress before, now seemed to be headed in the wrong direction.

This change on the world scene had a profound impact on the left in Latin America, including Brazil (Castañeda 1993). For instance, leading thinkers and strategists of the PT came to revalue the market, tone down demands for a revamping of the established socioeconomic order, and call for a thoroughgoing renovation of the party and its program (Genoíno 1992: 25–32; Leo 1991; see also Ridenti 1992). These proposals stimulated heated discussions among the left, which resulted in a slow tendency toward ideological moderation. This deradicalization of the left and the lack of any external sponsor for revolution eased fears among the right. A left that lacked a blueprint for systemic transformation could not lead Brazil into a radical experiment. And with the apparent turn in history's course, the right became more confident that it could protect its core interests. It now felt that it was sailing with the wind rather than paddling upstream against the current, as in the late 1980s.

With the end of the Cold War, powerful international actors – most importantly, the United States – also revised their priorities among competing goals. Until the late 1980s, the United States had often subordinated its desire to spread democracy to perceived strategic necessities, supporting, for instance, the ouster of a leftist government and the destruction of democracy in Brazil in 1964. With the implosion of the rival superpower, the United States no longer faced any security threats in the Western Hemisphere. Therefore, it came to concentrate much more on democracy promotion. As a result, efforts to overthrow civilian rule in Latin America have triggered a swift and strong response, which has successfully deterred and reversed coups and restored at least the basic outlines of democracy. Given its political and economic importance, Brazil would certainly face such pressure if democracy faced threats. Therefore, the end of the Cold War gave domestic political actors an important additional reason for not plotting any attack on the postauthoritarian regime.

Communism's fall and capitalism's perceived victory also gave additional impetus to market reforms, which had started in Latin America in the mid-1980s, but had progressed only sporadically. After President Sarney had taken some exceedingly cautious steps toward privatization and trade liberalization, President Collor decreed drastic adjustment and initiated bold, comprehensive market reforms upon taking office in March 1990. Even though several of these risky, costly measures elicited resistance even from businesspeople and conservative politicians, the overall effort to reduce state intervention and enhance the private sector's role and weight found much support: It promised to give capitalists a predominant place in the economy, to remove any threats to their property, to weaken trade unions and leftist parties, and to boost the political project of conservative parties. The advance of "neoliberalism" thus sealed the defeat of the radical left and strengthened the right, especially by giving its programmatic ideas political predominance. The most serious threats to Brazil's Second Wave democracy had emerged when challenges from the left induced the right to seek military intervention; consequently, the new "hegemony" of rightist ideas stabilized the postauthoritarian regime.

Initially, however, the enactment of neoliberalism exacerbated conflict and triggered new challenges to Brazilian democracy. President Collor pushed for numerous drastic measures with an imperious, arrogant strategy and style, despite his weak political base and the pronounced dispersal of power in Brazil. Collor's initiatives therefore triggered severe conflict, which caused a political stalemate from late 1990 onward. This deadlock produced a crisis atmosphere and provoked many proposals for institutional manipulation (Lamounier 1996: 179); it was resolved only by the president's impeachment in late 1992. The early 1990s, therefore, saw serious tension, which did not favor democratic consolidation. Only the use of fully democratic procedures – not extraconstitutional pressure – to oust Collor strengthened Brazilian democracy by proving its capacity to resolve a crisis.

When Fernando Henrique Cardoso – first as finance minister, then as president – resumed the push for market reform, he showed that he had learned from Collor's political failure. He, therefore, proposed less drastic measures, advocated a gradual reform process, and preferred negotiation to imposition. While not pushing for a full-scale free-market economy, Cardoso managed to enact a much wider range of structural reforms, especially deregulation and privatization, than Collor. These measures guaranteed business a central place in the economy and society, strengthened its clout by expanding its transnational links, and weakened its adversaries, especially trade unions. By weakening collective action among less well-off sectors, they also played into the hands of conservative and centrist parties. Because the center-right thus "won the war," it saw democracy no longer as a threat.

In fact, Cardoso's market reforms for years put the left on the defensive. Whereas the PT, in particular, had looked progressive and modern in the 1980s (Keck 1992), now the government aptly used the discourse of modernization to legitimate its reforms and depict the left as retrograde. Lacking a comprehensive, credible alternative to neoliberalism (Dulci 1997), the PT had difficulty responding to Cardoso's strategy (Nylen 2000: 138). For instance, by defending the losers from market reform – such as employees dismissed from the public administration or from privatized enterprises – the PT risked appearing as the protector of "special interests" that had enjoyed privileges not available to the large number of poor Brazilians. As a result of these quandaries, tensions inside the left increased; some sectors advocated a profound internal renovation and the acceptance of the basic outlines of market reform, whereas others dug in their heels and insisted on a socialist platform that sounded ever more obsolete (*Teoria e Debate* 1997, 17–28; Weyland 2002: ch 8). Weakened for years by infighting, the left seemed unable to promote any radical program that threatened the newly reinvigorated business sector and other conservative groupings. In fact, with the widespread acceptance of market reforms in Brazil, electoral incentives pulled the PT even more toward the center, and it further moderated its platform. Therefore, business and conservative politicians for the first time came to regard the party as acceptable for heading the government.

Whereas the prospect of a Lula victory had triggered panic in 1989 and stimulated threats of large-scale capital flight, by the late 1990s the PT came to be seen as a fully legitimate political force. The ideological spectrum in Brazilian politics narrowed decisively, and the deep gulf between left and center-right was bridged sufficiently to make alternation in power possible. Therefore, Lula's successful campaign for the presidency in 2002 and the PT's takeover of government power in January 2003 did not trigger any threat to Brazilian democracy. In fact, by charting a strikingly moderate and prudent economic policy course, the Lula administration quickly allayed the fears of investors, who had exacerbated economic problems with their defensive reactions in 2002. And by pursuing crucial items of President Cardoso's leftover structural reform agenda, especially an adjustment of Brazil's overly generous pension system for civil servants, the PT government ratified its ideological moderation and political reliability. Because all significant power contenders are now admitted to the political game and because conservative economic and political sectors that could bring down democracy no longer see their basic interests endangered, Brazilian democracy enjoys a high level of stability.

Market reform has also enhanced the external protection of democracy. Greater integration into the world economy exposes Brazil more to pressures from other democratic nations, especially the United States. The new international regime for safeguarding democracy commands powerful weapons against actors who seek to overthrow a civilian regime. Diplomatic isolation and economic sanctions could devastate the Brazilian economy, which is nowadays more dependent on short-term capital, long-term investments, and imports of technology. In addition to pressures emanating from the First World, Latin American countries themselves have constructed mechanisms for the collective defense of democracy, for instance in the Common Market of the South (MERCOSUL). Because Brazil has traditionally been eager to win international prestige and not become an outcast, it is particularly susceptible to these new constraints.

In sum, communism's collapse and the advance of market reform have secured democratic sustainability in Brazil. While social–structural developments, institutional changes, and political–cultural trends made the postauthoritarian regime more stable than the Second Wave democracy, these great transformations were decisive for immunizing the new civilian regime against threats.

CONCLUSION: A MULTIFACETED EXPLANATION

A wide range of factors have helped to make Brazil's new democracy much more stable than its predecessor (1946–64). First, social–structural developments have diminished the importance of the countryside with its endemic conflicts. Urban society has become more complex, confounding clear lines of class cleavage. For both reasons, socioeconomic and political elites nowadays face a lower threat of systemic transformation and can therefore accept democracy. Second, institutional changes – especially the left's inclusion in the party system – have moderated political conflict and forestalled polarization. And the strengthening of presidential prerogatives, particularly via extensive decree powers, has allowed chief executives to respond quickly and flexibly to crises and has lowered the danger of executive–legislative deadlock in Brazil's presidential system. Third, appreciation for democracy seems to have increased among elites. This value change may possibly prevent important political forces from single-mindedly pursuing their interests and risking dangerous conflict. At the mass level, however, democratic commitment remains weak. Finally, communism's fall and the progress of market reform have boosted democracy's sustainability by deradicalizing the left, reassuring the right, and thus leading to political convergence at the elite and mass level. The first three factors had a significant, yet limited impact by reducing the risk of a democratic breakdown; international developments were more decisive by precluding this danger and making the civilian regime highly stable. Whereas during the first decade of the New Republic important actors still worried about the survival of democracy, these concerns evaporated after the mid-1990s. In contemporary Brazil, democracy really is "the only game in town." Nothing demonstrates this process of democratic consolidation better than the undisturbed assumption of government power by Luiz Inácio Lula da Silva in 2002–03, whose prospective victory in 1989 could still have shaken the new civilian regime.

By stressing a variety of factors, this chapter proposes a complex explanation that combines elements of heterogeneous theories, hopefully in a systematic way. Social–structural arguments clarify the interests of political actors; political–institutional arguments elucidate the instruments and strategies that these actors use to pursue their interests; and cultural arguments analyze the normative constraints on the pursuit of these interests with those instruments and strategies. Finally, international developments affect the other three sets of factors.

While such a "catholic" approach may be anathema to purists, it embodies a notion of causality that is much more realistic for the political world, where several types of factors interact and the boundaries between domestic and international developments have become ever more porous. For instance, institutionalism – perhaps the predominant approach in contemporary political science – is obviously incomplete because it fails to elucidate the origin of actor preferences ("culture") and the underlying reasons for the institutional parameters of individuals' interaction ("structure"). Only explanations that take different kinds of factors into account can therefore be theoretically convincing (Lichbach 2003) and methodologically useful for unraveling the "multiple conjunctural causation" (Ragin 1987) that prevails in the political world.

4

The Demise of Mexico's One-Party Dominant Regime

Elite Choices and the Masses in the Establishment of Democracy

Beatriz Magaloni

The Mexican Partido Revolucionario Institucional (PRI; Institutional Revolutionary Party) was one of the most resilient autocrats in the world, holding office uninterruptedly for seventy years. Unlike single parties in most of Africa and the former Soviet bloc, the PRI stayed in power without constitutionally banning opposition parties or employing systematic repression. If we were to take Przeworski's dictum that "democracy is a system in which parties lose elections" (1991: 10), Mexico can unquestionably not be classified as democratic until 2000, when the PRI lost the presidency. Thus, from the onset of the democratization wave that swept the Latin American region starting in 1980, it took Mexico more than twenty years to democratize.

Why was the PRI so resilient? What accounts for its ultimate demise? In this chapter, I emphasize three sources of the PRI's capacity to survive: (a) the party's relative immunity to elite splitting; (b) the authoritarian nature of electoral institutions; and (c) the party's massive electoral support. I then explore how each of these pillars of the PRI regime was transformed, eventually leading to the establishment of democracy.

The chapter starts by placing the Mexican transition in comparative perspective. The democratization dynamics of one-party-dominant systems is different from other regime transitions. In transitions from military regimes and personal dictators, the main challenge the opposition faces is the threat of coercion. In transitions from one-party-dominant regimes, the opposition's main challenge is not coercion because opposition to the government is tolerated, as long as it takes established electoral means of contestation. The goal of the opposition is to defeat the party associated with the authoritarian past through the ballot box. Defeating the ruling party is extremely hard. The electoral arena is biased for two reasons. First, there are significant incumbency advantages, of which the most important is the ruling party's unilateral control of the state apparatus

The author thanks Frances Hagopian, Scott Mainwaring, and Alberto Diaz for comments and suggestions.

and the vast sources of patronage it can employ to deter voters from embracing the opposition camp. Second, the ruling party controls both the legislature and electoral institutions so that it can draft laws to raise the costs of entry to the opposition or, if need be, manipulate the voter registration, election procedures, and even the outcome of the elections.

The democratization of one-party-dominant autocracies requires, on the one hand, that voters defect to the opposition and, on the other, that the incumbent relinquishes its control of the electoral process so that some form of rule of law can emerge in the realm of elections. The granting of independence to the Federal Electoral Institute (Instituto Federal Electoral; IFE) through the 1994 electoral reform was a turning point in the Mexican democratization process because the PRI credibly tied its hands not to commit electoral fraud. What led the incumbent autocrat to renegotiate the existing rules of the game, relinquishing its control of the electoral process and delegating it to an independent electoral body? Through the use of a simple game theoretic model, the second section of this chapter answers this question. The model highlights why this form of political delegation was inconceivable when the opposition could not mount a serious challenge to the regime. Voters represented the main bargaining chips of the opposition to challenge the existing rules of the game. The last section of the chapter thus discusses how it was that voters ultimately defected from the ruling party. I end with a conclusion.

WHEN WAS DEMOCRACY ESTABLISHED?

Mexico became democratic sometime between the 1988 presidential election, when the PRI committed massive electoral fraud, and the 2000 presidential race. The PRI probably won the 1988 race, but massive fraud constitutes prima facie evidence that the incumbent was not ready to yield power peacefully (Przeworski et al. 2000). Moreover, back in 1988, only the Partido Acción Nacional (PAN; National Action Party) accepted the elections; the Cardenistas, who unified most of the left-wing opposition to the PRI into an electoral front, the so-called Democratic Front, did not. The balance of forces in society and the existing rules of the game changed between those two elections such that the PRI could no longer modify ex post facto the outcome of the electoral game, and *both* opposition parties chose to accept the existing electoral game as legitimate.[1] During those twelve years, the country crossed the threshold separating authoritarianism and democracy.

Unlike most transitions in Latin America, no one can provide a definite answer as to when exactly the Mexican one came about, however. The process of transition from one-party-dominant autocracies differs in significant ways

---

[1] I rely on Przeworski's (1991) definition of democracy as a system of *institutionalized uncertainty* where there are "ex ante uncertainty" (some positive probability that the incumbent will lose) *and* "ex post irreversibility" (outcomes of the elections are irreversible).

from the process of transition from military regimes and personal dictators.[2] The threshold that defines the passage from authoritarianism to democracy is easy to establish when the incumbent autocrat is the army or an individual dictator: Democracy is established when the army withdraws into the barracks or the dictator steps down, a founding election takes place, and the incumbent peacefully yields power to the opposition.

Transitions from one-party-dominant systems unravel in the electoral arena, where the party associated with the authoritarian past competes as a legitimate player and must be defeated through the ballot box. As elections become more competitive, the major political players tend to renegotiate the existing rules of the game so as to reflect the new balance of forces. A distinctive trait of this type of transition is that democratization might take place even without alternation of power in office. It is thus hard to establish the precise moment when democratization actually occurs.

The PRI unquestionably won the 1991 and 1994 federal elections. According to most political observers, the 1991 and 1994 elections were also relatively clean. In the 1994 presidential race, there were no significant allegations of fraud by the major contenders. Despite the transparency of the 1994 election, we do not know if the PRI would have peacefully stepped down from office had it actually lost. In 1997, the PRI lost the majority in the powerful Lower Chamber of Deputies for the first time and accepted its defeat. We do not know how this party would have behaved if the presidency had also been at stake in 1997 – although three years later, the PRI did yield power peacefully to the opposition's presidential candidate, Vicente Fox, suggesting that Mexico must have become a democracy sometime after 1988 and before 2000.

To avoid misclassifying a one-party-dominant authoritarian system as democratic, Przeworski et al. (2000) contend that one-party-dominant systems such as those existing in different historical moments in Taiwan, Malaysia, Mexico, and Botswana, to name a few, should be classified as authoritarian unless the incumbent actually loses and peacefully yields power. As the authors themselves recognize, the so-called alternation rule presents a problem, which is misclassifying a democratic system as authoritarian.[3] An additional drawback of this rule is that once an incumbent loses and accepts defeat, the authors classify the country as democratic for the whole period that the incumbent was in control of the government. However, because Mexico was autocratic during most of the years that the PRI ruled, it is not reasonable to count it as a democracy retroactively. We need additional criteria to be able to date the birth of democracy in Mexico.

There are other criteria that might help distinguish one-party-dominant autocracies from democracies. First, elections must be competitive such that there

---

[2] For the best existing cross-sectional empirical analysis of the different democratization dynamics of these regimes see Geddes (1999a). Karl and Schmitter (1991) discuss different "modes of transition" that are not necessarily related to regime type.

[3] The alternation rule creates some problems. For instance, if the authors had written their book ten years earlier, Japan and Italy both would have been classified as authoritarian.

is a real possibility that the incumbent might lose. Mexican scholars have employed a rule of thumb of winning with less than 65 percent of the vote to distinguish between "hegemony," where only one effective party exists and has a probability of winning, and "dominance," where elections are competitive despite having a major electoral force.[4] The threshold is obviously arbitrary, but it is useful in that it distinguishes among dramatically different party system configurations. For instance, the Mexican party system of the early 1970s differs from the party configuration of the late 1980s. In the seventies, the PRI won the overwhelming majority of races with more than 90 percent of the vote; it controlled virtually all the seats in the Lower Chamber of Deputies and 100 percent of the Senate; and no single governorship belonged to the opposition. Although still the dominant electoral force at the end of the eighties, in 1988 the PRI had lost the crucial supermajority (two thirds) of seats in the Lower Chamber needed to modify the constitution unilaterally; it had also, by 1989, lost two governorships, Chihuahua and Baja California; and over a third of elective offices in the country were won or lost by a small margin. The party system configuration of the late eighties was unquestionably competitive, although the PRI was still the dominant player.

Second, the opposition must accept electoral institutions as legitimate. As this chapter will make explicit, it was not until the 1994 and 1996 electoral reforms that all the major opposition contenders accepted the basic rules of the game as legitimate. The 1994 electoral reform established true independence for the IFE, and the 1996 reform made the playing field more level, as campaign financing and access to the mass media by opposition parties were dramatically increased. This criterion might help distinguish types of dominant party systems. Systems where there are exceptional allegations about the legitimacy of the basic rules of the game (e.g., Mexico until the early 1990s) should be classified as authoritarian in contrast to systems where the major contenders agree about the existing rules of the game and the electoral process itself (e.g., Italy or Japan).

Institutional compromises at the elite level thus played a crucial role in Mexico's democratization. However, as will become apparent in this chapter, they are not the ultimate cause of democracy. Electoral reforms were endogenous, the parties' strategic response to the changing balance of forces in society.

THE UNRAVELING OF THE ELITE-LEVEL COOPERATIVE EQUILIBRIUM

The PRI was quite successful at keeping its numerous factions united. Barbara Geddes (1999a: 11) attributes the resiliency of hegemonic party regimes to their relative immunity to elite splitting. In her view, what keeps a hegemonic coalition united is that everyone is better off if factions remain united despite

---

[4] Przeworski et al. (2000: 28) argue that a threshold of no more than two thirds of the vote screens out from the democracies similar countries as when they employ the strict criterion of an incumbent actually having lost power and yielded office.

ideological differences. The 1988 split within the PRI signals that something major in the system had changed that no longer allowed the hegemonic party to sustain the cooperative elite-level equilibrium. Why are hegemonic parties capable of solving elite divisions most of the time, and what triggers party splits? The literature does not provide clear answers.

The origins of the internal coordination of the governing coalition in Mexico can be traced to President Plutarco Elias Calles (1924–28). Calles came up with the idea of creating a political party that would draw into a single organization all of Mexico's then-relevant powerful revolutionary leaders, local bosses, and existing political parties, mostly regional ones. The then National Revolutionary Party (Partido Nacional Revolucionario; PNR), which was eventually transformed into the PRI, was crafted as an institutional solution to long years of political violence (Garrido 1982). The party soon became the most important national party organization. Lázaro Cárdenas (1934–40) extended the range of the party by incorporating interest groups into hierarchical organizations tied to the party, organizing workers into the National Confederation of Workers (Confederación de Trabajadores Mexicanos; CTM) and peasants into the National Confederation of Peasants (Confederación Nacional Campesina; CNC). He managed to obtain the loyalty of these groups by, among others things, providing them with direct material incentives.[5]

The PRI's relative immunity to elite splitting did not stem from ideological homogeneity. The party constituted an ideologically heterogeneous governing coalition.[6] Major splits did occur before the party consolidated its hegemony. The most important were by Juan Andreu Almazán in 1940, Ezequiel Padilla in 1946, and Miguel Henriquez Guzmán in 1952. Almazán headed the opposition against the PNR's nominee, Manuel Avila Camacho, in 1940. Almazán had support from some sectors in the army and from those who opposed the party's tilt toward the left during the Cárdenas years (Medina 1978). He obtained close to 6 percent of the vote. Padilla was nominated by the PDM (Partido Democrático Mexicano *or* Mexican Democratic Party). He had belonged to the ruling party, holding an important cabinet position during Avila Camacho's presidency. He obtained 19 percent of the vote. Henriquez Guzmán organized a strong opposition against the ruling party. He claimed to represent the "real" principles of the Mexican revolution, which according to him and his supporters, had been betrayed during Alemán's presidency. Henríquez Guzmán was at first supported by Lázaro Cárdenas himself. However, when Alemán named

---

[5] To peasants, Cárdenas gave land, dramatically increasing the number of hectares distributed through land reform, and to workers, he gave labor union rights and social security.

[6] Analysts traditionally distinguished two major wings in the PRI: (1) the left-wing, which like President Lázaro Cárdenas (1934–40) stressed income redistribution, land reform, and the party's commitment to social justice, and (2) the right-wing, which like President Miguel Alemán (1946–52) stressed the government's commitment to industrialization and state-led capitalist development (Hansen 1971: 110). Economic polices in Mexico tended to swing in a "pendular" fashion, from more rightist policies to more leftist ones and back again, from one presidential term to the other (Levy and Szekeley 1987).

Ruiz Cortinez as the presidential nominee, Lázaro Cárdenas publicly supported the PRI. Henríquez Guzmán nonetheless continued his campaign through the Frente Popular Mexicano. After the PRI won the presidency, these politicians came back to the party and were offered positions in the state. Henríquez Guzmán obtained 16 percent of the vote (Bruhn 1997).

After these elite-splitting episodes, the PRI made it even harder for independent candidates to compete in elections through subsequent electoral reforms. In 1946, the first major electoral reform, which according to Molinar (1991) marks the beginnings of the hegemonic era of the PRI, modified the electoral rules, prohibiting regional parties from competing in federal elections. The law required a legal registration to compete in elections. To obtain this registration, the parties had to form national organizations (which were required to possess 30,000 members in the whole country, and at least 1,000 members in no fewer than two thirds of the states) (Medina 1978). The new law also centralized the organizing, monitoring, and certifying of the electoral process in the federal government (Molinar 1991). After the split by Henríquez Guzmán, the laws were further modified to increase the requirements for obtaining a legal registration. The new laws of 1954 required at least 2,500 members in two thirds of the Mexican states and a total of 75,000 members in the entire country (Medina 1978: 28; Molinar 1991: 36).

After these electoral reforms, only the PRI, PAN, Partido Auténtico de la Revolución Mexicana (PARM; Authentic Party of the Mexican Revolution), and Partido Popular Socialista (PPS; Popular Socialist Party) survived as registered parties until 1979, when a new law allowed more parties to enter the electoral arena largely owing to the establishment of a mixed electoral system consisting of the original single-member districts, which entailed high barriers to entry, and multimember districts that significantly lowered entry costs (Diaz-Cayeros and Magaloni 2001).

Despite the heterogeneity of preferences, politicians had strong incentives to compete under a single-party label for three reasons (see Magaloni 1997: ch. 1). First, after the PRI established itself as a hegemonic party, it became the single most *efficient* path through which ambitious politicians could attain office. The opposition offered no real chance to office seekers.[7] Second, by offering a large number of attractive positions to its members, the PRI could make a political career available to a multitude of politicians. The rule of no consecutive reelection for all elective offices in the country,[8] plus the growth of state bureaucracies, allowed the party to distribute a sufficiently large number of attractive positions. Indeed, the Mexican PRI has been characterized by

[7] Those who cared more for office than for ideology invariably joined the PRI. During the years of party hegemony, those who joined the opposition did so knowing that they had no real chance of attaining office. Thus, this decision can only be understood as a product of intense ideological predispositions.

[8] Mexico instituted no-consecutive reelection for deputy, senator, municipal president, governor, and state legislature in 1933. Reelection of the president was not allowed, even when not consecutive, after the drafting of the 1917 Constitution, although this provision was temporarily modified to allow for Obregón's reelection in 1928. He was assassinated during the campaign.

constant elite circulation in a wide range of elective and nonelective offices (Smith 1979; Camp 1995). Third, the party offered those politicians who could reach political office or attain a bureaucratic position significant opportunities to further their own private economic goals (including corruption) while in office, thus making even short political careers attractive to most politicians.

The elite-level cooperative equilibrium seems to crucially depend on the interaction between elites and masses. A simple ambition theoretical framework, which draws on Cox (1997), helps explain why this is the case. Consider a politician who must decide whether to "cue" for the party's nomination or to join the opposition camp. The expected utility of joining the hegemonic party is given by multiplying the probability of winning under such party's label, P_I, by the likelihood of obtaining the party's nomination, N_I, times the utility of winning as a member of the hegemonic party, W_I, minus the costs incurred in running a campaign under the incumbent's label, C_I. The utility of winning as a member of the hegemonic party can be thought of as power plus the side-payments a politician receives in office (e.g., opportunities for corruption). Thus, the expected utility of running under the hegemonic party's label is defined as

$$E(U_I) = P_I N_I(W_I) - C_I$$

The expected utility of splitting or exiting is given by multiplying the probability of winning under an opposition party's label, P_o, by the probability of obtaining such party's nomination (or forming a successful ad hoc partisan organization), N_o, times the utility of winning as a member of the opposition, W_o, minus the costs incurred in campaigning under such party's label, C_o. The utility of winning as a member of the opposition relative to as a member of the hegemonic party can be thought of as power plus the policy utility that a politician receives for winning under the banner of a party whose policy proposals are closer to the politician's.[9]

$$E(U_o) = P_o N_o(W_o) - C_o$$

In this simple choice theoretic framework, splits are more likely when (1) the relative value of winning as a member of the opposition increases (e.g., when a politician has policy preferences that are dramatically different from those of the hegemonic party); (2) the relative value of winning as a member of the hegemonic party decreases (e.g., when the size of the pie to be distributed in the form of corruption decreases); (3) the probability of obtaining the hegemonic party's nomination decreases; (4) the politician can obtain nomination from another party or form his or her own ad hoc partisan organization; (5) the probability of winning under an opposition's party label's increases; and (6) the costs of campaigning as a member of the opposition decrease.

Using this framework, we can now analyze why the Cardenistas split when they did. Ideological considerations played a major role in the Cardenista splinter of 1988 (the difference between W_I and W_o was large). As it is clear in Bruhn's

---

[9] To simplify, the framework assumes no repetition of the decision problem. For a formalization of the repetitive decision problem, see Cox (1997).

(1997) account of the emergence of the Partido de la Revolución Democrática (PRD; Party of the Democratic Revolution), Cárdenas and his allies strongly disagreed with Miguel de la Madrid's economic polices. They strongly opposed the government's reduction of spending under the IMF stabilization package and the government's decision to continue to pay the foreign debt, and they were against trade liberalization and the privatization of state-owned enterprises. The Cardenistas instead still believed in the viability of import substitution industrialization and the need to maintain a strong, active, and nationalistic state.

However, Cuauhtémoc Cárdenas and the group of politicians that left the PRI with him in 1988 did not splinter from the ruling party for ideological differences only. Belonging to a radically different political group than the market-oriented technocrats that controlled the presidency, these politicians saw slim prospects of furthering successful political careers within the party (for them the likelihood of obtaining the party's nomination, N_I, was very slim). As Bruhn's study (1997) documents, the Cardenistas explicitly complained about a strong sense of exclusion during the De la Madrid presidency, arguing that the first circle of power was increasingly controlled by a small group of technocrats, which left the politicians, particularly those favoring another economic ideology, completely outside. Before splitting, the Cardenistas attempted to "democratize" the PRI – above all, they opposed the *dedazo* or having the incumbent president select his own successor and play a central role in the selection of gubernatorial, senatorial, and congressional candidates. When they realized their efforts had failed, they opted to exit the PRI. The split took place at the party assembly in March 1987, a couple of years after they had formed the Corriente Democrática to attempt to democratize the PRI's nomination procedures.

How could Cuauhtémoc Cárdenas overcome the barriers to running outside the PRI that were placed in the path of any of the party's potential defectors? Recall that the PRI had purposely created laws that made it very hard for politicians to form new parties. Cárdenas did not form a new political party prior to the 1988 presidential elections, however. Some preexisting political parties endorsed him (thus he could obtain an opposition party's nomination, N_O, at no cost). The first party to support his candidacy was the PARM, which is somehow paradoxical given that this old state-run party, together with the PPS and the Frente Cardenista de Reconstrucción Nacional (FCRN; Cardenista Front for National Reconstruction), were considered so-called *satellite* parties.[10] Most preexisting left-wing parties also supported Cárdenas.

But the nomination procedures within the PRI had always been hierarchical, and there had always been ideological battles within the PRI. What changed in 1988? One of the most consequential variables in the choice theoretic framework discussed earlier is the probability of winning as a member

---

[10] During the hegemonic era of the PRI, these parties had survived by fielding candidates for local elections and some senatorial, congressional, and gubernatorial races, but they always eventually came to support the PRI candidate for the presidential race.

of the hegemonic party, P_I, or as opposition, P_o. No matter how hierarchical nomination procedures are or how salient ideological divisions, if a politician is sufficiently ambitious, his dominant strategy seems to be not to split when there are no real chances of attaining office through other means. What was different in 1988, as we will see in the last section of the chapter, is the electoral discontent with the PRI. The anticipation of good electoral prospects is what ultimately provided Cárdenas and his allies the incentive to exit the party.

The 1988 presidential elections thus mark a turning point in Mexican politics. There is no doubt that massive electoral fraud was committed against Cárdenas, who claimed the victory. Whether electoral fraud was decisive in producing the PRI's victory in the presidential election is more debatable. It is impossible to know with precision what happened in those elections because the ballots were destroyed. One possibility, as Jorge Castañeda (2000) explains, is that the PRI employed electoral fraud to boost its electoral support above 50 percent so as to guarantee for itself a comfortable majority in the Electoral College of newly elected congressional members who were going to ratify their own election *and* the presidential election. Another possibility is that the electoral fraud was necessary for the PRI to retain the presidency.

The PRI managed to get away with electoral fraud because the opposition failed to present a unified front to challenge the official election results (Diaz-Cayeros and Magaloni 1995). The PAN seems to have cut an early deal with the incoming president, Carlos Salinas, a point to which I return later. The rest of the opposition parties that supported Cárdenas also refused to confront the results. As Bruhn (1997) documents, these parties were willing to defend their electoral victories in the Lower Chamber of Deputies, but they were not willing to defend Cárdenas's vote in the presidential race.

INSTITUTIONAL CHANGE

A central question of Mexico's transition is why the PRI agreed to renegotiate the existing rules of the game that had allowed it to commit fraud when needed. In particular, why did this party relinquish its control of the electoral process? The process of institutional reform[11] regarding organizing, monitoring, and sanctioning elections consisted of two distinctive stages presenting different types of logic. The first stage, from 1990 to 1993, consisted of piecemeal electoral reforms negotiated by a bipartisan coalition between the PRI and the PAN. The second stage, between 1994 and 1996, included the three main parties – PAN, PRD, and PRI. In this second stage, the PRI finally relinquished control of the electoral process. This section of the chapter focuses mainly on the second stage.

[11] Two sets of electoral rules are relevant for understanding the transition, rules for the translation of votes into seats, and rules regarding the organization and monitoring of elections. In Diaz-Cayeros and Magaloni (2001), we explore the process of institutional change with respect to the translation of votes into seats. Here I focus on the second set of rules.

First Stage of Institutional Reform

During the first stage, two electoral reforms were passed by the PAN and PRI, one in 1990 and the other in 1993. These came about as concessions given by Salinas to the PAN in exchange for its support in the Lower Chamber of Deputies of the president's economic agenda. Salinas needed the support of a party other than the PRI to carry out his economic agenda, which required the modification of the Constitution in fundamental ways (e.g., the privatization of the banking system and the restructuring of property rights in the country-side required constitutional changes). The natural congressional ally was the right-wing opposition party because it shared many of the goals of the market-oriented reforms.[12]

The PAN opted to support the presidential economic agenda in exchange for political reform. In the electoral reform of 1990, the PAN obtained the estab-lishment of a federal Electoral Tribunal.[13] The government, however, retained control of the electoral process. Although a separate Federal Electoral Institute was created, the government kept control of its board.[14] The 1993 electoral reforms went a little bit farther: They finally eliminated the "self-certification" by the Electoral College, granting the Federal Electoral Institute authority to certify electoral results. In addition, within the Electoral Tribunal, a second legal body for appeals was created (*Sala de Segunda Instancia*), whose decisions could not be appealed or reversed by any other authority.[15]

---

[12] Since its founding, this party had opposed excessive state intervention in markets, the increasing concentration of key industries in the government's hands and the overregulation of private property.

[13] An electoral tribunal existed before 1990, the *Tribunal de Lo Contencioso Electoral*. However, the decisions of this tribunal did not bind the Electoral College (composed of newly elected senators and deputies, who certified the election results). The Electoral Tribunal established in 1990 was very different. Its decisions could be modified but only by a two-thirds vote of the Electoral College. In addition, the electoral judges were also going to be elected by a two-thirds vote of the Lower Chamber of those candidates proposed by the president.

[14] The board was composed of the Secretario de Gobernación (as its president); four members of Congress (two belonging to the largest party and two the second largest party), party repre-sentatives (whose number varied according to the percentage of votes received by each party) and six *Consejeros Magistrados*, whose impartiality was severely questioned as they were elected from a list proposed by the president and ratified by a two-thirds vote of the Lower Chamber.

[15] The 1990 electoral reform did not modify the so-called governability clause, which gave the largest electoral party obtaining more than 35 percent of the vote an absolute majority of seats in the Lower Chamber, even if that party did not obtain the majority of the vote. In 1993, the electoral rule was changed. The new electoral rule for the translation of votes into seats in the Chamber of Deputies gave a more than proportional share of seats to the largest electoral party as long as it finished above some threshold with respect to the second largest party. The 1993 reform also changed the electoral rules for the composition of the Senate: Three senators were to be elected by plurality, and a fourth was to be given to the second largest party in the state. The rules for selecting the Senate largely benefited the PAN over the PRD. These rules for the selection of the Senate were later modified in the 1996 electoral reform, allocating the fourth senator by a form of proportional representation. On this occasion, the rule was meant to benefit the PRD (see Diaz-Cayeros and Magaloni 2001).

Salinas offered the PAN other side-payments in exchange for its acquiescence to the electoral fraud of 1988 and support for the regime. The president repeatedly intervened to force local PRI electoral machines to respect the PAN's electoral victories. On some occasions, the president even forced local PRI "elected" politicians to step down from office after the PAN contested the official results of the elections. This came to be known as the *concertacesiones* – postelectoral bargains among the PAN's leadership and the president that implied transferring elective office to the PAN when obscure local election results gave the victory to the PRI.[16]

During the Salinas presidency, Cárdenas and his new party, the PRD, were ostracized and on occasion openly persecuted. Most instances of political violence related to elections involved local races contested by the PRD, and this party claims to have lost around 300 activists to political violence during those years. The PRD took an increasingly antisystemic stand against the regime, opposing both the legitimacy of Salinas's presidency and the direction of economic policy.

Second Stage of Institutional Reform: The Establishment of an Independent Federal Electoral Institute

In the second stage of institutional reform, which included the 1994 and 1996 electoral reforms, the PRI relinquished its control of the Federal Electoral Institute. This time, the three major political players participated in the reforms.

The creation of the independent Federal Electoral Institute can be traced to the 1994 reforms, which took place just before the 1994 presidential elections. The Zapatista uprising in January of that year triggered this round of political negotiations, and the PRD participated in them. The three parties came together in the so-called *Acuerdos de Barcelona* to announce their commitment to peaceful means to attain office, and the last electoral reform during the Salinas presidency came as a result. The most significant aspect of the reform was that six *Consejeros Ciudadanos*, or citizen councilors, were to be elected to the new board of the Federal Electoral Institute by a two-thirds vote in the Lower Chamber. Each of the major parties – PRI, PAN, and PRD – had the right to propose two councilors. These six citizens joined four members of Congress, two of whom belonged to the PRI and two to the opposition parties. The political parties could be represented on the board, but they lost the right to vote. The board's president was the Interior Minister (Secretario de Gobernación). With this new arrangement, the government lost control of the Federal Electoral Institute's board, and the six citizens controlled much of the 1994 electoral

---

[16] The 1992 election in Guanajuato is an example of these *concertacesiones*. Vicente Fox ran as the PAN's candidate. After the PAN almost paralyzed the state with postelectoral protests, the PRI's newly elected governor, Ramón Aguirre, had to step down from office. The agreement between the PAN and Salinas was to name as governor the PAN politician Medina Placencia, instead of Vicente Fox.

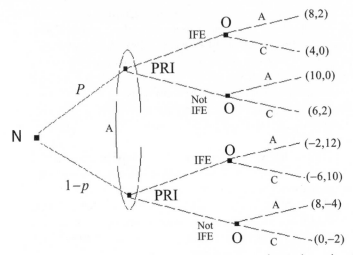

FIGURE 4.1. Extensive Form Game: The Creation of an Independent Electoral Institute.

process (Malo and Pastor 1996).[17] The 1994 electoral process was sufficiently transparent that the three main actors accepted the results with almost no complaint of electoral fraud.

What led the Salinas government to acquiesce to these reforms? Why was the PRD finally included in this last round of political negotiations, breaking Salinas's practice of dividing the opposition and isolating the PRD?

Figure 4.1 provides a game to answer these questions. For simplicity, the model assumes that there are only two players, the PRI and a united Opposition (O). The PRI has two available strategies: to create an independent Federal Electoral Institute (IFE) or to maintain the control of its board (not IFE). The opposition can then choose to contest the election results or not contest them. The opposition can contest the results through nonviolent means that seek to question the legitimacy of the electoral results such as massive demonstrations or hunger strikes. They can also contest through violent means. In this game Nature (N) decides the likelihood that the PRI will win (W) with probability p and the probability it will lose (L) the election with probability $1 - p$. The PRI must make its choice of whether to create an independent IFE before the election takes place. Because the party can't anticipate with certainty the elections results, the game is one of imperfect information.[18]

---

[17] In 1994, the voter registry was thoroughly revised and another set of registration cards, which included the voter's picture, signature, and thumbprint, were issued.

[18] The extensive form representation of the game depicts Nature choosing first and the PRI as the only actor not knowing the likely results of the elections. This assumption about informational asymmetries is not necessary for obtaining the results. I chose this representation for didactic purposes only because it makes very clear the concept of "subgame perfection" and the variables that drive the results of the model. If both actors do not know for certain the results of the elections, the most accurate representation of the model is one in which the PRI chooses first,

The actors' preference orders derive from the following set of simple assumptions: The PRI prefers winning to losing and having a submissive electoral institute to an independent IFE. But its payoffs also depend on what the Opposition does. The PRI prefers the Opposition to accept the election results rather than contest them because this entails legitimacy costs. In the specific numeric representation of the game in Figure 4.1, winning gives the PRI a payoff of 10; creating the IFE costs the PRI 2; committing electoral fraud costs 2; and the Opposition's challenge costs 4.

The Opposition prefers winning to losing; it prefers an independent IFE; and it makes its decision to accept or contest contingent on the PRI's choice to create an independent IFE or not. If the PRI creates the independent IFE, the Opposition accepts the results because contesting them is costly when the PRI no longer controls the electoral process and cannot commit fraud. Who is going to follow the Opposition into the streets against an adverse electoral outcome if there is no reason to believe that the PRI stole the elections? If the IFE remains subservient to the PRI, the Opposition contests the election results because they can more credibly argue before their supporters that the ruling party manipulated the elections. In the specific numeric representation of the game in Figure 4.1, winning gives a payoff of 10; obtaining an independent IFE gives a payoff of 2; losing because of electoral fraud costs −4; and contesting when the independent IFE is in place costs −2, while contesting when the IFE is not independent provides a benefit of 2.

I derive the payoffs for the PRI and the Opposition over the eight possible outcomes of this game from these simple assumptions. The probability that the PRI will win is consequential for the solution of the game. Suppose that the PRI anticipates an electoral defeat with certainty so that the actors know the lower "subgame" is being played. Anticipating electoral loss, the PRI will *not* relinquish its control of the IFE and "tie its hands" because in doing so it will not be able to commit electoral fraud and steal the elections from a winning Opposition. Keeping the control of the IFE generates costs because the Opposition will contest the election results. The PRI would much rather keep the control of the IFE, commit electoral fraud, and have the opposition accept the results, which provides a payoff of (8, −4), than have the Opposition contest fraudulent results, (0, −2). The difference between these payoffs for the PRI reflects the costs to the ruling party of keeping power through electoral fraud, which entices the Opposition to contest the election results, seriously damaging the legitimacy of the regime.

However, the outcome of losing, not delegating, and having the Opposition contest the results, is better for the PRI than what would ensue if it relinquished its control of the IFE. By relinquishing control of the IFE, the PRI "ties its hands" not to commit fraud. Delegating to the IFE entices the winning Opposition to

---

Nature moves second, and the Opposition chooses to contest or not the election results without observing the actual results of the elections, but only if an independent IFE is in place or not. The results of this second game, which is available upon request, are exactly the same.

accept the results, but the PRI loses power, which gives a payoff to the players of (−2, 12). This payoff is worse for the PRI than (0, −2), the outcome of not delegating power to the IFE, committing fraud, and having the Opposition contest the results. Indeed, in the lower subgame, delegating control of the electoral process to an independent IFE is a dominated strategy: No matter what the Opposition does, the PRI is always better off not delegating when this party knows it will lose the elections for certain.

Now suppose the PRI knows it will win for certain so that the upper subgame is being played. The PRI prefers retaining control of the IFE to relinquishing it. However, the cost of doing so, as the game makes explicit, is that the Opposition will then choose to contest the election results despite the fact that the PRI won the elections cleanly, which gives a payoff to the players of (6, 2). By contesting legitimate electoral results, the Opposition can question the legitimacy of the whole electoral process, and the PRI does not wish to run this risk if it knows it can win elections cleanly. The Opposition's threat to contest the election is credible because it is better for this player to contest when the PRI does not delegate to the IFE (6, 2), than to accept the results despite not having an independent IFE (10, 0). This is the PRI's most desirable outcome, namely win, not delegate, and get the Opposition to accept, but it is not attainable in equilibrium because without the IFE, the Opposition has a dominant strategy to contest the results.

It is this credible threat on the part of the Opposition that leads the PRI to delegate power to an independent IFE. By delegating power to the IFE, the PRI prevents the opposition from contesting the elections results *and* still keeps control of the government, which gives the players a payoff of (8, 2). This payoff is better for the PRI than (6, 2), the off-the-path payoff if the PRI does not delegate. And it is better because when an independent IFE exists, the Opposition faces no incentive to contest the election results despite having lost the election.

With the particular numeric payoff of the game proposed in Figure 4.1, the PRI chooses to delegate to an independent IFE when its probability of winning is larger than 1/2. However, the game could easily be presented in a more general algebraic format, allowing us to derive ceteris paribus conditions as to when delegation to an independent IFE would be more or less likely. I concentrate on two conditions: the PRI's ex ante probabilistic assessments about its chances of winning and the costs to the PRI of having the Opposition contest election results. As it should be clear, when the ex ante probabilistic assessments about the PRI's chances of winning decrease, so will the probability that delegation to an independent IFE would take place. Facing a higher electoral threat, the PRI's incentive to "tie its hands" not to commit fraud by delegating power to the IFE decreases, as this would entail the risk of losing power.

A key additional consideration for the PRI is the expected costs of facing the Opposition's challenge. In the game, the PRI chooses to delegate to the IFE not because of some supposed democratic credentials. It does so because it antic-ipates that the Opposition will be able to mount a serious challenge, possibly delegitimizing the whole electoral process. Now suppose that these costs drop from 4 to 1. Here, the PRI will not ever delegate power to an independent IFE, regardless of its chances of winning. If the costs to the PRI of having the opposition contest clean election results increase instead by 3 points, the likelihood of delegating will increase.

Thus, in the game, the PRI delegates to an independent IFE because, on the one hand, it calculates that its chances of winning elections cleanly are good and, on the other, because the opposition can mount a credible challenge to the PRI if it were to refuse to delegate power to an independent IFE. The game thus makes explicit why significant electoral reform in Mexico depended on having increasingly stronger opposition parties and why it was inconceivable in earlier years.

Returning to Mexico's real-life politics, we are now in a position to understand why Salinas decided to create an independent IFE several months before the 1994 elections. First consider the ex ante probability of winning the elections. Salinas was confident of the PRI's electoral strength. As I will discuss in the next section, by the 1991 midterm elections, the PRI had recovered most of the vote that had gone to Cárdenas in 1988. The ruling party had also managed to halt the advances of the PRD at the local level partly thanks to the National Solidarity Program (Programa Nacional de Solidaridad; PRONASOL), a poverty relief scheme that allowed the PRI to reshuffle its base of support from a corporatist to an increasingly territorial one. Furthermore, Salinas had managed to amass considerable support for the market-oriented reforms, privatization and NAFTA, in part because of the reforms themselves and in part because of the manner in which the president had employed the media to publicize them (Villarreal 1999). The president's approval ratings were astounding – at the beginning of the election year, close to 80 percent of respondents thought the president was doing a great job handling the economy. These early polls fueled the widespread belief that the PRI would win the coming presidential elections. Only the PRDistas had the unrealistic expectation that Cárdenas had a real chance of winning, a point to which I return later (Zinser 1994).

Now consider the anticipated costs of not delegating power to the IFE. With the Zapatista uprising of January 1994, political violence exploded in the country, and at that moment the government had limited information regarding the mass spread of the movement. One of the first demands of the movement was clean elections. Salinas needed to neutralize the Zapatistas with a nationwide political opening, one that included the PRD in particular. As Castañeda (1995: 95) makes explicit, there was a real risk of political explosion: "The dangers of fraud, postelectoral protests, and a second round were not the same before and after Chiapas. After January 1, weapons were involved – and the example of what could be accomplished with them."

There was a real question as to whether the PRDistas were going to join the Zapatistas in creating a united front against the regime, participate in the electoral process, and call the legitimacy of the elections into question after the fact. The creation of an independent IFE was a way to bring the PRDistas into the electoral contest, give them a legitimate chance, and, above all, commit them to the process. The independence of the IFE increased the costs to Cárdenas of claiming fraud after the fact. Who was going to believe him, and follow him into the streets, if the PRI was not in control of the process? The PRI thus accepted creating the IFE, expecting to be able to win a clean election.

The PRI was indeed able to win the 1994 elections, and there were no major allegations of fraud. The election year turned out to be more complicated than expected, however. The PRI's presidential candidate, Luis Donaldo Colosio, was assassinated in March, and two months after the election, the general secretary of the PRI was also assassinated. The peso crisis of 1994 erupted a few months after the elections, and with it the history of the PRI was altered, as it paved the way to the ruling party's losses of 1997 and 2000.

A possible objection to this model is that the PRI might falsely appear to be too shortsighted, delegating power to an independent IFE in 1994 without anticipating the possible costs of doing so in the near future.[19] Yet, experts and investors, let alone the PRI, did not predict the peso crisis. At the end of the Salinas presidency, expectations were extremely optimistic about the future of the Mexican economy among the international financial community. It was believed that the Salinas reforms had laid a solid foundation for future economic recovery and prosperity, and, at that time, the party anticipated profiting from these reforms for years to come.

The independent IFE was thus established in 1994, and it would become impossible to reverse it afterward. Any reform to the IFE required a constitutional reform, and the PRI no longer controlled the necessary majority to implement such a reform unilaterally.[20] The 1996 electoral reforms only fine-tuned this independence by, among other changes, granting the IFE the power to monitor and sanction campaign expenditures. Other very significant aspects of the 1996 electoral reforms were to level campaign financing and media access and to incorporate the Federal Electoral Tribunal into the judicial branch of government and allow for judicial review of electoral laws (Magaloni 2003; Magaloni and Sánchez 2001).

THE LOSS OF MASS SUPPORT AND THE EMERGENCE OF THE OPPOSITION

As important as electoral fraud was for the PRI's survival in 1988 and in many local elections, it is clear that fraud alone is insufficient to explain the party's hegemony. During the years of party hegemony, the PRI won the elections with

---

[19] The game could easily be drawn as a repetitive game to account for longer-term considerations.

[20] Beyond constitutional restrictions, the reason why the independence of the IFE could not be reversed after 1996 can be appreciated in the model. The costs of reversing the independence of the IFE once created could be visualized as a change in the PRI's payoff of not creating an independent IFE and getting the Opposition to contest the results. As demonstrated earlier, when these costs increase, so do the incentives to delegate.

substantial support, often more than 90 percent of the vote. The PRI did steal elections from the opposition but electoral fraud was more often carried out to boost the electoral support of the ruling party. The party increased barriers to entry that prevented some parties from emerging and slowed down the consolidation of the opposition. Nonetheless, as became clear in the 1988 presidential elections, barriers to entry were not infinite. When true discontent among the population emerged, it got translated into the party system. A central pillar to the PRI's hegemony, I argue, was mass support for the regime, and the process of democratization is deeply intertwined with the deterioration of the party's electoral base.

My analysis of voting patterns in Mexico highlights the following empirical correlations: (1) The PRI's electoral support begins to fall after the onset of the debt crisis, which for Mexico marks the beginning of more than twenty years of economic stagnation. (2) However, considering the depth and length of the recession, the deterioration of the PRI's base of support was gradual and protracted. (3) Modernization is a strong predictor of voter support for the opposition, yet development was not what ultimately brought democracy about: All the economic conditions had been ripe for democracy to emerge since the mid-1960s, but the authoritarian system survived for years despite the country's comparative wealth. (4) Democratization in Mexico must be understood in the context of Mexico's federalism, and the PRI's strategic use of the central government and its fiscal resources to punish localities that defected to the opposition. In doing so, the Mexican government could retard the establishment of democracy. (5) The liberalization of trade and the internationalization of the Mexican economy played a powerful role in enabling localities to defect to the opposition, both to the PAN and the PRD. (6) The 1994 peso crisis produced a "tipping phenomena": namely, localities began to defect from the PRI en masse after that date.

Economic Performance

From 1929 until 1982, the PRI was quite successful at generating political stability and economic growth. The party emerged as a compromise among warlords and revolutionary leaders to put an end to a long period of political violence. The compromise was successful, and for more than seventy years, political elites in Mexico settled their disagreements through the regime's institutional channels, seldom recurring to violence.

The PRI also produced economic growth. Before the PNR was founded in 1929, the economy was in dismal shape, which can be partly attributed to internal political instability. The economy began to grow after 1933, soon after Mexican politicians organized the party to put an end to violence. From 1933 until 1981, the Mexican economy had positive growth rates (an average of 6 percent a year).

The populist episode of the 1970s destroyed macroeconomic stability, and, despite the oil boom of the late seventies, the economy collapsed. Since 1982,

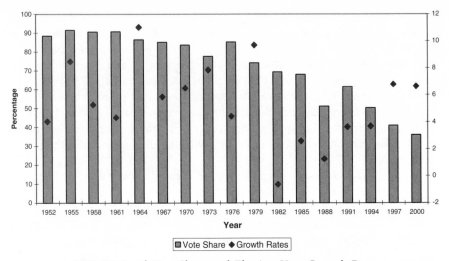

FIGURE 4.2. PRI's National Vote Share and Election Year Growth Rate, 1952–2000. Sources: Growth rates are from the Estadísticas Históricas de México (1993) and IFE.

Mexico experienced two economic recessions, first between 1982 and 1988 as a result of the debt crisis, and the second in 1995 and 1996 as a result of the devaluation of the peso. Both crises produced high inflation rates, devaluation, and a sharp decline in real wages and industrial production. Overall, from 1982 to 1997, the real minimum wage and the average industrial wages lost approximately 75 and 35 of their values, respectively.[21] Long-term growth collapsed during the eighties and nineties: From 1982 until 1989, the economy grew on average by 0.51 percent a year, and the average growth rate of the following decade was only 2.9 percent.[22]

Figure 4.2 graphs the vote for the PRI in federal elections from 1952 until 2000. Two general trends should be underscored. First, there is a secular decline in the vote for the PRI. The PRI's vote falls with the passing of time, with the exception of two elections: 1976, when the opposition did not even file a presidential candidate, and the midterm election in 1991, when Salinas managed to recover most of the vote that had gone to Cárdenas in the 1988 elections, an issue to which I return later. Second, the secular decline appears to accelerate after the debt crisis of 1982, and this pattern is even clearer in the local elections.

Closer analysis of the data reveals that voting trends are not strongly correlated with economic growth, however. Figure 4.2 also reports the election year growth rate. Although the correlation between annual election year growth rates and the vote is positive, it is quite low (0.23). The PRI received surprising support in the worst years of the recession of the eighties, namely 1982 and 1985, which seems to indicate that voters were not reacting in accordance

---

[21] These figures are from Banco de Mexico (www.banxico.org)
[22] Own calculations from data from INEGI's web page.

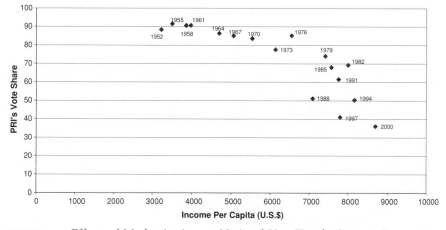

FIGURE 4.3. Effects of Modernization on National Vote Trends. Sources: Income per capita comes from Heston, Summers, and Aten (2002). Electoral data is from Presidencia de la República (1993) and IFE.

with the economic voting model. Limitations to this model also become apparent in 1997 and 2000, when the PRI was punished at the polls despite the relatively high growth rates of those two years (Magaloni and Poiré 2004b). Thus, while the economic collapse accelerated the decline at which the PRI was losing votes, the decline was too slow considering the depth and length of the economic recession.[23]

Modernization and Poverty

Development is a powerful predictor of the PRI's gradual loss of mass support. Can economic development also account for Mexico's democratization? Figure 4.3 shows a scatter plot of vote trends and income per capita in dollars from the Penn World Table. Economic development and national vote trends are highly intertwined (the correlation is −0.84).

Two rival interpretations can be given to the data. The first is that economic development is what ultimately brought democracy about, which would be consistent with endogenous modernization theory (Lipset 1959; Przeworski et al. 2000). Yet by comparative standards, the PRI survived for too many years after the country had reached the income threshold of $4,115, when according to Przeworski et al. (2000: 91), the probability of being democratic is above 0.50. If modernization theory is to have some predictive power, "there must be

---

[23] The literature on Mexican voting behavior has provided several accounts as to why the economic voting model confronts anomalies in the Mexican case. The seminal work is Domínguez and McCann (1995). See also Domínguez and Lawson (2004), Domínguez and Poiré (1999), and Magaloni (1997, 1999).

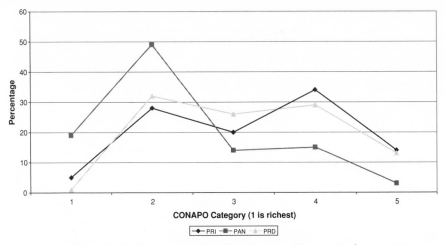

FIGURE 4.4. Municipal Governments by Deprivation Conapo Index, 1986–1999. Sources: Electoral data base of CIDAC and Consejo Nacional de Población (1990).

some level of income at which one can be relatively sure that the country will throw off its dictatorship" (Przeworski et al. 2000: 97).

The second interpretation of the data is that establishing democracy in Mexico was relatively more costly. All the economic conditions had been ripe for democracy to emerge since 1964, when the threshold was surpassed, but the authoritarian system survived for years despite the country's wealth by comparative standards.[24]

The PRI's long-lasting hegemony was solidly cemented on poverty and under-development. As study after study has shown, modernization and urbanization were correlated with a loss of support for the PRI (Ames 1970; Klesner 1996; Molinar 1991). Between 1940 and 1980, the Mexican economy did grow, but development was highly unequal and unbalanced. The PRI kept the support of the poorest localities and the prosperous and wealthiest regions defected to the opposition, most notably to the PAN (Magaloni 2000).

Figure 4.4 reports the levels of development of the municipalities governed by the PRI, the PAN, and the PRD between 1986 and 1999. Development is measured by the Conapo deprivation index.[25] The index groups localities

---

[24] In fact, by 1964 the country had reached the threshold above which, according to the results in Przeworski et al., the probability of democratic collapse is close to zero. Even the apparent high empirical correlation between development and democracy should be taken with caution. Przeworski et al. (2000: 97) suggest the following reason as to why this correlation might be spurious: Suppose that by the simple passing of time a regime faced each year some positive probability of dying for reasons not related to development. Thus, we might erroneously attribute the regime's collapse to development, when what really happened is that it dies because of the passing of time, including the accumulation of some random hazards.

[25] There are more than 2,400 municipalities in Mexico. The Conapo index, produced by the Mexican government, is a measure that reflects the level of deprivation per municipality. It

into five categories, from the wealthiest to the poorest. The wealthiest localities include, for example, Mexico City and many of the state capitals of the richer states in the north. The poorest localities are small, highly isolated and marginalized rural municipalities scattered around the country, many of them in the south.[26]

The PAN tended to win in the exact opposite type of localities from those of the PRI. Close to 70 percent of PAN's municipal governments were elected in localities classified by the Conapo index as the richest (1) and second richest (2). By contrast, only 33 percent of the PRI's municipalities were found in these categories. Less than 20 percent of PAN-governed municipalities were classified as poorest (5) or second poorest (4), whereas close to 50 percent of PRI-governed municipalities were from among these categories. An interesting pattern is that PRI- and PRD-governed municipalities, at least in this respect, were practically identical.

The PRD competed for the traditional base of support of the PRI, and to establish itself, it profited largely from ruling party splits, an issue to which I return later. Its original local base grew from the state of Michoacán, where Cárdenas had once been governor as a member of the PRI. During the Salinas presidency, the PRD managed to build some base of support in the southern states of Oaxaca, Guerrero, and Morelos and also to attract the support of the urban poor, state employees, students, and left-wing intellectuals. The PRD confronted colossal challenges. After the 1988 elections, Salinas created a government poverty relief program, PRONASOL, to recover the vote that had benefited Cárdenas in 1988 (Molinar and Weldon 1994; Magaloni, Diaz-Cayeros, and Estevez, forthcoming). The PRD had a hard time building its base largely as a consequence of this program (Bruhn 1997). During the administration of Ernesto Zedillo (1995–2000), the PRD's growth at the local level was more significant, and it largely came from ruling party splits.

By contrast, modernization can partly account for the gradual growth of the PAN at the local level. In 1980, the party governed only seven municipalities. By 1998, this party controlled 278 municipalities that comprised more than 30 percent of the population of Mexico (see Figure 4.5).[27] The expansion of the PAN significantly accelerated after the 1994 peso crisis. Whereas the party in 1994 governed only two state capitals, by 1998 it controlled twelve out of the thirty-two state capitals in the country.[28] The PAN was particularly strong in the North and in el Bajío.

---

is composed by a set of indicators such as percentage of employed population living under the minimum wage, illiteracy, housing with access to sewage, electricity, drinking water, and population living in rural localities.

[26] The data come from the municipal government political database compiled by Jacqueline Martínez at CIDAC.

[27] The data come from the municipal government political database compiled by Magaloni, Diaz-Cayeros, and Estevez. Electoral data are from Jacqueline Martinez at CIDAC.

[28] The data come from the municipal government political database compiled by Magaloni, Diaz-Cayeros, and Estevez. Electoral data are from Jacqueline Martinez at CIDAC.

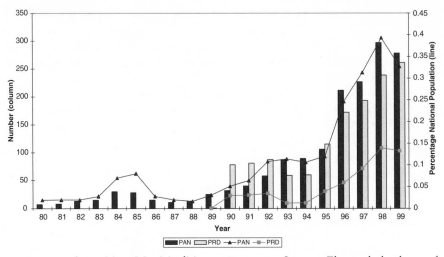

FIGURE 4.5. Opposition Municipalities, 1980–1999. Source: Electoral database of CIDAC.

The Liberalization of Trade

The internationalization of the Mexican economy played a significant role in the expansion of the opposition. Over the past two decades, Mexico's economy has become increasingly integrated with that of the United States. Many localities in Northern Mexico and el Bajío now possess vibrant economies with deep connections to the United States. Other poorer localities in the south have also developed extremely strong connections to the United States, mainly through intensive labor migration and the cash remittances migrant workers send to their families back home. In less than fifteen years, Mexico's economy experienced a dramatic transformation, and today it is the largest exporter of manufactured goods in Latin America.

The liberalization of trade has meant that the central government has increasingly lost control of the local economies. With import substitution industrialization (ISI) policies, local economies were geared toward the center, where markets for their goods and inputs concentrated. Policies such as multiple exchange rates, tariffs, permits, subsidized credit, strict regulations on foreign direct investment, and the transfer of technology all meant that producers had to court the central government. It is not surprising that the overwhelming majority of industry was concentrated in a single city, Mexico City, where the federal government operates.

Support for the opposition at the local level disproportionately came from localities that were more internationalized (Diaz-Cayeros, Magaloni, and Weingast 2002). The PAN, in particular, grew stronger in the northern and el Bajío localities, or those with higher levels trade with the United States. Support for the PRD, by contrast, disproportionately came from poorer localities that experienced more labor migration to the United States and that received higher remittances as a consequence (Diaz-Cayeros, Magaloni, and Weingast 2002). For these localities, the economic crisis of the 1980s and the subsequent implementation of orthodox stabilization during that decade intensified labor migration to the United States. In the worst years of the recession, labor migration might have alleviated social tension by giving the poor a possibility of exiting the country. Over time, however, labor migration worked against the PRI because remittances liberated communities from their dependence on the government. Indeed, remittances by migrant workers became a major source of capital for their communities back home, and the implication was that the livelihoods of these poorer, though internationalized localities, no longer were exclusively dependent on the PRI's patronage, which eventually gave them an alternative to defect to the opposition.

Why did the PRI adopt a policy, trade liberalization, that eventually contributed to its ultimate demise? As in other developing countries, trade liberalization came about because the old development model failed. ISI depended on continuous imports of intermediate and capital goods, which were financed first with agricultural exports and, when these dried up, with trade deficits. During the decade of the 1970s, intensive international borrowing, soft budget constraints, and oil exports allowed the government to sustain these policies for over a decade, despite huge inefficiencies. The debt crisis of the 1980s forced governments to alter existing policies.

The Tipping Phenomenon of the Post-1994 Peso Crisis

Figure 4.5 reports the municipalities won by the PAN and PRD in the course of these two decades. It took years for the opposition to achieve a national reach. Part of the reason why the opposition's electoral expansion at the local level was so slow is related to the centralization of fiscal resources (Diaz-Cayeros, Magaloni, and Weingast 2002). The PRI used its control of the national government to deploy these resources for political gain, strategically withdrawing funds from localities that were conquered by the opposition. In doing so, the national PRI was able to deter voters from defecting to the opposition. With few resources at their disposal, opposition parties were not very successful at governing localities. Voters were reluctant to support the opposition, and when they did, these parties had low reelection rates (Diaz-Cayeros, Magaloni, and Weingast 2002).

Note that the expansion of the opposition, and in particular the PAN, significantly accelerated after the 1994 peso crisis, a bust comparable to the downturn of the 1930s. In 1995 alone, GDP dropped by almost 7 percent, industrial wages declined by more than 30 percent in just two years, and the currency was devalued, overall, by around 250 percent. Between 1995 and 1997, the PRI lost three more gubernatorial races (Guanajuato, Jalisco, and Baja California) to the PAN as well as the majority of the vote in the deputy and/or municipal elections of Aguascalientes, Durango, Puebla, Sinaloa, Yucatán, Estado de México, Coahuila, and Morelos. The PAN won most of the important cities in which elections were held, including the capital cities of Jalisco, Baja California, Yucatán, Michoacán, Oaxaca, Chiapas, Puebla, Aguascalientes, Coahuila, Sinaloa, and Morelos.

The economic collapse also contributed to the growth of the PRD. The biggest prize for the PRD was Mexico City, which it won in 1997 after elections for governor were introduced for the first time. But the source of PRD's growth during the Zedillo administration is primarily related to PRI splits. Despite having no significant presence in the state of Zacatecas, the PRD won the gubernatorial election of 1998 when it supported Ricardo Monreal, who had split from the PRI when it denied him the nomination. Similarly, in Baja California Sur, when Cota lost the PRI's primary election, he joined the PRD and won the 1999 gubernatorial race. The PRD also won the gubernatorial elections of Tlaxcala and Nayarit. In those cases, a former PRIista was not only backed by the PRD but also by a coalition of all the state-level opposition parties.

Returning to the framework presented in the first section of this chapter, the PRI became so susceptible to party splits during the Zedillo administration because voters were willing to support whichever candidate ran under a non-PRI label.[29] The economic collapse created the necessary conditions for the mass public to be willing to vote against the PRI, something that occurred in one election after the other. And also consistent with this theoretical framework, the PRD was the main beneficiary of these splits, first, because this party was closer on the ideological spectrum to the PRI[30] and, second, because the PRD lacked local party organizations in many of the states. In the absence of local party organizations, disgruntled PRI politicians who joined the PRD did not have to compete with local opposition candidates for the nomination, as they would have needed to if they had decided to join the PAN.[31]

The defeat of the PRI in the midterm 1997 elections and later in the 2000 presidential race must be understood in the context of a series of precipitating events. The first was the economic collapse of 1995–96. Although short-lived, the crisis betrayed the public's expectations that the Salinas reforms had finally managed to put an end to economic misery and laid a solid foundation for future economic recovery. Instead of being perceived as the party that could best manage the economy, the PRI was seen as a major source of the country's economic difficulties (Magaloni and Poiré 2004b). A second contributing factor was the numerous and consecutive defeats at the local level, which created reasonable expectations among the public that the PRI could be defeated, generating a tipping phenomenon that enabled voters to coordinate against the ruling party. Third, the 1996 campaign finance and media access reforms also played a role (Lawson 1999). More access to the mass media allowed the opposition to disseminate information among the public, which contributed to

---

[29] P_0 was high because, thanks to the peso crisis, voters had signaled a clear disposition to vote against the PRI.

[30] The difference between W_I and W_0 is larger for PRD than for PAN.

[31] N_0 is less costly for PRD than for PAN.

reducing voter uncertainty about the opposition alternatives and enabled voters to coordinate. Fourth, strategic coordination among opposition voters played an important role in the PRI's defeat of 2000, as they were willing to set their ideological differences apart to cast a vote for the PAN candidate, who was most likely to defeat the PRI (Magaloni and Poiré 2004a).

FINAL REMARKS

In transitions from one-party-dominant systems, the opposition's main challenge is to defeat the party associated with the authoritarian past through the *ballot box*. The electoral arena is significantly skewed against opposition parties for two reasons: First, the incumbent party controls the existing electoral institutions so that it can draft laws to raise the costs of entry to the opposition or, if need be, manipulate the outcome of the elections. Second, the party associated with the authoritarian past enjoys significant incumbency advantages, the most important being its unilateral control of the state apparatus and its vast sources of patronage available to buy off mass support.

Thus, a central question is under what conditions one-party authoritarian incumbents relinquish their control of the electoral process, credibly delegating it to an independent electoral body. To understand democratization in one-party-dominant regimes, one needs to provide a theory of *endogenous* institutional change. The main contribution of the model presented in this chapter is to show that the creation of democratic institutions, most notably the independent IFE, ultimately depended on strategic choices made by the incumbent in response to its anticipation of electoral fortunes, and the expected reaction by opposition forces to the choice of retaining unilateral control of the elections, versus tying its hands not to commit fraud by delegating.

I have argued that the PRI chose to delegate independence to the IFE's board because it held a reasonable a priori expectation that it could win future elections and it wanted to deter the opposition from contesting the legitimacy of the electoral process in the present. The outcome thus depended, on the one hand, on the expectation of winning and, on the other, on the anticipation by the PRI that the opposition would mount a serious challenge to the legitimacy of the whole electoral process if it were to refuse to delegate authority to an independent IFE. The Chiapas uprising of January 1994, as I have argued, was a precipitating event because it generated a serious risk that the PRD would join the guerrillas in contesting the legitimacy of the entire electoral process after the fact. The creation of an independent IFE was a way to bring the PRDistas into the electoral contest, to give them a real chance, and, above all, to commit them to the process. The independence of the IFE increased the costs to Cárdenas of claiming fraud after the fact. The PRI thus accepted creating the IFE in the expectation that it would be able to win a clean election.

The decision to delegate depended upon the ability of the opposition to mount a credible challenge to the legitimacy of the electoral process, something that was inconceivable in earlier years when the opposition was weak. The balance of forces in society dramatically changed, and the new set of rules ultimately came to reflect that change.

My argument does not imply that the IFE became, so to say, an enforcer of democracy. This would be a naïve view of the role of institutions in democracy. As Przeworski (1991) argues, institutions cannot enforce democracy. Democracy, to be stable, must be self-enforcing, meaning that all relevant political players must have an interest in abiding by the election results, even if they lose. The IFE was designed to prevent the PRI from committing electoral fraud, but it would have not been able to *force* the PRI to step down from office had this party refused to accept defeat peacefully. After all, many autocrats around the world have opted to shut down democratic institutions such as electoral bodies, parliaments, and the like when the uncertain game of elections is adverse.

The PRI respected the 2000 defeat because it was in its interest to do so, partly because the IFE and other political players, including the media, opposition parties, and civil society, would have refused to accept an authoritarian imposition. In Przeworski's (1991) framework, by 2000 the costs of subverting the outcome of the elections were larger than the benefits of subverting. The cost of subverting were large because, on the one hand, the balance of forces in society had changed and, on the other, because, unlike 1988, this time the IFE had generated credible information that was available to all contenders about the actual results of the elections. With this information available to the public, it would have been too costly for the PRI to subvert the outcome of the 2000 elections. Common knowledge about the actual elections results served as a crucial social coordinating device, a focal point that would have united opposition parties and most of civil society against the PRI had it attempted to refuse to yield power to the PAN's winning candidate, Vicente Fox.

The IFE thus played a crucial role in Mexico's democratization. It was a pact among elites regarding their willingness to submit their struggles to the democratic process. And the IFE came to be because all political players, and mainly the PRI, regarded elections as their best channel to serve their goals. However, the independence of the IFE would have not been easy to conceive had the PRI anticipated the events that were to occur after 1994, including the peso crisis, which generated a tipping phenomenon against the ruling party in all subsequent local elections.

When the PRI granted independence to the IFE in 1994, this reform became irreversible because it required approval of the opposition since the ruling party no longer enjoyed the supermajority necessary for a constitutional change. Thus, through the 1994 electoral reforms, the PRI credibly "tied its hands" not to commit fraud because the opposition had become an effective veto player. Hence, institutions matter in the establishment of democracy as long as there are real political forces to back them up.

PART II

UNEXPECTED DEMOCRACIES IN UNLIKELY COUNTRIES

Bolivia, El Salvador, and Guatemala

5

Bolivia's Democracy at the Crossroads

René Antonio Mayorga

> That institutional reforms alter behaviour is an hypothesis, not an axiom.
>
> Robert Putnam, *Making Democracy Work (1993)*

This chapter addresses two key issues concerning the process of democratic development in Bolivia in the last two decades. First, I tackle the issue of why Bolivia, notwithstanding its previous authoritarian past and a series of harsh obstacles during the transition, succeeded in building a stable competitive regime in the post-1982 period. Second, I assess the democratic regime's major advances as well as its shortcomings and present challenges. I consider whether this process has laid the foundations for a stable and consolidated democracy and how much the regime's lingering problems affect democracy's future viability. The key question is whether sheer survival or durability has been the major achievement, or whether a political process has taken place that has given rise to the conditions for a self-sustaining democracy.

Scott Mainwaring (1999c: 104) has stressed that in Latin America's third wave of democratization, "no development is more surprising than Bolivia's democratic stability since 1982." Does this stability allow us to regard Bolivia's democracy as consolidated or moderately viable (Whitehead 2001: 3–20)? A consolidated democracy is one in which democracy as an intricate system of institutions, rules, and incentives has become "the only game in town" (Linz and Stepan 1996: 5). But consolidation does not involve a linear teleological process leading to a system capable of overcoming all challenges to its stability and precluding the possibility of future breakdown. Consolidation encompasses various interrelated arenas – party system, civil and economic society, rule of law – that strengthen each other, but this does not imply a priori determined teleological processes or development sequences.

I am very grateful to Frances Hagopian and Scott Mainwaring for their insightful comments on this chapter.

Democratic regimes evolve historically in different sequences and degrees and not in a systematic way as a historical and falsely teleological interpretation would suggest (Diamond 1999: 19). Because democratization is an uncertain and open-ended process vulnerable to reversals and erosions, a democracy that is considered consolidated can still die at any age (Przeworski et al. 1996). The bottom line is indeed crafting political democracy, and not just electoral democracy, through elected governments in an institutional context that guarantees reasonably free, competitive, and legitimate elections and the exercise of political and civil rights. Contingent on the abilities of political elites, governments and other democratic institutions may further reinforce democratization by enhancing the rule of law and citizenship and developing effective state management. But enhancing the quality of political democracy or deepening it should not be confounded with consolidation itself. Consolidation refers basically to a process in which a democratic regime is strengthened by significant political and social actors who accept the legitimacy of the democratic rules of the game.

In Latin America, there has been a convergence in some countries toward a semidemocratic, "noninstitutionalized" political form (O'Donnell 1993a, 1994). Bolivian democracy, however, steered its own course on the path of institution building and political stability (Mayorga 1991, 1997a). Political strategies and outcomes after 1985 pointed at a historically unprecedented watershed. My analysis of Bolivian democracy, therefore, starts from two basic claims: First, Bolivia's democratization did not lead to a type of delegative democracy, and, second, it was based on a complex and far-reaching process of institution building. I take issue with premature cyclical explanations that see Bolivia's democracy as another ephemeral, semidemocratic case that sooner or later was bound to collapse owing to a predominant pattern of cyclical alternation of democratic and authoritarian regimes. Cyclical approaches poured old wine in new bottles, hampering an adequate theoretical understanding of Latin American democracy (Remmer 1991a: 479–95).

Democratic consolidation as a historical process can come to a halt and be undermined if the outlook for economic development and social equity remains continuously bleak, if poverty and social exclusion persist, and if political parties cannot grapple with disruptive socioeconomic conflicts and delegitimate themselves as a result of poor performance, corruption, and clientelistic practices. Is this the case of Bolivia at present? Several strains facing Bolivia's democracy reveal that after eighteen years of structural adjustment policies (1985–2003) socioeconomic expectations of the population linked with the shift to democracy could not be met. In this regard, the double challenge to resume growth and consolidate political institutions simultaneously is still at the core of democracy.

Bolivia found a way to escape the pattern of noninstitutionalization leading to delegative democracy. Bolivia's democracy has been rooted in political reforms that helped rethink important implications of consensual politics and coalition governments on democracy and presidentialism. I explore why and how Bolivia's democracy developed political stability and democratic governance on the basis of substantial institutional reforms and behavioral changes including a shift to a market economy, the emergence of a moderate multiparty system, a constitutional reform, and popular participation. These reforms were preceded by significant behavioral changes in the 1980s – interparty bargaining, consensual politics, postelectoral coalition building, and election of the chief executive by Congress – based on new rules of political struggle, without altering existing institutions.

If the concept of institution is used as referring both to the rules of the game in extensive form and stable practices (Putnam 1993: 7), behavioral changes can also be regarded as a specific level of institutionalization that shapes the political process in new ways. Institutions without appropriate and compatible behavioral patterns do not work. Nobody in Bolivia or elsewhere expected far-reaching behavioral transformations as a probable outcome of a conflict-ridden transition. These changes caught most analysts by surprise. However, neither the protracted transition to democracy nor the serious crisis during the first democratic government a priori precluded successful political development.[1]

SHIFT TO A MARKET-CENTERED ECONOMY AND PACT FOR DEMOCRACY

The transition to democracy was a "transition through rupture" (Mayorga 1991: 214) with military power. It began with the overthrow of Banzer's dictatorship (1971–78), the longest dictatorship in the longest period of military governments in the twentieth century (1964–82). Beginning in 1977, an economic recession and an intensifying political opposition pressing for full democratization weakened Banzer's government and thwarted its initial liberalization strategy. At the same time, the international context shifted dramatically against Banzer as U.S. foreign policy under Carter (1977–81) turned toward the promotion of human rights and hastened the demise of military dictatorships in Latin America. The end of Banzer's dictatorship triggered a crisis of the military regime that became a full-blown crisis of the state-centered economy that had prevailed since the revolution of 1952. This crisis led to a vicious circle of repeated openings and closings in the transition process between January 1978 and October 1982; the country had two provisional civilian governments and three military governments and experienced two frustrated presidential elections and four coups d'état. Finally, given mass mobilizations, party opposition, splits within the armed forces and international pressure, the military had no other alternative but to relinquish power, making possible the rise to power of the center-left Unidad Democrática y Popular (UDP; Democratic and Popular Unity) coalition through constitutional means in October 1982.

---

[1] This called into question the traditional view that Bolivia was the quintessential example of political turmoil and military coups. Bolivia enjoyed extended periods of civilian government, first from 1880 to 1930 and then again from 1952 to 1964 (Mayorga 1999).

Strangled by the parliamentary opposition, the radical leadership of the Bolivian Workers' Confederation (Central Obrera Boliviana; COB) and the business associations, the UDP government soon failed in its attempts to govern through executive decree. State-owned enterprises went bankrupt, leading to the collapse of the economy and a bout with hyperinflation, which raged at 25,000 percent annualized between January and August 1985. As democracy was unraveling, the government was pressed by its partisan opponents to call new elections. The July 1985 elections helped to restore the viability of democracy. Although no party won a majority of votes, a minority MNR (Movimiento Nacionalista Revolucionario or National Revolutionary Movement) government was formed. The situation changed dramatically in August 1985 when President Paz Estenssoro (1985–89) launched a sweeping structural adjustment program known as the New Economic Policy (NEP), which was backed by former President Banzer's party, the Acción Democrática Nacionalista (ADN; Nationalistic Democratic Action). In October 1985, the ADN joined Paz Estenssoro's parliamentary alliance, which sustained the radical transformation of the economy. The historic Pact for Democracy inaugurated a majority government based on a parliamentary coalition. This pact ushered in an epoch of multiparty pacts and coalition governments that turned out to be the cornerstone of Bolivian democracy.

The NEP's astonishing success in producing an economic recovery had a strong positive effect on the stability and legitimacy of the democratic regime. Hyperinflation – the second highest inflation in twentieth-century Latin America – was curtailed. Inflation plummeted to 96 percent a year later, and then to only 3 percent. The NEP led to an average growth rate of 4 percent in the 1990s and an increase of domestic investment from 13.4 to 23.1 percent of gross domestic product. Foreign direct investment grew from 0.3 to 11.4 percent of GDP, and external debt decreased from 911 percent of GDP in 1986 to 522 percent in 1999. Exports grew from $US 587.5 million to $US 1.104 billion.

The breakdown of state capitalism, leftist populism, and fierce political antagonisms fostered an unexpected process of behavioral changes and institution building. Political and social actors reevaluated traditional patterns of action that had led to instability and ingovernability. They modified their behavior because of national and international constraints that initially pushed them toward a primarily instrumental – not principled – commitment to democracy. But, compelled by adverse circumstances to adapt to new challenges in order to survive, the major political parties and key social actors underwent a process of rule-altering, "experiential" learning. They drew some significant political lessons during the transition from the negative consequences of the prior destructive zero-sum games.

Thus, democratic development underwent a sea change, including (1) the shift to a market-centered economy; (2) a change of political culture from confrontational to consensual practices encompassing interparty bargaining and agreements on basic rules of the game; (3) the emergence of a moderate multiparty system able to tame and incorporate new antisystemic political forces; (4) the establishment of a government system of parliamentarized presidentialism based on political pacts and coalition governments; (5) the introduction of institution-building agreements leading to reform of the constitution and various state institutions, which strengthened the legitimacy of democracy and laid the foundations for salient changes in state structures and in the relations between state and society; and (6) the subordination of the military to the constitutional order, which was strengthened by the prosecution and conviction of the military dictator García Meza (1980–81).

THE RISE OF MODERATE MULTIPARTISM

Because the party system has not produced absolute majorities for the election of presidents since the transition to democracy, Article 90 of the Constitution, which requires that presidents be chosen by Congress when there is no popular-vote majority, has become the normal method for choosing the president. For the first time in its history, Bolivia has developed a moderate multiparty system capable of overcoming the polarized and weak party system that prevailed during the transition (Gamarra 1997; Mayorga 1991). Throughout the first half of the twentieth century, Bolivia had an exclusionary and oligarchic multiparty system. The revolution of 1952 destroyed this party system and gave rise instead to the dominance of a hegemonic party, the MNR. Only in the context of democratization beginning in 1979, and particularly after the key economic transformations from 1985 on, did the main features of a moderate multiparty system emerge. The system was based on five "relevant" (following Sartori's 1976 concept) parties with seats in Congress. The number of effective parties in the Chamber of Deputies rose from 2.04 in 1985 to 5.36 in 1997, although it fell slightly to 4.61 in 2002 (Table 5.1).

This increase, however, did not weaken the party system's vast political depolarization, which stemmed from three fundamental processes. First, the

TABLE 5.1. *Party System Characteristics, 1979–2002 (based on Lower Chamber and Senate results)*

Election	Number of Parties Participating	Effective Number of Parties (votes)	Number of Parties with Seats	Effective Number of Parties (seats)
1979	8	4.45	7	
1980	13	4.16	11	
1985	18	5.67	10	2.04
1989	10	5.97	5	3.92
1993	14	4.51	8	3.71
1997	10	5.93	7	5.36
2002	11	5.16	8	4.61

Source: Own calculations based on CNE (2001) figures.

switch to market-oriented adjustment policies prompted an extensive process of ideological transformation. The three main parties – MNR, ADN, and the Movimiento de Izquierda Revolucionario (MIR; Movement of the Revolutionary Left) – converged on two key principles: a representative democracy and a market economy. The MNR, the oldest party, created in 1941, abandoned its traditional populist ideology and nationalist program; the MIR, founded in 1971 as a leftist party with a Marxist–populist bent, did the same. From its inception in March 1979, the ADN was a rightist party committed to representative democracy and the market economy. Survey data on parliamentary elites provide evidence of this far-reaching ideological transformation. On a left–right scale from 1 to 10, the average ideological self-identification of deputies belonging to the five relevant parties was 6.1 (center-right) in 1997. Deputies of neopopulist parties placed themselves slightly to the left with an average of 5.2 on the same scale (Universidad de Salamanca 1997: 44–48).

Second, the failure of the UDP government (1982–85) and the crisis of the state economy caused the political defeat and waning of leftist, populist parties and of the labor movement. Third, a major shift in preferences and patterns of political culture in Bolivian society began to occur. This shift was neither linear nor irreversible because traditional values such as statism, intolerance, political participation through mass mobilization or corporatist engagement in decision making, and disregard for democratic institutions and the rule of law still persist. But centrist attitudes, gradualism as a mechanism of social and political change, and the demand for joint action between government, parties, and civil society aiming at policy making and social integration were gradually becoming ingrained patterns of political culture.

After 1985, Bolivia developed a relatively well institutionalized party system and not an inchoate, volatile system as Mainwaring and Scully (1995: 4–6) claim. The party system that emerged after the crucial elections of 1985 became a moderate multiparty system. Despite weak party identification and public distrust, parties channeled political preferences and mediated social interests. This was a major break with the recent past in which a divided society was dominated by a political system incapable of mediating conflict at the level of the state. Between 1979 and 2002, the number of legally registered parties fell from seventy-one to eighteen, and parties with representation in Congress fell from thirteen in 1980 to five in 1989, and then rose slightly to seven in 2002. The most important new parties were the ADN, the Unidad Cívica Solidaridad (UCS; Civic Union for Solidarity), the Movimiento al Socialismo (MAS; Movement towards Socialism), and Conciencia de Patria (CONDEPA; Conscience of the Nation). Although the party system displayed a high level of electoral volatility throughout this period, average volatility in elections for the Lower Chamber declined from 33.0 percent of seats in the period 1979–93 to 25.5 percent between the elections of 1993 and 1997. These rates were lower than in Brazil (40.9 percent) and Peru (54.4 percent) in the same period, and this volatility did not affect party-system legitimacy or government formation. The party system was based on two blocs, the ADN/MIR and the MNR, that were relatively stable (with two new neopopulist parties, the UCS and CONDEPA, joining two governments as minor coalition partners), and the effects of volatility were limited to reshuffling within blocs. Electoral processes and contending parties enjoyed ample legitimacy, and political elites adhered to the democratic rules of the game.

Beginning in 1991, key reforms that institutionalized electoral rules and procedures helped strengthen the party system. These changes included (1) the establishment of an autonomous, five-member National Electoral Court (NEC) comprising four nonpartisan figures chosen by two-thirds vote of Congress, plus one member appointed by the president; (2) the adoption of on-site vote validation at polling places; and (3) the abolition of mechanisms that made it possible for regional electoral courts to distort results. The constitutional reform package of August 1994 introduced a second wave of changes, of which the most important introduced a mixed-member proportional system based on the German model (Mayorga 2001b, 2001c). Of a constitutionally fixed number of 130 Congressional deputies, 68 are chosen by first-past-the-post voting in single-member districts, and the remainder (62) are chosen according to proportional representation in nine regional multimember districts. The overall allocation of seats is determined by the list vote obtained by each party. This reform also introduced the D'Hondt formula of proportional representation and established a 3 percent threshold for parties to gain seats in Congress.

Moderate multipartism was a crucial condition for the development of parliamentarized presidentialism and the set of state policies carried out after 1985. Because interparty competition shifted in favor of bargaining and coalition building, it became a driving force of government formation and political stability. A feedback relationship developed between strengthening the constitutional design, by which presidents would be elected in Congress, and postelectoral coalitions, which increased the incentives to bargain. Bargaining, in turn, induced parties to become more centrist. Given that no single party had majority status, majority formation was possible within a political axis dominated collectively by MNR, ADN, and MIR, each of which was the heart of a governing coalition. In the five general elections (1985, 1989, 1993, 1997, 2002), the total cumulative vote share of these three parties was between 73.6 and 42.2 percent (Table 5.2).

The Bolivian party system fit the model of a moderate, pluralist party system: There was a moderate ideological distance between major parties, a tendency on the part of the parties to form coalitions, and a predominantly centripetal pattern of competition (Sartori 1976). The development of this moderate multiparty system was paradoxical in that the system became more institutionalized and moderate even as new parties continuously arose. Democratic consolidation advanced primarily because of interparty competition, not because there was more democratic competition or openness within parties. Even as the party system modernized, the major parties themselves remained traditional in their internal structures and practices, despite launching internal democratization processes following a new political party law in 1999. Except for within the

TABLE 5.2. *Votes and Seats by Party in Bolivia, 1985–2002 (Chamber of Deputies)*

Party	July 14, 1985			May 7, 1989			June 6, 1993			June 7, 1997			June 7, 2002		
	% Votes	Seats	% Seats	% Votes	Seats	% Seats	% Votes	Seats	% Seats	% Votes	Seats	% Seats	% Votes	Seats	% Seats
ADN	32.8	41	31.5	25.2	38	29.2				22.26	32	24.62	3.40	5	3.18
MNR[a]	30.4	43	33.1	25.6	40	30.8	36.2	52	40.0	18.20	26	20.00	22.46	47	29.93
MIR	10.2	15	11.5	21.8	33	25.4				16.80	24	18.46	16.32	31	19.74
AP[b]							21.5	35	26.9						
CONDEPA				12.3	10	7.7	14.6	13	10.0	17.16	19	14.62	0.37		
UCS							14.0	20	15.4	16.11	21	16.11	5.51	5	3.18
IU	0.7			8.0	9	6.9	1.3			3.09	4	3.08			
PS	2.6	5	3.8	2.8									0.65	1	0.63
MRTKL	2.1	2	1.5	1.6											
MNRI	5.5	8	6.2												
MNRV	4.8	6	4.6												
FPU	2.5	4	3.1												
PDC	1.6	3	2.3												
FSB	1.3	3	2.3	0.7											
MBL							5.5	7	5.4	3.71	4	3.08			
ARBOL								1	1.8						
MAS													20.94	35	22.29
MIP													6.09	6	3.82
NFR													20.91	27	17.19
Others	5.5			1.9			5	2	1.5				3.35		
TOTAL	100	130	99.9	99.9	130	100	100	130	100	100	130	100	100	157	100

[a] Alliance with MRTKL in 1993.
[b] Alliance with ADN–MIR.

Source: Own calculations based on CNE (2002) figures.

MNR, this process of internal democratization was full of irregularities and did not achieve its goals.

One of the salient features of the political landscape in the late 1980s was the cleavage between these modernizing parties and two neopopulist political movements – CONDEPA and UCS. Neopopulism differed from traditional populism in two significant ways. First, while accepting representative democracy, neopopulists displayed an aggressive antiinstitutional bias, exalting as truly democratic the "will of the people," represented not by parties but by allegedly popular charismatic leaders. Second, neopopulists rejected traditional policies that called for state control of the economy and for a struggle against "imperialism." Both CONDEPA and UCS channeled the demands of the marginalized urban population – in the case of CONDEPA, the rural and migrant population in the department of La Paz – adversely affected by adjustment policies and not represented by centrist parties. Both CONDEPA and the UCS were led by authoritarian leaders. CONDEPA was founded by the owner of a television and radio network in La Paz, and the UCS was a political movement created by Max Fernández, the powerful stockholder of the country's most important brewery. Both had strong antiparty, antitraditional elite discourse and a personalistic and clientelistic style of politics that blended plebiscitary appeals to the masses with a commitment to market-oriented policies. These movements were led by "outsiders" who initially had antisystem tendencies. For a brief period, they counteracted the political depolarization taking place within the major parties and triggered a new tendency toward polarization. Ultimately, however, they did not have a negative effect on the party system's main tendencies nor did they undermine the legitimacy of democracy (Mayorga 1995).

CONDEPA and the UCS became predominantly "systemic" parties that integrated their constituencies into the political system, participated in the management of some important municipalities, entered into interparty agreements aimed at institutional reforms, and became coalition partners in various governments. The UCS gained votes and seats in the elections of 1989, 1993, and 1997, and it became a minor coalition partner in the governments led by Sánchez de Lozada (1993–97) and Banzer (1997–2001), holding the ministries of sustainable development and labor. CONDEPA also won a significant share of votes and seats in these elections and was a minor coalition partner in Banzer's government. Thus, although both parties emerged outside of and against the established party system, they soon became integrated. After the deaths of their leaders, these parties declined. CONDEPA suffered a catastrophic defeat in the municipal election of 1999 and disappeared in the 2002 general election. Given the persistent problem of poverty, however, the potential for neopopulist and antisystem actors remain, as evinced by the rise of the MAS. Despite the social reforms undertaken by the National Revolution, ethnic–cultural cleavages and the political representation of indigenous masses still constitute a major challenge to democratization. The biggest established parties were unable to build solid roots in the indigenous population, and several attempts to create indigenous parties since the end of the seventies have also been unsuccessful.

Despite the difficulty of organizing single-issue, indigenous parties, two new indigenous parties, the MAS and the MIP (Movimiento Indígena Pachakuti or Pachakuti Indigenous Movement), achieved a significant number of votes in the 2002 election, and advanced the cause of ethnic representation in Congress.

After the transformation of patterns of interparty competition and internal party organizations, parties became the targets of mounting disaffection owing to inefficient performance in government and growing corruption. Surveys show that parties earned consistently low scores, on a scale from 1 to 7, in regards to confidence in institutions. They received a score of 2.5 in 1992 and a score of 2.3, the lowest rating, in 2000 (ILDIS 1990, CNE 2001). These scores correlate with the phenomenon of increasing corruption. Fifty-two percent of the population considers corruption to be a major political and moral problem affecting the legitimacy of democracy. Apart from these perceptions, mobilizations and road blockades between 2000 and 2003 by several social sectors laid bare the weakness of political parties as mediating institutions, revealed the widening gap between society and the state, and provoked a profound political crisis, which nurtured the reemergence of antisystem tendencies and actors.

The party system also failed to integrate sufficiently the diverse social and ethnic–cultural identities and the interests of the rural population, despite the fact that the political and cultural inclusion of Indian peoples was one of the major endeavors of the MNR and the Movimiento Bolivia Libre (MBL). The Law of Popular Participation, passed in 1994, tried precisely to give voice to ethnic–cultural concerns and to create an institutional framework for political inclusion and participation. Bolivia undertook wide-ranging innovations in an attempt to be responsive to autonomous indigenous organizations and demands. Reforms of the constitution, the establishment of the mixed-member proportional system in the electoral system, the education system, and the Law of Popular Participation recognized the legitimacy of the traditional authorities and decision-making mechanisms of indigenous peoples, as well as the principle of cultural diversity and multilingual education. The municipal elections of 1995 and 1999, and particularly the general elections of 1997 and 2002, enhanced the representation of indigenous leaders in the political system. In the 2002 election, the MAS and the MIP together won 27 percent of the votes and 41 seats in Congress. By contrast, the separatist tendency toward an autonomous Aymara state, represented by the peasant leader Quispe, is a rather isolated phenomenon contested by other indigenous peasant movements in Cochabamba and Santa Cruz striving for integration into the nation state. Integration, not separation, is the driving force behind the peasant movements.

Since the transition, parties have become much less ideological, and the traditional left–right dimension has undergone a dramatic change. Ideological principles and political programs count for less than factors such as the defense of social interests, the record of government performance, and the quality of political leaders. The main parties uphold a liberal ideology, but they are pragmatically oriented and much less class-based than before. The MNR is no longer a popular party rooted in a broad class alliance as it was in the revolutionary era (1952–64), while the ADN has penetrated broader middle-class sectors. Both parties maintain strongholds in key regions of the country.

The main shortcomings of the parties are their weak, almost nonexistent linkages with civil society. As representative structures, parties have experienced such troublesome problems as electoral volatility and dealignment (Hagopian 1998). Two processes explain this complex scenario. First, the breakdown of the state-centered economy, the shift to a market economy, and insufficient economic diversification and growth has led to significant structural social changes. Working-class groups and unions have faded, while the informal sector has grown dramatically. In this context, parties have been unable to create new constituencies or reorganize old ones or in any way establish new roots in a society in which social forces are becoming deeply fragmented. Second, political parties have not sufficiently democratized their internal structures and developed new political styles and linkages with society. The main parties that play the key role of agents of political and economic modernization have not modernized themselves. The new political party law prompted parties to gradually begin to change their traditional authoritarian and centralist practices. Yet they are still linked with social organizations by traditional mechanisms of clientelism. Moreover, their key frame of reference seems no longer to be society but rather the state; they have become primarily state-linked organizations.[2] The MNR tried to rebuild its linkages with the rural population and recreate state–peasant relationships through the Law of Popular Participation. Other state policies changed for the better in response to the demands of indigenous populations and peasant organizations. However, whereas the Law of Popular Participation strengthened the representation of indigenous groups, the paradox is that parties did not benefit from it. Instead, their internal authoritarian structures and practices obstructed the thrust of Popular Participation. Unexpectedly, Popular Participation strengthened the autonomy of indigenous populations and increased the gap between these sectors, on the one hand, and the parties and the central government, on the other.

AN INSTITUTIONAL BLEND: PARLIAMENTARIZED PRESIDENTIALISM

Applied only once in the nineteenth century and twice in the 1940s, Article 90 of the Constitution became the key mechanism after the democratic transition for selecting the president and the institutional basis of parliamentarized presidentialism.[3] The Bolivian party system since the resumption of legitimate elections in 1979 has not produced a single predominant party or even engendered

---

[2] This transformation is similar to that of the emergence of cartel parties in Europe (Katz and Mair 1995).

[3] Since the constitutional reform of 1994, the provision has read: "If none of the candidates for the presidency obtains the absolute majority of votes, the Congress will hold an election by absolute majority of the votes among the two candidates who obtained the largest number of votes" (in the popular election).

alternating, absolute majorities. Siles Zuazo won a 38 percent plurality of the popular vote in 1981 and was chosen president by Congress, but he came into office as the head of a minority government. In contrast, since 1985, presidential elections have seen the forging of interparty agreements leading to majority-coalition governments. Article 90 makes no explicit provision for political pacts, but its requirement that presidents be chosen by Congress when there is no popular-vote majority made possible coalition building among political parties.

At the outset of the transition, parties were not very concerned with constitutional arrangements. The Constitution of 1967, which exhibited substantial continuity with earlier constitutions, seemed to be a "dead letter." After the turmoil of 1978–82, awareness grew about advantages to the constitutional framework that could prevent divided governments. By the time of Paz Estenssoro's election, the dead letter had become a driving force as key constitutional provisions regarding the creation and turnover of governments became effective rules of the democratic game. Consequently, crafting governments based on parliamentary majorities was the outcome both of the experience of destructive political deadlock and of the awareness of the incentives that Article 90 created for parties that hoped to gain power through coalition building.

Bolivia's government system requires coalition building *after elections* to select the president (Mayorga 1994). The proportional representation system that was in place until 1994 and the new mixed-member proportional system that has been used since 1994 guarantee a broad representation of parties in Congress, but they do not encourage as such negotiation and coalition building. Only the political need and will to craft majority governments has prompted parties and the Congress to choose from among the frontrunners. Most importantly, the Congress has not been bound to select the plurality winner, but rather the candidate who is able to build a parliamentary majority. In this way, the Bolivian system is quite different from the pre-1973 Chilean Congresses' practice of electing presidents who had received the largest plurality of the popular vote, a practice that often led to minority governments (Valenzuela 1994: 116–19). The Bolivian system's strong feature has been precisely to cope with problems of coalition building in a presidential system avoiding – in the context of a multiparty system generating pluralities – a zero-sum game and fostering instead cooperation and consensual practices between parties. This system, therefore, may be conceived of as *parliamentarized presidentialism* because of the Congress's decisive role in selecting presidents on the basis of parliamentary majorities that facilitates governability. Bolivia's democratic regime introduced mechanisms to solve some fundamental problems of presidential regimes such as minority governments, stalemate between the executive and legislative branches, policy immobilization, and governing by decree. Parliamentarized presidentialism permitted Bolivia to adopt adjustment policies, stick with the decision to move toward a market economy despite difficult circumstances, and transform its political system in a consensual direction. Certainly, confrontation between government and opposition parties over specific policies did not disappear. Legislation and decision making on a number of major issues regarding economic and state reforms were resolved by two-thirds votes of both houses of Congress. Many other Latin American presidential systems, in contrast, have encountered acute difficulties in producing legislative majorities because the direct and separate election of the president coexists with a fragmented multiparty system. The "difficult combination" of presidentialism, fragmented multiparty systems, and proportional representation has been an ongoing source of political conflicts in several countries, affecting democratic stability, governance, and institutionalization (Mainwaring 1993; Linz 1994).

In sum, the fundamental explanation for the stability of democratic governments in Bolivia was the institutional shift from presidentialism based on minority governments to a system of parliamentarized presidentialism based on majority governments. This system is a *mestizo* with both parliamentary and presidential features. It is presidential in that the president serves a fixed term that does not depend on the confidence of Congress and has the formal power to choose and dismiss cabinet ministers without Congressional approval. At the same time, this presidential regime is "parliamentarized" in its origin and its functioning because (1) the president is chosen by Congress on the basis of postelectoral interparty agreements; (2) the government rests on the same coalition that elects the president, ensuring both majority legislative support and the articulation of executive and legislative power; (3) consensualism is the predominant tendency in Congressional coalition building and decision making; (4) the Congress has authority not only to make laws and approve budgets but also to censure cabinet ministers and appoint other high-level officials; (5) the president's legislative powers are limited to an overrideable package veto plus the authority to declare a "state of siege"; and (6) there are informal restrictions on presidential discretion in making appointments (cabinet posts are shared among parties as part of the coalition-building process).

Parliamentarized presidentialism, however, does not entail the predominance of Congress or a balanced relationship between Congress and the president. As a result of the parliamentary majorities that presidents have enjoyed, the system can strongly enhance presidential powers, as it did under Sánchez de Lozada, who commanded a solid majority coalition centered around his own MNR in the face of a divided parliamentary opposition. Thus, depending on the coherence of coalitions and the strength of the president's party, the government system makes it possible to have a president with overwhelming power over the Congress.

As never before, the crafting of governments based on coalitions became the bottom line of democratic politics.[4] Since the politics of coalition – a dynamic

---

[4] Colombia and Venezuela experienced coalition governments from the mid-1950s through the early 1970s. Chile has had coalition governments as a result of preelectoral bargaining since the return of civilian rule in 1989, and Brazil has had them since 1994, but Bolivia has been unique in various aspects.

common in parliamentary regimes (Laver and Schofield 1991:1–14) – is the mainspring of this system, a "nested game" with a double logic of political competition underlies the struggle for power (Tsebelis 1990: 5–11). Parties strive to maximize their respective vote shares, but the popular balloting is a mere prelude to postelectoral bargaining among party leaders whose leverage determines who winds up in the Congressional majority, the cabinet, and the presidency. Thus, the game of interparty bargaining is nested within the prior and larger game of popular balloting. In these respects, Bolivian democratic governments since 1985 have come close to the logic of parliamentary multiparty governments in Western Europe. As Linz highlighted regarding the Bolivian case: "[T]he pure model of presidentialism in practice has been modified in ways that are more congruent with parliamentarism" (Linz 1994: 37). The rationale for characterizing the Bolivian government system as *parliamentarized presidentialism* is precisely to pin down the predominant working features of the Bolivian presidential system: interparty coalitions and Congressional election of presidents (Mayorga 2001a). Linz introduced the term "parliamentarized presidentialism" to emphasize the main thrust of a constitutional reform he was proposing that Bolivia adopt: the constructive vote of no confidence, a reform that would have strengthened even further the parliamentary features of the Bolivian government system.

Another essential feature of the government system has been the mechanism of governing by legislating through executive initiative supported by a parliamentary majority, rather than by decree, as in other Latin American countries (Carey and Shugart 1998a). The Constitution does not include provisions that allow the president to obtain emergency powers. Bypassing the legislature became a pointless temptation for presidents. Unlike the case of Menem's government in Argentina (Levitsky, this volume), "surplus majority governments" in Bolivia made it possible for the executive to govern without extensively negotiating policy issues with the opposition. Most coalition governments have passed the bulk of their laws in a fierce struggle against the opposition, as the legislation in the reform-intensive government of Sánchez de Lozada demonstrated.[5]

Consensual democracy based on pacts involved long-term agreements but faced severe obstacles when it became necessary to strike broad agreements for specific policy making in sensitive areas. In most cases, these conflicts arose because of tensions over the competing claims to legitimacy of consensual and majoritarian democracy. While coalition governments were convinced of their legitimate right to apply mechanisms of majoritarian democracy that barred opposition parties from legislative decision making, the opposition parties called such mechanisms into question, arguing that only consensual democracy could provide sufficient legitimacy for government policies. By insisting on overall agreements on legislation and government policies, opposition parties exerted veto power and rejected the principle of majoritarian decisions in Congress and

---

[5] The exception was Paz Estenssoro's government (1985–89), backed by ADN, the main opposition party, which did not formally join the government.

hence the fusion of executive power and parliamentary majority. Despite the experience of several coalition governments, democratic governance was not strengthened by deliberative decision making and cooperation on legislative policy between the executive and opposition.

ADVANCES AND PITFALLS OF THE DEMOCRATIC REGIME

The consolidation of the democratic regime in Bolivia was made possible by the emergence of new political practices and patterns of action, the development of a moderate multiparty system, and the advancement of a government system of parliamentarized presidentialism. Within this context, Bolivian democracy made other significant advances that also contributed to the sustainability of democracy. Among the most significant were the subordination of the military, the expansion of political participation, the routinization of political competition, the emergence of a democratic political culture, and the strengthening of Congress.

Since 1985, no military uprising or threat to the stability of the regime has occurred. The democratic regime has been successful in subordinating the armed forces to civilian authorities, although the military has maintained its autonomy in military affairs, and the Congress does not exercise oversight over the armed forces.[6] Moreover, until a few years ago, the armed forces stuck to the 1970s ideology of national security and, owing to its inability to adapt to democratic principles of citizenship, their acceptance of the rule of law and respect of human rights have been relative. By having the military broadly accept the democratic framework, democratic governments did not suffer from military interference in politics or tutelage by the armed forces as has occurred in Chile. The prosecution and conviction of the military dictator García Meza and his main collaborators was a historical milestone in the process of strengthening the subordination of the military (Mayorga 1997b). In short, the military has enjoyed no political leverage in political decisions, but it is not yet accountable to the legislature or even the executive in matters concerning military policy and military expenses. Because there is no institutionalized system of accountability for the institutions of public order, an essential prerequisite for democratic consolidation is missing (Rodríguez Veltzé 2001: 181).

Another institutional advance has been political participation in elections. Enfranchisement made substantial progress between 1979 and 2002, rising from 1,876,900 to 4,155,055 out of a population of 6 million and 8 million, respectively, and voter turnout, which was consistently above 70 percent, increased from 1,693,821 to 2,994,065 (IDEA 1997: 54, 84). Abstention rates increased, but in comparative perspective they are rather low, ranging from

---

[6] There are uncertainties about the role of the military. Should it restrict itself to the constitutional role of defending the country or instead play an active role in the struggle against drug trafficking as well as in productive activities? Should the military also be responsible for internal security, thereby usurping the role of the police?

9.8 percent in 1979 to 18.0 percent in 1985 to 27.9 percent in 2002. Although some obstacles remain, such as an inadequate system of electoral inscriptions – as of 1997 only 80 percent of the urban population and 60 percent of the rural population had the identity card necessary for electoral registration – barriers to universal suffrage have been eliminated.

After a party-dependent NEC allowed blatant vote rigging in the presidential elections of 1989, setting the stage for the disputed Congressional election of Paz Zamora, the democratic legitimacy of successive governments was enhanced by the accepted rules of the game and the transparency of electoral processes. Mass surveys provide evidence that political and social actors have committed themselves to the support of democracy: 68.9 percent (Latinobarómetro 1998), 82 percent (CNE 2001), and 71.6 percent (Seligson 1999) of respondents support democracy as being preferable to an authoritarian regime and would be willing to defend democracy if it were threatened. These percentages are among the highest in Latin America. Thus, both turnout and surveys point to a remarkable shift in attitudinal change that is comparable to that witnessed in Argentina (Levitsky, this volume) and differs from the case of Brazil (Weyland, this volume). Paradoxically, these data contrast with data on confidence in political and social institutions. Political parties have been among the institutions with the lowest confidence rating since the first survey in 1990. On a scale of 1 to 7, political parties received a score of 3.3 in 1990 (ILDIS 1990) and a score of 2.5 in 1999, even lower than those obtained by the armed forces and the police. The trend toward growing distrust of political parties and politicians has continued. In a 2001 survey, 60 percent of the people responded that there would be no serious consequences for democracy if political parties were to disappear or be eliminated (CNE 2001).

The regime's stability and the routinization of political competition up to 2002 are evidenced by four consecutive cases of constitutional transfers of power and formation of coalition governments. With the exception of the Banzer (1997–2001), Quiroga (2001–02), and the second Sánchez de Lozada (2002–03) governments, coalitions were surprisingly stable. Coalitions were predominantly based on policy-oriented motivations and interests, not merely on office seeking and patronage. Paz Estenssoro's (1985–89) Pacto por la Democracia and Sánchez de Lozada's (1993–97) Pacto de Gobernabilidad were mainly policy-based coalitions, while Paz Zamora's (1989–93) Acuerdo Patriótico and Banzer's (1997–2001) Compromiso por la Democracia were patronage-based coalitions. Coalition building made it possible for political parties to share power in government and have access to spoils and patronage. Coalitions played a contradictory role: they allowed governments to stabilize democracy, implement long-term policies, and carry out institutional reforms that weakened the spoils system, but they also legitimized patronage to a great extent. Coalition governments endured because of a stable democratic system rooted in interparty pacts – "democracy by pacts" (Mayorga 1991: 245–75; 2001a) that established a framework for governability and institutional innovation. Three crucial agreements – the Pact for Democracy in August 1985, the

Agreement for the Reform of the Electoral System and the NEC in February 1991, and the Agreement for the Modernization of the State in July 1992, which led to constitutional and electoral reforms in 1994 – have underpinned Bolivian democratic politics.

Although the democratic process has strengthened the Congress, institutional change in the legislature has been limited, especially in comparison with the NEC. The paramount role of Congress has been to select presidents, support the executive, and promote the consensus needed for institutional reforms. Yet this role was not matched by other important functions the Congress should perform, above all, exercising oversight over the executive branch. The modernization of Congressional structures and management resources – the task of a modernization committee set up in 1993 – has been limited, in large part because of their partial scope, the lack of continuity in reform efforts, and the lack of political will to eliminate pork-barrel politics in Congress. A stable, efficient bureaucracy based on a merit career system is missing. Deputies and senators do not have specialized professional and staff support for their activities. This deficiency weakens Congress's ability to play an effective role in representing constituencies and in legislating.[7] Given the support of a parliamentary majority and the weakness of the opposition, the executive has not been accountable to the Congress in many areas of policy making.

Horizontal accountability – the ability of state institutions such as Congress and the Supreme Court of Justice to make public officials accountable for their actions – therefore, remains one of the crucial challenges for Bolivia's democratic regime. Although progress has been made in some areas – in budget oversight and in building support for legal reforms in areas such as environmental law, for example – coalition governments have weakened Congressional powers and prevented a system of checks and balances from coming into being. Parliamentarized presidentialism has given rise to an overwhelming predominance of the executive over the legislature both in proposing legislation and in ensuring disciplined voting in the legislature. Congress has mostly tended to serve as an executive rubber stamp rather than as a forum for discussion and deliberation. Paradoxically, this predominance has not entailed a central policy-making role for coalition parties. To the contrary, policy-making has been the domain of independent experts working closely with the president. The role of politicians who belong to coalition parties has been limited mainly to supporting the executive in Congress.

The judiciary lags even further behind in fostering horizontal accountability. Bolivia's administration of justice has traditionally been slow, corrupt, inconsistent, unreliable, and party-dependent. The judiciary has been unable to protect citizen rights through the impartial administration of justice and to address the acute problems of public corruption by prosecuting and holding

---

[7] This problem has been compounded by the mixed-member electoral system, which prompts single-seat district deputies to confuse their role as municipal councilors and to overemphasize constituency-serving patronage politics at the expense of national politics (Mayorga 2001c).

corrupt politicians accountable. Following the 1994 constitutional reform, the Congress overhauled the judicial system. They established a Judicial Council, a Constitutional Tribunal, and later, in 1998, an Ombudsman (Defensor del Pueblo) to participate in judicial review and to defend human rights. But the reform of the Supreme Court and the Judicial Council, which was responsible for personnel selection, financial management, and disciplinary action in the lower court system, has faced great obstacles. Political parties stacked both institutions with their own appointees. Despite the reform laws and a constitutional provision establishing the judiciary's autonomy, the Supreme Court of Justice and especially the lower courts continue to be dependent on the executive because governing political parties have persistently nominated subservient appointees to these institutions. In fact, the return to democracy appears to have increased the desire of politicians to seek to control the judiciary, rather than to respect its autonomy, nurturing asymmetric relationships between the executive and the judiciary (Rodríguez Veltzé 2001: 189).

The recent judicial reform has been beset with massive problems in implementation. Existing patronage networks within the judiciary and the political parties have been extremely resistant to the reforms. Given the subordination of the administration of justice to the executive and party politics, the rule of law is not sufficiently guaranteed. Impunity of corrupt government officials has been a pressing but unresolved issue, eroding the legitimacy of politicians and parties. Two different sets of events, however, have set significant precedents for judicial autonomy. First, the trial of ex-dictator García Meza by the Supreme Court demonstrated that it could play a decisive constitutional role by prosecuting and condemning the former military dictator for violations against the Constitution and human rights. Second, alternation in power and political stability unintentionally advanced the institutional autonomy of the Supreme Court to the point where governments clashed with the Supreme Court on several occasions in the 1990s. When the magistrates' terms of office began to diverge from the terms of the president and Congress, the executive on more than one occasion attempted – arbitrarily and unsuccessfully – to submit the Supreme Court to its authority by appointing new members loyal to the government. The most serious conflict arose in 1990 when the Acuerdo Patriótico government (1989–93) dismissed eight of twelve members of the Supreme Court on the charge of corruption and of a judicial decision that it alleged jeopardized the financial stability of the country. A similar conflict broke out when the same government decided to prosecute the Court's president and a senior official for alleged bribery and corruption.

Institutional deficiencies and social constraints diminish the full protection of citizens' rights, but democratic governments have widely complied with constitutional provisions protecting the rights of citizens. In comparison with past authoritarian regimes, democratic governments have enhanced the respect for human rights. Freedom House scores on political and civil rights such as freedom of speech, freedom of the press, and freedom of association corroborate Bolivia's progress in strengthening democratic institutions. In 1980–81, the rating was an extremely high 7 for political rights and 5 for civil liberties. In the 1992–93 survey, by contrast, the rating was 2 for political rights and 3 for civil liberties, putting the country within Freedom House's category of "free." The 1999–2000 survey assigns Bolivia's democracy an even better rating of 1.3 (Freedom House 2001). Nonetheless, the institutions of public order such as the police and the armed forces constitute a permanent threat to the rule of law and the respect for human rights. Although they have supported democratization, their authoritarian practices persist and are at odds with human rights and citizens' guarantees. Human rights associations have brought to light several violations stemming from repressive action by the police and the armed forces, most of which occurred during states of siege.

THE IMPACT OF INSTITUTIONAL REFORMS ON SOCIETY

The main reasons for Bolivia's success in building a competitive democratic regime were crucial institutional reforms and behavioral changes. But to assess whether democracy also took root in society, it is necessary to address the extent to which institutional innovations have permeated Bolivian society. The issue is twofold: To what extent has civil society contributed to democracy's sustainability, and has the successful democratization of the political system spread throughout society and fostered democratic state–society relationships.

During the transition, civil society was split into three different types of organizations with diverse and contradictory orientations toward democratization. The popular sectors – mainly workers, teachers, and peasants – were represented by the powerful leftist COB, which had an ambiguous attitude toward representative democracy (Mayorga 1991: 143–206). The COB made a major contribution in the struggle against the military dictatorship, but its support for representative democracy, which it viewed as merely an intermediate instrumental step toward socialism, was halfhearted. Its strategy, aimed at toppling the UDP government, provoked instead the irreparable decline of the labor movement (Mayorga 1991: 143–67). Regional interests and business groups, represented by civic committees and the national peak organization – the Confederation of Private Entrepreneurs (Confederación de Empresarios Privados de Bolivia, CEPB) – became a major prodemocratic force, but they, too, displayed an ambiguous stance toward democracy. During the transition of 1978–82, they were suspicious of democracy and hence supported military coups d'état.

While the CEPB's political clout came to the fore in the shift to a market economy, popular actors such as peasant organizations, worker unions, and associations of informal workers have been fragmented. These organizations have weakened in the last decade as a result of great structural changes in the economy caused by economic adjustment policies, which had profound effects on the labor force, employment, and worker organizations. The informal sector grew to about 65 percent of the labor force. The collapse of the state tin mining companies and the shift from a state-led economy to a market economy caused the dissolution of the powerful mining proletariat, changing the political and social scenario. The downfall of mining also led to a persistent economic depression in two key regions (Oruro and Potosí), fostering the migration of miners' and peasant families to the coca regions of the Chapare and the eastern lowlands of Santa Cruz. Only the peasant organizations of the Chapare and the Northern Altiplano have retained their strength in articulating interests and demands. Other social organizations also became influential. A panoply of non-governmental organizations, human rights organizations, and the media reinforced civil society. Civil society organizations went beyond class-based issues and fought for the defense of human rights, women's rights, the fair administration of justice, and the struggle against corruption. The media evolved as a strong countervailing power to the executive, exerting oversight functions over policies, management, and politicians – albeit often accusing politicians and other citizens without sufficient evidence.

To address the question whether the democratization of the political system extended to civil society, fostering democratic state–society relationships, I will focus on the most relevant institutional reform: the Law of Popular Participation, promulgated in 1993. To widen the scope of representative democracy, this law aimed at promoting democratic state building and citizen participation. It transferred responsibility for the administration of health, education, and infrastructure services to municipal governments and expanded municipal jurisdiction to rural areas. The management of municipal governments was complemented by a mechanism of participatory democracy – the oversight committees – composed of local grassroots organizations that participate in the planning, public investment, and evaluation of municipal policies. The law also recognized the territorial authority of indigenous organizations and their traditional decision-making mechanisms rooted in communitarian consensual practices and entrenched in the constitutional reform of 1994, which established Bolivia as a multiethnic and multicultural country. The Law of Popular Participation intended to accomplish as a nation-building project what the National Revolution (1952–64) could not achieve: to reconcile and integrate the rich ethnic–cultural diversities of Bolivian society into a democratic system, asserting the rights of individuals and peoples that do not belong to a homogeneous culture and nation.

Paradoxically, this ambitious law was a reform from above. It did not respond to effective mass demands of citizen participation at the local level. It was designed and implemented at a conjuncture in which the indigenous and peasant movements did not exert any pressure toward this specific juridical and constitutional reform. The law was opposed by powerful regional organizations such as the civic committees, which favored a radical decentralization approach at the departmental rather than the municipal level. The law introduced a model of participation by creating new territorial actors. This altered profoundly not only the role of traditional social actors but also the corporatist forms of direct participation of labor unions at the national level in managing state enterprises. Initially, both the opposition parties and the unions clashed with the government over the law on the grounds that the government intended to strengthen the MNR at the local level and thereby dominate municipalities. But distrust against the law soon faded because the distribution of national resources and the structure of public investment dramatically changed in favor of rural municipalities. All parties embraced the law because they found new incentives for pursuing their interests and expanding their political opportunities.[8]

Political and social actors realized the financial and political benefits provided by the law. Before the Law of Popular Participation, 91 percent of fiscal resources were concentrated in the departmental capitals. By 1999, the distribution of revenue had doubled the transfer of state income to municipalities from 10 to 20 percent of total tax revenue, benefiting rural municipalities on the basis of a per capita distribution formula. The increase of municipal revenues was not the only critical change. Political transformations have been as important as the fiscal changes and the redefinition of municipal responsibilities. Local politics became a new field of political action as rural municipalities became centers of local power. In their electoral strategies, parties began to target rural municipalities. This crucial transformation transpired in the 1995 and 1999 municipal elections in which new local leaders achieved access to rural municipalities, for example, in the Chapare. Already in the 1995 elections, one out of four municipalities elected indigenous mayors. Indigenous councilors won seats in 210 municipal governments, or two thirds of the total. This process of political inclusion counteracted tendencies toward political autonomy expressed by radical Katarista parties at the beginning of the democratic process and recently by peasant leader Quispe. Rural municipalities in Quechua, Aymara, and Guarani regions have become core elements of an emerging multiethnic and democratic state based on social participation, indigenous rights, and ethnic–cultural interests and identities.

Thus, the Law of Popular Participation unleashed a process in which traditional state–society relationships began to change. New social actors emerged, local democracy was enhanced, and indigenous participation developed within the framework of new forms of social participation. The relationships between parties and new social actors at the local level have evolved in different ways. Because parties have traditionally been weak at the local level, the new dynamics of municipal politics are exerting pressure on party structures. Parties are trying to adjust to the new forces and demands. Some local parties have rented their labels to peasant organizations or invited peasant leaders to run in municipal elections on their slates. This was the case of small parties such as the Izquierda Unida (IU: United Left) and the MAS in the Chapare region. Another party strategy has been to nominate party members with roots in local politics as candidates in municipal elections.

Owing to major regional and ethnic–cultural diversities and to different levels of social organization, the outcomes of the Law of Popular Participation regarding the democratization of state–society relationships have greatly varied.

---

[8] The Law of Popular Participation established a new strategic context for rational political behavior and unleashed dynamics consistent with the institutionalist hypothesis about the consequences of change (Grindle 2000: 144).

In some regions, parties have hindered the development of social participation by incorporating oversight committees into their clientelistic networks. This is the case of some municipalities in the Altiplano where communities and peasant unions are fragile. In other cases in the valleys and tropics, oversight committees have strengthened their role vis-à-vis parties, thereby enhancing local organizations and social participation (Gray-Molina 2001). Given these contradictory tendencies, the unresolved question is whether popular partici- pation is strengthening social organizations rather than political parties. The thrust of the Law of Popular Participation lies precisely in decentralizing state structures and democratizing political power at the local level. In the nine years since its implementation, its most important outcomes have been the regionally differentiated, party-mediated strengthening of indigenous and peasant repre- sentation in local politics; greater citizen participation in public decision mak- ing, especially in rural areas; and significant urban-to-rural redistribution of fiscal resources. Some analysts assert that the Law of Popular Participation did not bring about the strengthening of local society and politics, but rather the extension of the state based on the hegemony of parties over local society and local politics. Critical assessments have also pointed out that the Law of Popu- lar Participation rests on a radical municipalist concept of autonomy that lacks a coherent framework of decentralization and subsidiarity.

In addition to the constraints originating in traditional party politics – mainly clientelistic patterns of action – serious shortcomings have hampered the en- hancement of local politics and social participation. These shortcomings stem both from the traditionally weak managerial and administrative capacities of most municipalities and from the flaws in the design of many municipal dis- tricts, which are too small and not sustainable (more than 30 percent of the 314 municipalities). Moreover, economic development has not bolstered backward rural areas. The Law of Popular Participation is not embedded in a dynamic economic development of rural areas. In this regard, so far it has been an "empty box": It has triggered a unique transformation of local politics, but it has not provided development policies needed to reduce rural poverty (Gray-Molina 2001: 64). Thus, crucial problems rooted in gaps of the institutional frame- work, traditional patterns of action, legislative flaws, and economic factors are affecting the institutionalization of local governments and undermining their efficacy in enhancing social participation and reducing poverty and exclusion. Although its outcomes are mixed and not consistent enough, the Law of Popu- lar Participation has been widely accepted by Bolivian society as a far-reaching institutional reform that fosters more democratic state–society relationships.

SHORTCOMINGS AND GOVERNABILITY CRISIS

Democratic advances thanks to institution building and economic reforms were remarkable. Between 1988 and 1998 the New Economic Policy managed to achieve economic stability and a noteworthy average growth rate of 4 percent. A key problem, though, has been that this performance was not enough to lower unemployment (65 percent of urban jobs are informal), to reduce poverty (two thirds of the population is poor), and to improve education, health, and nutrition (infant mortality stands at sixty-nine per thousand live births), as well as to lessen income concentration (10% of the population earns 58% of all income). However important to attract foreign investment and to raise technological standards in oil and telecommunications, privatization policies have not had substantial spillover effects and have been unable to meet the rising socioeconomic expectations of a poverty-ridden country, benefiting only some middle-class and business groups.[9] So, democratic governments have faced serious pitfalls in tackling several structural problems that affect the economy and the state, such as social exclusion, economic dependency on the export of raw materials, an insufficiently diversified economy, a narrow internal market, a weak entrepreneurial class, and inefficient state management. Bolivia faces a crucial challenge stemming from historical and structural problems of the society and the economy left unresolved by different models of government since the National Revolution. The long-term prospects for the consolidation of Bolivian democracy remain heavily contingent on the country's ability to bring about a reasonably efficient blend of democracy, economic development, and equity. The key task is still democracy's legitimation by state and economic performance.

Like most Latin American countries, Bolivia has been hit since 1999 by economic stagnation, unemployment, and deteriorating living conditions, both as a consequence of an international recession and as the result of the crackdown on coca production. Between 1999 and 2002, real GDP grew only 1.46 percent per year on average. From 1997 to 2000, the coca eradication policy, under U.S. pressure, provoked a reduction of about 8 percent of the GDP. The slump was the background for growing social unrest, mass mobilizations, and road blockages beginning in April 2000. Banzer's government (1997–2001)[10] was overwhelmed by the economic and social crisis, which rapidly turned into a deep crisis of government and state that reached a climax in the forced resignation of President Sánchez de Lozada in October 2003. This is a paradox: Politically and economically, Bolivia has been one of the most aggressive reformers in Latin America since the 1980s, but there seem to be signs that the structural adjustment model and the process of political institutionalization have reached their limits.

Since Banzer's government (1997–2001), political mismanagement, insufficient economic growth, social exclusion, corruption, and contentious social

---

9 Unlike orthodox privatization, the Bolivian privatization, called capitalization and implemented by Sánchez de Lozada's government, transformed six state enterprises, the most important being in the energy and telecommunication sectors, into joint stock companies by selling new shares (equivalent to 50 percent of the existing share capital) to strategic transnational companies, which assumed management functions (Morales 2001: 53–54). The state was barred from the administration of these funds since they were handed over to private pension funds.

10 As a result of illness, Banzer stepped down on August 6, 2001, and was replaced by Vice President Jorge Quiroga.

movements have put democracy in jeopardy. Institutional and economic re-forms have failed to deliver better living conditions to the poor and excluded. As a consequence of a decade of institution building that was not backed by sufficient economic growth and reduction in poverty, Bolivia now faces serious strains. The fundamental question is whether this crisis is a conjunctural cri-sis of government or a deep structural crisis stemming from the institutional weaknesses of the state, or both. Following the collective frustration of the past years, a widely held perception was not that the government had failed but that the economic model and the democratic system as a whole had failed. Neverthe-less, the sociopolitical crisis during Banzer's government reflects a complex mix-ture of conjunctural and structural problems. The structural problems include fragile state structures, economic weaknesses, constitutional shortcomings, and traditional patterns of party politics.

State reforms were hampered by the lack of development of a modern bureau-cracy and efficient state structures. Patronage politics have strongly impinged on policy performance and on state capabilities and management. Policies aimed at the development of an efficient bureaucracy were weak, discontinuous, and con-tradictory. Paz Estenssoro's administration (1985–89) made an initial attempt to rationalize public employment. Paz Zamora's government (1989–93) timidly tried to introduce the principle of merit into the civil service, but patronage, bureaucratic inefficiency, and bloated state payrolls remained serious problems. Modernization of the state apparatus has been dominated by a contradictory logic of reform and politicization of the public administration and strangled by patronage networks and a spoils system that are still driving forces in Bolivian politics. As a recent study puts it, "the price for reforms under this system has been and is likely to continue to be a measure of plunder" (Guevara 2000: 2). Key state institutions – the Central Bank, the Office of the Controller General, the National Electoral Court, and the former state-owned enterprises – were taken out of the spoils system. This process paradoxically dried up the sources of plunder, and the remaining sources have increased in value for parties. But the risk has been that government parties tried to undo or at least thwart some of the modernizing reforms that they themselves had fostered. In short, despite reforms, state organizations did not sufficiently adapt to the new institutional framework; therefore, they did not enhance efficiency. On the contrary, despite the fact that a regulatory system was put into effect, the structural adjustment and the privatization of state enterprises have undermined the state and its ability to cope with the economic crisis and to manage social conflict.

Parliamentarized presidentialism lacks a constitutional mechanism for han-dling severe government crises that evolve into a state crisis. There is no mech-anism for a government to change when the president loses majority support in Congress or proves incapable of coping with government problems. Banzer's coalition found itself in this situation and became increasingly incapable of dealing with the socioeconomic crisis and its political consequences. Lacking a constructive vote of no confidence, this politically exhausted government had to finish its term.

Deep disenchantment with political parties as representative institutions and government agents spawned a widespread perception that political decision making can no longer be restricted to parties. Since the mass popular upheavals of April and September 2000, the discontent with politics and parties has generated an even more aggressive repudiation of both. Emerging antiparty tendencies questioned "the party monopoly of politics," proposing instead a fuzzy and unfeasible model of participatory democracy based mainly on corporatist mechanisms of social control over the state administration. Before the 2002 election, the most radical tendencies were expressed by the peasant movements of Morales and Quispe. As in the process of the National Revolution, there has been a strong demand for direct participation in policy making. These groups conceive of politics as a realm for the direct intervention of social movements in state affairs, making political representation unnecessary. This is the most troubling aspect of this appeal to an utterly utopian direct democracy, which can itself be understood as a reaction to the failure of political parties to meet the demands of social participation in policy making.

The nature and performance of Banzer's government greatly exacerbated the structural problems underlying the state and the economy. The most severe sociopolitical crisis since the UDP government (1982–85) also had homegrown causes. Banzer's government was unable to implement efficient policies to reduce poverty and fight against corruption. Underlying this failure was a coalition overwhelmingly based on rent seeking and patronage, giving rise to a fragile government. The nemesis of this government was a dramatic lack of political program, governing capacity, and leadership. Paradoxically, it began as an allegedly powerful "megacoalition" formed by five parties that controlled more than two thirds of seats in Congress. Nevertheless, this oversized majority did not result in an efficient executive capable of decision making, or anticipating and resolving social conflicts rooted mainly in economic problems. On the contrary, deadlock and disagreements were constant problems within the coalition, and thwarted effective governmental responses to the economic crisis. The coalition split up between August 1999 and January 2000 when two minor parties, CONDEPA and Nueva Fuerza Republicana (NFR; New Republican Force), were ousted from the government. Their defection put the coalition in a precarious position in Congress.

To offset its lack of a program and to initiate a new governing style based on agreements with civil society, the government summoned all leading social and regional organizations as well as political parties to a National Dialogue in October 1997. The National Dialogue aimed to work out guidelines for state policies on economic development, institution building, human development, and the struggle against drug trafficking. The key objective was to create interactive mechanisms of semidirect and deliberative democracy so as to integrate social organizations into the process of policy making.[11] Unfortunately, the

---

[11] This was an important conclusion of the National Dialogue of October 1997, but it had no impact on policy making.

government wasted the political capital achieved in the National Dialogue by riding roughshod over its conclusions on policies to which it had committed itself. Initially, the government's target was to do away with state reforms carried out by Sánchez de Lozada's government (1993–97), such as the privatization of state enterprises. Yet it was unable to reverse the reforms, either because they had gained ground in Bolivian society or because international organizations and companies were fiercely opposed to the reversals. The privatization policy was reluctantly accepted. Other reforms such as Popular Participation were discontinued and stunted. Banzer's government dangerously undermined institutions while keeping up the appearance of reinforcing them.

The inability to govern became dramatically manifest in the social crisis that crippled the country after April 2000. This crisis revealed the government's inability to deal with the extreme fragmentation of social organizations and the multiplicity of conflicts that had emerged in the last decade. About seventy multifarious demands were put forward by three different contentious actors: the Chapare's federations of coca-growing peasants, who opposed the sweeping coca eradication policy and demanded permission to continue limited coca production; poor sectors and rural irrigation cooperatives of the city of Cochabamba organized in a "water committee" that rejected an increase in water prices and called for the cancellation of the water supply contract with an international company; and the Aymara peasants of the Northern Altiplano, who were protesting against their poverty and social exclusion. Taking advantage of the critical situation, other organizations such as rural teachers' unions and even rioting police joined the protests and mobilizations and demanded wage increases. Some organizations, especially the peasants' confederation, went beyond economic demands and pursued forms of ethnic autonomy that would entail radical changes of the legal order and the state.

Despite their fragmentation, the peasant organizations paralyzed the country's economy and besieged the government, taking it hostage. Neither repressive actions nor a state of siege imposed in April 2000 could deter protesting actors as a clash loomed between the armed forces and the police. Conflicts became locked into a perverse logic. An aimless government was forced to cave in to economic and political demands that exceeded its capacity to meet them. In turn, this inability fueled a never-ending spiral of radical pressures and demands ranging from constitutional changes to the acquisition of tractors. In a sign of political bankruptcy, the government surrendered in a way that subverted the legal structure and the authority of the state by agreeing, for example, to revoke an agrarian law that had been the result of a complex bargaining process.

In this context, the crisis of Banzer's blundering government triggered three far-reaching political consequences for the party system and the state. First, it deepened the gap between society, on the one hand, and parties and the state, on the other. The politicization of social conflicts demonstrated that parties have declined as crucial mediating structures. Direct confrontation between the state and contentious social actors became a constant, echoing the political pattern of unmediated social conflicts during the transition (1978–82). Second, the major parties have deteriorated and lost their capacity to articulate and aggregate demands of the sectors that did not benefit from economic development. The peasant movements under Morales's and Quispe's command repudiated the neoliberal economic model, pressed the government to restore the state enterprises, and adopted an antisystem strategy that threatens the basic tenets of representative democracy.[12] Increasing dissatisfaction with the economy's performance and the emergence of a new radical leadership put serious strains on the political system. As the capabilities of the government and the state fell behind social demands, democracy entered a stage of intense politicization of social conflicts, engendering a crisis of governability.

The third consequence was the erosion of consensus policies and the return to confrontation between Banzer's coalition and the main opposition party, the MNR. Several attempts by both sides to work out a plan to address the economic crisis failed. In 2000, a standoff made the situation worse when the MNR refused to resume negotiations with the government because of the political damage caused when the government appointed forty-one new party-dependent members to the regional electoral courts. The coalition parties had dealt a harsh blow to Article 266 of the Constitution, which established the autonomy and impartiality of electoral courts. They also broke key tenets of the 1992 interparty agreement for state reform. But given the strong opposition of the MNR, the Catholic Church, and the media, this assault against the National Electoral Court's institutional stability backfired. Congress removed the Banzer government's appointees to the regional electoral courts.

At the end of Banzer's government, the loss of the mediating capacities of both governing and opposition parties became apparent when the Catholic Church resumed its role as arbiter in deepening political and social conflicts and helped the government to find shaky solutions to the conflicts in 2000.[13] In 2001, the Church again helped to strike an important agreement with the opposition aimed at restoring consensual politics to tackle the economic recession and widespread corruption. However, persistent disagreements and the government's inefficacy led to disappointing results and a worsening socioeconomic crisis.

The June 2002 general election gave the party system another chance. Yet it did not create political conditions for overcoming the national crisis. On the contrary, the election had three long-term, disruptive effects. First, the party system was substantially undermined. The three major parties – MNR, MIR, and ADN – gathered only 42.18 percent of the vote and 52.85 percent of seats, while the indigenous movements – MAS and MIP – won 27.03 percent of the vote

---

[12] Indigenous movements are not per se strategic political actors with a strongly institutionalist orientations, as Foweraker (1995: 64) contends.

[13] Banzer launched the National Dialogue II in May 2000. Politically disappointing, it did not contribute to preventing or defusing the crisis of September 2000. Its fundamental goal was to formulate policies against poverty. It also proposed a questionable agenda of constitutional reforms that reflected the growing antisystem feelings of the population (Mayorga 2001d).

and 26.11 percent of seats (Table 5.2). Second, although the effective number of parties fell to 4.61 (Table 5.1), the emergence of these antisystem political movements transformed the moderate party system into a polarized one, fractured by new and old ethnic cleavages. Neopopulist and ethnic leaders articulated demands for the demise of representative democracy, participation of popular organizations independent of parties in political decision making, the control over state institutions and policies by social organizations, and the return to a state-led economy. The parliamentary and mobilization power achieved by these movements dangerously polarized the party system. The newcomers had persistent normative and political disagreements with the established parties on democratic principles, rules of the game, and policy objectives.

Third, the stability of the democratic regime and democratic governance was jeopardized as a result of the formation of a precarious coalition government by the MNR and the MIR. Sánchez de Lozada's second term, inaugurated in August 2002, could not curb the political and socioeconomic crisis because the polarization of the party system triggered a dangerous deadlock between the government and indigenous political movements. Aiming to substitute a state-centered economy and direct democracy based on Indian community structures for representative democracy and a market economy, the MAS's antiinstitutional strategy, dubbed a "siege strategy," successfully blocked the government by using both popular mobilizations and the veto power against government initiatives.

Polarization and stalemate intensified the protracted crisis of government and state whose functioning was hampered by a pernicious coalition that sought patronage and rent seeking over crisis management and policy. In February 2003, a disturbing process of political decomposition was already underway as a violent clash between the armed forces and a rebellious police force occurred in the context of antigovernment protests against an income tax. Relying on the military, the government reacted only by shoring up the coalition and by pointless bickering in Congress, whereas the MAS launched an offensive against planned natural gas exports and free trade policies. By October 2003, the mobilizations turned into a triumphant uprising of marginalized but well-organized sectors of El Alto (the large satellite city on the periphery of La Paz) and peasant unions of some Aymara provinces in the Department of La Paz. President Sánchez de Lozada was forced to step down. Just fourteen months into its five-year term, the coalition government was overthrown. The MAS and the MIP apparently had a preconceived scheme to bring down the government, but the uprising did not respond to unified leadership. Capitalizing on the government's failure to reach agreements with contentious political and social movements, the revolt demonstrated the extent to which persistent unemployment, impoverishment, and social exclusion nurtured an explosive situation. Fragmented but increasingly resourceful social movements and popular organizations fiercely opposed liberal economic reforms, plans to export natural gas, the integration of Bolivia's economy into global free trade, and coca eradication.

Thus, the democratic regime went through its most serious crisis. The constitutional transfer of power to Vice President Mesa permitted democracy's arduous survival, at the expense of the governing parties, which suffered a devastating blow as Mesa decided to build a government above partisan politics. Dependent on party support, Mesa's supraparty government faces the daunting challenge of defusing the veto power of radical sociopolitical movements and of reformulating economic policies while restructuring the state through a highly controversial Constituent Assembly that the antisystem leaders demanded.

CONCLUSION

Bolivia's democratic development faced weighty structural obstacles stemming from a weak economy, social exclusion, and a political system prone to authoritarianism and confrontation. Against this backdrop, political elites after 1985 laid the foundations of a strikingly stable political system by carrying out crucial institutional reforms including the shift to a market economy, the development of a moderate multiparty system, the growth of multiparty government coalitions, and the development of municipal structures. Nevertheless, lingering socioeconomic problems, political mismanagement, corruption, and contentious social movements have put democracy in jeopardy. Although there is theoretically and empirically no strong correlation between economic performance and regime stability, Bolivia's crisis seems to prove that, in a situation of a relatively protracted economic crisis, the key question is "whether the citizens believe that the democratic government is doing a credible job in trying to overcome economic problems" (Linz and Stepan 1996: 80).

Two decades after the transition, democracy has reached a turning point. Democracy has suffered critical setbacks that cast serious doubts on the regime's sustainability. The insurmountable problems of Banzer's and Sánchez de Lozada's governments – a deepening economic recession, intense social conflicts, shaky and inefficient coalitions – caused a crisis of the state and of democracy, compounded by a failed state decentralization that is contested by economically strong regions, which demand greater autonomy. Since 2000, the government, the Congress, and the party system have undergone a political crisis that reveals a long-term crisis of leadership, a decline of consensus building and cooperation practices among political elites, and diminished capacity to channel escalating social conflicts. Mobilization and violent protests prevailed over institutional conflict solving through parties and other democratic institutions. Moreover, as a result of the 2002 general election, political stability was fractured by the party system's polarization and the deadlock between the executive and the new indigenous opposition parties. Consequently, antisystem actors emerged demanding the demise of representative democracy; the participation, independent of political parties, of popular organizations in political decision making; the control over state institutions and policies; and the return to a state-led economy.

In the face of the seeming exhaustion of economic policies and the confluence of a deep economic crisis and political destabilization, the governing parties were incapable of providing solutions. This failure was the fundamental cause for the breakdown of Sánchez de Lozada's government in October 2003 and the establishment of a government independent of parties led by President Carlos Mesa. This breakdown had the far-reaching and destructive consequences of discrediting the ruling parties – and eventually, perhaps, of their collapse. Parties lost their grip on executive power and retained Congress as their last refugee. Democracy's sustainability is again shrouded in uncertainty. Bad state performance and the economic crisis have eroded the party system's legitimacy and party politics itself, provoking a profound crisis of governability. As the main established parties have deteriorated, the threat of plebiscitary alternatives – such as Morales's ethnic–populist fundamentalism and tendencies toward corporatist and ethnic-based representation – have become stronger, engendering a bleak scenario for democracy's viability.

6

Challenges to Political Democracy in El Salvador

Elisabeth Jean Wood

As El Salvador descended into civil war, few observers expected that political democracy would result. With a brief exception in the 1940s, El Salvador's regime had been authoritarian for decades prior to the civil war: Although elections were held, political competition was strictly limited, and the outcome was merely an endorsement of the continued rule of the official military party. The longstanding alliance between agrarian elites and the military meant that even modest attempts at reform were repeatedly vetoed, as hardline elements of the military carried out coups against reformist military elements and violently suppressed nascent social movements demanding change. Rather than bringing political development in its wake, economic diversification after World War II was accompanied by renewed political exclusion and economic concentration. The regime met the widespread social mobilization of the mid-1970s with brutality and violence rather than compromise. That the only contender for power in the aftermath of the repression was a revolutionary guerrilla movement also did not augur well for a democratic outcome.

Nonetheless, a negotiated peace settlement not only ended the civil war in 1992 but brought democratizing reforms to the regime and state, culminating in the country's first inclusive elections in 1994. Since then, political competition has increased as the erstwhile guerrilla movement gradually solidified its new identity as a political party: It became the leading party in the national legislature in the 2000 elections and maintained that position in the 2003 elections. The required reforms to military, police, judicial, and electoral institutions have been carried out to a significant degree. And in some areas of the countryside, an unprecedented civil society actively lobbies for local interests.

I thank Katherine Andrade, William Barnes, Charles Call, David Holiday, Hector Lindo-Fuentes, Vince McElhinny, Barry Shelley, and Jack Spence for facilitating access to data and documents, and William Barnes, Fran Hagopian, Scott Mainwaring, Jack Spence, and Rubén Zamora for comments on an earlier version of this paper.

Yet such "war transitions" – dual transitions from war to peace and from authoritarianism to democracy (Karl, Maphai, and Zamora 1996; Call 1999a) – in unequal and exclusionary polities leave legacies that limit the quality of democracy. Although reforms may liberalize police, judicial, and electoral practices to a significant extent and political competition may ensue, the long history of rule in the service of the few rather than the many is not easily superceded. Not only does the recent history of violence pose immediate challenges of demobilizing armed combatants and accounting for human rights violations, the negotiated agenda of institutional reform may prove inadequate to the longer-term challenges of the postwar period, particularly to reduce longstanding patterns of social and economic exclusion and to confront the escalation of criminal (not political) violence. While the extraordinary influx of remittances from Salvadorans in the United States continues to provide resources to families and the economy generally, rates of poverty and extreme poverty remain high, particularly in areas hard hit by the two major earthquakes of early 2001. Voter turnout in elections since the founding 1994 elections has been quite low.

In this chapter, I first broadly contrast Salvadoran politics before and after the civil war, analyzing the fundamental changes in agrarian labor relations and class structure, the political regime, elite political culture and representation, and insurgent political culture and organization. After briefly describing the implementation of provisions of the peace agreement essential for the country's transition to political democracy, I discuss the principal advances in democracy during the postwar period. I then analyze the principal challenges to improving the quality of democracy in El Salvador, namely, declining participation in elections, still-high rates of poverty, and extraordinarily high levels of crime and nonpolitical violence. Throughout the paper I use material from fieldwork carried out in the department of Usulután between 1991 and 1996 to illustrate the argument, as well as documents and interviews with political elites in San Salvador.[1]

SALVADORAN POLITICS BEFORE AND AFTER THE CIVIL WAR

Politics in El Salvador have changed profoundly since the beginning of the civil war. Even though significant challenges remain before the postwar quality of democracy meets the high hopes that many Salvadorans held at the end of the war, the contrast is nonetheless very sharp. Before the war, the country was governed by political parties controlled by the military that came to power through uncompetitive electoral processes in which either other parties could not compete or, if they did, they were not allowed to win. An authoritarian political culture and coercive state institutions long ensured the self-censorship of nascent dissent and the suppression of expressed dissent. The widespread social movements of the 1970s were crushed by state violence with tens of

---

[1] See Wood (2000a and 2003).

thousands of casualties. Even reformist military factions that came to power were quickly deposed.

In contrast, after the war, electoral processes were very competitive locally as well as nationally, there were no ideological constraints on political party formation, the police force was separate from the military (although the military did still carry out some policing activities in the countryside), and political violence largely vanished. The contrasts before and after the civil war in agrarian labor relations and class structure, the political regime, elite political culture, and rural political culture and organization illustrate the principal changes in the polity.

Agrarian Labor Relations, Class Structure, and Elite Economic Interests

The civil war broke a longstanding pattern of state enforcement of coercive agrarian labor relations and an extremely rigid class structure, which had been forged in the late nineteenth and early twentieth centuries as coffee cultivation rapidly expanded in areas of dense indigenous settlement, a pattern unique in Latin America (Roseberry 1991: 359). In El Salvador, the factors of production for the expansion of coffee were secured not in land or labor markets but by a deliberate redefinition of property rights by coercion (Lindo-Fuentes 1990; Williams 1994; Stanley 1996). Thus in El Salvador, along with Guatemala and Honduras, national police forces were founded *before* the institutional consolidation of the armed forces, with deleterious consequences for development of the rule of law autonomous from landed interests (Kincaid 2000).

By the 1920s, the landed elite together with immigrant families that invested in coffee mills and export firms began to coalesce into an oligarchy of a few dozen families. Although the economy grew more diverse and oligarchic families became more numerous after World War II, economic power remained extremely concentrated as this expanding but still small elite controlled the financial sector, the agricultural sector, and the slowly growing manufacturing sector (Colindres 1976 and 1977; Sevilla 1985; Paige 1987). Although patron–client relations were gradually replaced by wage labor, close relations between local landlords and military commanders, which included the permanent billeting of state security forces on some individual estates, endured until the outbreak of civil war.

One result of this pattern of development was a highly unequal distribution of land and a high incidence of rural poverty. In 1971, farms larger than 200 hectares constituted a half of a percent (0.5 percent) of all farms, but they held over a third of farmland; farms smaller than a hectare comprised 50 percent of farms but held just 4 percent of farmland (Dirección General de Estadística y Censos 1974, vol 2: 1). Population increases were one reason for increasing landlessness after World War II, but the landless fraction of the rural population rose much faster because cotton and sugar cultivation were expanding and the concentration of property rights throughout the export agriculture sector was increasing (Durham 1979: 47–8). The proportion of the economically active agricultural population that was landless increased – in just a decade – from 40.0 percent in 1961 to 51.5 percent in 1971, and the proportion with access to more than 1 hectare declined from 28.5 percent to 14.4 percent (Seligson 1995: 62). Access to land declined still further after 1971 with the return of a hundred thousand Salvadorans from Honduras after the brief "Soccer War" between the two countries.

The civil war dramatically reshaped the economic structure of the country, including significant changes in this pattern of class exclusion and coercive labor relations. Insurgency, together with the state's counterinsurgency policies, had two primary economic effects. First, national output rapidly declined from the 1978 peak: the (real) per capita domestic product fell 28 percent between 1978 and 1982.[2] Even though a further decline was arrested (in part by massive international assistance), production stagnated between 1982 and 1989. Second, a very significant shift in the relative contributions of economic sectors to the gross domestic product took place: Export agriculture comprised 13 or 14 percent of GDP in the early 1970s, increased to almost 25 percent in 1978, declined sharply to less than 5 percent by 1989, and fell to about 3 percent by 1992.[3] As agriculture declined, the commercial sectors (but not manufacturing) surged: commerce increased from prewar levels ranging from 20 to 25 percent of GDP to over 36 percent in 1992.

This sectoral shift occurred for several war-induced reasons. The guerrilla forces targeted export crops for sabotage and extracted "war tax" payments that eroded profits. The 1980 counterinsurgency land reform resulted in the expropriation of about a quarter of all farmland in the country, including some of the most productive farms. Moreover, in a classic instance of "Dutch disease," an extraordinary inflow of dollars (both official U.S. transfers and a growing flood of remittances from Salvadorans relocated to the United States to avoid the war) distorted relative prices, further undermining the export sector and increasing the value of other sectors.[4] As a result, the profitability of the agro-export sector declined sharply during the years of the war. The decline would have been even greater had it not been for the labor policies maintained throughout the war: Real wages for agricultural workers declined by 63 percent between 1980 and 1991 (calculated from Paus 1996: Table 12.4).

As a result of this structural transformation, by the late 1980s, economic elites in El Salvador drew much more of their income from the commercial sector than from traditional export agricultural production and processing.[5] At the end of the war, economic elites were doing very well, capturing a

---

[2] Unless otherwise noted, all data are calculated from the national accounts data published by the Central Reserve Bank in its quarterly *Revista Trimestral*.

[3] Export agriculture is defined here as the sum of the value added to GDP by the production of coffee, cotton, and sugar, including the initial processing of coffee and sugar, but not coffee roasting, beverage production, or other food processing.

[4] The agricultural price index increased by a factor of 6 from the early 1970s to the end of the war: That of commerce increased by a factor of 34 and that of manufacturing, by 15.

[5] Data on individual portfolios are not available: In El Salvador, such information is extremely closely guarded, even within families.

remarkable share of national income: Profit rates for nonagricultural enterprises increased from less than 10 percent in 1980 to well over 20 percent by 1991.[6] Interviews with wealthy Salvadorans (Wood 2000a: 64–7) indicate that most families that had failed to diversify were marginalized economically and politically. The prospect of increased investments through participation in free trade agreements was an incentive to resolve the war lest trade and investment go to other countries (Paus 1996: 270).

The war also accelerated urbanization in El Salvador as families and especially young men fled the violence of contested areas of the countryside for the relative safety and anonymity of the cities. In 1975, 41.5 percent of the population lived in urban areas; in 2001, 61.3 percent did (UNDP 2003: Table 5). Remittances from the United States led to an unprecedented degree of class mobility as some families were able to buy land or houses and to fund more grades of schooling for their children. Thus, although the exodus of Salvadorans to the United States imposed hardships on individual families and entailed a significant flight of human capital, it also brought important economic resources for the postwar period. Urbanization probably contributed to the decline in the total fertility rate (per woman) from its average of 6.1 from 1970 to 1975 to 2.9 from 2000 to 2005 (UNDP 2003: Table 5).

The Political Regime

State and regime formation in El Salvador as in Guatemala and Nicaragua was shaped by the exclusionary nature of the political economy of export agriculture. Not only were police forces founded to patrol the class boundaries of this political economy as coffee expanded, but between the draconian suppression in 1932 of a largely indigenous rural uprising until the civil war (with a brief exception in 1944), military officers (or former officers) ruled the polity. They usually did so through a veneer of tightly controlled elections always won by the official party, the Partido de Conciliación Nacional (PCN; Party of National Conciliation) and its antecedents. Economic elites controlled economic policy as ministers of various cabinet posts. Though riven by divergent interests on some issues, this oligarchic alliance agreed on the bottom line: the maintenance of the country's rigid class structure and exclusionary political regime. While reformist factions of the military occasionally attempted to modernize land tenure and labor relations (in 1944, 1960, 1972, and 1976), the core alliance of landlords and military hardliners repeatedly defeated such attempted reforms (Stanley 1996).

Nonetheless, an extremely limited process of regime liberalization did occur in the decades after World War II. A few minor parties with little organization or widespread appeal were tolerated after the 1940s. More significantly, after the introduction of proportional representation for the 1964 election, opposition

---

[6] Harberger (1993, Table 6). In contrast, between 1980 and 1991, average real wages for workers affiliated with the social security institute (i.e., wages in the formal private sector) fell 58 percent (calculated from Paus 1996: Table 12.4).

parties competed for seats in the national legislature and some mayoral offices, including San Salvador. The Christian Democratic Party (Partido Demócrata Cristiano; PDC) built up a significant party apparatus through José Napoleon Duarte's three terms as mayor of San Salvador (Karl 1986a; Eguizábal 1992). When widespread fraud denied candidate Duarte the presidency in 1972, political disaffection rapidly increased, leading a few urban youth and intellectuals to found or join guerrilla movements.

Widespread political mobilization in the 1970s by *campesinos* – workers and students calling for political and economic reform – was met by brutal state violence, which led more activists to support the hitherto tiny guerrilla forces. The threat posed by mobilization, repression, and the growing potential for armed conflict led to a coup by reformist officers in 1979. While the reformists were soon marginalized, the deepening insurgent threat led to the formation in 1980 of a new governing alliance between the military and the PDC, supported by the United States (Stanley 1996). As a condition of receiving U.S. military and economic aid, the military not only carried out the agrarian reform but agreed to liberalize the political regime, a process that led to a more liberal constitution and more competitive elections, culminating in the 1984 election of Christian Democrat Duarte as president – the first time in decades that a nonmilitary candidate took office. In contrast to previous initiatives, these reforms endured: In the eyes of the United States and Salvadoran policy makers, reform was necessary because of the ongoing military capacity of the Frente Farabundo Martí para la Liberación Nacional (FMLN; Farabundo Martí National Liberation Front).

However, the breaking of the ruling alliance did not displace the will and capacity of the security forces for violence against popular organizations: Violence worsened in the wake of the coup, culminating in the assassination of several opposition political leaders in November 1980. The indiscriminate nature of the violence, as well as its brutality, led still more people to support the guerrilla groups, allied as the FMLN. After an attempted "final offensive" failed in 1981 and ongoing state violence decimated urban opposition groups, the guerrilla organizations consolidated their forces in the countryside. Despite billions of dollars of U.S. assistance, by the mid-1980s a military stalemate was in place, as was made dramatically clear in 1989 when the FMLN attacked San Salvador and occupied a number of wealthy neighborhoods for several days (Gibb and Smyth 1990). The offensive brought home the realization that the insurgents would not disappear with the end of the Cold War. Subsequently, negotiations to end the war began in earnest under UN mediation. These led to a series of interim accords that culminated in the signing of the final peace agreement on January 16, 1992.

Elite Political Culture and Representation

Of course, a transformation of elite economic interests and military stalemate does not in itself lead to political compromise: There must emerge elite political actors who recognize that in the country's new situation, they would be better off with peace than continued war. Ironically, an organization that came to recognize this change emerged from origins in the profound political violence of the early years of the war. In the late 1970s and early 1980s, rightist hardliners led by Roberto D'Aubuisson with the financial help of wealthy Salvadoran exiles in Miami developed death squads to deter political mobilization through intimidation and violence. Most such squads were not private groups but members of state security and intelligence forces. The rightists also founded the National Republican Alliance (Alianza Republicana Nacionalista; ARENA) to contest power in elections rather than relying on the military – a new development in El Salvador.[7] The subsequent limited electoral competition under conditions of civil war had unintended outcomes, however. ARENA won the 1982 constitutional assembly elections (i.e., a win for precisely those hardline elements that the liberal reforms were designed to undermine).[8] After the United States made clear its strong opposition to D'Aubuisson's nomination as interim president, a compromise was reached whereby ARENA gave up the presidency but took control of the Ministry of Agriculture and the agrarian reform institutions, effectively ending agrarian reform.

No longer able to rely on military allies to govern, ARENA leaders sought to broaden the electoral base of the party by appealing to new constituencies, including middle-class voters and small businesspeople. A significant step in this process occurred in September 1985 when Alfredo Cristiani replaced D'Aubuisson as party president, signaling a shift within the party away from the hardliners of the Miami group. Cristiani's faction with its diversified economic interests was more tolerant of democratic norms and aspirations than were those members of the elite with interests narrowly based on coffee cultivation, as documented by Paige (1997) in his extensive interviews with Salvadoran elites.[9] For these moderate elites, the decline of export agriculture lessened their reliance on coercive labor practices.

With the help of a U.S.-funded think tank, the Cristiani faction developed and proposed a set of neoliberal policies (Johnson 1993). Neoliberalism was attractive to these elites for several reasons: Its emphasis on private sector innovation could justify reprivatizing the nationalized sectors, its agenda of neoliberal reforms would render the state incapable of threatening elite economic interests even if a party hostile to elite interests later governed, and liberalization of capital flows would discipline the state against redistributive measures (Wood 2000a: 244–6). In the 1989 presidential elections, the revamped ARENA party

---

[7] The Truth Commission (1993) and later the Joint Group for the Investigation of Illegal Armed Groups (1994) documented the close ties between the leaders and funders of ARENA and the death squads.

[8] ARENA won only a plurality, but with the support of allied parties it commanded a majority.

[9] Revelations that a ring of kidnappers that had preyed on the elite included military officers associated with D'Aubuisson also contributed to the transition in leadership (Stanley 1996: 238–40).

appealed to voters more than the PDC or the social democratic alternatives, and Cristiani was elected president.

Thus, a fundamental change wrought by the civil war was the emergence of factions of Salvadoran elites who agreed that renewed war should be avoided even if uncomfortable compromises might have to be made in the implementation of the peace agreement. The unprecedented acceptance of electoral competition by many actors on the right reflected not only the structural changes in the political economy but also the process of political learning during the course of the war. Involvement with liberal international actors, initially as a result of U.S. insistence on liberalizing the political regime and promoting neoliberal policies in the 1980s and later as a result of UN mediation and peace building, was essential to this increasing acceptance of liberal political norms (Peceny and Stanley 2001).[10] By the early 1990s, ARENA had built a formidable party base and had proved very successful in competing on the new electoral terrain.

Insurgent Political Culture

One consequence of El Salvador's long history of political and economic exclusion – particularly the extreme violence with which state forces suppressed the 1932 uprising – was a political culture among *campesinos* of apparent quiescence, in which attitudes of self-deprecation, fatalism, conformism, and individualism were pervasive (Martín-Baró 1973; Montes 1986). Given the high degree of social control in the countryside, *campesinos* had little reason to expect any change in life circumstances. Schooling provided little opportunity for social mobility as few attended school past the first or second grade, as indicated by the 63 percent illiteracy rate in 1971 (Montes 1986: 98, citing the 1971 population census).

Pastoral practices informed by liberation theology overcame peasant quiescence in many areas of the countryside, impelling a wave of popular mobilization (Cabarrús 1983; Cardenal 1985; Gordon 1983; Montgomery 1995; Pearce 1986). By the late 1970s, networks of church workers, PDC members, and covert members of the guerrilla organizations provided the political coordination for massive demonstrations and marches in the streets of San Salvador. In response to the state violence of the late 1970s and early 1980s, a subset of those *campesinos* that participated in the earlier social movement joined the FMLN. Some were driven by moral outrage at the violence, some judged violence a legitimate means toward the realization of social justice in the circumstances of extreme state violence, some grasped the opportunity to defy oppressive social authority, and some undoubtedly sought vengeance (Wood 2003).

---

[10] Rubén Zamora (1998: 312–15) argues for a more complex interpretation: While acknowledging the emergence of a degree of liberal consensus among the political elite, he documents an enduring strong difference of political opinion between ARENA, on the one hand, and the FMLN, PDC, and PCN, on the other.

Drawing on unprecedented networks of insurgent *campesinos*, the FMLN maintained a significant presence in widespread areas and developed a rural intelligence capacity that outperformed – by far – that of the government (Bacevich et al. 1988). Even some agrarian reform beneficiaries continued to support the insurgents covertly; this was true, for example, of many members of agrarian reform cooperatives located on the coast plain of the municipality of Jiquilisco, Usulután. The government responded to the insurgency's growing military capacity by increasingly, if sporadically, following a counterinsurgency strategy that emphasized civic actions to win civilian hearts and minds.[11] The FMLN responded in turn with a new strategy, dispersing guerrilla forces in smaller, more mobile units to strengthen or develop civilian organizations, such as the insurgent cooperatives that claimed land throughout the contested areas in the late 1990s (Wood 2003).

Thus, among some residents (about a third in the contested areas of Usulután) in some areas, more than a decade of political mobilization left behind a legacy of political participation, a network of civic organizations, and a new political culture based on values of citizenship and entitlement and a rejection of deference toward rural elites (Lungo Uclés 1995; Hammond 1998; Wood 2003).[12] In interviews in the contested areas of Usulután, for example, civilian activists and supporters of the FMLN expressed a profound sense of pride in their collective achievements during the war and asserted an unprecedented claim to political equality (Wood 2003). Several erstwhile landlords of properties in Usulután recognized this transformation of rural culture, expressing concern that should they return to their properties after the war, they would face assertive and well-organized workers supported by a panoply of new organizations.

However, the importance and strength of this participatory legacy varied significantly even across areas whose wartime history was similar. For example, in an area of Usulután known as "Las Marías," where many *campesinos* actively supported the FMLN during the war, networks of activists continue to organize collectively, bargaining with various agencies and non-governmental organizations (NGOs) over the terms of development assistance. In contrast, insurgent *campesinos* in the coastal municipality of Jiquilisco became deeply disillusioned within a few years of the peace agreement as a result of the extensive manipulation of local organizations by the resident guerrilla faction. Only in the wake of the January 13, 2001, earthquake did local organization reemerge

---

[11] After the 1983 visit to El Salvador by Vice President Bush to warn the Salvadoran military that the United States would not provide significant aid if human rights violations continued at the high levels of 1980–82, civilian casualties dropped significantly and remained low until the end of the war with the exception of the 1989 FMLN offensive on San Salvador and other major cities.

[12] Additional evidence for this transformation of rural political culture in some areas of El Salvador comes from surveys of living conditions carried out after the war (discussed in Wood 2003: Chapter 7).

to any significant degree. Even in this case, voters elected FMLN mayors in 1997, 2000, and 2003.

IMPLEMENTING THE PEACE AGREEMENT

Despite the country's history of agrarian elite recalcitrance, political exclusion, and economic inequality, El Salvador's civil war culminated in a transition to democracy. In polities such as El Salvador, victory by the insurgents is highly unlikely given the cohesiveness of economic and regime elites (in contrast to countries with personalist regimes such as Nicaragua under Somoza). While falling short of revolutionary success, insurgent mobilization may nonetheless culminate in a negotiated transition to democracy. Thus, El Salvador is an unusual case in which a transition to democracy was forged from below (Wood 2000a, 2001). The outcome – capitalist democracy – is an instance of the classic democratic bargain in which both parties gain something valued by their adherents: Insurgent forces achieve political inclusion and agree to politics by democratic means, while economic elites protect their control of assets through constitutional provisions that (in a liberal world economy) diminish any prospect for widespread nationalization even if the erstwhile insurgents came to power through elections.

Elite compromise occurred because the changes in the political economy of the country lessened elite dependence on coercive labor institutions and because elite political leaders had learned they could compete well in elections. Of course, other factors also contributed. The regional peace process provided additional impetus for compromise. The killing of the six Jesuit priests by the government's Atlacatl Battalion during the FMLN's 1989 offensive resulted in renewed Congressional opposition to U.S. funding of the Salvadoran military (Whitfield 1994). Because (thanks to the insurgent threat) the military was dependent on U.S. funding, a shift in U.S. policy toward negotiation ensured the military's compliance. As the military stalemate dragged on, FMLN moderates willing to compromise gained influence. The end of the Cold War reinforced the *domestic* dynamics pushing the parties toward compromise.

Thus the core of the peace agreement consisted of reforms intended to create a transition to a democratic political regime. The guerrilla organization would lay down its arms and pursue its political agenda as a political party in competitive elections (and some members of the FMLN would join the new civilian police force), while the government agreed to carry out reforms to the military, judicial, and electoral institutions that would make political competition possible. The peace agreement (and preliminary agreements) defined constitutional reforms to the mission and prerogatives of the military as well as to the judicial and electoral systems, including the founding of a human rights office, the Procuraduría Nacional para La Defensa de los Derechos Humanos (National Ombudsman for the Defense of Human Rights); the strengthening of the election supervisory body toward broader political party representation and increased autonomy from the executive; and the strengthening of the autonomy of the National Judicial Council. The peace agreement also mandated the founding of a new, *civilian* police force (PNC or Policía Nacional Civil) and a new police academy, as well as the dissolution of two infamous security forces. The parties also agreed that two extraordinary commissions would assess human rights violations during the course of the war. As a result, the "Ad-hoc Commission" recommended that more than a hundred officers be purged from the ranks of the military. The Truth Commission documented the pattern of human rights violations by all parties and recommended further reforms to judicial institutions.

The legacy of the country's long history of exclusionary economic and political development and the civil war posed daunting challenges to the implementation of the agreement. Yet the war and its negotiated resolution left positive legacies as well, including those discussed previously. The peace agreement itself served as a key resource for sustaining the democratic compromise in the postwar period because it served as a touchstone (an evolving one) of agreed-upon reforms and provided the initial legitimacy and mandate for the United Nation's extraordinary mission in El Salvador, the United Nations Observer Mission in El Salvador (ONUSAL, 1990–95, thereafter smaller missions with changed names).

ONUSAL's role evolved during the peace process from mediating the negotiations, to verifying human rights conditions, to verifying compliance with the peace agreement, to institution building through detailed involvement in several key institutions and processes (Burgerman 2000; Holiday and Stanley 1993; Montgomery 1995; Peceny and Stanley 2001; Stanley and Holiday 1997). Other international actors also contributed: Bilateral and multilateral donors committed significant financial resources for spending on the peace process and reconstruction (Boyce 1996; Orr 2001). Even though coordination between the various international actors was sometimes inadequate (Boyce 1996; de Soto and del Castillo 1994), international actors met many of the costs of the peace and reinforced its benefits through ongoing scrutiny of compliance with the peace agreement.

The provisions of the peace agreement were largely implemented by 1995, though unevenly and incompletely.[13] In 1994, the first inclusive elections in El Salvador's history led to a victory by the presidential candidate of the incumbent political party (after a second round of voting). The FMLN made a respectable showing, winning 25 percent of the vote in the first round. The demobilization of combatants went forward, although with significant delays. Crises occurred around the government's apparent reluctance to dissolve the National Guard and Treasury Police; the scope and pace of the transfer of land to insurgent supporters; the role of NGOs in reconstruction; the transition to the new police force; and the discovery of a large covert FMLN weapons depot in Managua.

---

[13] For details of the implementation of the peace agreement, see the various documents produced by ONUSAL and the series of reports published by Hemisphere Initiatives; see also Call (1994 and 1999b), Montgomery (1995), Stanley (1995 and 1999), and Wood (2000a).

The recommendations of the Ad-hoc and Truth Commissions also brought political crises in their wake. Extraordinary international pressure was brought to bear on Cristiani before he carried out the Ad-hoc Commission's recommendation that he dismiss many military officers for human rights violations. The Truth Commission's report caused further furor (particularly on the right) after its release in March 1993, as it held government and allied forces responsible for 85 percent of human rights violations, named those deemed responsible for well-documented cases of violations, and recommended that those named be excluded from political office for 10 years.[14] Perhaps ironically, the most overt conflict took place over the scope and terms of demobilization benefits for members of the various government forces as thousands of ex-members of the National Police, security forces, and civil defense patrols repeatedly paralyzed the government from 1993 to 1995, demanding land, severance indemnity, and other benefits (del Castillo 1997: 355–56; Stanley and Holiday 1997: 32–3).

These crises were addressed in a wide variety of fora during the first years of the peace process. The National Commission for the Consolidation of Peace – a group composed of representatives of political parties, the FMLN, and the government – was mandated by the peace agreement to supervise the implementation of the agreements, verify compliance, and draft necessary legislation. Increasingly, however, discussions by the commission were superceded by private bilateral negotiations between the government and the FMLN mediated by ONUSAL, with ongoing extraordinary involvement by other actors including the United States, the UNDP, and the office of the UN Secretary General.

ADVANCES IN DEMOCRACY IN EL SALVADOR

Thus, the changes wrought by the civil war made possible a transition to democracy despite the country's long history of authoritarian rule. The two principal achievements of the peace process were the withdrawal of the military from politics and the inclusion of the political left in democratic political competition for electoral offices – both unprecedented and essential prerequisites for a democratic political regime.

While the military retains a high degree of institutional autonomy (Stanley 1996; Williams and Walter 1997), both the military as an institution and individual military officers appear to have little influence on government policy or within the main political parties. Since 1992, the military has accepted an unprecedented civilian purging of its officer corps, a limited degree of civilian input into military training, and a significant reduction in size, budget, and mandate. This sea change in Salvadoran politics is in sharp contrast to the continuing role

---

[14] The Truth Commission also recommended various reforms to the judicial system, including that the entire Supreme Court resign. The judicial reforms were only carried out after long delays (Popkin, Spence, and Vickers 1994; Popkin 2000). By mid-1994, a new Supreme Court was inaugurated with an unprecedented breadth of political representation.

of the military in Guatemalan politics in the postwar period where although the military is smaller than during its civil war, officers continue to exert power over civilian governments and to enjoy unusual prerogatives (Seligson, this volume). One exception to the declining role of the military is its ongoing participation in internal security in the form of patrolling areas against crime, usually jointly with the PNC, a practice justified in the eyes of many elites and civilians by the country's high crime rate.

Political inclusion and competition, the sine qua non of democracy, is the second principal achievement of the past decade. Two presidential elections have been held, and democracy seems to be the "only game in town" (Przeworski 1991). Few influential voices at national or local levels call for any abrogation or lessening of elections as the principal of governance: ARENA has accepted the results of elections that sharply reduced its control of the legislature and most social mobilization is channeled through democratic institutions via strikingly ordinary processes of coalition building and lobbying, as in the campaign for the forgiveness of agrarian debt.[15] Democratic values such as political tolerance and support for the (democratic) system increased strongly between 1991 and 1999 (Seligson, Cruz, and Córdova Macías 2000: 58–61, 78–86). Moreover, irrespective of political party membership, Salvadorans polled in 1997 strongly agreed with the statement that even if people do not vote intelligently everyone should be allowed to vote (IUDOP 1997: Table 5).

Not only is the left now pursuing political power via elections, the degree of electoral competition is increasing at both the national (in legislative though not in presidential elections) and the municipal levels. In coalition with other parties, the FMLN made a respectable showing in the 1994 presidential elections, forcing the presidential election into a runoff round (which it lost to ARENA by a wide margin). On its own, the FMLN won 21 of the 84 seats in the legislature.

However, the FMLN split soon after the elections, when the leadership of one guerrilla faction (the Ejército Revolucionario del Pueblo or Revolutionary Army of the People) together with some leaders of a second faction (the Resistencia Nacional or National Resistance) dramatically broke with the FMLN in the inaugural session of the new legislature. The group subsequently founded a new party, the Democratic Party (Partido Democrático or PD); the FMLN lost seven of the twenty-one seats in the split. However, this proved a severe miscalculation as most supporters remained with the FMLN, or switched back to the FMLN after the PD leadership entered into a pact with ARENA to support an increase in the value-added tax. The party's share of valid votes in 1997 was an abysmal 1.2 percent for the legislature and 1.0 percent for mayoral elections (Acevedo 1998: 217). Nor did its record improve in the subsequent election: In 2000, in coalition with the small Convergencia Demócrata (CD; Democratic Convergence), the PD won only three seats and four municipalities, even

---

[15] One exception was the mobilization by ex-soldiers and civil defense patrol members who occupied the legislature in 1995.

TABLE 6.1. *Legislative and Municipal Elections, 1994–2003*

	Seats (out of 84)				Mayors (out of 262)			
	1994	1997	2000	2003	1994	1997	2000	2003
ARENA	39	28	29	28	207	160	132	117
FMLN	21	27	31	31	13	48	71	67
FMLN coalition	–	–	–		3	6	2	–
PCN	4	11	14	15	10	17	33	52
PDC	18	7	5	5	28	16	16	20
PDC-PD	–	3	–	–	–	4	–	–
CD (&PD 2000)	1	2	3	5	0	0	4	–
Other	1	6	2	–	1	11	4	6

Sources: Legislature: For 1994, 1997, and 2000, Spence, Lanchin, and Thale (2001: 5); for 2003, *www.asamblea.gob.sv*. Municipal: For 1994, 1997, and 2000, personal communication from Jack Spence, April 18, 2001; for 2003, data from the Supreme Electoral Tribunal.

losing nearly all municipal contests in its traditional stronghold of northern Morazán. A second split occurred in 2002, when Facundo Guardado led his *renovador* faction out of the FMLN, with equally poor results in the subsequent election.

Despite these splits, the FMLN has made a surprisingly effective transition from a guerrilla army to a political party, increasing or retaining its share of votes (except in presidential races), legislative seats, and municipalities from election to election (Table 6.1). In 1997, the FMLN won twenty-seven seats in the legislature, only one less than ARENA's twenty-eight seats. The party performed poorly in the 1999 presidential election, failing even to force a second round, perhaps because of the well-publicized conflict between the two party factions in choosing a candidate (Spence et al. 2001). After the March 2000 elections, however, it was the leading party in the national legislature, holding thirty-one seats to ARENA's twenty-nine. However, this lead position did not translate proportionally into power over policy as the recovering PCN voted with ARENA, as did the still-declining PDC. In 2003, the FMLN retained its thirty-one seats (indeed, it recovered those lost after the *renovador* faction left), while ARENA lost one seat.

Particularly striking is the FMLN's increasing ability to compete in municipal elections. The fraction of municipalities the party governed (either solely or in coalition) increased from just over 6 percent in 1994 to 21 percent in 1997, to 28 percent in 2000, and to 26 percent in 2003. There appear to be two underlying patterns to the FMLN's growth at the municipal level. The party has broad appeal in urban areas (Zamora 1998: 265–67): For example, in coalition with other parties, it has governed San Salvador since 1997. The party won the 2000 municipal elections in thirteen of the fifteen largest municipalities, while ARENA did not win in *any*. And the party has increasing appeal in some ex-conflictive zones: Of the 115 municipalities that were conflicted during the war, the FMLN (by itself or in coalition) won fourteen in 1994, thirty in 1997, and thirty-seven in 2000.[16]

The FMLN's growing control of political offices reflects to some extent its ability to take advantage of ARENA's decline. ARENA lost more than 200,000 votes between 1994 and 1997, a decrease of 34.6 percent, whereas those of the FMLN increased about 82,000 (22.2 percent), significantly more than the increase in other parties (Cruz 1998a: Table 20; see also Cruz 1998b: 140).[17] Where the FMLN's vote share is growing most strongly – in urban areas – is precisely where ARENA's votes are declining (Zamora 1998: 88–89). Other opposition parties have proven significantly less appealing to voters than the FMLN. The PDC's vote shares, legislative seats, and municipalities governed have declined nearly monotonically from the mid-1980s; however, between 1997 and 2000, the party appears to have stabilized its shares, albeit at a low level. While the CD increased its votes by 50 percent between 1997 and 2000 (Spence et al. 2001: 4), the center-left party struggles to convert the high – and urban – visibility of its leaders into votes (Zamora 1998: 296). Party leader Rubén Zamora lost his seat when the coalition between the CD and the PD failed to win more than one seat in San Salvador, which went to PD leader Juan Ramón Medrano, who was first on their joint list. An exception to this trend of declining appeal of political parties (other than the FMLN) is the PCN, which appears to be recovering a degree of electoral appeal after its eclipse on the right by ARENA in the 1980s.[18]

SHORTCOMINGS OF DEMOCRACY IN EL SALVADOR

Despite these achievements, the quality of democracy in El Salvador remains weak. Four difficult challenges – low and declining rates of voting, institutional weakness that appears to undermine the value of democracy to ordinary people, extraordinarily high rates of crime and (nonpolitical) violence, and continuing

---

[16] Calculated from TSE (Tribunal Suprema Electoral or Supreme Electoral Tribunal) electoral data using coding of municipalities as conflicted zones from Checchi and Company Consulting, Inc., and Daniel Carr and Associates, "Final Report. Evaluation of the Social Stabilization and Municipal Development Strengthening Project," San Salvador, February 1994, reprinted in Seligson and Córdova Macías (1995: Appendix 2).

[17] Of course, this does not imply that the same voters who stopped voting for ARENA were those that subsequently voted for the FMLN. There is, however, evidence that some voters have switched between the FMLN and ARENA (Cruz 1998b: 142–44).

[18] There appear to be two reasons for this increase in vote share. Conflict within ARENA (concerning among other things its abandonment of policies to promote agriculture and hardliners' perceptions that the government had been overzealous in implementing the peace accords) culminated in the departure in 1997 from the party of a group of prominent leaders who joined the PCN (Acevedo 1998: 211–13; Ramos 1998: 12–16, 23–24). Seventy-five ARENA mayors as well as some prominent businesspeople followed them into the PCN (Acevedo 1998: 212). Second, the party's share of seats in the legislature is significantly higher than its vote share, reflecting its "leveraging" of a bias of El Salvador's proportional representation system that gives small departments a disproportionate number of seats (Spence et al. 2001: 6–7).

poverty and social exclusion – confront postwar El Salvador. These challenges raise questions about citizen perceptions of the principal achievements of the peace process (the withdrawal of the military from governance and political democracy), which appear not to be highly valued by ordinary people who frequently and increasingly do not vote. Because citizens' perceptions of their quality of life appear to be closely tied to perceptions of (the elected) government's performance in addressing crime and poverty, these challenges are closely intertwined. (There are, of course, other reasons to care about these issues, but here I focus on their implications for democracy.)

Declining Voter Participation

Voting rates as measured as the ratio of voters to registered voters declined from 52.8 percent in the first round of the presidential election in 1994 to 38.6 in the 1999 contest; voting rates in legislative contests declined similarly until 2000 when they reached a low of 37 percent before increasing to 41 percent in the 2003 election.[19] The more fundamental ratio of voters to the voting age population (VAP) declined from rates of about 53 percent in the first round of the 1994 presidential election to about 34 percent in the 2000 elections.[20]

Of course, voting rates are similarly low in a few other countries; for example, in the United States, where the ratio of voters to the VAP in presidential elections fell to 55.1 percent in 1992 and to 49.0 percent in 1996, and rates in nonpresidential contests fell to 36.6 percent in 1994 and to 32.9 percent in 1998 (*Statistical Abstract of the United States* 2000: Table 479).

However, low voting rates are arguably more troubling in El Salvador's immediate postwar context. The peace agreement revolves around the premise that elections are the first and only form of legitimation of rule in postwar El Salvador (Dada Hirezi 1998: 215). In the aftermath of a civil war among whose causes was the "transcendent" one of creating political space for political opposition, support for democratic institutions and political tolerance are fundamental prerequisites for democratic stability, according to Seligson and Córdova Macías (1995: 4–5). This latter claim may be too strong: Given the military's withdrawal from politics, regime stability does not seem to be the issue, but until the FMLN wins a presidential election, it is an open question.

Institutional Weaknesses

Two schools of thought have emerged to explain this low and declining participation rate (Cruz 1998a; Seligson et al. 2000). One school stresses the

[19] The 1994 and 1999 presidential figures are from Seligson et al. (2000: 112); the 2000 figure is from William Barnes, personal communication; the 2003 figure was widely reported in the Salvadoran press.

[20] The 1994 figure is from Barnes (1998: 92); the 2000 figure is from William Barnes, personal communication.

obstacles to voting that exist in El Salvador. Registering to vote is tedious and time-consuming, requiring several trips to the municipal center, along with the birth certificate that not all Salvadorans have. One study estimated that about 150,000 voters applied to register but did not receive their electoral carnet in time to vote in the 1994 elections (FLACSO Programa El Salvador 1995: 171–72). Nor did the process improve before the 1997 elections; ongoing procedural problems kept hundreds of thousands from being properly registered in time to vote (Peñate and Díaz Rodríguez 1998: 73–74).[21] Voting itself poses significant logistical problems, particularly in large cities: For example, in the 1997 elections, there were only eight voting sites in San Salvador, each with hundreds of voting tables. Each voter was assigned to a particular table on an alphabetical basis, with the result that many voters traveled across the city to then engage in a frustrating search to find the correct table (Barnes 1998: 73).

Public opinion polls provide some support for this school of thought.[22] When asked in public opinion polls why they or others might not vote, Salvadorans of voting age give various answers, among them the lack of a carnet. For example, in a survey carried out before the 1997 elections, of those who stated they did not intend to vote (17.2 percent), about a quarter of them (26.7 percent) gave as their reason that they did not have a carnet (IUDOP 1997: Table 10). However, the same survey found that 82 percent *did* have their carnets (IUDOP 1997: Table 14), so this does not explain the low voter turnout rates in the 1997 and 2000 elections of 35–40 percent.

The same survey also provides support for the second school of thought, which argues that the low voter turnout rate reflects a fundamental disenchantment with the postwar political process: Of those who did not intend to vote, 22.5 percent said that no party appealed to them, 15.8 percent said that nothing would change, and 13.8 percent stated that it did not interest them (IUDOP 1997). Confirming evidence comes from the indirect (and probably more telling) responses to the question why respondents thought *others* would not vote: In 1999, 86.4 percent answered that it was because of a lack of confidence or interest (Seligson et al. 2000: 117–18).

Analysts vary in the reasons why such a disenchantment with democracy has taken place. José Miguel Cruz (1998b: 149–51) argues that many people perceived that peace brought few changes in the difficult conditions of their everyday life in that they were still economically and socially excluded (more later in this section). As a result, they were disillusioned not just with ARENA policies but also with the peace process and therefore the political system itself: Despite several elections, for many poor people, little had changed in terms

---

[21] A new identity document should replace the electoral carnet before the 2004 elections, which may increase participation. However, ARENA and PCN legislators blocked the implementation of residential voting (rather than birthplace voting), which would have also increased participation.

[22] As nonvoting is tremendously underreported in surveys (William Barnes, personal communication), evidence on voting patterns reported in surveys should be interpreted cautiously.

of opportunities for schooling, employment, and access to medical services. Carlos Acevedo (1998: 200) agrees: Procedural democracy without effective democratization of the social and economic order leads to a withdrawal of participation that expresses the growing lack of credibility of political parties.

Other scholars argue that democratic disenchantment reflected ongoing problems with El Salvador's political party system. Rubén Zamora (1998: 319–22) suggests that political parties lack credibility because of their social isolation from the population, in part because political parties have not superceded wartime patterns of extremely polarized discourse and an absence of interparty cooperation (see also Cruz 1998a). The nature of the transition – negotiated between the two principal parties to the war with UN mediation with little participation by civil society organizations – is another factor contributing to this isolation of political parties from the citizenry (Dada Hirezi: 1998: 219–21). The ongoing upheaval within the political party system probably also contributes to this disenchantment. Since the end of the civil war, two processes fundamentally reorganized the configuration of political parties (Ramos 1998). A series of new parties have been founded (more than a dozen parties competed in the 1997 elections), while bitter struggles for leadership racked traditional parties – such as the ongoing conflict within the leadership of ARENA between "*fundadores*" (founders) and financial interests, and the interminable struggles within the PDC that often appear more driven by opportunism than ideological differences – culminating in schisms, scandal, and declining support.[23]

Some analysts (e.g., Acevedo 1998 and Barnes 1998) see as central to the crisis of the political party system the absence of a strong center party. However, the comparative record does not support this argument, as democracy has been stable for decades in a number of countries without such parties (Germany and Britain are examples), and strong centrist parties do not always ensure democratic stability (as in Chile).[24] Moreover, there is no persuasive reason why the FMLN could not play the role of a democratizing political force in the future as in the past.

Evaluating the conflicting explanations for declining voter turnout is difficult given available evidence, in part because in the experience of ordinary people various processes may be closely intertwined. For example, the difficulties in obtaining a carnet and actually voting probably gives rise to a sense that political party elites are little concerned with ordinary people.

Other institutional problems also undermine the quality of democracy in El Salvador. While elections may be free, they are far from fair for several reasons. Campaign finance regulation is weak, which advantages ARENA and the PCN given the relative wealth of their members compared to the FMLN. Further, the

---

[23] In the aftermath of the schism, tension between *ortodoxos* and *renovadores* continued (Zamora 1998: 257–63). One result was that it took three conventions to choose a candidate in the 1999 presidential election. The two "tendencies" were abolished as formal entities within the party in December 2000 (Spence et al. 2001: 9).

[24] I am indebted to Frances Hagopian and Scott Mainwaring for this point.

winner-take-all nature of municipal elections (candidates for mayor and other positions on the municipal council run together as a slate, and the winning slate takes over all municipal offices) may undermine the quality of democracy because it lessens the opportunity for local political leaders to experience the ordinary give-and-take of representative government with members of other parties.

Additionally, as in many other countries, the political processes internal to political parties in El Salvador has been far from democratic: Control was centralized with little role for the party rank and file, and there was little transparency concerning party financing (Zamora 1998: 215–217). In 2003, both ARENA and the FMLN introduced more democratic internal procedures. In particular, members of the FMLN *elected* Shafik Handal to be the party's presidential candidate (with a low rate of participation, however).

Crime and Violence

High postwar crime rates pose a sharp challenge to the quality of democracy in El Salvador, as does the inability or unwillingness of postdemocratic transition governments to address long-standing patterns of poverty and social exclusion (a pattern shared with many other Latin American countries). I discuss each in turn.

Crime rates in postwar El Salvador were extraordinarily high, particularly the homicide rate, which was 138 per 100,000 inhabitants in 1994 and 1995, compared to prewar rates of 33 and *exceeding* the rate at the height of the war violence of 55.3 in 1982 (Cruz and González 1997; see also Call 1999c). El Salvador's postwar homicide rate was (along with Colombia and South Africa) among the world's very highest, sixteen times the U.S. rate (Spence et al. 2001: 17). In a 1998 survey, 25.7 percent of those polled reported that their families had been the victims of assault in the previous four months (IUDOP 1998: Table 2). Crime rates appear to have declined since then (in 1997, the homicide rate was 111; Seligson et al. 2000: 144), but they remain very high.

High violent crime rates are of course troubling in themselves; they also may undermine support for democracy. In a 1999 survey, many more Salvadorans (55 percent) stated that crime would justify a coup compared to any other issue (the nearest competing response was unemployment at 28 percent; Seligson et al. 2000: 156). Moreover, Salvadorans who had been the victims of crime felt significantly less confident in the functioning of the system, were more likely to support a coup for reasons of high crime rates, and ranked higher in support for an authoritarian regime. More specifically, in regressions the level of insecurity felt by respondents was a strong and significant predictor of support for an authoritarian regime; those who had been victimized were more likely to feel a high level of insecurity (Seligson et al. 2000: 153–54, 164–65, 179, 180).

Various factors appear to contribute to these extraordinarily high crime rates (Cruz 1997; Call 1999c). Charles Call (1999c: 1) argues that certain various aspects of "war transitions" explain the puzzle that "peace can be more violent than war." El Salvador, like other post–civil war countries, suffers from the consequences of the rapid demobilization of two armies, a social habituation to violence, the ready availability of arms, and a process of restructuring of police forces. Such transitions are negotiated settlements between armed parties to a civil war, with the result that not only are arms abundant, but the negotiating parties are likely to be preoccupied with their own security in bargaining rather than the general security of individuals and society. Wartime processes of physical and social dislocation exacerbate prewar social conditions such as political and social exclusion and may render legal institutions weak.[25]

Despite the high crime rate, the postwar security institutions do not provide an entirely bleak picture. William Stanley (1999) argues that the PNC is a mixed picture of success and failure as the new force is better educated and trained, is more respectful of human rights, is more transparent in its procedures, and has exhibited a degree of independence in investigating actors who would have enjoyed impunity. However, while political violence by the new police force is nothing like that of the former security forces, nonetheless a troubling pattern of human rights violations (including occasional incidents of torture and beating of suspects) and corruption among members of the police force is apparent (Spence et al. 2001: 17–22; Call 1999b; Stanley 1995).[26] A presidential commission was named in 2000 to recommend measures to address police abuses; the ensuing process appears to have led to the dismissal of dozens and perhaps hundreds of corrupt or abusive officers (judicial appeals are still pending).

In contrast to this emphasis on institutional reform, José Miguel Cruz (1997) emphasizes the culture of violence: The civil war deepened and made universal an existing culture of violence as it militarized society, devalued human life, legitimized violence as the means toward personal ends, and left a generation of combatants with no history of or preparation toward a nonviolent way of life, given the widely acknowledged inadequacies of the "reinsertion" programs for demobilized combatants. An additional factor often advanced as contributing particularly to urban crime is the emergence of street gangs as a result of the deportation of young Salvadorans with experience of gang culture from the United States.

As a result of these various factors, policing in El Salvador – despite the promise of the peace accords of a new democratic and civilian police force – has converged toward the new Latin American model of public security (Kincaid 2000). There are three characteristics of this new model: militarization whereby the military supplements and sometimes replaces police forces in some domestic spheres; informalization whereby neighborhood watch committees and sometimes gangs provide neighborhood "security" and mobs lynch alleged criminals; and privatization whereby wealthier individuals and organizations

---

[25] Other analysts concur that these factors all contribute to the high violent crime rate (Cruz 1997; Stanley 1999; Spence et al. 2001).

[26] See the annual reports of human rights organizations such as the Procuraduría, Human Rights Watch, and Amnesty International for details.

hire private security firms to protect their personnel and assets. In a 1998 survey, 51.9 percent of the Salvadorans surveyed stated that they supported reclaiming the "right" to take justice into their own hands; 48.9 percent supported the formation of armed neighborhood groups; and 36.9 percent supported illegal armed groups (IUDOP 1998: Table 4).

Economic and Social Exclusion

We have already seen that the persistence of poverty appears to be a principal reason for democratic disenchantment among Salvadoran citizens. It is important, however, to note that poverty rates have declined since the end of the war. Official poverty rates show a decline in total poverty (combining relative and extreme poverty rates) from 58.7 percent in 1992 to 44.6 in 1998; in relative poverty (household income less than twice the cost of a basic food basket but more than the cost of one basket) from 31.0 to 25.6 percent; and in extreme poverty (household income less than the cost of a single basket) from 27.7 to 18.9 percent (Conning, Olinto, and Trigueros 2000: Table 2). The under-five mortality rate (per 1,000 live births) fell from 162 in 1970 to 39 in 2001 (UNDP 2003: Table 8). The urban rates declined particularly dramatically, from 52.9 to 36.0 percent for the total rate; from 31.0 to 23.1 for relative poverty; and from 21.9 to 12.9 percent for extreme poverty.[27] One reason for rapidly declining urban poverty is the relatively low unemployment rate of 6.5 percent in 2000 (for men the rate was 8.1 percent; for women, 4.0 percent; Trigueros, Vega, and Lazo Marín 2001: Figure 2).

This decline in poverty reflects both the ongoing influx of remittances from the United States and reasonably high postwar growth rates. Remittances have increased annually since the end of the civil war, comprising 49 percent of exports (fourth highest in the world) and 11 percent of GNP (fifth highest) in 1998 (Spence et al. 2001: 14–15, drawing on World Bank figures). Despite the "Dutch disease" consequences of remittances (an overvalued exchange rate,[28] terms of trade unfavorable to the agricultural sector, and high interest rates), the economy grew in the postwar period: from 1992 to 1995, the growth rate averaged 6.8 percent, then declined to an average of 3.2 percent from 1996 to 1999).[29] Despite these growth rates, income per capita in purchasing power parity terms had not reached prewar levels by 2001 (UNDP 2003: Table 12). One reason was the growth in exports: nontraditional exports grew by 71 percent between 1994 and 1999, while *net* maquila exports grew by 250 percent over

[27] However, the official rates underestimate the poverty rate as they are based on a count of households rather than individuals (poorer households have more people); correcting for this discrepancy gives a higher urban rate of total poverty in 1998 of 40.6 percent (and of 64.0 percent in rural areas; Conning et al. 2000: 10).

[28] The real effective exchange rate appreciated more than 50 percent from 1990 to 1999 (Conning et al. 2000: Table 5).

[29] Calculated from Trigueros et al. (2001: Table 2).

the same period (calculated from Banco Central de Reserva figures reprinted in Trigueros et al. 2001: Table 16).

Despite this decline in urban poverty, poverty rates remain very high, particularly in the countryside. Rural rates fell much less, from 65.0 percent in 1992 to 58.6 in 1998 for total poverty, from 31.1 to 29.9 for relative poverty, and from 34.0 to 28.7 for extreme poverty. Significant disparities exist between urban and rural life expectancy and adult literacy rates, which in 1996 varied between 70.4 years and 90.1 percent, respectively, in San Salvador to 64.8 years and 55.4 percent in Morazán.[30] According to Conning et al. (2000: 10), the human development index (HDI) rankings for San Salvador are comparable to Cuba, Peru, and Jordan, while those of the three poorest departments are similar to Kenya and Pakistan (a difference in the HDI of 50 points).[31] The ongoing decline in rural wages – the real minimum wage for coffee and sugar harvests fell 12.1 percent and 11.0 percent, respectively, between 1993 and 1998 – and worsening terms of trade for agricultural goods also contributed to enduring rural poverty (Conning et al. 2000: 9).[32] Rural landlessness remained very high after the war, despite the distribution of about 30 percent of farmland through the 1980 agrarian reform and the land transfer program after the peace agreement (Seligson 1995).

In early 2001, two earthquakes devastated significant areas of El Salvador. The first quake alone left about 681 people dead, and more than 20,000 homes destroyed (CIDAI 2001a: 16).[33] In February 2001, the government estimated accumulated damages at about $3 billion, or about 22 percent of GDP (CIDAI 2001b: 6). A later and more conservative estimate puts the accumulated damage at 12 percent of GDP (Spence et al. 2001: 1). Undoubtedly, current poverty figures are significantly higher than those given earlier in this chapter to the damage to infrastructure and the displacement of families from their work and homes. The response of the government was, in the judgment of many observers, distinctly partisan: The president named only members and supporters of ARENA (all bank owners and large capitalists) to the government commission to receive, distribute, and regulate official aid in its aftermath (CIDAI 2001d: 2–3).

CONCLUSION

To live in El Salvador is so difficult that its habitants abandon the country. The population has lost confidence; they (the people) don't believe in El Salvador enough to stay here. ("La Tragedia Social De El Salvador" 2000)

---

[30] From Table 3 of Conning et al. (2000).

[31] The overall HDI ranking for El Salvador is quite low; among Latin American countries, only Honduras, Guatemala, Nicaragua, and Haiti are lower (Conning et al. 2000: 8).

[32] Recent analyses of panel data from two surveys of households in 1995 and 1997 illuminate these patterns. See Beneke de Sanfeliú (2000); Briones and Andrade-Eekhoff (2000); Conning et al. (2000); and Larde de Palomo and Arguello de Morera (2000). Papers are available at *www.wisc.edu/ltc/baspubca.html*.

[33] See CIDAI (2001c: Figure 1) for a detailed estimate of the costs of the first earthquake.

Despite significant advances in ideological pluralism and political tolerance, declining rates of poverty, increasing political competition, and the gradual strengthening of the new institutions founded by the peace agreement to ensure democratic rule, the quality of democracy in El Salvador in the decade after the end of the war was only moderate. Rates of voter participation were low, the political party system was less than stable, economic and social exclusion undermined democratic rights, and crime terrorized all. The postwar political process has not yet healed the legacy of inequality, political exclusion, terror, and poverty. Of course, disenchantment with political parties and processes and enduring structural inequalities are also characteristic of many other Latin America countries. El Salvador has thus joined modern Latin America in the aftermath of its civil war. It appears that not only are there various routes to democratic governance (as Charles Tilly once wrote, "democracy is a lake"), but there are also various routes to low-quality democracy. In contrast to cases of redemocratization discussed in this volume, however, these challenges to the quality of democracy cannot be characterized as setbacks: Even low-quality democracy marks a fundamental sea change in Salvadoran politics.

This fundamental transformation in Salvadoran politics is in marked contrast to the continuity in Guatemalan politics despite civil war and a degree of democratization there (see Seligson, this volume). Guatemala is in many ways historically similar to El Salvador: In both countries, a political and economically exclusive polity developed around the political economy of export agriculture, protest was met by state violence, and the civil war was resolved through negotiations. However, the insurgent threat was weak in Guatemala: No agrarian reform was carried out, few landlords were displaced from their property, and rather than stalemate, the war ended in the defeat of the insurgents. As a result, the interests of agrarian economic elites were not transformed, and the process of political learning on the part of elites was sharply circumscribed. The military continues to play a significant role in Guatemalan politics, and political violence continues to threaten political opposition.

In contrast to the grim situation in Guatemala, there are several reasons to hope for ongoing improvement in the quality of democracy in El Salvador. The present freedom of expression and organization are absolutely without precedent, particularly in the countryside. Democratization at the municipal level is another favorable development, even given the problems discussed in this chapter. Progress in ending social exclusion is being made in a few spheres, as more children complete school than ever before. While difficult to quantify, tens of thousands of poor rural Salvadorans have come to an unprecedented sense of citizenship and entitlement.

7

Democracy on Ice

The Multiple Challenges of Guatemala's Peace Process

Mitchell A. Seligson

This chapter focuses on Guatemala, a country that has experienced a breath-taking shift from decades of coups, repressive military regimes, and protracted civil war to the establishment of electoral democracy, which began in 1986 and culminated with the signing of the final peace accords in 1996. Regular, free, and fair elections are today the rule, and former guerrilla leaders hold elected office at both the local and the national level. Moreover, indigenous groups have emerged from the shadows and are in the process of forging a new Mayan ethnic identity.

These changes in Guatemala represent a stunning advance in democracy in a country where few scholars would have predicted them. It is even more difficult to explain why they have occurred. This chapter will review those advances, but it will also highlight the several major challenges Guatemala must overcome if democracy is to deepen and the promises of the peace accords are to be fulfilled. The chapter argues that unless these challenges are met, not only will further progress be denied, but the chances for serious setbacks will increase.

ADVANCES IN GUATEMALAN DEMOCRACY

The striking advances that Guatemala has made in democracy since the mid-1980s stand in such bold relief largely because of the dismal state of affairs that had prevailed for much of the prior two centuries. In terms relative to the rest of Latin America, Guatemala is still far behind; it was ranked nineteen out of twenty countries (only Haiti ranked lower) in the Fitzgibbon-Johnson study of the opinions of Latin Americanist experts for the year 2000 (Kelly 2001), and Freedom House classifies Guatemala, notwithstanding fifteen years of regular free and fair elections, as only "partly free" (Piano and Puddington 2001).

I thank Dinorah Azpuru, Siddhartha Baviskar, Susanne Jonas, and Fabrice LeHoucq for their very helpful comments on a draft version of this paper.

Independence from Spain in 1821 brought about a protracted struggle between liberals and conservatives in Guatemala. Conservatives dominated the country up through the early 1870s, but then in the so-called "Liberal Revolution" of 1871, power shifted to the Liberals. Yet, this shift had no effect on stimulating the emergence of democracy, and the country remained dominated by *caudillos* who ruled for the benefit of a tiny, but very powerful elite. Central to elite power was the domination of the indigenous majority, comprised largely, but not exclusively, of a large number of Mayan Indian groupings. During this period the indigenous population survived largely as indentured servants to the *ladino* minority. Export agriculture dominated the economy, first heavily controlled by the export of *añil* dye, and later focused on coffee and bananas. Repressive laws, which tied Indians to the land, systematically denied democratic rights and liberties to much of the population.

The twentieth century brought to power a series of unsavory dictators who gave rise to the horrific image painted in Miguel Asturias's famous novel, *El Señor Presidente*. Elections, when they were held, were won by fraud, or were often overturned by coups. In the background loomed the United States and its interventionist policy in the Central American region (Pérez-Brignoli 1989). U.S. policy at the time supported strongman rule, so long as those strongmen favored U.S. policy interests both domestically and internationally.

It was not until 1944, as the United States was occupied in its struggles in both Europe and Asia, that a combination of a more benign "Good Neighbor" policy, along with the rise of democratic political stirrings, made it possible for a reformist president to come to power. Juan José Arévalo, who ruled from 1944 to 1951, introduced Guatemala's first, albeit tentative, social reforms and expansion of the political arena. Among the most important advances were the introduction of social security and a new labor code, although large elements of the population were excluded from their protections. Political parties began to organize more freely, and the electorate was expanded. In 1951, the more sharply reformist regime of Jacobo Arbenz was elected to power, and it immediately sought more extensive reforms, especially in rural areas. Arbenz engineered an extensive land reform that resulted in the expropriation of large banana plantations owned by the United Fruit Company (Handy 1994). This was the "Prague Spring" of Guatemala's tortured political history, but it was soon to end by the realities of the Cold War. Reforms, such as the ones being undertaken in Guatemala, were seen as challenging to U.S. interests in the region, and particularly worried the Eisenhower administration in Washington when it thought it saw evidence that Arbenz was attempting to spread his ideas to other countries in the region (Schifter 1980). The CIA planned, funded, and armed a small invasion force that carried out what was widely claimed at the time to be a "textbook" case of unseating a "communist regime." Later, on closer inspection, this "flawless operation" proved to be so deeply flawed it seemed more like a Keystone Kops operation than a model to be emulated elsewhere (Cullather 1999).

The aftermath of the invasion brought with it unspeakable repression and violations of human rights, giving rise to anthropologist Richard Adams's (1970) classic and aptly titled monograph, *Crucifixion by Power*. In this context, guerrilla movements developed, which gave the army the justification it needed to apply a scorched earth policy that was largely directed at indigenous communities in the highlands. The general context of the Cold War continued to justify the repression, which increased in intensity after the Sandinistas took over Nicaragua in 1979 and full-scale civil war broke out in El Salvador at about the same time. Probably the darkest period occurred in the early 1980s when massacres of Indian villages became commonplace.

Despite these negative events, Guatemala proved not to be insulated from the broader Latin America–wide pattern of a transition to democracy in the late 1980s. The democratization process took place in three basic stages. First, in 1985, competitive elections were held, and the elected president, Vinicio Cerezo, was able to serve out his term. As he was leaving office in 1991, the Sandinistas had been voted out of power in Nicaragua, and peace was coming to El Salvador's decade-long conflict. Those two changes took place in the context of the fall of the Berlin Wall and the greatly reduced East–West tensions. All these factors together began to deprive the Guatemalan military of the justification for its repressive policies and enabled normal electoral processes to take root.

The second stage in the democratization process began inauspiciously in 1993, when President Jorge Serrano, victor in the 1991 elections, attempted to stage an executive coup to resolve a series of problems he was confronting but found that his actions were resisted by the international community, now firmly committed to democracy, and sectors of the Guatemalan elite and public. In contrast to its long-standing interventionist tradition, the military in this case opted not to support the coup and allowed the Congress to appoint none other than Ramiro de Leon Carpio, who had served as the Guatemalan human rights ombudsman. This was certainly a landmark event in that it seemed to ring the death knell of irregular transfers of power that had been so common over the centuries in Guatemala.

The third stage in the democratization process began in 1994 when the government signed the first of what was to be several peace accords with the guerrilla movement, now fused into the Unidad Revolucionaria Nacional Guatemalteca (URNG; Guatemalan National Revolutionary Unit). Without an end to the thirty-year-long civil war, the consolidation of democracy was clearly impossible. International pressures to do something to end the war were growing, including pressure from other countries in the region, led by Nobel Peace Prize laureate Oscar Arias. Those negotiations were protracted because motivations to grant concessions to the other side were very limited. On the one hand, it was clear to the government that militarily the guerrillas had been defeated and had no prospect of receiving extensive international support to continue their struggle. Major concessions to the URNG did not seem necessary. On the other hand, the guerrillas knew that the government needed to put the civil war behind it or face the prospect of a continued, albeit low-intensity conflict; therefore, they sought the upper hand in the negotiations. Detailed discussion of the give and take of those negotiations is beyond the scope of this chapter, but the topic has been covered by Jonas (2000a) and Azpuru (1999b). Suffice it to say that the accords were developed piecemeal, with a series of accords being developed and signed, culminating in the final signing in December 1996.

Beginning in 1997, then, all of the elements were in place for a deepening of democracy. The terms of the peace accords specified a multitude of steps that were to be carried out over the next several years that, if realized, would both reign in the military and establish durable democratic rights for Guatemalan citizens, especially its indigenous population. Free and fair elections had already become routinized, and most sectors of the military were prepared to accept a far more limited role in politics than they had enjoyed for over a century. In addition, opposition groups were now able to organize and run candidates for local and national office. In effect, these advances in democracy led to an opening of the political process, such that dissident voices were no longer immediately accused of being disloyal or subversive. The press gained previously unrealized freedom to report on taboo subjects, especially criminal acts alleged to have been committed by members and former members of the armed services. In addition, reports of corruption by elected officials became commonplace. For the first time, the heretofore consistently pusillanimous office of the state prosecutor found the courage to take on a limited number of controversial cases involving the military, and in a small number of very high profile cases the judiciary actually convicted them. Sadly, however, many of the judges who stood firm and convicted these military men later had to flee the country because of multiple threats on their lives. Finally, forensic pathologists began the gruesome task of exhuming the mass graves of victims of massacres of civilians, largely Indians, that had taken place during the long civil war. This process not only convincingly demonstrated the culpability of the military in these violations of human rights, but it also helped to bring cloture to the open wounds of thousands of families whose relatives had disappeared in the dark of night never to be seen again (Sanford 2003).

The transformation of Guatemala from an authoritarian, war-wracked society into an electoral democracy in which the guerrilla war is a fading memory has been nothing short of miraculous. Yet, these achievements have simultaneously created new challenges, which thus far have proven largely unmet. Specifically, the peace accords, the very centerpiece of the democratization process, officially recognized that the long period of authoritarian rule was a product of deep structural problems in Guatemalan society that needed to be remedied if democracy was to take permanent hold. As will be detailed in the pages that follow, Guatemalan citizens were promised a great deal by the accords, but few concrete steps have been taken to deliver on those promises. The result is that the democratization process has become frozen, as the title of this chapter suggests, producing the risk that gains from the peace process may be eroded by a growing impatience with unfulfilled promises. There is evidence, as will be shown later, that Guatemalan "consumers" are beginning to ask for a "rebate" on their newly purchased model of governance we call "democracy," while others are asking for a complete "recall."

POTENTIAL FOR STAGNATION OR SETBACKS IN GUATEMALA'S DEMOCRATIZATION PROCESS

For many countries around the world, the "great wave of democratization" seems frozen in suspended animation, caught on a plateau of democratic formalism that over time does not seem to widen or deepen. In a broad-ranging look at worldwide consolidation of Third World democracies, Larry Diamond sees a pattern of emerging "illiberal democracies," political systems that are more democratic in form than in substance (1999: 42–50), while Guillermo O'Donnell (1994) sees the emergence of "delegatory democracies" in which elected officials have little accountability to their citizens. In the most recent Freedom House surveys, whereas twenty-five countries experienced gains in freedom in 1999–2000, another eighteen saw losses (Piano and Puddington 2001).[1] From a longer-term perspective, the last decade of the twentieth century experienced an increase in the percentage of countries rated by Freedom House as "free," from 39.3 to 44.8 percent, but the period also saw an *increase* in the absolute number of "partly free" and "not free" countries, from 100 in 1990 to 106 in 2000 (Piano and Puddington 2001).[2] In the Latin American region, the major positive shift was in Mexico, where the first clearly free, fair, and competitive election since the 1930s brought the opposition candidate, Vicente Fox, to power. On the other hand, Ecuador experienced a brief coup and has been embroiled in deep political turmoil; the results of Haiti's election in 2000 are widely disputed; Venezuela's President Hugo Chávez continued to expand his powers and limit many democratic processes; and the abrupt resignation of Peru's President Alberto Fujimori (himself the winner in an election of highly dubious legitimacy) and the accompanying revelations of the depth and breadth of the corruption of that system by his secretive henchman, Vladimiro Montecinos, left most Peruvians deeply distrustful of their "democracy."

It is difficult, when we are so close to the events at hand, to know what direction democracy is taking worldwide, or in Latin America in particular. It is impossible to predict with any degree of certainty the long-term outcomes for the great bulk of newly democratizing countries. Political scientists, however, are capable of enumerating and highlighting the challenges faced by nations undergoing democratization. That is the task facing the contributors to this volume.

[1] For an analysis of biases in democracy measures, see Bollen and Paxton (2000). The Freedom House measure has some right-wing bias, which would mean that in the case of Guatemala, the scores may be higher (more democratic) than they would be absent that bias.

[2] The total number of countries in the Freedom House surveys increased from 165 in 1990 to 192 in 2000, largely as a result of the expansion of the number of world states.

In the case of Guatemala, most analysts are not optimistic about the future of democracy, in spite of the major transformations that have already occurred since 1986. In 2000, Guatemala ranked nineteenth out of twenty countries (Kelly 2001) on the "Fitzgibbon-Johnson Index of Democracy in Latin America," a ranking carried out regularly since 1945 that gives the average perceptions of over 100 U.S.-based academic experts on the region.[3] Only Haiti ranked lower (Kelly 2001). Indeed, Guatemala's ranking among Latin American countries today is far lower than it was in the 1950s, 1960s, and 1970s, when it ranked between tenth and thirteenth out of twenty, signaling that these experts view Guatemala's advance as relatively less impressive than that of its peers. While these views reflect those of Latin Americanists generally, experts on Guatemala in particular are also pessimistic. Long-time observer of Guatemalan politics Susanne Jonas writes in her most recent work, "As I was in the last few months of finalizing this book, which has been my daily companion for nearly ten years, Guatemala once again dashed my hopes" (2000a: 10).

Although there are regular rumors of coup plots, few observers take those seriously, and there seems little reason to doubt that electoral democracy is secure. Moreover, the political arena has clearly been widened to include the left; in the 1999 presidential election the URNG fielded a presidential candidate (Alvaro Colom Caballeros) who won 12 percent of the vote and candidates for deputy who won 9 out of the 113 seats in the unicameral legislature.

The ending of military rule and the establishment of electoral democracy was a crucial first step in the democratization process. But electoral democracy alone is insufficient to guarantee long-term democratic stability. A narrow view, focused on elections alone, threatens to become reductionist by avoiding key questions of class and ethnic exclusion that are so central to the Guatemalan case. As Diamond (1999: 9) has argued, even when definitions of electoral democracy are corrected to exclude cases in which true power continues to reside with the military, "such formulations may still fail to give due weight to political repression and marginalization, which exclude significant segments of the population – typically the poor or ethnic and regional minorities – from exercising their democratic rights." In Guatemala there has emerged a series of five challenges, which threaten to undermine the democratization process. These are (1) the dilemma of peace accords that go too far; (2) the paradox of neoliberalism imposed upon a classic liberal economy; (3) the expansion of ethnic rights while intraethnic conflict increases; (4) the paradox of winning the war but losing the peace; and (5) the difficulty of building institutional democracy unsupported by a democratic political culture. I will examine each of these challenges in terms of the obstacles they present to long-term democratic

---

[3] The ranking, like all others, carries with it numerous biases and is a measure of *perception* rather than an actual measure of democracy. Moreover, it is a ranking; therefore, one country will always end up at the top and another at the bottom, even if in absolute terms all have become more democratic. Yet, the index is an excellent way to learn about expert views as to how democratic Guatemala is *relative* to other countries in the region.

stability. I make no effort to predict the future. Unless these obstacles are over-come, however, Guatemala cannot be protected from either remaining caught on a plateau of electoral democracy, or even reverting to its authoritarian, po-litically unstable past.

The Dilemma of Peace Accords That Do Too Much

It is conventional wisdom that pioneers pay the price of inexperience and those who follow learn from the errors of their predecessors. Applying this generaliza-tion to peace accords that resolve long-standing national conflicts, Guatemala has benefited from watching the peace process embarked upon by its neighbor, El Salvador, a process that was concluded on January 1, 1992. When I was in Guatemala City after the signing of the Salvadoran peace accords, I recall seeing a full-page advertisement in the local press paid for by the government of El Salvador. It read: "We did it . . . now it's your turn." That sort of pressure, along with the other factors mentioned in the introduction of this chapter, made Guatemala seriously turn toward peace negotiations.

What were the lessons of the Salvadoran peace accords?[4] For many, the Salvadoran accords were too narrowly drawn. The Salvador accords are re-viewed in Elisabeth Wood's chapter in this volume, but suffice it to say that they were chiefly intended to open political space for the opposition (the Farabundo Martí National Liberation Front or Frente Farabundo Martí para la Liberación Nacionla; FMLN), and they did so by demilitarizing society and reconfiguring the various repressive arms of the state. In addition, the Salvadoran accords mandated some judicial reforms, principally by establishing an office for pros-ecuting violations of human rights and by increasing the budget of the judicial branch of government. In the economic and social sphere, however, the goals of the accords were quite limited (Córdova Macías 1999; Karl 1992). The Salvadoran accords did not demand transformations in the social structure of the nation but instead sought benefits largely narrowly directed at those who had fought in the nation's armed conflicts (reeducation and training programs, land transfers, etc.). Guatemalans who came to the table to negotiate the ac-cords for their country in 1994 sought much more and, in my view, got much less. The Guatemalan accords were drawn so broadly, and promised to do so much, that in many respects their goals were unrealistic, especially in the con-text of a state committed to neoliberal economic policies, as will be described later.

It is hard to overstate the breadth of the Guatemalan accords (Azpuru 1999b). The number of commitments exceeds 300.[5] Agreed to over a period of several years, the Guatemalan accords began with the human rights accord

---

[4] See Vinegrad (1998) for a good comparison of the Guatemalan peace process with that in El Salvador and other Latin American countries.

[5] According to one source, the commitments number 317 (Gallego 2001: 29), but others have argued that the number exceeds 600.

signed in March 1994.[6] This document created the UN Verification Mission, known as MINUGUA, and charged it with monitoring and documenting human rights violations in Guatemala. A truth commission was also approved in June 1994, but its effectiveness was largely undermined by the granting of amnesty for crimes that occurred during the protracted period of internal warfare. In addition, the Guatemalan truth commission, while it did clearly convey the message that the military bore the large share of the blame for the human rights abuses committed during the war, was not able to name names, as its counterpart had in El Salvador, and thereby allowed the guilty on both sides to remain comfortably anonymous.[7] This accord was followed with the Agreement on the Resettlement of Populations Uprooted by the Armed Confrontation, which provided for the peaceful return of internal and international exiles (many living in Southern Mexico).

In March 1995, the Accord for the Identity and Rights of Indigenous Peoples that redefined Guatemala as a "multiethnic, multicultural, and multilingual nation" was signed. This recognition was a crucial step forward in dealing, at least in theory, with the problem of a nation divided along ethnic lines. According to the view of many *ladinos*, classically incorporated into the public education system, Guatemala was a Catholic, European society in which the indigenous population was an unwelcome guest.

Many see the next accord, signed in September 1996, as the most important because it limits the role of the army to defending the nation from external attacks. At the same time, it mandated the consolidation of the several existing police forces into a "National Civilian Police" force, which was to be professionalized and trained in a national police academy and to have no fewer than 20,000 members. This agreement, called The Accord on the Strengthening of Civil Power and the Functioning of the Army in a Democratic Society, clearly linked the reduction in the role of the military to democratization of the Guatemalan political system. The accord also abolished the so-called civilian patrols, which was little more than a highly effective system of military social control at the village level, extending down even to the level of the family. This accord also cut the size and budget of the army by one third.

The September 1996 accord went far beyond the issue of the military, however, and concerned itself with the legislature and the judiciary as well. It demanded, for example, that the Constitution be amended to prevent deputies from serving more than two consecutive terms, in effect establishing term limits for office. Other required changes were set out in such broad terms that it is difficult to see how they could be practically implemented. Article II 6b of this accord, for example, provided for measures to

Control the Executive Branch to ensure public policies are sufficiently clear; verify the consistency of programs; ensure honesty in the programming and implementation of the

---

[6] See Jonas (2000a, 2000b) for an extensive review of the accords.
[7] Another report, issued in 1998 by the Catholic Church, did name names, but this second report was not the official truth commission report.

nation's budget; examine and evaluate the administrative actions or omissions of ministers of state and other top officials; and follow up on government actions to safeguard the general interests of the population and to preserve the legitimacy of institutions.

When it came to the judiciary, similar language was used in Article III 10: "A priority in this area is the reform to the administration of justice in order to reverse ineffectiveness, eradicate corruption, guarantee free access to justice, its impartial application, judicial independence, ethical authority, the probity of the system as a whole, and its modernization."

This accord also mandated some specific changes to the Constitution, such as the following: "Art. 203: The article should have an initial reference to the guarantees for the administration of justice, and as such, should include: free access to it in the native language; respect for the country's multi-ethnic, pluricultural, and multilingual nature; defense for those unable to pay for it; the judge's impartiality and independence; reasonable and prompt solution of social conflicts and the opening of alternate mechanisms to settle conflicts." Implementation of such constitutional changes was left to legislative debate, to be followed by a national referendum.

A key difference between the Guatemalan and Salvadoran accords may be found in the 1996 agreement on "Socioeconomic and Agrarian Issues." This agreement goes far beyond the goal of ending the war in that it seeks to make fundamental transformations in Guatemalan economic policy. It rejects the longstanding laissez-faire role of the state in favor of one that carries responsibility for its citizens' social welfare. Specifically, the accord requires an increase in tax revenues from the traditional 8–9 percent level to 12 percent by the year 2000. In addition, it set a target for economic growth of an annual rate of 6 percent by the year 2000. This contrasts with a growth rate of 1.0 percent in the period 1980–89, and 3.9 percent for 1990–96 (World Bank 1997: Statistical Appendix Table 1). By 2000, public spending was to have increased by 50 percent over 1995 levels; public health expenditures were to be shifted from curative to preventive; and 1.5 percent of tax revenue was to be spent on low-income housing beginning in 1997.

The accords went even further. They specified an annual public investment program on rural development of Q300 million a year (about $43 million), the provision of at least three years of primary education to all children between the ages of seven and twelve, and an increase in literacy to 70 percent of the population by the year 2000. In addition, by the same year, infant and maternal mortality was to be cut by 50 percent, and poliomyelitis and measles were to be eradicated.

These illustrations are sufficient to give the reader a sense of the extensiveness of the Guatemalan peace accords. Even though there have been undeniable successes emerging from those accords – not the least of which is the cessation of armed conflict – and the size of the military budget and the armed forces have in fact been trimmed to levels established by the accords, the many failures significantly complicate the road to democratic consolidation. First is the stark difference between the role of the army in post-peace El Salvador and Guatemala. In El Salvador, the army not only was reduced in size but also went through an extensive process of "purification" in which a great number of senior military men who were held to be the fundamental driving force behind repression, were cashiered (most belonging to the infamous *tandona*), and the key battalions that had been responsible for a long list of massacres and human rights violations were abolished. In Guatemala, however, the army, while smaller, remains largely unaltered in its role and mission as an institution.[8] Indeed, the Guatemalan army sees itself, and is seen by many Guatemalans, as having won the war against the guerrillas and "communist insurgency," largely without assistance from the United States. Many of the men who led the army at the height of its human rights abuses are still in place, while the 1999 election brought to civilian political power "former army officials who had been key players in the scorched-earth 'dirty-war' of the 1980s, not to mention [Efraín] Ríos Montt himself, who was to preside over Congress" (Jonas 2000b: 31). Ríos Montt was initially barred from running for the office of President, but in a protracted conflict involving his party, the electoral tribunal and the national Supreme Court, he eventually won that right in 2003. In the election itself, however, he was defeated.

Another major problem of the peace accords emerged when a series of constitutional reforms specified in the peace accords was rejected in the *consulta popular* of May 1999. The peace accords specified changes to be made in the Guatemalan Constitution, which, if approved, could have redefined the political system in many vital ways. Some of these changes were noted in the preceding discussion on the accords. Others of them dealt with the way the legislative and judicial branches of government were organized. These reforms were debated by the legislature for over a year and finally won legislative approval in late 1998. Unfortunately, the reforms had become complicated by many other issues, which meant that by the time they came before the public, some fifty different reforms, divided into four major categories, were to be voted upon. These categories were (1) the rights of indigenous people, (2) reforms of the legislature, (3) reforms of the executive, and (4) reforms of the judiciary. Some of these reforms were only tangentially related to the peace accords and democracy (such as establishing worker's compensation rights for dismissed government employees), while others were central to the democratization process. Among the key reforms was the recognition of the multilingual, multiethnic nature of the Guatemalan nation including granting official status to a long list of indigenous languages, recognizing indigenous law in certain cases, and imposing the requirement that the indigenous population would be consulted directly when legislation that would affect them is considered. The reforms also required the professionalization of the judiciary, setting new requirements for minimum levels of training for judicial officials.

---

[8] President Portillo did manage to retire over 100 officers shortly after he took office, but the impact on the military of that effort is unknown.

The entire *consulta* process proved to be confusing even to highly educated members of the public, let alone the great bulk of the Guatemalan people, who, on average, have fewer than four years of education. Partially as a result of this confusion, only 18.5 percent of registered voters cast their ballots in the referendum. But, most importantly, the constitutional reforms were defeated 55 to 45 percent, leaving in suspended animation the key elements of the peace agreements noted previously (see Arnson 1999). While the more general principles of the agreements, such as recognizing the multiethnic nature of Guatemalan society, stand on their own as part of the peace accords without the constitutional revisions, most of the others could not. For example, the changes in the judiciary and the military require constitutional revisions, as does the requirement that indigenous languages can be used for official transactions. Without a constitutional reform, these important elements of the peace agreements that would have reined in the military and helped level the playing field for the indigenous population have been left as hollow achievements of the peace process. It is doubtful that public support to make these changes can be generated.

One survey of 1,200 Guatemalans (conducted jointly by the University of Pittsburgh Latin American Public Opinion Project and ASIES, a Guatemalan think tank),[9] found that although the uneducated rural poor were more supportive of constitutional reforms than more highly educated and urban Guatemalans, support even among this group barely reached 50 percent. And even though 42 percent of the indigenous population that cast a vote supported the reforms (compared to 32 percent of the *ladinos* who supported it), the majority of the indigenous population that cast a vote opposed the reforms (Seligson et al. 2000). As late as 1999, Guatemalans were not yet ready to accept the key transformations required by the peace process.

So much of the success of the commitments made in the economic portion of the accords depends upon expanding state capacity by expanding state revenue. The accords mandated that increases in spending on social programs were to be accomplished largely through increased tax revenues rather than cutbacks in other areas (the reduced military budget notwithstanding). One key mechanism was to have been a change in the property tax law that would have made tax collection more progressive in that reforms were mainly directed toward large rural landowners. The reform was approved by Congress in 1997 but was met with a storm of protests, much of it coming from the indigenous population itself and led by Nobel Laureate Rigoberta Menchú. There was concern that the new tax law would somehow reduce local and municipal autonomy and strengthen the central government. The protests grew so loud and widespread that the government of President Arzú, in February 1998, had the law repealed by the Guatemalan Congress. This action undermined another element of the peace accords.

An overall assessment of goals and accomplishments through the year 2000, the year in which the main goals of the peace accords were to have been met,

---

[9] Based on a 1999 national probability survey.

appears in Table 7.1. The results are mixed, with some notable successes. For example, the military police have disappeared, the army has been cut from nearly 47,000 troops to just over 31,000, and the civil patrols and forced military conscription have been abandoned, although some still operate without government approval. The literacy target of 70 percent seems to have been nearly achieved, an almost 6 percent increase since 1995 (although percentages for the most recent years are estimates, and many are skeptical of the quality of those numbers). Gains have been made in education, with increased coverage of the population. Infant mortality appears to have come down, from nearly 40 per 1,000 to 33.5, although the entire data series for 1997–2000 are only estimates.[10] These signs are all evidence that the quality of Guatemala's human capital is improving.

Guatemala's macroeconomic program, the sine qua non for generating the funds necessary to increase and sustain social spending, has not done nearly as well. The improvements reported earlier have largely been made possible by the flood of international donations that were made to support the peace process. Those donations, however, are not long-term, and indeed the failure of Guatemala to fulfill its part of the peace bargain has already caused some donors to curtail their support. To achieve its goals without vastly expanding taxation, not a politically possible solution in any event, strong economic growth was seen as necessary and indeed required by the peace accords. The growth rate, which was targeted by the accords to reach 6 percent by 2000, is far below its goal. According to the World Bank, for Guatemala to reduce the number of its poor, economic growth must be at least at 5.8 percent per year (World Bank 2000a: 33). Reducing the number of poor people also depends on income distribution because the impact of growth is reduced in direct proportion to the degree of income inequality. But Guatemala's income distribution is the third most unequal in the world; the richest 20 percent of the population earned 63 percent of the income, a figure nearly identical to Brazil's (at 63.8 percent) and only slightly below that of South Africa, the world's most unequal country (at 64.8 percent) (World Bank 2001c: 282–83).

Moreover, inequality in income distribution makes it far more difficult to reduce the number of Guatemala's poor in comparison to most other nations; growth must reach high levels and stay there over long periods before its effects can "trickle down" to the poor. Given the present limitations of Guatemala's human capital, however, it is difficult to imagine how that growth rate could be achieved. For example, while Guatemala has increased health spending from 0.9 percent of GDP to 1.3 percent in 2000, the average for Latin America as a whole was 3.0 percent. Similarly, education spending, which was 1.6 percent of GDP in 1995 and targeted to rise to 2.5 percent (but only reached 2.2 percent) in 2000, compares unfavorably with the Latin American average of 4.3 percent. Finally, if Guatemala follows the pattern of other Latin American countries, it

[10] The most recent World Bank data (2001a: 20), lists a 1999 infant mortality rate for Guatemala of 40, showing no decline at all.

TABLE 7.1. *Key Targets and Accomplishments of the Guatemalan Peace Accords*

	Fiscal (% of GDP)	Base 95	1997	1998	1999	2000
1. Growth rate (%)		Target	4.2	5.1	6.0	6.0
		Actual	4.3	5.1[p]	**3.6[f]**	**4.0[f]**
2. Tax ratio	7.6	Target	8.6	10.0	11.4	12.0
		Actual	8.8	**8.9[p]**	**9.4**	**9.1[f]**
3. Health spending	0.9	Target	1.0	1.1	1.2	1.3
		Actual	1.0	1.1[p]	1.2[f]	1.3[f]
4. Education spending	1.6	Target	1.9	2.1	2.3	2.5
		Actual	**1.8**	**2.2[p]**	**2.1[f]**	**2.2[f]**
5. Public security spending	0.3	Target	0.3	0.4	0.4	0.5
		Actual	0.3	0.5[p]	0.6[f]	**0.6[f]**
6. Judicial/public ministry spending	0.3	Target	0.3	0.4	0.4	0.5
		Actual	0.3	0.4[p]	**0.3[f]**	**0.5[f]**
7. Military spending	1	Target	0.9	0.8	0.7	0.7
		Actual	0.9	0.7[p]	0.6[f]	0.6[f]
8. Preventive care *(% of health budget)*	38	Target	–	–	>50.0	>50.0
		Actual	43.0	46.0[p]	49.0[f]	52.0[f]
9. Low-income housing budget *(% of tax revenues)*	–	Target	–	1.5	1.5	1.5
		Actual	–	1.5[a]	1.6[f]	1.5[f]
10. Investment on rural development *(million of Q.)*	–	Target	50.0	50.0	50.0	50.0
		Actual	–	265.9[e]	329.3[a]	>300.0[f]
11. Investment on rural infrastructure *(million of Q.)*	–	Target	300.0	300.0	300.0	300.0
		Actual	–	>300.0[e]	>300.0[a]	>300.0[f]
Social / Security Measures						
12. Literacy rate (%) *(INE – 1994 Census)*	64.2	Target	–	–	–	70.0
		Actual	66.4[e]	67.4[e]	68.6[f]	69.3[f]
13. Primary education coverage *(3 years – gross rate)*	84	Target	–	–	100.0	100.0
		Actual	86.0[e]	89[e]	91.0[f]	92.0[f]
14. Primary education coverage *(3 years – net rate)*	69	Target	–	–	100.0	100.0
		Actual	71.0	72.9[e]	75.1[f]	77.0[f]
15. Infant mortality rate *(deaths per 1,000 living births)*	39.9	Target	–	–	20.0	20.0
		Actual	38.5[e]	37.0[e]	35.3[f]	33.5[f]
16. Maternal mortality rate *(deaths/100,000 women giving birth)*	97	Target	–	–	48.5	48.5
		Actual	97.9[e]	97.7[e]	97.5[e]	97.2[f]
17. Poliomyelitis cases *(vaccination coverage)*	80	Target	85.0	85.0	85.0	85.0
		Actual	**74.0[e]**	88.0[e]	88.0[f]	88.0[f]
18. Measles cases *(vaccination coverage)*	83	Target	–	–	–	–95.0
		Actual	74.0[e]	79.0[e]	84.0[f]	87.0[f]
19. Army reduction *(number of troops)*	46,900	Target	31,423.0	31,423.0	31,423.0	31,423.0
		Actual	31,270.0	–	–	–
20. Military police *(number of members)*	2,421	Target	Nil	Nil	Nil	Nil
		Actual	Nil	Nil	Nil	Nil

Note: Preventive health includes water and sanitation. Bold means underachievement. a, assigned; e, World Bank staff estimate; f, World Bank staff forecasts PIB (GNP) 99: Q134,301.7 million (quetzales); p, projected.
Source: World Bank (2000a).

will take fifteen years to cut its infant mortality rate in half, not the five years programmed in the peace accords (World Bank 2000a: 35).

As a practical matter, all parties realized that the fiscal targets specified in the accords could not be met by 2000, so they were rescheduled for 2002, but those goals have not yet been met. In fact, there seems to be no reasonable chance that tax reforms will enable the government to increase revenue to 12 percent of GDP in the foreseeable future, striking a blow to some of the central elements of the peace accords on which so much of the future of Guatemalan democracy depends. To deal with the new realities, a "fiscal pact" was agreed to on May 25, 2000. The pact involves increasing the marginal tax brackets for those with the highest incomes from 25 to 31 percent, but it provides a loophole: Taxes are reduced for those who can show proof of having paid the VAT (value-added tax). Thus, those who are the wealthiest, and who can afford to spend the most, will pay the lowest taxes (Hernández Pico 2000b). The pact ended up in a shambles, however, when in July 2000 the ruling Guatemalan Republican Front (Frente Republicano Guatemalteco; FRG) decided it could not go ahead with most of the tax increases, and a scandal erupted as a result of an apparent alteration of the approved law to satisfy pressures from the liquor industry (hence the term for the scandal, "boozegate") (Hernández Pico 2000a). As of this writing, most changes in the tax code have been postponed, and all attention has been placed on increasing the VAT, which if accomplished would produce new revenue, but it would also add a further regressive element to the tax structure, impacting the poor the most. Thus, ironically, the poor may suffer economically more under democracy than they did under dictatorship, leaving many to wonder what gains have been made by the peace agreements that can help in the long-term solution to democratize Guatemala through incorporation of the poor into the political process.

The Paradox of Neoliberalism in a Classically Liberal Economy

Guatemala is a divided nation, split between an impoverished indigenous population that comprises a near majority of the population[11] and a *ladino* population that on the whole enjoys a higher standard of living. According to the most recent, preliminary findings of the World Bank (2001a), carried out in 2001, while the poverty rate in Guatemala City is 11 percent and in the country as a whole, 54.3 percent, that in the indigenous regions varies from 65 to 79 percent. Perpetuation of this split, after the establishment of electoral democracy and the signing of the peace agreements, does not bode well for the deepening of Guatemalan democracy because that division has been central to the exclusion of the indigenous population from positions of political power since the days of the Spanish conquest and colonization. Yet, macro-level economic policy,

---

[11] The census data show that about two fifths of the population self-identify as indigenous, but many experts on Guatemala refer to the "Indian majority." Because ethnicity is a socially defined characteristic, one cannot provide a universally accepted percentage of Indians in Guatemala.

as will be shown in this section of this chapter, has thus far proven unwilling to make the serious reallocations needed to overcome this division. In that sense, the pathway that has been taken by the political economy threatens to undermine the promises made in the peace accords.

Worldwide, nations have been adopting neoliberal economic policies for well over a decade. A central feature of these policies has been shrinking the size of government so that the "invisible hand" of competition will be less hampered by regulatory controls that inevitably seem to favor rent-seeking behaviors at the cost of the entire economy's welfare. The so-called Washington consensus on neoliberalism is backed up by credible threats to cut off access to international loans and investment capital. It is thus ironic that Guatemala is among the relatively small group of countries that have out-liberalized the neoliberals. Worldwide, government income averages 20.1 percent of GDP, and with a standard deviation of 9.8 percent. Guatemala's government revenue, however, is only 8.7 percent of GNP, a figure that did not change between 1980 and 1998. This means that Guatemala is more than one standard deviation below the worldwide mean, and a small portion of the 23.5 percent its Central American neighbor, Costa Rica earns (World Bank 2000a: Appendix Table 8; World Bank 2000c: 230–31, 256–57). While Costa Rica's social democracy may not be a good yardstick for comparison, a worldwide look reveals that in *only six countries in the world* (for which 1997 government revenue data are available) does government income comprise a smaller portion of the national economy. Nepal's government income, at 8.9 percent, is closest to that of Guatemala. No Latin American government is as small as Guatemala's. These figures actually understate the degree of Guatemala's low level of spending because they are limited to central government income and exclude subnational government income. In Guatemala, such income is very low – only 1.7 percent of total tax revenues (World Bank 2000c: 216), compared to far higher levels in federal systems such as Mexico (20.6 percent), Brazil (31.3 percent), Argentina (41.1 percent), and the United States (46.4 percent). Indeed, most countries in the world spend more on local government than does Guatemala; only Botswana and the Dominican Republic spend a lower percentage of total tax revenues on local government (World Bank 2000c: 216–17).

Because Guatemala is a relatively poor country, it is not surprising that it has a small government. Yet, even when national income is partialed out of the equation, Guatemala is found to be an outlier, with government revenue far lower than might be predicted by national wealth (as measured by purchasing power parity [PPP] GNP). If the Guatemalan government's share of national income were in line with its GNP, that level would be about 17 percent, or about twice as high as it actually is (see Figure 7.1). Guatemala's low level of government revenue, then, is not merely a product of economic underdevelopment but is a function of policy choices that have constrained the size of government below a level that its economy could afford. Moreover, this pattern has been a constant for decades, well before neoliberal policies forced governments to contract worldwide.

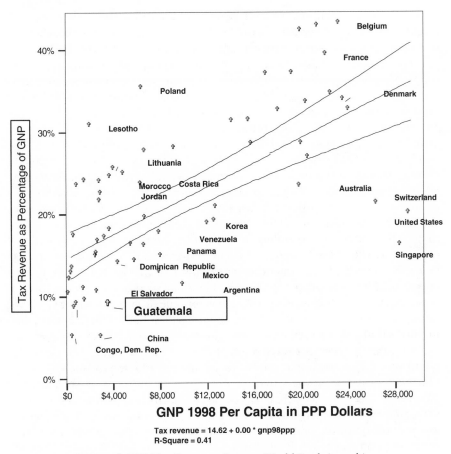

FIGURE 7.1. GNP and GDP Tax Revenue. Source: World Bank (2001b).

Small government is not new to Guatemala, but it has been preserved at the cost of human capital development. As extensive studies on human capital formation have shown, countries can transcend their level of income; low GNP and low human capital do not necessarily go hand-in-hand (UNDP 2000: 157–60). Guatemala is not only a poor country (GNP in PPP dollars 1999 = $3,517), but also one in which human capital is woefully underdeveloped. The mortality rate for children under the age of five in 1998 was 52 per 1,000, compared to 36 per 1,000 in neighboring El Salvador and 15 per 1,000 in Costa Rica (World Bank 2001c: 276). According to the most recent estimates by the World Bank, 58 percent of Guatemala's population, and 71 percent of its rural population, live in poverty (World Bank 2000b: 9). Forty percent of Guatemalan adult women were illiterate as late as 1998, a rate exceeded in the Americas only by Haiti (World Bank 2001c: 276).

Research clearly shows that human capital formation requires investment in health and education, and that without adequate human capital, a nation's economic development will be constrained (Birdsall, Ross, and Sabot 1995). A recent study by the Inter-American Development Bank, for example, shows a strong positive association between education and level of GDP (IDB 2000b: 12). Given Guatemala's long-term policy of keeping government very small, it comes as no surprise that the country presents an extreme case of under-investment in human capital.[12] Clearly, Guatemala is in dire need of additional revenues to spur human capital development.

Extremely low levels of government spending has been shown to have a neg-ative impact on human capital formation, which in turn is linked to slow eco-nomic growth (Rotberg 2001). For example, Goldin and Katz (2001) highlight the significance of the increase in secondary school enrollment in the United States between 1910 and 1940 as an essential ingredient in the growth of the economy in subsequent decades. Because of limited government revenues, so-cial spending is constrained. However, social spending in Guatemala amounted to 39.3 percent of total spending in 1997, a level far higher than the extreme cases of China and the Congo, and about on par with El Salvador. Yet, it is far lower than in other Latin American states. Consider Mexico, which has central government revenue of 12.8 percent of GNP but spends 50.1 percent of that on social services, or Argentina, which has revenue of 11.2 percent of GNP but spends 63.6 percent on social services. In fact, within Latin America, according to the World Bank data set, only El Salvador (at 37.7 percent) spends a smaller portion of its government revenue on social services, and the Dominican Re-public (at 41.5 percent) is the only other country, in addition to Guatemala and El Salvador, that spends less than 50 percent of its revenues on such services (World Bank 2000a, 2000c). There is, therefore, an evident interaction effect in Guatemala – extremely low government revenues combined with a relatively low proportion of the budget dedicated to social services, a combination that constrains human capital development.

An excessively small government makes it very difficult to achieve the goals set out in the peace process. Consider the problem of illiteracy. The propor-tion of the population that is illiterate has been declining in Guatemala since the baseline year of 1994, dropping from nearly 39 to 32 percent of the total population, but the national population has grown so rapidly that the *absolute* number of illiterates was nearly the same in 1999 as it was five years earlier (1994), or about 1.8 million adults (Ralón 1998: 28). For the absolute numbers to diminish in a population that from 1990 to 1999 was growing at an annual rate of 2.6 percent (World Bank 2001c: 278), the relative increases would have to be far steeper than they have been. It also should be stressed that more Guatemalan women are illiterate than men. According to the United Nations, 25.1 percent of Guatemalan males and 40.3 percent of females could not read or write in 1998 (UNDP 2000: 163). Among the indigenous population,

---

[12] Guatemala, like the other countries in Central America, is a unitary system of government. Local government income as a proportion of total income is very small, only 2.1 percent in 1996 (Gutiérrez Saxe 1999: 237), and 1.7 percent in 1997 (World Bank 2000c: 216).

illiteracy was 72 percent in 1995 (World Bank 2000a: 33). Solving the illiteracy problem would be neither technically complex nor costly. An investment of $4.4 million annually between 1999 and 2006, or 0.8 percent of Guatemala's total education budget for the year 2000 (World Bank 2000a: Statistical Appendix Table 5), would produce an absolute decline in the number of illiterates from 1.8 million to 1.5 million (still 22 percent of its projected population in the year 2006). Yet, given the anemic financial capabilities of the state, even such a modest reduction in the number of illiterates remains an elusive goal.

An examination of public health conditions produces similar findings. Maternal mortality per 100,000 live births was 190 in 1998, greater than that of Vietnam (160 per 100,000), a country with a PPP GNP half that of Guatemala (UNDP 2000: 188). Intestinal parasites, a set of diseases that are virtually entirely a function of poor public water and sanitation facilities, account for 28 percent of all morbidity (Ministerio de Salud Pública y Asistencia Social 1997). Yet, total public health expenditures were only 1.3 percent of the total budget for the year 2000 (World Bank 2000a: Statistical Appendix Table 6). Amazingly, even this small budget was systematically *underspent;* in the second half of the 1990s, public health budget expenditures for preventive measures never exceeded 58 percent of the budgeted amount (Ministerio de Salud Pública y Asistencia Social 1997).

In its fiscal situation, Guatemala today is caught between a rock and a hard place. It is a country that historically has constrained government to a minimal role, especially in social services. The negative impact of these policies is evident in its underdeveloped human capital. The peace accords commit Guatemala to overcoming its legacy of underinvestment in human capital, but to do so it will have to make substantial increases in the national budget because reallocation within an inadequate budget would be of only limited utility. Increasing the national budget implies raising taxes, greater indebtedness, or both – all policies that are anathema to most powerful political elites in Guatemala, yet that is precisely what the peace accords require. How, then, can Guatemala both invest in its population and remain within the fiscal boundaries imposed by neoliberalism, and still adhere to the accords? This challenge will not be easy to overcome.

The Expansion of Ethnic Rights While Increasing Intraethnic Conflict

Barrington Moore (1966: 480), in his classic work on the social origins of democracy and dictatorship, found that while peasants provide "the dynamite to bring down the old building," they are also inevitably "its first victims." In Guatemala, it was indeed the peasants, especially indigenous peasants, who were the first victims, but ironically they did not bring down the old order and may not even have had much to do with providing the social dynamite. David Stoll (1993) makes it clear that for the "Ixil Triangle," one of the most violent regions involved in the conflict, revolutionary elements were not centrally or perhaps even marginally drawn from the indigenous populations of Guatemala.

Rather, external elements implanted themselves in heavily indigenous areas, and the military, seeking to employ the counterinsurgency doctrine of removing the "water" from the "fish," attacked indigenous populations mercilessly (Seligson 1996). Research on the origins of the guerrilla war in Guatemala suggests that it began in the early 1960s with a secret military club to protest corruption within the military. The group attracted student leaders and attempted to implement Ché Guevara's *foco* strategy of guerrilla warfare (Landau 1993). Indians, for the most part, were far removed from these activities.

The war, while doing enormous physical damage to Guatemala's indigenous populations, also served to spark a sense of "Mayan" ethnic identity. When I first traveled to Guatemala in the 1960s, Indians identified themselves by their language and territory, but by the 1980s the term "Maya" was being used by some Indians to identify themselves. Anthropologists have long debated the meaning of ethnicity and the mechanism by which it is formed (Wilson 1995: 3–19), but all observers agree that Mayan activism has exploded in recent years in Guatemala. As Fischer and McKenna Brown (1996: 1) note, many terms have been used to characterize the new phenomenon, including "Mayan nationalism," "the Pan-Maya movement," and the "Maya revitalization movement," but they all refer to a new form of identity that has sprung up in the highlands of Guatemala.

The long war, largely fought at the cost of the indigenous population, helped to catalyze this sense of ethnic identity, but the peace process itself, which was often couched in terms of a struggle for indigenous rights, was perhaps even more central. Important role models emerged, not only the best-known one of Rigoberta Menchú but also local political leaders as well as national deputies. The widening use of "civic committees" at the municipal level, which enabled local party-like structures to form and to run candidates for office at both the municipal and deputy level, further spurred this identification. Kay Warren, an astute observer of this process, stresses the international dimension to this ethnic awakening (1998: 4):

Quite unexpectedly, the peace process brought about a striking transformation in the terms of debate for indigenous issues in national politics. Most recently, Pan-Mayanism has experienced the contradictory pressures of international funders who in the name of neoliberalism pressure the government to trim bureaucracies and social services and in the name of peace offer very specific kinds of support for the strengthening of civil society and democracy.

Warren also realizes that ethnic mobilization often produces serious "side effects." She notes: "At the center of many observers' reservations about ethnic mobilizing are two expressed fears: that calls for self-determination inexorably lead to the destructive breakup of existing states and that ethnic violence is the sign of our times" (Warren 1998: 5). Ethnic resurgence can, of course, have a positive impact on democratization, helping to overcome a long history of exclusionary politics and empowering ethnic groups who are in the political minority (even if they represent a numerical majority, as they come close to doing in Guatemala).[13] This is the argument made forcefully by Yashar (1996) in a study of ethnicity and democratization.

The strongest concern is that Guatemala's transition to democracy might ultimately be responsible for widespread ethnic-based violence, perhaps concentrated on ethnic rivalries between subdivisions of the Mayan population or even spilling over into Maya–*ladino* conflicts. It is now well established in the political science literature that unconsolidated democracies are most prone to civil conflicts (Hegre et al. 2001). In a broad-ranging theoretical and empirical study of the subject, Jack Snyder (2000:15) points to the fundamental paradox between "the claim that promoting the spread of democracy would also promote peace" and the fact that "rocky transitions to democracy often give rise to warlike nationalism and violent ethnic conflicts."[14] Certainly, the breakup of the former in postcommunist Yugoslavia, in which elected officials inspired and directed brutal ethnic conflicts that emerged, is a good example. Although Gurr and Moore (1997) show that, in transitions resulting in (what might be considered) consolidated democracies, the rights of ethnic minorities have been closely protected, the record in countries such as Guatemala, where major problems remain after the cessation of open warfare, is not as good. Some of the cases that Snyder mentions are ethnic groups in the former Yugoslavia, the Armenians in Azerbaijan, the Chechens in Russia, and the horror story of the 1993 conflict between Hutus and Tutsis in Burundi.[15] For Snyder (2000: 32), the process of democratization itself increases nationalist and ethnic appeals, as it has in Guatemala.

What do Guatemalans think about the prospect for ethnic conflict? We asked them directly in the 1999 survey carried out by the University of Pittsburgh: "How probable do you think it is that Guatemala will have an ethnic conflict in the future?" Of the 83 percent of the sample who responded to this question, 28.5 percent felt that such ethnic conflict was "very probable," 33.1 percent felt that it was somewhat probable, while 38.5 percent thought that it was not probable. In other words, only a minority rejects the possibility of ethnic conflict, while 62 percent believed that such conflict could occur. These percentages

---

[13] Warren (1998: 8, 12) claims that Guatemala has an indigenous majority of about 60 percent, the second largest indigenous proportion in Latin America. However, the Guatemalan census data from 1994 (the most recent census available) puts the figure far lower, at 43 percent. For much of Guatemala's history, the census taker decided the ethnic group of the respondent. In recent years, however, self-identification has been the norm. I find self-identification to be the most useful, since in survey work, this variable, rather than language or dress, seems the best way to distinguish relevant groupings in Guatemala. In the surveys I have conducted in Guatemala, self-identification produces results in the 41–45 percent range, nowhere near the claimed 60 percent. Yet, this percentage is high in comparative terms. In Bolivia, a country widely acknowledged to have an indigenous majority, only 13 percent of respondents in the University of Pittsburgh Latin American Public Opinion Project identify themselves as indigenous, and only 3 percent, as *cholos*.

[14] On the other hand, Cleary (2000) argues that democracy results in decreased instances of ethnic rebellion in Latin America, although he does not address the issue of intraethnic conflict.

[15] A list of all such conflicts in the period 1945–99 appears in Snyder (2000: 355–60).

did not vary significantly by gender, education, wealth, or ethnicity (Seligson et al. 2000).

We must keep in mind, however, that in Guatemala while some anthropologists and NGOs dedicated to promoting pan-Mayanism see the Indian population as all one big family of "Mayans," many if not most Indians still are more firmly tied to their own far smaller ethnic group, defined largely by language. There are twenty-eight Mayan languages, and several other non-Mayan languages. Has the withdrawal of threats of military/guerrilla violence led to an increase in tensions among these different groupings? It is difficult to say, but one disturbing piece of evidence of incipient growing violence among the indigenous population in Guatemala has been the emergence of what Guatemalans call "lynchings." While these so-called lynchings are not usually murders by hanging, as has happened so often in the United States, they do involve vigilante actions that frequently end in single or multiple deaths, often by immolation or mob beatings. In a recent study of the phenomenon by MINUGUA, the organization monitoring the UN peace accords, the first systematically recorded cases began in 1996, perhaps not coincidentally the year the final peace accords were signed (MINUGUA 2000: 6). There had been some prior instances of lynchings, especially one infamous case of a North American woman accused of attempting to steal a child, but these were clearly isolated instances and not part of the wave that emerged in 1996.

According to MINUGUA, between 1996 and 2000, there were no fewer than 337 recorded cases of lynchings, averaging well over one a week. Of those cases, with a total of 635 victims, 187 of the victims died (see Table 7.2). The actual pace of lynchings has accelerated since the peace began, going from only 35 cases in 1996 to 105 in 1999, but then it seemed to decline in 2000, the last year for which data are available.

Unfortunately, MINUGUA has not documented the ethnicity of the perpetrators or the victims. Hence we do not know if these lynchings are conflicts entirely confined within ethnic groupings or if they cross ethnic lines. Even if we had that data, we would not know about clan-level violence that proved so critical in the slaughter in the Ethiopia–Eritrea conflict. All we do know is that lynchings are not only becoming a way of life in Guatemala, but they

TABLE 7.2. *Lynchings in Guatemala, 1996–2000*

Year	Lynchings	Lynching Attempts	Total Lynching	Persons Murdered	Persons Wounded	Total Victims
1996	21	14	35	23	24	47
1997	22	56	78	30	80	110
1998	38	29	67	54	73	127
1999	71	34	105	48	188	236
2000	24	28	52	32	83	115
Totals	176	161	337	187	448	635

Source: MINUGUA (2000: 6).

have widespread popular support. In the 1999 University of Pittsburgh survey mentioned previously, Guatemalans were asked about their support for vigilante justice. The question read: "In various communities, suspected criminals have been lynched. Some say that when the authorities do not fulfill their responsibilities the people can take justice into their own hands, while others say that these means should not be resorted to. With which view are you more in agreement?" Nearly one third of the respondents see the lynching of suspected criminals to be an acceptable form of "justice." While 36 percent of the *ladino* population, excluding the nonrespondents from the results, approve of lynchings, 41 percent of the self-identified indigenous population approve, a difference that, while not statistically significant, shows the broad support for the phenomenon across the ethnic divide in Guatemala.

In March 2001 a radical change occurred in the pattern of lynchings. Up until that time, all victims were alleged criminals, but on March 13 a mob murdered a *ladino* judge in Alta Verapaz, a department whose population is 89 percent indigenous (World Bank 2000a: Statistical Appendix Table 39). It is too early to tell whether this case represents a new trend of *ladino*–indigenous conflict, but such an action against a quintessential representative of state authority is certainly a new and ominous development for democracy, indicating a breakdown in respect for the official legal authorities.

My data analysis suggests that these lynchings have occurred all over the country, but they are especially heavily concentrated in the highly indigenous areas of the *zonapaz*, that is, the former zone of military conflict. Observers have gone to great lengths to negate this connection. MINUGUA (2000: 7) notes, for example, that while many of the lynchings have taken place in highly indigenous departments, a large number have also taken place in the Department of Guatemala, which is highly *ladino*. The UN did not, however, per capitize the data, perhaps forgetting that the Department of Guatemala has a far larger population than other departments. If that is done, a very clear pattern linking the lynchings to concentrations of indigenous populations emerges, as is shown in Figure 7.2. The Department of Guatemala, for example, has a very low per capita number of lynching victims and a low percentage of indigenous people. The percent indigenous in the department explains 49 percent of the variance in the lynchings. Put in other terms, the regression shows that for each 10 percent increase in the indigenous population, lynching victims increase by 3 per 100,000, an important figure when the national murder rate is about 50 per 100,000. Only El Petén is not well predicted by this model, having a lynching rate far higher than its percentage of indigenous persons would predict. Yet, the ethnic data, which are based on the 1994 population census, probably miss the mark for this department far more than others because of the very large migration of indigenous populations to the Petén in recent years. Indeed, it is these very areas in which major land-based conflicts have broken out between the newcomers and residents of longer duration, a factor that may be in part responsible for the lynchings. The United Nations argues that the lynchings are directly linked to the now largely demobilized civil defense patrols set up by

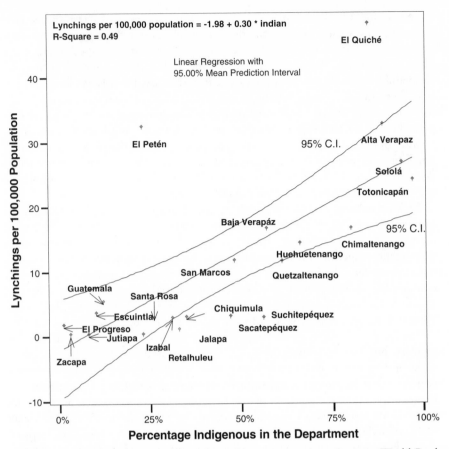

FIGURE 7.2. Indigenous Population and Lynchings, 1996–2000. Sources: World Bank (2001b), MINUGUA (2000).

the military during the insurgency as an auxiliary branch of the armed services. However, because these patrols were most commonly established in indigenous areas, it is very difficult to separate the impact of ethnicity from the impact of the civilian defense patrols as a causal factor in the lynchings. In effect, there is a problem of multicollinearity that cannot be corrected because the two variables, ethnic identification and the presence of civil patrols, are highly associated with each other. What we know from the analysis presented in Figure 7.2 is that high concentrations of indigenous populations are strongly associated with a high frequency of lynchings, which does not bode well for a deepening of democracy in Guatemala.

The Paradox of Winning the War but Losing the Peace

Closely related to the potential for violent ethnic conflict is the growing nationwide problem of crime in Guatemala. There is historical evidence from

Europe that increased crime threatens the survival of democracy. Many theories have been advanced to explain the breakdowns of half of Europe's parliamentary democracies between 1920 and 1938, with economic crisis cited most frequently as the cause. Most familiar is the argument that Germany's democracy broke down because of the extreme inflation suffered prior to the election of Hitler. Nancy Bermeo (1999: 1) shows, however, that this explanation simply does not work because the democracies that survived in Europe in the 1930s suffered no less economically than those that broke down. Bermeo's important insight is that what clearly distinguishes the surviving democracies from those that collapsed is the crime rate. Her data show that in democracies that broke down, homicides occurred at three times the rate of the surviving democracies. Others who support this view have also studied the German case and argue persuasively that voters who brought Hitler to power believed that they were supporting a "law and order" candidate (Altemeyer 1996: 91).

If Bermeo is correct in arguing that social disorder in the form of crime is a significant factor driving voters to support authoritarian solutions, and thus is a cause of the ultimate breakdown of democracy, then Latin America is a good place to test the thesis. Taking homicide rates, which are usually considered to be the most reliable indicator of crime since few murders go unreported, in Bermeo's interwar data set, the homicide rate for the countries in which democracy broke down averaged 7 per 100,000 population. By contrast, researchers estimate that the annual homicide rate in Latin America is 30 murders per 100,000 persons, whereas it is now about 7 in the United States and about 2 in the United Kingdom, Spain, and Switzerland.[16] This means that there are 140,000 homicides each year in the region. According to Gaviria and Pagés (1999), not only are homicide rates consistently higher in Latin America, but also the differences with the rest of the world are growing larger. Using 1970–94 data from the United Nations World Crime Surveys, Fajnzylber, Loayza, and Lederman (1998) find that Latin America and the Caribbean nations have the world's highest homicide rates, followed by sub-Saharan African countries.[17] According to this and other indicators, violence in Latin America is five times higher than in other places in the world.

---

[16] The Pan American Health Organization reports a lower average murder rate for Latin America as a whole of 20 per 100,000 people. According to the United Nations Global Report on Crime (United Nations 1999: 12–13), health statistics as a basis for measuring homicide significantly underreport the total homicide level because they are based on the classification of deaths made by physicians rather than by the police. Health-based homicide rates average about half those of Interpol or UN statistics (Pan American Health Organization press release, July 17, 1997. *www.paho.org/english/DPI/rl970717.htm*).

[17] Thirty-four countries are included in the study described in Fajnzylber et al. 1998. The Latin American and Caribbean countries included are Mexico, Colombia, Brazil, Venezuela, Ecuador, Uruguay, Argentina, Chile, Peru, Bahamas, Jamaica, Nicaragua, Barbados, Costa Rica, Trinidad and Tobago, Bermuda, Suriname, Honduras, Antigua, Dominica, Belize, Panama, Guyana, Cuba, and El Salvador.

If Latin America is a good place to study the chilling impact of violent crime on support for democracy, Guatemala is an ideal case. According to the Centro de Investigaciones Económicas Nacionales (CIEN 1999), the national violent death rate for 1996 was calculated at 58.68 per 100,000 inhabitants. That is a level *eight times* higher than in the European democracies that broke down in the 1920s and 1930s and fifty times higher than in the ones that survived. These violent deaths include deaths caused by guns, knives, or other causes (Seligson and Azpuru 1999). These rates of homicide are high even in the far longer historical international perspective provided by Ted Robert Gurr's (1981: 306) classic study. In that study, one has to go back to fourteenth-century London, at a time prior to the establishment of regular police forces, to find historical homicide rates as high as found in contemporary Guatemala.[18] According to Kincaid, "Some 60 gangs were operating in Guatemala City in mid-1998; among them were several chapters of the largest Salvadoran gang, Salvatruchas" (2000: 49). The Inter-American Development Bank reports that in Guatemala crime victimization is higher than in any other country in Latin America, with El Salvador in second place (IDB 2000b:13).

The growing fear of crime has placed in jeopardy what was perhaps one of the most important reforms agreed to in the peace accords, and that is limiting the army to defending the nation from external attack. Using the army for internal security purposes has been one of the most important impediments to democratization in Latin America for many decades (Loveman 1993, 1999; Loveman and Davies 1997). Such a restricted role for the Guatemalan military, as specified by the peace accords, conflicted with the 1985 Constitution, as amended in 1993, which itself had been drawn up by the military regime. That Constitution defined the military's mission to include an internal security role (Kincaid 2000: 47). Specifically, the Constitution states in Article 244: "The Army of Guatemala is an institution dedicated to maintaining the independence, sovereignty, and honor of Guatemala, its territorial integrity, peace, and internal and external security." Because the constitutional reform was defeated in the national referendum referred to earlier, the military still retains its dual role. The reform would have made two key changes in the role of the military. First, the following language would have been inserted in Article 244: "The Army of Guatemala is an institution permanently at the service of the State." Second, "It has the function of defending the sovereignty of the state, its territorial integrity, and its external security."

Although key military counterinsurgency bases were to have been closed, some have remained open in order to facilitate the military's internal policing function, which it still retains. About one third of the army, Kincaid (2000) estimates, serve in police roles. Moreover, the great bulk of the members of the "new" civilian police force are merely recycled members of the outlawed National Treasury Police. This is a clear signal that the "civilian" police force mandated by the peace accords involved changing insignias and uniforms,

---

[18] Gurr (1981) reports a rate for the first half of the fourteenth century as somewhere between 36 and 52 per 100,000.

but little else. Yet, public support for the military's role in fighting crime is overwhelming: 79 percent of the population in the 1999 University of Pittsburgh survey supported this role (Seligson et al. 2000).

Another item in the University of Pittsburgh Latin American Public Opinion Project gives further reasons to be concerned with crime and its threat to democracy in Guatemala. In response to the question, "Do you think that in our country what is needed is a strong-hand government [*gobierno de mano dura*] or do you think that the problems can be resolved by the participation of everyone?" (which was asked in national samples in 1993, 1995, 1997, and 1999), there was more support for strong-hand rule than for popular participation in politics (48 versus 40 percent, the rest "don't know"). Moreover, support for strong-hand rule was very stable from 1993 through 1997, but then it increased significantly in 1999 (to 60 percent) (Seligson et al. 2000). This increase occurred in the context of a presidential campaign in which law and order became a central issue. The victor in that campaign not only advocated a tough stand on crime but also admitted to personally having killed two men in self-defense some years earlier while in Mexico. Pollsters claimed that this incident provided a "macho" image for the candidate, one whom voters could trust to be "tough on crime."

This finding is reinforced by responses to another item that was used for the first time in the 1999 survey. Respondents were asked: "What do you think is better: To live in an orderly society, even though some liberties are limited, or respect all of the rights and liberties, even if this causes some disorder?" For the national sample as a whole, 70 percent of the respondents preferred order to rights. Further analysis of the data finds that these preferences are linked, as one would suspect, to education, with the less well educated being more likely to be willing sacrifice rights for order than the better educated. What is surprising is that even among the university-educated portion of the sample (only 7 percent of the respondents had some education beyond high school), nearly two thirds of them would be willing to sacrifice liberty for order (Seligson et al. 2000). We do not know the level of crime in contemporary Latin America that might cause citizens to demand that the military take over. Indeed, we do not know if there is any level of crime that would cause this to happen. Yet, the evidence presented earlier, while not suggesting that democracy in the form of regular competitive elections would be overthrown in Guatemala, does suggest that high levels of crime could stimulate support for restrictions on civil liberties. Might governments get into the habit of restricting democracy in order to deal with crime? If the answer is "yes," the future of democracy in Guatemala is grim indeed.

The Difficulty of Building Institutional Democracy Unsupported by a Democratic Political Culture

Guatemala's peace accords attempted to construct the institutional basis for democratic consolidation. Dahl, in his classic book on polyarchy (1971), argued forcefully that institutions alone are not enough to ensure a democratic

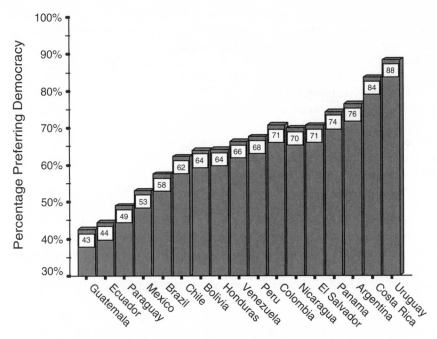

FIGURE 7.3. Preference for Democracy: Guatemala in Comparative Perspective.

outcome. Only when citizens of a nation embrace democratic values can democracy survive and prosper. Looking at the data for Guatemala, there is reason to be concerned. In the 1997 Latinobarómetro, a question asked respondents to select among three alternatives: (1) "Democracy is preferable to any other form of government;" (2) "Under certain circumstances, a dictatorship is preferable to democracy;" (3) "For people like me, a democratic or a nondemocratic regime are the same;" or (4) "Don't know" (Latinobarómetro 1997).

The bars in Figure 7.3 represent those who chose the *democracy* response, and the rest chose between the other responses (i.e., a preference for authoritarianism, indifference, or don't know). As is clear from this comparison, Guatemala scores at the bottom in Latin America.[19] When the identical question was asked in the 1999 University of Pittsburgh survey of Guatemala, the results were virtually identical, with only 43.5 percent of respondents preferring democracy. Among those with the lowest level of education, just over one third of the respondents prefer democracy, and among those with primary or less education,

[19] Unfortunately, the Latinobarómetro suffers from a number of problems in sample design that vary from country to country. The results presented here are based on weighted results that attempt to correct for the serious overrepresentation of highly educated respondents in many countries. If those corrections are made, the series is more homogenous in design than the original database. The Latin Barometer results for other years show fluctuation in these results, but as the raw data are not publicly available for those years, we cannot make the appropriate weighting adjustments and draw any conclusions from them.

who comprise 74 percent of the sample, only two fifths support it. Only among the tiny minority of Guatemalans with at least some university education is there a strong preference for democracy over authoritarianism (Seligson et al. 2000).

One might hope that as democracy takes hold in Guatemala, there will be an increase in support for it. Yet, analysis of the data reveals that *younger* Guatemalans are no more likely to support democracy than older Guatemalans. Perhaps this is because so many young people have not experienced the full impact of the repressive period, or perhaps they are more seriously affected by problems of low income, unemployment, and crime that have accompanied democratization. Whatever the reasons, the young are not the hope for the future in terms of support for Guatemala's democracy. Guatemalan democracy has been weakened by low levels of political participation. Citizens have been able to go to the polls regularly and choose candidates for both local and national office for fifteen years, and since the signing of the peace agreements, their choices have included representatives of the former guerrilla groups. Nonetheless, voter turnout in Guatemala, which historically has been low (Boneo and Torres-Rivas 2000: 2), remains among the very lowest in Latin America (IDB 2000b: 178). Other forms of political participation, such as paying attention to political news, rank second lowest in the region (IDB 2000b). Table 7.3 shows the long-term trends in voting in Guatemala. It is notable that in the most

TABLE 7.3. *Voter Turnout in Guatemala for Presidential Elections, 1950–1999*

Year	Vote as Percentage of Registered Voters	Vote as Percentage of Voting-Age Population
1950	71.5	30.4
1954	69.5	32.5
1958	66.8	28.3
1959	44.6	18.0
1961	44.5	19.0
1966	55.0	23.7
1970	53.3	25.9
1974	46.4	25.5
1978	40.0	22.9
1982	45.6	30.6
1985	69.3[a]	49.9
1990	56.4	43.8[b]
1995	46.7	33.3
1999	53.8	44.0

[a] First-round results.

[b] The main source for this table seems to be in error (with a significant underestimate) for these data points, so results from Córdova Macías (2001) are substituted.

Source: Boneo and Torres-Rivas (2000: 2); Córdova Macías (2001).

recent two elections there has been a substantial increase in turnout, which is certainly a positive sign, indicating greater citizen involvement, at least in elections. One wonders if this trend will continue. It is well known that institutional/structural factors such as whether elections are held on a weekday or a weekend, and whether or not voting is compulsory, heavily influence voting turnout. More recently, a study by IDEA (1997) found a very strong linear association between government expenditure as a percentage of GNP and voter turnout, and Guatemala ranks the lowest on both measures in Latin America. Thus, the macro-level problems I have identified earlier seem to have other adverse effects on democracy. But the impact of low government spending is not limited to low turnout. In the 1999 University of Pittsburgh survey cited previously, there is a significant association between nonregistration and voting abstention, on the one hand, and lack of support for democracy, as measured by the three-choice question discussed earlier. So there is a vicious circle here, with low spending linked to low support for democracy, which in turn discourages democratic political participation in the form of voting.

GUATEMALAN DEMOCRACY: ADVANCES AND SETBACKS

Achieving democratization in Guatemala is going to be a long and difficult process. It is impossible to predict the ultimate outcome, yet when compared to the darkest days of the long period of repression, prospects for the future certainly look brighter. Today, elections are free, fair, and regular, and Guatemala is no longer laboring under the burdens of a protracted civil war. The peace agreements, in theory, at least, guarantee citizenship rights that were unthinkable only a decade earlier.

Yet, this chapter has emphasized the many and serious challenges to democracy that Guatemala is facing. It is clear from the analysis presented here that many of the fundamental elements of the peace agreements, aimed at breaking down the barriers to full participation by the indigenous population, by stimulating development of their human capital, have not been realized, and it is difficult to imagine how and when they could be achieved. The changes needed require a major reorientation of the political economy, one that would emphasize substantially increased investment in human capital, along with increased taxation. The prospects for such a reorientation seem dim indeed. Failures to implement key constitutional changes through the referendum process leave the role of the military unchanged, constitutionally allowing it to continue to play a role as a central player in maintaining domestic order.

Equally troubling are the issues of violence raised in the chapter. Democracy is a system of government with many strengths and weaknesses, but, for many observers, the "bottom line" is that democracies, unlike dictatorships, do not regularly kill their citizens. According to an extensive study carried out by Rummel (1994), worldwide some 170 million people were murdered by their governments for other than criminal acts during the period 1900–87, a number he calculates as five time higher than the number of deaths attributed to international or civil wars. The 170 million total includes some 40 million foreign civilians killed by governments. Excluding the killing of foreign civilians (e.g., the attempt to exterminate Jews by Nazi Germany) leaves a total of 130 million domestic civilians who were killed by their governments for political reasons from 1900 to 1987. Dictatorships and authoritarian governments were responsible for over 129 million of those deaths. The rest, 158,000 citizens, or 0.12 percent of the total, were murdered by democratic governments. Democratically elected governments thus have been extremely unlikely to exterminate their own citizens during the twentieth century, as they account for a minuscule 0.1 percent of the total number of citizens killed for political reasons by their government.

What we learn from Rummel's study is that while democracies do not kill their own citizens, Guatemalan democracy is allowing them to be killed by criminals or vigilante mobs. It appears that what has happened in Guatemala is that one kind of violence, largely carried out by the state, is being replaced by another that is being carried out by its citizens. The result is that physical security, a fundamental benefit of democracy, if not *the* fundamental benefit of democracy, is not being enjoyed by Guatemalans. Indeed, one could go further and argue that a fundamental benefit of states of any kind, since state organization first emerged on the global scene, is the physical protection of its citizens from violence, a feature that has been and remains sadly lacking in Guatemala, both during the decades of dictatorial rule and during its present period of electoral democracy.

Much of the future of Guatemala's democratic prospects will depend upon resolving the paradoxes I have enumerated. If social spending remains low, violence continues to be a serious threat (or becomes even worse), vigilante justice grows, and support for democracy remains low, the prospects are grim indeed. On the other hand, virtually no social scientist would have predicted in the 1980s that Guatemala would one day sign a peace treaty with the guerrillas and that the agreements would specify such a broad range of measures to help democratize the system. The problem remains, however, of turning those agreements into reality.

PART III

DEMOCRATIC EROSIONS IN THE THIRD WAVE

Colombia, Peru, and Venezuela

8

From "Restricted" to "Besieged"

The Changing Nature of the Limits to Democracy in Colombia

Ana María Bejarano and Eduardo Pizarro

Colombia's democracy has always been a democracy with adjectives.[1] Recently, references to its "controlled" or "restricted" nature have been replaced in the literature with descriptions of this democracy as "besieged" (Archer 1995) or "under assault" (Kline 1995). The shift in semantics is revealing. In this chapter, we argue that democracy in Colombia is still limited by a series of characteristics that merit the continued use of adjectives. Nevertheless, given that these limits have changed in nature, any adjectives used to characterize the current political regime in that country must be fundamentally different from those employed during the three decades spanning 1958 to 1991.

As Collier and Levitsky have pointed out (1997: 432), a good description is indispensable to evaluating the origins and consequences of any political regime. We have adopted the term "besieged"[2] to describe the current state of democracy in Colombia. While previous adjectives emphasized internal or endogenous limits on the political regime, this definition highlights exogenous factors – that is, external forces that make it difficult for democracy to function adequately. During the National Front period, democracy's limitations resulted from restrictions on political participation and political competition. In the present era, its limitations are rooted in the impact of various forces on democracy: the erosion of the state, the expansion of violence, and the rise of powerful extrainstitutional actors who constrain the space needed to consolidate a free democratic playing field.

A COMPLEX CLASSIFICATION

Colombia's government is a civilian one, and elections have been held at regular intervals with little interruption since Gran Colombia's dissolution in 1830.

---

[1] "Most analysts have viewed Colombia since 1958 as a qualified democracy, using adjectives such as 'controlled,' 'oligarchic,' 'traditional bipartisan elitist,' 'near polyarchy,' or 'restricted'" (Hartlyn and Dugas 1999: 251).

[2] Inspiration comes from the title of Ron Archer's article (1995).

The country's record of periodic elections that have brought civilian rulers to power (see Posada-Carbó 1996) has led to its repeated classification as a democracy. Yet, a closer look at current indicators reveals a number of paradoxes. True, elections are held on a regular basis – but candidates and elected politicians are also regularly assassinated. The press is free from state censorship, but journalists and academics are systematically murdered. Electoral authorities recognize a growing number of political parties and minorities have increasing participation in representative bodies. The constitution and the law explicitly address the opposition's rights and responsibilities. At the same time, the killings of opposition leaders multiply. For a century and a half, control of the state has been in civilian hands except for a few short and exceptional periods. Nevertheless, the military has retained a high degree of autonomy in matters of internal public order, as well as a series of prerogatives that place it above civilian control. The state claims that it alone can exercise legitimate use of force, while at the same time admitting its inability to contain one of the world's highest murder rates. Can this legitimately be called democracy?

In our opinion, it would be a misinterpretation to cross the border that separates democracies from nondemocracies and classify Colombia as an authoritarian regime. Instead, we adopt the three-part classification proposed by Mainwaring et al. (2001), which provides a clearer typology for borderline cases such as Colombia's. Based on quantitative indicators, Mainwaring (1999a), and Altman Olin and Pérez-Liñán (2002) show no hesitation in classifying Colombia as a semidemocracy since 1958,[3] with the exception of a short democratic period between 1974 and 1990 (see Mainwaring and Pérez-Liñán, this volume, and Table I.1).

These authors' quantitative data are useful for dating and describing important changes in political regimes that are generally classified as democratic. Yet, it is important not only to date and describe processes of change but also to understand their nature. It therefore seems worthwhile to point out that in the Colombian case, the nature of restrictions has changed from one semidemocratic period to another. Mainwaring (1999a), for example, correctly classifies the Colombian regime as "semi-democratic" in two different periods of its contemporary history.[4] The problem lies in the lack of differentiation between these two periods, which in our judgment seems critical. While the first period (1958–74) was fundamentally characterized by restrictions on competition resulting from the 1957 institutional pact, restrictions during the second period

---

[3] "A semi-democratic government or restricted democracy refers to a civilian government elected under reasonably fair conditions, but with significant restrictions in participation, competition and/or the observance of civil liberties" (Mainwaring 1999a: 14).

[4] His decision to classify the Colombian regime as "democratic" between 1974 and 1990 is somewhat questionable, given that many of the formal and informal restrictions put in place by the National Front were still in place after 1974 and were only abolished with the 1991 Constitution. Despite this, we basically agree with his classification of Colombia as semidemocratic during most of the second half of the twentieth century.

(1990–97) are related to the Colombian state's inability to guarantee basic civil rights and liberties.

Rather than unify in a single index the multiple dimensions that are critical to democracy, it seems best to consider each dimension separately in order to distinguish the nature of threats to, and limitations on, our democracies. The measurement approach offered by Freedom House[5] is an example that can be applied to the Colombian case. A careful look at Table 8.1 clearly shows that while the country's general rating has worsened notably since 1989–90, the deterioration of civil liberties has been more marked and sustained than that of political rights. In fact, the latter dimension presents variations that are difficult to interpret as a steadily worsening trend: There have been improvements after 1991 and irregular variations since 1994.

Among the alternative types proposed by Collier and Levitsky (1997), the subtype of "illiberal" democracy perhaps best defines the current situation of Colombian democracy. It alludes to the absence of a state capable of guaranteeing a constitutional order – that is, the absence of the rule of law, which makes the liberal dimension of modern democracy possible. Colombia's regime is a democracy whose faults are not to be located at the level of the typical dimensions of polyarchy (i.e., participation and opposition, according to Dahl, 1971), but whose main failure is related to the lack of the rule of law.[6] Based on the preceding discussion, we propose to reformulate the classification of Colombia's political regime during the twentieth century as follows (see Table 8.2).

The current state of Colombia's democracy can be conceived as a game being played simultaneously on two fields. There is an electoral field – where the rules of the democratic game are largely respected among legally recognized political actors – and an extrainstitutional field – where the rules of war rather than the rules of democracy apply, including the accumulation of instruments of force such as men, territory, and arms. The electoral game is in a way "suspended" over the field of extrainstitutional forces, which have a powerful impact on its outcome. This impact comes not only from the interconnections between institutional and extrainstitutional actors but also from the fact that the space available for the electoral game depends upon the expansion or contraction of the space designated for the second game: war. This is why we have adopted the metaphor of "besieged democracy."

---

[5] Given the difficulties of creating complex indices to measure the various dimensions of democracy, Mainwaring recommends using the data produced by Freedom House. Every year since 1972, Freedom House has assigned each country a grade between 1 (best) and 7 (worst) and measures its performance on two aspects: political rights and civil liberties. Although we agree with some of Munck and Verkuilen's criticisms (2002) of Freedom House's approach, such long-term series of data are difficult to find. For more information on Freedom House's methodology and sources, and for the conceptual distinction between political rights and civil liberties, see *http://freedomhouse.org*.

[6] The claim of liberal democracies to be such rests on their well-established and accessible procedures for protecting the liberties of individual citizens. (Alan Ware 1992, as cited in O'Donnell 1999a: n.16, 156).

TABLE 8.1. *Colombia: Freedom House Scores, 1972–2000*

Year	Political Rights	Civil Liberties	Combined Index[a]	Status[b]
1972–1973	2	2	4	F
1973–1974	2	2	4	F
1974–1975	2	2	4	F
1975–1976	2	3	5	F
1976–1977	2	3	5	F
1977–1978	2	3	5	F
1978–1979	2	3	5	F
1979–1980	2	3	5	F
1980–1981	2	3	5	F
1981–1982	2	3	5	F
1982–1983	2	3	5	F
1983–1984	2	3	5	F
1984–1985	2	3	5	F
1985–1986	2	3	5	F
1986–1987	2	3	5	F
1987–1988	2	3	5	F
1988–1989	2	3	5	F
1989–1990	3	4	7	PF
1990–1991	3	4	7	PF
1991–1992	2	4	6	PF
1992–1993	2	4	6	PF
1993–1994	2	4	6	PF
1994–1995	3	4	7	PF
1995–1996	4	4	8	PF
1996–1997	4	4	8	PF
1997–1998	4	4	8	PF
1998–1999	3	4	7	PF
1999–2000	4	4	8	PF

[a] Combining Freedom House's two measures in a single index, Mainwaring creates a scale that goes from 2 (best performance) to 14 (worst). Democracies are usually rated between 2 and 5; 7 corresponds to his category of semidemocratic governments; authoritarian regimes fall between 9 and 14; numbers 6 and 8 denote borderline cases with the former between democracy and semidemocracy and the latter between semidemocracy and authoritarianism (Mainwaring 1999a: 22).

[b] The designation of status as "free" (F), "partially free" (PF), or "not free" (NF) indicates the general degree of freedom in a country or territory.

Source: Mainwaring (1999a) and Freedom House.

"NOT ALL GOOD THINGS GO TOGETHER . . ."

Four attributes constitute the core of the contemporary consensus about democracy understood in procedural terms. These are (1) inclusion of the majority of the adult population through universal suffrage; (2) selection of top political leaders (president and parliament, at least) through competitive, free, clean, and regular elections; (3) respect for and effective protection of civil rights

TABLE 8.2. *Colombia: Regime Subtypes in the Twentieth Century*

Period	1910–1949	1949–1958	1958–1974 (1986)	1985–2000
Missing Attribute	Full suffrage	All	Full contestation	Civil liberties
Democratic Subtype	"Oligarchic" democracy[a]	None (authoritarian)	"Restricted" democracy[b]	"Besieged" (illiberal) democracy[c]

[a] The original concept is from Alexander Wilde (1982).
[b] The original concept is from Francisco Leal Buitrago (1984).
[c] The original concept is from Ronald Archer (1995).

and liberties; (4) the ability of elected authorities to govern without being subject to external controls or vetoes by nonelected actors (such as the military).[7] Nevertheless, as the Colombian case illustrates so well, the holding of competitive and fraud-free elections in which the whole adult population has the right to participate is not always accompanied by the other essential attributes of democracy. As suggested by the Freedom House data, it is conceivable that the various dimensions associated with democracy may evolve following variable rhythms and, sometimes, even in opposite directions. Consequently, it does not seem appropriate to speak of advances and setbacks of democracy as a whole because one case may present advances in some dimensions alongside setbacks in others. Even worse: efforts to improve some critical aspects of democracy (such as electoral reforms, for example) may have a negative impact on other crucial dimensions (such as governability).

Colombia has fulfilled the first of these attributes (universal suffrage) since the 1957 plebiscite, when women exercised the right to vote for the first time. The second attribute, which deals with the quality of the electoral process, suffered serious restrictions between 1958 and 1974, especially with regard to political competition. Since the National Front pacts not only excluded third parties but also limited competition between the two majority parties (Liberal and Conservative), the regime at the time has been correctly described as semicompetitive, restricted, or limited.[8] The situation between 1974 and 1986 is difficult to define with any precision, since the majority of formal restrictions were gradually lifted after the National Front period ended.[9] And yet, many informal restrictions remained – an inescapable legacy of the formal limits placed

---

[7] These four basic requirements condense the list proposed by Dahl (1971) and coincide with many contemporary definitions of liberal, representative, and procedural democracy (Collier and Levitsky 1997; Mainwaring 1999a; and Mainwaring et al. 2001).

[8] The best study of the period is Hartlyn (1988).

[9] Following the 1968 constitutional reform (which dismantled the National Front), restrictions on competition at the local level were lifted in 1970. Restrictions that limited competition in congressional and presidential elections were eliminated in 1974. The rule requiring partisan parity (power sharing) in the executive branch was formally extended until 1978 and practiced

on the democratic playing field. From 1986 onward (with the decision on the part of President Barco's government to put together an exclusively Liberal administration and the Conservatives' concomitant decision to oppose it as a party), the last of the remaining restrictions related to the composition of the executive branch fell away. Delegates to the 1991 Constituent Assembly legalized this situation, and the new constitution ratified that year finally eliminated all vestiges inherited from the National Front pacts.

Simultaneous to these political reforms, between 1989 and 1994, successful negotiations took place with five guerrilla movements – including the April 19 Movement (Movimiento 19 de Abril or M-19); the Revolutionary Workers' Party (Partido Revolucionario de los Trabajadores or PRT); the Quintín Lame Armed Movement (Movimiento Armado Quintín Lame or MAQL); the Socialist Renovation Current (Corriente de Renovación Socialista or CRS); and the Popular Liberation Army (Ejército Popular de Liberación or EPL).[10] As a result of these negotiations, some 4,000 excombatants were reincorporated into civilian life (Palacios 2000: 362).

Consequently, from the beginning of the 1990s, we can speak of the existence in Colombia of a democracy that – unambiguously – meets the first two requirements of any contemporary definition of democracy: broad participation and free competition.[11] From that time on, it is impossible to argue for this regime's classification as some subtype of authoritarianism. It seems best, instead, to classify it as a subtype (albeit "diminished") of democracy (see Collier and Levitsky 1997).

In spite of these advances, Colombia has not been able to achieve the consolidation of a full democracy. Despite efforts to incorporate armed rebels and to broaden the legal political space, the regime has deteriorated since the mid-1980s. Yet the nature of democracy's erosion during the most recent period is, as we have argued, fundamentally different from that experienced by the regime during the period that began with the National Front. The causes of the current situation are found primarily in the state's inability to guarantee civil rights and liberties effectively. If there is a crisis of democracy in Colombia, it is the result of the deterioration of the last two basic attributes of democracy rather than those related to political inclusion via elections.

---

informally thereafter for eight more years, until 1986. At the same time, the rule requiring partisan parity in judicial branch appointments remained in place until 1991 – that is, for thirty-three years.

[10] Only two guerrilla groups remain active – Fuerzas Armadas Revolucionarias de Colombia (Revolutionary Armed Forces of Colombia) or FARC (created in 1964), and Ejército de Liberacíon Nacional (National Liberation Army) or ELN (created in 1965).

[11] An era of political reform began during the Betancur government (1982–86) and ended with the writing of the new constitution. The "Basic Statute of Political Parties" (Law 58/1985) was approved in 1985; municipal reforms and the popular election of mayors were approved in 1986; and the 1991 Constitution eliminated all remaining restrictions, while broadening the channels and opportunities for political participation and competition. For a summary of party reforms, see Dugas (2000). For an evaluation of political reform, see Pizarro and Bejarano (2001). For the 1991 Constitution, see Dugas (1993), Gómez (2000), and Bejarano (2001).

Any discussion about the question of civil rights and liberties in Colombia must begin with a look at the country's gruesome human rights record, which demonstrates the state's growing inability to protect its citizens' lives, rights, and freedoms. "In Colombia, between October 1999 and March 2000, on average, nearly 14 persons were victims of sociopolitical violence every day. Of these, more than eight were victims of extra judicial executions and political homicides; close to one was forcibly disappeared; there was one homicide every two days committed against socially marginal persons; and more than four people died in combat each day" (Colombian Commission of Jurists 2000: 9). Between 1994 and 1998, the annual average number of homicides reached approximately 26,000. During the same period, 7,022 people were kidnapped. In addition, approximately 1,350,000 people were forcibly displaced between 1985 and 1998 (Zuluaga 1999: 50–53).

On the other hand, when speaking of the capacity of elected officials to govern effectively, we argue that Colombia does not deserve any of the adjectives usually applied to facade democracies – in which the military holds the real power over civilian puppets – such as "guarded" or "tutelary" democracy. The Colombian military has not occupied the political center stage for a number of reasons that will not be analyzed here.[12] Yet, even though the military has not obstructed the civilian government's ability to govern, since 1958 it has enjoyed a high degree of autonomy and an increasing number of prerogatives. Specifically, the Colombian military has enjoyed a great deal of latitude in defining policies for external defense and internal security, both of which have become critical given the situation of protracted internal conflict.

Rather than apply the term "tutelary democracy" to the Colombian case, we would rather employ Samuel Valenzuela's framework (1992), which highlights the military's "tutelary powers" and "reserved domains" as perverse elements impeding the consolidation of democracy. These prerogatives and reserved domains grew as the war expanded and the military's involvement in antidrug efforts increased (see Pizarro 1996b). The process became evident from 1977 onward[13] and continued without pause during the Turbay Ayala administration (1978–82). Efforts by the next three governments (1982–94) to subordinate the military were only partly successful and were greatly reversed during the Samper administration (1994–98).

As a result, two contradictory tendencies have been at work simultaneously in Colombia: a tendency toward greater democratization – with the elimination of prior restrictions and the broadening of the space for political participation and competition – as well as a tendency toward deterioration of the indicators

[12] The reasons include the history of state and party formation in the nineteenth century. For more on the Colombian military, see Leal Buitrago (1984) and Dávila (1998).

[13] This date marks a breaking point in the country's recent history. In September 1977, organized labor led a broad movement of social protest that culminated with a nationwide general strike. Reacting to the mobilization, the military sent a memorandum to President López Michelsen asking for a "strong hand" against social unrest. The state's harsh response became evident during the Turbay administration (1978–82), which issued the Security Statute.

of "civility," of respect and protection of basic citizens' rights and liberties,[14] and of civilian control of the military. That said (and despite our argument that the central problems of Colombian democracy relate to accountability and civil rights and liberties), we also realize that the second tendency has a negative impact on the components of participation and competition that are typical in any democracy. Neither competition nor participation can be complete in a context of widespread-armed conflict, as is the case in Colombia. Even though massive electoral fraud does not exist, distortions in the electoral process – especially at the local and regional levels – are very serious. Since the end of the 1980s, and especially since the first popular election of mayors in 1988, local and regional elections have been increasingly subject to limitations on competition resulting from the actions of different types of armed actors who seek to capture and control territory and population.[15] Numerous Colombian government officials have been assassinated following their election. According to Echandía (1999a), between 1989 and 1999, 138 mayors and 569 members of either parliament, departmental assemblies, or city councils were assassinated, along with 174 public officials in other positions. Simultaneously, the electorate's ability to vote "freely" (i.e., free from fear and/or coercion) has also decreased as the areas controlled by one armed actor or another have expanded – and above all, in those areas where armed actors compete bitterly for the control of territory and people. Violence distorts democracy's participatory and competitive dimensions, both before and after elections.

It is difficult to pinpoint an exact date or specific event that marked the beginning of this contradictory process of democratic erosion. In contrast with other cases where an attempted military coup, popular insurrection, or some other major event led to a crisis, Colombia has witnessed a process of gradual erosion, rather than a sudden breakdown of democracy.[16] The process began in the mid-to-late 1980s, although some prefer to date its origins to late 1989, early 1990.[17] In Coppedge and Reinecke's analysis of the year 1985, Colombia

---

[14] Just as some (e.g., Hershberg 1999: 292) argue that the exercise of citizenship is incomplete or impractical when there is socioeconomic exclusion or inequality, we would argue that there is a fundamental dimension of citizenship that has not been adequately considered, which is mostly related to its juridical or normative component, and is defined as the universal access to certain basic rights (such as the right to life, to physical integrity, and to safety), regardless of the distribution of socioeconomic rights and opportunities.

[15] It would be worthwhile to classify Colombian municipalities according to Oquist's methodology (1978), who distinguished those municipalities where a single party was hegemonic or in control from those that experienced real two-party competition between 1930 and 1946. The big difference is that control and hegemony today are in the hands of armed actors – rather than in those of the two traditional parties. In fact, the struggle for control among armed actors has greatly diminished the space for democratic political competition, particularly at the local level.

[16] As Mainwaring (1999a: 37) points out, it is important to distinguish between the processes of breakdown and the erosion of democracy. The Colombian case is very clearly one of gradual erosion, or "slow death" of democracy (O'Donnell 1992) and not one of an unexpected return to authoritarianism.

[17] Between August 1989 and April 1990, three presidential candidates were assassinated. Among these was the Liberal candidate with the greatest chance of becoming president: Luis Carlos

is classified as a democracy (1990: 63). Some years later, Mainwairing classified Colombia as a "semi-democracy," marking the turning point at 1990 (1999a: 16). Freedom House's data indicates that the passage from "free" to "partially free" status took place between 1989 and 1990. In Hartlyn and Dugas's judgment (1999), the period of crisis began in the mid-1980s, with some ultimately failed attempts at recuperation in the early 1990s. After two decades of steady deterioration, perhaps the most surprising aspect of the Colombian case is not the fact that its democracy is in crisis but rather the fact that it has survived, given the very formidable political – rather than structural or economic – challenges confronting it.

EXPLAINING THE EROSION OF COLOMBIAN DEMOCRACY

In his article "Democratic Survivability in Latin America," Mainwaring (1999a) argues that three factors help explain the vicissitudes of democracy in Latin America, including the scope and duration of the last wave of democratization in the region (1999a: 12). The first factor relates to the transformations unleashed by modernization. Structural changes related to urbanization, expanded literacy, the growth of the working and middle classes, and the reduction of the land-owning class's power constitute fertile ground for the growth of more democratic forms of government. Mainwaring's second factor, democracy's increasing international support, has also contributed to the emergence and durability of democratic regimes in Latin America and elsewhere.

He also argues that a third factor favoring democracy since the 1980s is related to changes in the political attitudes of actors placed both on the right and the left of the political spectrum. Democracy became more valued, and the political environment less polarized than it had been in the sixties and seventies (1999a: 12). To support his thesis, Mainwaring documents an important change in attitudes toward democracy, especially among leftist political actors throughout the region (1999a: 42–43). It is perhaps here that Colombia has distanced itself radically from the rest of the region. In the Colombian case, five guerrilla groups were reincorporated into civil society between 1990 and 1994, but notably, two groups remained active: Fuerzas Armadas Revolucionarias de Colombia (the Revolutionary Armed Forces of Colombia or FARC) and the Ejército de Liberación Nacional (National Liberation Army or ELN). Far from changing their views of democracy and revolution, these two groups deepened the more radical aspects of their discourse and their perception of reality. This radicalization not only robbed the moderate, legal left of political space but also produced an equally extreme radicalization of the right, which was channeled not through a legal political party but through multiple "paramilitary"

Galán. After his assassination, apparently planned by the drug-mafia, the Barco government unleashed a major offensive against drug trafficking (the "war on drugs"). This in turn led to a bloody wave of "narcoterrorism" against the Colombian government and society.

groups. Consequently, this factor, which has favored democracy's survivability in the rest of Latin America, has evolved in the opposite direction in Colombia.

Of the three factors cited by Mainwaring (1999a), the first (economic modernization) and the second (international factors) serve to explain the resilience of Colombia's democracy despite the twin threats of guerrilla warfare and violence from the right. The third factor (attitudes of political actors) may count, instead, as one of the possible causes explaining its erosion. Increasing ideological polarization has had a negative impact on the political regime. Yet, this factor alone seems insufficient to explain the regime's dramatic erosion and its failure to meet some of the fundamental requirements of any democracy.

Some authors have sought to explain the erosion of Colombia's democracy with cultural arguments. Not many have volunteered macroeconomic explanations because it is obvious that the Colombian political crisis is the cause, rather than the consequence, of the recent economic crisis. Others have insisted on highlighting inequality and poverty as structural impediments to democracy. Still others have blamed the drug trade and its effects as the cause of all ills. Without discounting the multifaceted nature of the current crisis, we would like to propose a fundamentally political explanation that is based upon a set of variables related to both the regime and the state. The first set of variables highlights the defects, vacuums, and institutional distortions inherent in the political regime. The second set focuses on aspects associated with the state, emphasizing its historic weakness, its recent erosion, and its partial collapse.

The Crumbling of the System of Political Representation

From its beginnings in 1958, critics decried the bipartisan institutional arrangement of the National Front as being antidemocratic. Alfonso López Michelsen, one of the first to criticize the National Front pacts, founded a dissident faction of the Liberal Party (the Liberal Revolutionary Movement or Movimiento Revolucionario Liberal, MRL), based on his opposition to the rules of the game imposed by the pacts enshrined by the 1957 plebiscite and Legislative Act No. 1 of 1959. The communist left was at first ambivalent but quickly became very critical of the restrictions that grew out of the agreement, in particular of the exclusion of third parties from political competition. As a result of the electoral fraud allegedly committed against the National Popular Alliance (Alianza Nacional Popular; ANAPO) in the 1970 elections, criticism of the National Front's institutional arrangement became more radical. Many joined the ranks of the armed left with the argument that they had been excluded from access to the state through the established institutional channels.[18]

---

[18] Although all guerrilla groups fed upon this radicalization of the anti–National Front critique, the M-19 (which took its name from the 1970 electoral fraud) was the clearest representative of this segment of the left – opposing the antidemocratic restrictions of the institutional pacts and speaking out in favor of a democratic opening.

Throughout the 1970s and 1980s, social scientists made this critique of the restrictions on government their own.[19] Reforming the regime became a shared cause among leftists, intellectuals, and reformist politicians. Many diagnoses of Colombia's democratic crisis and armed conflict were based on the argument of a "restricted democracy," which, while formally democratic, was stifled by the remnants of a series of exclusionary, even if informal, practices. Inherited from the National Front, they restricted free competition and gave traditional parties a near-monopoly on political life, closing off any possibility for the emergence and consolidation of a democratic leftist opposition. The proposals for reform that proliferated during the 1980s (many of which grew out of peace negotiations with the guerrillas) had their roots in this diagnosis, which also served as the cornerstone of the constitution-making process of 1991. A central objective of the 1991 Constitution, was to dismantle the restrictions on Colombian democracy once and for all.

From the mid-1980s until the mid-1990s, the rules of the political game were fundamentally transformed in Colombia, allowing an opening in the channels of access to power that led to a broader representation of society in the state. All formal restrictions on democratic competition were abolished with the 1991 Constitution, allowing the establishment of an extremely lax electoral system that imposed almost no institutional barriers to entry. The opening of the channels of political representation at a time when the two-party system was showing signs of exhaustion was one positive effect of the 1991 constitutional reform. The extreme atomization of political representation was an important negative effect. The overall result of the reforms was therefore ambiguous.

Today, it seems impossible to argue that restrictions on the political regime are still the source of the problems of democracy in Colombia. It is also unconvincing to maintain that informal rules of the game or specific political practices (clientelism, patronage, and other types of "particularism"[20]) undermine the regime's democratic character, as some authors have maintained following the thesis of Leal Buitrago (1984) and later Leal Buitrago and Dávila (1990). Evidently, such practices and their frequency affect the "quality" of democracy. Yet undesirable as they are, the mere existence of particularistic practices does not prohibit the possibility of classifying the Colombian political regime as democratic.[21]

The main element related to the regime's institutional design that helps explain the recent crisis is no longer associated with its "restrictions" but instead with the excessive opening that began in the 1980s culminating in 1991. The

---

[19] The most influential text was Francisco Leal Buitrago's "La crisis del regimen bipartidista" (1984).

[20] The term coined by O'Donnell to name these political practices, which are so common throughout Latin America.

[21] Moreover, recent studies show that the independent ("untied") urban vote has increased, especially but not exclusively in presidential elections. Additionally, political, ethnic, and religious minorities – which don't base their vote on clientelism or the use of public resources – have had increasing access to the representative system since 1991. See Bejarano and Dávila (1998).

TABLE 8.3. *Number of Parties and Lists Presented in Congressional Elections,*
1990–1998

Year	Number of Parties	Number of Lists for Senate	Number of Lists for Chamber of Deputies
1990	8	213	351
1991	22	143	486
1994	54	251	628
1998	80	319	692

Source: Pizarro and Bejarano (2001).

pendulum has swung to the opposite side. Taken to the extreme, this "logic of incorporation" (see Pizarro and Bejarano 2001), led to the design of an extremely lax electoral system[22] that produced enormous disorganization among parties (both new and traditional) as well as in the system of political representation. Some would argue, correctly, that Colombian parties have always lacked organization and discipline, and that their tendency toward dispersion and fragmentation is nothing new. Our argument is that the institutional reforms taking place since 1985 – above all, those related to the electoral system and the statute on parties[23] – reinforced these historical tendencies among Colombian parties by creating additional incentives for fragmentation and atomization. These incentives have become so strong that they have also led the new political parties and movements in this direction.

As Table 8.3 shows, both the number of political parties and movements registered with the National Electoral Council as well as the number of lists of candidates for the Senate and the Chamber of Deputies have dramatically increased in the last decade. The situation has given rise not to a diffuse multiparty system (as in Ecuador) but to an attenuated (and highly atomized) two-party system accompanied by a motley collection of "third forces" (which are also highly fragmented).

[22] A document commissioned by the Ministry of the Interior, authored by a prestigious group of consultants (Arturo Valenzuela, Josep Colomer, Arend Lijphart, and Matthew Soberg Shugart), states that "Colombia's current electoral system is the most 'personalistic' in the world" (1999: 237). The Colombian electoral system is based on proportional representation, with a Hare distribution formula and closed and blocked lists. However – and herein lies the main problem – each party or movement can put forth an indefinite number of lists or candidates in each electoral district. In a context of party disorganization, this leads to a widespread "war of residuals" that aims to obtain the largest possible number of seats with the fewest votes. By presenting multiple lists in various electoral districts, each party or movement splits its own vote, "giving up the possibility of obtaining seats by quotient but maximizing the possibility of obtaining them by residual" (Gutiérrez 1998: 222).

[23] According to current laws governing parties, a party needs the support of one member of Parliament, 50,000 votes, or 50,000 signatures to be legally recognized by the National Electoral Council. Thanks to this lax requirement, any electoral microenterprise (whether a Liberal or Conservative personalistic faction or a "third force") can have free access to television, obtain state financing, and indiscriminately issue endorsements for electoral campaigns.

This disarray of the parties and the party system has had an enormously negative impact on effective governance because it is impossible to obtain minimal party discipline at the various levels of political representation (Congress, departmental legislatures, or municipal councils), given the relative autonomy of each of the many dozens of "electoral microenterprises" that have captured the country's representative political space. Party-based lists and party-appointed candidates are gradually disappearing in Colombia. This atomization has generated enormous obstacles to coordination between the executive and legislative branches and made the task of governance much more difficult. It has also hindered the formation of a coherent opposition capable of keeping a check on government and becoming a genuine political alternative. Since the mid-nineteenth century, the Colombian state has compensated for its weakness, at least partly, by exercising indirect control at the local and regional levels through political parties (González 1989, 1997). In this sense, the weakening of the political parties and of their organizational capacity adds one more dimension to the Colombian state's loss of control over the country.

The democratic reforms of the 1980s and 1990s have had additional perverse effects on the state and democracy in Colombia (see Bejarano 2002). Decentralization has weakened the central government and devolved power to actors who control regional and local governments, among them – in some regions – the very rivals of the state (guerrillas and drug traffickers). Partly because of the transfer of resources from the center to the periphery mandated by the 1991 Constitution, the fiscal deficit has seriously deepened. The executive branch has also seen its power diminish vis-à-vis Congress and the courts since 1991. All these reforms, while desirable and convenient from a democratic point of view, have nevertheless added new burdens and difficulties to the central state as it attempts to recover and affirm its authority throughout the territory. In a different context, perhaps, such effects could have been considered as a necessary trade-off in exchange for the political opening in place since the mid-eighties. Nevertheless, at times when the drug trade, paramilitary, and far-left groups have intensified their siege of Colombian democratic institutions, some of these reforms have instead contributed to their decay. These examples illustrate the paradoxical situation in which efforts to strengthen democracy can have perverse and unexpected results, thereby contributing to its erosion rather than its consolidation.

The Erosion and "Partial Collapse" of the State

The multiple problems besieging Colombia's democracy are located not only in the most visible dimension of its political regime but also at the level of its foundations, in the place where every democracy finds indispensable support: the effective exercise of basic civil rights and liberties. These rights and liberties are violated daily by each and every one of the armed actors engaged in the ongoing conflict. The common cause of these violations is the loss of the Colombian state's coercive and normative capacities – that is, the collapse

TABLE 8.4. *Colombia: Total Violent Deaths and Population Growth, 1970–1997*

Year	Total Violent Deaths[a]	Population (in thousands)[b]
1970	4,445	23,132
1980	9,122	29,719
1987	17,419	n.a.
1989	23,312	n.a.
1991	28,872	34,970 (1990)
1997	27,085	41,564 (1999, est.)

[a] Colombian Commission of Jurists (2000), Table 1: "Evolution of the Situation of Human Rights and Socio-political Violence in Colombia, 1970–1997."

[b] IDB (2000a: 141).

of those state organizations that must guarantee the effective exercise of full citizenship throughout the national territory.

Historians have frequently pointed to the fact that since its creation in the early nineteenth century, the Colombian state has traditionally been small, weak, and poor. Historically, the difficult task of state consolidation in Colombia has been compounded by a daunting geography; a weak, outwardly oriented economy with a very small domestic market; and a very precarious national identity that was fractured by deep regional and party cleavages. Its traditional weakness took a downward turn in the last two decades of the twentieth century, reaching a point of "partial collapse" in the late 1980s and beginning of the 1990s.

One of the crudest and most dramatic indicators of state decay is the number of homicides. In 1960, when the "La Violencia" came to an end, Colombia still had the highest rate of nonaccidental deaths in the world (see Oquist 1978: 11). Around the mid-1960s the homicide rate decreased, reaching an annual level of about 20 homicides per 100,000 inhabitants. It remained relatively stable at that point until the beginning of the 1980s.[24] Since the mid-1980s, the homicide rate experienced a dramatic increase, reaching a new peak of about 80 homicides per 100,000 inhabitants in 1991. Since that time it has decreased only slightly.[25] According to a report by the Institute of Legal Medicine and Forensic Sciences, "approximately 500,000 people, the majority civilians, died violently in Colombia during the last two decades.... The figure is equivalent to more than 1 percent of the current Colombian population, which is estimated at 41 million." (*El Tiempo*, October 13, 2000).[26] The available data on violent deaths in Colombia are undoubtedly alarming (see Table 8.4). Between 1970

[24] Between 1963 and 1983, the homicide rate per 100,000 inhabitants averaged 24.8.

[25] Levels of violence in Colombia are unusually high, even compared to other Latin American countries. Only El Salvador's homicide rate surpassed that of Colombia in the 1990s. See Levitt and Rubio (2000: 3–4).

[26] See *http://eltiempo.terra.com.co/13-10-2000/judi_1.html* According to Paul Oquist (1978: 11), between 1946 and 1966, the conflict "left at least 200,000 people dead." Between 1980 and 2000 in Colombia, two and one half times more people died violently than during "La Violencia."

and 1980, the number of violent deaths doubled. The figure doubled again around 1987. In 1989, the number was five times that of 1970, and the figure from 1991 is six and one half times the number of violent deaths recorded at the beginning of the 1970s. The population has, of course, grown in the last three decades, but certainly not at the same pace as the homicide rate.

By the mid-twentieth century, the intraparty warfare known as "La Violencia" (1948–58) brought about a serious decay and crisis of the state's authority and capacity, that Oquist (1978) labeled as the first "partial collapse" of the Colombian state. The National Front period (1958–74) gave way to a process of selective reconstruction and strengthening of the state (Bejarano and Segura 1996). In the 1980s, severe erosion took place again as the result of two main factors: a divided elite and the emergence of powerful competitors, to the left and to the right, both of them financed by the rents accruing from the drug trade. Elite divisions contributed to the erosion of the state "from within," while the expansion and consolidation of its competitors meant a gradual erosion "from outside." Both trends contributed to a spiral of state decay that led to a major contraction of the state's capacity to "broadcast its power" (Herbst 2000) throughout the national territory and society.

This partial collapse of the state can be read as having two meanings: one is geographical; the other is functional. In geographical terms, the adjective "partial" refers to the fact that the central state is unable to extend its reach throughout the territory, particularly in the peripheral zones beyond the agricultural frontier. The Colombian state has never been able to broadcast its power throughout its entire territory. This is a fact widely recognized and documented by geographers, historians, and sociologists, particularly those who have devoted their studies to the *zonas de colonización* or regions of recent settlement. But it is also a fact that such capacity has shrunk in the last two decades, as a result of the capacity of rival armed organizations (the guerrillas and the paramilitaries) to occupy and control ever-increasing portions of the national territory.

The problem, therefore, is not only that the Colombian state has historically failed to control the territory under its jurisdiction but also that its capacity to do so has increasingly "contracted" in the last two decades. In some regions, the state has delegated the fulfillment of basic functions to right-wing organizations such as the United Self-Defenses of Colombia (Autodefensas Unidas de Colombia; AUC), thus clearly abdicating its power in their favor. This is the case in various regions within the mid Magdalena, in the north of Antioquia and the department of Córdoba. In other areas, the state's control is seriously challenged by rival armed organizations (the guerrillas), as in the zones where coca growing has expanded during the last two decades (the lowlands east of the Andean range, including the Orinoco and the Amazon basins). This geographic contraction of the Colombian state has happened in tandem with the growth and expansion of the state's organized rivals, who have been successful at challenging the state's control over an increasing portion of the territory under its formal control and jurisdiction.

In a functional sense, the collapse of the Colombian state is also "partial" in that while some state organizations (i.e., the bureaucracy, the technocracy, the administration, the representative bodies) retain a certain coherence and capacity for action, some other crucial state agencies have become increasingly unable to fulfill their functions and deliver the services that are expected of them (most notably security and justice) or have become totally disfigured with reference to their constitutional functions (e.g., the armed forces).

Finally, by making an argument about the "partial collapse" of the state, we want to differentiate the Colombian case from those instances where there has been a total collapse of the state, such as Somalia and other cases treated in the contemporary literature on "failed states" (see Rotberg 2003 and Zartman 1995).

Proximate Causes of State Erosion and Contraction

Guerrilla warfare started in Colombia a decade before the Cuban revolution (Pizarro 1991, 1996a). In contrast to the rest of Latin America, the Colombian guerrillas avoided being exterminated in the 1960s and managed to consolidate in the 1970s. This consolidation is, in fact, evidence of the secular weakness of the Colombian state. Beyond the emergence and eventual consolidation of the guerrillas, the recent erosion of state authority in Colombia is explained by the exhaustion caused by more than three decades of internal armed conflict. The amount of resources spent for counterinsurgency purposes, added to the organizational and budgetary distortions implied by the need to maintain an army fighting an internal war for more than thirty years, partly explains the current configuration of the Colombian state, the enlargement of its armed forces, and the weakness of other crucial state components such as the judiciary.

In addition to the protracted conflict with the guerrillas, a second cause of state weakness stems from the lack of consensus among elites (political, economic, and military) on the appropriate strategy to confront this armed opposition. As suggested by Mauceri (2001: 1–2, 11–14), the absence of a coherent political project shared by the elites is perhaps one of the most important causes of the weakness of the Colombian state. Starting with the Betancur government (1982–86), and because of the negotiation policy advocated by the president, a deep division among the elites became evident: While some sectors insisted on a negotiated settlement of the armed conflict, others preferred to privatize and decentralize the counterinsurgency effort by supporting paramilitary groups and bypassing the role of the state in keeping order within its borders. Within the state itself, while some sectors have insisted on a political exit to the armed impasse, others (particularly in the armed forces) have offered these private justice groups (paramilitaries, self-defense groups, death squads, etc.) the legal coverage and logistical support needed to carry out their counterinsurgency strategy. Clearly, the so-called paramilitary armies in Colombia and the abdication of power by some sectors within the state are the consequence of a political split among the elites.

The 1980s also witnessed the expansion of a market for illegal drugs in the United States and the increasing role of Colombian entrepreneurs in these transnational drug circuits. Drugtrafficking certainly occupies an important place in any explanation of the Colombian crisis, not in and of itself, as a phenomenon exogenous to politics, but instead precisely on account of its multiple economic, social, and political ramifications, particularly its impact on the process of state erosion and decay. The criminal organizations linked to the drug business have had immense and devastating consequences for society and politics in Colombia (see López 1998; López and Camacho 2001). On the one hand, the drug dealers have sought to translate their enormous fortunes into political influence and have gained access to political decision-making processes via multiple paths – including creating personal electoral vehicles, openly participating in the traditional political parties, financing electoral campaigns,[27] and wielding enormous power in local politics. On the other hand, to combat the U.S.-backed antinarcotic policies implemented by the state, the narcotraffickers have resorted to all kinds of means: from bribery and corruption all the way to death threats, assassination of state officials (prison guards, police officers, judges, magistrates, military officers, and politicians), and the use of large-scale terrorism.

Besides its direct impact on the state, the rents produced by the drug trade have fed all armed actors in Colombia. Private militias guarding the drug dealers, paramilitary groups, and even the guerrillas have all based their expansion on the resources extracted from the drug business. The boom in the drug trade in the 1980s and 1990s changed the magnitude of the armed conflict in Colombia. Thanks to the impact of drug trafficking, the state has seen its capacity diminish not only in absolute terms – as a result of corruption and the threat and use of force – but also in relative terms: The rents accruing from drugs have allowed its rivals to expand their reach and their operational capacity at the same time that the state is losing its own.

Additionally, since the beginning of the 1980s, the United States' antidrug policies in the Andean region have also contributed to the deterioration of state authority in Colombia (see Mason 2000). This policy, aimed at cutting off the supply of drugs from South America, has limited the autonomy of the Andean states and made it impossible for them to design alternative strategies for combating the production and trade of narcotics. Perhaps the most perverse effect of the policy, in the Colombian case, has been the increasing militarization of the fight against drugs (involving first the police and now the army). This militarization has placed additional pressure on the state to increase the resources, prerogatives, and hardware available to the military to the detriment of support for other key branches of government such as the judiciary.[28] Imbalances within the state have become deeper as a result.

---

[27] The most renowned case but by no means the only one was the presidential campaign of Ernesto Samper in 1994, which was partially funded by the Cali Cartel.

[28] This trend toward militarization of the fight against drugs has gone even further since the U.S. Congress approved the funding of "Plan Colombia" in the year 2000.

In his article "War Making and State Making as Organized Crime," Charles Tilly draws a bold picture of the state-making process. According to Tilly, states perform four basic tasks: (1) Through "war making," they eliminate or neutralize their foreign enemies; (2) "state making," in turn, implies the elimination of their rivals within the territory; (3) "protection," relates to their capacity to eliminate or neutralize the enemies of their clients; and, finally (4) "extraction" allows them to acquire the resources needed to fulfill the other three tasks (1985: 181). All four activities depend on the capacity of the state to monopolize the concentrated means of coercion. They may overlap and cross each other, but most importantly, success in fulfilling one of them generally reinforces the rest. In Tilly's own words, "a state that successfully eradicates its internal rivals strengthens its ability to extract resources, to wage war, and to protect its chief supporters" (Tilly 1985: 181).

Inversely, we argue, the incapacity to fulfill any one of them tends to weaken all the rest. A state like the Colombian one, incapable of eliminating or neutralizing its rivals within its territory, is neither able to eliminate or neutralize the enemies of its potential clients (the citizens) nor to extract the resources needed in order to perform its basic functions. Therefore, the inability of the state to monopolize the means of coercion gives rise to a vicious circle, which keeps on debilitating it, while its rivals find a fertile terrain in which to grow and thrive. As a result, Colombia has experienced, in the last two decades, the emergence and expansion of a panoply of groups with diverse ideological views, apparently rival proto-states that accumulate power given their capacity to provide the basic political goods that the state, by definition, should be able to provide: protection and justice.

The Consequences of State Erosion and Decay

As the central state loses its monopoly of coercion and becomes, as a consequence, less able to offer protection to the citizenry, alternative suppliers of protection come onto the scene. The "partial collapse" of the Colombian state and the strategic location of Colombia in the international narcotics market have cleared the way for the emergence and expansion of many different political entities that include criminal bands, "warlords" or "coercive entrepreneurs," and "aspiring state-makers." For the purposes of this chapter, we will concentrate our attention on three of them: the two guerrilla groups that still remain active, FARC and the ELN, and the recently formed umbrella organization that comprises many of the right-wing paramilitary groups, the AUC.

In contrast with the rest of Latin America, the guerrilla experiments of the 1960s not only survived in Colombia but also solidified. Moreover, in the 1970s and 1980s, a new series of "second generation" armed movements appeared (Pizarro 1996a). The second-generation groups negotiated their reincorporation into civilian life during the first half of the 1990s, as did one of the 1960s-era groups, the EPL. However, the two largest and best-armed guerrilla groups, the

FARC and the ELN, remained active.[29] These two groups have grown exponentially in the last two decades,[30] confirming the loss of the state's monopoly on the use of force described previously.

On the other hand, there are the so-called "paramilitary" groups, best characterized as "vigilantes" in that they are organized, extralegal groups that take the law into their own hands (Cubides 1999). These groups employ different operational tactics and are of diverse social origin, ranging from peasants legitimately organized in "self-defense" against the guerrilla's predatory practices to random hired killers and mercenaries. There are also "social cleansing" groups (primarily in urban areas), death squads, and bands of right-wing rural guerrillas (in the style of the Nicaraguan "Contras"). The most notable process related to the development of paramilitary groups – apart from their unusual growth (estimates are that they increased their ranks from 650 men in 1987 to 8,000 in 2000)[31] – has been the emergence of an organization attempting to centralize and control these unruly vigilante groups. Since the late-1990s, the AUC has emerged as a coordinator of anti–guerrilla forces (similar to the former Simón Bolívar Guerrilla Coordinating Group). The AUC serves as an umbrella organization for small and large vigilante groups acting with similar goals: to combat the guerrillas and defend the "establishment" at all costs.

The paramilitaries' preferred tactic has been to carry out massacres of large groups of people with the aim of terrorizing the population.[32] They have also engaged in selective assassination and sporadic combat with the guerrillas. Paramilitary groups are estimated to have an armed presence in 409 municipalities (40 percent of all the municipalities in the country), mostly in rural areas of the departments of Antioquia (Urabá) and Córdoba, the departments that border the midsection of the Magdalena River, and north and south Santander. More recently, they have entered such cities as Barrancabermeja, Montería, Medellín, and Bogotá. Their participation in politics has not been limited to war: The groups have also exercised their influence through elections by supporting candidates for city council, mayor, departmental assemblies, and Congress. In the areas they control, paramilitary groups (like guerrillas) have become true "proto-state" actors. According to one account, they "safeguard local morality (in Tierralta, Córdoba, the local paramilitary commander gave the men one month to decide whether they would stay with their wives or

---

[29] On the FARC, see Pizarro (1991) and Rangel (1999). Echandía (1999a, 1999b) traces the process of guerrilla expansion in Colombia.

[30] In 2001, it was estimated that the FARC had approximately 18,000 armed combatants, including 6,000 lightly armed urban militia. They were divided into some 70 "fronts," each averaging about 250 combatants. As for the ELN, the figure is approximately 3,500 men in arms (*The Economist* 2001: 11–13).

[31] In 1987, the government revealed for the first time before Congress the existence of 138 self-defense groups whose membership included 650 men. Today, it is estimated that these groups have a membership of up to 8,000 combatants (Dirección de Inteligencia EJC 2000).

[32] In 2000, they assassinated 988 unarmed civilians, according to Ministry of Defense data. Statistics on massacres during the second half of the 1990s are found in Zuluaga (1999).

their lovers), implement local development projects ... and mete out the death penalty, without a trial, to thieves, prostitutes, homosexuals and drug addicts" (*Semana* 2001).

As the capacity of the Colombian state to monopolize power dwindled in the late 1980s, the size of these illegal forces increased. Both the guerrillas and the paramilitaries have expanded enormously since the early 1980s, but the latter seem to be growing at a greater pace. The growth of these two groups throughout the 1980s and 1990s is also associated with their access to the rents accruing from the drug trade. Their political influence has gone beyond their territorial strongholds and extends throughout the national territory by way of capturing or otherwise influencing the structures and relations of power at the local level. Out of a total of Colombia's 1,092 municipalities, at least 600 (more than half) are being targeted "politically" by one group or the other (Forero 2000), causing much of the current violence. In these municipalities, the guerrillas and/or the paramilitaries give open or tacit approval to candidates, force some to withdraw, and assassinate others. During the campaign preceding local elections in the year 2000, 36 candidates for mayor, council, or other offices were killed, and another 50 were kidnapped. Twenty-four mayoral candidates and 64 candidates for town councils withdrew after meddling by armed groups. And 29 towns have registered only one candidate for mayor, "a sign that the tampering has frightened away other candidates" (Forero 2000).[33]

There are at least three degrees of local control by the armed actors, as indicated by their capacity to sabotage, control, or otherwise influence the electoral process: Elections are routinely sabotaged in approximately 10 percent of municipalities every election round; control of candidates and influence over elections happens in another 10 to 20 percent of the territory; and violence encompasses a much wider portion of the territory, making evident the existence of a fierce competition between the state and its armed rivals (as well as between the rivals themselves) for the control of local political power (Bejarano and Dávila 1998).

Tilly's description of "war-makers" and "state-makers" as "coercive and self-seeking entrepreneurs" (1985: 169) seems quite apt for explaining the interactions that take place today in Colombia between a semicollapsed state and these "aspiring state-makers" – the guerrillas (especially the FARC) and the paramilitary groups (especially the AUC). These groups, which are conceived

---

[33] And yet, contrary to most apocalyptic accounts of the Colombian situation, we would argue that the central government still controls more than half of the total territory, including the bigger and medium-sized cities, where over 70 percent of the Colombian population lives. Even though it is true that a big portion of the territory, sparsely populated and beyond the agricultural frontier (starting in the lowlands of the Eastern-most mountain range and extending all the way to the borders of Venezuela, Brazil, Peru, and Ecuador), is not fully controlled by the central government, it is neither under the grip of the guerrillas, nor the paramilitaries. In this part of the country, the state, the guerrillas, and the paramilitaries sharply compete to control some strategic economic enclaves (such as Arauca and Putumayo where there is both petroleum and coca). The rest of the country, however, is very sparsely populated and inhospitable territory.

as "coercive entrepreneurs" (Tilly 1985), exercise "coercive exploitation" in the regions they dominate and compete among themselves for the monopoly of the means of coercion. The Colombian war can thus be explained on the basis of the effort that each of these groups of entrepreneurs makes in controlling or defeating its competitors in order to enjoy the advantages of power over a secure, expanding territory (Tilly 1985: 172).

The Impact of State Erosion on Democracy

The state's diminished control over the means of coercion also has a negative impact on its capacity to deliver justice. Impunity is yet another face of state weakness and failure (Méndez 1999: 20). It goes hand in hand with the other phenomena we have included here as symptoms of the state's erosion and "partial" collapse. Levels of criminality skyrocket when the state is unable to prevent or contain them. Criminal organizations charged with taking justice "into their own hands" tend to mushroom. To put it in Juan Méndez's words (1999: 21),

private armies and vigilante squads complicate the matter of assigning responsibility. It is not always clear that their actions are conducted under color of authority, or even that they are officially tolerated, although in certain regions evidence to that effect is not lacking. Yet, even if no policy exists of encouraging these actions, their existence and growth demonstrate a signal weakness in the ability of the state to keep peace and maintain order.

The weakness of state institutions in protecting citizens from potential abuses of their rights – joined with the state's inability to punish the guilty and provide effective mechanisms for conflict resolution – is one of the biggest threats to democracy in Colombia and in the rest of Latin America. Much of this weakness is attributable to the deplorable situation of the justice system throughout the continent. In nearly all of Latin America, the justice system lacks independence from the executive branch. In Colombia, the problem of judicial independence was solved thanks to the National Front pacts that established a system for appointing judges, which guaranteed their autonomy in relation to politicians for many years (until the 1991 Constitution). Nevertheless, along with the rest of Latin America, Colombia shares a need to modernize its justice system and adapt it to new situations and changing problems. Throughout the region, the judiciary suffers from a lack of budgetary support, technical and administrative backwardness, and a backlog of cases. Yet, in Colombia, the greatest problem lies in its incapacity to deal with social conflict – and particularly with conflicts that tend to turn violent. The Colombian judiciary is simply overwhelmed. Since the early 1980s, the country has experienced a real increase in levels of criminality associated with both the growth in armed groups and the explosion in drug trafficking. At the same time, the impact of corruption, intimidation, threats, and violence by armed actors (in particular by drug traffickers) against members of the judiciary has been devastating.

The statistics presented by Mauricio Rubio in this regard are extremely alarming. In 1987, following the assassination of 53 members of the judiciary, "a survey of judges revealed their worry about the 'insecurity of members of this branch.' Twenty-five percent of those surveyed stated that they or their families had been threatened as a result of their official activities. [. . .] Judges have been more affected by violence than other citizens, even more than those who live in the most violent areas of the country and more than members of the armed forces" (Rubio 1999: 213–14). This systematic attack on members of the judiciary partly explains the Colombian state's growing inability to punish those who are guilty of abuses and to provide justice. Systematic intimidation, along with threats and attacks on judges throughout the country, represent a fundamental cause of the process of state deterioration described earlier. More than any other sector of the state, the judiciary has truly been besieged during the last two decades.

The deterioration of the state's ability to provide justice is not an isolated fact. As Rubio has shown, there is

a negative relationship between violence, measured by the homicide rate, armed groups and various indicators of performance in the area of criminal justice. In the last two decades, the Colombian homicide rate has more than quadrupled. The influence of the main armed organizations has increased in a parallel fashion. During the same period, the criminal system's capacity to investigate homicides has been reduced to one-fifth of what it was previously. (Rubio 1999: 214–15)

In the 1970s, more than 60 percent of homicides led to the arrest of suspects. In the 1990s, this proportion fell to less than 20 percent. In the 1970s, more than 35 percent of homicides went to trial; in the 1990s, less than 6 percent ended in trial. In the 1970s, more than 11 percent of homicides ended with a conviction; in the 1990s, less than 4 percent did (Rubio 1999: 215). These alarming rates of impunity have continued to worsen despite the judicial reform launched by the 1991 Constitution and the fiscal effort made since the early 1990s in terms of expenditures for justice.[34] With rates of impunity that surpass 96 percent (Ariza, Barreto, and Gaitán 1999; Ariza, Barreto, and Iturralde 2000; García and Santos 2001; García and Uprimny 2000), we can undoubtedly affirm that the criminal justice system and the state's capacity to deliver justice have collapsed in Colombia.

This affects a crucial dimension of the state, the rule of law,[35] whose erosion threatens the very foundations of democratic rule. A democratic state not only

[34] The average expenditure on justice, expressed as a percentage of GDP, increased from 0.5 percent between 1970 and 1979, to 0.6 percent between 1980 and 1989 and to 0.99 percent between 1990 and 1998. Spending has doubled in the last thirty years. The annual real rate of growth was 4.36 percent in the 1970s, 5.8 percent in the 1980s, and 11.11 percent in the 1990s. The crisis in the justice system and the 1991 Constitution explain the notable increase of the 1990s. See Ariza et al. (2000: 77–78).

[35] According to O'Donnell, a "democratic rule of law" should be defined as the legally based rule of a democratic state. For O'Donnell, a legal system is democratic if it: (1) upholds the political freedoms and guarantees of polyarchy; (2) upholds the civil rights of the entire population; and (3) establishes networks of responsibility and accountability by which all public and private agents, including the highest placed officials of the regime, are subject to appropriate, legally established controls of the lawfulness of their acts. As long as it fulfills these conditions, "such

claims a monopoly on violence in society but, more importantly, claims that this monopoly is a necessary condition for effectively guaranteeing the rights and freedoms of the citizens under its jurisdiction. However, the state's inability to provide protection and justice limits the democratic regime's performance and inhibits its capacity to carry out the promises of greater equality and freedom, effective representation, and universal participation.

In Colombia, the very existence of the rule of law is called into question by the degree to which the state has lost its monopoly of violence. The contraction of the state's capacity in this regard precedes and is perhaps more serious than its inability to provide certain services and satisfy certain basic material needs. O'Donnell's depiction of the process of erosion of some Latin American states aptly describes the Colombian case:

In these situations, ineffective states coexist with autonomous, also territorially based, spheres of power. States become ostensibly unable to enact effective regulations of social life across their territories and their stratification systems. Provinces or districts peripheral to the national center . . . create (or reinforce) systems of local power which tend to reach extremes of violent, personalistic rule . . . open to all sorts of violent and arbitrary practices. (1999a: 138)

The shrinking of state authority has propelled the guerrillas, paramilitary groups, and drug lords to organize "proto-states" both in the coercive and normative senses of the word in regions such as northern Antioquia, a large portion of Córdoba, areas of Magdalena Medio, and the cocaine-growing zones of the eastern foothills and Amazon basin. "These are subnational systems of power that, oddly enough for most extant theories of the state and of democracy, have a territorial basis and an informal but quite effective legal system and that coexist with a regime that, at least at the center of national politics, is polyarchical" (O'Donnell 1999b: 314). These regions, the majority of which are rural, are far from functioning as "polyarchies" or democracies at the regional and local levels. National elections (i.e., presidential and Congressional elections) may function in a more or less transparent way.[36] But local and regional elections generally are much less clean, free, and competitive; intimidation, threats, and the use of force play a very important role (Dávila and Corredor 1998; García 2000a, 2000b).

As inappropriate use of force or simple threats by state or nonstate actors become widespread, fewer people participate in elections. Even when they participate, the result of the electoral process is distorted because of either threats before, or assassinations after, elections. At the same time, the proliferation of armed actors and their capacity to act on their threats reduces the presence of alternative parties, and when the latter dare to compete, they are eliminated, either before or after elections. The situation leads to a vicious circle that has

---

a state is not just a state ruled by law; it is a democratic legal state, or an *estado democrático de derecho*" (O'Donnell 1999b: 318–19).

[36] It is worth remembering that during the 1990 presidential campaign in Colombia, three presidential candidates were assassinated: Luis Carlos Galán, Carlos Pizarro, and Bernardo Jaramillo. Another, Jaime Pardo Leal, had been assassinated two years earlier, in 1987.

terribly pernicious effects on democracy. In the absence of necessary guarantees, experiments aimed at broadening democracy can lead to even greater levels of violence. This is especially true if the opening of spaces that were previously closed to political competition (e.g., the popular election of mayors) provides a new incentive for the state's rivals to extend and deepen strategies to control territory and population.

This situation, as remarked upon by O'Donnell, "highlights the question of who represents and what is represented in the institutions of the national regime and, more specifically, of how one conceptualizes a polyarchical regime that may contain regional regimes that are not at all polyarchical" (1999b: 315). The Colombian case not only shows concrete evidence of this paradox but also demonstrates the necessity to theorize about this situation's impact on democracy. Undoubtedly, "our theories must come to terms with . . . the extent to which a polyarchical regime coexists with a properly democratic rule of law (or an *estado democrático de derecho*)" (O'Donnell 1999b: 325).

CONCLUSION

The Colombian case proves that democracy's various dimensions can evolve at different paces, sometimes even in opposing directions. It is, therefore, not accurate to speak of advances or setbacks in democracy as a whole because a single case may reveal advances in some dimensions alongside setbacks in others. Moreover – and this is perhaps one of the most troubling findings of this study – it is possible for efforts that enhance some aspects of democracy (i.e., opening the electoral arena) to have a negative impact on its other crucial dimensions (i.e., effective governance). For these reasons, it is important to remain aware of the trade-offs involved in any major democratization effort.

During the last decade and a half, Colombia has witnessed both an improvement in the dimensions of political participation and contestation and a severe deterioration in the dimensions related to effective protection of civil liberties and subordination of the military. Consequently, the Colombian political regime is difficult to classify because it is neither a full democracy nor an authoritarian regime. The term "semidemocracy" seems most appropriate to us. Yet we also point out that the restrictions that made the Colombian regime semidemocratic during the second half of the twentieth century have changed in nature. Between 1958 and 1986, restrictions were placed mostly on the competitive dimension of democracy. From the mid-1980s onward, the regime's shortcomings stem more clearly from the weakness of the state, the emergence of powerful armed actors (guerrillas and paramilitary groups), and the absence of the rule of law. Thus, we have classified Colombia as a "besieged democracy."

Searching for an explanation for this recent process of democratic erosion, we have built an argument that hinges mainly on political variables, even as it takes into account the enormously deleterious impact of drug trafficking on the Colombian state, society, and politics. At the regime level, we claim that it is no longer the system's "closed" nature that affects prospects for democratic consolidation, but that it is instead the excessively lax rules of the game created during a long process of political reform that began in the mid-1980s and culminated with the new 1991 Constitution. This set of rules, resulting from what we have called the "logic of incorporation," has created additional incentives for party fragmentation, leading to an extremely atomized and personalistic party system that makes the task of effective governance extremely difficult.

Yet, at another level, we argue that the Colombian state has undergone a severe erosion that led to its partial collapse in the late 1980s. This collapse is partial in the geographical sense and in the sense that while some state agencies (i.e., the bureaucracy, the technocracy, the administration, the representative bodies) have retained certain coherence and capacity to act, other crucial branches have either collapsed (i.e., the criminal justice system), become almost totally ineffective (i.e., the police), or become totally disfigured in relation to their Constitutional functions (i.e., the armed forces). This "partial collapse" of the state is the result of challenges posed by very powerful criminal organizations (the drug-dealing cartels) upon a state that was historically weak to begin with and that had been confronting a guerrilla insurgency for over three decades.

Theoretically, we aim to emphasize the role of the state and find a proper place for it in discussions of the conditions and prospects for democracy, not only in Colombia but also in other countries in the region. We have presented evidence to sustain our thesis about the partial collapse of the Colombian state, particularly concerning its normative and coercive dimensions. What seems evident in the Colombian case is the absence of a state in which, according to Kriegel, "the sovereign's confiscation of all acts of war, his monopoly on the sword of justice, brings about individual security by means of the rule of law"(cited in Posada-Carbó 1998: 14). And without a solid, democratic rule of law, democracy becomes impossible. The absence of a properly democratic rule of law not only threatens citizens' individual security and the exercise of minimal human and civil rights but also calls into question the dimensions of participation and competition that characterize all democratic political regimes.

In the best of cases, the state's glaring incapacity to provide security and justice leads to a paradoxical situation in which democratic rights (participation and competition) are respected while democracy's liberal components (human rights and civil liberties) are systematically violated. Ultimately, however, the absence of effective guarantees on the exercise of basic human and civil rights – joined with an excess of autonomy and prerogatives granted to the military – end up affecting the participatory and representative dimensions of democracy. In other words, the very existence of polyarchy – using the term in its most minimal and procedural sense – is compromised by the absence of a properly democratic rule of law.

Clearly, the reconstruction of the state is the sine qua non prerequisite for recovering and consolidating Colombia's political democracy (Bejarano 1994).

Nevertheless, as difficult as it may sound, we propose that these two tasks be carried out not sequentially but simultaneously. We do not want to argue for the rebuilding of the state as a priority that should precede democracy. Such an exercise could lead to the reconstruction of an authoritarian state that would be hostile to the democratic order. The struggle to rebuild the state must be closely tied to the struggle to rebuild and deepen democracy. In short, the goal is to rebuild authority without authoritarianism. The result must be a democratic state whose central authority is simultaneously reconstructed and democratically controlled.

9

Peru 1980–2000

Chronicle of a Death Foretold? Determinism, Political Decisions, and Open Outcomes

Martín Tanaka

Peru is a revealing case for assessing the advances and setbacks of democratization in Latin America because it challenges conventional interpretations, questions the role of structural variables or social prerequisites in explaining the different routes the countries in the region have followed in their democratic histories, and illustrates the importance of decisions taken by political actors. In theoretical terms, my analysis of the Peruvian experience follows the line of reasoning set out by Juan Linz in analyzing the breakdown of democracies (1978) and by O'Donnell and Schmitter (1986) in analyzing the transitions from authoritarian rule.[1] It also challenges conventional interpretations of the Peruvian case that commit what Bendix (1964) calls the fallacy of "retrospective determinism" – biasing the analysis of the case by looking only at the elements that fit with the final outcome – by summoning the shortcomings of democracy during the 1980s to explain the collapse of the party system and the democratic regime in 1992 or by focusing on the elements that characterize the Fujimori regime as corrupt to explain its fall in 2000. These facile interpretations ignore the complexity of the Peruvian case, the fact that these were unexpected outcomes, and the fact that Peru's history was, and still is, open to diverse outcomes.

The conventional view maintains that Peru was unlikely to consolidate democracy from the very beginning of the Third Wave of democratization, given its history of absence of democratic institutions and its structural constraints. From this perspective, Peru was quickly beset by huge problems, mainly an economic crisis that reached hyperinflationary levels and a bloody armed

[1] On the social requisites for democracy and the importance of political action, see Lipset (1996). I am grateful to Gretchen Helmke for her comments on a first draft of this study, and very especially to Frances Hagopian and Scott Mainwaring, for all their suggestions for improving it for this volume. I also appreciate the criticism and comments of Carlos Contreras, Julio Cotler, Carlos Iván Degregori, and Romeo Grompone at a meeting held at the Institute of Peruvian Studies in August 2001. Any shortcomings are the result of my own stubbornness.

internal conflict that discredited political parties and the precarious democratic institutions. These flaws during the 1980s created a crisis of representation, which made possible in 1990 the emergence of an authoritarian leader with an antipolitics discourse – Alberto Fujimori – who ultimately established a regime that exemplified a reversal of democratization. Peru became the only case of a clear democratic breakdown in the Third Wave of democratization. The Fujimori government eventually became so corrupt and discredited that it allowed opposition forces to advance, which led to a democratic transition, however precarious.

This conventional view is misleading. The Peruvian case is not one of expected outcomes; on the contrary, it is an intriguing case of unexpected twists and surprising finales. Peruvian democracy certainly exhibited significant shortcomings during the eighties, but did not deviate so far from other countries that did not experience major setbacks in the 1990s. All the countries in the region experienced the pressure of the exhaustion of the "statist national popular sociopolitical matrix" (Garretón et al. 2003) and the difficulties of adopting a neoliberal model. Although Peru belongs to a group of countries where this exhaustion was especially painful, others – Bolivia, Argentina, and Brazil – experienced hyperinflation in the 1980s but did not experience the kind of setback that Peru suffered in the nineties. Similarly, Colombia eloquently shows that political violence – even an intense and bloody armed conflict – does not necessarily lead to the collapse of democratic rule.

Peru's uniqueness during the nineties was not a consequence of structural legacies or of the poor performances of the two democratic governments during the 1980s. The Peruvian party system, until even 1990, showed signs of evolving in a similar manner as other countries in the region not on the verge of collapse. Additionally, Peru's political system during the 1980s showed important signs of being a democracy in the making. I will show that even in the context of a severe economic crisis and increasing political violence, democratic rule in Peru was basically the "only game in town" – despite various degrees of commitment from the political actors. What distinguished Peru from Brazil, Argentina, Bolivia, and Colombia in the 1990s was that Peru had a successful antiestablishment leader (Fujimori), with an antipolitics, antiinstitutional discourse and practice. Antiestablishment politicians in other countries also exploited situations of crisis and instability, but they either failed in their confrontation with the political system (Collor in Brazil in 1992, Bucaram in Ecuador in 1997, and Serrano in Guatemala in 1993), or they finally reached some degree of understanding with systemic forces (Caldera in Venezuela in 1993 and recently Uribe in Colombia and Gutiérrez in Ecuador). Only in Venezuela (after 1998) did the party system break down and the democratic regime suffer a comparable erosion. In Venezuela, as in Peru, profound mistakes by the main political actors allowed the consolidation in power of an outsider (Hugo Chávez), who destroyed the prevailing political order and its main actors and established a government with authoritarian characteristics.

Fujimorismo was a consequence, then, of actions taken by the main political actors under particular circumstances, not a story predetermined by the
problems that Peru faced during the eighties. Fujimori's rise to power did not
necessarily imply the destruction of the political party system and the institutional order then in place. Even in 1990, the most likely scenario was one
of negotiation between Fujimori and the "traditional" parties, as occurred in
other countries in the region, or, if Fujimori tried to confront them, his failure,
given his lack of experience and an organized party supporting him. Fujimori
succeeded in a confrontational strategy where most others failed because the
main political actors committed mistakes and, crucially, because he was able
to stop hyperinflation, an achievement that enabled him to build a coalition
and consolidate his power. This coalition included the groups that supported
the neoliberal reforms and the popular groups that benefited from the social
programs that were distributed under clientelistic schemes.

The Latin American leaders who were able to arrest hyperinflation –
Fujimori, Paz Estenssoro in Bolivia (1985–89), Menem in Argentina (1989–99),
and Cardoso in Brazil (1995–2002) – ultimately led a profound reconfiguration
of the statist, national popular social and political order and instituted a new,
neoliberal one. The effects of this "critical juncture" (Collier and Collier 1991)
were long lasting and profound. But whereas Paz Estenssoro, Menem, and
Cardoso were part of their political establishments and the success of their governments also gave stability to democracy and the political system as a whole,
in Peru, Fujimori's success consolidated not only the neoliberal order but also
a personalistic and authoritarian regime with an antiinstitutional, antiparty
discourse and practice that thoroughly weakened democratic institutions.

This does not mean that Fujimori was plainly a dictator or merely the head
of a "mafia regime." Fujimori's government was a dictatorship only between
April (April 5th was the date of the *autogolpe* [self coup]) and November 1992,
when a new Congress was elected. In November 1993, a new constitution was
approved by referendum, and in 1995 Fujimori was reelected in free and fair
elections with 64 percent of the vote. However, despite having elections and
democratic institutions, Peru did not return to democratic rule because there
were no effective checks and balances or mechanisms of horizontal accountability. Peru thus clearly fits within what others have labeled as *competitive author-
itarianisms* (Diamond 2002; Levitsky and Way 2002; Schedler 2002). Fujimori
undermined the advances in democratic institutionalization between 1993 and
1995 with his campaign, starting in 1996, for a second, unconstitutional reelection in 2000. This campaign coincided with a cycle of economic recession
that weakened Fujimori; however, he was successful in his reelection attempts
because of the extreme weakness of the opposition forces and their inability to
surmount their collective action problems.

Fujimori consolidated power, but he did not build an alternative institutional
order. He did not even abide by the rules created by his own government and the
1993 Constitution, or create a party that could extend his rule beyond his term
in power. In this sense, Peru was the exact opposite of Mexico under the rule

of the Institutional Revolutionary Party (Partido Revolucionario Institucional; PRI). Fujimori's power was highly personalistic and concentrated in his own person and in his intelligence adviser, Vladimiro Montesinos, who ran government operations through political negotiations, bribery, and extortion. Once their association was severed in 2000, Fujimori could not remain in power. Peru witnessed an unexpected breakdown of the Fujimori government precisely when it was beginning to overcome the widespread condemnation after the questionable 2000 reelection, and Peru experienced a surprisingly peaceful transition to a democratic rule in 2001 with the election of a new president, Alejandro Toledo.

The current prospects for democracy in Peru look uncertain, but not necessarily grim. On the one hand, President Toledo has inherited a troubled legacy: a party system in shambles, weak democratic institutions, and weak political actors. On the other hand, Peru has learned through bitter experience that it must build democratic institutions, the conditions for popular participation and transparent governance, and mechanisms of horizontal accountability. In a salutary development, Peruvian politics has also become characterized by a centripetal logic of competition in which most actors vie to occupy the political center. Moreover, Peru currently exhibits more economic and political stability than its neighbors. However, as in the entire region, democracy must survive the pressures emanating from high levels of poverty and mediocre growth rates.

PERUVIAN DEMOCRACY IN THE 1980S

Peru's new democracy emerged in 1980[2] after twelve years of military dictatorship, with unprecedented, historic opportunities to consolidate democracy and a representative party system. For the first time in its history, Peru established a completely inclusive democracy in which illiterates were allowed to vote. Parties such as Alianza Popular Revolucionaria Americana (APRA; American Popular Revolutionary Alliance) that had historically been banned for questioning the status quo and diverse groups of the Marxist left that appeared in the 1970s became protagonists of the democratic game. The party system that emerged after the 1978 transition consisted of three large political blocks. The United Left (Izquierda Unida or IU) occupied the left side of the spectrum; the Popular Christian Party (Partido Popular Cristiano or PPC) and Popular Action (Acción Popular or AP) were on the right; and APRA occupied the center. These three blocks had roots in important political and intellectual traditions dating back to the 1920s. In the effervescent political atmosphere of the 1980s, these parties attempted to carry out programs and advance ideologies that had been postponed during the military rule. In contrast to previous decades, the political system now interacted with an increasingly active and mobilized civil society, represented by business interests, workers, and new social movements. In short, Peru had an unprecedented opportunity to build a fully representative party

---

[2] A more extensive development of these ideas can be found in Tanaka (1998).

system. Yet the 1980s ended with an inflation rate of 7,481.7 percent. During the decade, there were a huge number of deaths in a decade of armed conflict. In 1990, the GDP fell 12.9 percentage points, and the outsider Alberto Fujimori was elected president. The 1990s began with an *autogolpe* in April 1992 that won the approval of more than 80 percent of the population. The country's authoritarian leader was reelected in 1995 and established a regime that finally sank to levels of corruption almost unprecedented in Peruvian history.

According to the predominant view, serious weaknesses made the country's democratic consolidation highly uncertain from the outset. Peru started out with major structural problems, institutional and state fragility, weakness of the main political and social actors, a lack of democratic culture, and the persistence of a culture of conflict among the elite (Cotler 1994, 1995). This same elite, isolated in the old, oligarchic Creole culture, lost touch with an increasingly mestizo, "informal" population that had gradually begun to seek new paths (Degregori and Grompone 1991). The weight of history expressed itself in conflicts that unleashed economic crisis, political violence, and a growing ideological and social polarization. The main political parties alternated in government and time after time proved incapable of solving problems. In the long run, this situation caused a crisis of representation involving the entire political class, and the failure of the traditional elite allowed Fujimori to attain power (Kenney 2000; López 1992; Lynch 1999). Acting in an authoritarian fashion, Fujimori successfully trespassed against the institutional restrictions of the 1979 Constitution and defeated its authors, the political parties, which by this time were utterly lacking in legitimacy. In this sense, the success of his April 1992 *autogolpe* was understandable as was the approval citizens gave it.

This reasoning is certainly plausible. Between 1980 and 1985, during the administration of Fernando Belaúnde, Peru had an average inflation rate of 97.3 percent and a GDP growth rate of only 0.7 percent. Between 1986 and 1990, during the administration of Alan García, Peru had an average inflation rate of 1,662.5 percent, and a growth rate of 2.0 percent. With respect to the political violence, most of the estimated 69,280 deaths calculated by the Commission for Truth and Reconciliation (Comisión de la Verdad y Reconciliación, CVR, 2003) occurred during the two democratic governments of Belaúnde and García; almost one third of them were caused by state agents. The Truth Commission concluded that these two democratic governments abdicated their responsibility to direct countersubversive actions and left the issue instead in the hands of the military. At the same time, they also abdicated their responsibility to enforce the rule of law and especially the respect for human rights for the civilian population. According to the Truth Commission, in certain periods and in certain areas, the armed forces and other state agents systematically abused human rights.

From this perspective, the collapse of the party system and the breakdown of democratic rule between 1990 and 1992 were the logical consequences of the terrible economic performance and the political violence during the eighties. However, this is a misleading conclusion. The Peruvian performance was not unlike that of other countries that consolidated their democracies during the nineties. At the same time, a careful analysis of the Peruvian situation up to 1989 shows no signs of an imminent breakdown or a crisis of representation; to the contrary, there was an advance of very strong and mobilized political actors.

Peru is not that different from Argentina, Bolivia, and Brazil, countries that also suffered especially painful economic situations during the eighties and nineties. All these countries went through a very conflictive exhaustion of the "statist national popular sociopolitical matrix" that pervaded the region (Garretón et al. 2003). Peru's inflation rate surpassed the average inflation rate of the four countries for only three years, between 1989 and 1991. Regarding GDP growth, Peru looks very bad when compared to the others in 1983, and between 1988 and 1992. But Argentina looks very bad in 1981, 1982, 1985, 1988, and 1989; Bolivia, between 1982 and 1986; and Brazil, between 1990 and 1992. However, the paths that these four countries followed in political terms are quite different.

One might say that the Peruvian case was peculiar because, in addition to a dismal economic performance, there was a bloody armed internal conflict. However, despite the vast scale of violence, one of the most striking conclusions of the CVR is that most of the nearly 70,000 deaths went unnoticed. Prior to the work of the CVR, the most frequently used estimate was 25,000 deaths, a number shared by official statistics and also by independent human rights non-governmental organizations. The discrepancy between the official 25,000 and the true total of nearly 69,280 is explained by the fact that most of the victims lived in rural and marginal areas, with almost no connections to the state (e.g., with no documentation or registration of any kind). Forty percent of the victims lived in the rural department of Ayacucho; 75 percent of the victims spoke Quechua (the native pre-Hispanic language) as their mother tongue; 68 percent were illiterate or had not completed a primary education; and 79 percent of the victims lived in rural areas. The real drama of the political violence in Peru was that, despite the huge numbers of victims, as long as it took place in isolated and circumscribed rural areas it did not have an important impact on the functioning of the political system. (Colombia's violence can be analyzed in similar terms.) As Carrión (1992) and others have showed, lack of public support for presidents Belaúnde and García cannot be explained by the dynamic of terrorist actions or the number of registered victims but rather by economic performance, specifically by inflation rates.

In conclusion, the collapse of the party system and the breakdown of democracy in Peru cannot be explained by bad government performance in the 1980s. As of 1990, we were not at the brink of "a death foretold," taking the title of a García Márquez novel. The party system seemed to be taking root, as in other countries of the region. Despite all the problems, democracy was considered "the only game in town" for the main political actors, as McClintock correctly suggested in an article in 1989. Facing the 1990 general elections, most observers worried not about the possible rise of an antiparty candidate taking advantage of a crisis of legitimacy or representation but about a growing polarization between ideological actors similar to the situation that Chile faced in the early 1970s. The main concern was that the crisis of the center (APRA) could lead to unmanageable infighting between the two extremes of the political spectrum, a situation that could pave the way for a rightist and repressive military coup.

Until the 1990 elections, Peruvian democracy had certainly experienced very difficult moments, but it also registered important advances, contrary to conventional wisdom. In three critical areas – the electoral strength of the political parties, the organization and mobilization of civil society organizations, and the level of commitment on the part of political actors to the democratic system – the achievements in the 1980s were not negligible. I examine each in turn.

The Parties

From 1978 until the first round of the 1990 presidential election, the four main political groups (IU, PPC, AP, and APRA) captured over 70 percent of the vote (Figure 9.1). In the Constituent Assembly elections of 1978, these four major groups received 88.5 percent of the vote; from then until the 1989 municipal elections, this figure surpassed 90 percent. In the 1989 elections, the percentage decreased to 71.5 percent, and in the first round of the 1990 presidential election, which Mario Vargas Llosa won, the figure dropped a bit more, to 68 percent. Although electoral volatility was high from the outset of the democratic regime, electoral preferences were always expressed – even in 1990 – within the confines of the party system.

In retrospect, the electoral decline of the four major parties began with the 1989 municipal elections; however, up until the 1990 presidential election, the party system still showed significant strength. Moreover, one of the factors leading to the 1992 coup was the weakness of the government's bloc in Congress (elected in 1990), its minority position, and the corresponding strength of the

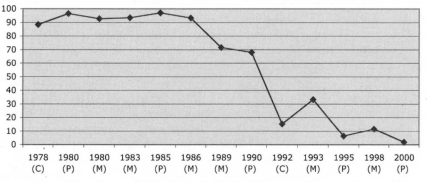

FIGURE 9.1. Vote Share of "Traditional" Political Parties, Peru, 1978–2000. Source: ONPE (Oficina Nacional de Procesos Electorales or National Office of Electoral Processes).

"traditional" parties. Cambio 90, Fujimori's movement, held fewer seats in Congress than APRA.

The respectable showing of the major parties in 1990 – they won 68 percent of the vote in the first round of the presidential election – did not in any way presage the system's future collapse. On the contrary, their electoral performance was comparable to that of parties in other countries throughout the region. In Bolivia, the Movimiento Nacionalista Revolucionario (MNR; National Revolutionary Movement), Acción Democrática Nacionalista (ADN; Nationalist Democratic Action), and Movimiento de Izquierda Revolucionaria (MIR; Revolutionary Leftist Movement) obtained 63.9 percent of the vote in the 1985 presidential election, 65.3 percent in 1989, and 54.1 percent in 1993. In 1993, Conciencia de la Patria (CONDEPA; Conscience of the Nation) garnered 13.6 percent of the vote and the Unión Cívica Solidaridad (UCS; Civic Union for Solidarity) received 13.1% (Gamarra and Malloy 1995). In Argentina, the Peronist and Radical parties together won 92.2 percent of the vote in the 1983 presidential election, 79.9 percent in 1989, and 66.9 percent in 1995, when Frente por un País Solidario (FREPASO; Front for a Country in Solidarity) surpassed the Radical Party (Gervasoni 1997).[3] Despite the sharp decline in the vote share of the major parties, no one would have argued that the Peronists or Radicals were about to disappear from Argentina's political map.

Civil Society

A second indication that Peruvian democracy was functioning despite its difficulties was the organization and mobilization of civil society, and its links with the party system. Within the popular sectors, strong labor organizations that developed under the military regime (more precisely under the Velasco administration of 1968–75) reached levels of influence and collective action never seen before in Peruvian history. Especially important were the General Confederation of Workers of Peru (Central General de Trabajadores del Perú; CGTP) and the teachers' union, the Union of Peruvian Education Workers (Sindicato Único de Trabajadores de la Educación Peruana; SUTEP). Rural workers and peasants were organized in the Peruvian Peasant Confederation (Confederacíon Compesina del Perú; CCP) and the National Agrarian Confederation (Confederación Nacional Agraria; CNA). But Peruvian popular sectors had more than strong "traditional" workers' organizations. During the 1980s, strong organizations developed mainly in urban areas among shantytown dwellers, women who ran popular kitchens and other state-sponsored social programs, and others that were labeled "new social movements" and "constructors of a new order" by sociologists in Peru (Ballón 1986). These "traditional" and "new" popular organizations had strong ties with parties of the left that belonged to the IU, to the point that the political and social spheres overlapped almost

---

[3] The results of legislative and constituent Congressional elections show a similar tendency.

completely (Gonzales de Olarte and Samamé 1991).[4] This representation of popular organizations was complemented by the United Left's solid electoral support among the popular sectors.[5]

Business groups also showed increasing levels of organization. At the beginning of the 1980s, an umbrella organization of entrepreneurs was constituted (Confederation of Private Entrepreneurial Institutions or Confederacíon de Instituciones Empresariales Privadas, CONFIEP) that became increasingly professional and participated actively in the production of ideas and policy proposals between 1984 and 1993. Business groups had strong ties with the parties of the right, especially the PPC, throughout the 1980s. During Alan García's administration (1985–90), the relationship between business and right-wing parties was even closer, especially after July 1987, when García announced plans to nationalize the financial system. The PPC and AP fought the proposed legislation in Congress and organized rallies and street demonstrations along with the leaders of business associations. In early 1988, the Democratic Front (Frente Democrático; FREDEMO) was born, composed of the Liberty Movement (Movimiento Libertad, led by Mario Vargas Llosa and a group of independents), AP, and the PPC. Relations between business and these parties were never closer. Many well-known leaders of business associations went on to become leaders and congressional candidates of the Movimiento Libertad (Durand 1995, 1999).

Commitment to Democracy

A third key criterion for evaluating the performance of democracy in Peru is the degree of commitment on the part of the main social and political actors to the rules of the democratic game, expressed by their respect for the political pact laid out in the 1979 Constitution. Following Linz and Stepan (1996), a key indicator of democratic consolidation is that for all main actors democracy is "the only game in town." In this case, "respect" does not mean scrupulous compliance with each and every one of its articles but rather, more realistically, the degree to which party actors behaved strategically – and assuming that the rules of alternation and of the democratic game would be the principal mechanisms for settling political differences – without resorting to antisystem strategies. Despite the fact that polarization occurred, it did not strain the system's limits. The left employed revolutionary and antisystem rhetoric and maintained a certain ambiguity in its defense of the democratic regime, but in practice most organizations of the left followed the rules of the game and distanced themselves from the antisystem terrorist organizations Shining Path and the Túpac Amaru Revolutionary Movement (Movimiento Revolucionario Túpac

---

[4] This evidence fits with Touraine's (1989) observations about Latin American political dynamics. One characteristic he noted was society's lack of autonomy in relation to politics.

[5] Cameron (1994) and Dietz and Dugan (1996) establish that there was a high correlation between voting for the IU and belonging to the popular sectors.

Amaru; MRTA). The right abandoned its traditional path of knocking on the doors of the barracks to solicit a military coup to prevent the advances of leftist or antisystem forces, and upper- and middle-class demands were channeled through the party system. Especially revealing is the fact that some military coups were plotted during the 1980s but never came to fruition because the political class defended the constitutional order. The period from mid-1988 to early 1989 was especially difficult in this sense, characterized by the crisis and virtual decomposition of the APRA government.[6]

In conclusion, Peruvian democracy during the 1980s functioned according to basic minimum requirements, and the Peruvian situation was not radically different from that of other countries in the region that did not experience a democratic breakdown during the 1990s. Even until 1990, Peru's party system was beginning to become institutionalized, in line with regional trends, despite the severity of the crisis. The main challenge to the party system at the end of the 1980s was not a problem of representation resulting from a legitimacy crisis but rather the polarization of strong ideological actors.

THE COLLAPSE OF THE PARTY SYSTEM AND DEMOCRATIC BREAKDOWN

By the end of the 1980s, then, Peruvian democracy was not doomed, although the party system was indeed vulnerable. Fujimori's election to the presidency is better explained not by the crisis of the 1980s but by the 1990 electoral process.

The protagonists of the 1990 election appeared to be relatively strong. The right, which had become a minority political bloc after the AP–PPC government (1980–85), rapidly reconstituted itself in FREDEMO in 1988. It experienced an ideological renewal in terms of its neoliberal program and gained a renowned leader in the writer Mario Vargas Llosa. By the 1989 municipal elections, the right was once again the country's strongest political force. FREDEMO was favored to win the 1990 general election, and Vargas Llosa did win a plurality of the first-round vote with 32.6 percent of the vote to Fujimori's 29.1 percent.[7] Without an absolute majority, however, he was forced to compete

---

[6] In 1988 there were persistent rumors that a military coup was being prepared against President García. The two main presidential candidates, Mario Vargas Llosa (FREDEMO) and Alfonso Barrantes (IU), as well as all major political actors, explicitly rejected the idea of a coup. Lynch (1999) and Cotler (1995) emphasize the dominance of noncooperative behavior and the parties' lack of adherence to democratic values. Such arguments correctly call attention to problems of governability that existed within the system, but they do not help to explain democracy's persistence over a ten-year period and the crisis of *representation* that led to the system's collapse. Therefore, those arguments illustrate the fallacy of retrospective determinism. Leading actors were not strongly committed to the ideals of democracy, but they acted strategically within its limits. Moreover, in the period preceding the 1992 *autogolpe*, parties arrived at important agreements on the main issues of public interest (a counterterrorism strategy is one example) for the first time.

[7] Some have erroneously hailed the victory of "independent" candidate Ricardo Belmont, who became mayor of Lima in the November 1989 municipal elections, as a clear sign of party weakness

in a runoff election, which Fujimori won. Despite the crisis of its administration from 1988 onward, APRA remained an important electoral option. In the 1989 municipal elections, the party obtained almost 20 percent of the vote. Moreover, in the 1990 election, APRA presidential candidate Luis Alva Castro came close to reaching the runoff. He ended up with 22.5 percent of the vote. Finally, the left was also a very competitive actor. Led by Alfonso Barrantes, the United Left throughout 1988 and much of 1989 was favored to win the 1990 election. Barrantes would have been the first Marxist president to be elected in Peru's history and the second in Latin America after Salvador Allende.

However, the IU's chances shrank because it divided after its "unity" congress in January 1989. The real possibility of seizing power in the 1990 election in a polarized context exacerbated internal conflicts, which led to a division between a reformist and a revolutionary wing. Especially contentious were the discussions about the IU's position on political violence. One segment completely opposed violence as a strategy for obtaining power, while another refused to rule it out for ideological reasons. These contradictions became exacerbated as the dynamic of violence intensified. The IU split boosted FREDEMO's public support, and it even seemed that Vargas Llosa was going to win in the first round election in 1990 with an outright majority of the vote. However, major campaign errors by FREDEMO (which in large part resulted from the belief that it would be a sure winner) unexpectedly created a representation vacuum that the APRA candidate, Luis Alva Castro, could not fill because of APRA's internal divisions. Alan García did not support the party candidate for fear that Alva Castro might threaten García's leadership and control over the party. García in the end supported the independent Alberto Fujimori. Fujimori took advantage of the division of the IU, the mistakes of FREDEMO, and the internal conflicts within APRA. In a context of crisis, these circumstances created a vacuum that was finally and incredibly occupied by the outsider Fujimori, who was a virtual unknown just weeks before the election. In the runoff election, Fujimori obtained 62.4 percent of the vote, and Vargas Llosa garnered 37.6 percent.

In spite of Fujimori's victory, the four largest post-1978 parties still controlled Congress and continued to be the most significant actors. Together, FREDEMO, APRA, and two leftist groups (IU and IS, or Socialist Left, a split from the IU) held 182 seats in Congress out of a total of 242 in the two chambers (or 75.2 percent of the total). Cambio 90 held 46 seats, far fewer than FREDEMO (84) and APRA (70). Faced with this situation, Fujimori followed a strategy of confrontation with the parties and the institutional order. They, in turn, tried to manage the weak and inexperienced president, looking ahead to the 1995 election in which Fujimori would not be allowed to compete because of the 1979 Constitution's prohibition on the immediate reelection of the incumbent president. The opposition parties encouraged organized protest

and of the advance of leaders from outside the system. Belmont explicitly and enthusiastically supported Mario Vargas Llosa, which demonstrates that system actors still had the power to bring in independents.

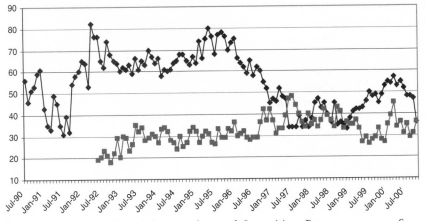

FIGURE 9.2. Approval Levels for President and Opposition, Peru, 1990–2000. Source:
APOYO.

against economic adjustment policies, and mobilizations were intense throughout 1991.

How was it that the weak and inexperienced Fujimori – facing serious problems, with a minority in Congress, heading an improvised political movement,
besieged by social protest, limited by the opposition and the institutional order –
masterminded a successful *autogolpe* in 1992? His triumph can be contrasted to
the failures of presidents Bucaram in Ecuador (1997), Collor in Brazil (1992),
and Serrano Elías (1993) in Guatemala, who also faced off against legislative bodies utilizing antipolitical discourse in a context in which politicians
had lost legitimacy, but ultimately were forced to resign (Pérez-Liñán 1998,
2000). Fujimori's success is even more puzzling given that approval levels for
his administration dropped from an average of 54 percent between August
and December 1990 to 38.5 percent between January and September 1991
(Figure 9.2). Although inflation had fallen substantially, it was still rather high;
in 1991 the rate was 139.2 percent. Moreover, with the inflationary flare-ups
of December 1990 (23.7 percent) and January 1991 (17.8 percent), there was
a general feeling that the economic program had failed. By early March 1991,
public disapproval for Fujimori was around 50 percent, and approval was only
around 33 percent, according to various polls. Meanwhile, the violence continued, and the Shining Path terrorist movement claimed to have reached what it
called a "strategic equilibrium" – the phase leading to the offensive that would
bring it to power. In addition, responding to the president's belligerent rhetoric
against Congress, his opponents began in March 1991 to discuss the possibility
of deposing Fujimori and replacing him with Máximo San Román, the first vice
president and the president of the Senate.

Thus, during the first half of 1991, it seemed probable that the Congress
would depose Fujimori, or – in the best-case scenario – Fujimori would end up
making major concessions to the opposition. Given the context, the decision
of the opposition parties to confront Fujimori and try to place limits on the

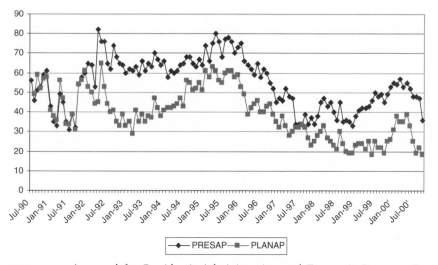

FIGURE 9.3. Approval for President's Administration and Economic Program, Peru, 1990–2000. Source: APOYO.

president seemed rational. Yet Fujimori overcame his isolation, built a coalition of interests that supported his administration after April 5, 1992, and stayed in power when Collor in Brazil and Bucaram in Ecuador failed. The key difference is that he managed to stabilize the economy in time. The monthly inflation rate, which was around 7.7 percent between January and September 1991, declined consistently after October. Between October 1991 and February 1992, it dropped to an average of 3.9 percent. There is a clear correlation between the rate of inflation and the government's approval ratings during this period. The latter went from an average of 38.5 percent between January and September 1991 to an average of 60 percent between October 1991 and February 1992 (Figure 9.3).

Economic stabilization allowed Fujimori to win the increasingly high-stakes battle for public opinion. Structural changes that grew out of the period of hyperinflation between 1988 and 1991 undermined the foundations for *movimientista* politics in Peru, particularly with respect to popular organizations. Unlike the late 1970s when mass mobilizations paved the way for the transition to democracy, between 1988 and 1991 power no longer depended on the capacity to mobilize social actors. Hyperinflation and structural adjustment policies destroyed formal employment, swelled the informal sector, and enormously weakened the capacity for mobilization and protest. As Figure 9.4 shows, after 1988 (following the adjustment program launched by APRA minister Abel Salinas), the decrease in formal employment diminished the ability of organized workers to strike. The opposition, which had deeply rooted relationships with social actors and interest groups, bet on being able to limit Fujimori's power through mobilization and social protest. Nevertheless, with time it became apparent that the capacity to influence organized sectors of the population did not translate into power. Gradually, power was best gained in a critical new

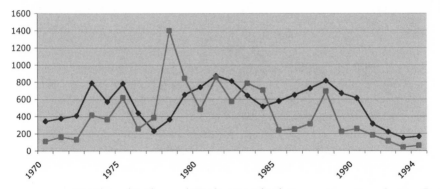

FIGURE 9.4. Number of Strikes and Workers Involved, Peru, 1970–1994. Source: *Perú en Números* (various years).

arena: that of public opinion. At the same time, the success of orthodox adjustment policies enabled Fujimori to gain support among such key actors as entrepreneurs, the military, and multilateral organizations.

Had Fujimori attempted his *autogolpe* in mid-1991, he would have failed. His situation would have been similar to that of Serrano Elías in Guatemala in 1993, where parties were no stronger than in Peru but prevailed against the attacks of an antiparty president. But in April 1992, thanks to his control of the hyperinflationary process and its destabilizing effects, Fujimori found himself in favorable circumstances and those circumstances – marked by economic stability and the expectation of future improvement – allowed him to legitimize his actions. The parties' attempts to limit Fujimori's power by a combination of actions in institutional spaces (Congress) and on the streets were insufficient to counter the legitimacy he enjoyed from public opinion and key actors.

By consolidating his government, Fujimori also consolidated an authoritarian order; he legitimized antiinstitutional discourse and practices and, consequently, dislocated and forced the collapse of parties and the party system of the 1980s. In other countries – including Paz Estenssoro's Bolivia (1985–89), Menem's Argentina (1989–99), and Cardoso's Brazil (1995–2002) – presidents also successfully stabilized their economies by adopting neoliberal policies, as did Fujimori. But in these cases, the prevailing economic model was changed within the framework of the party system. For Menem and Paz Estenssoro, the main challenge was to transform their traditional party identities. In Peru, by contrast, the unexpected arrival of an outsider to the presidency and the establishment of a completely different political dynamic placed his government in opposition to the party system and democratic institutions.

THE CONSOLIDATION OF *FUJIMORISMO*

From April 1992 onward, Fujimorism underwent a process of consolidation on both the economic and counterterrorism fronts. In the economic realm,

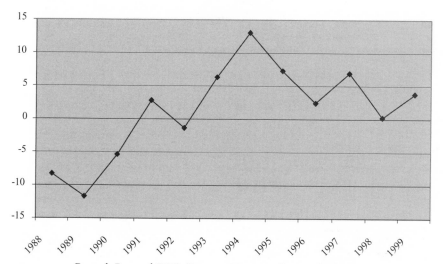

FIGURE 9.5. Growth Rate of GDP, Peru, 1988–1999. Source: INEI.

the government achieved a substantial and sustained reduction in inflation. After the four-digit annual rates of 1988–90 and even 139 percent in 1991, inflation declined to 57 percent in 1992, 40 percent in 1993, 15 percent in 1994, and finally single digits by 1997. In 1999, inflation was only 3.2 percent (Instituto Nacional de Estadística e Informática; INEI). Peru's GDP also grew significantly between 1993 and 1995 (Figure 9.5), making the country's average growth between 1993 and 1998 among the highest in Latin America.[8]

The government also defeated the two terrorist movements, the Shining Path and MRTA. Terrorist attacks declined in 1993 (Figure 9.6), after the April 1992 coup and the September capture of the Shining Path's leader, Abimael Guzmán, suggesting that the government's successful antisubversive strategy was not what lent legitimacy to the 1992 coup but helped to consolidate it afterward (Carrión 1999; Weyland 2001).

Fujimori's visible successes afforded him great popular support, as expressed in high approval ratings for his administration. As Figure 9.2 demonstrates, between 1992 and 1996, the administration's approval levels almost never dropped below 60 percent and throughout 1995 surpassed 70 percent. From October 1991 to October 1996, the administration averaged a 66 percent approval rating in metropolitan Lima (Table 9.1).

Fujimori exploited this public support to consolidate a personalistic, authoritarian leadership style characterized by confrontation with the institutional order and an antipolitical, antiparty discourse. The political parties that had won more than 90 percent of the vote in nearly every election held in Peru during the 1980s practically disappeared (with the partial exception of APRA,

---

[8] For further development of the ideas discussed in this section, see Tanaka 1999b and 2003.

TABLE 9.1. *Percentage of Lima Residents Who Approve of the President's Administration, by Social Sector, 1990–2000*

Period	Average	A	B	C	D
1. July–Dec. 1990	54	45	47	56	61
2. Jan. 1991–Sept. 1991	38	36	36	39	38
3. Oct. 1991–Oct. 1996	66	68	62	62	63
4. Nov. 1996–Dec. 1998	40	39	34	38	43
5. Jan. 1999–Apr. 2000	48	41	38	46	54

Note: Sector A is the most affluent; Sector D is the poorest.
Source: Data from APOYO for metropolitan Lima area.

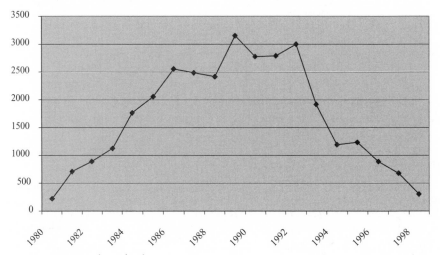

FIGURE 9.6. Number of Subversive Actions, Peru, 1980–1998. Source: *Perú en Números* (various years).

which reappeared on the national scene with Alan García's return in the 2001 election). Fujimori began a deep neoliberal restructuring of the country, closing a chapter in the long battle to control the nation's path that had begun with the crisis of the oligarchical order. The new government combined a first generation of structural reforms with neopopulist practices that symbolically incorporated popular sectors through clientelistic mechanisms (Kay 1995; Roberts 1995; Tanaka 2003; Weyland 1996b).

At this point, a broad coalition of interests coalesced around Fujimori, beginning with the winners in the process of structural reform: the hegemonic business sector, comprised of large mining companies, financial interests, and importers who had benefited from trade liberalization, privatization, and foreign investment (Cotler 1998, 1999; Gonzales de Olarte 1998). At the same time, Fujimori enjoyed important international support, from multilateral institutions and the U.S. government, which considered Fujimori an effective ally in the fight against drug trafficking (Cotler 1999).

These sectors, while powerful, were extremely small in social terms and insufficient to guarantee electoral victories. Therefore, the government developed a social policy to win popular support, especially after 1993. Throughout his administration, Fujimori significantly increased social spending on a per capita basis, as a percentage of GDP, and as a percentage of total public expenditure. Social spending per capita rose from $12 in 1990 to $63 in 1993, $75 in 1994, $145 in 1995, and $158 in 1996 (INEI); as a percentage of GDP, by Fujimori's second administration, social spending had reached its highest level in two decades. As a percentage of total public expenditure, it doubled from 17 percent in 1990 to 35 percent in 1996, before falling off to 28 percent in 1999. Moreover, between 1997 and 2000 the percentage of persons in extreme poverty (approximately 15 percent of the population) who received government-donated food increased from 71.4 percent to 75.5 percent (O'Brien 2001).

Fujimori won a comfortable reelection in 1995. He obtained 64 percent of the vote for president, and his movement received 52 percent of the votes in the Congressional races. His nearest competitor, Javier Pérez de Cuéllar, obtained only 22 percent of the presidential vote and his movement, Union for Peru (Unión Por el Perú; UPP), 14% of the Congressional vote. These lopsided results did not allow for the reconfiguration of a new party system. If the opposition had fared better at the polls, there could have emerged a bipartisan format with two large blocs, one linked to Fujimori and the other to a democratic opposition. Instead, Fujimori's landslide victory in 1995 dealt a blow to the development of a balanced party system, a system of checks and balances, and the hope of a return to a more competitive democracy.

With no significant counterweights to his power, Fujimori maintained and later deepened an authoritarian dynamic, extending the post-1992 coup scenario to a great extent. This fact is important to our understanding of democratic regimes. It is not enough for governments to originate with reasonably clean elections – institutions must also function at a certain level, and there must be some degree of political competition (Tanaka 1999a). Peru eloquently demonstrates that without these factors, democracy lacks authenticity. Peru had a government with important political support, capable of winning elections, but functioning as an authoritarian regime, given the lack of autonomous institutions and effective mechanisms of checks and balances (McClintock 1999a; Tanaka 1999a); this is what Levitsky and Way (2002) have characterized as "competitive authoritarianism."[9]

Fujimorism took on an increasingly authoritarian character after 1996, when Fujimori began the maneuvers that led to his reelection in 2000. His goal of

---

[9] See also Schedler (2002) and Diamond (2002). The importance of including in a conception of democracy not merely elections but also mechanisms of horizontal accountability is crucial for analyzing other cases such as Venezuela under Chávez.

winning reelection led him to seek control over almost all state institutions and to erase the differences between state and government. Given that the institutional structure created by Fujimori himself from 1993 onward would impede his reelection, the government began to violate this structure to its own advantage. In August 1996, Congress passed the "Law of Authentic Interpretation of the Constitution" (Law 26657),[10] which violated the 1993 Constitution, the spirit of the Constituent Assembly debate, and the jurisprudence of the National Elections Board (Jurado Nacional de Elecciones; JNE)[11] – all of which the regime itself had established as its legal foundations. The government intervened in the judicial branch (June 1996) and the attorney general's office (January 1997); deactivated the Constitutional Tribunal and dismissed three of its seven members (May 1997); curbed the powers of the National Magistrates' Council (March 1998); maneuvered to stop Congress's call for a referendum on presidential reelection (August 1998); and took actions to limit the power of electoral bodies to declare Fujimori's candidacy illegal (May 1999). Practically every state institution was tampered with to remove every obstacle that might stand in the way of Fujimori's reelection.[12] With democratic institutions functioning only in a superficial sense, Fujimori's government descended into an authoritarian regime.

Fujimori built a personalistic regime; he did not build a real party or movement that could benefit from his political capital. All of the movements linked to the government – Cambio 90, New Majority, Let's Go Neighbors, and Peru 2000 – lacked organic life and organization. Moreover, there were no bases or organized social sectors that could be clearly considered constituents of the regime. Fujimori's personalistic order was the opposite of the traditional PRI order in Mexico. Fujimori opted to weaken popular organizations and establish loose clientelistic networks. Because the key to success with popular sectors was the clientelistic use of state resources, by necessity, the regime's survival depended on Fujimori's personal continuity in power. His base of support relied increasingly on manipulation; his dependency on the state made it impossible for him to subject himself to the uncertainty of electoral mechanisms, unless he could manipulate these to ensure the regime's continuity, as he did in 2000. Because Fujimori could not deal with reelection through institutional means (with a referendum to change the 1993 Constitution), he simply violated the juridical order. Because Fujimori could not count on a political apparatus to

---

[10] According to the 1993 Constitution, immediate reelection can only take place once. The new law established that Fujimori's first term had begun in 1995 rather than 1990 (because in 1990 Fujimori had been elected under the 1979 Constitution).

[11] The Constituent Assembly debate and the National Elections Board established that Fujimori could be a presidential candidate in 1995 *with the understanding that* in so doing, he was aspiring to reelection as permitted by the 1993 Constitution.

[12] Because the government controlled every institution, including the attorney general's office and the judicial branch, it is easy to understand how it sank to levels of corruption rarely before seen in Peruvian history. The situation was the result of the state's enormous (by national standards) access to resources (generated principally by privatizations) and the absence of effective counterweights and controls.

put these actions into practice, he relied more and more on the state apparatus and in particular on the National Intelligence Service (Servicio de Inteligencia Nacional; SIN) and his advisor Vladimiro Montesinos.[13] Behind the scenes was a vast network of pressure and corruption.

Could the road to the consolidation of an authoritarian regime have been avoided? Contrary to the conventional wisdom that portrays Fujimori as invincible, and his regime powerful and impregnable, the situation was always open to different outcomes, depending upon the decisions of the principal political actors.

FUJIMORI'S WEAKNESS, THE OPPOSITION'S WEAKNESS, AND THE 2000 ELECTION

The Fujimori government, from the second half of 1996 through the end of 1998, steadily lost popular support (see Figure 9.3). By December 1998, when his approval rate was 33 percent, Fujimori's prospects for reelection in 2000 seemed doomed. Some authors have stressed that the Fujimori government based its popularity on the control of the media and the manipulation of public opinion (Arias 2001; Cotler 2000; Degregori 2000; Grompone 2000; Quijano 2000; Vega Centeno 2000). However, the volatility of the president's approval ratings suggests that Fujimori's support was not immovable. The key to explaining the recovery of Fujimori's popularity during the course of 1999, which ultimately allowed his second reelection, is the fact that he faced an extremely weak opposition as a result of actors' decisions and the legacy of party system collapse. More specifically, the political movements that replaced "traditional" parties were guided by a very shortsighted logic that facilitated the success of Fujimori's maneuvers, even when there were opportunities to take advantage of the rejection that many of his actions generated.[14]

Immediately following the April 1992 *autogolpe*, the government felt obliged by international pressure to seek a return to constitutional normality. Fujimori had to call elections for a new Congress. In November 1992, an election was held for the Democratic Constituent Congress (CCD), which both served as a Congress and drafted a new constitution. The main opposition political actors abstained from the election, calling for a nullification of ballots. The vote for the opposition was 25 percent, but it was divided among five groups. The CCD election ended up giving Fujimori a narrow majority and a significant increase in the size of his Congressional delegation. In the 1990 election, Cambio 90 won 21.7 percent of the votes for Senate and 16.5 percent for the Chamber of Deputies. In 1992, New Majority–Cambio 90 obtained 49.2 percent of the vote, which translated into forty-four out of eighty Congressional seats. In November 1993, a referendum was held to approve the new constitution. Contrary to what one would expect from the image of an invincible Fujimori, the

---

[13] The National Intelligence Service (SIN) carried out the functions that a political committee would have had within a political party. On Montesinos and the SIN, see Rospigliosi (2000).

[14] This section follows ideas developed in Tanaka (2003).

referendum ended in a technical draw amidst serious denunciations of fraud and irregularities.[15] The referendum campaign was important for several reasons, including the fact that it established a basis for potential unity among government opposition forces. A broad group of opposition forces joined together in the "'No' Campaign Command." This movement effectively raised regional demands for decentralization and called for defense of the social rights that had been supported by the 1979 Constitution but reduced in the 1993 Charter. Despite the victory of the "yes" vote, the "no" campaign demonstrated a unity that paved the way for a series of conversations to select a single candidate for the 1995 presidential election or at least to develop a common strategy for opposing Fujimori.

Fujimori's vulnerability was manifest not only in the November 1993 referendum but also in local elections. In January 1993, just two months after the CCD election, government-backed candidates were soundly defeated in municipal elections. The government's mayoral candidate in Lima, Pablo Gutiérrez, was forced to bow out weeks before the election to avoid an expected loss. In the provinces, the few government candidates were also defeated. In the 1995 and 1998 municipal elections in Lima, government candidates were again beaten. In 1995, Jaime Yoshiyama, who was considered Fujimori's heir apparent, was defeated in his bid to become mayor of Lima by independent candidate Alberto Andrade from the "We Are Lima" movement. Several analysts concluded that Fujimori's attempt to create an heir to succeed him also failed here.[16] Fujimorism as a movement never took hold.

These losses in local elections show that Fujimori never built a political movement, relying instead on personal, not institutional, power. Since 1990, Fujimori had been alone – without a party or organization – and he chose to build a personalistic apparatus. This helps to explain why Fujimori chose to elect the Congress in 1995 and 2000 through a single national district, a highly proportional system, rather than through small electoral districts, which in theory would have been better for him.[17] Elections involving diverse electoral districts imply negotiation with regional leaders, even when the national leadership controls the candidate selection process. A single national district, in contrast, allows a central power to manage the list of candidates with almost complete discretion.

---

[15] The "yes" vote on the new constitution was 52.3 percent, and the "no," 47.7 percent. The "yes" vote was higher in Lima, but almost all the provinces and poorest areas, which had not benefited as much from stabilization policies and were more critical of the government, voted "no." This situation began to change in 1993, however, when the economy improved and the government began to increase social spending.

[16] Yoshiyama lost by a narrow margin. Andrade obtained 52.1 percent of the vote, and Yoshiyama won 47.9 percent.

[17] Peru 2000 obtained fifty-two seats in the April 2000 election. According to various proposals to reform the electoral system with regional, departmental or provincial electoral districts (all presented by opposition members of Congress), Peru 2000 would have obtained between seventy-one and eighty-one seats. See *Datos para la democracia*.

Fujimori's election in 1995 – despite his administration's high approval ratings – was not a foregone conclusion. During 1993 and much of 1994, opposition candidate Javier Pérez de Cuéllar fared better than Fujimori in preelection polls. Pérez de Cuéllar and his movement, Union for Peru, could have helped to constitute a party system with two fairly balanced forces. Fujimori's opposition could have conceivably formed a unitary bloc, given the precedent of the 1993 "No" Campaign Command. Nevertheless, the opposition set aside this valuable experience and faced the electoral process divided. Underestimating how deeply Fujimori had changed Peruvian political life, and captivated by the mirage of their representation prior to 1990, the parties believed they could regain their previous strength by putting forth candidates who were strongly identified with their organizations. They paid dearly for their mistakes, suffering a shocking defeat in 1995. Together, they earned only 6.3 percent of the votes for president and only 14.8 percent of the votes for Congress (Schmidt 1999).

Even given the results of the 1995 election, the opposition still might have coalesced around the UPP, led by Javier Pérez de Cuéllar. Fujimori's government was in crisis beginning in late 1996, and the regime's main opponents could have capitalized on his decline. Instead, the UPP began to weaken. Like Mario Vargas Llosa in 1990, the former UN secretary general left the country in 1995, depriving the main opposition party of identity and leadership and unleashing a series of internal conflicts for the vacant leadership. The movement, which had relied so much on Pérez de Cuéllar, was as vulnerable as all movements that depend on a single personality. The UPP's congressional delegation and political capacity diminished with time; it had seventeen members of Congress in 1995, but ended with only two in 2000.

The opposition squandered other opportunities beginning in 1996, when public disapproval of Fujimori's performance began to increase, until mid-1999, when his disapproval rating still surpassed his approval ratings. Beginning in the last quarter of 1996, the opposition's approval ratings increased, eventually matching the president's approval ratings by mid-1997. From then until mid-1999, this parity continued (Figure 9.2). The same period also witnessed the dismissal of judges from the constitutional tribunal, student protest marches in response, and the opposition's campaign for a referendum against Fujimori's third term. This period differed radically from that of 1992 to 1996. Diverse sectors of the opposition converged around a single cause and substantive issues.

In late 1998, after the municipal elections, it seemed reasonable to expect that Alberto Andrade, the recently reelected mayor of Lima, would win the April 2000 election and impossible that the worn-out Fujimori regime would be capable of rebounding from its systematic three-year decline. Despite this, the opposition was unable to win the battle for political hegemony. Throughout 1999 Fujimori won back public approval, to the point that he nearly won an outright majority in the 2000 presidential election. On average, the president's approval ratings rose from 40 percent in 1998 to 45 percent in 1999, and again to 50 percent between January and July 2000. Why did the opposition's tendency to grow in strength over the years, and Fujimori's to decline, change drastically during 1999? Why did Fujimori's declining approval levels and the errors and political scandals associated with his reelection bid not translate into stronger support for the opposition?

This question has a three-part answer. First, and most importantly, the opposition that was built around the 1996 referendum had developed a negative identity; it opposed Fujimori, but left unanswered the question of who should run the country and how. As Przeworski (1986) argued, an authoritarian regime's crisis of legitimacy does not necessarily lead to a transition process: For this to happen, a clear alternative must appear. In Peru, Fujimori had lost strength but no clear alternative surfaced. This was particularly clear in the economic realm. During Fujimori's crisis period, when the effects of recession were of critical concern to most citizens, the opposition focused on the referendum and the presidential reelection, brandishing arguments based on abstract principles amidst a confusing juridical debate. This caused the opposition's support to increase among the upper and middle classes, while Fujimori gained strength among the popular sectors through the clientelistic practices described previously. Table 9.1 shows that during the preelection period between January 1999 and April 2000, Fujimori's approval in sector "D" was six points above average, and sixteen points above his approval ratings among sector "B," which corresponded to the middle class.

Second, the opposition went into the 2000 election divided and without a common strategy, which scattered the anti-Fujimori vote. Although total electoral support for opposition candidates evenly matched Fujimori's support in preelection polls, the opposition was unable to stitch together an electoral coalition similar to the Alliance that took shape in Argentina around the same time. Their failure to do so can be explained in part by Peru's electoral system and in part by the nature of Peru's opposition political movements. According to the 1993 Constitution, if no candidate obtains an absolute majority of the vote, the two leading candidates must go head-to-head in a second-round election. Although Fujimori appeared to be close to winning an absolute majority, most analysts predicted that he would not do so. Reasoning that in a second-round election the total votes for the opposition would outstrip Fujimori's, all of the opposition candidates concentrated their efforts on winning the battle for second place, which was hotly disputed from mid-1999 to just one month before the April 2000 election. The nature of Peru's opposition movements also explains the dispersion of opposition forces. These movements were new, weak, and inexperienced; consequently, they viewed a small representation in Congress as sufficient reward for their efforts. The electoral system fostered this logic: In 1995 and 2000 Congress was elected from a single national district, with no entry barriers, under a highly proportional system in which a candidate could win a seat with just 0.8 percent of the vote.[18]

---

[18] Argentina also elects its president in runoff elections, but it is not necessary, as in Peru, to achieve more that 50 percent of the vote. But more importantly, in Argentina the cost of staying out of power, for a party like the Radical Party, with strong constituencies to satisfy, is far higher

TABLE 9.2. *Vote Intention for President, Peru, 1999–2000*

	Oct. 1999	Jan. 2000	Feb. 2000	Mar. 2000	Apr. 9, 2000
Fujimori	36	41	39	38	46
Andrade	19	16	14	8	2.8
Castañeda	19	14	12	5	1.7
Toledo	6	7	10	27	37

Source: National surveys carried out by APOYO for October 1999 to March 2000. The data for April 9 are the final official election results based on the total number of votes cast, including blank and spoiled ballots.

Fujimori's recovery was not merely the result of the opposition's miscalculations and mistakes. A third reason for his rebound at the polls was his achievements in office, most notably his government's success at stimulating a modest economic recovery in 1999; a peace treaty with Ecuador that ended decades of disputed borders; the resolution of ongoing border disputes with Chile; and the capture of "Comrade Feliciano," the main Shining Path leader still at large. The combination of opposition weakness and government success allowed Fujimori to succeed in a series of authoritarian and dirty maneuvers, including such tactics as the use of state resources in the election campaign, the control of most of the press, and smear campaigns against opposition candidates in the tabloids.

Elections were carried out in a highly irregular fashion; clearly they did not meet international standards for free and fair elections. The regime's smear tactics against the opposition gradually weakened the two main opposition candidates (Alberto Andrade and Luis Castañeda), but they also produced, unexpectedly, just weeks before the election, "the Toledo phenomenon." Alejandro Toledo, another independent, a technocratic-style economist who had run unsuccessfully for the presidency in 1995,[19] rose quickly in preelection polls, from 10 percent six weeks before the election to 37 percent of the votes cast on April 9 (Table 9.2). Toledo embodied a hope for renewal based on a centrist program "to continue what was good about the government," to correct its errors, and to create jobs, without getting too involved in institutional issues. In an impressive show of voter autonomy, practically the entire opposition vote concentrated quickly and spontaneously on a single candidate, achieving the collective unity that opposition leaders had previously been unable to forge.

than the cost for new and inexperienced parties like the ones in Peru. At the same time, for the Radicals the alliance was useful because, given they had the more powerful organization, they were going to head it; for FREPASO, a new and inexperienced organization, it was attractive to be part of a strong coalition with a good chance of winning the elections. In Peru, on the contrary, we had new, small, and weak parties that were satisfied with only a small representation in Congress; they lacked incentives to unite and act collectively.

[19] In 1995, Toledo obtained 3.2 percent of the vote for president, and his candidates for Congress obtained 4.1 percent.

The results of the April 9 vote are impressive because of both the very high number of votes cast for Fujimori after ten years in power and Toledo's completely unexpected, sudden, and spontaneous rise. Also remarkable is the very poor showing of other candidates, revealing the extreme volatility of the opposition vote.[20] In the end, the regime was electorally vulnerable despite its authoritarianism and maneuvering, but it still came within just tenths of a percentage point of winning an absolute majority of the valid vote.[21] Even so, the government's legitimacy was weakened, and Toledo's growth was significant. Toledo united opposition groups and citizen protest movements, amidst general allegations of fraud and serious irregularities in the vote count.[22]

In the second round, despite the fact that he found himself at the head of a vast protest movement, Toledo's candidacy was limited to institutional demands. He committed the same error that the opposition had years before in the fight against Fujimori, and he lost much of the status that had made him attractive in the first round. The absence of concrete policy proposals for a country battered by economic crisis meant that just days before the second round, most opinion polls gave Fujimori a ten-point advantage over Toledo, although many voters were still undecided. The government's refusal to postpone the second-round election, which the Organization of American States (OAS) had requested in order to check the software used in the disputed vote-counting system, gave Toledo the opening to boycott an election plagued by irregularities. In the voting held on May 28, which took place with a single candidate and without Peruvian or foreign election observers or opposition delegates, Fujimori received 51 percent of the votes cast, and Alejandro Toledo, 18 percent.[23]

Between the May 28 vote and the start of Fujimori's third term on July 28, a battle was launched on three fronts: in the international arena, in Congress, and in the streets. The opposition sought to discredit Fujimori's victory in all three places, but the Fujimori regime succeeded in weathering the storm. On the international front, it achieved recognition of the new government in exchange for

---

[20] The validity of these figures has been widely debated, and there have been insistent, generalized allegations of fraud. Although the electoral process was full of irregularities, as is characteristic of any election organized by an authoritarian regime, the results cited do not differ substantially from the vote counts arrived at by unquestionably independent groups of electoral observers, such as Transparencia. The process as a whole was flawed, and there was no regulation and control of the process of counting ballots, but nonetheless a flagrant case of fraud was not perpetrated on April 9.

[21] Discounting null and blank ballots, Fujimori was just 0.13 of a point away from winning in the first-round election.

[22] Eduardo Stein, who headed the Organization of American States' observation team, described the vote computation process as a "black box" and pointed out on the night of April 9 that "something sinister was happening." Just one of the many irregularities in the computation process was that at times, the more votes that were counted, the more the absolute number of votes for some opposition groups *decreased.*

[23] The proportion of nullified votes reached nearly 30 percent, and the abstention rate was 17 percent – just above what it had been in the first round.

the establishment of a permanent OAS mission in the country to seek "democratization." In Congress, the government rapidly managed to add twelve members to Peru 2000's fifty-two-seat delegation (out of a Congress of 120 seats) to achieve a four-seat majority. On July 27, the government's candidate obtained seventy votes in the election of the new president of the Congress, and the opposition candidate received only forty-six votes.[24] Finally, some believed that the mobilization of citizens in the streets could topple the regime, but such a view was naïve and evinced nostalgia for *movimientista* politics that had come to an end in Peru between 1988 and 1991. It was no longer possible, as it had been in the 1980s, to build real power on the basis of popular mobilization. The mobilizations that occurred in protest of Fujimori's third term were spontaneous and unorganized and had little capacity to disrupt production or the provision of essential services. Thus, their ability to pressure the government was only symbolic.[25] In sum, although Fujimori began his third term besieged by a serious legitimacy crisis and with a democratizing agenda on the horizon, the government had basically succeeded in overcoming every obstacle confronting it immediately after the elections.

THE COLLAPSE OF FUJIMORISM: "INCOMPLETE LEARNING" AND THE CHALLENGE OF RECONSTRUCTING DEMOCRATIC INSTITUTIONS

Precisely when Fujimori seemed to have surmounted the problems of the legitimacy of his second reelection, his government unexpectedly collapsed. Understanding why Fujimorism collapsed is important for understanding the challenges that Alejandro Toledo's government and Peruvian democracy face today. This collapse cannot be deduced from what happened in elections and postelectoral conflicts or from its loss of legitimacy. Those factors are certainly important, but only as intervening or contextual variables. The fall of a regime supported by the logic of raw power cannot be explained in terms of legitimacy or the interventions of rather weak social and political actors; rather, it must be explained according to this logic of power, in this case, its internal divisions (expressed by the rupture between Fujimori and Montesinos) which were precipitated by internal and external pressures.[26]

After dispelling all questions about his third term, Alberto Fujimori surprisingly called new elections on September 16, 2000, as a consequence of his break with Montesinos. The rupture seems to have been precipitated after a press conference held on August 21, when Fujimori and Montesinos announced the dismantling of an arms smuggling network that had sold weapons to Revolutionary Armed Forces of Colombia (FARC). In the following days, it became

---

[24] Today we know that many of the members of Congress who supported the government had been bought off by Vladimiro Montesinos.

[25] The fragility of Peruvian mass mobilizations is apparent when compared with those that took place in Ecuador and Bolivia in recent years.

[26] See Cotler (2000), who also emphasizes the weight of external factors.

known that high officers of the Peruvian army and Montesinos himself had been directly implicated in the sale. This placed the regime in open conflict with the United States' strategic interests in the region. The scandal marked a de facto change in the regime's foreign policy and put it on a collision course with the United States. These and other actions on the part of his adviser led Fujimori to decide to exclude Montesinos from the circle of power. Nevertheless, Montesinos enjoyed solid support among the highest ranks of the armed forces, which might have staged a coup against Fujimori.[27]

As soon as the divorce between Fujimori and Montesinos was set in motion, the nucleus of power interests and the heart of this highly personalistic regime were destroyed – as were its chances for survival. Only in this context can it be understood why Fujimori voluntarily gave up power after having prepared his reelection bid for years. In a surprise move, Fujimori called for elections as a preventive measure in order to redefine the political scene, avoid a probable coup d'etat, and attempt to lead the transition process. Nonetheless, the conflict with Montesinos made Fujimori lose control of the political process. The opposition censured Fujimori's president of the Congress on November 13. (Weeks earlier an attempt to do so had failed, before Fujimori had shown these signs of extreme weakness.) On November 16, Valentín Paniagua was elected the new president of Congress, which opened up the possibility of declaring the presidency vacant or at least initiating investigations against Fujimori on different charges. On November 20, Fujimori resigned as president. On November 22, Paniagua was sworn in as president of the Republic after accepting the resignations of the two *Fujimorista* vice presidents. The Fujimori regime, which had been so strong, collapsed in a quick, unexpected, and shocking manner. A coalition of heterogeneous interests structured around a personalized power that was articulated through access to clientelistic benefits, the regime's whole body decayed once its head was cut off.

The nature of Fujimori's collapse has important consequences for the challenges that Alejandro Toledo's government and Peruvian democracy face today. The collapse of the Fujimori regime left a legacy of institutional destruction, distrust, and discouragement among citizens, weak and disorganized social actors, and equally precarious political actors who have suddenly found themselves faced with the enormous task of rebuilding the country.

The members of the political elite now in power in Peru have undergone a process of "incomplete learning."[28] Precisely when the regime's unmasked authoritarianism made these actors value democracy and consensus in dealing with problems, Fujimorism suddenly collapsed. This situation has encouraged elites to overestimate their abilities and their role in the demise of Fujimori's regime and to underestimate the challenges they now face. Now that the force

---

[27] The fact that Montesinos was preparing plans for a coup against Fujimori has since been documented; Carlos Boloña (former economy minister) was to have been named provisional president.

[28] See McCoy (1999).

against which the opposition fought has disappeared, tendencies toward dispersion and confrontation may prevail.

The 2001 election proved much of this to be true. Nine political movements ran presidential candidates in the 2000 election; just one year later, in the 2001 election, eight movements participated but only two had been present the year before (Peru Posible and APRA). The parties (with the relative exception of APRA) were little more than election-year configurations, with little substance. During the 2001 campaign, there were sharp confrontations and even a "dirty campaign" between Peru Posible and National Unity, whose leaders had very recently led the struggle against the Fujimori government. These conflicts allowed the surprising return of Alan García to national politics as APRA's candidate, where he took a conciliatory posture and tried to assume the role of a statesman who had learned from his past errors. Alejandro Toledo, who had unexpectedly, unintentionally, led the struggles against Fujimori, finally assumed the presidency on July 28, 2001.[29] Whether Toledo, who is inexperienced, leads an ad hoc, heterogeneous coalition, and lacks a majority in Congress, can successfully tackle the numerous challenges ahead is an open question.[30]

There are reasons to be optimistic, especially if we examine the current situation in light of Peru's experience of the past few decades. The programmatic convergence among the main political actors, which represents a major shift from recent history, is particularly positive. In the last few decades, the extreme precariousness, weakness, fragility, lack of durability, and volatility of the political actors and their games have stood out. Each has championed widely divergent political projects and exhibited great ideological differences, and their interactions have been polarized. Consequently, their politics have swung back and forth and their efforts have been interrupted and disjointed, never consolidating an order of any kind.

For most of the twentieth century, the Peruvian oligarchy constituted an order – albeit an unjust one. After it disappeared and its basis of support was destroyed by General Velasco's military government (1968–75), a stable alternative order did not emerge. The 1980s witnessed a struggle for hegemony and a reconfiguration of the country following the fall of the old order. In this conflict, we find the proposed liberalism of the Belaúnde government and later of Vargas Llosa's FREDEMO, the rejuvenated populism of APRA, a Marxist left, and important antisystem challenges expressed in the totalitarian project of the Shining Path and in the repressive projects of sectors of the armed forces. These disputes were resolved in the 1990s with a profound neoliberal restructuring

---

[29] In the first electoral round, Toledo obtained 36.6 percent of the vote; García, 25.9 percent; and Lourdes Flores, 24.2 percent. In the second round, Toledo won with 53.1 percent, and García received 46.9 percent of the valid votes.

[30] In the 120-member Congress, Peru Posible has 45 seats, APRA has 28, National Unity has 17, and the Independent Moralizing Front (Frente Independiente Moralizador, or FMI) has 11. Peru 2000 and Popular Solution, two movements identified with Fujimori, have just 3 and 1 representatives, respectively. This confirms the extremely personalistic nature of Fujimorism – without the leader, the movement does not exist.

process. A first generation of reforms was achieved, but the second-generation agenda was never implemented in large part because of the personalism, sectarianism, lack of vision, and corruption of Fujimori's government. In short, neither Peru's military government nor the democracy of the 1980s nor Fujimori succeeded in building a stable order.

The situation is not all bleak. In contrast to recent decades in Peruvian history, a wide consensus has emerged on several major issues. This consensus, a consequence of the terrible experience left by Fujimorism, promotes and defends democratic values and favors horizontal accountability mechanisms, transparency, civil society participation, and the struggle against corruption and authoritarianism. Never before has there been such a degree of programmatic convergence around the political center on the proposals of key actors and a recognition of the limits of both the old populist model and the neoliberal one. There is also agreement on the necessity to rebuild the state's capacity to intervene in order to make the market economy more competitive and to reduce its social costs. The situation is certainly complicated. As in the entire region, the main challenge for Peruvian democracy is how to make compatible the people's hopes and expectations and their support for democracy in the midst of very high poverty levels and a recession. Still, the possibilities are open for political action. Now, as before, everything depends on the decisions of the main actors.

10

Explaining Democratic Deterioration in Venezuela through Nested Inference

Michael Coppedge

From a Latin American perspective, Venezuela has often been a contrary case. It was one of the last major South American countries to give any kind of democracy a try (1946); democracy took firmer root in the early 1960s, just as authoritarian regimes were beginning to sweep most of South America; and it was reputed to be an old and well-established democracy by the time its neighbors underwent their democratic transitions in the late 1970s and early 1980s. During these periods, Venezuela was so out of step with its neighbors that it tended to be written off as an exceptional case. Its concerns were not on the regional research agenda, and the theories developed for other countries were assumed not to apply to Venezuela.[1] In the 1990s, however, observers began to wonder whether Venezuela was a harbinger of its neighbors' political future. Violent repression in 1989, two coup attempts in 1992, and the rise of an anti-system president with authoritarian proclivities in 1998 presaged or coincided with setbacks in democracy in Peru, Guatemala, Paraguay, Ecuador, Colombia, and the Dominican Republic. Now we commonly assume that the influential theories do apply to Venezuela and that whatever explains Venezuela's crisis may be relevant for other countries. Venezuelan exceptionalism is over.

It is time, therefore, to reinsert Venezuela in the major theoretical debates. Here I do that by first examining how well general theories – not developed with Venezuela in mind – explain Venezuela's regime changes. I then examine how much the literature specifically about Venezuela adds to our understanding of its regime changes. I conclude with some suggestions for improving general theory that are inspired by the Venezuelan experience. Beginning with general theory is essential for identifying what it is that demands explanation. From a global perspective, for the three decades after 1958 Venezuela was actually *more* democratic than the most general theories of democratization would have led one to expect. From this perspective, its recent setbacks are better understood as

---

[1] Venezuela was included as a case in the *Transitions from Authoritarian Rule* series, but only with reference to its transition in 1958 (Karl 1986b).

reversions to a level of democracy that is more appropriate for a country in its situation. From a Latin American perspective, however, Venezuela's past is less puzzling and its recent changes more surprising. But neither general perspective would have predicted the magnitude or the timing of the change in Venezuela; only close attention to the case can do that. However, the general theories are still useful for highlighting the arguments in the literature on Venezuela that contribute the most to our understanding. Among those arguments are those pointing to the nature of political parties, the growth of waste and corruption in an oil economy, and civil–military relations. Together, in context, these factors yield a fairly comprehensive explanation for both the rise and the decline of democracy in Venezuela.

THE NATURE OF THE SETBACK IN VENEZUELA

Before beginning the analysis, however, it is necessary to establish that Venezuela suffered a setback. This is not as easy as it might seem because of the different criteria people use to evaluate democracy. Most observers consider the 1958–98 regime to have been a democratic regime, but not a perfect one, and some critics judge its flaws more harshly than others. Since 1999 Venezuela has had a different constitution and a different regime. Some observers consider the new regime more democratic than its predecessor and others, less so. However, all agree that Venezuela's political regime, democratic or not, is less institutionalized than it used to be.

Venezuela had no experience with democracy before 1958 aside from the eight-month presidency of Rómulo Gallegos, who was deposed in 1948 in an atmosphere of intense polarization between the nationalist, anticlerical, and overbearing Acción Democrática (AD; Democratic Action) government and a threatened Catholic and conservative-led opposition, led by the Social Christian party COPEI (Comité de Organización Política Electoral Independiente). Military rule followed for the next decade. During this time, some leaders of AD and COPEI agreed that to give democracy a chance, they would share power and keep the most polarizing issues off the political agenda (Levine 1973). A mass uprising against dictator Marcos Pérez Jiménez in 1957 gave them their chance. The interparty agreement was formalized in the 1958 Pact of Punto Fijo and led to the national unity government of AD's Rómulo Betanourt (1959–64).

The first years of the regime were shaky. But by 1969, it had weathered several coup attempts, defeated a communist guerrilla insurgency, carried out a far-reaching land reform, and survived several major party splits and the succession of COPEI founder Rafael Caldera to the presidency. In the 1973 election, AD and COPEI emerged as the two jointly dominant parties, and they maintained this dominant position for the next two decades. They alternated in the presidency in 1969, 1974, 1979, and 1984. Few observers questioned the integrity of elections. Most observers considered Venezuela a consolidated democracy during these years, especially in contrast to its authoritarian contemporaries in Brazil, Argentina, Bolivia, Peru, Ecuador, Chile, and Uruguay.

Nevertheless, it was a flawed democratic regime. The bureaucracy was extremely inefficient, the courts were corrupt, and most important institutions and political actors were excessively partisan (Crisp 2000). AD and COPEI (and some smaller parties) struggled for control over government appointments, judges, the electoral council, military officers, unions, students, peasants, professional guilds, and neighborhood associations. Party militants were subject to tight discipline in the service of a small inner circle of leaders at the head of each party. Venezuelan critics began to call their system a *partidocracia* (partyarchy) rather than a *democracia* (democracy) (Coppedge 1994). Corruption worsened in the 1970s when the oil shocks flooded Venezuela with petrodollars, and the two parties colluded in protecting each other's members from prosecution (Karl 1997).

In reaction to these flaws, the regime became less institutionalized in the 1980s. Electoral abstention rose from single digits before 1978 to 12.4 percent in 1978, 12.3 percent in 1983, 18.1 percent in 1988, and 39.8 percent in 1993. The announcement of an economic shock program in 1989 sparked a three-day spate of riots and looting that was ended only with brutal repression. Two coup attempts followed in 1992 (both unsuccessful), and President Carlos Andrés Pérez was impeached in 1993. Finally, the party system itself began to fragment. AD and COPEI, which had consistently shared about 80 percent of the legislative vote and 90 percent of the presidential vote since 1973, fell to just 46 percent of the legislative vote in 1993 and lost the presidency to Rafael Caldera, who ran as an independent that year. During the second Caldera presidency (1994–99), the bastions of the first democratic regime, its political parties, continued deteriorating. By the 1998 election, neither party even ran a candidate of its own. Both backed an independent, who was defeated by Hugo Chávez Frías, the leader of the February 1993 coup attempt.

Chávez led the transition to a new regime. Whether it was democratic or not was especially controversial. Despite some breaks with the Constitution of 1961, and despite the loud complaints of the opposition, Venezuela in 2003 still had a democratic constitution, an elected president and national legislature, a vocal opposition, a lively press, and all other minimal requirements for democracy. Moreover, President Hugo Chávez Frías claimed to be deepening democracy, not destroying it. By his account and that of his many supporters, Venezuela was not democratic before 1998; rather, it was a corrupt, unresponsive *partidocracia*. Therefore, he argued, all of the transformations he achieved – revising the constitution, prosecuting corrupt officials, forcing elections in the Venezuelan Workers Confederation (Confederación de Trabaja dores de Venezuela; CTV), promulgating a new electoral law, and appointing a new electoral council – were necessary steps to uproot the old, undemocratic bosses and make the government responsive to the great, long-suffering, and much-abused majority.

Although there is some truth to this argument, the emphasis on executing the will of the current majority distracted attention from a more important and more conventional version of democracy – liberal democracy. Chávez's version of democracy, popular sovereignty, tends to degenerate into the tyranny of the majority or worse. For this reason, scholars and policy makers for the past two centuries have preferred liberal democracy, which tempers the will of transient majorities by adding checks and balances and guarantees of fundamental civil liberties and political rights to the definition of democracy. As long as popular sovereignty was the standard for democracy, the concern was more about what might happen after 2000 than about what had happened up to that year. But if liberal democracy is the standard, then the setback was an accomplished fact by 2000. Venezuela had ceased to be an adequately liberal democracy.

The Chávez "revolution" (he and his followers did frequently refer to their "revolution") systematically removed all the checks and balances required for liberal democracy (Coppedge 2003). This was achieved in two stages: eliminating the old actors in a position to check the president and then ensuring the loyalty of the new actors to the president. In the first stage, the National Constituent Assembly (Asamblea Nacional Constituyente; ANC), which was authorized by referendum in April 1999 and elected in July 1999, drafted a new constitution in three months, had it ratified on December 15, 1999, and disbanded itself on January 31, 2000. The ANC delegates took their work seriously, but the greatest advantage to the ANC was its ability to eliminate checks on the president in the short term. Only a constituent assembly would have the power to neutralize the opposition-controlled Congress elected in November 1998. This it did in short order. The old Congress allowed itself to be marginalized soon after the ANC was seated, and it formally ceased to exist the day the 1999 Constitution was ratified. That date also marked the elimination of the Supreme Court (Corte Suprema de Justicia; CSJ) and the beginning of the second stage, for the ANC appointed a new Tribunal Supremo de Justicia (TSJ; Supreme Tribunal of Justice), a new electoral council, and a new Comptroller general, all of whom cooperated with Chávez. At the same time, the ANC designated an unelected National Legislative Committee to take the place of the legislature until new elections could be held and appointed a commission that purged hundreds of judges from the courts.

This transitional regime continued in power until August 2000, when new officials elected in July were seated. Chávez himself was reelected with a 56.9 percent landslide, and his allied parties won at least 99 of 165 seats in the new National Assembly (now sans senate). In November 2000, they granted the president sweeping powers to issue decree-laws in a wide range of areas. A few governors remained affiliated with opposition parties, but the federal government undermined their power by reducing funding for state and local governments. Between December 1998 and August 2000, therefore, Chávez removed, coopted, or severely weakened all possible checks from other branches and levels of government.

By late 2001, President Chávez had alienated three powerful groups with his high-handed style of governing. Business leaders were incensed that he had abused powers delegated by the National Assembly to decree two dozen important laws, including a land reform and a law on hydrocarbons, without adequate consultation. The CTV felt threatened by his attempt to coopt unions into an officialist "Bolivarian Labor Front." Some high-ranking military officers protested his pro-Cuba tilt, his tolerance of FARC (Fuerzas Armadas Revolucionarias de Colombia or Revolutionary Armed Forces of Colombia) guerrillas inside Venezuelan territory, and the rank-jumping implicit in a lieutenant colonel (Chávez's rank) giving orders to generals. In addition, Chávez lost the popular support of all but his hard core, who comprised less than a third of the population. Using a melee that broke out during massive anti-Chávez demonstrations as a pretext, a business–military–labor plot seized power for two days beginning April 12, 2002. However, the conspiracy fell apart even before junta president Pedro Carmona Estanga announced the dissolution of the National Assembly and Supreme Court, repudiated the 1999 Constitution, and began arresting pro-Chávez governors. The plotters were unable to persuade Chávez to resign and therefore could not take power without violating the constitution. Military commanders – partially influenced by Latin American condemnation of the coup – rallied in support of the constitutional line of succession and pro-Chávez demonstrations filled the streets. Soon Chávez was back in power.

However, the experience left the country more deeply divided than before. In December 2002, oil workers and managers went on strike, and they were soon joined by a general labor-and-business strike calling for Chávez to resign or for a referendum to demand his resignation. He refused, even though the general strike lasted until the end of January 2003, carrying with it severe economic hardships. Mediation by the Organization of American States and the Carter Center produced an agreement that a binding referendum could be held after August 2003. Although the government erected all possible barriers to such a referendum, the opposition came to believe that eventually President Chávez would be removed by peaceful, constitutional means.

Liberal democracy had already been severely eroded well before 2003. But even from the standpoint of popular sovereignty, democracy was at risk in Venezuela, as the 2002 coup demonstrated. Without popular support, Chávez's democratic legitimacy evaporated. What saved him from exile in 2002 was not popular sovereignty but, ironically, the liberal constitutional principle that a president stays in office until constitutionally replaced, even if he becomes unpopular.

WHAT GENERAL MODELS SAY ABOUT VENEZUELAN DEMOCRACY

In this section, I go to unusual lengths to situate Venezuela's setback in comparative perspective. Although many scholars try to keep their cases in comparative perspective, few have gone to the extreme of estimating the predictions of general theories based on a large sample, as I do here, in order to see how well the general theories explain a particular case. The procedure that I will follow is to (1) explain as much as possible of the variation in Venezuelan democracy since 1973 using quantitative variables; (2) note what aspects of the variation are well explained by general theories; and then (3) isolate the aspects that are not explained well (the residuals) in order to highlight the research tasks that remain for qualitative analysis. I believe that this procedure, called "nested inference," is the best way to achieve analytic control when combining quantitative and qualitative explanatory factors. This procedure allows one to hold the quantitative factors constant before developing a complementary qualitative explanation.

Applying controls aids the accumulation of general theoretical knowledge by evaluating *which* cases a theory explains (how well it "travels") and assessing *how well* a theory explains them, both in absolute terms and relative to other theories. For those who are concerned with building general theory, this is no small advantage. However, these controls are also useful for those who care more about explaining a specific case than about building general theory. General theories sometimes point to explanatory factors that are taken for granted by those who are focused on a single case. Often it is only with a large sample of countries that there is sufficient variance on such factors to realize that they may matter and to estimate how much they matter. Controlling carefully for general causes helps one to avoid the pitfall of "myopia": overestimating the uniqueness of a case and underestimating the explanatory power of general theory. Without controls for general factors, case-specific factors get some of the credit for processes that are in fact general; consequently, their importance is exaggerated, and the general factors are underrated. Nested inference lessens this selection bias by giving the case study the job of explaining only the aspects of the phenomenon of interest that cannot be well explained by general factors.[2]

When one is able to distinguish well between the general and the specific, then aspects that are well explained by general theory can be treated cursorily, and more attention can be focused on explaining the unexpected deviations from the predictions – the residuals, and especially the extreme residuals known as outliers. This exercise can frame the research agenda in a case study – sometimes in a very different and surprising way, as we will see here.

Because democratization has been a favorite object of study since the birth of comparative politics, comparativists have proposed quite a few theories, which have been used to generate too many hypotheses to list here. In this section, I will limit the discussion to a few hypotheses that can be tested with the data at my disposal. The dependent variable is a modified Freedom House score

---

[2] This can be only a provisional solution because it assumes that the general and case-specific variables are completely independent. If there is an association between them, then the general variables will be credited with any impact that they share with case-specific variables. However, even though nested inference is an imperfect solution in such cases, there is no practical way to do better until all the associated variables can be measured and included in a large-sample study. In this case, nested inference would help to identify which case-specific factors should have a high priority for inclusion in the larger dataset.

for all countries for the years 1973–96 (through 1999 for Venezuela only).[3] It was constructed by adding the Political Rights and Civil Liberties indexes and subtracting the sum from 16, which results in an index ranging from 2 (least "free") to 14 (most "free").[4] The dataset also includes independent variables measuring wealth, economic growth, and a dummy variable for the Latin American region.[5] Omitted explanatory factors are discussed, when they seem to be relevant, in the case study portion of the paper.

Economic Explanations: A Paradox

The Venezuelan economy has not achieved sustained growth since 1979. In fact, real per capita GDP in 1992 was about the same as it was in 1963. The most obvious hunch about Venezuela's democratic deterioration, therefore, is that it has something to do with bad economic performance. But rigorous tests of this notion produce a paradox: Economic explanations seem to work very well and in multiple ways for Venezuela alone, yet they are not powerful enough to explain the deterioration in comparative perspective. This section elaborates on this paradox; the next section explains it.

The hypothesis that wealthier countries tend to be more democratic is the most frequently and consistently confirmed proposition in quantitative studies of democratization (Diamond 1992; Rueschemeyer 1991; Przeworski and Limongi 1997). The reasons for this association remain uncertain, however, because this hypothesis is consistent with several different theories. All of these theories, or just one, could be true.[6] Empirically they are difficult to distinguish and will remain so until more and better data become available. For clarity, I will distinguish among six strands of thinking about economic causes of democratization or breakdown (Lipset 1959).

The first strand holds that increasing wealth transforms social structure. As a society becomes wealthier, *new social groups* are created, and these groups constitute a natural constituency for democracy. The earliest theorists emphasized the growth in numbers of the middle class (Tocqueville 1969; Lipset 1959; Johnson 1958); more recently others have argued that the working class was the true bearer of democracy (Rueschemeyer et al. 1992). The second strand,

---

3 The Freedom House variable is a reliable enough indicator of democracy for large-N comparisons. At any rate, for a study examining worldwide changes in democracy over several decades to the present, there is no alternative.

4 I am grateful to Ross Burkhart and Michael Lewis-Beck for sharing their Freedom House indicator for the years 1973 to 1989. I and various research assistants added in the observations for 1990–96.

5 These independent variables were gathered primarily by Daniel Brinks, aided by a grant from the World Society Foundation. For more detailed information, see Brinks and Coppedge (1999).

6 One major theory holds the opposite: that the more developed Third World countries were likely to become more authoritarian, not more democratic (O'Donnell 1973). Mainwaring (1999c) has recently shown that level of development explains less in Latin America than it appears to in other world regions, and that the relationship may be weakening as Latin American democracies have survived for a surprising length of time.

closely related to the first, holds that the *resources* that accrue to certain social actors, not simply their numbers, are crucial for democratization. Such
resources include literacy, education, and information about politics; access to
mass media; rapid transportation; money to finance political activity; leisure
time to take political advantage of any of these; and even control of a strategic
sector of the economy. The third strand argues that a high or rising standard
of living fosters a *political culture* that favors democracy. It refers most commonly to the values of moderation and tolerance, which make conflicts less
likely to arise and easier to resolve (Verba, Nie, and Kim 1978).[7] A fourth
strand combined all of these to argue that newly empowered classes would
form and support *moderate political parties* rather than the extreme right-wing
parties that destroyed the Weimar Republic or the extreme left-wing parties
that fomented communist revolutions. Fifth, a recent argument holds that
wealth extends the *life expectancy* of democratic regimes (or any regime, for
that matter) but does not affect the probability that a country will become
democratic in the first place (Przeworski and Limongi 1997; Przeworski et al.
2000).

The sixth strand focuses on short-term *growth and crisis.* Modernization is
best understood as a long-term process; year-to-year changes probably would
not have much of an impact on social structure, group resources, political culture, party stances, or even the probability of a regime surviving one more year.
Nevertheless, several scholars have hypothesized that economic growth and
crisis are associated with democratic change in the shorter term (Haggard and
Kaufman 1995; Remmer 1991b).[8] If democracy is not thoroughly institutionalized, then the legitimacy of the regime could rise and fall rapidly in response to
economic performance, especially to rates of inflation and unemployment and
changes in per capita income. A growing economy is a positive-sum game in
which tolerance and compromise are easy; a shrinking economy is a zero-sum
game in which resentment and intransigence are more likely. Such an environment creates an incentive for the politics of outbidding by populist politicians
who promise to alleviate the suffering of the innocent majority in short order. It also serves as an incubator for crime, demonstrations, and violence. If
such extremes become common, they could grow into what Linz (1978) called
"unsolvable problems," which drive politicians and voters into increasingly
desperate acts, some of which could do away with democracy.

Taken together, these six propositions suggest a plausible economic explanation for the rise and fall of Venezuelan democracy. Venezuela was an extremely
poor, rural country before the oil industry developed. As oil exports boomed,
oil wealth was invested in the rest of the economy, creating an industrial working class and a sizable middle class, which provided support for two large,

[7] Some of this theory, now discredited, once also argued that economic development was associated
with secularization and a diminution of ethnic identities.
[8] Again, Mainwaring (1999c) has observed that short-term economic crises have had little impact
on Latin American democratic regimes.

moderate, catch-all parties. These parties (AD and COPEI) were exemplary practitioners of moderation and compromise, first in the once-celebrated, now maligned Pact of Punto Fijo, and later in their alternation in power and habit of consulting frequently on important legislation. During the oil boom years, when growth was extremely rapid and optimism ran high, these groups were content and remained loyal to the democratic regime. But when the oil economy went bust, the middle class shrank and working-class unions lost membership and clout. The political culture became less moderate and more radical. Venezuelans withdrew some support for the regime and the moderate parties and turned instead to leftist parties and an immoderate, intransigent, and intolerant politician – Hugo Chávez Frías. Even if the earlier strands of modernization theory are rejected in favor of the more recent belief that wealth merely helps a regime survive, Venezuela's recent political instability is consistent with the secular decline in the standard of living.

In a loose way, therefore, Venezuela's political decline is consistent with any and all of the strands of economic explanation. The data used here do not make it possible to test rigorously each separate strand of theory. However, one can depict the relationship between per capita GDP and democracy in Venezuela. Figures 10.1a and 10.1b suggest the intuitive relationship since the 1940s. The Polity 98 data are used as the democracy indicator in Figure 10.1a to show the trends before the first year of Freedom House data, 1973. Both figures suggest that some strand or strands of modernization theory would do a good job of explaining what happened to Venezuelan democracy because the direction and timing of change in the economy closely tracks the direction and timing of change in the political system. The association appears to be tight in Venezuela, aside from the persistence of democracy for a decade after the economic decline began in 1979.

Unfortunately, these economic explanations do not work as well in comparative perspective. Models 1.1 and 1.2 in Table 10.1 report the impact of logged per capita GDP and changes in per capita GDP on Freedom House (FH) scores as estimated in a worldwide sample for 1973–96. Both explanatory variables are statistically significant and have appropriate signs: The wealthier the average person in a society is, and the more positive the growth rate is, the more democratic the country is likely to be. Expressed verbally, this relationship seems to be identical to the economic hypotheses just described. Expressed numerically, however, there are three crucial differences. First, the verbal explanation refers only to the direction of change, while the statistical estimates match up certain *levels* of wealth with certain levels of democracy: They establish benchmarks. Second, the statistical estimates measure the *magnitude* of the impact of changes in wealth on changes in democracy (the slope). Finally, the statistical estimate does not avoid the question of how well the whole model explains the phenomenon in question; rather, it tells us the percentage of the variance explained, in this case, 0.310 (31 percent). This is basic information for those who do statistical research, but its implications for explaining a specific case are rarely spelled out.

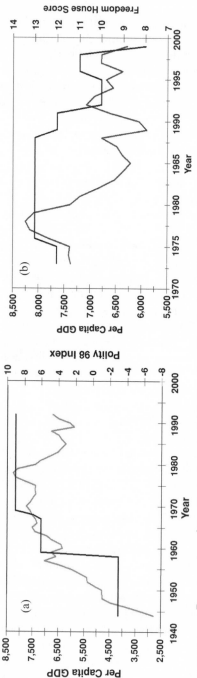

FIGURE 10.1. Democracy and Per Capita Income. (a) Polity 98 and Per Capita Income. (a) Polity 98 and Per Capita GDP in Venezuela, 1944–1992. (b) Freedom House and Per Capita GDP in Venezuela, 1973–1999. Sources: Jaggers and Gurr (1995). Polity 98: *http://lk.gleditsch.socsci.gla.ac.uk/polity.html.* Freedom House score: calculated from Political Rights and Civil Liberties indexes available at *www.freedomhouse.org.* Real per capita GDP 1944–92: calculated from Maddison (1995: Table D-1d); adjusted to chain smoothly with Penn World Tables 5.6 data. Per capita GDP 1973–99: Penn World Tables 5.6 (Heston et al. 1995).

TABLE 10.1. *General Models of Democratization (Dependent variable: Freedom House scores for all countries, 1973–1999)*

Model	1.1	1.2	1.3
N	4068	4050	4050
R-squared	.307	.310	.343
F (i, 198)	107	70	72
Constant	−7.67	−7.51	−7.5
	(1.44)	(1.45)	(1.44)
ln (per capita GDP)	1.99	1.96	1.93
	(.192)	(.194)	(.195)
Economic growth		6.20	6.33
(Δ per capita GDP)		(2.80)	(2.71)
Latin American			2.78
Presidentialism			(.45)

Table entries are unstandardized regression coefficients. All coefficients are significant at far better than the customary 0.05 level. Standard errors (in parentheses beneath) are estimates that are robust with respect to countries. This panel's – robust estimation procedure affects only the standard errors, not the coefficient estimates. It is highly preferable for this purpose because confidence intervals for Venezuela are extremely and implausibly narrow without it.

Fixed Effects

Venezuela's intercept is an invariant parameter, the same for every year Venezuela is in the sample. It is therefore most likely to be associated with invariant characteristics of Venezuela.

There are several easily testable theories that involve such "fixed effects." For example, it has been argued that Latin America's political culture – Thomist and corporativist in Wiarda's view – makes the region poor soil for cultivating democracy (Wiarda 1996). On the other hand, Scott Mainwaring (1999c) has noted the surprising persistence of democracy in Latin America during the Third Wave. Juan Linz (1978) has also proposed that presidentialism tends to undermine new democratic regimes. These ideas are easy to test, but hard to test *separately* because they are relatively fixed and covarying characteristics of the Latin American region: There is little variance to analyze. This not only makes it virtually impossible to separate the impact of culture from the impact of presidentialism but also makes it hard to separate the impact of these two characteristics from the impact of any other fixed characteristic of the region. Other characteristics could include having a (state) capitalist economy (outside Cuba), being in the Western Hemisphere with the Colossus of the North, and having a predominantly Western political culture (at least at the elite level). No purely cross-national analysis that is limited to a Latin American sample can say much about which of these characteristics affect democracy or how much of an impact they have.[9]

With a global sample, however, it is a simple matter to create a dummy variable that will test for any systematic difference in democracy between the countries that possess this bundle of characteristics and those that do not. It is not a problem if some of the characteristics tend to favor democracy while the others tend to work against it, because the impact of the dummy variable can be interpreted as the net impact of all these characteristics together. Such impacts have been called "specific ignorance" because they narrow the set of possibilities without decisively confirming or rejecting any of the possibilities remaining in the set (Maddala 1977).

Model 1.3 in Table 10.1 reports that the net effect of "Latin Americanism" (and all other shared characteristics) is strongly positive and highly significant. This is probably surprising to readers who are familiar with arguments about the burdens of Latin American political culture and the "failure of presidential democracy" (Linz and Valenzuela 1994). But this estimate based on global data is a very useful reminder of a fact that Latin Americanists often take for granted: Latin American countries tend to be more democratic than countries outside the region at a comparable level of economic development.[10] This finding is the flip side to the debate about the incompatibility of Islam or "Asian values" with democracy. Whether one says that Islamic and Asian countries are less likely than normal to be democratic, or that Latin American countries are more likely than normal to be democratic depends on what one considers a "normal" baseline level of democracy to be. And it also suggests (but does not prove) that we should shift some explanatory weight to the aspects of the region that might favor democracy, such as Western culture, capitalism, and proximity to the United States.

Figure 10.2 spells out the implications by superimposing Venezuela's *actual* Freedom House scores (in black) on Model 1.3's *predictions* of its scores. The two gray lines are the predictions (i.e., the upper and lower 95 percent confidence intervals for the predictions). These predictions are based on the association between per capita GDP and growth, on the one hand, and Freedom

---

[9] Much *can* be learned by shifting to a subnational level of analysis, where it becomes possible to compare individuals with differing cultural attributes and possibly even variation over time in the type of presidentialism. But this is no longer a purely cross-national analysis, and it is insufficient for estimating the full impact of these characteristics from a global perspective.

[10] Two alternative interpretations cannot be ruled out. The first is that this is a temporary phenomenon, limited to the Third Wave; in earlier historical periods, there may have been a negative net impact in Latin America. If so, this finding merely restates the question that Mainwaring (1999c) has posed. The second alternative is that the positive coefficient is picking up a pro-Latin American bias in the Freedom House scale. Kenneth Bollen has shown that Freedom House ratings do tend to rate Latin American countries as more democratic than they should be, but his estimates of the bias are not large enough to account for a 2.78-point difference (Bollen 1993).

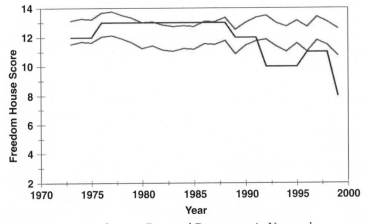

FIGURE 10.2. Actual versus Expected Democracy in Venezuela.

House scores, on the other, in more than four thousand country-years all over the world, not just in Venezuela. It is perfectly appropriate to estimate this relationship with such a large sample because we are interested in building general theory and in seeing how well general explanations account for what has happened in Venezuela. If the relationship that holds in a very large sample is different for Venezuela, then we need to discover what other factors make the pattern different for Venezuela.

These confidence intervals are satisfyingly narrow: They make predictions to within about 1.5 points on this thirteen-point scale, and because they are 95 percent confidence intervals, they mean that nineteen out of every twenty actual scores should fall inside this predicted interval. What is striking about Figure 10.2 is that many of Venezuela's scores do not. In fact, none of them do after 1992. What this means is that – in line with an R^2 of .498 – the economic theories plus fixed effects do not explain Venezuela's setback well in worldwide perspective. From 1973 to 1992 (with a small exception), the country was about as democratic as its standard of living would have predicted. The exception is the brief 1982–85 period, when it was more democratic than predicted. After 1992, Venezuela's level of democracy declined to levels well below the range predicted by economic theories, but this *change* was not predicted by the economic theories alone. Some other reason must be sought.

How can the economic explanations be regarded as incomplete, when Figures 10.1a and 10.1b seem to vindicate the predictions of economic theories so closely and in so many respects? The answer is that Figures 10.1a and 10.1b made arbitrary assumptions about two key parameters of the explanation – the intercept and the slope. Both parameters have to be defined before the explanation that works for Venezuela can be correctly incorporated into more general comparative theory. The intercept is the baseline level of democracy: the degree of democracy that would be average for a country owing to any causes that are not explicitly modeled. Figures 10.1a and 10.1b were misleading because they arbitrarily assumed that the intercept would be whatever level that would make the democracy curve overlap the per capita GDP curve as much as possible. The true intercept could have placed considerable vertical distance between the two curves. The slope is the ratio of a change in democracy to a unit change in per capita GDP, or how dramatically the democracy curve bounces up and down as wealth changes. Here again, the figures were misleading because they were drawn to make it look like changes in wealth and democracy were of similar size. In reality, no slope was estimated. Figure 10.2, by contrast, incorporates the intercept and slope estimates of Model 1.3. The result is that the predicted values in Figure 10.2 are flatter than the actual democracy curve. They are flatter as a result of the size of the slopes for wealth and growth. If the slopes were larger, the predicted lines would rise and fall more dramatically and possibly do a better job of explaining the actual freedom scores. But according to the estimate of Model 1.3, even the large swings in per capita GDP observed in Figure 10.1 have only a weak effect on Venezuelan democracy. The standard of living did indeed decline in the 1980s, but the predicted impact was surprisingly modest – a difference of about one point. Democracy, wealth, and growth moved in the same direction in 1976, 1989, and 1999, but it moved in opposite directions in 1993 and 1996. These economic variables by themselves are simply not sufficient to explain Venezuela's political dynamics.

This does not mean that economic performance did not play an important role in the deterioration of the democratic regime in Venezuela. On the contrary, Figures 10.1 and 10.2 together suggest that economic variables had a *more powerful* impact in Venezuela than they typically do in other countries. The implication of the paradox is, rather, that this Venezuelan evidence holds no clear lesson for general comparative theory until we can specify why the impact of the economy was unusually powerful there in this period. The remainder of this paper proposes answers to these two questions.

To summarize, Figure 10.2 makes three important points about advances and setbacks in Venezuelan democracy. First, the fixed effect suggests that some of the reasons for Venezuela's high level of democracy before 1992 were not unique to Venezuela; rather, they were a combination of Venezuela's high standard of living and rapid growth with characteristics that Venezuela shared with other Latin American countries, although this analysis cannot pinpoint them. Second, the 1982–85 period was a small exception to this. Democracy persisted in Venezuela despite its economic decline in the early 1980s for reasons that go beyond its shared Latin American heritage. Some characteristic less typical of the region was partially responsible for Venezuela's political success during those years. Third, Models 1.2 and 1.3 both make very flat predictions. (There is a slight decline in predicted democracy, but it does not begin to account for the much larger actual decline.) Therefore, the big change between 1987 and 1992 is not adequately explained by Venezuela's per capita GDP, economic growth or crisis, or the characteristics it shares with other Latin American countries. To understand why the economy had such devastating consequences for the

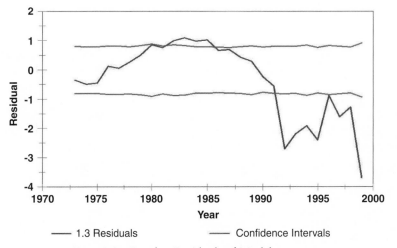

FIGURE 10.3. Remaining Puzzles: Residuals of Model 1.3.

political regime in Venezuela, we must focus attention on other explanatory factors.[11] And because data to do this are not easily available for many countries, the best way to proceed from here is to carry out a more qualitative case study.[12]

Reframing the Puzzle

Now that general models have explained some aspects of Venezuela's democratic record, the focus shifts to explanations that are specific to Venezuela and that explain what has not been explained already. In statistical terms, this means that we should try to explain just the residuals: the differences between the actual and the predicted scores. The black line in Figure 10.3 plots the residuals from Model 1.4; gray lines delimit the width of the 95 percent confidence intervals. The years between the gray lines have been adequately explained by the general theories. What remain unexplained are the segments of the black line that lie above the top gray line (1982–85) or below the lower gray line (1992–99). I intend to show that the best explanation for these residuals is the rise and decline of the backbone of Venezuela's stability – its partyarchy.

---

[11] Other models confirm that two diffusion effects are significant: global trends in democratization and the average Freedom House score of each country's geographic neighborhood. However, neither variable has a substantively strong impact on the predictions, so these variables are omitted from the model reported here.

[12] Lagging the dependent variable seems to be a good idea because doing so forces the other independent variables to explain the difference between a country's current level of democracy and its level in the year before – in other words, to explain change. Such a model fits the years of no change extremely well, but it is caught flat-footed whenever there is a change. It adjusts to the new level quickly but never anticipates change, and so tells us nothing but to expect the status quo ante.

Explanations that were developed by scholars focused primarily on Venezuela (or in some cases, Latin America) may both fill in gaps and add flesh to the general skeleton developed in the first half. In order to take the best advantage of the quantitative analysis, I will evaluate the case literature with respect to five criteria. First, the most useful explanatory factors are those that explain the residuals (Figure 10.3) rather than the raw, uncontrolled political dynamics. Second, I will privilege explanations that can explain both the surprisingly high level of democracy in 1982–85 and the surprisingly low level of democracy after 1992. Any factor that changed dramatically, in that direction, at that time, is highly likely to have had a crucial causal impact. Third, I will discard static factors, both because I have already controlled for fixed effects and because conditions that did not change during this period logically cannot explain the dramatic changes in the residuals. Fourth, I will rule out proposed factors that changed in the wrong direction during this period. Finally, I will discount factors that can be equated with the general variables already held constant – wealth, growth and crisis, and Latin American heritage. Attributing additional influence to them at this stage of the analysis would result in either exaggerating their importance or failing to specify omitted variables with which they implicitly interact.

Some Easily Discarded Explanations

Several explanatory factors can be ruled out quickly because they are static. One points to aspects of Venezuela's political culture. Richard Hillman (1994), for example, has argued that Venezuela was never very democratic. Its democratic regime was only a facade that protected a corrupt, authoritarian oligarchy and engendered frustration that finally broke through the surface in the 1989 riots (Hillman 1994). If he had argued that the culture he describes had become greatly accentuated between 1982 and 1992, then Venezuelan culture could be an acceptable explanation. But Hillman portrays a culture that was born many decades ago and that intensified gradually over a long period of time. By itself, this adds little to an understanding of this crisis. A similar argument proposed decades ago was that Venezuela became unusually democratic in the 1960s in reaction to the Cuban revolution (Alexander 1964). This argument also fails to account for the change in orientation. At best, one could claim that these attributes (if they are even validly characterized) are Venezuelan variations on Latin American fixed effects and that they reduce the prodemocratic tendencies associated with the region.

A different set of explanatory factors that seem useful for understanding the surprising persistence of democracy in Latin America moves in the wrong direction for explaining the contrary case of Venezuela. These include some of the same factors that have been used to explain both the Third Wave of democratization in Latin America and elsewhere (Huntington 1991) and the resilience of democracy in Latin America in the 1980s and 1990s (Mainwaring 1999c). One is the reorientation of U.S. foreign policy away from propping up anticommunist dictatorships and toward support for human rights and free and fair elections. If this policy had an impact on Venezuela, it was only as a policy that backfired. The United States tended to be supportive of Pérez's Great Turnaround in the face of massive popular rejection in Venezuela; it was disappointed in the Caldera administration for the very economic policies that gave Venezuelans hope; and Chávez has gone out of his way to show solidarity with Fidel Castro, Saddam Hussein, and fellow OPEC members and to refuse cooperation with Plan Colombia. A second factor is the Catholic Church's shift in favor of human rights and democracy. The Venezuelan Church has not been a powerful political actor since it applauded the breakdown of Venezuela's first democratic regime in 1948 (Levine 1973). Few human rights groups today, for example, have religious ties. And to the extent that the bishops have been politically involved in recent years, they have been on poor terms with the Chávez government (Smilde 2000). Finally, the collapse of the Soviet Union and the corresponding lack of legitimate alternatives to political democracy came too late to explain the weakening of Venezuelan democracy that was already visible before 1989. All these shifts would lead one to expect more democracy in Venezuela, not less. These factors may help explain why the setback has not been more serious so far, but they do not explain why there has been a setback in the first place.

So what factors could have magnified the political impact of economic decline in Venezuela? One might surmise that indicators of aggregate economic growth and per capita GDP are too crude to have a powerful impact on the regime. Some more socially meaningful indicators might have had a more direct impact. This possibility can be tested over time within the Venezuelan case, as relevant indicators that would not be available worldwide are available for Venezuela over varying periods of time. Table 10.2 reports coefficients estimated by regressing the Venezuelan residuals from Model 1.3 on several such variables: percentage change in per capita GDP, the real value of the official minimum wage, the percentage of the labor force that is unemployed, the size of the informal sector, social spending as a percentage of GDP, and the percentages of households living in critical and extreme poverty. Unfortunately, data on economic inequality per se are too scarce and static even for Venezuela alone to test the thesis that democracies with unequal societies have a shorter "regime life expectancy" (Muller 1995, Burkhart 1997). However, the households in critical or extreme poverty should serve as good proxies for inequality.

Table 10.2 also reports the same statistics for various indicators of fiscal crisis. These indicators can test a different hypothesis: that Venezuela's powerful economic elites withdrew their support from the democratic regime when it proved incapable of managing the economy. This scenario, too, would tend to magnify the impact of poor economic performance. The indicators tested under this heading include urban consumer price inflation, government spending as a

TABLE 10.2. *What Magnified the Impact of the Economy in Venezuela? (Dependent variable: Residuals from Model 1.3)*

Independent variable	Years	Bivariate		Controlling for AD/COPEI Vote	
		Slope	T	Slope	T
Social variables					
Change in per capita GNP (%)	1973–98	−0.005	−0.11		
Value of minimum wage	1979–93	0.019*	2.18	−0.001	−0.357
Unemployed (% of laborforce)	1978–94	0.120	1.14		
Informal sector (% of employment)	1983–98	−0.174*	−2.30	0.105*	2.08
Social spending (% of GDP)	1981–92	0.012	1.77		
Households in critical poverty (%)	1980–96	−0.163*	−3.07	0.017	0.465
Households in extreme poverty (%)	1980–96	−0.096	−1.92		
Fiscal variables					
Inflation	1973–99	−0.021	−1.93		
Government spending (% of GDP)	1973–95	−0.083	−0.92		
Central government revenues (m Bs.)	1984–96	−0.36	−1.46		
Central government spending (m Bs.)	1984–96	−0.52	−1.79		
Tax revenues (m Bs.)	1984–96	−0.91	−1.62		
Fiscal deficits (m Bs.)	1984–96	−0.30	−0.25		
Public employment (% of workforce)	1983–98	0.568*	4.90	0.020	0.116
AD/COPEI vote	1973–99	0.113*	8.86	0.12*–0.17*	3.6–9.1

* Significant at 0.05 level or better.

The "Bivariate" column reports coefficients and T-statistics from bivariate regressions of the residuals from Model 1.3 on each of the independent variables in the first column. The "Controlling for AD/COPEI Vote" column reports coefficients and T-statistics from regressing the residuals from Model 1.4 on both the AD/COPEI vote and one social variable.

Source: Value of minimum wage, unemployment, informal sector, critical poverty, extreme poverty: Oficina Central de Estadísticas e Información (OCEI), *Estimaciones y proyecciones de población, 1950 a 2025;* change in per capita GNP, inflation, government spending, revenues, central government spending and reveunes, social spending, tax revenues, fiscal deficits, public employment: Banco Central de Venezuela. The foregoing data are available from datasets maintained by the Instituto de Estudios Superiores de la Administración (IESA) at *http://servicios2.iesa.edu.ve/macroeconomia/.* (This website has been taken off-line, but the data used in the analysis are available from the author on request.) AD/COPEI vote: Consejo Supremo Electoral and Consejo Nacional Electoral. This variable reflects actual votes in election years and interpolations for nonelection years.

percentage of GDP, central government revenues, central government spending, and fiscal deficits as a percentage of GDP. Finally, Table 10.2 also tests for the impact of changes in public employment. Some scholars have argued that the Venezuelan democratic regime was propped up by massive patronage and clientelism, and that the regime was weakened when it could no longer afford to buy support in this way.

Only three of the fifteen variables reported in Table 10.2 have a statistically significant association with the residuals from Model 1.4: inflation, households in extreme poverty, and the size of the workforce employed in the informal economy. The other variables add nothing new to the explanation (although they are probably correlated with per capita GDP, and to that extent they would be valid parts of the economic part of the explanation). And even these three significant variables cease to have a credible impact when we control for the political variable to be discussed next: the vote for the two establishment parties. The right-hand column of Table 10.2 shows that all of these coefficients take on the wrong sign when controlling for the two-party vote. If these were real relationships, it would mean that Venezuelan democracy was favored by high inflation, widespread poverty, and the growth of the informal economy. It is far more likely that these relationships were spurious all along.

The Pivotal Role of Parties

The explanatory factor that best fits the pattern of the residuals is the strength of AD and COPEI. These two parties once had a formidable capacity to mobilize voters, but that capacity eroded after the election of 1983, first with the growth in abstention, and then by both abstention and a loss of vote share to third parties and personalist candidates. This trend is well operationalized by the combined vote for these two parties in legislative elections as a percentage of total population.[13] If the goal of this chapter were merely to explain variances in Venezuela's Freedom House scores, Figure 10.4 would mark the completion of the task. Both variables rise from 1973 to 1983, decline moderately in the 1980s, plummet by 1993, and remain low until the present. The little variance left to explain could be written off as measurement error. One may object that using the decline of these two parties that were so identified with the democratic regime to explain the decline of the regime borders on circularity. However, a comparable change in the party system of a different country (such as Italy, Japan, and Canada in the 1990s) would not necessarily coincide with a deterioration of its democratic regime. The fact that these trends did coincide in Venezuela is exactly my point: The tight association is empirical and causal, not definitional.

---

[13] I use percentage of total population rather than percentage of eligible or registered voters because total population figures are probably more reliable. However, to the extent that estimates of the number of eligible voters are accurate, an alternative measure would be proportional to the statistic used in Figure 10.4.

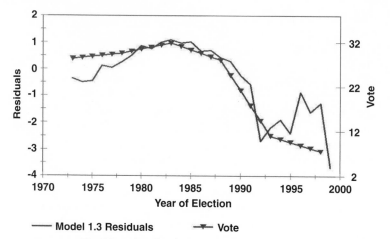

FIGURE 10.4. The Pivotal Role of Parties in Venezuela's Democratic Deterioration.

It should not be surprising that the health of the democratic regime was so closely tied to the health of the two parties. For many people, AD and COPEI *were* equated with democracy. These were the two most important parties that set aside old animosities and in 1958 signed the Pact of Punto Fijo, which helped ensure a successful transition (Karl 1986b). They were the only two parties that elected presidents for the first thirty-five years of the regime. When they were relatively small and divided (1958–68), democracy was threatened by guerrilla insurgency and several coup attempts; when they were strong (1973–88), people considered Venezuela a consolidated democracy.

These two parties were the founders of the regime and its guarantors against internal threats from the left and the right, so there was some justification for equating their success with democracy. Nevertheless, it would be more accurate to equate their success with the *institutionalization* of democracy rather than the quality of democracy. The regime that they founded, which Venezuelans call *partidocracia* and I call partyarchy, was lacking in "democraticness" in several respects. (Perhaps for these reasons, Venezuela never was assigned the maximum score of fourteen on the Freedom House scale.) It continually satisfied the minimal requirements for democracy as defined in Dahl's concept of polyarchy – free and fair elections of the effective policy makers, freedom of political organization, freedom of expression, broad suffrage and eligibility for public office, and lively media that provided alternatives to official sources of information (Dahl 1989).[14] However, the parties monopolized nominations and choices on the ballot, controlled legislators tightly, penetrated most civil society organizations and politicized them along party lines, and centralized authority in a small

---

[14] Polyarchy does not require an independent judiciary. If judicial independence is a requirement for democracy, then Venezuela should never have been considered a democracy, nor should other Latin American countries except Chile and Costa Rica.

inner circle at the top. They did these things to such an extreme that citizens had to be represented through these parties or not at all; and the chances of being represented well through the parties were slim, given their top-down, centralized, hierarchical organization (Coppedge 1994). Furthermore, the Congress was frequently marginalized by the concentration of policy-making authority in the executive, which preferred to deal almost exclusively with a small number of officially recognized interest groups (Crisp 2000), and the bureaucracy was grossly inefficient and ineffective at implementing whatever policies were adopted (Naím 1993). But Venezuela's basic democratic institutions – parties, elections, Congress, and the like – were well institutionalized as long as AD and COPEI were successful.

The first symptoms of the democratic setback in Venezuela were symptoms of weakened institutionalization, not of less democracy. The rise in electoral abstention in 1988 showed that the authorities were losing their ability to enforce the mandatory voting requirement; the riots and looting of 1989 were an extreme example of the state's inability to maintain public order; the coup attempts of 1992 demonstrated that the subordination of the armed forces to civilian control could no longer be taken for granted; and the fragmentation of the party system in 1993 was the byproduct of weakened party loyalties. None of these signs of diminished institutionalization constituted an unambiguous decline in the quality of democracy.[15] However, the weakening of the partyarchic regime opened political space that was filled by forces dedicated to the elimination of the checks and balances required for liberal democracy. If AD and COPEI had not lost support after 1988, then Chávez could not have won the presidency in 1998 or won support of his agenda in three subsequent referendums.

The decline of partyarchy permitted the rise of other forces, but some other cause must explain why the vacuum was filled by antiliberal forces. This question can be answered by explaining why AD and COPEI lost support because the support for Chávez was a direct reaction against the drawbacks of the partyarchic regime.

Why the Parties Lost Support

Figures 10.1a and 10.1b suggest that economic decline had something to do with the regime crisis in Venezuela, yet Figure 10.2 casts doubt on any purely economic explanation. How can this paradox be resolved? The answer is that the cause was not economic decline alone, but how Venezuelans understood economic decline. They reacted to it with feelings of moral outrage, and this reaction magnified the impact of economic decline. We should not expect such a powerful reaction to economic crisis in all countries, and indeed as Figure 10.2

---

[15] The brutal repression of the 1989 riots certainly violated basic human rights, but a callous disregard for human life and due process was already a feature of the regime, as seen in neighborhood "sweeps" for criminals and the treatment of prison inmates.

shows, we do not observe it. But when fundamental principles of justice and fairness are violated, then an exaggerated reaction is to be expected (Scott 1976).

The fact that the Venezuelan state has long been dependent on oil exports is partially and indirectly responsible for both the economic decline Venezuela experienced in the late 1980s and the extreme reaction to it. The oil economy had three effects. First, it created a popular perception that Venezuela was a wealthy country. This impression was reinforced by the economy's 6 percent growth rate sustained throughout the 1950s and 1960s and intensified by accelerated growth during the OPEC oil embargo of 1973–74, when the international price of crude oil more than tripled (Naím 1993: 22).

Second, this oil-led rapid growth, especially during the boom years created an irresistible temptation to overlook state inefficiencies, waste, and corruption. Terry Karl (1997) has argued that Venezuela, like other oil exporters with a high ratio of population to oil revenues, faced powerful pressures to spend these revenues quickly in an attempt to develop other sectors of the economy. Countries that achieved a high degree of "stateness" before oil revenues became available (Norway and Indonesia) succeeded in investing enough of these profits abroad to avoid "Dutch disease." States that were less developed before oil (Venezuela, along with Algeria, Nigeria, and Iran) succumbed to the pressures and created sprawling bureaucracies prone to waste and corruption. Whether one accepts the general validity of this theory of commodity determinism or not, it fits Venezuela well. For example, during Carlos Andrés Pérez's first five-year government (1974–79), the Venezuelan state received 54 percent more revenues from oil than were received by all Venezuelan governments from 1917 to 1974 combined (Karl 1982: 17). Despite this enormous windfall, the Venezuelan state had contracted $33 billion in international debt by 1982. There is simply no way that all of these funds could have been spent wisely. The number of public employees tripled during the first Pérez administration, and the resulting inefficiencies in public administration have been well documented ever since (Naím 1993; Angell and Graham 1995).

Third, the tendency of capital-dependent oil exporters to spend quickly rather than stabilizing income by investing abroad leaves them at the mercy of fluctuating international commodity prices, subjecting them to severe boom-and-bust cycles (Karl 1997). Venezuela went through a particularly dramatic cycle in the 1970s and 1980s, with oil prices soaring in 1973–76, falling in 1977–78, soaring again in 1979–81, falling again in 1982–83, and plummeting in 1986. Per capita oil revenues fell from $1,700 in 1981 to $382 in 1992 (Naím 1993: 25–29, 37–38). All Latin American countries experienced the debt crisis that hit in 1982, but in Venezuela it was preceded by an oil bust and followed by an even bigger oil bust.

These three conditions – economic decline, the belief that Venezuela was a rich country, and knowledge that corruption was rampant – would be enough to create frustration and disappointment. However, in comparative perspective, the anger seems disproportionate. Venezuela never suffered the most traumatic kind of economic crisis – hyperinflation – as Argentina, Brazil, and Bolivia did, yet the repudiation of incumbent parties was stronger. Also, the experience of other countries is more in line with the small estimate of the impact of economic performance in Model 1.3. Therefore, we need to add to the explanation something different about Venezuela that would explain the extra charge that the economy acquired in voting decisions starting in the mid-1980s. Several scholars have pointed to the abrupt policy switch in 1989: Pérez's *Gran Viraje* (Great Turnaround) to drastic economic liberalization, and especially to the manner in which it was done. Some argue that the public reaction would not have been so negative and violent if the rationale for the policies had been explained better in advance to the public and in particular to governing party leaders (Naím 1993: 150–51; Corrales 1997). Weyland (1996c) argues that it was the timing that mattered. Unlike Bolivia, Mexico, and Argentina, Venezuela had not experienced an economic crisis deep enough to make voters take a "wait-and-see" attitude toward a shock program, so their reaction was immediately negative.

I believe that both arguments are valid but insufficient. During his 1988 campaign, Pérez allowed voters to believe that he would be the same old populist he was the first time around, and the fact that he turned out to be just the opposite surely contributed to feelings of betrayal and cynicism in the electorate. This would account for rejection of Pérez, but not his party, and not COPEI (which has suffered the bigger loss), and I doubt that any communication strategy would have made a big difference. Weyland's argument is more plausible. In fact, when President Caldera finally attempted a shock program in April 1996, voters reacted with resignation because by that time the crisis had deepened far more. Nevertheless, when poll after poll shows Venezuelans blaming the economic crisis on waste and corruption rather than the debt or falling oil prices, it seems likely that a perceived moral dimension of the economic decline was a more important cause of the loss of support for AD and COPEI (Templeton 1995: 87, 90–91). A large percentage of Venezuelans came to believe that the economy declined because the politicians had stolen from the national patrimony of a fundamentally rich country (Naím 1993: 127; Templeton 1995).

A more complete explanation for the sense of moral outrage that Venezuelans felt by 1989 requires taking partyarchy into account. (Please refer to the diagram in Figure 10.5.) Indirectly, partyarchy permitted corruption and made it less tolerable by institutionalizing impunity. Impunity was the rule, and punishment was the rare exception for alleged corruption at least until the early 1990s. The existence of corruption would probably be tolerable to voters if its practitioners were usually caught and prosecuted. But if they routinely go free, then moral indignation increases. AD and COPEI made impunity the rule first by protecting their own members and secondly by protecting each other's members. Without it, corruption would have been far less common and extensive. Partyarchy also contributed directly to the moral outrage of some citizens. The hierarchy, discipline, and penetration sought by AD and COPEI alienated many

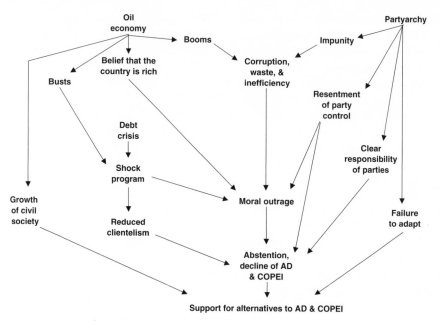

FIGURE 10.5. Paths to Major Party Decline.

Venezuelans who experienced them personally or heard about them, especially when the parties resorted to secret deals, cooptation, bribery, or intimidation to achieve their ends.[16]

Partyarchy also helped channel this moral outrage into a rejection of AD and COPEI at the polls. The downside to being so much in control for so many years is that everyone knows whom to blame when things go wrong. (Of course, voters could have blamed the International Monetary Fund or oil buyers, but they were not on the ballot.) Venezuela had AD presidents from 1959 to 1969; then, Copeyano Rafael Caldera from 1969 to 1974. Venezuelans returned to

[16] I doubt that most Venezuelans felt directly critical of these party practices before the late 1980s. Only citizens with a certain level of political experience and sophistication would have been able to attribute blame to something as abstract as *partidocracia*. However, I believe that many of the more educated or politically active (outside AD and COPEI) Venezuelans viewed the situation in these terms early on. For example, all observers of neighborhood associations and other civil society associations note that they strove to keep party politics out of their organizations (often without success) (Crisp and Levine 1998). This was a guiding principle of a Venezuelan youth group in which I participated during my first stay in Venezuela in 1975. Also, out of eight countries for which Latinobarómetro survey evidence is available for 1995, Venezuela had the highest proportion (29 percent) of respondents who believed that political parties are powerful but should not be powerful. This opinion is correlated significantly with education (author's own analysis). In the late 1990s, these opinion leaders, and especially *commandante* Chávez, promoted this diagnosis of Venezuela's political ills, to the point that it is repeated as dogma by the pro-Chávez majority today.

AD during good times in 1973. When prosperity was marred by corruption and inflation in 1978, they elected Luis Herrera of COPEI. But Herrera blew hot and cold, starting out with a monetary strictness and then overspending during the second oil shock and finally authorizing a traumatic devaluation in 1983. The voters then elected Jaime Lusinchi of AD in a landslide. He stopped the decline but never produced recovery. Voters then gave AD a second chance by electing Pérez, from whom they expected a restoration of good times; instead, he delivered in 1989 the worst economic performance in the postwar period. Voters need to see some improvement from time to time in order to keep believing that their vote helps. By 1989, they had experienced three administrations in a row from two parties in fifteen years without any sustained economic improvement. At that point, they gave up hope that alternation between AD and COPEI would solve their problems, and there was no one else to blame.

This effect was augmented by an economic factor as well. A great deal of the parties' mobilization success had always come from the diversion of public funds for partisan purposes. When the federal budget had to be cut in the late 1980s and after, it cut into a kind of informal public financing for political parties and undercut their ability to get out the vote (Bland 1997).

Lost support does not always stay lost, however. Sometimes parties adapt in ways that appeal to voters and recover their electoral appeal. AD and COPEI did not, and partyarchy helps explain their failure to adapt. In a party that is hierarchical and disciplined, leadership tends to turn over slowly; new leaders must rise slowly through the ranks, "paying their dues" along the way. New ideas and new ways of running the party are discouraged because they imply that those in charge of the party have something to learn. Upstarts are resented. COPEI always chose as its presidential candidate Rafael Caldera or his protégé du jour until 1993, when he was 77 years old; and when his own party rejected him, he ran as an independent and took a sizable portion of the party leadership with him. AD ran a relatively young and programmatically different presidential candidate (Claudio Fermín) in 1993; but when he lost, the party machine marginalized and expelled his supporters. The uncharismatic general secretary, Luis Alfaro Ucero, tightened his control over the organization and engineered his own nomination for president in 1998, not because he had a chance of being elected, but because it was his turn. It would be hard to find a better example of a stubborn refusal to adapt.

Because the voters made AD and COPEI the focus of their outrage, and because neither party adapted in any way that would win these voters over again, voters searched for an alternative who would be all the things than AD and COPEI were not: an incorruptible antiparty politician who could bring economic recovery and put an end to impunity. Demand for such a candidate was boosted by the slow transformation of society as a result of past economic growth. Voters in 1998 were better educated than those thirty years earlier, and more worked in professional occupations; more participated in civil society organizations that tried to stay independent of political parties (Crisp and

Levine 1998).[17] Still, the explanation is incomplete because there is nothing in this profile that specifies demand for a military candidate with a questionable commitment to liberal democracy.

Why Chávez?

Two additional questions must be answered to complete the explanation. First, why were there military plots to overthrow the government in 1992? Second, how did the leader of one of those attempts come to be the most popular politician in Venezuela?

Military plots arose because there were both motives and opportunities. The goals of Chávez and his principal co-conspirator, Francisco Arias Cárdenas, were fundamentally the same as those of many civilians in 1992: to remove Carlos Andrés Pérez from office, to end impunity, and to restore prosperity. Just as the Brazilian military saw itself as *o pôvo fardado* (the people in uniform), these junior officers in the Venezuelan army felt that they shared in the suffering of the Venezuelan people (Stepan 1971: 43). Military salaries had not kept up with inflation; their purchasing power had eroded so badly (by 90 percent according to one source) that even junior officers sometimes had to live in shantytowns or move in with relatives (Burggraaff and Millett 1995: 62). The difference was that the conspirators had more elaborate and ambitious goals than most civilians and had been working toward them longer. Chávez and Arias had worked out a detailed diagnosis of Venezuela's problems that put the blame squarely on a corrupt AD–COPEI political class; their prescription called not just for the removal of Pérez, but for the forcible dismantling of partyarchy itself. Once in power, they hoped to restore prosperity, eliminate corruption, redistribute wealth, and reorient the nation along patriotic, nationalistic lines. All of this they had amalgamated with their interpretation of the works of the national patriarch Simón Bolívar, creating a loose ideology they called Bolivarianism. Other versions of Bolivarianism have also stressed national unity forged by a bond between a paternalistic leader and the *pueblo* (the lower and middle classes) (Coronil and Skurski 1991: 296–97). The plotters also had other goals of exclusively military concern, such as granting the suffrage to soldiers, relieving them of nonmilitary duties, and ending the politicization of military promotions.

This conspiracy had existed for a long time. The Movimiento Bolivariano Revolucionario 200 was founded in 1983. That year was both the 200th anniversary of Simón Bolívar's birth and the year of *Viernes Negro* (Black Friday), the traumatic and drastic devaluation of the Bolívar – the first in many years and the first of many to come – which symbolized the end of Venezuela's prosperity.

---

[17] The impact of this societal change should not be exaggerated. AD and COPEI did not merely fail to win over emerging segments of the population; they actually *lost* voters who once were loyal. Furthermore, the politically independent stance of the emerging civil society organizations was itself a reaction against partyarchy, and thus is not a fully independent causal factor.

The conspiracy survived because civilian officials at first did not take it seriously, and then stopped keeping tabs on it. After the guerrilla insurgency ended in the late 1960s, the Venezuelan armed forces were fragmented by service, each of which was allowed to become highly autonomous within its narrow sphere of activity. Civilians at first took pains to ensure generous salaries, benefits, and perquisites for soldiers, but they soon began to take the military's loyalty for granted. Both military and civilian agencies reported to presidents on the faction's existence and aims, but no president took action against it after 1984. Instead, its leaders were allowed to rise normally through the ranks, and by 1992 the conspirators were in command of a sufficient number of bases, men, and weapons to mount a serious coup attempt (Trinkunas 2002).

In this way, officers sympathetic to widely shared civilian concerns came to lead a coup attempt in 1992. Their attempt was defeated (as was a second attempt by a different conspiracy nine months later), but it brought Chávez and Arias into the national spotlight as instant heroes to a surprisingly large number of Venezuelans. Initially, support for them was based on superficial details: that they had tried to do *something* to get rid of a despised president (who was impeached fourteen months later); that they belonged to the most respected institution; that they appeared to be honest and professional. They also received a boost in legitimacy from a live televised speech by Senator Rafael Caldera just days after the coup attempt, expressing sympathy for their cause but not their methods. This speech also revived Caldera's political career and was an important stepping stone in his return to the presidency in 1994. Chávez and Arias had been explaining their cause to reporters from prison in the meantime, but President Caldera pardoned them and their co-plotters. Once free, Chávez began to organize an electoral movement. For quite a while he was descending into obscurity. But as the 1998 presidential election began to come closer, more and more Venezuelans began to rally around him. The race was shaping up as a contest between the establishment parties, on the one hand, and anyone but them, on the other. Still, Chávez was not the most popular candidate in the polls for many months.

All during 1997, the frontrunner was Irene Sáez Conde, the mayor of Chacao and former Miss Universe. It was already clear that neither AD nor COPEI would win this election, but it was not inevitable that a semiloyal ex-military leader would win. However, the political situation became increasingly polarized in late 1997 and early 1998, for a variety of reasons: Colombian guerrillas were crossing the frontier into Venezuela, President Caldera's structural adjustment program had failed to renew economic growth after nearly two years, oil prices fell from $26.55 per barrel in January 1997 to $13.41 in mid-March 1998, and the federal budget was cut in February. Polls showed support beginning to shift toward Chávez, the more radical candidate. By March 1998, Chávez was the clear frontrunner, and he held that position to the end. Chávez's successful assault on liberal democracy since that date is best explained by his political skills. He makes an ambitious promise that raises expectations, actually carries it out, and then parlays that momentum and credibility into a victory on his next project – calling a constituent assembly, getting the new constitution ratified, getting decree powers, forcing union elections.

The arguments developed in this Venezuelan case study were not formally derived, but they fit together in a logical argument that makes the deterioration of Venezuelan democracy appear to have been nearly a necessity. If citizens anywhere believe that their economic decline is unnecessary and caused by corruption, they are likely to punish the incumbents; if one or two parties exercised great power over a long span of time, it will be perfectly clear whom to punish; if extremely powerful parties central to the working of the political system are marginalized, there will be a power vacuum; and if that vacuum is filled by a charismatic leader who cares much more about implementing his populist agenda than about respecting democratic institutions, then democratic institutions are in jeopardy.

CONCLUSION: VENEZUELAN LESSONS FOR GENERAL THEORY

One of the benefits of nesting a qualitative, case-specific explanation inside a quantitative, general one is that it applies the theory in a way that best sheds light on the case. Another benefit is the reverse: It helps to identify the aspects of the case that suggest the most useful ways to modify the general theory. This conclusion addresses the latter task. This is an "iffier" task because there is no way to ensure that the "right" lessons are being derived from the exercise. Nevertheless, the preceding analysis suggests the following propositions.

1. Latin American countries are able to attain, though perhaps not sustain, some degree of democracy at a level of socioeconomic development lower than that expected for other world regions. However, it is not clear what it is about Latin America that produces this tendency.
2. The generic impact of year-to-year changes in per capita GDP is too small to affect a country's political regime, at least in the span of a decade or so. However, there are probably other conditions that can magnify the impact of economic performance enough to make a big difference in a short time. One such magnifying condition appears to be corruption. Citizens can tolerate corruption if the economy is growing rapidly, and they can tolerate a contraction if they believe their representatives have done everything possible to prevent it or stop it. But when a contraction coincides with known corruption, the political consequences are magnified.
3. The stronger a political party is, and the clearer the connection between the nature of the party or party system and corruption, the more likely it is that it will be electorally punished when such a crisis hits.
4. When large, important political parties are discredited, there is a danger that the resulting political vacuum will allow demagogues to rise to power.

PART IV

CONCLUSIONS

11

Conclusions

Government Performance, Political Representation,
and Public Perceptions of Contemporary Democracy
in Latin America

Frances Hagopian

A quarter century after the Third Wave of democratization began in Latin America, democratic regimes have never been as prevalent or even as secure in Latin America. There have been no reversals of democracy to speak of in the past quarter century – only in Peru in 1992 was there a partial exception to democratic rule, and only in Cuba today is an authoritarian leader so firmly entrenched that uncertainty remains about the way to effect a democratic transition. In most of the continent, that transition took place so long ago that an entire generation cannot remember living at a time when they could not vote for their leaders.

Yet, all is not well. Public support and enthusiasm for democracy is as weak as it has perhaps ever been. When asked specifically whether or not they prefer democracy to any other form of government, Latin Americans manifest high rates of ambivalence. Latinobarómetro data – published annually in *The Economist* magazine – shows that Latin America is replete with "doubting democrats."[1] On average, in 2003 only slightly more than half of Latin Americans agreed with the statement that "democracy is preferable to any other kind of government" (*The Economist* 2003: 33),[2] and 52 percent of respondents across the region agreed that they would "not mind a non-democratic government in power if it could solve the economic problems" (Latinobarómetro 2003: 12). Only in Honduras, Venezuela, and Mexico has public support for democracy not eroded in the past seven years (see Table 1.11). Forty-four percent of Paraguayans, a third of Ecuadorians, and about a fifth of Bolivians, Peruvians, Brazilians, Argentines, and Panamanians even went so far as to say that, in certain circumstances, an authoritarian government could be preferable to a democratic one (*The Economist* 2003: 33). If one wonders whether or not to believe polls, and what precisely it means when people aren't quite sure

---

[1] A table in one of these published surveys (*The Economist*, 2002) carries the tag, "Still doubting democrats."

[2] This average is weighted.

whether they prefer democracy as a political regime type, the trends visible in polls are confirmed by a general rise in electoral abstentions, electoral volatility, and new parties and antisystem political leaders. In the past five years, several elected presidents, among them Jamil Mahuad (Ecuador, 2000), Fernando de la Rua (Argentina, 2001), Gonzalo Sánchez de Lozada (Bolivia, 2003), and Jean-Bertrand Aristide (Haiti, 2004) were forced by public protests to leave office ahead of the expiration of their terms. In a 2004 report, the United Nations Development Programme warned that after 25 years of progress toward elected civilian government, Latin American democracies are suffering from a deep crisis of confidence (UNDP 2004).

Thus we are faced with a paradox: The military has stayed in its barracks, and civilian elites seem to want to keep them there, yet, support for democracy and its institutions is diminishing. Unlike the 1960s and 1970s, when democracies were weakened by the clash of ordinary people demanding the rights that elites were reluctant to grant – to *become* citizens – today the crisis of democracy in the region is one of the widespread and deep disillusion of those who *are* citizens. Mass disaffection has led to low levels of public trust in political institutions and political parties, to mass support for strong-arm democrats – the "neopopulist" leaders – and even to such popular subversions of the rule of law as mass lynchings.

One could object that mass satisfaction or disaffection with democracy does not matter, and anyone interested in projecting the future stability of democracy in Latin America should look elsewhere. Yet, democracy in the Third Wave of democratization is a broader affair than was democracy in the second, postwar wave of democratization, when many observers feel that democracies broke down precisely because they could not handle – either structurally or institutionally – the demands for redistribution and a share of political power that emanated from the popular classes. The political rights of citizenship – in particular voting rights – have expanded since the 1960s. Illiterates won the vote in Chile in 1970, in Peru in 1980, and in Brazil in 1985.[3] Indeed, the electorate expanded considerably in most of the countries included in this volume. Mass democracy today carries with it a set of demands on government that are greater than ever before.

Skeptics could also rightfully claim, moreover, that democracies in Latin America are not the only ones that are "troubled," and our paradox is not unique to the region. If citizens in Latin America are worried about unemployment and corruption and the quality of health care and education, and they vote

---

[3] To give a sense of the immediate impact of this reform, in Chile, those voting as a percentage of the *voting age population* rose from 46 percent in the 1969 parliamentary election to 63 percent in the 1973 election. In Peru, the percentage of those voting in presidential elections rose from 36 percent in 1973 to 59 percent in 1980 to 73 percent in 1985. In Brazil, 33 percent of the voting age population cast a ballot for president in 1960, compared to 79 percent in 1989. Data are from the Institute for Democracy and Electoral Assistance (IDEA): *http://www.idea. int/voter_turnout/southamerica/chile.html*; *http://www.idea.int.voter_turnout/southamerica/peru.html*; *http://www.idea.int/voter_turnout/southamerica/brazil.html*.

on that basis – if they are "critical" – then this makes them pretty much like citizens elsewhere, as one recent book title, *Critical Citizens* (Norris 1999), implies. In fact, citizens around the world do defer to and trust their governments less. Democracies in the former communist bloc have seen increases in citizen disaffection as the memory of communism fades, unemployment rises, and social services decline. Moreover, not merely new democracies, but established democracies, too, seem to be afflicted, as attested to by one prominent recent volume – *Disaffected Democracies* (Pharr and Putnam 2000). Yet, even with this important caveat, levels of public support for democracy are far lower in the newer Latin American democracies than in the established democracies of the Trilateral region, and skepticism about government in the Trilateral countries has not produced the same degree of regime instability.

This chapter takes up the question of why, on the one hand, democracy has survived so well for so long, even in the far reaches of the continent where it has no roots, and why, on the other, such pessimism about democracy and its prospects abounds. Why support for democracy is declining is not an easy question to answer. Our sense of "strong" and "fragile" democracies shifts quickly, making it difficult to draw conclusions and establish causal patterns. Drawing from the collective wisdom of the authors of the chapters in this volume, I contend that the same factors that keep political regimes safe – such as international support for democracy and value change, or even the proper functioning of political institutions that can overcome the constraints of divided government and fragmented party systems – are not enough to ensure citizen support for democracy. To explain democracy's erosion, we must move beyond the paradigms on which we have largely relied in our studies of regime transition and democratization. Many scholars, including Scott Mainwaring and Aníbal Peréz-Liñán in this volume, have forcefully argued that the performance of democratic governments, specifically to generate jobs, reduce poverty and inequality, and establish the rule of law, has been woefully inadequate where democratic regimes have tottered. I build on this insight and connect it to a second theme that recurs throughout this volume: the importance of the expectations, participation, and political representation of citizens in stabilizing democracy. Whether or not governments perform well, citizens must *perceive* that their elected leaders are governing in a clean, transparent, and effective way, and above all, that their voices are being heard.

My thesis is that in an era of mass democracy, these perceptions – both of what citizens expect as well as what their political leaders deliver – often depend critically on the functioning of the institutions of political representation. Where institutions of political representation are vibrant, and where parties are responsive and accountable to the preferences of citizens that can associate in the terrain of civil and political society, democracy is somewhat inoculated from setbacks, even when banking systems collapse and corruption scandals are brought to light. But where these channels have decayed and do not function well, or civil society is strong but political institutions are weak, antisystem leaders may successfully mobilize support, and the future is far more uncertain.

Of course the crucial question that this analysis raises, but I do not pretend to answer in this chapter, is whether democracy can continue to survive without popular support. Mainwaring and Pérez-Liñán analyze the impact of other variables on the survivability to date of democratic regimes, but the world of mass public opinion is a brave new one. Absent hard data that would permit us to test empirically past patterns, and dependent only on historical accounts and passing observations of the public mood, the past may, or may not, be an accurate guide to the future.

I proceed as follows. First, I attempt to summarize what we have learned about democracy's advance. Next, I map out where – in what countries and in what areas – we see signs of vitality and where we see signs of affliction. Notwithstanding the Latin American trend toward popular (and middle-class) protest against the economic policies of democratic regimes and the early exit of sitting presidents, we see considerable diversity today in how citizens perceive the effectiveness of their democratic governments to administer social and economic policy, and on the basis of those evaluations, we also see wide variation in their subjective support for democracy and levels of voter turnout. In the next section, I examine two hypotheses about why support for democracy may be eroding, globalization and neoliberalism, and the gap between government performance and citizen expectations in the three areas of highest salience to Latin American voters: economic security, personal security, and corruption. In the final section, I contend that the link between a healthy democracy and less than perfect government performance is the effective functioning of the institutions of political representation. I conclude with a series of unanswered questions that call for more research.

WHAT HAVE WE LEARNED ABOUT DEMOCRACY'S ADVANCE?

Several key theses have emerged in this volume to account for the dramatic change in Latin American politics of the past quarter century. In Chapter 1 of this volume, Scott Mainwaring and Aníbal Pérez-Liñán identify the key factors accounting for democratic survivability. Their research, echoed in the country chapters by various authors, including Kurt Weyland, Elisabeth Jean Wood, and Michael Coppedge, confirms empirically that international change was crucial in insulating new democracies from potential authoritarian reversals. There are at least three reasons for believing that international change was so important in advancing and safeguarding the Third Wave of democratization in Latin America. The first relates to the shift in U.S. foreign policy away from supporting friendly dictatorships toward insisting that its allies remain democracies, and the role of hemispheric institutions such as the Organization of American States and Mercosur in making plain that democracy was a continuing criterion for membership. Signals from the international community provided powerful disincentives to would-be coup plotters in Peru (1992), Guatemala (1993), and Paraguay (1996) (Valenzuela 1997). Both U.S. and international organizations pushed warring sides toward peace in those countries that had been wracked by civil war. As Wood explains it in her chapter, in El Salvador, international actors such as the United Nations observer mission (ONUSAL) "met many of the costs of the peace and reinforced its benefits through ongoing, comparatively close scrutiny of compliance with the peace agreement."

Second, along with changed international norms there has been a change in regional mentalities. The international environment was radically altered by the collapse of communism in Europe, as well as by cultural change in the Catholic Church, which of course had long been a pillar of the conservative order. In their chapter, Mainwaring and Pérez-Liñán also demonstrate that the collapse of the communist bloc and the experience in exile of so many members of Latin America's left – an experience that tamed their passions for socialism and led them to appreciate the inherent value of democracy (cf. Hite 2000) – was certainly instrumental in securing the Third Wave. Continuing with the Salvadoran case, Wood asserts that involvement with international actors, initially as a result of U.S. insistence on liberalizing the political regime in the 1980s and later as a result of UN mediation in fostering the peace process, was essential to an increasing acceptance of liberal political norms, which led to the "unprecedented acceptance of electoral competition by actors on the right." Steven Levitsky, in his chapter, makes a similar observation about Argentina, where, he claims, the 1976–83 dictatorship produced a "profound metamorphosis of Argentine political culture." He contends that as a result of the horrors of dictatorship, issues of human rights and democracy gained unprecedented salience among the electorate in the 1980s, an elite consensus formed around the rules of the game, and in the 1990s the mass-level commitment to democracy also grew.

While democracy-enabling value change generally caught on across the region, it has not done so everywhere. In one of the most dramatic cases – Colombia – four guerrilla groups were reincorporated into civil society in the early 1990s, but the Revolutionary Armed Forces of Colombia (Fuerzas Armadas Revolucionarios de Colombia; FARC) and the National Liberation Army (Ejército de Liberacíon Nacional; ELN) actually *deepened* their radical discourse, as Ana María Bejarano and Eduardo Pizarro are quick to note in Chapter 8. The stubborn radicalism of the left in turn radicalized the right, fueled the growth of paramilitary groups, and rocked the foundations of one of the longest standing democratic regimes in Latin America. The case of Brazil is less clear. In his chapter, Weyland downplays the importance for democratic stability of value change in Brazil: He characterizes the elite commitment to democracy as only "somewhat stronger" under the postauthoritarian regime than under the Second Wave democracy and value change at the mass level as "even weaker." Yet, he concedes (p. 93) that Brazilian democracy has been "virtually secure" in Brazil since 1995 (ten years after the military left power) owing to "ideological convergence brought about by the fall of Communism." If such convergence cannot be directly linked to attachments to democracy per se on the part of elite actors on the right, it has been facilitated by the spread of neoliberal economics in the Third Wave of democratization, a third international change that altered the trajectory of Latin American regimes.

Many scholars believe that the introduction of market-oriented reforms in Latin America has eroded democratic institutions and popular support for democracy. The reforms are believed to have had this effect because they cause unemployment to rise, more families to fall into poverty, and income disparities to widen – and also because they constrain the policy choices of governments, making impossible badly needed and anticipated social reform. The evidence for this position is not as persuasive as one might expect, however. Weyland and Wood have stressed the positive effects of these reforms for the survival of democratic regimes. For Weyland, the collapse of communism and the spread of neoliberalism have narrowed the ideological spectrum inside Brazil, put political and socioeconomic elites "at ease," and stimulated greater acceptance of the uncertainty created by democracy. Wood makes a similar argument about El Salvador. After charting the economic diversification of the Salvadoran coffee elite in the 1980s, she recounts that the Cristiani faction of ARENA developed and proposed a set of neoliberal policy reforms, which were attractive to the elite for at least three important reasons: They could justify reprivatizing nationalized sectors; they would render the state incapable of threatening elite economic interests even if a party hostile to elite interests later governed; and the liberalization of capital flows specifically would discipline the state against redistributive measures. The same arguments could well be made across the Latin American continent. From Mexico to Argentina, the adoption of market reforms and the opening of Latin American economies to trade and capital flows has had the effect of attenuating the great postwar conflicts between capital and labor, restricting the capacity of governments to enact redistributive policies, and halting the politically expedient practice of passing along the costs of inflation.

International change, value change, and the diminished threat of communist subversion or even radical redistributive policies have in turn been reflected in perhaps the most dramatic difference between the past and the present to anyone who has studied Latin America over this quarter century and earlier – the retreat of the military. No longer do civilian elites seek out the military to settle scores with their opponents – not after the long, dark night of authoritarian rule. The prosecution and conviction of top military officers under the Alfonsín government in Argentina and the military dictator Gen. Luis García Meza (1980–81) and some of his colleagues in Bolivia (Mayorga, this volume) has served to raise the bar for future military intervention. Weyland attributes the diminished propensity of the Brazilian military to intervene in politics (as it had in 1955–56, 1961, and 1964) to the reorganization of the military during the military regime, and its greater unity. The admonitions of some about the great reserve of military power aside (see especially Stepan 1988, but also Hagopian 1990), since 1985 there have been no military uprisings, and no saber rattling in Brazil, even when a more radical Workers' Party (PT) appeared it might win the presidential election in 1989 and the president was impeached in 1992 for gross corruption. Most impressively, both the administrations of Fernando Collor de Mello and Fernando Henrique Cardoso made great strides in subordinating the military to civilian direction (Hunter 2000: 116), most prominently by establishing a unified defense ministry in 1999 and placing it under the direction of a civilian minister.[4]

But perhaps the most spectacular differences between civil–military relations in the Second and Third Waves of democracy are evident in Argentina and El Salvador, two countries in which the military had been deeply entrenched in politics since the Great Depression. In El Salvador, as Wood puts it, between 1932 (when the military perpetrated one of the most dramatic peasant massacres in the history of the twentieth century) and the civil war of the early 1980s, active duty or retired military officers "ruled the polity" in alliance with economic elites (through the National Conciliation Party or Partido de Conciliación Nacional; PCN), and this oligarchic alliance of hardline officers and landlords, moreover, was able repeatedly to thwart attempts at reform of land tenure and labor relations by other military factions (as it did in 1944, 1960, 1972, and 1976). Against this backdrop, the accomplishments of the peace process, including the introduction of constitutional reforms to the mission and prerogatives of the military, the dissolution of the National Guard and the Treasury Police and the founding of a new civilian police force, and the purging of more than a hundred officers from the ranks of the military for human rights abuses, are nothing short of remarkable.

In Argentina, the great change began with the prosecution of top military officers by the Alfonsín government for human rights abuses in the 1976–83 period. Although the scope of these trials was later circumscribed as a result of the *carapintada* rebellion of April 1987 (with the "due obedience" clause), and convicted officers later (controversially) pardoned by the Menem government, the principle of civilian control over the military in Argentina was unquestionably established – to a greater extent than at any time since 1930 – and the military's presence in politics reduced to insignificance. Since that time, the military has had no role in the cabinet, military officers have not issued proclamations, and there has been no military show of force in the streets. The 1988 Defense Law denied the military command any policy-making role and prohibited the armed forces from intervening in matters of internal security. Key areas of military decision making, including the budget, procurement, and national defense strategy, were placed under the civilian-led defense ministry. The Menem government slashed the military budget by a third, abolished the draft, and privatized military-owned enterprises. The bottom line has been

---

[4] One prominent Brazilian scholar, Jorge Zaverucha, would give a decidedly more pessimistic view of the containment of military influence in contemporary Brazilian democracy. For Zaverucha (2000), Brazilian democracy is fragile, and the military is only partially under civilian control. The armed forces are not as powerful as they were under the authoritarian regime, but they are nonetheless still the "fourth branch of government." More specifically, he claims (2000: 10) that thirteen years after the assumption of the presidency by a civilian, the military continue to maintain many authoritarian enclaves, or, reserved domains of power in the state apparatus. Perhaps most provocatively, he claims (2000: 12) that the power of the Brazilian military was less subtle, but no less powerful, than it was in Chile. His reservations aside, I stand by my overall interpretation.

summarized by Levitsky in his chapter: By the late 1990s, "military spending was under the exclusive control of the economic ministry, responsibility
for determining the missions and deployment of the armed forces was in the
hands of the foreign ministry, and the 'bulk of serious military effort' was being devoted to external peacekeeping missions." Most telling, perhaps, is what
appears to be the permanent fracture of the half-century military–elite alliance.
Citing Gibson (1996), Levitsky underscores that conservatives who had previously turned to the military for protection invested instead in electoral politics.
From Buenos Aires to Guatemala, the fracture of the civilian–military elite is
why, in the words of Carlos Acuña, "the future is no longer what it used to be"
(Acuña 1994).

There is also a greater resolve to make political institutions work. During
their transitions from authoritarian rule, several countries, including Chile and
Brazil, entertained proposals to shift from presidential to parliamentary democracies. These proposals were ultimately not accepted, but the elite and public
debates about their merits did shine attention on the need either to reform
other institutions or to develop informal ones to overcome the most pernicious
effects of divided government. Several countries discussed in this volume *did*
institute significant reforms. New electoral institutions were created in Mexico
and Bolivia, electoral reforms in Chile and Bolivia attenuated polarization in the
party system, and the executive was strengthened in relation to the legislature
in Brazil – a development that facilitated the legislative process.

These reforms were each, in their own way, hugely consequential. In her
chapter, Beatriz Magaloni explains with elegant precision the calculations in the
Mexican case that led to the creation of institutions for a democratic transition,
especially the Federal Electoral Institute (IFE). She explains why, given voter
preferences, the PRI had little choice but to cede authority to the IFE, and as she
contends, this decision paved the way for the erosion of the one-party dominant
authoritarian regime. In Chile, the binomial electoral system instituted in 1989
(by the outgoing Pinochet regime) has had the effect of attenuating polarization
in the political system. Because deputies are elected in two-member districts
from lists within which votes are pooled, and only candidates from the top
two lists can win representation in any district, the overwhelming incentive has
been for parties to band together in coalitions. The electoral law, as much as any
structural or ideological factor, is believed by most observers of Chilean politics
to be responsible for the redefinition of the Chilean party system from one of
polarized to moderate pluralism. In the Brazilian case, although some observers
view the executive decree authority to issue "provisional measures" enshrined
in the 1988 Constitution as pernicious because the president can use them to
circumvent Congress, Weyland emphasizes the governability-enhancing effects
of this institution, and its contribution to the substantive performance of the
new democracy. In particular, the prerogative to issue even temporary decrees
can help the executive to set the agenda for parliamentary deliberation because
Congress must afford the provisional measures priority attention.

The Bolivian reforms are particularly illustrative. In his chapter, René
Mayorga credits the emergence of a moderate multiparty system with three

major parties – the MNR (Movimiento Nacionalista Revolucionario or National Revolutionary Movement), ADN (Acción Democrática Nacionalista or Nationalist Democratic Action), and MIR (Movimiento Izquierda Revolucionario or Movement of the Revolutionary Left) – to the creation of an autonomous National Election Commission in 1991 and the adoption in 1994 of a mixed-member proportional electoral system modeled on the German system. The new system reserves seats for 68 deputies (of 130) chosen by first-past-the-post voting in single-member districts and 62 for deputies selected by party-list voting according to proportional representation in nine multimember regional districts. (The overall allocation of seats is determined by the list vote obtained by each party, with seats determined by the d'Hondt formula for parties whose vote total meets a 3 percent threshold.) Added to these and other institutional changes were behavioral changes that produced in the 1980s a system of what Mayorga calls "parliamentarized presidentialism." Article 90 of the Constitution (in force since 1851 but applied only three times in Bolivian history prior to the current democratic period – once in the nineteenth century and twice in the 1940s) required that presidents be chosen by Congress when there is no popular vote majority but made no explicit provision for the process by which that coalition would be generated and did not specify that the top vote-getter should be selected. In the 1980s, in the context of a terrible economic crisis, Bolivia's parties learned to select the president by bargaining votes in Congress and building postelectoral parliamentary governing coalitions. The practice of forming a postelection coalition to select the president, which forms the basis of a majority government, has persisted and provided a strong base of support for presidential initiatives in the Congress. Mayorga credits the process of bargaining that generated consensus and strong coalition governments with enabling Bolivia's presidential democracy in the 1990s to escape the sort of exercise of presidential power elsewhere in Latin America during times of economic reform that eroded democratic institutions.

In some cases where new democratic institutions were created or existing democratic institutions were fruitfully redesigned, democracies outperformed their pasts. Adjustments to and investments in political institutions have enabled the "right" legislation – economic reforms and policies, and even moderate environmental protection policies and educational reforms but not radical, redistributive reforms – to get passed. In the Third Wave, institutional development was not uniformly positive, however, and where institutions atrophied, as was the case with Venezuelan and Peruvian political parties, or were revised in ways that unwittingly undermined their effectiveness, as was true with Colombia's party reform of 1991 that resulted in an enormous disorganization among parties and an extreme atomization of political representation (Bejarano and Pizarro, this volume), democracies became destabilized. If representative parties and presidents with Congressional support are essential to democratic stability, deinstitutionalization can put democracy in grave peril.

In these countries where institutions faltered, the Third Wave of democratization started to recede beginning in 1992, the year of two coup attempts in Venezuela and the Peruvian *autogolpe*. In Peru, we know, this interruption of democracy was temporary. Elsewhere, the loss of faith has mercifully not resulted in a breakdown of democracy, but it has set it back. Our task is to understand when fragile democracies will limp along and when they can become vulnerable to creeping authoritarian incursions, if not coups. It is to this question that I next turn my attention.

WHERE IS DEMOCRACY FLOURISHING, AND WHERE IS IT IN TROUBLE? PERFORMANCE AND PERCEPTIONS

Impressionistically, most observers today would doubtless say that Latin America's most successful democracies are Costa Rica, Uruguay, and Chile. Costa Rica has remained a model democracy for more than five decades, and military regimes in Uruguay and Chile, however brutal, are now seen as blips on the longer trajectory of stable, democratic governance. Although this volume did not examine the cases of Costa Rica, Uruguay, and Chile because we did not view successful democratic governance in these cases as particularly surprising, reinserting these cases into our analysis would now enable us to identify the key factors sustaining and nourishing democracy in Latin America today.

In order to advance our understanding of the diversity of Latin America's experiences with democracy, a more systematic assessment of democratic performance and its role in explaining how much and why citizens support their democracies is warranted. The first obligation of democratic regimes is to guarantee political rights and civil liberties. Of the twelve countries included in this sample, three – Chile, Costa Rica, and Uruguay – were scored by Freedom House as free in each of the eleven years from 1992 through 2003 (Table 11.1). El Salvador has been free since 1997; Mexico, since its transition to democracy in 2000; and Peru, since 2001 (and Alberto Fujimori's exit from the presidency). Brazil has also moved toward becoming a freer country since 2003, without a change of regime. Argentina experienced two years of partial freedom during the country's 2001–02 crisis, but in 2003 it moved back into the "free" column. Scored free for every year except 1995, Bolivia was downgraded to "partly free" in 2003. Most disturbingly, Colombia and Guatemala have been only partly free in each of the eleven years covered. Colombia has especially experienced a sustained deterioration of civil liberties.

A broader evaluation of democratic performance would take into account the extent to which democratic regimes are responsive and accountable to their citizens, which is notoriously hard to measure, as well as how effectively, transparently, and cleanly they govern. Table 11.2 summarizes estimates of six dimensions of governance developed by the World Bank's Global Governance project that attempt to capture many of the indicators in which we are interested: voice and accountability, political stability, government effectiveness, regulatory quality, rule of law, and control of corruption (Kaufmann, Kraay, and Mastruzzi 2003). The first two – voice and accountability and political stability – generally capture the strength of democracy; the second two – democratic governance and regulatory quality – its effectiveness; and the last

TABLE 11.1. *Freedom House Ratings of Political Rights and Civil Liberties: Twelve Latin American Countries, 1993–2003*

Country	1993	1994	1995	1996	1997	1998	1999	2000	2001	2002	2003
Argentina	5	5	5	5	5	6	5	3	6	6	4
Bolivia	5	5	6	5	4	4	4	4	4	5	6
Brazil	7	6	6	6	7	7	7	6	6	5	5
Chile	4	4	4	4	4	5	4	4	4	3	2
Colombia	6	7	8	8	8	7	8	8	8	8	8
Costa Rica	3	3	3	3	3	3	3	3	3	3	3
El Salvador	6	6	6	6	5	5	5	5	5	5	5
Guatemala	9	9	9	7	7	7	7	7	7	8	8
Mexico	8	8	8	7	7	7	7	5	5	4	4
Peru	9	9	9	7	9	9	9	6	4	5	5
Uruguay	4	4	4	3	3	3	3	2	2	2	2
Venezuela	6	6	6	5	5	5	8	8	8	7	7

Notes: Scores provided represent combined ratings for political rights and civil liberties. Both are measured on a one-to-seven scale, with one representing the highest degree of freedom and seven the lowest. Until 2003, countries whose combined average ratings for political rights and for civil liberties fell between 1 and 2.5 were designated "free"; between 3.0 and 5.0, "partly free"; and between 5.5 and 7.0, "not free." Beginning with the ratings for 2003, countries whose combined average ratings fall between 3.0 and 5.0 are "partly free," and those between 5.5 and 7.0 are "not free." Countries receiving the "partly free" label were: Argentina: 2001–02; Bolivia: 1995, 2003; Brazil: 1993–2001; Colombia, 1993–2003; El Salvador, 1993–96; Guatemala: 1993–2003; Mexico: 1993–99; Peru: 1993–2000; and Venezuela: 1993–95, 1999–2003.

Source: Data are from annual editions of Freedom House, *Freedom in the World*, available as an Excel spreadsheet, "Annual Freedom in the World Country Scores, 1972 through 2003," at *http://www.freedomhouse.org/ratings/index.htm* (retrieved on March 11, 2004).

TABLE 11.2. *Democratic Governance in Twelve Latin American Countries, 2002*

Country	Voice and Accountability		Political Stability		Government Effectiveness		Regulatory Quality		Rule of Law		Control of Corruption		Point Estimate Sum
	Point Estimate	Percentile Rank	Point Estimate	Percentile Rank	Point Estimate	Percentile Rank	Point Estimate	Percentile Rank	Point Estimate	Percentile Rank	Point Estimate	Percentile Rank	
Chile	+1.12	84.3	+1.04	85.9	+1.19	86.6	+1.50	90.2	+1.30	87.1	+1.55	90.7	+7.7
Costa Rica	+1.16	84.8	+1.06	86.5	+0.37	66.6	+0.74	72.7	+0.67	72.2	+0.88	79.4	+4.88
Uruguay	+0.95	77.8	+0.91	79.5	+0.51	68.6	+0.48	67.0	+0.56	69.1	+0.79	75.8	+4.2
Mexico	+0.33	59.6	+0.22	50.8	+0.15	61.9	+0.49	68.0	-0.22	52.1	-0.19	52.1	+0.78
Brazil	+0.28	58.1	+0.17	48.1	-0.22	50.0	+0.26	63.4	-0.30	50.0	-0.05	56.7	+0.14
El Salvador	+0.06	51.5	+0.35	56.8	-0.53	35.6	+0.04	56.2	-0.46	39.7	-0.54	36.6	-1.08
Peru	+0.22	57.6	-0.67	25.4	-0.47	38.7	+0.24	62.9	-0.44	40.7	-0.20	51.5	-1.32
Bolivia	+0.01	50.0	-0.20	36.8	-0.53	34.5	-0.11	50.5	-0.60	32.5	-0.82	25.3	-2.25
Guatemala	-0.48	35.4	-0.43	32.4	-0.61	32.0	-0.09	52.1	-0.84	21.6	-0.71	30.9	-3.16
Argentina	+0.12	52.5	-0.74	23.8	-0.49	37.6	-0.84	19.6	-0.73	27.8	-0.77	27.8	-3.45
Colombia	-0.55	30.8	-1.78	4.9	-0.39	45.4	-0.04	53.1	-0.75	26.8	-0.47	38.7	-3.98
Venezuela	-0.41	38.9	-1.20	17.3	-1.14	10.3	-0.54	34.5	-1.04	13.4	-0.94	18.6	-5.27
Standard Error	.17-.18		.19-.25		.15-.18		.17-.19		.13-.16		.14-.18		

Notes: Indicators are based on several hundred individual variables measuring perceptions of governance, drawn from twenty-five separate data sources constructed by eighteen different organizations. Authors assign these individual measures of governance to categories capturing key dimensions of governance and use an unobserved components model to construct six aggregate governance indicators in each of the four periods. The authors also present the point estimates of the dimensions of governance as well as the margins of error for each country. Margins of error are calculated separately for each indicator in each country. For the countries in our sample, they range from .17 to .18 for voice and accountability, .19 to .25 for political stability, .15 to .18 for government effectiveness, .17 to .19 for regulatory quality, .13 to .16 for rule of law, and .14 to .18 for control of corruption. In each of these cases, the highest standard error is recorded for El Salvador.

Source: Kaufmann, Kraay, and Mastruzzi (2003).

two – rule of law and control of corruption – the transparency and fairness of democratic regimes. Country rankings are provided along with the point estimates. The estimates are based on a weighted average of the sources for each country (which combined several hundred variables drawn from twenty-five separate data sources constructed by eighteen different organizations, including Freedom House, *The Economist* Intelligence Unit, Gallup International, Latinobarómetro, and Standard and Poor's DRI McGraw-Hill) and have an expected value across countries of zero and a standard deviation of one; thus the scores lie between −2.5 and 2.5.[5] I have simply summarized the point estimates to provide a scale of the quality of democratic governance in the countries in our sample.

The countries that we typically classify as strong, high-quality democracies – Chile, Costa Rica, and Uruguay – also score the highest on the World Bank's six indicators of governance. They clearly receive the highest percentile ranking on voice and accountability, political stability, government effectiveness, rule of law, and control of corruption, and, along with Mexico, on regulatory quality. Mexico and Brazil are middling democratic performers. Both are perceived as providing a reasonable degree of voice and accountability, and both are comparatively effective states, at least as measured by their regulatory quality. Mexico's government is rated as significantly more effective than Brazil's, though Brazil is perceived as having achieved a greater degree of control of corruption. The performance of these regimes varies considerably, but both are considered to be positive.

The next set of countries shows promise and flaws. At the top of this group is El Salvador, which overall scores better perhaps than the impression left us by Wood's sober account of the flaws of Salvadoran democracy; its weakest areas are government effectiveness, rule of law, and control of corruption. Though both are considered less than politically stable, Peru is perceived to have a higher-quality democracy than Bolivia. Such a conclusion may have seemed surprising just a few years ago given that democracy in Peru appeared to be imperiled under Fujimori and in Bolivia, more stable than any other in the Andean region. Yet, in retrospect, Bolivia's democratic regime was precariously perched on a foundation of perceived corruption, weak rule of law, and a relatively weak (by Latin American standards) degree of voice and accountability, which may have led to the ouster of President Gonzalo Sánchez de Lozada. Peru, by contrast, has improved the control of corruption[6] (at this point the difference between the two countries is vast), regulatory quality, and even the rule of law.

---

[5] These measures are not perfect. Some components of "voice and accountability" actually measure freedom and rights (including survey responses to the question of the extent to which the state and/or its allied groups engage in repression of its citizens as well as Freedom House's measures of civil liberties, political rights, and press freedom) and stability (including responses to questions such as "how likely is the government to remain in power") (Kaufmann, Kraay, and Mastruzzi 2003: 91). Needless to say, a government may protect freedom and be stable, but not give voice to citizens and be accountable to them.

[6] One reason may be because of the highly regarded performance of the office of the ombudsman.

Argentina, which in previous years had unambiguously been perceived as the next strongest, most effective, and transparent democracy in the region after Chile, Costa Rica, and Uruguay, has now fallen to one of the worst democratic performers in the region, especially because of political instability, poor regulatory quality, and the relative absence of the rule of law.[7] Finally, Guatemala, Colombia, and Venezuela score toward the bottom of Latin America's democracies on most measures. The problematic nature of Guatemala's democracy underscored by Mitchell Seligson in his chapter is most evident in low scores on voice and accountability and the rule of law. The years of political violence in Colombia and the erosion of democracy in Venezuela during the Chávez administration have dropped two of the region's oldest democracies to the bottom of the list. While its democratic governments have long been perceived as reasonably effective and capable of regulation, Colombia is especially penalized for political instability. Venezuela's scores are particularly abysmal along the dimensions of political stability, government effectiveness, rule of law, and corruption.

How significant is the performance of democratic regimes in explaining citizen support? One recent scholarly thesis holds that countries in the Third Wave of democratization that have introduced competitive elections before establishing the basic institutions of the modern state, including the rule of law – these "incomplete" democracies – run the risk of falling into a "low-level equilibrium trap in which the inadequacies of elites are matched by low popular demands and expectations" (Rose and Shin 2001: 331).[8] We might logically ask whether this has happened in Latin America, and if there is a correlation between the quality of democratic governance and the support for democracy. The most commonly used comparative referent for the extent of citizen support for democracy is the level of agreement with the statement, "Democracy is preferable to any other form of government." By this measure, public support for democracy in Latin America is highest in Uruguay, Costa Rica, Argentina, and Venezuela, where 78, 77, 68, and 67 percent of respondents, respectively, agreed with this statement in 2003 (Table 1.11). Mass support for democracy lies in a medium range in Mexico (53 percent), Peru (52 percent), Chile (50 percent), and Bolivia (50 percent). At the other end of the spectrum, only 46 percent of Colombians, 45 percent of Salvadorans, 35 percent of Brazilians, and 33 percent of Guatemalans could agree that democracy was their preferred form of government. In 2002, citizens of each of these four countries were the most open to a nondemocratic government, if it could solve the country's economic problems (62 percent of Brazilians, 64 percent of Guatemalans, 57 percent of Colombians, and 55 percent of Salvadorans were open to such a possibility). Yet, one of the highest levels of support for democracy was

---

[7] In 2000–01, Argentina received scores of .57 for voice and accountability, .55 for political stability, .18 for government effectiveness, .25 for regulatory quality, .22 for rule of law, and −.36 for control of corruption (Kaufmann, Kraay, and Zoido-Lobatón 2002).

[8] Many scholars will find this argument similar to Zakaria's well-known thesis of "illiberal democracy" (Zakaria 1997).

found in Venezuela – 67 percent of Venezuelans supported democracy (only in Uruguay, Costa Rica, and Argentina was support for democracy higher) – but Venezuela's ranking on governance indicators was across the board the lowest in Latin America. On the whole, the correlation between this measure of support for democracy and the quality of democratic governance is not statistically significant.

There are other reasons why faith in these responses would be misplaced. Public support for democracy is notoriously highly volatile.[9] Presumably, public support for democracy does not evaporate from one month to the next, though that is precisely how this loss of support often manifests itself. Of the countries under examination here, the greatest percentage point declines in public support for democracy in the years from 1996 to 2003 were registered in El Salvador (11), Peru (11), Bolivia (14), Colombia (14), and Guatemala (18). Rates of decline were even higher in Paraguay and Panama (19 and 24 percentage points, respectively). In Mexico, public support for democracy dropped in a single year from 63 (2002) to 53 percent (2003). (See again Table 1.11.) Moreover, it is often difficult to make sense of public responses to this question on its own. In a recent Eurobarometer survey of twenty-one postcommunist countries, the correlation between each country's Freedom House score and aggregate satisfaction with democracy found in surveys was .001, and more Albanians (76 percent) were satisfied with their democracy than Britons (46 percent) (Rose and Shin 2001: 339–41). Apparently, the comparative measure on which we most rely for citizen attitudes toward democracy is volatile and barely correlated to "real" levels of democracy.

From what measures of public attitudes or behavior – if not support for democracy – can we then infer something meaningful about the health of democracy? Inevitably, when working with a small set of countries, answers to any one survey item in a single year may reflect national idiosyncrasies and provide an inadequate foundation upon which to draw broader comparative conclusions. To compensate for the weakness of these measures, I created an index of citizen satisfaction with democracy for the twelve Latin American countries in our sample comprised of an average of six indicators: levels of support for democracy (2000–04 average), satisfaction with democracy (2000–04 average), and trust in government (2003); numbers responding that democracy is the best governmental system (2003–04 average) and that voting can make a difference (2004); and valid votes as a percentage of the voting age population (1990–2002 average) (Table 11.3). The first five are captured from responses to the surveys of public opinion, and the sixth, an average of turnout in democratic elections, matches opinion with the most fundamental act of citizenship in a democracy.

---

[9] Cynthia McClintock (1999b: 342) has appropriately pointed out that from 1982 to 1994 Peruvians consistently supported democracy even when real alternatives – a military dictatorship (which earlier had distributed land, nationalized oil, and brought workers into management of state enterprises) and revolution (in the guise of the Maoist Shining Path) – were available. Yet in 1992, 88 percent of Limeños also backed Alberto Fujimori's *autogolpe*.

TABLE 11.3. *Citizen Perceptions of Democracy in Latin America, 2000–2004*

Country	Support for Democracy[a]	Satisfaction with Democracy[b]	Importance of Voting[c]	Valid Votes/VAP[d]	Trust in Government[e]	Democracy is the Best System[f]	Index
Uruguay	79	53	71	92	19	84	66
Costa Rica	75	56	51	67	23	80	59
Argentina	65	28	65	71	45	80	59
Chile	52	32	53	67	46	71	53
Panama	53	34	72	68	20	71	53
Venezuela	67	43	68	36	28	74	53
Honduras	56	41	49	64	25	72	51
Brazil	36	23	59	54	42	69	47
Nicaragua	52	30	50	74	12	66	47
Mexico	52	23	52	57	24	75	47
El Salvador	45	31	61	37	21	61	42
Colombia	43	20	57	30	33	64	41
Peru	56	15	54	49	14	59	41
Bolivia	53	21	37	52	14	62	40
Ecuador	47	19	45	53	10	55	38
Paraguay	41	10	50	52	16	55	38
Guatemala	38	26	54	32	7	46	34
Latin America	54	30	60	56	24	68	49

[a] Percent agreeing with statement, "Democracy is preferable to any other kind of government," 2000–04 average.
[b] Percent responding they are "very satisfied" and "fairly satisfied" with the functioning of democracy, 2000–04 average.
[c] Percent responding "How one votes can make things different in the future," 2004.
[d] Valid votes as percent of voting age population, 1990–2002 average.
[e] Percent expressing "a lot of confidence" and "some confidence" in government, 2003.
[f] Percent agreeing with the statement, "Democracy may have problems, but it is the best system of government," 2003–04 average.

Sources: Latinobarómetro 2003, 2004; UNDP 2004: 87.

While not perfect, this index solves for some anomalies. If we look only at the response to the single question of support for democracy, Brazil appears to be one of the two weakest democracies in Latin America. But by taking into account trust in government, satisfaction with democracy, the opinion that democracy is better than the alternatives, and the rate at which Brazilians actually turn out to vote, Brazil's democracy appears stronger, and the contrast with Guatemala, the other country at the bottom of the support for democracy column, is now stark. When these indicators are factored in, Guatemala falls to the bottom of the index, a view that conforms to Seligson's interpretation of the state of Guatemalan democracy, and in Brazil, Mexico, and El Salvador, all things considered, democracy may be as strong as it has ever been. The best supported democracies are Uruguay, Costa Rica, and Argentina.

What explains these broader public perceptions about democracy and the importance citizens attach to voting participation? Although many scholars and pollsters believe that support for democracy may be correlated with the performance of the government of the day and especially the popularity of the president, in fact, the lowest presidential approval ratings in Latin America in 2003 were in Uruguay and Costa Rica (the countries with the highest support for democracy). The quality of democratic governance more broadly gives us greater leverage over our question. The correlation between the index of satisfaction with democracy and the quality of democratic governance (Table 11.2) is .57 (significant at the .05 level). When this relationship is mapped (Figure 11.1), we see that most countries can be fitted in a predictable pattern:

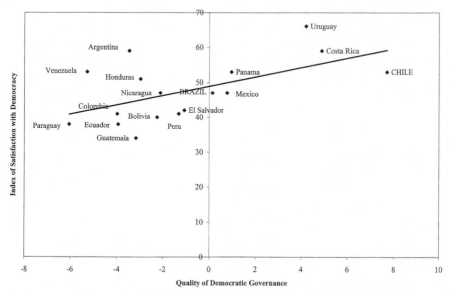

FIGURE 11.1. Democracy in Latin America: Performance and Perceptions.
Sources: Tables 11.2 and 11.3.

Support for and satisfaction with democracy and trust in its institutions tends to rise along with the quality of democratic governance. There are, however, outliers. In Venezuela, Argentina, and even Uruguay, satisfaction with democracy clearly outperforms the quality of democratic governance; in Chile and in Guatemala, it falls far short. Clearly, we still need to discover the variables that attenuate the impact of regime performance and that explain democracy's advances and setbacks.

EXPLAINING DEMOCRACY'S SETBACKS

The great trends that explain the surprising wave of democratization in the region do not explain democracy's setbacks where an elite consensus in favor of democracy was strong and political institutions appeared to be functioning well. The collapse of communism and the transformation of the left cannot in and of themselves guarantee quality democratic governance. International support for democracy cannot inspire citizen loyalty, participation, and confidence in democratic government. And political institutions reformed to overcome deadlock, polarization, and fragmentation might smooth out the governing process, but it cannot ensure that citizens will endorse all policy courses set by their governments. These factors alone cannot enhance the quality of democracy in contexts where it can be perilously low, especially when economic and social inclusion so palpably lags behind.

These shortcomings suggest that we need to move beyond the study of regime transition and political institutions that has dominated much political science scholarship of the past decade and a half. These frameworks served us well when we were attempting to explain exits from authoritarian rule and the capacity of democratic political systems to build an elite consensus for democracy. But in this era of mass democracy in which democratic regimes benefit from an international protection racket, if we are to explain the solidity or fragility of democratic regimes we will need to treat democratic governance not merely as the ability of the executive to get a reform agenda or a budget proposal through Congress, but also as the responsiveness of governments to constituent demands. We will need to assess how well the outputs of public policy – well-paying jobs, safe streets, and access to quality schools and health care, delivered by governments that are perceived to be clean and fair – meet the expectations of constituents. We will also need to reconnect the legislative process to citizen participation, government responsiveness, democratic accountability, and the quality of political representation. We need, in other words, to build a new approach to studying democratic regimes.

Beyond Transitions and Institutions: What Role for Citizens?

If citizen support makes democratic regimes in the Third Wave solid and the loss of that support makes them vulnerable to erosion, then we need to understand citizen expectations of government, perceptions of the policy course that governments set, and evaluations of the success of those policies. The conventional wisdom maintains that high expectations followed transitions from authoritarian rule, and the results of market-oriented reforms have generated potentially destabilizing disappointment. Such a view recalls the paradigmatic argument advanced three decades ago by Michel Crozier, Samuel Huntington, and Joji Watanuki (1975), who in a justifiably influential work admonished that the democracies in Western Europe, North America, and Japan – the Trilateral region – were being "overloaded" with the demands of an array of citizens' groups. States that caved were stretched beyond their capacities, ran deficits that fueled inflation, and, in turn, generated more discontent and a sense that governments could not govern. The notion that there was a tradeoff between democratic participation and democratic governance, advanced by Huntington (1968) years earlier, was challenged a quarter century later when Robert Putnam, Susan Pharr, and Russell Dalton (2000), asking whatever happened to the overload problem in advanced industrial democracies, found that where there had once been intense citizen mobilization and strong engagement with political institutions, there were now unmistakable signs of malaise and political disaffection: declining attachments to political parties, low rates of approval of parliaments, negative assessments of the "political class," and declining levels of trust in government and elected officials. Such an interpretation built on the Putnamesque (and Tocquevillian) notion that government works best, and democracy is at its healthiest when government is engaged and held to account by its own civil society (Putnam 1993).

The question of how much participation on the part of civil society is ideal in a mass democracy and how it should best be channeled is at least as significant in Latin America today, where at stake is not just this year's budget deficit or the functioning of regional governments but democracy itself, as in advanced industrial society then and now. On the one hand, inflated expectations on the part of mobilized voters are alleged to have fueled neopopulist politics that undermine fiscal discipline, democratic institutions, and the rule of law. On the other hand, the experience of the Latin American cases in the Third Wave of democracy examined in this volume may reveal a more dangerous side effect of the democratic dilemma than heretofore appreciated: What "works" when government is performing well – that is, a low level of popular mobilization and a low level of demands – may leave democracy vulnerable when government performance falters. Loss of confidence in government and political institutions, once eroded, may not be easily recouped.

While there are many possible explanations for the magnitude and the causes of citizen support for and disaffection with their democratic regimes, two stand out for the frequency and vehemence with which they have been asserted, and for the logically intuitive nature of their arguments. The first concerns the impact of globalization and the adoption of neoliberal economic policies. If neoliberalism is claimed to have contributed to the longevity of the Third Wave of democratization by calming nervous *elites*, it is also alleged to have jeopardized it by eroding *popular* support for democracy in Latin America today.

The second concerns the gap between government performance and citizen expectations. I do not pretend to test these hypotheses adequately, but I examine each in light of what we do know, and I raise questions for further research.

Globalization and Neoliberalism

Writing of the Trilateral countries, Alesina and Wacziarg (2000) conjectured that the secular decline in public support for democratic governments in advanced industrial society could be caused by globalization. The increased openness of countries to global trade and the rapid mobility of international capital is alleged to have constrained OECD (Organisation for Economic Co-operation and Development) governments from adopting policies that conform to the position of the median voter, which in turn has increased public dissatisfaction with government. The idea is theoretically appealing but probably exaggerated in the case of the advanced industrial societies, where such externally imposed constraints are not hard (Garrett 1998; Mosley 2003). However, recent research has shown that governments in developing countries are subject to more constraints than their OECD counterparts (Kaufman and Segura-Ubiergo 2001; Mosley 2003). Kaufman and Segura-Ubiergo (2001: 554) find that trade integration has had a consistently negative effect on aggregate social spending, and this is compounded by openness to capital markets. The negative effect of international economic integration operates primarily in the area of social security transfers (mainly pensions), while health and education expenditures are far less vulnerable. In Latin America, the conversion to neoliberalism is alleged to have enhanced these constraints. Latin American countries are now as open to trade as at any time since the Great Depression, and financial mobility has so reduced the scope of financial policy that Ecuador and El Salvador have joined Panama in dollarizing their economies, and Argentina and Brazil both adopted currency reforms that pegged the peso and the real to the dollar (with the Argentine policy a far stricter variant), until these exchange rates became unsustainable. Brazil let the real float in early 1999 (resulting in a huge devaluation), and Argentina abandoned its currency board and convertibility plan after its banking system collapsed in December 2001.

Have the constraints of globalization dampened levels of public support for democratic regimes and governments? Do mass publics that reject globalization and neoliberal market reforms, and that identify democratic governments as responsible for ushering in those reforms, penalize those governments, as this thesis expects? In fact, on the one hand, Latin Americans are generally supportive of increased openness to international trade and foreign investment. In a Market and Opinion Research International (MORI) poll conducted in 1998, 85 percent of respondents in fourteen Latin American countries supported free trade, and 60 percent reported that foreign direct investment was good because it promotes economic growth (cited in Magaloni and Romero

2004: 11).[10] On the other hand, on average, citizens are skeptical of state retrenchment. Support for private ownership in seven key sectors (oil, electricity, airlines, mines, telephone, water, and TV) in 1998 was lukewarm at best, and citizens in all fourteen Latin American countries included in the MORI survey expressed a preference for greater, not lesser, state involvement in the provision of education, health care, and pensions. Since then, support for privatization of state companies has eroded in every country in the region. In Latinobarómetro polls taken in 2003, support for privatization had fallen since 1998 by 24 percentage points, to its current low level of 22 percent (Table 11.4). Polls show that Latin Americans *generally* support a market economy, on average, 57 percent of Latin Americans agree with the statement "Only with a market economy can (country) become a developed country," but only 16 percent were very or fairly satisfied with how the market economy worked in their country. Nearly three quarters were less satisfied with the delivery of privatized public services than they were before (Table 11.4). Magaloni and Romero (2004: 27) confirm that economic performance can dramatically shape citizen evaluations of neoliberal policies. Where the economy grew in the 1990s relative to the 1980s, respondents supported globalization. Where short-term inflation was high in the late 1990s relative to the 1980s, survey respondents embraced state retrenchment, but when macroeconomic stabilization had been achieved, they preferred state expansion.

Does increasing skepticism about state retrenchment from key industries and especially social services, then, translate into a loss of support for democracy? Do citizens who object to neoliberal *policies* penalize either their government or their democracy? For better or for worse, mass publics do not ascribe blame for their country's economic problems to the impersonal forces of globalization, but rather they put the blame squarely on the doorstep of their governments. When asked in 2003 which of a list of institutions and actors were responsible for the economic problems, 63 percent of Latin Americans cited the "government's economic policy," but only 14 percent held the International Monetary Fund (IMF) responsible; 14 percent, "globalization"; 12 percent, "the banks"; and 8 percent, the World Trade Organization (WTO) (Latinobarómetro 2003: 17). The key question, of course, is whether voters assess a penalty merely in response to survey questions, or whether they impose an *electoral* penalty as well? If dissatisfaction *is* expressed politically at the ballot box, does it take the form of support for a democratic opponent, or an antisystem alternative?

Globalization, Neoliberalism, and Democracy

To begin, is satisfaction with market reform correlated with support for democracy? The short answer, in aggregate terms, is no. The correlation

---

[10] The countries included ten of the twelve countries examined in this chapter: Argentina, Bolivia, Brazil, Chile, Colombia, Costa Rica, Guatemala, Mexico, Peru, and Venezuela. Also included were Dominican Republic, Ecuador, Panama, and Paraguay. El Salvador and Uruguay were omitted.

TABLE 11.4. *Popular Perceptions of Market-Oriented Reforms: Latin America, 2003*

	Privatization of State Companies[a]			Market Economy		Satisfaction with Privatization of Public Services		State Problem-Solving Capacity[b]	
	1998	2003	Change	Support[c]	Satisfaction[d]	Decrease[e]	Increase	Only a Few	Not Any
Argentina	32	12	−20	51	15	69	25	37	3
Bolivia	49	19	−30	54	11	75	21	47	19
Brazil	51	33	−18	69	25	69	26	43	7
Chile	51	29	−22	52	23	67	22	42	7
Colombia	39	24	−15	56	16	67	21	43	15
Costa Rica	–	–	–	64	17	–	–	60	15
El Salvador	54	15	−39	56	23	81	11	50	13
Guatemala	62	16	−46	33	15	69	15	27	26
Mexico	49	31	−18	65	17	60	35	53	11
Peru	44	22	−22	61	7	67	28	50	17
Uruguay	29	16	−13	59	11	–	–	19	5
Venezuela	51	32	−19	50	18	64	33	30	10
Latin America	46	22	−24	57	16	71	22	43	13

[a] Q. Do you strongly agree, somewhat agree, somewhat disagree, or strongly disagree with each of the following phrases that I am going to read: "The privation of state companies has been beneficial to the country." Percent responding "strongly agree" and "somewhat agree."

[b] Q. It is said that the state can solve our society's problems because it has the resources to do so. Would you say that the state can solve: All the problems/The majority of the problems/Quite a lot of problems/Only a few problems/The state cannot solve any problems.

[c] Q. Do you strongly agree, somewhat agree, disagree, or strongly disagree with the following statement? Only with a market economy can (country) become a developed country. Percent responding "strongly agree" and "agree."

[d] Q. In general, would you say that you are very satisfied, fairly satisfied, not very satisfied or not at all satisfied with the way market economy works in (country)? Percent responding "very satisfied" and "fairly satisfied."

[e] Q. Public services like water, and electricity have been privatized. Considering price and quality, are you much more satisfied, more satisfied, less satisfied, or much less satisfied than you were before with these privatized services? Percent responding "less satisfied" and "much less satisfied."

Source: Latinobarómetro (2003: 14, 57, 58, 59, 16, 17).

between satisfaction with the market and both the simple measure of support for democracy and the composite index of citizen support for democracy is negative and insignificant.

Argentina's drama is illustrative. Although the Convertibility Plan imposed hard constraints on Argentine government policy for a full decade after its implementation in 1991 and before its abandonment in 2001, public support for this tight restraint (perceived as responsible for taming inflation) remained firm, and support for democracy was fairly high in Argentina by regional standards in 1995–96. Levels of satisfaction with the performance of the market economy understandably plunged after unemployment continued to be high and the banking system collapsed, taking with it many families' life savings. In 2002, a mere 2 percent of Argentines were satisfied with the functioning of the market. But even amid tightly constrained macroeconomic policy and rising poverty, ordinary Argentines continued to support democratic governance; support for democracy remained steady at high levels by regional standards. In 2002, voters turned to Nestor Kirschner, who campaigned against the neoliberal model and IMF policies, but who represented the most important Argentine political party – the Peronists.

The other question to address is whether the openness to the world economy emblematic of globalization affects citizen support for democracy. El Salvador and Mexico are among the most open economies in Latin America; their trade as a percentage of GDP is in the same range as Chile (roughly 55 percent) (Table 11.5), but both are doing reasonably well in terms of citizen support for democracy. Such a finding is consistent with work that has shown that public confidence levels have remained high in some of the smaller Trilateral democracies (i.e., those most dependent on the global economy and most affected by internationalization or globalization) (Katzenstein 2000) – at least if they continue to provide protection against the risks that follow from exposure to trade. In our Latin American sample, trade openness is not significantly correlated with market satisfaction or support for democracy. There is also no correlation between openness to capital markets and foreign investment and citizen support for democracy.

Although globalization, understood as increased trade and capital flows, and neoliberalism are often used interchangeably in the popular (and especially opposition) discourse, they are distinct phenomena. Given higher levels of public support for globalization than for state retrenchment, it is possible that not globalization, but neoliberal state reform, might erode support for democracy. Satisfaction with the quality of public services narrowly misses a statistically significant correlation with the composite index of citizen support for democracy. To explore this hypothesis more fully, we would want to consider whether opposition to neoliberalism is evident at the polls.

From Opinions to Votes

It is almost a truism that the people in Latin America won't stand for neoliberalism. Reality is more complicated. Latin American voters have shown that they

TABLE 11.5. *Globalization and Economic Openness: Latin America*

	Trade Openness[a]	Net Private Capital Flows (% GDP)	Foreign Direct Investment (% GDP)	Capital Account Liberalization Index[b] (1995)
Argentina	17.5	6.2	4.3	0.99
Bolivia	36.8	11.6	9.2	0.89
Brazil	23.2	9.1	6.5	0.64
Chile	54.8	7.6	5.8	0.75
Colombia	30.4	3.8	2.8	0.73
Costa Rica	28.3	3.8	2.5	1.0
El Salvador	56.5	2.4	1.3	0.92
Guatemala	39.1	.9	1.1	0.95
Mexico	54.2	1.9	2.2	0.88
Peru	29.2	2.9	1.3	0.91
Uruguay	71.6	3.1	1.6	0.84
Venezuela	37.0	4.4	3.6	0.93
Latin America		6.2		

[a] Trade openness represents the sum of exports plus imports expressed as a percentage of GDP.

[b] The capital account (or international financial) liberalization index represents the average of four components, which reflect the sector control of foreign investment; limits on profit and interest repatriation; controls on external credits by national borrowers; and capital outflows. The index is normalized to be between zero and one, with one being the most reformed or free from distortion or government intervention. The difference between each country's "raw" index and the least liberalized country observation is expressed as a percentage of the difference between the maximum and minimum observations for all the countries over the entire period from 1970 to 1995. The maximum value of the index is the level actually attained in Costa Rica in 1990 and 1995 (Morley, Machado, and Pettinato 1999: 11, 9).

Sources: World Bank (2003: 238–41); Morley et al. (1999: 32).

are willing to mete out punishment for sluggish growth, high unemployment, and declining real income – as they did quite dramatically in Mexico in 1988. When economic reforms seem to work, however, they tend to reward incumbents. The reelection of Carlos Menem (1995), Alberto Fujimori (1995), and Fernando Henrique Cardoso (1998) may be attributable to the success of their governments in controlling inflation. In this volume, Martín Tanaka attributes Fujimori's ability to build a coalition to consolidate his power to his timely control of inflation. Mayorga credits the success of the Paz Estenssoro administration's NEP (New Economic Policy) in stabilizing the Bolivian economy and later generating an economic recovery with helping to solidify and legitimize the Bolivian democratic regime. These elections demonstrate a growing political sophistication on the part of Latin American voters.

The success of neoliberal reforms may be especially important when voters feel deceived. Stokes (2001) finds that although voters tend to support a government that changes course in office from what it promised in its electoral campaign when outcomes are sufficiently good, as they were in Argentina under Carlos Menem, they abandon a government that does the same when the outcomes of unmandated policies are bad, and this is what she contends happened in Venezuela. The outcome of elections may also be sealed by the ability of governments to focus voters on issue areas other than the one where the government imposed unmandated policies. In Peru, the Fujimori government successfully diverted attention from the economy to peace and rallied support by defeating the Shining Path guerrilla rebellion and embarking on a spending program just before election time. At minimum, the impact of economic constraints on democracy are complicated and probably attenuated by the way they are presented (a point Moisés Naím [1993] made about Venezuela under Carlos Andres Pérez), and perceived.

The process by which reform is generated, and the results of reform, can also be significant. Drawing from the Polish experience, Adam Przeworski argued that when reforms are ushered in by stealth by insulated technocrats, when, in other words, policy makers circumvent representative institutions in order to speed the reform process, the public "learns" that important decisions are made outside the framework of representative institutions. "Repeated surveys show that people do not see the locus of power in the properly constituted institutions.... If decisions are made elsewhere, representative institutions wilt" (Przeworski 1995: 80–82). Although the Argentine case is often cited as an example of reform by presidential decree, Levitsky points out – correctly – in his chapter that after the first year of his government, Menem consulted widely with Congress, which had significant influence over the package of economic reforms (a point reinforced by Corrales 2002). He sees the strength of the (Peronist) Justicialista Party (PJ) as facilitating smooth executive–legislative relations. As he rightly points out, Argentina combined economic liberalization and democracy in a way that was unparalleled in Latin America. Among fully democratic cases (e.g., Costa Rica, Uruguay, Venezuela, and Brazil), Argentina's economic reforms were more rapid and far-reaching, and among cases of deep crisis and radical reform (i.e., Chile, Mexico, and Peru), Argentina's regime was the most democratic. Even Bolivia under Paz Estenssoro relied on a stage of siege and harsh labor repression.

Finally, globalization is perceived to have destabilized democracies in two ways: by creating economic dislocation and by engendering a cultural reaction as people struggle to maintain their distinctive national, religious, and ethnic identities – in the words of one popular writer, they fight for their "olive trees" (Friedman 2000). This claim may assume greater salience in the Andean region, where ethnic grievances have come to the fore in recent years. In Bolivia, Evo Morales's Movement to Socialism won 21 percent of the vote in the 2002 election, and the Pachakutik party of Felipe Quispe won another 6 percent; together, they captured 33 percent of the seats in the lower Chamber (*The Economist* 2004: 36). Although Deborah Yashar has downplayed the impact of globalization, per se, on the emergence of ethnic movements and political parties in Ecuador and Bolivia, she does attribute great weight to the redefinition of rights and representation that has accompanied neoliberal economic reforms (Yashar 2005).

Citizen Expectations and Government Performance

Our second thesis was that citizen disillusion with democracy might be attributable to a gap between government *performance* and what citizens *expect* of government. If citizen expectations are unrealistically high, something that scholars feared in the 1980s as democratic governments were poised to inherit bankrupt states and promissory notes to citizens deprived of material well-being – as well as freedom – by authoritarian regimes, it could result that no government could match inflated and unrealistic expectations. Supporting such a view, Malone, Baviskar, and Manel (2003: 23) find that the higher that citizens in Argentina, Brazil, Chile, and Guatemala rank what they call the "all-embracing" elements of democracy (in an ideal democracy, public security is maintained, the well-being of citizens is protected, all citizens have access to education and health care, no one goes hungry, and everyone has work and a minimal standard of living), the *less likely* they are to support democracy unequivocally (i.e., respond that "democracy is preferable to any other form of government"). They find that the gap between expectations and performance is substantially wider in the newer democracies of Latin America than in the established democracies of Germany, Denmark, and the United States (2003: 20).

If expectations are important in explaining citizens' declining confidence, so, too, is performance. For Newton and Norris (2000: 72), the performance of governments and political institutions is critical, and several authors in this volume highlight the performance side of the equation. Reflecting on the rather sudden erosion of the democratic regime in Bolivia after 2000, Mayorga called attention to the fact that democratic governments in Bolivia have performed poorly, and have been unable to meet the socioeconomic expectations of a poverty-ridden country – with 65 percent of all urban jobs in the informal sector, two thirds of the population being poor, and persistently low levels of education, health, and nutrition. Mainwaring and Pérez-Liñán contend that poor government performance since 1992 is perhaps the single most important variable accounting for democratic erosion in the region. Indeed, the record of democratic governments has been dramatically poor in several key areas. In 2003, 225 million Latin Americans had incomes that fell below the poverty line (UNDP 2004), leading the UNDP to conclude: "Slow economic growth, profound inequalities, and ineffective legal systems and social services are triggering popular unrest and undermining confidence in electoral democracy."

Many authors treat citizen expectations of government as general. But might poor performance in some areas weigh more heavily in public dissatisfaction with and indifference toward democracy than overall macroeconomic stability and growth, as Naím (1993) poignantly argued was the case in Venezuela in 1991 when the economy grew by 10 percent, but an angry public penalized their government nonetheless for a sharp deterioration in the quality of public services? With the advantage of more sophisticated polling of public opinion in Latin America than ever before, we can reasonably accurately identify those problems that citizens perceive are important and that government is not handling well at any given time. A volume on Latin American democracy appearing in the late 1980s would undoubtedly have highlighted inflation as public enemy number one. With inflation generally under control across the continent by the late 1990s (Table 1.12), that issue is no longer cited by survey respondents as one of the most urgent facing their families, their localities, or their countries.

In recent years, three issues have topped the charts (Table 11.6). The first is *economic security*, understood principally as unemployment and secondarily as poverty. To a more limited extent, some citizens also expressed concern with "economic crisis," and real incomes and the cost of living, indicating that the desire for a well-paying job is a far more salient concern today than inflation and even overall growth rates. Although growth and employment are surely related, "jobless recoveries" do exist. The second major policy area is *public security*, especially violent crime but sometimes including drug trafficking, gangs, and guerrillas. The third most salient issue is *corruption*. Access to quality social services (health and education) is less salient. I examine the first three areas in turn. Although perceptions about corruption could color evaluations of government performance in managing the economy and providing order – that is, citizens might penalize governments more if they attribute the performance-expectations gap to malfeasance rather than structural constraints, wrong policies, or even mere incompetence – I treat corruption as a separate issue.

Economic Security

Alesina and Wacziarg (2000) place great emphasis on government performance in the areas of growth, inflation, and unemployment. Because they are explaining a secular trend over the course of a half century, they are most interested in the dramatic drop-off in the performance of governments in the Trilateral Democracies before and after the 1973–74 oil shock. Prior to this, growth was more robust, inflation was lower, and unemployment rates were more modest. After the oil shock, the reverse was true in each area.

In Latin America, it is also true that growth was more robust in the period prior to 1974, when world trade expanded and commodity prices for Latin America's main exports were high. Certainly the 1980s are considered the "lost decade" in Latin America, so called because standards of living at the end of the decade were lower than they were at the beginning, and in most countries equal to levels in 1970. In other words, economic contraction in the 1980s eroded the gains produced by growth in the 1970s. At the same time, inflation in the 1980s was extraordinarily high, fueled by the astronomical burden of debt service.

In the 1990s, things generally turned around. Inflation rates fell to rates lower than they had been even during the period of growth in the Second Wave democracies. In Argentina, Peru, Brazil, and elsewhere, voters tended in the Third Wave to reward governments that could impose price stability. But on the other hand, unemployment has risen in most countries with scant signs of abating.

TABLE 11.6. *Most Salient Problems in Twelve Latin American Countries (percent responding most important problem facing country or sum of responses)*

Country	Date of Poll	Economic Security				Personal Security		Access to Social Services		Government/ Corruption
		Unemployment	Poverty	Economic Crisis	Cost of Living/Wages	Public Security/Crime	Specific Problems	Health	Education	
Argentina	May 2003	82(1)	27(4)			39(2)		22(5)	29(3)	
Bolivia	Dec. 2003	63(1)	45(3)							57(2)
Brazil	Dec. 2002	63(1)				35(4)	41(2)[a]	41(2)		
Chile	Jan. 2002	63(1)	45(3)							57(2)
Colombia	Dec. 2003	40(1)					24(3)[b]			29(2)
Costa Rica	Oct.–Dec. 2002	18(2)	8(5)	11(4)	19(1)	16(3)	8(6)[a]			
El Salvador	Nov.–Dec. 2003	22(1)	19(3)	15(4)		22(1)	8(5)[c]			
Guatemala	Oct. 2001	16(2)	15(3)		40(1)	18(3, 4)[d]				
Mexico	Feb. 2004	22(2)	15(3)	24(1)	13(4)					7(5)
Peru	Aug. 2003	24(1)	13(4)	21(2)		7(6)[e]				15(3)
Uruguay	Jan. 2004	44(1)			9(5)					
Venezuela	Aug. 2003	38(1)		13(2)	15(2)	15(2)				22(3, 4)[f]

[a] Drugs. [b] Guerrillas. [c] Gangs.

[d] "Common crime," was cited by 11 percent of respondents, and "violence in general," by 7 percent.

[e] The fifth most important problem was a "crisis of values," cited by 9 percent of respondents.

[f] "The executive does not govern well" was cited by 12 percent of respondents, and "Congress does not function; politicians don't agree," by 10 percent.

Sources:

Argentina: Ipsos–Mora y Araujo (2003). Based on a national sample of 1,200 cases.

Bolivia: Encuestas & Estudios (2003). Based on a sample of 1,500 urban and rural residents.

Brazil: IBOPE (2002). Based on a nationwide sample of 2,000 adults.

Chile: Centro de Estudios Públicos (2002).

Colombia: *Revista Semana* (2004).

Costa Rica: Latin American Public Opinion Project, Vanderbilt University (2002). Based on a national sample of 1,016 adults.

El Salvador: IUDOP (2003).

Guatemala: ASIES (2001). I am grateful to Dinorah Azpuru for making these data available.

Mexico: Consulta Mitofsky (2004). Based on a sample of 1,200 adults over the age of 18.

Peru: Grupo de Opinión Pública de la Universidad de Lima (2003). Based on a sample of 518 persons in Lima-Callao.

Uruguay: Cifra/González, Raga y Asociados (2004). Based on a sample of urban areas with more than 2,000 inhabitants.

Venezuela: Alfredo Keller y Asociados (2003). Based on a national sample of 1,200 and groups in twelve cities.

In one recent survey, 54 percent of Latin Americans – *not counting those who are already unemployed* – expressed concern that they will be left without work or become unemployed during the next twelve months (Table 11.7).

What has been the impact on elections and democracy of persistent government impotence in generating employment? In the years from 1982 to 1990, Remmer (1991b) found that crisis conditions, as indicated by inflation, economic growth, and exchange rate depreciation, undermined support for incumbents and provoked high levels of electoral volatility, but without necessarily fostering growth of political extremism or exhaustion of the elite consensus for democracy. But how long the pass to failing democratic governments and the era of good feeling following from the victory over inflation lasts is not clear. Perhaps predictably, in Argentina, voters turned out the Peronist government that had conquered hyperinflation (and even recorded a 50 percent expansion of the economy in the early 1990s) after unemployment rose above 17 percent and stayed there. On the other hand, in this volume Magaloni argues that in Mexico voting trends are not strongly correlated with economic growth. The PRI recovered surprising support in the worst years of the recession of the 1980s (when the economy grew on average by only 0.5 percent per year and real minimum wages and average industrial wages lost around 75 percent and 35 percent of their value, respectively), and in 1997 and 2000, the PRI was punished at the polls despite an improvement in growth rates to 2.9 percent per year. Venezuela's severe economic decline (from 1993 to 2002, the economy shrank by 18 percent and urban unemployment averaged 20 percent, the worst performance in Latin America [Table 1.12]) certainly contributed to the collapse of the Venezuelan party system, but Coppedge argues that this powerful political effect was unusual. As he puts it, rising unemployment, falling real incomes, and even economic contraction, as was true in Venezuela, may result in the rejection of an incumbent government or party at the polls, but not typically in a grave crisis of the democratic regime. Consistent with Magaloni and Coppedge's insights, neither rates of unemployment nor economic growth are significantly correlated with the index of citizen perceptions of democracy.

Along with growth, inflation, and unemployment, particularly in Latin America, looms the question of inequality. Inequality in Latin America has worsened over the course of the Third Wave, probably as a result of both stagnant economies and neoliberal reforms. Might persistent inequality be a cause for public disaffection from democracy in societies where disparities in wealth and life chances are as dramatic as they are anywhere in the world, as suggested recently by *The Economist* (2004)? Here, the aggregate evidence is inconclusive. Two countries in our sample with among the most severe inequalities in the world – Brazil and Guatemala (along with South Africa) – display quite different levels of composite support for democracy.

Public Security and Crime

In several Latin American countries, crime and violence are serious problems and highly salient political issues. The case of Colombia, where the state has

TABLE 11.7. *Popular Experience with Salient Problems: Latin America, 2003*

	Fear of Unemployment[a]	Victim of Crime[b]	Drug Consumption[c]	Satisfaction with Access to Health	Satisfaction with Access to Education	Awareness of Corruption[d]	Progress in Reducing Corruption in State Institutions[e]
Argentina	55	42	19	48	52	19	26
Bolivia	57	31	9		52	20	17
Brazil	63	36	41	38	50	56	28
Chile	40	34	19		43	6	36
Colombia	57	36	18		54	11	57
Costa Rica	47	33	31		74	18	–
El Salvador	60	39	14	51	58	20	24
Guatemala	66	32	11	42	49	10	10
Mexico	53	60	57		58	53	29
Peru	50	37	15		21	14	24
Uruguay	40	26	10		57	11	36
Venezuela	59	44	29	44	56	23	22
Latin America	54	36	21		49	21	28

Notes:

[a] Q. How concerned would you say you are that you will be left without work or unemployed during the next 12 months? Very concerned, concerned, a little concerned, or not at all concerned? Percent responding "very concerned" and "concerned."

[b] Q. Have you, or someone in your family, been assaulted, attacked, or been the victim of a crime in the past 12 months? Percent responding "yes."

[c] Q. Have you known if any of your friends or someone in your family has consumed drugs in the past 12 months. Percent responding "yes."

[d] Q. Have you, or someone you know, been aware of an act of corruption in the past 12 months? Percent responding "yes."

[e] Q. How much do you think that there has been progress in reducing corruption in state institutions during the last two years? Percent responding "a lot" and "some."

Source: Latinobarómetro (2003: 10, 51, 52, 50, 30).

clearly failed to exercise a monopoly on violence in society, particularly stands out in this respect. In their chapter, Bejarano and Pizarro argue that the capacity of the Colombian state to control its jurisdiction contracted over the course of two decades in favor of armed groups on both the left and right, and the state even abdicated some of its functions and power to right-wing organizations like the United Self-Defense Forces of Colombia. Their evidence is persuasive: Paramilitary groups operated in 40 percent of all Colombian municipalities, and hundreds of mayors, members of parliament and departmental assemblies, and other public officials were assassinated in the decade from 1989 to 1999. Tragically, there have been half a million violent deaths in the past twenty years.

Where citizens crave security against violence, they clearly have cause to lose faith in the effectiveness of their governments. In his chapter, Mitchell Seligson brings to our attention a recent paper by Nancy Bermeo about the breakdown of democracy in interwar Europe, a time in which, like in the Third Wave of democratization in Latin America, "never before had so many citizens in so many nations been accorded so many formal rights" (Bermeo 2003: 21). Revising the conventional wisdom that rampant inflation and economic depression caused fragile democracies to crack wide open, Bermeo (1999, cited in Seligson, this volume) contends that what distinguishes the surviving democracies from those that collapsed is the crime rate. Her data show that from 1920 to 1938 in democracies that broke down, homicides (the least underreported crime) occurred at three times the rate of the surviving democracies.

Against this backdrop, the data reported by Seligson (this volume) are sobering: According to the United Nations Global Report on Crime, the estimated homicide rate in Latin America is 30 per 100,000, compared to 7 per 100,000 in the United States (the rate in those European countries in which democracy broke down in the interwar period), and 2 per 100,000 today in the United Kingdom, Spain, and Switzerland. Guatemala's homicide rate – 58.68 per 100,000 – is at a level eight times higher than in the European democracies that broke down in the 1920s and 1930s, and fifty times higher than in the ones that survived. Wood reports that El Salvador's homicide rate in 1994 and 1995 was an astronomically high 138 per 100,000. The significance of this figure – the world's highest along with Colombia (80 per 100,000 in 1991) and South Africa – can perhaps best be appreciated by contrasting it to the prewar rate (33 per 100,000), and the rate in 1982 (at the height of the war) – 55.3. According to the IADB (Inter-American Development Bank), crime victimization more generally is higher in Guatemala and El Salvador than in any of the other Latin American countries. In 1998, 25.7 percent of Salvadorans polled reported that their families had been victims of an assault in the previous four months. In public opinion surveys since 1994, more Salvadorans judged crime to be the principal problem facing the country, more so than any other issue, including the economy. The Salvadoran case is not unique. Across the region, more than one third of Latin Americans (and 60 percent of Mexicans) in 2003 reported that they or someone in their family had been the victim of a crime in the previous twelve months (Table 11.7).

When citizens perceive their (democratic) governors cannot handle a serious problem, they look elsewhere. One possibility is the military. Public support for the military's role in fighting crime is overwhelming: Seligson's data from the 1999 University of Pittsburgh survey show 79 percent of the Guatemalan population supported this role (this volume). He speculates that high levels of crime could stimulate support for restrictions on civil liberties, a speculation that is well supported by a disturbing pattern of rising support for the *mano dura* (strong-hand government) over the "participation of everyone" as a means of solving the country's problems. Support for the *mano dura* rose from 48 percent of respondents in 1993 to 60 percent in 1999, while those who favored broad participation shrunk from 40 percent in 1993 to 29 percent in 1999. Seventy percent of respondents preferred order to rights. More starkly, in 1999, 55 percent of Salvadorans stated that crime would justify a coup (Wood, this volume). Another possibility is to take "justice" into their own hands: One of the most disturbing trends in the otherwise salutary move toward democracy in Central America has been the spread of mob justice to close the public security gap. "Lynchings" – not hangings, per se, but more frequently death by immolation or mob beatings – have become problematic in El Salvador and rampant in Guatemala (Mendoza and Torres-Rivas 2003). From 1996 to 2000, there were 337 lynchings in Guatemala, with a total of 185 deaths, and 448 persons were wounded for a total of 635 victims (Seligson, this volume). In the Pittsburgh surveys reported by Seligson, 29 percent of Guatemalans approved of the lynchings, and 12 percent approved of the lynchings some of the time; only just under half of respondents always rejected this practice.

The Salience of Corruption

At the same time that new entrants to the political arena may wish greater outputs of government – cheaper goods, neighborhoods free of drug dealers and gangs, access to quality health care, better schools for their kids, a real roof over their heads – citizens also generally wish for cleaner government. They want to know that public officials, from chief executives and government ministers to the local police officer on the block, are not skimming off the public purse. Susan Pharr (2000) found that misconduct in office is a far more powerful predictor of Japanese confidence levels over the past two decades than a number of other possible causes. Both *actual* and *perceived* levels of corruption may be important. Actual corruption may be responsible for worsening government performance, thus reducing trust in government's capacity to address citizens' demands, as Donatella della Porta (2000) shows is true in the Trilateral democracies. Perceptions of corruption could be at least as important in that they shape citizens' views about their democracies and their democratic institutions as much as or more than the reality.

Does corruption, as widely presumed, indeed erode trust in government or destabilize democracy? By one measure, voting, it is not at all clear that citizens turn to antisystem options when they perceive their officials are corrupt. In one recent study, Seawright (2004: 25–27) finds that in the two cases when voters abandoned established political parties in droves and destabilized democracy – Peru and Venezuela – at the aggregate level, perceptions of corruption were only in the upper third of all countries included in the 1995–97 World Values Survey, and not as high as in other countries such as Argentina where democracy has fared much better. At the individual level, he finds that voters who believed corruption to be prevalent abandoned the governing party in favor of candidacies he calls "insurgent" only in the 1990 local elections; in the 1983 presidential election, they tended to reject the incumbent Social Christian (COPEI) party but to the benefit of its established opposition, the Acción Democrática (AD), and in 1998, perceptions of corruption appear to have played no role in voters' decisions to vote for or against the traditional parties (Seawright 2004: 36).

The timing of the "corruption penalty" in Venezuelan elections, and the targeted beneficiaries suggest that the corruption penalty may have been applied to the traditional parties in sequence. It is also entirely possible, as Michael Coppedge suggests in his chapter, that there is an interaction effect between perceptions about corruption and economic performance. If economic performance explains no more than about a third of the vote shift away from the traditional parties, as Seawright argues, Coppedge's identification of corruption as a "magnifying condition" becomes highly relevant. Coppedge argues (p. 314) that corruption "can magnify the impact of economic performance enough to make a big difference [in a country's political regime] in a short time. . . . Citizens can tolerate corruption if the economy is growing rapidly, and they can tolerate a contraction if they believe their representatives have done everything possible to prevent it or stop it. But when a contraction coincides with known corruption, the political consequences are magnified." For Coppedge, this was how Venezuelans understood economic decline: Venezuelans believed that their country was rich, and that corruption was rampant. In this volume (p. 311) he writes, "Poll after poll showed Venezuelans blaming the economic crisis on waste and corruption rather than the debt or falling oil prices. . . . A large percentage of Venezuelans came to believe that the economy declined because the politicians had stolen from the patrimony of a fundamentally rich country." The key for Coppedge is that the two major parties – the AD and COPEI – tolerated corruption, institutionalized impunity, and permitted corruption to become commonplace and widespread. They protected their own and each other's members and made punishment the rare exception for alleged corruption – at least until the early 1990s. Impunity also had the effect of making corruption less tolerable.

The link between perceptions of corruption and support for democracy, however intuitive, has not been an easy one to establish empirically (see Seligson 2001: 92–93 for a discussion of the claims advanced in World Bank papers in recent years). Such a link needs to be made at the individual level, which requires appropriate survey data. Based on such surveys, Seligson (2001: 115–16) did find evidence in Bolivia of an inverse relationship between having been a victim of corruption and support for democracy; higher rates of victimization were correlated with higher levels of support for an authoritarian regime and government *de mano dura*, and with lower levels of satisfaction with democracy. This finding was replicated in El Salvador, Nicaragua, and Paraguay[11] (Seligson 2002: 424).

With strong reason to believe that high levels of corruption erode support for the legitimacy of the political system, we would want to know how severe the problem of corruption is perceived to be in Latin America in recent years. One fifth of Latin Americans (21 percent) claim to have been aware of an act of corruption in the preceding twelve months, or know someone who was (Table 11.7). Again, the countries that are perceived to be the least corrupt are those we consider to have the strongest democracies – Chile, Costa Rica, and Uruguay. Of the nine cases studied in this volume, Brazil and Peru receive the highest scores from both Transparency International (Table 1.12) and the World Bank Global Governance Indicators project (Table 11.2), with the greater improvement in Brazil. Mexico, Colombia, El Salvador, and Argentina follow, and of these, Argentina shows the most precipitous decline, suggesting that more corruption scandals have come to light in Argentina in recent years. Venezuela, Guatemala, and Bolivia are perceived to be the most corrupt; in these, democracy is perceived by many scholars to be fragile.

Is there, then, a strong link between perceptions about corruption and support for democracy? Much more research is clearly needed. Our cases and research suggest that the answer may depend on the interaction of corruption with economic performance, whether corruption is perceived to be grand theft – a spectacular gain on the part of a president (such as Collor de Mello) or simply "malfeasance" (the charge against Carlos Andres Perez) – or widely practiced on a petty level by government bureaucrats and police officers, and especially whether or not citizens care. In Brazil in 2002, corruption was cited as only the sixth most important problems facing the new Lula government, behind unemployment, health, drugs, public security, and inflation, despite the fact that more Brazilians (56 percent of respondents) showed awareness in the most recent Latinobarómetro poll of an act of corruption in the preceding twelve months than any other country (Table 11.7). Similarly, Mexicans, who also were aware of corruption in high numbers, did not identify the issue as salient. By contrast, Chileans, with the most favorable Transparency International rating in the region and the lowest public experience with corruption, rated corruption as the second most important problem facing the country. Most telling, the identification of corruption as one of the most serious problems facing the country among Bolivians rose from 14 percent of respondents to a

---

[11] This survey consisted of 2,914 randomly selected interviews in El Salvador, 2,410 in Nicaragua, 2,970 in Bolivia, and 1,463 in Paraguay. All fell into the bottom half of countries on Transparency International's corruption index (Salvador, 49th; Nicaragua, 70th; Bolivia, 80th; and Paraguay, 90th). Experiences with corruption were ascertained by responses to a battery of eight questions that asked if the respondent had been stopped by a police officer and asked to pay a bribe, had observed a bribe being paid to a police officer or public official, or had been asked to pay a bribe to a public office, municipal government, place of work, or the court system (Seligson 2002: 418–19).

national poll in January 1995 to 57 percent of 1500 respondents in December 2003 (Encuestas & Estudios 2003), just two months after Sánchez de Lozada's ouster.

In sum, the relationship between faltering government performance and loss of support for democracy is strong but certainly not perfectly linear. Unemployment has been as high in Argentina and Uruguay in the past decade as anywhere in Latin America except for Venezuela and Colombia, but democracy in these countries appears to be about as solid as can reasonably be expected. We have known at least since the Great Depression – when a ravaged German economy paved the way for Nazism but equally dire circumstances in the United States and Sweden did not – that political systems can navigate perilous economic waters or sink in them. Dizzying crime rates and levels of violence have been more threatening to democracy in Guatemala and Colombia than in El Salvador. Corruption appears to erode public confidence in democracy, but on its own cannot accurately predict the loss of public support for democratic institutions. Something, then, mediates the effects of inadequate government performance in some countries, and insulates others from truly spectacular crises. What prompts citizens to look the other way, to trust their government and their leaders?

WHEN DO CITIZENS FORGIVE POOR GOVERNMENT PERFORMANCE? THE ELUSIVE DIMENSION OF POLITICAL REPRESENTATION

In his chapter on Argentina, Steven Levitsky attributes the surprising success of the Menem government in maintaining Argentine democracy, even amid 20 percent unemployment, to a layer of political representation that socialized citizens, cushioned the blows of deprivation, and organized consent. He contrasts Argentina to Peru, where the reservoir of Peronist organizations was not present, and where the sole political party to survive – Alianza Popular Revolucionaria Americana (APRA; American Popular Revolutionary Alliance) – never had that reach into the countryside. Levitsky's evidence is compelling and his argument is persuasive. In his detailed surveys of Peronist unions and neighborhoods in the late 1990s, he found that more than 80 percent of national unions, and more than 90 percent of local unions, participated in Justicialista Party (PJ) activities. He also found that the PJ maintained close ties to a range of other civic and social organizations. In 1997, more than half of 112 local party branches maintained ties to civil associations, clubs, or other social organizations, and more than a third possessed ties to at least two such organizations. Levitsky's survey found 96 percent of local PJ branches engaged in some form of social assistance: Nearly 70 percent of these local branches distributed food or medicine, and more than half regularly organized child care and tutoring services, as well as social and cultural activities in their neighborhoods. Slightly less than half offered programs for the elderly. Levitsky's research is consistent with that of Auyero (2000), who found that neighborhood-level Peronist "problem solving networks" interceded with state authorities to obtain wheelchairs, disability pensions, scholarships, funeral expenses, and odd jobs for their constituents. The PJ's strong ties to working- and lower-class society, Levitsky argues, prevented the sort of mass urban looting and protest over economic reforms witnessed elsewhere in Latin America in the 1990s, and it helped the PJ to retain its traditional and lower-class electorate in the 1990s, even amid soaring rates of unemployment, which in turn served to limit the prospects for the sorts of antireform and antisystem appeals that took hold in other countries. Such prospects were real, not hypothetical, in the Argentine case: The electoral challenge of Movement for Dignity and Independence (MODIN; Movimiento por la Dignidad y la Independencia), which had seemed viable in 1994, collapsed in 1995. As Levitsky correctly points out, even Front for a Country in Solidarity (Frente por un País Solidario; FREPASO) drew primarily middle-class, not lower-class support.

To generalize such a promising argument is difficult. We must first of all be able to recognize a network when we see one, and most scholars have not engaged in the kind of fieldwork that Levitsky and Auyero have conducted in Argentina. In their place, we may rely on the density of party networks or even membership in organizations of civil society, but we would have no way of knowing how vibrant or moribund such organizations really are. We would also need to know what *kind* of networks of representation are most effective in bonding citizens to their democratic institutions. Some linkages may be more effective and enduring than others. At times, networks that deliver to citizens particularistic benefits – be they patronage, goodies from the pork-barrel, clientelism and social assistance, or even resolution of personal problems with the bureaucracy – can be especially effective in organizing consent, and at other times, parties that rely on these compensation mechanisms may find themselves suffering massive voter rejection at the polls. In other contexts, networks that allow for genuine popular participation in real decision making may be more resilient. It is not at all clear that networks based on compensation and participation are interchangeable from the standpoint of democratic stability, especially since networks that allow for genuine participation may be more difficult for governments to manage.

In order for connections to preserve citizen trust in government and support for democracy, must they be personal? On the one hand, the contemporary debate about "social capital" suggests that the answer should be yes. On the other, a long tradition in political science that focuses on the responsiveness and accountability of representatives to citizens suggests that if parties offer ideologies, programs, or policies that conform to voters' wishes, they may continue to enjoy citizen support, even in the absence of personal attention, particularistic benefits, and social ties, whereas if they do not, they may suffer electoral penalty, even if these are offered. This discussion adds a wrinkle to the unresolved Huntington–Putnam debate. If civil society organizations can either buttress parties or, as Berman (1997) has shown was true of Weimar Germany, compete with them and even undermine democracy, then is a well-mobilized civil society an asset for democracy *independent* of the strength of political parties and partisan–citizen linkages, or is it beneficial for democracy only when it is anchored to strong political parties?

To begin, let us consider first the impact of the unmediated mobilization of civil society on democracy. Levitsky assigns great weight to the flourishing of Argentine civil society *as a counterweight to state authority* in the preservation of Argentine democracy. He credits not merely or especially the organized labor movement, which was always strong in Argentina, but also the "second-wave" human rights-oriented organizations and Argentina's print and electronic media with providing the sort of societal accountability that held regional and national governments to account for the deaths of the Catamarcan teenager María Soledad Morales (cf. Smulovitz and Peruzzotti 2003) and the investigative journalist José Luiz Cabezas. Civil society also blossomed in Brazil during the Third Wave of democratization; indeed, this may be one of the most dramatic differences distinguishing Brazil's contemporary democracy from its postwar variant. Weyland acknowledges that both trade union density and participation in voluntary associations is rising in Brazil. In one recent survey, two thirds of respondents reported membership in voluntary associations, a percentage that is significantly higher than that of Spain (McDonough et al. 1998). Some of these organizations contribute to local and state-level decision making through the practice of "participatory budgeting," an experiment that originally took shape in southern Brazil and that has since been emulated elsewhere in Brazil and abroad as one of the most vibrant democratic experiments of the Third Wave. Political participation may be more widespread, independent, and active in Brazil today than it has ever been.

There is also evidence that social organizations served as schools of democracy in war-torn El Salvador. Citing surveys conducted by Seligson and Córdova Macías in 1995, Wood reports that participation in municipal meetings was much higher in areas in which the Farabundo Martí National Liberation Front had been active than elsewhere. Residents of FMLN zones were also more politically tolerant, attended municipal meetings at a much higher rate, and characterized municipal services – even where they were seriously deficient – more favorably than other groups. In an area of Usulután in which Wood did her own field research, where *campesinos* had supported the FMLN during the war, networks of activists continue to organize collectively and bargain with various agencies and non-governmental organizations over the terms of development assistance.

One of the most important contemporary claims about the import of the independent association of citizens in civil society and civic involvement is that it builds "social capital" (Putnam 1993), the social ties and trust that make governments more effective and responsive to their constituents. Newton and Norris (2000: 72) find that "aggregate level social trust and confidence in government and its institutions are strongly associated with each other." Their claim is that social trust can help build effective social and political institutions, which can help governments perform effectively, and this in turn encourages confidence in civic institutions.

TABLE 11.8. *Interpersonal Trust, Trust in Government, Trust in Political Institutions: Latin America, 2003*

	Interpersonal[a]	Political Parties[b]	Vote for a Political Party[c]	Government[b]	Recovering Credibility[d]
Argentina	17	8	44	45	59
Bolivia	21	6	46	14	47
Brazil	4	16	44	42	66
Chile	10	13	45	46	39
Colombia	13	9	31	33	34
Costa Rica	11	10	39	23	46
El Salvador	12	11	42	21	50
Guatemala	18	8	22	7	39
Mexico	19	10	55	24	65
Peru	15	8	40	14	54
Uruguay	36	18	53	19	48
Venezuela	13	14	47	28	53
Latin America	17	11	42	24	49

Notes:
[a] Q. Generally speaking, would you say that you can trust most people, or that you can never be too careful when dealing with others? Percent responding "You can trust most people."
[b] Q. Please look at this card and tell me how much confidence you have in each of the following groups/institutions. Would you say you have a lot, some, a little, or no confidence? Political Parties. Government. Percent responding "A lot" and "Some."
[c] Q. If elections were held this Sunday, which party would you vote for? (Percent responses that mention a political party.)
[d] Q. Some people say politics and politicians have lost credibility and it seems like they cannot recover it. Other people say that politics depends on the people that are in charge and each one has the opportunity to recover that credibility. Percent responding "Politics depends on the people that are in charge and each one has the opportunity to recover that credibility."
Source: Latinobarómetro (2003: 27, 47, 46, 40, 48).

In Latin America, it is not at all clear that interpersonal trust engenders greater trust in government and political institutions. The highest rates of interpersonal trust in the 2003 Latinobarómetro poll were registered in Uruguay (Table 11.8), where 36 percent of those surveyed responded "You can trust most people," followed by Bolivia (21 percent), Mexico (19 percent), and Guatemala (18 percent). Both Bolivia and Guatemala have large indigenous populations, and it is possible that the dimension of interpersonal trust is capturing communal solidarities. Yet, Guatemala and Bolivia (along with Peru) had the lowest levels of trust in government (only 7 and 14 percent, respectively). Conversely, Brazil and Chile, two of the three countries with the highest levels of trust in government (along with Argentina), where 46 and 45 percent of respondents, respectively, expressed a lot of or some confidence in government, had the lowest levels of interpersonal trust (4 and 10 percent, respectively). With less than one fourth the level of interpersonal trust, Brazilians placed six times more trust in government than Guatemalans. In fact, the correlation between interpersonal trust and trust in government is negative and not significant.

Similarly, there is no apparent link between interpersonal trust and trust in political parties. Latin Americans generally exhibit little trust in political parties, though such low scores are fairly typical in comparative terms. In a recent survey, the percentage of citizens trusting political parties in Austria, Korea, the Czech Republic, and Russia were 17, 21, 15, and 7 percent, respectively (Rose and Shin 2001: 345). Having said this, there are intraregional differences. In 2003, the lowest rate of trust in parties was registered in Bolivia (where only 6 percent of the population expressed trust in parties), Peru, Guatemala, and Argentina (where 8 percent did so) – countries with relatively high rates of interpersonal trust (Table 11.8). At the opposite end of the spectrum, the highest rates were recorded in Uruguay and Brazil (18 and 16 percent, respectively). Brazilians had twice the level of trust in political parties and were twice as likely to be able to identify a party for which they intended to vote as Guatemalans, who exhibited more than four times more interpersonal trust. Although Uruguayans had nine times the level of interpersonal trust that the Brazilians did, they had nearly the same level of trust in political parties (Table 11.8). Although Brazilians exhibited the lowest levels of interpersonal trust in Latin America, by far, they were also the most willing to concede that politicians had the opportunity to recover their credibility (Table 11.8). Two thirds agreed that such a recovery was possible.

If interpersonal trust predicts little about trust in political institutions, then we should ask more precise questions about the conditions under which social organizations are linked to political representatives in ways that strengthen democracy.[12] In particular, we would want to return to the question of whether civil society should be connected to political parties, and whether democracy is healthier when it is. Here, our authors offer divergent answers. Levitsky is quite clear in the importance he attaches to the continuing strength of political parties in Argentina in accounting for the resilience of Argentine democracy. In his chapter on Brazil, Kurt Weyland views civil society in precisely the opposite way. For Weyland, Brazil's democracy survives because it is of "low quality." People make few demands, or few demands that can be met by government, so the potential supporters of an authoritarian order are satisfied to let democracy ride. Because we know that membership in organizations is high, his argument hinges on the incapacity of Brazilian civil society to voice effectively its demands that government redress inequality. Weyland insists that Brazilian civil society is fragmented in ways that make coordinated, class-based action

---

[12] Robert Fishman (2004: 107), drawing from extensive survey research in a number of Spanish towns and cities, has recently argued that mere membership in any social organizations, what he calls *total organizations*, is not nearly as productive a concept as membership in *useful organizations*, those identified by respondents as useful in pursuing collective objectives. Useful organizations exert a far greater impact on what he calls "globally discursive horizons," or, the capacity of cities and citizens to transcend the defense of specific local interests and instead address more widely experienced problems and processes.

in favor of redistributive policies difficult. The labor movement is divided between the more radical Central Única dos Trabalhadores (CUT) and the more
moderate Força Sindical, which mitigates class conflict, and the popular sectors
are divided and weakened by pronounced organizational fragmentation. But
crucially, he also sees (p. 105) parties as lacking firm links with social groups,
which "disables the main institutional mechanism that could in principle advance bottom-up pressure for a systemic transformation." Thus mass poverty
and egregious social inequality do not translate into open political contention.

René Mayorga's analysis of Bolivian society straddles both sides of this de-
bate. On the one hand, he speaks of the decline of labor union influence in
Bolivia in much the same way that Weyland does for Brazil and that Carlos
Waisman (1992) did in describing the effect of the weakening of the Argentine
labor movement in the 1980s for Argentina's economic and political recovery and its escape from the destructive cycle of the preceding Peronist era.
For Mayorga, the practical elimination of the Bolivian Workers' Confederation
(Central Obrera Boliviana; COB) (which had an ambiguous commitment to
democracy) as a political actor and as an agent of political representation for
the popular classes, and the erosion of corporatist, class-based interest representation served to attenuate political conflict in Bolivia. In this respect, Mayorga
joins the view that a well-organized civil society can overload government,
throttle economic reforms, and frighten elites to the point that they seek out
antidemocratic alliances.

But another way to read Mayorga is that the most dangerous development
in Bolivia has been a mobilized civil society that is unconnected to, deeply disenchanted with, and certainly not represented by political parties. In Mayorga's
account, the capacity of Bolivian political parties to serve as mediating structures and to articulate and aggregate the demands of the sectors that did not
benefit from economic development – to represent them – declined during the
administration of Hugo Banzer. The best evidence of this, for Mayorga, was the
politicization of social conflicts during Banzer's term, and the constant, direct
confrontation between the state and contentious social actors. The leading edge
of civil society today is the peasant movements of Chapare and the Northern
Altiplano, represented by ethnic leaders Evo Morales and Felipe Quispe, which
reject the "party monopoly of politics" (as well as the neoliberal model) in favor
of a "fuzzy model" of participatory democracy in which popular organizations
and social movements intervene directly in state affairs and exert corporatist
mechanisms of social control over the state administration.

This discussion returns us to the starring role of political parties in securing
representative democracy. If most scholars and aid agencies are already per-
suaded of the value of a vibrant civil society, they are now becoming aware
that political parties are allowed to rot at democracy's peril. The recent United
Nations project on citizens' democracy (UNDP 2004) highlighted that 59 percent of 231 political leaders interviewed (including almost all sitting presidents
and living former presidents in Latin America) lamented that political parties
are failing to fulfill their necessary role. Where citizens trust parties and believe

they can recover their credibility, support for democracy across a series of measures is stronger. What keeps parties vibrant as representatives of citizens?

The Latin American cases examined in this volume point in two directions. One is for parties to maintain effective linkages with social organizations, or to be inclusive. When parties were linked to social organizations in Venezuela, democracy was by all accounts quite robust (Levine 1973), but when these links frayed, Venezuelan democracy was left quite hollow and defenseless when oil prices fell and belts had to be tightened. Recent events in Brazil confirm such a view. The 2002 vote for Lula in the presidential election cannot be viewed as an expression of distrust in traditional parties and a vote for an insurgent, or antisystem, party and candidate – turnover rates in the legislative elections were very similar to the past, and while the Partido dos Trabalhadores (PT; Workers' Party) gained some seats, the partisan balance in the legislature was not noticeably upset, and gubernatorial elections confirmed the stature of governors of the Party of Brazilian Social Democracy (Partido da Social Democracia Brasileira; PSDB) and the Party of the Liberal Front (Partido de Frente Liberal; PFL). Arguably, the PT succeeded where other parties of the "establishment left" in Latin America failed because of the party's close connections, built up over a course of two decades, with Brazil's civic organizations. In this feature of Argentina's party–civil society relations may lie the key to its democratic overachievement.

A second key to party effectiveness may be the representation of policy alternatives. Seawright (2004) argues that party system collapse in Peru and Venezuela was a product of genuine policy divergence between traditional parties and the electorate. If we continue with the logic of this argument, we may note that where there are more partisan policy differences and more real opportunities for parties on both the left and right to gain local and national power than ever before, democracy may be more robust. This may be especially evident in Mexico, where serious political contenders have emerged to the left *and* right of the PRI, and El Salvador, where the left has gained in electoral strength since the first post–civil war elections. Uruguayan democracy is also arguably more responsive and flexible for having moved from a two-party system of the traditional Colorados and Blancos to a three-party system now including the leftist Frente Amplio. The Brazilian party system is also stronger not merely because of the growing strength of the PT but also because parties more generally are decidedly stronger than their reputation.

The new mix of parties in these countries raises the question of what is the "right" degree of partisan difference and electoral change. Obviously, in order for new alternatives to emerge and become electorally viable, there must inevitably result a certain degree of polarization and volatility, two conditions that ordinarily cause concern among political scientists. Rising rates of electoral volatility can be a sure sign that something is amiss in a party system: The massive rejection of Venezuela's COPEI and Peruvian political parties in the mid-1990s, for example, constitutes perhaps our best indication that something was terribly wrong with democracy in these countries. Also, persistently high rates of volatility may signal a failure of a new, stable party system to take root. On the other hand, opening up parties and political systems to new actors may be precisely what keeps them vibrant, and moderate volatility for a delimited period may be a salutary development for democracy if it permits a party system to realign and develop new partisan options. Venezuela's low electoral volatility in the 1980s may have concealed voter frustration, which led first to the rise of Causa R and other third-party alternatives, and eventually to Hugo Chávez's Bolivarian movement. To his supporters, Chávez may have given voice to long-standing frustrations, and despite Chávez's apparent disregard for Venezuela's democratic institutions, Venezuelans evince reasonably high levels of support for democracy. And Chileans, who do not value their democracy to nearly the same degree that we would expect given the highest scores on democratic governance of any country in Latin America, may be bristling precisely at the narrowing of the scope of partisan policy difference on key issues since the transition to democracy.[13] The party that has performed well in recent years, the Independent Democratic Union (Unión Demócrata Independiente; UDI), has staked out clear positions on the far right of the political spectrum and established close connections with citizens at the grassroots level.

In sum, the weight of the evidence in this volume suggests that over the long haul, a robust civil society, given links to political institutions and a chance to participate, may serve as the best inoculation that democracy has against disappointing economic performance, especially when caused by exogenous shocks. There is an inherent danger in basing legitimacy on performance, as every exdictator knows. Where political representation is weak, the survival of governments is dependent on performance, and poor performance may erode democratic regimes, as evidenced in Haiti, Paraguay, Ecuador, and Peru. Even given a similar set of economic problems, democracy has remained more solid in those countries that can count on mature – or maturing – networks of political association, participation, and representation. Where layers of political representation effectively texture the political process, democracy today appears stronger than where these layers have frayed or never existed. Of course, it is very possible that I have reversed the causal arrows, and that declining performance erodes trust in parties, which severs these connections. But that is a question for further research.

---

[13] In the mid-1990s, Juan Linz and Alfred Stepan (1996: 222–23) attributed the relatively low and declining levels of support for democracy in Chile (in 1995, 52.2 percent of Chileans agreed that democracy was preferable to any other form of government, down from 63.8 percent in 1991) to "the *incompleteness* of the Chilean transition, the ... place of the military in Chilean ... society ... , and the constraints under which Chilean democracy has been operating." Given the movement toward the resolution of the role of the military since the arrest in Britain of Augusto Pinochet, it seems plausible that we consider further the nature of the perceived constraints on Chilean democracy. Ideological polarization, or the distance between the ideological self-placement of members of the leftmost and rightmost parties (the Socialists and the Independent Democratic Union), is fairly narrow in comparative terms (Martínez Rodríguez 1998: 61), and party positions are fairly close on the most important economic issues of the day.

CONCLUSIONS

This chapter began by asking why in the past quarter century democracy has endured longer in Latin America than ever before, and, under those circumstances, why it appears to be so poorly supported by its own citizens. In contrast with earlier eras, when ordinary Latin Americans struggled for the rights and benefits of citizenship, mass publics today appear disaffected, disenchanted, and, at times, even available to support politicians whose democratic credentials are dubious at best. With the benefit of the contributions to this volume, the first question was relatively simple to address: International support for democracy, value change among Latin American elites and the left, the fracture of the civil–military alliance, the narrowing of the scope for redistributive measures that has accompanied the adoption of neoliberal economic policies, and the reform of political institutions have maintained the momentum of a wave that might have otherwise crashed like those that came before.

Explaining the gradual and sporadic receding of this wave, however, is more difficult. Unlike in other contexts, in Latin America in the Third Wave, support for democracy is nearly impossible to predict, interpersonal trust is not strongly associated with trust in government and political institutions, and globalization and neoliberalism have not condemned democracy to a poor quality of life, as alleged. We should not be daunted by a lack of fit between comparative trends and the politics of Latin America's Third Wave. Regime change in Latin America has previously informed comparative theories about political regimes and the sources of their stability and instability, teaching us that democracy in middle-income countries can break down (O'Donnell 1973) and that authoritarian regimes can fall apart, not because of structural conditions but because of strategic splits within ruling circles (O'Donnell and Schmitter 1986). Latin American cases have also instructed us that the Roman Catholic Church can be a force for democracy, and that militaries can be tamed. In the best tradition of Latin American politics, we should use the experience of the Third Wave democracies in the region in the past quarter century as a window on how citizens evaluate their governments and their democracies.

This volume has highlighted the relationship between faltering government performance and the erosion of public support for democracy. We are not the first to do so. The shortcomings of government in responding to citizen needs are widely known in Latin America and the United States among elites, mass publics, international aid agencies, and the academic community. For international aid agencies, the solution is perceived to be to empower civil society to perform a watchdog role. For some academics, the solution is to insulate decision makers, attenuate polarization and conflict, and inoculate governments from populist pressures that can only derail governments from pursuing the tough but correct policies. Yet a third approach has been to reform political institutions. It is now apparent that these approaches taken individually cannot stabilize the rapidly shifting sands on which Latin American democracy is standing.

The relationship between faltering government performance and the erosion of the Third Wave of democratization is expressed in declining public support for democracy. But this erosion is not directly linear. In this chapter, I have suggested that the key variable mediating the relationship between government performance and citizen attachment to democracy is the nature and quality of political representation, and specifically, the linkages between citizens, civic organizations, and political parties. In making this argument, I have undoubtedly raised many more questions than I have resolved. Nonetheless, if this volume sparks more analysis of individual level attitudes and behavior and more research on the connection between citizens and national political institutions in this era of mass democracy, it will have made an important contribution. And if this analysis turns out to be correct, as we go forward we should bear in mind that the various strands of political representation are worth connecting, and the networks themselves are worth deepening and extending, if mass democracy is to survive in hard times like ours.

References

Abente Brun, Diego. 1999. "People Power in Paraguay." *Journal of Democracy* 10 No. 3: 93–100.

Acevedo, Carlos. 1998. "Las limitaciones del sistema de partidos para enfrentar los problemas fundamentales del país." In Héctor Dada Hirezi, ed., *Las Elecciones de 1997: Un Paseo más en la Transición Democrática?*, pp. 195–238. San Salvador: FLACSO.

Acuña, Carlos. 1994. "Politics and Economics in the Argentina of the Nineties (Or, Why the Future No Longer Is What It Used to Be)." In William C. Smith, Carlos H. Acuña, and Eduardo A. Gamarra, eds., *Democracy, Markets, and Structural Reform in Latin America: Argentina, Bolivia, Brazil, Chile, and Mexico*, pp. 31–73. Miami: North–South Center and Boulder, CO: Lynne Rienner Publishers.

Adams, Richard Newbold. 1970. *Crucifixion by Power: Essays on Guatemalan National Social Structure, 1944–1966*. Austin: University of Texas.

Aguilar Zinser, Adolfo. 1994. *Vamos a Ganar*. Mexico City: Cal y Arena.

Alesina, Alberto, and Romain Wacziarg. 2000. "The Economics of Civil Trust." In Susan J. Pharr and Robert D. Putnam, eds., *Disaffected Democracies: What's Troubling the Trilateral Democracies?*, pp. 149–170. Princeton, NJ: Princeton University Press.

Alexander, Robert J. 1964. *The Venezuelan Democratic Revolution*. New Brunswick, NJ: Rutgers University Press.

Alfredo Keller y Asociados. 2003. "Condiciones del Escenario Político de Venezuela: En base a los resultados de la encuesta nacional y de los focus groups de Agosto 2003." Caracas.

Altemeyer, Bob. 1996. *The Authoritarian Specter*. Cambridge, MA: Harvard University Press.

Altman Olin, David, and Aníbal Pérez-Liñán. 2002. "Assessing the Quality of Democracy: Freedom, Competitiveness and Participation in 18 Latin American Countries." *Democratization* 9 No. 2: 85–100.

Ames, Barry. 1970. "Bases of Support for Mexico's Dominant Party." *American Political Science Review* 64 No. 1: 153–67.

2001. *The Deadlock of Democracy in Brazil*. Ann Arbor: University of Michigan Press.

Angell, Alan, and Carol Graham. 1995. "Can Social Sector Reform Make Adjustment Sustainable and Equitable? Lessons from Chile and Venezuela." *Journal of Latin American Studies* 27 No. 1: 189–211.

APOYO. "Informe de Opinión Mensual." Lima: Instituto APOYO.

Archer, Ronald. 1995. "Party Strength and Weakness in Colombia's Besieged Democracy." In Scott Mainwaring and Timothy R. Scully, eds., *Building Democratic Institutions: Party Systems in Latin America*, pp. 164–99. Stanford, CA: Stanford University Press.

Arias, César. 2001. "El gélido invierno del fujimorato." *Nueva Sociedad* 171: 4–11.

Ariza, Libardo, Antonio Barreto, and Olga Lucía Gaitán. 1999. "La justicia en 1998." In Luis Alberto Restrepo, ed., *Síntesis 1999. Anuario Social, Político y Económico de Colombia*, pp. 87–94. Bogotá: IEPRI – Fundación Social–Tercer Mundo Editores.

Ariza, Libardo, Antonio Barreto, and Manuel Iturralde. 2000. "La administración de justicia." In Luis Alberto Restrepo, ed., *Síntesis 2000. Anuario Social, Político y Económico de Colombia*, pp. 77–88. Bogotá: IEPRI – Fundación Social–Tercer Mundo Editores.

Arnson, Cynthia. 1993. *Crossroads: Congress, the President, and Central America, 1976–1993*. University Park: Pennsylvania State University Press.

1999. ed. "La Consulta Popular y el Futuro del Proceso de Paz en Guatemala." Working Paper No. 243, Woodrow Wilson International Center for Scholars, Washington, DC.

ASIES (Asociación de Investigación y Estudios Sociales). 2001. "Democratic Indicators Monitoring System (DIMS) Project." ASIES – University of Pittsburgh Latin American Opinion Project (October).

Auyero, Javier. 2000. *Poor People's Politics: Peronist Survival Networks and the Legacy of Evita*. Durham, NC: Duke University Press.

Azpuru, Dinorah. 1999a. "The *Consulta Popular*: A Vote Divided by Geography." In Dinorah Azpuru, Demetrio Cojtí Cuxil, Carroll Ríos de Rodríguez, Bernardo Arévalo de León, and Edelberto Torres-Rivas. *The Popular Referendum (Consulta Popular) and the Future of the Peace Process in Guatemala*. Washington, DC: Woodrow Wilson International Center for Scholars, The Latin American Program.

1999b. "Peace and Democratization in Guatemala: Two Parallel Processes." In Cynthia J. Arnson, ed., *Comparative Peace Processes in Latin America*. Washington, DC, and Stanford, CA: Woodrow Wilson Center Press and Stanford University Press.

Bacevich, A. J., James D. Hallums, Richard H. White, and Thomas F. Young. 1988. "American Military Policy in Small Wars: The Case of El Salvador." Paper presented at John F. Kennedy School of Government, Harvard University.

Ballón, Eduardo, ed. 1986. *Movimientos sociales y democracia: la fundación de un nuevo orden*. Lima: DESCO.

Baloyra, Enrique A. 1983. "Reactionary Despotism in El Salvador: An Impediment to Democratic Transition." In Martin Diskin, ed., *Trouble in Our Backyard: Central America and the United States in the Eighties*, pp. 101–23. New York: Pantheon.

Banks, Arthur S. 1976. *Cross-National Time Series, 1815–1973* [Computer file]. ICPSR ed. Ann Arbor, MI: Inter-university Consortium for Political and Social Research [producer and distributor].

Barnes, William A. 1998. "Incomplete Democracy in Central America: Polarization and Voter Turnout in Nicaragua and El Salvador." *Journal of Interamerican Studies and World Affairs* 40 No. 3: 63–101.

BCR (Banco Central de Reserva de El Salvador). 2000. "Revista Trimestral." San Salvador: BCR.

Bejarano, Ana María. 1994. "Recuperar el estado para fortalecer la democracia." *Análisis Político* No. 22 (May–August): 47–79.

2001. "The Constitution of 1991: An Institutional Evaluation Seven Years Later." In Charles Bergquist, Ricardo Peñaranda, and Gonzalo Sánchez, eds., *Violence in Colombia, 1990–2000: Waging War and Negotiating Peace*, pp. 53–74. Wilmington, DE: Scholarly Resources, Inc.

2002. "Buenas intenciones y efectos perversos. Los límites del reformismo institucional en Colombia y Venezuela." *Comentario Internacional* No. 4, II semestre: 177–86.

Bejarano, Ana María, and Andrés Dávila, eds. 1998. *Elecciones y Democracia en Colombia, 1997–1998*. Bogotá: Universidad de los Andes, Departamento de Ciencia Política – Fundación Social – Veeduría Ciudadana a la Elección Presidencial.

Bejarano, Ana María, and Renata Segura. 1996. "El fortalecimiento selectivo del Estado durante el Frente Nacional." *Controversia* No. 169, Segunda Etapa (November): 9–35.

Bellin, Eva. 2000. "Contingent Democrats." *World Politics* 52 No. 2: 175–205.

Bendix, Reinhard. 1964. *Nation Building and Citizenship: Studies of Our Changing Social Order*. New York: John Wiley and Sons.

Beneke de Sanfeliú, Margarita. 2000. "Dinámica del Ingreso de las Familias Rurales en El Salvador: Estudio de Panel, 1995–1997." Documento de Investigación BASIS (Broadening Access and Strengthening Input Market Systems Collaborative Research Support Program) No. 1. San Salvador: FUSADES (Fundación Salvadoreña para el Desarrollo Económico y Social).

Benevides, Maria Victória de Mesquita. 1981. *A UDN e o Udenismo: Ambigüidades do Liberalismo Brasileiro (1945–1965)*. Rio de Janeiro: Paz e Terra.

Berman, Sheri. 1997. "Civil Society and the Collapse of the Weimar Republic." *World Politics* 49 No. 3: 401–29.

Bermeo, Nancy. 1999. "Getting Mad or Going Mad: Citizens, Scarcity and the Breakdown of Democracy in Interwar Europe." Working Paper, Center for the Study of Democracy, University of California at Irvine.

2003. *Ordinary People in Extraordinary Times: The Citizenry and the Breakdown of Democracy*. Princeton, NJ: Princeton University Press.

Birdsall, Nancy, David Ross, and Richard Sabot. 1995. "Inequality and Growth Reconsidered: Lessons from East Asia." *The World Bank Economic Review* 9 No. 3: 477–508.

Bland, Gary. 1997. "Political Brokers Revisited: Local Government, Decentralization, and Democracy in Chile and Venezuela." Ph.D. dissertation, The Paul H. Nitze School of Advanced International Studies.

Blanes, José. 2000. *Mallkus y Alcaldes*. La Paz: CEBEM.

Bollen, Kenneth A. 1980. "Issues in the Comparative Measurement of Political Democracy." *American Sociological Review* 45 No. 2: 370–90.

1993. "Liberal Democracy: Validity and Method Factors in Cross-National Measures." *American Journal of Political Science* 37 No. 4: 1207–30.

Bollen, Kenneth A., and Robert W. Jackman. 1985. "Economic and Noneconomic Determinants of Political Democracy in the 1960s." *Research in Political Sociology* 1: 27–48.

Bollen, Kenneth A., and Pamela Paxton. 2000. "Subjective Measures of Liberal Democracy." *Comparative Political Studies* 33 No. 1: 58–86.

Boneo, Horacio, and Edelberto Torres-Rivas. 2000. *¿ Por qué no votan los Guatemaltecos?* Guatemala City, Guatemala: Tribunal Supremo Electoral and United Nations Development Program.

Boron, Atilio. 1992. "Becoming Democrats? Some Skeptical Considerations on the Right in Latin America." In Douglas A. Chalmers, Maria do Carmo Campello de Souza, and Atilio Boron, eds., *The Right and Democracy in Latin America*, pp. 68–95. New York: Praeger Publishers.

Boyce, James K. 1996. "External Resource Mobilization." In James K. Boyce, ed., *Economic Policy for Building Peace: The Lessons of El Salvador*. Boulder, CO: Lynne Rienner Publishers.

Brener, Jayme, Luciano Suassuna, and Hélio Contreiras. 1993. "Quepe no Topete." *Veja* No. 1263 (15 December): 23–25.

Brinks, Daniel, and Michael Coppedge. 1999. "Patterns of Diffusion in the Third Wave of Democratization." Paper presented at the Annual Meeting of the American Political Science Association, Washington, DC.

Briones, Carlos, and Katherine Andrade-Eekhoff. 2000. "Participación en los Mercados Laborales de los Residentes en las Areas Rurales: Limitaciones y Desafíos." Documento de Investigación BASIS (Broadening Access and Strengthening Input Market Systems Collaborative Research Support Program), No. 2. San Salvador: FUSADES (Fundación Salvadoreña para el Desarrollo Económico y Social).

Brown, Archie. 2000. "Transnational Influences in the Transition from Communism." *Post-Soviet Affairs* 16 No. 2: 177–200.

Bruhn, Kathleen. 1997. *Taking on Goliath: The Emergence of a New Left Party and the Struggle for Democracy in Mexico*. University Park: Pennsylvania State University Press.

Bunce, Valerie. 2000. "Comparative Democratization: Big and Bounded Generalization." *Comparative Political Studies* 33 No. 6/7: 703–34.

Burgerman, Susan D. 2000. "Building the Peace by Mandating Reform: United Nations-Mediated Human Rights Agreements in El Salvador and Guatemala." *Latin American Perspectives* 27 No. 3: 63–87.

Burggraaff, Winfield J., and Richard L. Millett. 1995. "More than Failed Coups: The Crisis in Venezuelan Civil–Military Relations." In Louis W. Goodman, Johanna Mendelson Forman, Moisés Naím, Joseph S. Tulchin, and Gary Bland, eds., *Lessons of the Venezuelan Experience*, pp. 54–78. Washington, DC, and Baltimore, MD: The Woodrow Wilson Center Press and Johns Hopkins University Press.

Burkhart, Ross E. 1997. "Comparative Democracy and Income Distribution: Shape and Direction of the Causal Arrow." *Journal of Politics* 59 No. 1: 148–64.

Burkhart, Ross E., and Michael Lewis-Beck. 1994. "Comparative Democracy: The Economic Development Thesis." *American Political Science Review* 88 No. 4: 903–10.

Burrell, Jennifer, and Michael Shifter. 2000. "Estados Unidos, la OEA y la promoción de la democracia en las Américas." In Arlene B. Tickner, ed., *Sistema interamericano y democracia: Antecedentes históricos y tendencias futuras*, pp. 27–50. Bogotá: Ediciones Uniandes.

Cabarrús, Carlos Rafael. 1983. *Génesis de una revolución*. Mexico City: Ediciones de la Casa, Centro de Investigaciones y Estudios Superiores en Antropología Social.

Call, Charles T. 1994. *Recent Setbacks in the Police Transition. El Salvador Peace Plan Update 3*. Washington, DC: Washington Office on Latin America.

1999a. "From Soldiers to Cops: 'War Transitions' and the Demilitarization of Public Security in El Salvador." Ph.D. dissertation, Stanford University.

1999b. "Assessing El Salvador's Transition from Civil War to Peace." Paper contributed to the Stanford University Center for International Security and Cooperation/ International Peace Academy Project on Implementing Peace Agreements after Civil Wars, Stanford University.

1999c. "Crime and Peace: Why Successful Peace Processes Produce the World's Most Violent Countries." Paper presented at the Annual Conference of the International Studies Association, Washington, DC, February.

Cameron, Maxwell. 1994. *Democracy and Authoritarianism in Peru: Political Coalitions and Social Change.* New York: St. Martin's Press.

Camp, Roderic Ai. 1995. *Political Recruitment Across Two Centuries: Mexico 1884–1991.* Austin: University of Texas Press.

Cardenal, Rodolfo. 1985. *Historia de una esperanza: vida de Rutilio Grande.* San Salvador: UCA Editores.

Carey, John M., and Matthew Soberg Shugart. 1998a. "Calling Out the Tanks or Filling Out the Forms?" In John M. Carey and Matthew Soberg Shugart, eds., *Executive Decree Authority*, pp. 1–29. Cambridge: Cambridge University Press.

1998b. *Executive Decree Authority.* Cambridge: Cambridge University Press.

Carothers, Thomas. 1991. "The Reagan Years: The 1980s." In Abraham F. Lowenthal, ed., *Exporting Democracy: The United States and Latin America, Themes and Issues*, pp. 90–122. Baltimore, MD: Johns Hopkins University Press.

Carrión, Julio. 1992. "Presidential Popularity in Peru, 1980–1992." Paper delivered at the XVII Congress of the Latin American Studies Association, Los Angeles.

1994. "The 'Support Gap' for Democracy in Peru." Paper presented at the XVIII Congress of the Latin American Studies Association, Atlanta, March 10–12.

1999. "La popularidad de Fujimori en tiempos ordinarios, 1993, 1997." In Fernando Tuesta, ed., *El juego político. Fujimori, la oposición y las reglas*, pp. 231–46. Lima: Fundación Friedrich Ebert.

Castañeda, Jorge. 1993. *Utopia Unarmed: The Latin American Left After the Cold War.* New York: Alfred A. Knopf.

1995. *The Mexican Shock.* New York: The New Press.

2000. *Perpetuating Power: How Mexican Presidents Were Chosen.* New York: The New Press.

Catterberg, Edgardo. 1991. *Argentina Confronts Politics: Political Culture and Public Opinion in the Argentine Transition to Democracy.* Boulder, CO: Lynne Rienner.

Cavarozzi, Marcelo. 1983. *Autoritarismo y democracia (1955–1983).* Buenos Aires: Centro Editor.

1986. "Political Cycles in Argentina Since 1955." In Guillermo O'Donnell, Philippe C. Schmitter, and Laurence Whitehead, eds., *Transitions from Authoritarian Rule: Latin America*, pp. 19–48. Baltimore, MD: Johns Hopkins University Press.

Centro de Estudios Públicos. 2002. "Estudio Nacional de Opinión Pública No. 14." Tercera Serie (Diciembre–Enero). Documento de Trabajo No. 329 (February).

CEPAL. Various years. Anuario Estadístico de América Latina y el Caribe. Santiago: CEPAL.

Chalmers, Douglas A. 1977. "The Politicized State in Latin America." In James M. Malloy, ed., *Authoritarianism and Corporatism in Latin America*, pp. 23–45. Pittsburgh: University of Pittsburgh Press.

Cheibub, José Antonio. 2002. "Minority Governments, Deadlock Situations, and the Survival of Presidential Democracies." *Comparative Political Studies* 35 No. 3: 284–312.

CIDAC (Centro de Investigación para el Desarrollo). *www.cidac.org*.

2001a. "Terremoto del 13 de enero en El Salvador. Resumen de información." *El Salvador Proceso* 935: 14–16.

2001b. "Los terremotos de enero y febrero: implicaciones económicas." *El Salvador Proceso* 940: 6–7.

2001c. "Consideraciones Económicas, Sociales y Políticas del Terremoto del 13 de Enero." *Estudios Centroamericanos* 56 No. 627–28: 29–58.

2001d. "Cae la fachada democrática." *El Salvador Proceso* 935: 2–3.

CIEN (Centro de Investigaciones Económicas Nacionales). 1999. "Investigando la violencia en Guatemala: Algunas consideraciones conceptuales y metodológicas." Guatemala City, Guatemala: CIEN (June).

Cifra/González, Raga y Asociados. 2004.

Cleary, Matthew R. 2000. "Democracy and Indigenous Rebellion in Latin America." *Comparative Political Studies* 33 No. 9: 1123–53.

CNE (Corte Nacional Electoral). 2001. *Encuesta sobre Democracia y Cultura Política en Bolivia*. La Paz: CNE.

2002. *Elecciones Generales de junio de 2002*. La Paz: CNE.

Cohen, Youssef. 1994. *Radicals, Reformers, and Reactionaries*. Chicago: University of Chicago Press.

Colindres, Eduardo. 1976. "La Tenencia de la Tierra en El Salvador." *Estudios Centroamericanos* 31 (335–36): 463–72.

1977. *Fundamentos Económicos de la Burguesía Salvadoreña*. San Salvador: UCA Editores.

Collier, David, and Steven Levitsky. 1997. "Democracy with Adjectives: Conceptual Innovation in Comparative Research." *World Politics* 49 No. 3: 430–51.

Collier, Ruth Berins. 1999. *Paths Toward Democracy: The Working Class and Elites in Western Europe and South America*. Cambridge: Cambridge University Press.

Collier, Ruth Berins, and David Collier. 1991. *Shaping the Political Arena: Critical Junctures, the Labor Movement, and Regime Dynamics in Latin America*. Princeton, NJ: Princeton University Press.

Colombian Commission of Jurists (Comisión Colombiana de Juristas). 2000. *Panorama de derechos humanos y derecho humanitario en Colombia. Informe de avance sobre 2000*. Bogotá: Comisión Colombiana de Juristas.

Comisión de la Verdad y Reconciliación (CVR). 2003. "Informe Final." Lima. *www.cverdad.org.pe*.

Conaghan, Catherine. 1995. "Polls, Political Discourse, and the Public Sphere." In Peter Smith, ed., *Latin America in Comparative Perspective*, pp. 227–55. Boulder, CO: Westview Press.

Conning, Jonathan, Pedro Olinto, and Alvarado Trigueros. 2000. "Land and Labor Adjustment Strategies during an Economic Downturn in Rural El Salvador." University of Wisconsin Land Tenure Center, Broadening Access and Strengthening Input Market Systems Program. Unpublished paper.

Consejo Nacional de Población. 1990. *www.CONAPO.gob.mx*.

Consulta Mitofsky. 2004. "XIII Evaluación del Presidente Vicente Fox, Encuesta Nacional en Viviendas." (February). *www.consulta.com.mx*.

Coppedge, Michael. 1994. *Strong Parties and Lame Ducks: Presidential Partyarchy and Factionalism in Venezuela.* Stanford, CA: Stanford University Press.

——— 1997. "Modernization and Thresholds of Democracy: Evidence for a Common Path and Process." In Manus I. Midlarsky, ed., *Inequality, Democracy, and Economic Development*, pp. 177–201. Cambridge: Cambridge University Press.

——— 1998. "The Dynamic Diversity of Latin American Party Systems." *Party Politics* 4 No. 4 : 547–68.

——— 2003. "Venezuela: Popular Sovereignty versus Liberal Democracy." In Jorge I. Domínguez and Michael Shifter, eds., *Constructing Democratic Governance*, 2nd ed. Baltimore, MD: Johns Hopkins University Press.

Coppedge, Michael, and Wolfgang H. Reinicke. 1990. "Measuring Polyarchy." *Studies in Comparative International Development* 25 No. 1 : 51–72.

Córdova Macías, Ricardo. 1999. "Comentarios en torno a la implementación de los acuerdos de paz en el caso de Salvador" (El Salvador: An Assessment of the Implementation of the 1992 Peace Accords). Lecture, U.S. Institute of Peace, Washington, DC, December 8.

Córdova Macías, Ricardo. 2001. "Who Votes in Central America." Ph.D. dissertation, University of Pittsburgh.

Coronil, Fernando, and Julie Skurski. 1991. "Dismembering and Remembering the Nation: The Semantics of Political Violence in Venezuela." *Comparative Studies in Society and History* 33 No. 2: 288–337.

Corradi, Juan E. 1985. *The Fitful Republic: Economy, Society, and Politics in Argentina.* Boulder, CO: Westview Press.

Corrales, Javier. 1997. "Do Economic Crises Contribute to Economic Reform? Argentina and Venezuela in the 1990s." *Political Science Quarterly* 112 No. 4: 617–44.

——— 2002. *Presidents without Parties: Economic Reforms in Argentina and Venezuela in the 1990s.* University Park: Pennsylvania State University Press.

Cotler, Julio. 1994. "Crisis política, *outsiders* y autoritarismo plebiscitario: el fujimorismo." In *Política y sociedad en el Perú: cambios y continuidades*, pp. 165–235. Lima: IEP.

——— 1995. "Political Parties and the Problems of Democratic Consolidation in Peru." In Scott Mainwaring and Timothy R. Scully, eds., *Building Democratic Institutions: Party Systems in Latin America*, pp. 323–53. Stanford, CA: Stanford University Press.

——— 1998. "Los empresarios y las reformas económicas en el Perú." Documento de Trabajo No. 91. Lima: IEP.

——— 1999. *Drogas y política en el Perú. La conexión norteamericana.* Lima: IEP.

——— 2000. "La gobernabilidad en el Perú: entre el autoritarismo y la democracia." In Julio Cotler and Romeo Grompone, eds., *El fujimorismo: ascenso y caída de un régimen autoritario*, pp. 13–75. Lima: IEP.

Cox, Gary. 1997. *Making Votes Count.* Cambridge: Cambridge University Press.

Crisp, Brian F. 2000. *Democratic Institutional Design: The Powers and Incentives of Venezuelan Politicians and Interest Groups.* Stanford, CA: Stanford University Press.

Crisp, Brian F., and Daniel H. Levine. 1998. "Democratizing the Democracy? Crisis and Reform in Venezuela." *Journal of Interamerican Studies and World Affairs* 40 No. 2: 27–61.

Crozier, Michel J., Samuel P. Huntington, and Joji Watanuki. 1975. *The Crisis of Democracy: Report on the Governability of Democracies to the Trilateral Commission.* New York: Trilateral Commission/New York University Press.

Cruz, José Miguel. 1997. "Los factores posibilitadores y las expresiones de la violencia en los noventa." *Estudios Centroamericanos* 52 No. 588. *http://www.uca.edu.sv/publica/eca/ecaind.html.*

1998a. "Por qué no votan los salvadoreños?" *Estudios Centroamericanos* 53 No. 595–96.

1998b. "Elecciones y pensamiento social: opinión pública en los comicios 97." In Héctor Dada Hirezi, ed., *Las Elecciones de 1997: Un Paseo más en la Transición Democrática?*, pp. 79–158. San Salvador: FLACSO.

Cruz, José Miguel, and Luis Armando González. 1997. "Magnitud de la violencia en El Salvador." *Estudios Centroamericanos* 52 No. 588. *http://www.uca.edu.sv/publica/eca/ecaind.html.*

Cubides, Fernando. 1999. "Los paramilitares y su estrategia." In Malcolm Deas and María Victoria Llorente, eds., *Reconocer la guerra para construir la paz*, pp. 151–99. Bogotá: Ediciones Uniandes – Editorial Norma.

Cullather, Nick. 1999. *Secret History: The CIA's Classified Account of Its Operations in Guatemala, 1952–1954*. Stanford, CA: Stanford University Press.

Dada Hirezi, Héctor. 1998. "Las elecciones de 1997: sus resultados y la nueva distribución política." In Héctor Dada Hirezi, ed., *Las Elecciones de 1997: Un Paso más en la Transición Democrática?* pp. 239–70. San Salvador: FLACSO.

Dahl, Robert. 1971. *Polyarchy: Participation and Opposition.* New Haven, CT: Yale University Press.

1989. *Democracy and Its Critics.* New Haven, CT: Yale University Press.

Datos para la democracia Year 1 No. 2. Asociación Civil Transparencia. *http://www.transparencia.com.pe.*

Dávila, Andrés. 1998. *El juego del poder. Historia, armas y votos.* Bogotá: Uniandes – CEREC.

Dávila, Andrés, and Ana María Corredor. 1998. "Las elecciones del 26 de octubre: ¿Cómo se reprodujo el poder local y regional?" In Ana María Bejarano and Andrés Dávila, eds., *Elecciones y Democracia en Colombia, 1997–1998*, pp. 77–140. Bogotá: Universidad de los Andes, Departamento de Ciencia Política – Fundación Social – Veeduría Ciudadana a la Elección Presidencial.

Degregori, Carlos Iván. 2000. *La década de la antipolítica. Auge y huida de Alberto Fujimori y Vladimiro Montesinos.* Lima: IEP.

Degregori, Carlos Iván, and Romeo Grompone. 1991. *Elecciones 1990: Demonios y redentores en el nuevo Perú. Una tragedia en dos vueltas.* Lima: IEP.

Del Castillo, Graciana. 1997. "The arms-for-land deal in El Salvador." In Michael W. Doyle, Ian Johnstone, and Robert C. Orr, eds., *Keeping the Peace: Multi-dimensional UN Operations in Cambodia and El Salvador*, pp. 342–65. Cambridge: Cambridge University Press.

Della Porta, Donatella. 2000. "Social Capital, Beliefs in Government, and Political Corruption." In Susan J. Pharr and Robert D. Putnam, eds., *Disaffected Democracies: What's Troubling the Trilateral Democracies?*, pp. 202–28. Princeton, NJ: Princeton University Press.

De Soto, Alvaro, and Graciana del Castillo. 1994. "Obstacles to Peacebuilding." *Foreign Policy* 94: 69–83.

De Souza, Amaury, and Bolívar Lamounier. 1992. *As Elites Brasileiras e a Modernização do Setor Público.* São Paulo: IDESP.

Diamond, Larry. 1992. "Economic Development and Democracy Reconsidered." In Gary Marks and Larry Diamond, eds., *Reexamining Democracy: Essays in Honor of Seymour Martin Lipset*, pp. 93–139. Newbury Park, CA: Sage.

1996. "Democracy in Latin America: Degrees, Illusions, and Directions for Consolidation." In Tom Farer, ed., *Beyond Sovereignty: Collectively Defending Democracy in the Americas*, pp. 52–104. Baltimore, MD: Johns Hopkins University Press.

1999. *Developing Democracy: Toward Consolidation*. Baltimore, MD: Johns Hopkins University Press.

2002. "Thinking About Hybrid Regimes." *Journal of Democracy* 13 No. 2: 21–35.

Diamond, Larry, and Juan J. Linz. 1989. "Introduction: Politics, Society, and Democracy in Latin America." In Larry Diamond, Juan J. Linz, and Seymour Martin Lipset, eds., *Democracy in Developing Countries: Latin America*, pp. 1–58. Boulder, CO: Lynne Rienner Publishers.

Diaz-Cayeros, Alberto, and Beatriz Magaloni. 1995. "Transition Games: Initiating and Sustaining Democracy." Paper presented at the American Political Science Association Meeting, Chicago, IL, September.

2001. "Party Dominance and the Logic of Electoral Design in Mexico's Transition to Democracy." *Journal of Theoretical Politics* 12 No. 3: 271–93.

Diaz-Cayeros, Alberto, Beatriz Magaloni, and Barry Weingast. 2002. "Democratization and the Economy in Mexico: Equilibrium (PRI) Hegemony and its Demise." Stanford, CA: Hoover Institution. Unpublished manuscript.

Dietz, Henry, and William Dugan. 1996. "Clases sociales urbanas y comportamiento electoral en Lima: un análisis de datos agregados." In Fernando Tuesta, ed., *Los enigmas del poder, Fujimori 1990–1996*, pp. 251–76. Lima: Fundación Friedrich Ebert.

Dimenstein, Gilberto, and Josias de Souza. 1994. *A História Real*. São Paulo: Ática.

Di Palma, Giuseppe. 1990. *To Craft Democracies: An Essay on Democratic Transitions*. Berkeley: University of California Press.

Dirección de Inteligencia EJC. 2000. "Folleto Evolución y Composición Grupos Terroristas" (June).

Dirección General de Estadística y Censos. 1974. *Tercer Censo Nacional Agropecuario, 1971*. San Salvador: Dirección General de Estadística y Censos.

Di Tella, Torcuato. 1968. "Stalemate or Coexistence in Argentina." In James Petras and Maurice Zeitlin, eds., *Latin America: Reform or Revolution*, pp. 249–63. Greenwich, CT: Fawcett Publishers.

Domínguez, Jorge I. 1993. "The Caribbean Question: Why Has Liberal Democracy (Surprisingly) Flourished?" In Jorge I. Domínguez, Robert A. Pastor, and R. Delisle Worrell, eds., *Democracy in the Caribbean: Political, Economic, and Social Perspectives*, pp. 1–25. Baltimore, MD: Johns Hopkins University Press.

1998. *Democratic Politics in Latin America and the Caribbean*. Baltimore, MD: Johns Hopkins University Press.

Domínguez, Jorge I., and Chappell H. Lawson. 2004, eds. *Mexico's Pivotal Democratic Election: Candidates, Voters, and the Presidential Campaign of 2000*. Stanford, CA: Stanford University Press.

Domínguez, Jorge, and James McCann. 1995. "Shaping Mexico's Electoral Arena: The Construction of Partisan Cleavages in the 1988 and 1991 Elections." *American Political Science Review* 89 No. 1: 34–48.

Domínguez, Jorge, and Alejandro Poiré, eds. 1999. *Toward Mexico's Democratization: Campaigns, Elections and Public Opinion*. New York: Routledge.

Doorenspleet, Renske. 2000. "Reassessing the Three Waves of Democratization." *World Politics* 52 No. 3: 384–406.

Dos Santos, Wanderley Guilherme. 1986. *Sessenta e Quatro: Anatomia da Crise*. São Paulo: Vértice.

———. 1992. "Fronteiras do Estado Mínimo." In João Paulo dos Reis Velloso, ed., *O Brasil e as Reformas Políticas*, pp. 49–94. Rio de Janeiro: José Olympio.

Dugas, John, ed. 1993. *La Constitución de 1991: ¿ Un pacto político viable?* Bogotá: Universidad de los Andes and Fondo Editorial CEREC.

Dugas, John. 2000. "Sisyphus in the Andes? The Quest for Political Party Reform in Colombia." Unpublished manuscript, Kalamazoo College.

Dulci, Luiz. 1997. "Por uma Nova Estratégia." *Teoria & Debate* 10 No. 34: 25–28.

Durand, Francisco. 1995. "From Fragile Crystal to Solid Rock. The Formation and Consolidation of a Business Peak Association in Peru." In Ernest Bartell and Leigh Payne, eds., *Business and Democracy in Latin America*, pp. 141–78. Pittsburgh: University of Pittsburgh Press.

———. 1999. "La democracia, los empresarios y Fujimori." In Fernando Tuesta, ed., *El juego político. Fujimori, la oposición y las reglas*, pp. 165–200. Lima: Fundación Friedrich Ebert.

Durham, William H. 1979. *Scarcity and Survival in Central America: The Ecological Origins of the Soccer War*. Stanford, CA: Stanford University Press.

Echandía, Camilo. 1999a. *El conflicto armado y las manifestaciones de violencia en las regiones de Colombia*. Bogotá: Presidencia de la República, Oficina del Alto Comisionado para la Paz.

———. 1999b. "Expansión territorial de las guerrillas colombianas: geografía, economía y violencia." In Malcolm Deas and María Victoria Llorente, eds., *Reconocer la guerra para construir la paz*, pp. 99–150. Bogotá: CEREC, Ediciones Uniandes – Editorial Norma.

ECLAC (Economic Commission for Latin America and the Caribbean). 2001. *Economic Survey of Latin America and the Caribbean: Current Conditions and Outlook*. Santiago: United Nations, ECLAC.

———. 2003. *Economic Survey of Latin America and the Caribbean: Current Conditions and Outlook*. Santiago: United Nations, ECLAC.

The Economist. 2001. "A Survey of Colombia." April 21.

———. 2002. "The Latinobarómetro Poll: Democracy clings on in a cold economic climate." August 17: 29–30.

———. 2003. "The Latinobarómetro Poll: The stubborn survival of frustrated democrats." November 1: 33–34.

———. 2004. "A Political Awakening: Indigenous People in South America." February 21: 35–37.

Eguizábal, Cristina. 1992. "Parties, Programs, and Politics in El Salvador." In L. W. Goodman, W. M. LeoGrande, and J. Mendelson Forman, eds., *Political Parties and Democracy in the United States and Central America*, pp. 135–60. Boulder, CO: Westview Press.

Encuestas & Estudios. 2003. La Paz, Bolivia. December.

Escolar, Marcelo, and Ernesto Calvo. 2003. "Últimas imágenes antes del naufragio: las elecciones del 2001 en Argentina." *Desarrollo Económico* 42 (January–March).

Estadísticas Históricas de México. 1993. Instituto Nacional de Estadística, Geografía e Informática. *www.INEGI.gob.mx*.

Etchemendy, Sebastián, and Vicente Palermo. 1998. "Conflicto y concertación: Gobierno, Congreso y organizaciones de interés en la reforma laboral del primer gobierno de Menem." *Desarrollo Económico* 37 No. 148: 559–90.

Fajnzylber, Pablo, Norman Loayza, and Daniel Lederman. 1998. *Determinants of Crime Rates in Latin America and the World: An Empirical Assessment.* Washington, DC: The World Bank.

Ferreira Rubio, Delia, and Matteo Goretti. 1998. "When the President Governs Alone: The *Decretazo* in Argentina, 1989–93." In John M. Carey and Mathew Soberg Shugart, eds., *Executive Decree Authority*, pp. 33–61. Cambridge: Cambridge University Press.

2000. "Executive–Legislative Relationship in Argentina: From Menem's *Decretazo* to a New Style?" Paper presented at the conference, Argentina 2000: Politics, Economy, Society and International Relations, Oxford University, May 15–17.

Figueiredo, Argelina, and Fernando Limongi. 1997. "O Congresso e as Medidas Provisórias." *Novos Estudos CEBRAP* No. 47: 127–54.

2000. "Presidential Power, Legislative Organization, and Party Behavior in Brazil." *Comparative Politics* 32 No. 2: 151–70.

Fischer, Edward F., and R. McKenna Brown, eds. 1996. *Maya Cultural Activism in Guatemala.* Austin: University of Texas Press.

Fishman, Robert. 2004. *Democracy's Voices: Social Ties and the Quality of Public Life in Spain.* Ithaca, NY: Cornell University Press.

Fitch, J. Samuel. 1998. *The Armed Forces and Democracy in Latin America.* Baltimore, MD: Johns Hopkins University Press.

FLACSO (Facultad Latinoamérica de Ciencias Sociales) Programa El Salvador. 1995. *El Proceso Electoral 1994.* San Salvador: FLACSO.

Forero, Juan. 2000. "Behind Colombia's Election Hoopla, Rebels Wield Power." *New York Times*, October 29.

Foweraker, Joe. 1995. *Theorizing Social Movements.* London: Pluto Press.

Fraga, Rosendo. 1995. *Argentina en las Urnas, 1916–1994.* Buenos Aires: Editorial Centro de Estudios Unión para la Nueva Mayoría.

Freedom House. *http://freedomhouse.org.*

Freedom House. 2001. "Annual Survey of Freedom House Scores from 1972–73 to 1999–2000." New York: Freedom House.

French, John. 1992. *The Brazilian Workers' ABC.* Chapel Hill: University of North Carolina Press.

Friedman, Thomas. 2000. *The Lexus and the Olive Tree.* New York: Anchor Books.

Fukuyama, Francis. 1989. "The End of History?" *National Interest* No. 16 (Summer): 3–18.

Gallego, Rosa María. 2001. *El Programa de Incorporación: Un Camino Pendiente para los Ex-Combatientes, 1997–2001.* Guatemala City: Unión Europea, Cruz Roja Española, and ASIES.

Gamarra, Eduardo. 1997. "Hybrid Presidentialism and Democratization: The Case of Bolivia." In Scott Mainwaring and Matthew Soberg Shugart, eds., *Presidentialism and Democracy in Latin America*, pp. 363–93. Cambridge: Cambridge University Press.

Gamarra, Eduardo, and James Malloy. 1995. "The Patrimonial Dynamics of Party Politics in Bolivia." In Scott Mainwaring and Timothy R. Scully, eds., *Building Democratic Institutions: Party Systems in Latin America*, pp. 399–433. Stanford, CA: Stanford University Press.

García, Mauricio, and Boaventura de Sousa Santos. 2001. *El caleidoscopio de las justicias en Colombia*, 2 vols. Bogotá: Colciencias.

García, Mauricio, and Rodrigo Uprimny. 2000. "El nudo gordiano de la justicia y la guerra en Colombia." In Alvaro Camacho Guizado and Francisco Leal Buitrago, eds., *Armar la paz es desarmar la guerra*, pp. 33–72. Bogotá: CEREC–DNP–PNUD, FESCOL, IEPRI, Presidencia de la República.

García, Miguel. 2000a. "Elección popular de alcaldes y terceras fuerzas. El sistema de partidos en el ámbito municipal, 1988–1997." *Análisis Político* No. 14 (September–December): 84–97.

——— 2000b. "Elecciones municipales. Bipartidismo, un paso atrás." *U.N. Periódico* No. 16 (November 19).

Garretón, Manuel Antonio, Marcelo Cavarozzi, Peter Cleaves, Gary Gereffi, and Jonathan Hartlyn. 2003. *Latin America in the 21ˢᵗ Century: Toward a New Sociopolitical Matrix*. Miami: North–South Center Press at the University of Miami.

Garrett, Geoff. 1998. "Global Markets and National Politics: Collision Course or Virtuous Circle." *International Organization* 52 No. 4: 787–824.

Garrido, Luis Javier. 1982. *El Partido de la Revolución Institucionalizada*. Mexico City: Siglo XXI.

Gasiorowski, Mark J. 1995. "Economic Crisis and Political Regime Change: An Event History Analysis." *American Political Science Review* 89 No. 4: 882–97.

——— 1998. "Macroeconomic Conditions and Political Instability: An Empirical Analysis." *Studies in Comparative International Development* 33 No. 3: 3–17.

——— 2000. "Democracy and Macroeconomic Performance in Underdeveloped Countries: An Empirical Analysis." *Comparative Political Studies* 33 No. 3: 319–49.

Gasiorowski, Mark J., and Timothy J. Power. 1998. "The Structural Determinants of Democratic Consolidation – Evidence from the Third World." *Comparative Political Studies* 31 No. 6: 740–71.

Gastil, Raymond D. 1991. "The Comparative Survey of Freedom: Experiences and Suggestions." In Alex Inkeles, ed., *On Measuring Democracy: Its Consequences and Concomitants*, pp. 21–46. New Brunswick, NJ: Transaction Publishers.

Gaviria, Alejandro, and Carmen Pagés. 1999. "Patterns of Crime Victimization in Latin America." Inter-American Development Bank Conference on Economic and Social Progress in Latin America, Washington, DC, April.

Geddes, Barbara. 1999a. "Authoritarian Breakdown: Empirical Test of a Game Theoretic Argument." Paper presented at the American Political Science Association Meeting, Atlanta, GA, September.

——— 1999b. "What Do We Know about Democratization after Twenty Years?" *Annual Review of Political Science* 2: 115–44.

Genoíno, José. 1992. *Repensando a Esquerda*. Brasília: Câmara dos Deputados.

Gervasoni, Carlos. 1997. "La sustentabilidad electoral de los programas de estabilización y reforma estructural: los casos de Argentina y Perú." Paper presented at the XX Congress of the Latin American Studies Association, Guadalajara, Mexico.

Gibb, Tom, and Frank Smyth. 1990. "El Salvador: Is Peace Possible?" Washington Office on Latin America (April).

Gibson, Edward. 1996. *Class and Conservative Parties: Argentina in Comparative Perspective*. Baltimore, MD: Johns Hopkins University Press.

Gillespie, Richard. 1982. *Soldiers of Perón: Argentina's Montoneros*. Oxford: Clarendon Press.

Gleditsch, Kristian Skrede. 2002. *All International Politics is Local: The Diffusion of Conflict, Integration, and Democratization.* Ann Arbor: University of Michigan Press.

Global Financial Database. *http://www.globalfindata.com/.*

Goldenberg, Boris. 1971. *Kommunismus in Lateinamerika.* Stuttgart: Kohlhammer.

Goldin, Claudia, and Lawrence F. Katz. 2001. "Human Capital and Social Capital: The Rise of Secondary Schooling in America, 1910–1940." In Robert I. Rotberg, ed., *Patterns of Social Capital: Stability and Change in Historical Perspective*, pp.295–336. Cambridge: Cambridge University Press.

Gómez, Juan Gabriel. 2000. "Sobre las constituciones de Colombia (incluida la de papel)." In Instituto de Estudios Políticos y Relaciones Internacionales (IEPRI), *Colombia: Cambio de siglo. Balances y Perspectivas*, pp. 255–92. Bogotá: Planeta Colombiana Editorial S.A.

Gonzales de Olarte, Efraín. 1998. *El neoliberalismo a la peruana. Economía política del ajuste estructural, 1990–1997.* Lima: IEP.

Gonzales de Olarte, Efraín, and Lilian Samamé. 1991. *El péndulo peruano. Políticas económicas, gobernabilidad y subdesarrollo, 1963–1990.* Lima: IEP.

González, Fernán. 1989. "Aproximación a la configuración política de Colombia." *Controversia* Nos. 153–54: 19–72.

  1997. *Para leer la política. Ensayos de historia política colombiana*, 2 vols. Bogotá: CINEP.

Gordon, Sara R. 1983. "La Transformación Agraria en El Salvador: Un Conflicto Interburgués." *Estudios Sociales Centroamericanos* 36: 13–37.

Gray-Molina, George. 2001. "Exclusion, Participation and Democratic State-building." In Laurence Whitehead and John Crabtree, eds., *Towards Democratic Viability: The Bolivian Experience*, pp. 63–82. London: Palgrave.

Grindle, Merilee. 2000. *Audacious Reforms: Institutional Invention and Democracy in Latin America.* Baltimore, MD: Johns Hopkins University Press.

Grompone, Romeo. 2000. "Al día siguiente: el fujimorismo como proyecto inconcluso de transformación política y social." In Julio Cotler and Romeo Grompone, eds., *El fujimorismo: ascenso y caída de un régimen autoritario*, pp. 77–178. Lima: IEP.

Grupo de Opinión Pública de la Universidad de Lima. 2003. *Estudio 209, Barómetro.* (December). Lima: Metropolitana y Callao.

Guevara Anaya, Walter. 2000. "Depolarization of Public Institutions. How the Spoils System Exacts a Tribute for Reforms in Bolivia." La Paz. Unpublished manuscript, Department of the Civil Service.

Gurr, Ted Robert. 1981. "Historical Trends in Violent Crime: A Critical Review of the Evidence." In Michael Tonry and Norval Morris, eds., *Crime and Justice Review: An Annual Review of Research*, pp. 295–353. Chicago: University of Chicago Press.

Gurr, Ted Robert, and Will H. Moore. 1997. "Ethnopolitical Rebellion: A Cross-Sectional Analysis of the 1980s with Risk Assessments for the 1990s." *American Journal of Political Science* 41 No. 4: 1079–1103.

Gurr, Ted Robert, Keith Jaggers, and Will Moore. 1990. "The Transformation of the Western State: The Growth of Democracy, Autocracy, and State Power since 1800." *Studies in Comparative International Development* 25 (Spring): 73–108.

Gutiérrez, Francisco. 1998. "Rescate por un elefante. Congreso, sistema y reforma política." In Ana Maria Bejarano and Andres Dávila, eds., *Elecciones y democracia en Colombia 1997–1998*, pp. 215–53. Bogotá: Universidad de los Andes.

Gutiérrez Saxe, Miguel, ed. 1999. *Estado de la Región.* San José, Costa Rica: Proyecto Estado de la Nación.

Gwartney, James, Robert Lawson, and Walter Block. 1996. *Economic Freedom of the World, 1975–1995.* Vancouver, British Columbia: The Fraser Institute.

Haggard, Stephen, and Robert R. Kaufman. 1995. *The Political Economy of Democratic Transitions.* Princeton, NJ: Princeton University Press.

Hagopian, Frances. 1990. "'Democracy by Undemocratic Means?' Elites, Political Pacts, and Regime Transition in Brazil." *Comparative Political Studies* 23 No. 2: 147–70.

1996a. *Traditional Politics and Regime Change in Brazil.* Cambridge: Cambridge University Press.

1996b. "Traditional Power Structures and Democratic Governance in Latin America." In Jorge I. Domínguez and Abraham F. Lowenthal, eds., *Constructing Democratic Governance: Latin America and the Caribbean in the 1990s – Themes and Issues*, pp. 64–86. Baltimore, MD: Johns Hopkins University Press.

1998. "Democracy and Political Representation in Latin America in the 1990s: Pause, Reorganization, or Decline?" In Felipe Agüero and Jeffrey Stark, eds., *Fault Lines of Democracy in Post-Transition Latin America*, pp. 99–144. Miami: North–South Center Press at the University of Miami.

Hammond, John L. 1998. *Fighting to Learn: Popular Education and Guerrilla War in El Salvador.* New Brunswick, NJ: Rutgers University Press.

Handy, Jim. 1994. *Revolution in the Countryside: Rural Conflict and Agrarian Reform in Guatemala, 1944–1954.* Chapel Hill, NC: University of North Carolina Press.

Hansen, Roger D. 1971. *The Politics of Mexican Development.* Baltimore, MD, and London: Johns Hopkins University Press.

Harberger, A. C. 1993. "Measuring the Components of Economic Growth in El Salvador." San Salvador: FUSADES. Mimeo.

Hartlyn, Jonathan. 1988. *The Politics of Coalition Rule in Colombia.* Cambridge: Cambridge University Press.

Hartlyn, Jonathan, and John Dugas. 1999. "Colombia: The Politics of Violence and Democratic Transformation." In Larry Diamond, Jonathan Hartlyn, Juan J. Linz, and Seymour Martin Lipset, eds., *Democracy in Developing Countries: Latin America*, pp. 249–307. Boulder, CO: Lynne Rienner Publishers.

Hegre, Håvard, Tanja Ellingsen, Scott Gates, and Nils Petter Gleditsch. 2001. "Toward a Democratic Civil Peace? Democracy, Political Change and Civil War, 1816–1999." *American Political Science Review* 95 No. 1: 33–48.

Helmke, Gretchen. 2003. "Checks and Balances by Other Means: The Argentine Judiciary in the 1990s." *Comparative Politics* 35 No. 2: 213–30.

2005. *Courts Under Constraints: Judges, Generals, and Presidents in Argentina.* Cambridge: Cambridge University Press.

Herbst, Jeffrey I. 2000. *States and Power in Africa: Comparative Lessons in Authority and Control.* Princeton, NJ: Princeton University Press.

Hernández Pico, Juan. 2000a. "Boozegate: A Revealing Ethical – Political Earthquake." *Envio* 19 No. 231: 23–31.

2000b. "Fiscal Pact a Major Achievement: Tax Reform Next in Line." *Envio* 19 No. 229: 24–31.

Hershberg, Eric. 1999. "Democracy and Its Discontents: Constraints on Political Citizenship in Latin America." In Howard Handelman and Mark Tessler, eds., *Democracy and Its Limits: Lessons from Asia, Latin America and the Middle East*, pp. 290–320. Notre Dame, IN: University of Notre Dame Press.

Heston, Alan, Robert Summers, and Bettina Aten. 2002. *Penn World Table*, Version 6.1, Center for International Comparisons at the University of Pennsylvania (CICUP).

Heston, Alan, Robert Summers, Daniel A. Nuxoll, and Bettina Aten. 1995. *Penn World Table* Version 5.6, Center for International Comparisons at the University of Pennsylvania (CICUP).

Hillman, Richard S. 1994. *Democracy for the Privileged: Crisis and Transition in Venezuela.* Boulder, CO: Lynne Rienner Publishers.

Hite, Katherine. 2000. *When the Romance Ended: Leaders of the Chilean Left, 1968–1998.* New York: Columbia University Press.

Hochstetler, Kathryn. 2000. "Democratizing Pressures from Below?" In Peter Kingstone and Timothy Power, eds., *Democratic Brazil: Actors, Institutions, and Processes*, pp. 167–82. Pittsburgh: University of Pittsburgh Press.

Holiday, David, and William Stanley. 1993. "Building the Peace: Preliminary Lessons From El Salvador." *Journal of International Affairs* 46 No. 2: 415–38.

Htun, Mala. 2003. *Sex and the State: Abortion, Divorce, and the Family Under Latin American Dictatorships and Democracies.* Cambridge: Cambridge University Press.

Hunter, Wendy. 1992. "Back to the Barracks?" Ph.D. dissertation, University of California, Berkeley.

1997. *Eroding Military Influence in Brazil.* Chapel Hill: University of North Carolina Press.

2000. "Assessing Civil–Military Relations in Postauthoritarian Brazil." In Peter Kingstone and Timothy Power, eds., *Democratic Brazil: Actors, Institutions, and Processes*, pp. 101–25. Pittsburgh: University of Pittsburgh Press.

Huntington, Samuel P. 1968. *Political Order in Changing Societies.* New Haven, CT: Yale University Press.

1984. "Will More Countries Become Democratic?" *Political Science Quarterly* 99 No. 2: 193–218.

1991. *The Third Wave: Democratization in the Late Twentieth Century.* Norman: University of Oklahoma Press.

Huntington, Samuel P., and Joan M. Nelson. 1976. *No Easy Choice: Political Participation in Developing Countries.* Cambridge, MA: Harvard University Press.

IBGE (Instituto Brasileiro de Geografia e Estatística). 1998. *Pesquisa Nacional por Amostra de Domicílios.* Brasil, vol. 20. Rio de Janeiro: IBGE.

1999. *Síntese de Indicadores Sociais 1998.* Rio de Janeiro: IBGE.

IBOPE. 2000a. *Pesquisa de Opinião Pública sobre Assuntos Políticos/Administrativos* (May). OPP 145. São Paulo: IBOPE.

2000b. *Pesquisa de Opinião Pública sobre Assuntos Políticos/Administrativos* (August). OPP 333. São Paulo: IBOPE.

2002. OPP 570 (December). *www.ibope.com.br.*

IDB (Inter-American Development Bank). 1997. *Latin America after a Decade of Reforms: Economic and Social Progress.* Washington, DC: IDB.

2000a. *Annual Report 1999.* Washington, DC: IDB.

2000b. *Development Beyond Economics: Economic and Social Progress in Latin America, 2000 Report.* Washington, DC: Johns Hopkins University Press.

IDEA (International Institute for Democracy and Electoral Assistance). 1997. *Voter Turnout from 1945 to 1997: A Global Report on Political Participation.* Stockholm: IDEA.

2004. "Voter Turnout from 1945 to Date: A Global Report on Political Participation." South and Central America. *http://www.idea.int/voter_turnout/southamerica.html* (March 11).

IFE (Instituto Federal Electoral). *www.ife.org.mx.*

ILDIS. 1990. "Encuesta sobre Instituciones Democráticas." La Paz: ILDIS.

INEI (Instituto Nacional de Estadística e Informática). Lima: INEI. *www.inei.gob.pe.*

Ipsos–Mora y Araujo. 2003. "Inseguridad, la gran preocupación." *La Nación,* June 8.

IUDOP (Instituto Universitario de Opinión Pública). 1997. "La opinión pública sobre las elecciones de 1997." *Estudios Centroamericanos* 52 No. 581–82. *http://www.uca.edu.sv/publica/eca/ecaind.html.*

— 1998. "Delincuencia y opinión pública." *Estudios Centroamericanos* 53 No. 599 (September). *http://www.uca.edu.sv/publica/eca/ecaind.html.*

— 2003. "Evaluacíon del país a finales de 2003 y perspectives electorales para 2004: Encuesta de opinión pública." Boletín de prensa 38 No. 4.

Jackman, Robert 1973. "On the Relation of Economic Development to Democratic Performance." *American Journal of Political Science* 17 No. 3: 611–21.

Jaggers, Keith, and Ted Robert Gurr. 1995. "Tracking Democracy's Third Wave with the Polity III Data." *Journal of Peace Research* 32 No. 4: 469–82.

Johnson, John J. 1958. *Political Change in Latin America: The Emergence of the Middle Sectors.* Stanford, CA: Stanford University Press.

Johnson, Kenneth. 1993. "Between Revolution and Democracy: Business Elites and the State in El Salvador during the 1980s." Ph.D. dissertation, Tulane University.

Joint Group for the Investigation of Illegal Armed Groups. 1994. *Report of the Joint Group for the Investigation of Illegal Armed Groups with Political Motivation in El Salvador.* San Salvador (28 July). Mimeo.

Jonas, Susanne. 2000a. *Of Centaurs and Doves: Guatemala's Peace Process.* Boulder, CO: Westview Press.

— 2000b. "Democratization Through Peace: The Difficult Case of Guatemala." *Journal of Interamerican Studies and World Affairs* 42 No. 4: 9–38.

Jones, Mark P. 1995. *Electoral Laws and the Survival of Presidential Democracies.* Notre Dame, IN: University of Notre Dame Press.

— 1997. "Evaluating Argentina's Presidential Democracy." In Scott Mainwaring and Matthew Soberg Shugart, eds., *Presidentialism and Democracy in Latin America,* pp. 259–99. Cambridge: Cambridge University Press.

Karl, Terry Lynn. 1982. "The Political Economy of Petrodollars: Oil and Democracy in Venezuela." Ph.D. dissertation, Stanford University.

— 1986a. "Imposing Consent? Electoralism Vs. Democratization in El Salvador." In Paul Drake and Eduardo Silva, eds., *Elections and Democratization in Latin America,* pp. 9–36. San Diego: Center for Iberian and Latin American Studies, University of California.

— 1986b. "Petroleum and Political Pacts: The Transition to Democracy in Venezuela." In Guillermo O'Donnell, Philippe C. Schmitter, and Laurence Whitehead, eds., *Transitions from Authoritarian Rule: Latin America,* pp. 196–219. Baltimore, MD: Johns Hopkins University Press.

— 1992. "El Salvador's Negotiated Revolution." *Foreign Affairs* 71 No. 2: 147–64.

— 1997. *The Paradox of Plenty: Oil Booms and Petro States.* Berkeley: University of California Press.

Karl, Terry Lynn, Vincent Maphai, and Rubén Zamora. 1996. "War Transitions: Ending Armed Conflict and Starting Democracy in 'Uncivil' Societies." Unpublished research proposal. Stanford University.

Karl, Terry L., and Philippe Schmitter. 1991. "Modes of Transition in Latin America, Southern and Eastern Europe." *International Social Science Journal* 43 No. 128: 269–84.

Katz, Richard, and Peter Mair. 1995. "Changing Models of Party Organizations and Party Democracy: The Emergence of the Cartel Party." *Party Politics* 1 No. 1: 5–28.

Katzenstein, Peter J. 2000. "Confidence, Trust, International Relations, and Lessons from Smaller Democracies." In Susan J. Pharr and Robert D. Putnam, eds., *Disaffected Democracies: What's Troubling the Trilateral Democracies?* pp. 121–48. Princeton, NJ: Princeton University Press.

Kaufmann, Daniel, Aart Kraay, and Massimo Mastruzzi. 2003. *Governance Matters III: Governance Indicators for 1996–2002*, World Bank Policy Research Working Paper 3106. *http://www.worldbank.org/wbi/governance/govdata2002/*.

Kaufmann, Daniel, Aart Kraay, and Pablo Zoido-Lobatón. 2002. *Governance Matters II: Updated Indicators for 2000/01*. World Bank (January). *http://www.worldbank.org/wbi/governance/govdata2001.htm*.

Kaufman, Robert R., and Alex Segura-Ubiergo. 2001. "Globalization, Domestic Politics, and Social Spending in Latin America: A Time-Series Cross-Section Analysis, 1973–97." *World Politics* 53 No. 4: 553–87.

Kay, Bruce. 1995. "Fujipopulism and the Liberal State in Peru, 1990–1995." Paper given at the Congress of the Latin American Studies Association, Washington, DC, September 28–30.

Keck, Margaret. 1992. *The Workers' Party and Democratization in Brazil*. New Haven, CT: Yale University Press.

Keck, Margaret E., and Kathryn Sikkink. 1998. *Activists Beyond Borders: Advocacy Networks in International Politics*. Ithaca, NY: Cornell University Press.

Kelly, Phil. 2001. "The Fitzgibbon-Johnson Index: Specialists' View of Democracy in Latin America, 1945–2000." Emporia State University, Emporia, KS. Unpublished paper.

Kenney, Charles. 2000. "The Collapse of the Peruvian Party System: Cleavages, Institutionalization, and Political Elites." University of Oklahoma. Unpublished paper.

2004. *Fujimori's Coup and the Breakdown of Democracy in Latin America*. Notre Dame, IN: University of Notre Dame Press.

Kincaid, A. Douglas. 2000. "Demilitarization and Security in El Salvador and Guatemala: Convergences of Success and Crisis." *Journal of Interamerican Studies and World Affairs* 42 No. 4: 39–58.

King, Gary, and Langche Zeng. 2001a. "Logistic Regression in Rare Events Data." *Political Analysis* 9 No. 2: 137–63.

2001b. "Explaining Rare Events in International Relations." *International Organization* 55 No. 3: 693–715.

Kingstone, Peter. 1999. *Crafting Coalitions for Reform: Business Preferences, Political Institutions, and Neoliberal Reform in Brazil*. University Park: Pennsylvania State University Press.

Klesner, Joseph. 1996. "¿ Realineación o Desalineación? Consecuencias de la Crisis y la Reestructuración Económica para el Sistema Partidiario Mexicano." In Maria Lorena Cook, Kevin Middlebrook, and Juan Molinar, eds., *Las dimensiones políticas de la reestructuración económica*. Mexico City: Cal y Arena.

Kline, Harvey. 1995. *Colombia: Democracy Under Assault*, 2nd ed. Boulder, CO: Westview.

Kornblith, Miriam, and Daniel H. Levine. 1995. "Venezuela: The Life and Times of the Party System." In Scott Mainwaring and Timothy R. Scully, eds., *Building Democratic Institutions: Party Systems in Latin America*, pp. 37–71. Stanford, CA: Stanford University Press.

Laakso, Markku, and Rein Taagepera. 1979. "'Effective' Number of Parties: A Measure with Application to Western Europe." *Comparative Political Studies* 12 No. 1: 3–27.

Lagos, Marta. 2001. "Between Stability and Crisis in Latin America." *Journal of Democracy* 12 No. 1: 137–45.

Lamounier, Bolívar. 1979. "Representação Política: A Importância de Certos Formalismos." In Bolívar Lamounier, Francisco Weffort, and Maria Victória Benevides, eds., *Direito, Cidadania e Participação*, pp. 230–57. São Paulo: Tao.

1996. "Brazil: The Hyperactive Paralysis Syndrome." In Jorge I. Domínguez and Abraham F. Lowenthal, eds., *Constructing Democratic Governance: South America in the 1990s*, pp. 166–87. Baltimore, MD: Johns Hopkins University Press.

Lamounier, Bolívar, and Amaury de Souza. 1991. "Democracia e Reforma Institucional no Brasil." *Dados* 34 No. 3: 311–47.

Lamounier, Bolívar, and Alexandre Marques. 1992. "A Democracia Brasileira no Final da 'Década Perdida'." In Bolívar Lamounier, ed., *Ouvindo o Brasil*, pp. 137–58. São Paulo: Sumaré.

Landau, Saul. 1993. *The Guerrilla Wars of Central America: Nicaragua, El Salvador and Guatemala*. London: Weidenfeld and Nicolson.

Landman, Todd. 1999. "Economic Development and Democracy: The View from Latin America." *Political Studies* 47 No. 4: 607–26.

Larde de Palomo, Anabella, and Aida Arguello de Morera. 2000. "Integración a Los Mercados de los Hogares Rurales y Generación de Ingresos." Documento de Investigación BASIS (Broadening Access and Strengthening Input Market Systems Collaborative Research Support Program), No. 3. San Salvador: FUSADES (Fundación Salvadoreña para el Desarrollo Económico y Social).

Larkins, Christopher. 1998. "The Judiciary and Delegative Democracy in Argentina." *Comparative Politics* 30 No. 4: 423–42.

Latin American Public Opinion Project. 2002. Vanderbilt University.

Latin American Weekly Report. 1980–2001.

Latinobarómetro. 1997. *Informe de Prensa Latinobarómetro 1997*. Santiago, Chile: Latinobarómetro.

1998. "Encuesta sobre la democracia en América Latina." Santiago, Chile: Latinobarómetro.

2002. *Informe de Prensa Latinobarómetro 2002*. Santiago: Latinobarómetro.

2003. "Summary – Report. Democracy and Economy." October. *www.latinobarometro.org*.

2004. "Informe – Resumen: Una Década de Mediciones." August. Available at *www.latinobarometro.org*.

Lavareda, Antônio. 1991. *A Democracia nas Urnas*. Rio de Janeiro: Rio Fundo.

Laver, Michael, and Norman Schofield. 1991. *Multiparty Government: The Politics of Coalition in Europe*. Oxford: Oxford University Press.

Lawson, Chappell. 1999. "Why Cárdenas Won." In Jorge Domínguez and Alejandro Poiré, eds., *Towards Mexico's Democratization: Campaigns, Elections and Public Opinion*. New York: Routledge.

Leal Buitrago, Francisco. 1984. *Estado y política en Colombia*. Bogotá: Siglo XXI Editores.

Leal Buitrago, Francisco, and Andrés Dávila. 1990. *Clientelismo. El sistema político y su expresión regional*. Bogotá: Tercer Mundo Editores/IEPRI.

Lemke, Christiane, and Gary Marks. 1992. "From Decline to Demise?" In Christiane Lemke and Gary Marks, eds., *The Crisis of Socialism in Europe*, pp. 1–20. Durham, NC: Duke University Press.

Leo, Sérgio. 1991. "Mercado Não É Pecado." *Veja* No. 1136 (3 July): 3–6.

Levine, Daniel H. 1973. *Conflict and Political Change in Venezuela*. Princeton, NJ: Princeton University Press.

1978. "Venezuela since 1958: The Consolidation of Democratic Politics." In Juan J. Linz and Alfred Stepan, eds., *The Breakdown of Democratic Regimes*, Vol. 3, *Latin America*, pp. 82–109. Baltimore, MD: Johns Hopkins University Press.

1981. *Religion and Politics in Latin America: The Catholic Church in Venezuela and Colombia*. Princeton, NJ: Princeton University Press.

Levitsky, Steven. 2001. "An 'Organized Disorganization': Informal Organization and the Persistence of Local Party Structures in Argentine Peronism." *Journal of Latin American Studies* 33 No. 1: 29–66.

2003. *Transforming Labor-Based Parties in Latin America: Argentine Peronism in Comparative Perspective*. Cambridge: Cambridge University Press.

Levitsky, Steven, and Maxwell A. Cameron. 2003. "Democracy without Parties? Political Parties and Regime Change in Fujimori's Peru." *Latin American Politics and Society* 45 No. 3: 1–33.

Levitsky, Steven, and Lucan A. Way. 1998. "Between a Shock and a Hard Place: The Dynamics of Labor-Backed Adjustment in Argentina and Poland." *Comparative Politics* 30 No. 2: 171–92.

2002. "The Rise of Competitive Authoritarianism." *Journal of Democracy* 13 No. 2: 51–65.

Levitt, Steven, and Mauricio Rubio. 2000. "Understanding Crime in Colombia and What Can Be Done About It." Working Paper Series No. 20 (August), Fedesarrollo, Bogotá.

Levy, Daniel, and Gabriel Szekeley. 1987. *Mexico: Paradoxes of Stability and Change*. Boulder, CO: Westview Press.

Lichbach, Mark. 2003. *Is Rational Choice Theory All of Social Science?* Ann Arbor: University of Michigan Press.

Lijphart, Arend. 1977. *Democracy in Plural Societies: A Comparative Exploration*. New Haven, CT: Yale University Press.

Lindo-Fuentes, Hector. 1990. *Weak Foundations: The Economy of El Salvador in the Nineteenth Century*. Berkeley: University of California Press.

Linz, Juan. 1978. *The Breakdown of Democratic Regimes: Crisis, Breakdown, and Reequilibration*. Baltimore, MD: John Hopkins University Press.

1994. "Presidential or Parliamentary Democracy: Does It Make a Difference?" In Juan Linz and Arturo Valenzuela, eds., *The Failure of Presidential Democracy: Comparative Perspectives*, Vol. 1, pp. 3–87. Baltimore, MD: Johns Hopkins University Press.

Linz, Juan J., and Alfred Stepan, eds. 1978. *The Breakdown of Democratic Regimes*. Baltimore, MD: Johns Hopkins University Press.

1989. "Political Crafting of Democratic Consolidation or Destruction: European and South American Comparisons." In Robert A. Pastor, ed., *Democracy in the Americas: Stopping the Pendulum*, pp. 41–61. New York: Holmes and Meier.

1996. *Problems of Democratic Transition and Consolidation: Southern Europe, South America, and Post-Communist Europe*. Baltimore, MD: Johns Hopkins University Press.

Linz, Juan J., and Arturo Valenzuela, eds. 1994. *The Failure of Presidential Democracy.* Baltimore, MD: Johns Hopkins University Press.

Lipset, Seymour Martin. 1959. "Some Social Requisites of Democracy: Economic Development and Political Legitimacy." *American Political Science Review* 53 No. 1: 69–105.

——— 1996. "Repensando los requisitos sociales de la democracia." *Ágora* No. 5: 29–65. [Originally appeared in *American Sociological Review* 59 (February 1994): 1–22.]

Lipset, Seymour Martin, K. Seong, and John Charles Torres. 1993. "A Comparative Analysis of the Social Requisites of Democracy." *International Social Science Journal* 45 No. 136: 155–75.

Llanos, Mariana. 2001. "Understanding Presidential Power in Argentina: A Study of the Policy of Privatization in the 1990s." *Journal of Latin American Studies* 33 No. 1: 67–99.

Londregan, John B., and Keith T Poole. 1996. "Does High Income Promote Democracy?" *World Politics* 49 No. 1: 1–30.

López, Andrés. 1998. "Narcotráfico y elecciones: delincuencia y corrupción en la reciente vida política colombiana." In Ana María Bejarano and Andrés Dávila, eds., *Elecciones y Democracia en Colombia, 1997–1998*, pp. 35–50. Bogotá: Departamento de Ciencia Política, Universidad de los Andes – Fundación Social – Veeduría Ciudadana a la Elección Presidencial.

López, Andrés, and Alvaro Camacho. 2001. "From Smugglers to Drug-Lords to 'Traquetos': Changes in the Colombian Illicit Drug Traffic." Paper presented at the conference Democracy, Human Rights, and Peace in Colombia, Kellogg Institute for International Studies, University of Notre Dame, March 26–27.

López, Sinesio. 1992. "Fujimori y la crisis de la civilización del siglo XX." In Juan Abugattás, Rolando Ames, and Sinesio López, eds., *Desde el límite. Perú, reflexiones en el umbral de una nueva época*, pp. 221–34. Lima: Instituto Democracia y Socialismo.

Loveman, Brian. 1993. *The Constitution of Tyranny: Regimes of Exception in Spanish America.* Pittsburgh: University of Pittsburgh Press.

——— 1999. *For la Patria: Politics and the Armed Forces in Latin America.* Wilmington, DE: Scholarly Resources.

Loveman, Brian, and Thomas M. Davies, eds. 1997. *The Politics of Antipolitics: the Military in Latin America.* Revised and updated. Wilmington, DE: Scholarly Resources.

Lowenthal, Abraham F. 1991. "The United States and Latin American Democracy: Learning from History." In Abraham F. Lowenthal, ed., *Exporting Democracy: The United States and Latin America, Themes and Issues*, pp. 243–65. Baltimore, MD: Johns Hopkins University Press.

Lungo Uclés, Mario. 1995. "Building an Alternative: The Formation of a Popular Project." In Minor Sinclair, ed., *The New Politics of Survival: Grassroots Movements in Central America*, pp. 153–79. New York: Monthly Review Press.

Lynch, Nicolás. 1999. *Una tragedia sin héroes. La derrota de los partidos y el origen de los independientes. Perú 1980–1992.* Lima: UNMSM.

Maddala, G. S. 1977. *Econometrics.* New York: McGraw-Hill.

Maddison, Angus. 1995. *Monitoring the World Economy, 1820–1992.* Paris: Development Centre of the Organisation for Economic Co-operation and Development.

Magaloni, Beatriz. 1997. "The Dynamics of Dominant Party Decline: The Mexican Transition to Multipartysm." Ph.D. dissertation, Duke University.

1999. "Is the PRI Fading? Economic Performance, Electoral Accountability and Voting Behavior." In Jorge I. Domínguez and Alejandro Poiré, eds., *Toward Mexico's Democratization: Parties, Campaigns, Elections and Public Opinion*, pp. 203–36. New York: Routledge.

2000. "Multiple Party Systems, Coordination Dilemmas and Federalism: Mexico 1985–1998." Paper presented at the 96th American Political Science Association Meeting, Washington, DC, August 31–September 3.

2003. "Authoritarianism, Democracy and the Supreme Court: Horizontal Exchange and the Rule of Law in Mexico." In Scott Mainwaring and Christopher Welna, eds., *Democratic Accountability in Latin America*, pp. 266–305. Oxford: Oxford University Press.

Magaloni, Beatriz, and Alejandro Poiré. 2004a. "Strategic Coordination in the 2000 Mexican Presidential Race." In Jorge I. Domínguez and Chappell H. Lawson, eds., *Mexico's Pivotal Democratic Election: Candidates, Voters, and the Presidential Campaign of 2000*, pp. 269–92. Stanford, CA: Stanford University Press.

2004b. "The Issues, the Vote and the Mandate for Change." In Jorge I. Domínguez and Chappell H. Lawson, eds. *Mexico's Pivotal Democratic Election: Candidates, Voters, and the Presidential Campaign of 2000*, pp. 293–319. Stanford, CA: Stanford University Press.

Magaloni, Beatriz, and Vidal Romero. 2004. "Support for Globalization and State Retrenchment in Latin America: Economic Performance and Partisanship." Paper presented at the Workshop on the Analysis of Political Cleavages and Party Competition, Duke University, April 2–3.

Magaloni, Beatriz, and Arianna Sánchez. 2001. "Empowering Courts as Constitutional Veto Players: Presidential Delegation and the New Mexican Supreme Court." Paper presented at the 2001 Annual Meeting of the American Political Science Association, San Francisco, August 30–September 2.

Magaloni, Beatriz, Alberto Diaz-Cayeros, and Federico Estévez. Forthcoming. "The Erosion of Party Hegemony, Clientelism and Portfolio Diversification." In Herbert Kitschelt and Scott Wilson, eds. *Clientelistic Linkages in Comparative Perspective*.

Mahoney, James, and Richard Snyder. 1999. "The Missing Variable: Institutions and the Study of Regime Change." *Comparative Politics* 32 No. 1: 103–22.

Mainwaring, Scott. 1986. *The Catholic Church and Politics in Brazil, 1916–1985*. Stanford, CA: Stanford University Press.

1987. "Urban Popular Movements, Identity, and Democratization in Brazil." *Comparative Political Studies* 20 No. 2: 131–59.

1993. "Presidentialism, Multipartism, and Democracy – The Difficult Combination." *Comparative Political Studies* 26 No. 2: 198–228.

1997. "Multipartism, Robust Federalism, and Presidentialism in Brazil." In Scott Mainwaring and Matthew Soberg Shugart, eds., *Presidentialism and Democracy in Latin America*, pp. 55–109. Cambridge: Cambridge University Press.

1999a. "Democratic Survivability in Latin America." In Howard Handelman and Mark Tessler, eds., *Democracy and Its Limits*, pp. 11–68. Notre Dame, IN: University of Notre Dame Press.

1999b. *Rethinking Party Systems in the Third Wave of Democratization: The Case of Brazil*. Stanford, CA: Stanford University Press.

1999c. "The Surprising Resilience of Elected Governments." *Journal of Democracy* 10 No. 3: 101–14.

Mainwaring, Scott, and Aníbal Pérez-Liñán. 2003. "Level of Development and Democracy in Latin America: Latin American Exceptionalism, 1945–1996." *Comparative Political Studies* 36 No. 9: 1031–67.

Mainwaring, Scott, and Timothy R. Scully, eds. 1995. *Building Democratic Institutions: Party Systems in Latin America.* Stanford, CA: Stanford University Press.

Mainwaring, Scott, and Mathew Soberg Shugart, eds. 1997. *Presidentialism and Democracy in Latin America.* Cambridge: Cambridge University Press.

Mainwaring, Scott, Daniel Brinks, and Aníbal Pérez-Liñán. 2001. "Classifying Political Regimes in Latin America, 1945–1999." *Studies in Comparative International Development* 36 No. 1: 37–65.

Malo, Verónica, and Julio Pastor. 1996. "Autonomía e Imparcialidad en el Consejo General del IFE, 1994–1995." Tesis de Licenciatura, Instituto Tecnológico Autónomo de México.

Malone, Mary Fran T., Siddhartha Baviskar, and David Manel. 2003. "As Good As It Gets? Citizens' Expectations and Support for Democracy." Paper presented at the 2003 Graduate Student Conference on Latin American Social and Public Policy, Pittsburgh, February 20–21.

Marques, Carlos. 1993. "O Bicho-Papão Vira Príncipe." *IstoÉ* No. 1259 (17 November): 74–76.

Martín-Baró, Ignacio. 1973. "Psicología del campesino salvadoreño." *Estudios Centroamericanos* 28 (297–98): 476–95.

Martínez Rodríguez, Antonia. 1998. "Parliamentary Elites and the Polarisation of the Party System in Mexico." In Mónica Serrano, ed., *Governing Mexico: Political Parties and Elections*, pp. 58–68. London: Institute of Latin American Studies, University of London.

Mason, Ann C. 2000. "The Colombian Security Crisis: International Causes and Consequences of a Failing State." Paper presented at the Research Workshop Civil Conflict in Colombia: The Challenges of Peacemaking and Reconciliation, Princeton University, September 22.

Mauceri, Philip. 2001. "State, Elites and Counter-Insurgency: Some Preliminary Comparisons Between Colombia and Peru." University of Northern Iowa. Unpublished manuscript.

Mayorga, René Antonio. 1991. *De la Anomia Política al Orden Democrático? Democracia, Estado y Movimiento Sindical.* La Paz: CEBEM.

1994. "Gobernabilidad y Reforma Política: La Experiencia de Bolivia." *HOY. Revista de Ciencias Sociales* No. 8 (Junio): 35–62.

1995. *Antipolítica y Neopopulismo.* La Paz: CEBEM.

1997a. "Bolivia's Silent Revolution." *The Journal of Democracy* 8 No. 1: 142–56.

1997b. "Democracy Dignified and an End to Impunity: Bolivia's Military Dictatorship on Trial." In A. James McAdams, ed., *Transitional Justice and the Rule of Law*, pp. 61–92. Notre Dame, IN: University of Notre Dame Press.

1999. "La Democracia o el Desafío de la Modernización Política." In Fernando Campero, ed., *Bolivia en el Siglo XX: La Formación de la Bolivia Contemporánea*, pp. 329–58. La Paz: Harvard Club de Bolivia.

2001a. *Desmontaje de la Democracia. Crítica de las propuestas de reforma política del Diálogo Nacional 2000 y las tendencias antisistémicas.* La Paz: CEBEM.

2001b. "La democracia en Bolivia: Presidencialismo parlamentarizado y gobiernos de coalición." In Jorge Lanzaro and René Antonio Mayorga, eds., *Presidencialismo y Gobiernos de Coalición en América Latina*, pp. 101–36. Buenos Aires: CLACSO.

2001c. "Electoral Reform in Bolivia: Origins of the Mixed-Member Proportional System." In Matthew Soberg Shugart and Martin Wattenberg, eds., *Mixed-Member Electoral Systems: The Best of Both Worlds?*, pp. 194–208. Oxford: Oxford University Press.

2001d. "The Mixed-Member Proportional System and Its Consequences in Bolivia." In Matthew Soberg Shugart and Martin Wattenberg, eds., *Mixed-Member Electoral Systems: The Best of Both Worlds?*, pp. 432–46. Oxford: Oxford University Press.

McClintock, Cynthia. 1989. "The Prospects for Democratic Consolidation in a 'Least Likely' Case: Peru." *Comparative Politics* 21 No. 2: 127–48.

1999a. "¿Es autoritario el gobierno de Fujimori?" In Fernando Tuesta, ed., *El juego político. Fujimori, la oposición y las reglas*, pp. 65–96. Lima: Fundación Friedrich Ebert.

1999b. "Peru: Precarious Regimes, Authoritarian and Democratic." In Larry Diamond, Jonathan Hartlyn, Juan J. Linz, and Seymour Martin Lipset, eds., *Democracy in Developing Countries: Latin America*, 2nd ed., pp. 309–65. Boulder, CO: Lynne Rienner Publishers.

McCoy, Jennifer. 1999. "Comparative Lessons." In Jennifer McCoy, ed., *Political Learning and Redemocratization in Latin America: Do Politicians Learn from Political Crisis?*, pp. 131–48. Miami: North–South Center Press.

McDonough, Peter, Doh Shin, and José Álvaro Moisés. 1998. "Democratization and Participation: Comparing Spain, Brazil, and Korea." *Journal of Politics* 60 No. 4: 919–53.

McGuire, James W. 1995. "Political Parties and Democracy in Argentina." In Scott Mainwaring and Timothy R. Scully, eds., *Building Democratic Institutions: Party Systems in Latin America*, pp. 200–46. Stanford, CA: Stanford University Press.

1997. *Peronism Without Perón: Unions, Parties, and Democracy in Argentina*. Stanford, CA: Stanford University Press.

Medina, Luis. 1978. *Evolución Electoral en el México Contemporáneo*. Mexico City: Gaceta Informativa de la Comisión Federal Electoral.

Méndez, Juan. 1999. "Problems of Lawless Violence: Introduction." In Juan E. Méndez, Guillermo O'Donnell, and Paulo Sergio Pinheiro, eds., *The (Un)Rule of Law and the Underprivileged in Latin America*, pp. 19–24. Notre Dame, IN: University of Notre Dame Press.

Mendoza, Carlos, and Edelberto Torres-Rivas. 2003. *Linchamientos: ¿barbarie o justicia popular?* Guatemala: Colección Cultura de Paz.

Meseguer, Covadonga. 2002. "Bayesian Learning about Policies." Ph.D. dissertation, Instituto Juan March de Estudios e Investigaciones.

Mettenheim, Kurt von. 1990. "The Brazilian Voter in Democratic Transition, 1974–1982." *Comparative Politics* 23 No. 1: 23–44.

Ministerio de Salud Pública y Asistencia Social. 1997. *Guatemala: Los Contrastes del Desarrollo Humano*. Edición 1998. Sistema de las Naciones Unidas para Guatemala.

MINUGUA (United Nations Verification Mission in Guatemala). 2000. *Los linchamientos: un flagelo contra la dignidad humana*. Guatemala City: United Nations.

Moisés, José Álvaro. 1995. *Os Brasileiros e a Democracia*. São Paulo: Ática.

Molinar Horcasitas, Juan. 1991. *El Tiempo de la Legitimidad. Elecciones, Autoritarismo y Democracia en México*. Mexico City: Cal y Arena.

Molinar Horcasitas, Juan, and Jeffrey A. Weldon. 1994. "Electoral Determinants and Consequences of National Solidarity." In Wayne A. Cornelius, Ann L. Craig, and Jonathan Fox, eds., *Transforming State–Society Relations in Mexico: The National*

Solidarity Strategy, pp. 123–41. La Jolla, CA: Center for U.S.–Mexican Studies, University of California, San Diego.

Montes, Segundo. 1986. *El Agro Salvadoreño (1973–1980)*. San Salvador: Colección: Estructuras y Procesos.

Montgomery, Tommie Sue. 1995. *Revolution in El Salvador: From Civil Strife to Civil Peace*, 2nd ed. Boulder, CO: Westview Press.

Moore, Barrington, Jr. 1966. *Social Origins of Dictatorship and Democracy: Lord and Peasant in the Making of the Modern World*. Boston: Beacon Press.

Mora, Frank O. 2000. "Paraguay y el sistema interamericano: Del autoritarismo y la parálisis a la democracia y la aplicación de la Resolución 1080." In Arlene B. Tickner, ed., *Sistema interamericano y democracia: Antecedentes históricos y tendencias futuras*, pp. 235–57. Bogotá: Ediciones Uniandes.

Morales, Juan Antonio. 2001. "Economic Vulnerability in Bolivia." In Laurence Whitehead and John Crabtree, eds., *Towards Democratic Viability: The Bolivian Experience*, pp. 41–60. London: Palgrave.

Morley, Samuel A., Roberto Machado, and Stefano Pettinato. 1999. *Indexes of Structural Reform in Latin America*. Santiago, Chile: United Nations Economic Commission for Latin America and the Caribbean. Economic Reforms Series 12 (January).

Mosley, Layna. 2003. *Global Capital and National Governments*. Cambridge: Cambridge University Press.

Muller, Edward N. 1988. "Democracy, Economic Development, and Income Inequality." *American Sociological Review* 53 No. 1: 50–68.

   1995. "Economic Determinants of Democracy." *American Sociological Review* 60 No. 4: 966–82.

Munck, Gerardo. 1998. *Authoritarianism and Democratization: Soldiers and Workers in Argentina, 1976–1983*. University Park: The Pennsylvania State University Press.

Munck, Gerardo, and Jay Verkuilen. 2002. "Conceptualizing and Measuring Democracy: Evaluating Alternative Indices." *Comparative Political Studies* 35 No. 1: 5–34.

Murillo, María Victoria. 1997. "Union Politics, Market-Oriented Reforms, and the Reshaping of Argentine Corporatism." In Douglas A. Chalmers, Carlos M. Vilas, Katherine Hite, Scott B. Martin, Kerianne Piester, and Monique Segarra, eds., *The New Politics of Inequality in Latin America: Rethinking Representation and Participation*, pp. 72–94. Oxford: Oxford University Press.

   2001. *Partisan Coalitions and Labor Competition in Latin America: Trade Unions and Market Reforms*. Cambridge: Cambridge University Press.

Muszynski, Judith, and Antonio Teixeira Mendes. 1990. "Democratização e Opinião Pública no Brasil." In Bolívar Lamounier, ed., *De Geisel a Collor*, pp. 61–80. São Paulo: Sumaré.

Naím, Moisés. 1993. *Paper Tigers and Minotaurs: The Politics of Venezuela's Economic Reforms*. Washington, DC: Carnegie Endowment for International Peace.

Newton, Kenneth, and Pippa Norris. 2000. "Confidence in Public Institutions: Faith, Culture, or Performance." In Susan J. Pharr and Robert D. Putnam, eds., *Disaffected Democracies: What's Troubling the Trilateral Democracies?*, pp. 52–73. Princeton, NJ: Princeton University Press.

Norden, Deborah L. 1996. *Military Rebellion in Argentina: Between Coups and Consolidation*. Lincoln: University of Nebraska Press.

Norris, Pippa, ed. 1999. *Critical Citizens: Global Support for Democratic Government*. Oxford: Oxford University Press.

Novaro, Marcos. 1994. *Pilotos de Tormentas: crisis de representación y personalización de la política en Argentina (1989–1993)*. Buenos Aires: Ediciones Letra Buena.

Nylen, William. 2000. "The Making of a Loyal Opposition." In Peter Kingstone and Timothy Power, eds., *Democratic Brazil*, pp. 126–43. Pittsburgh: University of Pittsburgh Press.

O'Brien, Eduardo. 2001. "Informe sobre programas sociales." Mesa de Concertación de Lucha Contra la Pobreza. Lima: PROMUDEH.

O'Donnell, Guillermo A. 1973. *Modernization and Bureaucratic-Authoritarianism: Studies in South American Politics*. Berkeley: Institute for International Studies, University of California.

1978a. "Permanent Crisis and the Failure to Create a Democratic Regime." In Juan J. Linz and Alfred Stepan, eds., *The Breakdown of Democratic Regimes*, Vol. 3, *Latin America*, pp. 138–77. Baltimore, MD: Johns Hopkins University Press.

1978b. "Reflections on the Patterns of Change in the Bureaucratic-Authoritarian State." *Latin American Research Review* 13 No. 1: 3–38.

1978c. "State and Alliances in Argentina, 1956–1976." *Journal of Development Studies* 15 No. 2: 3–33.

1979. "Tensions in the Bureaucratic-Authoritarian State and the Question of Democracy." In David Collier, ed., *The New Authoritarianism in Latin America*, pp. 285–318. Princeton, NJ: Princeton University Press.

1988. *Bureaucratic Authoritarianism: Argentina, 1966–1973, in Comparative Perspective*. Berkeley: University of California Press.

1992. "Transitions, Continuities and Paradoxes." In Scott Mainwaring, Guillermo O'Donnell, and J. Samuel Valenzuela, eds., *Issues in Democratic Consolidation: The New South American Democracies in Comparative Perspective*, pp. 17–56. Notre Dame, IN: University of Notre Dame Press.

1993a. "Estado, democratización y ciudadanía." *Nueva Sociedad* No. 128 (November–December): 62–87.

1993b. "On the State, Democratization and Some Conceptual Problems – A Latin–American View with Glances at Some Postcommunist Countries." *World Development* 21 No. 8: 1355–69.

1994. "Delegative Democracy." *Journal of Democracy* 5 No. 1: 55–69.

1999a. "On the State, Democratization and Some Conceptual Problems: A Latin American View with Glances at Some Postcommunist Countries." In *Counterpoints: Selected Essays on Authoritarianism and Democratization*, pp. 133–57. Notre Dame, IN: University of Notre Dame Press.

1999b. "Polyarchies and the (Un)Rule of Law in Latin America: A Partial Conclusion." In Juan E. Méndez, Guillermo O'Donnell, and Paulo Sergio Pinheiro, eds., *The (Un)Rule of Law and the Underprivileged in Latin America*, pp. 303–37. Notre Dame, IN: University of Notre Dame Press.

2003. "Democracia, desarrollo humano y derechos humanos." In Guillermo O'Donnell, Osvaldo Iazzeta, and Jorge Vargas Cullell, eds., *Democracia, desarrollo humano y ciudadanía*, pp 25–147. Rosario, Argentina: Homo Sapiens.

O'Donnell, Guillermo, and Philippe C. Schmitter. 1986. *Transitions from Authoritarian Rule: Tentative Conclusions about Uncertain Democracies*. Baltimore, MD: Johns Hopkins University Press.

Oliveira, Jane Souto de, ed. 1993. *O Traço da Desigualdade Social no Brasil*. Rio de Janeiro: IBGE.

Ollier, María Matilde. 1998. "The Political Learning Process among the Argentine Revolutionary Left, 1966–1995." Ph.D. dissertation, University of Notre Dame.

Olson, Mancur. 1982. *The Rise and Decline of Nations: Economic Growth, Stagflation, and Social Rigidities*. New Haven, CT: Yale University Press.

1986. "A Theory of the Incentives Facing Political Organizations." *International Political Science Review* 7 No. 2: 165–89.

Ondetti, Gabriel. 2002. "Opportunities, Ideas and Actions: The Brazilian Landless Movement, 1979–2001." Ph.D. dissertation, University of North Carolina, Chapel Hill.

ONPE (Oficina Nacional de Procesos Electorales). *www.onpe.gob.pe.*

Oquist, Paul. 1978. *Violencia, Conflicto y Política en Colombia*. Bogotá: Instituto de Estudios Colombianos – Biblioteca Banco Popular.

Orr, Robert C. 2001. "Building Peace in El Salvador: From Exception to Rule." In Elizabeth M. Cousens and Chetan Kumar, eds., *Peacebuilding as Politics: Cultivating Peace in Fragile Societies*. Boulder, CO: Lynne Rienner Publishers.

Ostiguy, Pierre. 1998. "Peronism and Anti-Peronism: Class–Cultural Cleavages and Political Identity in Argentina." Ph.D. dissertation, University of California, Berkeley.

Packenham, Robert A. 1986. "The Changing Political Discourse in Brazil, 1964–1985." In Wayne Selcher, ed., *Political Liberalization in Brazil: Dynamics, Dilemmas, and Future Prospects*, pp. 135–73. Boulder, CO: Westview.

1992. *The Dependency Movement: Scholarship and Politics in Development Studies*. Cambridge, MA: Harvard University Press.

Paige, Jeffrey M. 1987. "Coffee and Politics in Central America." In Richard Tardanico, ed., *Crises in the Caribbean Basin*, pp. 141–90. Newbury Park, CA: Sage Publishers.

1997. *Coffee and Power: Revolution and the Rise of Democracy in Central America*. Cambridge, MA: Harvard University Press.

Palacios, Marco. 2000. "La solución política al conflicto armado, 1982–1997." In Alvaro Camacho Guizado and Francisco Leal Buitrago, eds., *Armar la paz es desarmar la guerra*, pp. 345–401. Bogotá: CEREC–DNP–PNUD, FESCOL, IEPRI, Presidencia de la República.

Pastor, Robert A., ed. 1989a. *Democracy in the Americas: Stopping the Pendulum*. New York: Holmes and Meier.

1989b. "How to Reinforce Democracy in the Americas: Seven Proposals." In Robert A. Pastor, ed., *Democracy in the Americas: Stopping the Pendulum*, pp. 139–55. New York: Holmes and Meier.

Paus, Eva. 1996. "Exports and the Consolidation of Peace." In James K. Boyce, ed., *Economic Policy for Building Peace: The Lessons of El Salvador*, pp. 247–78. Boulder, CO: Lynne Rienner Publishers.

Payne, Leigh. 1994. *Brazilian Industrialists and Democratic Change*. Baltimore, MD: Johns Hopkins University Press.

Pearce, Jenny. 1986. *Promised Land: Peasant Rebellion in Chalatenango, El Salvador*. London: Latin American Review.

Peceny, Mark, and William Stanley. 2001. "Liberal Social Reconstruction and the Resolution of Civil Wars in Central America." *International Observation* 55 No. 1: 149–82.

Peñate, Tomás Samuel, and Francisco Díaz Rodríguez. 1998. "Reforma electoral, legal e institucional: avances y retrocesos." In Héctor Dada Hirezi, ed., *Las Elecciones de 1997: Un Paso más en la Transición Democrática?*, pp. 59–78. San Salvador: FLACSO.

Pereira, Anthony W. 1997. *The End of the Peasantry: The Rural Labor Movement in Northeast Brazil, 1961–1988.* Pittsburgh: University of Pittsburgh Press.

Pereira, Carlos, and Bernardo Mueller. 2004. "The Cost of Governing: Strategic Behavior of the President and Legislators in Brazil's Budgetary Process. *Comparative Political Studies* 37 No. 7: 781–815.

Pérez-Brignoli, Héctor. 1989. *A Brief History of Central America.* Berkeley: University of California Press.

1997. *Breve Historia Contemporánea de Costa Rica.* Colección Popular. México: Fondo de Cultura Económica.

Pérez-Liñán, Aníbal. 1998. "Presidential Crisis and Political Accountability in Latin America (1990–1997)." Paper presented at the Latin American Studies Association meeting, Chicago.

2000. "The Institutional Determinants of Impeachment." Paper presented at the Latin American Studies Association meeting, Miami.

2003. "Pugna de Poderes y Crisis de Gobernabilidad: ¿Hacia un Nuevo Presidencialismo?" *Latin American Research Review* 38 No. 3: 149–64.

Perina, Rubén M. 2000. "El régimen democrático interamericano: El papel de la OEA." In Arlene B. Tickner, ed., *Sistema interamericano y democracia: Antecedentes históricos y tendencias futuras,* pp. 311–76. Bogotá: Ediciones Uniandes.

Perú en Números. Various years. Lima: Instituto Cuánto.

Peruzzotti, Enrique. 2001. "The Nature of the New Argentine Democracy: The Delegative Democracy Argument Revisited." *Journal of Latin American Studies* 33 No. 1: 133–55.

2002. "Towards a New Politics: Citizenship and Rights in Contemporary Argentina." *Citizenship Studies* 6 No. 1: 77–93.

Pevehouse, Jon C. 2002. "With a Little Help from My Friends? Regional Organizations and the Consolidation of Democracy." *American Journal of Political Science* 46 No. 3: 611–26.

Pharr, Susan J. 2000. "Officials' Misconduct and Public Distrust: Japan and the Trilateral Democracies." In Susan J. Pharr and Robert D. Putnam, eds., *Disaffected Democracies: What's Troubling the Trilateral Democracies?*, pp. 173–201. Princeton, NJ: Princeton University Press.

Pharr, Susan J., and Robert D. Putnam, eds. 2000. *Disaffected Democracies: What's Troubling the Trilateral Democracies?* Princeton, NJ: Princeton University Press.

Piano, Aili, and Arch Puddington. 2001. "The 2000 Freedom House Survey: Gains Offset Losses." *Journal of Democracy* 12 No. 1: 87–92.

Pizarro, Eduardo. 1991. *Las FARC 1949–1966: De la autodefensa a la combinación de todas las formas de lucha.* Bogotá: IEPRI–Tercer Mundo Editores.

1996a. *Insurgencia sin revolución. La guerrilla colombiana en perspectiva comparada.* Bogotá: IEPRI–Tercer Mundo Editores.

1996b. "La reforma militar en un contexto de democratización política." In Francisco Leal Buitrago, ed., *En busca de la estabilidad perdida,* pp. 159–208. Bogotá: Tercer Mundo Editores–IEPRI.

Pizarro, Eduardo, and Ana María Bejarano. 2001. "La reforma política después de 1991: ¿Qué queda por reformar?" Paper presented at the conference Democracy, Human Rights, and Peace in Colombia, Kellogg Institute of International Studies, University of Notre Dame, March 26–27.

Polity 98. *http://k.gleditsch.socsci.gla.ac.uk/polity.html.*

Polity IV Project. 2000. Polity IV Dataset. [Computer file; version p4v2000] College Park, MD: Center for International Development and Conflict Management, University of Maryland.

Popkin, Margaret. 2000. *Peace Without Justice: Obstacles to Building the Rule of Law in El Salvador*. University Park: Pennsylvania State University Press.

Popkin, Margaret, with Jack Spence and George Vickers. 1994. *Justice Delayed: The Slow Pace of Judicial Reform in El Salvador*. Washington, DC: Washington Office on Latin America and Hemisphere Initiatives.

Posada-Carbó, Eduardo, ed. 1996. *Elections before Democracy: The History of Elections in Europe and Latin America*. London: Macmillan Press Ltd.

    1998. "Reflections on the Colombian State: In Search of a Modern Role." In Eduardo Posada-Carbó, ed., *Colombia: The Politics of Reforming the State*, pp. 1–17. New York: St. Martin's Press.

Power, Timothy. 1997. "Parties, Puppets and Paradoxes." *Party Politics* 3 No. 2: 189–219.

    1998. "The Pen is Mightier Than the Congress." In John Carey and Matthew Soberg Shugart, eds., *Executive Decree Authority*, pp. 197–230. Cambridge: Cambridge University Press.

    2000. *The Political Right in Postauthoritarian Brazil*. University Park: Pennsylvania State University Press.

Power, Timothy, and Timmons Roberts. 2000. "A New Brazil?" In Peter Kingstone and Timothy Power, eds., *Democratic Brazil*, pp. 236–62. Pittsburgh: University of Pittsburgh Press.

Powers, Nancy R. 2001. *Grassroots Expectations of Democracy and Economy: Argentina in Comparative Perspective*. Pittsburgh: University of Pittsburgh Press.

Presidencia de la República. 1993. *V Informe de Gobierno*. Mexico City: Presidencia de la República.

Pridham, Geoffrey, ed. 1991. *Encouraging Democracy: The International Context of Regime Transition in Southern Europe*. New York: St. Martin's Press.

Przeworski, Adam. 1986. "Some Problems in the Study of the Transition to Democracy." In Guillermo O'Donnell, Philippe C. Schmitter, and Laurence Whitehead, eds., *Transitions from Authoritarian Rule: Comparative Perspectives*, pp. 47–63. Baltimore, MD: Johns Hopkins University Press.

    1991. *Democracy and the Market: Political and Economic Reform in Eastern Europe and Latin America*. Cambridge: Cambridge University Press.

    1995. *Sustainable Democracy*. Cambridge: Cambridge University Press.

Przeworski, Adam, and Fernando Limongi. 1997. "Modernization: Theories and Facts." *World Politics* 49 No. 2: 155–83.

Przeworski, Adam, Michael Alvarez, José Antonio Cheibub, and Fernando Limongi. 1996. "What Makes Democracies Endure?" *Journal of Democracy* 7 No. 1: 39–55.

    2000. *Democracy and Development: Political Institutions and Well-Being in the World, 1950–1990*. Cambridge: Cambridge University Press.

Putnam, Robert. 1993. *Making Democracy Work: Civic Traditions in Modern Italy*. Princeton, NJ: Princeton University Press.

Putnam, Robert D., Susan J. Pharr, and Russell J. Dalton. 2000. "Introduction: What's Troubling the Trilateral Democracies?" In Susan J. Pharr and Robert D. Putnam, eds., *Disaffected Democracies: What's Troubling the Trilateral Democracies?*, pp. 3–27. Princeton, NJ: Princeton University Press.

Quijano, Aníbal. 2000. "La alternativa: gobierno provisional de los concejos municipales." *Nueva Sociedad* No. 168 (July–August): 63–66.

Ragin, Charles. 1987. *The Comparative Method: Moving Beyond Qualitative and Quantitative Strategies.* Berkeley: University of California Press.

Ralón, Carlos. 1998. *Revisión del Programa de Inversión Pública: Sector Educación.* Guatemala City: CIEN.

Ramos, Carlos Guillermo. 1998. "Los actores de la contienda electoral: trayectorias y comportamientos políticos." In Héctor Dada Hirezi, ed., *Las Elecciones de 1997: Un Paso más en la Transición Democrática?*, pp. 1–58. San Salvador: FLACSO.

Rangel, Alfredo. 1999. "Las FARC–EP: una mirada actual." In Malcolm Deas and María Victoria Llorente, eds., *Reconocer la guerra para construir la paz*, pp. 21–51. Bogotá: CEREC–Ediciones Uniandes–Editorial Norma.

Reis, Elisa, and Zairo Cheibub. 1995. "Valores Políticos das Elites e Consolidação Democrática." *Dados* 38 No. 1: 31–56.

Remmer, Karen L. 1991a. "New Wine or Old Bottlenecks? The Study of Latin American Democracy." *Comparative Politics* 23 No. 4: 479–95.

1991b. "The Political Impact of Economic Crisis in Latin America in the 1980s." *American Political Science Review* 85 No. 3: 777–800.

1996. "The Sustainability of Political Democracy." *Comparative Political Studies* 29 No. 6: 611–34.

Revista Semana. 2004. (January 2).

Ridenti, Marcelo. 1992. "Os Comunistas Brasileiros e a Crise do Socialismo." Paper presented at the XVII Congress of the Latin American Studies Association, Los Angeles, September 24–27.

Roberts, Kenneth. 1995. "Neoliberalism and the Transformation of Populism in Latin America: The Peruvian Case." *World Politics* 48 No. 1: 82–116.

1998. *Deepening Democracy? The Modern Left and Social Movements in Chile and Peru.* Stanford, CA: Stanford University Press.

Rodríguez Veltzé, Eduardo. 2001. "Legal Security in Bolivia." In Laurence Whitehead and John Crabtree, eds., *Towards Democratic Viability: The Bolivian Experience*, pp. 179–94. London: Palgrave.

Rose, Richard, and Doh Chull Shin. 2001. "Democratization Backwards: The Problem of Third-Wave Democracies." *British Journal of Political Science* 31 No. 2: 331–54.

Roseberry, William. 1991. "La Falta de Brazos: Land and Labor in the Coffee Economies of Nineteenth-Century Latin America." *Theory and Society* 20 No. 3: 351–81.

Rospigliosi, Fernando. 2000. *Montesinos y las Fuerzas Armadas. Cómo controló durante una década las instituciones militares.* Lima: IEP.

Rotberg, Robert I., ed. 2001. *Patterns of Social Capital: Stability and Change in Historical Perspective.* Cambridge: Cambridge University Press.

2003. *When States Fail: Causes and Consequences.* Princeton, NJ: Princeton University Press.

Rubio, Mauricio. 1999. "La justicia en una sociedad violenta." In María Victoria Llorente and Malcolm Deas, eds., *Reconocer la guerra para construir la paz*, pp. 201–35. Bogotá: Ediciones Uniandes–CEREC–Editorial Norma.

Rueschemeyer, Dietrich. 1991. "Different Methods, Contradictory Results? Research on Development and Democracy." *International Journal of Comparative Sociology* 32 No. 1: 1–2, 9–38.

Rueschemeyer, Dietrich, John Stephens, and Evelyne Huber Stephens. 1992. *Capitalist Development and Democracy.* Chicago: University of Chicago Press.

Rummel, R. J. 1994. *Death by Government*. New Brunswick, NJ: Transaction Press.

Samuels, David, and Richard Snyder. 2001. "The Value of a Vote: Malapportionment in Comparative Perspective." *British Journal of Political Science* 31 No. 4: 651–71.

Sanford, Victoria. 2003. *Buried Secrets: Truth and Human Rights in Guatemala*. New York: Palgrave Macmillan.

Sani, Giacomo, and Giovanni Sartori. 1983. "Polarization, Fragmentation, and Competition in Western Democracies." In Hans Daalder and Peter Mair, eds., *Western European Party Systems*, pp. 307–40. Beverly Hills, CA: Sage.

Sartori, Giovanni. 1976. *Parties and Party Systems: A Framework for Analysis*. Cambridge: Cambridge University Press.

Schedler, Andreas. 2002. "The Menu of Manipulation." *Journal of Democracy* 13 No. 2: 36–50.

Schifter, Jacobo S. 1980. *Populismo Versus Transformismo: Fase Oculta de la Guerra Civil en Costa Rica*. San José, Costa Rica: EDUCA.

Schmidt, Gregory. 1999. "Crónica de una reelección." In Fernando Tuesta, ed., *El juego político. Fujimori, la oposición y las reglas*, pp. 97–130. Lima: Fundación Friedrich Ebert.

Schmitter, Philippe. 1983. "Democratic Theory and Neocorporatist Practice." *Social Research* 50 No. 4: 885–928.

Scott, James C. 1976. *The Moral Economy of the Peasant: Rebellion and Subsistence in Southeast Asia*. New Haven, CT: Yale University Press.

Seawright, Jason. 2004. "The 'Demand Side' of Party System Collapse: Political Preferences and Votes for Insurgent Parties." Paper presented at the Workshop on the Analysis of Political Cleavages and Party Competition, Duke University, April 2–3.

Seligson, Mitchell A. 1995. "Thirty Years of Transformation in the Agrarian Structure of El Salvador." *Latin American Research Review* 30 No. 3: 43–76.

    1996. "Agrarian Inequality and the Theory of Peasant Rebellion." *Latin American Research Review* 31 No. 2: 140–57.

    1999. *La cultura política de la democracia boliviana*. La Paz: Encuestas & Estudios.

    2001. "La Cultura Política de la Democracia en Bolivia: 2000." La Paz: Universidad Católica Boliviana (UCB).

    2002. "The Impact of Corruption on Regime Legitimacy: A Comparative Study of Four Latin American Democracies." *Journal of Politics* 64 No. 2: 408–33.

Seligson, Mitchell A., and Dinorah Azpuru. 1999. "The Demography of Crime in Guatemala and Its Political Impact." Paper delivered at International Seminar: The Population of the Central American Isthmus at the End of the Millennium, Jacó, Costa Rica, October 20–22.

Seligson, Mitchell A., and Ricardo Córdova Macías. 1995. *De la Guerra a la Paz: Una Cultura Política en Transición*. El Salvador: IDELA/University of Pittsburgh/ FUNDAUNGO.

Seligson, Mitchell A., José Miguel Cruz, and Ricardo Córdova Macías. 2000. *Auditoria de la Democrácia: El Salvador 1999*. San Salvador: IUDOP/UCA, University of Pittsburgh and FUNDAUNGO.

Seligson, Mitchell A., Malcolm Young, Max Eduardo Lucas, and Dinorah Azpuru. 2000. *La Cultura Política de los Guatemaltecos: Cuarto Estudio, 1999*. Guatemala City: ASIES.

Semana. 2001. "La guerra de los paras." *Semana.com*. April 5: 3.

Sevilla, Manuel. 1985. *La Concentración Económica en El Salvador*. Managua: Instituto Investigaciones Económicas y Sociales.

Shugart, Matthew Soberg, and John M. Carey. 1992. *Presidents and Assemblies: Constitutional Design and Electoral Dynamics.* Cambridge: Cambridge University Press.

Shugart, Matthew Soberg, and Scott Mainwaring. 1997. "Presidentialism and Democracy in Latin America." In Scott Mainwaring and Matthew Soberg Shugart, eds., *Presidentialism and Democracy in Latin America*, pp. 12–54. Cambridge: Cambridge University Press.

Skidmore, Thomas. 1967. *Politics in Brazil, 1930–1964.* London: Oxford University Press.

    1977. "The Politics of Economic Stabilization in Postwar Latin America." In James Malloy, ed., *Authoritarianism and Corporatism in Latin America*, pp. 149–90. Pittsburgh: University of Pittsburgh Press.

Smilde, David. 2000. "Evangelicals Bring Chávez's Message to the People." *Oxford Analitica* (January 28).

Smith, Peter H. 1979. *Labyrinths of Power. Political Recruitment in Twentieth-Century Mexico.* Princeton, NJ: Princeton University Press.

Smith, William. 1990. "Democracy, Distributional Conflicts and Macroeconomic Policymaking in Argentina, 1983–1989." *Journal of Inter-American Studies and World Affairs* 32 No. 2: 1–36.

Smulovitz, Catalina, and Enrique Peruzzotti. 2000. "Societal Accountability in Latin America." *Journal of Democracy* 11 No. 4: 147–58.

    2003. "Societal and Horizontal Controls: Two Cases of a Fruitful Relationship." In Scott Mainwaring and Christopher Welna, eds., *Democratic Accountability in Latin America*, pp. 309–31. Oxford: Oxford University Press.

Snyder, Jack. 2000. *From Voting to Violence: Democratization and Nationalist Conflict.* New York: W. W. Norton.

Snyder, Richard. 2001. *Politics after Neoliberalism: Reregulation in Mexico.* Cambridge: Cambridge University Press.

Soares de Lima, Maria, and Renato Boschi. 1995. "Democracia e Reforma Econômica." *Dados* 38 No. 1: 7–30.

Soares de Lima, Maria, and Zairo Cheibub. 1994. *Elites Estratégicas e Dilemas do Desenvolvimento.* Rio de Janeiro: IUPERJ.

Spence, Jack, Mike Lanchin, and Geoff Thale. 2001. *From Elections to Earthquakes: Reform and Participation in Post-War El Salvador.* Cambridge, MA: Hemisphere Initiatives.

Spiller, Pablo T., and Mariano Tommasi. 2000. "Los Determinantes Institucionales del Desarrollo Argentino: Una Aproximación Desde la Nueva Economía Institucional." Centro de Estudios para el Desarrollo Institucional Working Paper No. 33 (May), CEDI, Buenos Aires.

Stanley, William. 1995. "International Tutelage and Domestic Political Will: Lessons from El Salvador's Civilian Police Project." *Studies in Comparative International Development* 30 No. 1: 30–58.

    1996. *The Protection Racket State: Elite Politics, Military Extortion, and Civil War in El Salvador.* Philadelphia: Temple University Press.

    1999. "Building New Police Forces in Guatemala and El Salvador: Learning and Counter-Learning." *International Peacekeeping* 6 No. 4: 113–34.

Stanley, William, and David Holiday. 1997. "Peace Mission Strategy and Domestic Actors: UN Mediation, Verification, and Institution-Building in El Salvador." *International Peacekeeping* 4 No. 2: 22–49.

Starr, Harvey. 1991. "Democratic Dominoes: Diffusion Approaches to the Spread of Democracy in the International System." *Journal of Conflict Resolution* 35 No. 2: 356–81.

Stepan, Alfred. 1971. *The Military in Politics: Changing Patterns in Brazil.* Princeton, NJ: Princeton University Press.

   1978. "Political Leadership and Regime Breakdown: Brazil." In Juan J. Linz and Alfred Stepan, eds., *The Breakdown of Democratic Regimes*, Vol. 3, *Latin America*, pp. 110–37. Baltimore, MD: Johns Hopkins University Press.

   1988. *Rethinking Military Politics: Brazil and the Southern Cone.* Princeton, NJ: Princeton University Press.

Stepan, Alfred, and Cindy Skach. 1994. "Presidentialism and Parliamentarism in Comparative Perspective." In Juan J. Linz and Arturo Valenzuela, eds., *The Failure of Presidential Democracy*, Vol. 1, *Comparative Perspectives*, pp. 119–36. Baltimore, MD: Johns Hopkins University Press.

Stokes, Susan C. 1996. "Economic Reform and Public Opinion in Peru, 1990–1995." *Comparative Political Studies* 29 (October): 544–66.

   2001. *Mandates and Democracy: Neoliberalism by Surprise in Latin America.* Cambridge: Cambridge University Press.

Stoll, David. 1993. *Between Two Armies in the Ixil Towns of Guatemala.* New York: Columbia University Press.

Tanaka, Martín. 1998. *Los espejismos de la democracia. El colapso del sistema de partidos en el Perú, 1980–1995, en perspectiva comparada.* Lima: IEP.

   1999a. "La consolidación democrática en América Latina y la importancia de la competencia política. Lecciones desde la experiencia peruana." In Fernando Tuesta, ed., *El juego político. Fujimori, la oposición y las reglas*, pp. 43–64. Lima: Fundación Friedrich Ebert.

   1999b. "Los partidos políticos en el Perú, 1992–1999: estatalidad, sobrevivencia y política mediática." Documento de Trabajo no. 108. Lima: IEP–The Japan Center for Area Studies.

   2003. "The Political Constraints on Market Reform in Peru." In Carol Wise, Riordan Roett, and Guadalupe Paz, eds., *Post-Stabilization Politics in Latin America: Competition, Transition, Collapse*, pp. 221–48. Washington, DC: Brookings Institution Press.

Templeton, Andrew. 1995. "The Evolution of Popular Opinion." In Louis W. Goodman, Johanna Mendelson Forman, Moisés Naím, Joseph Tulchin, and Gary Bland, eds., *Lessons of the Venezuelan Experience*, pp. 79–114. Washington, DC, and Baltimore, MD: The Wilson Center Press and Johns Hopkins University Press.

"Tendências – Eleições Presidenciais. Brasil 1950–1994." 1994. Encarte de Dados. *Opinião Pública* 2 No. 2.

"Tendências – Reforma Agrária no Brasil: 1962–1995." 1996. Encarte de Dados. *Opinião Pública* 4 No. 1.

Teoria e Debate. 1997. 10 No. 34.

Tilly, Charles. 1985. "War Making and State Making as Organized Crime." In Peter B. Evans, Dietrich Rueschemeyer, and Theda Skocpol, eds., *Bringing the State Back In*, pp. 169–91. Cambridge: Cambridge University Press.

Tocqueville, Alexis de. 1969. *Democracy in America.* Trans. by George Lawrence. Garden City, NY: Doubleday.

Touraine, Alain. 1989. *América Latina. Política y Sociedad.* (First edition published in French, 1988). Madrid: Espasa-Calpe.

"La Tragedia Social de El Salvador." 2000. *Estudios Centroamericanos* 55 No. 621–22: 669–84.

Transparency International. 2000. "Transparency International Releases the Year 2000 Corruption Perceptions Index." *www.transparency.de/documents/cpi/2000/cpi2000.html*.

———. 2003. *Global Corruption Report 2003*. London: Profile Books.

Trigueros, Alvaro, Lilian Vega, and Francisco Lazo Marín. 2001. "Análisis de la coyuntura económica: segundo semestre del año 2000." *Estudios Centroamericanos* 56 No. 627–28: 59–83.

Trinkunas, Harold. 2000. "Crafting Civilian Control in Emerging Democracies: Argentina and Venezuela." *Journal of Interamerican Studies and World Affairs* 42 No. 3: 77–110.

———. 2002. "The Crisis in Venezuelan Civil–Military Relations: From 'Punto Fijo' to the Fifth Republic." *Latin American Research Review* 37 No. 1: 41–76.

Truth Commission. 1993. "From Madness to Hope: The 12 Year War in El Salvador." Report of the Commission on the Truth for El Salvador. New York and San Salvador: United Nations.

Tsebelis, George. 1990. *Nested Games: Rational Choice in Comparative Politics*. Berkeley: University of California Press.

———. 1995. "Decision Making in Political Systems." *British Journal of Political Science* 25 No. 3: 289–325.

UNDP (United Nations Development Programme). 2000. *Human Development Report, 2000*. New York: Oxford University Press.

———. 2003. "Human Development Indicators: El Salvador." In *Human Development Report 2003*. UNDP. *www.undp.org/hdr2003/indicator/cty_f_SLV*.

———. 2004. "Democracy in Latin America: Towards a Citizens' Democracy." *http://www.undp.org/dpa/pressrelease/releases/2004/april/0421/proda*.

UNICAMP–AEL, IBOPE. 1952. *Coleção IBOPE: Boletim das Classes Dirigentes 1952*: 99–111 (23–29 November). Archived in CESOP/UNICAMP.

United Nations. 1999. *Global Report on Crime and Justice*. Graeme Newman, ed. New York: Oxford University Press.

Universidad de Salamanca. 1997. *Elites Parlamentarias Iberoamericanas*. Vol. 11: *Bolivia*. Madrid: CIS.

Valenzuela, Arturo. 1978. *The Breakdown of Democratic Regimes: Chile*. Baltimore, MD: Johns Hopkins University Press.

———. 1994. "Party Politics and the Crisis of Presidentialism in Chile: A Proposal for a Parliamentary Form of Government." In Juan J. Linz and Arturo Valenzuela, eds., *The Failure of Presidential Democracy: The Case of Latin America*, Vol. 2, pp. 91–150. Baltimore, MD: Johns Hopkins University Press.

———. 1997. "Paraguay: The Coup That Didn't Happen." *Journal of Democracy* 8 No. 11: 43–55.

Valenzuela, Arturo, Josep Colomer, Arendt Lijphart, and Matthew Soberg Shugart. 1999. "Sobre la reforma política en Colombia. Informe de la Consultoría Internacional". In *Reforma Política. Un propósito de nación*, Serie Documentos, No. 17, pp. 209–311. Bogotá: Ministerio del Interior.

Valenzuela, Arturo, and J. Samuel Valenzuela. 1983. "Los orígenes de la democracia: Reflexiones teóricas sobre el caso de Chile." *Estudios Públicos* 12: 5–39.

Valenzuela, J. Samuel. 1992. "Democratic Consolidation in Post-Transitional Settings: Notion, Process and Facilitating Conditions." In Scott Mainwaring, Guillermo

O'Donnell, and J. Samuel Valenzuela, eds., *Issues in Democratic Consolidation: The New South American Democracies in Comparative Perspective*, pp. 57–104. Notre Dame, IN: University of Notre Dame Press.

Varshney, Ashutosh. 1998. "Why Democracy Survives." *Journal of Democracy* 9 No. 3: 36–50.

Vega Centeno, Imelda. 2000. "Drama o sainete en dos vueltas." *Nueva Sociedad* 168 (July–August): 67–71.

Verba, Sidney, Norman Nie, and J. Kim. 1978. *Participation and Political Equality*. Cambridge: Cambridge University Press.

Villarreal, Andrés. 1999. "Public Opinion of the Economy and the President among Mexico City Residents: The Salinas Sexenio." *Latin American Research Review* 34 No. 2: 132–51.

Vinegrad, Anna. 1998. "From Guerrillas to Politicians: The Transition of the Guatemalan Revolutionary Movement in Historical and Comparative Perspective." In Rachel Sieder, ed., *Guatemala after the Peace Accords*. London: Institute of Latin American Studies, University of London.

Waisbord, Sylvio. 2000. *Watchdog Journalism in South America: News, Accountability, and Democracy*. New York: Columbia University Press.

Waisman, Carlos. 1987. *Reversal of Development: Postwar Counterrevolutionary Policies and their Structural Consequences*. Princeton, NJ: Princeton University Press.

Waisman, Carlos. 1992. "Argentina's Revolution from Above: State Economic Transformation and Political Realignment." In Edward C. Epstein, ed., *The New Argentine Democracy: The Search for a Successful Formula*, pp. 228–43. Westport, CT: Praeger.

Walker, Ignacio. 1990. *Socialismo y democracia: Chile y Europa en perspectiva comparada*. Santiago: CIEPLAN/Hachette.

Warren, Kay B. 1998. *Indigenous Movements and Their Critics: Pan-Maya Activism in Guatemala*. Princeton, NJ: Princeton University Press.

Weaver, Frederick Stirton. 1994. *Inside the Volcano: The History and Political Economy of Central America*. Boulder, CO: Westview Press.

Weffort, Francisco. 1986. *Por Que Democracia?*, 4th ed. São Paulo: Brasiliense.

Weyland, Kurt. 1996a. *Democracy Without Equity*. Pittsburgh: University of Pittsburgh Press.

1996b. "Neo-Populism and Neo-Liberalism in Latin America: Unexpected Affinities." *Studies in Comparative International Development* 31 No. 3: 3–31.

1996c. "Risk Taking in Latin American Economic Restructuring: Lessons from Prospect Theory." *International Studies Quarterly* 40 No. 2: 185–208.

1998. "The Politics of Corruption in Latin America." *Journal of Democracy* 9 No. 2: 108–21.

1999. "Neoliberal Populism in Latin America and Eastern Europe." *Comparative Politics* 31 No. 4: 379–401.

2001. "¿La paradoja del éxito? Los determinantes de apoyo político al presidente Fujimori." *Debates en Sociología* No. 25–26: 213–44. Lima: PUCP.

2002. *The Politics of Market Reform in Fragile Democracies*. Princeton, NJ: Princeton University Press.

Whitehead, Laurence. 1986. "International Aspects of Democratization." In Guillermo O'Donnell, Philippe Schmitter, and Laurence Whitehead, eds., *Transitions from Authoritarian Rule: Prospects for Democracy*, Part III, pp. 3–46. Baltimore, MD: Johns Hopkins University Press.

1991. "Democracy by Convergence and Southern Europe: A Comparative Politics Perspective." In Geoffrey Pridham, ed., *Encouraging Democracy: The International Context of Regime Transition in Southern Europe*, pp. 45–61. New York: St. Martin's Press.

1996. ed. *The International Dimensions of Democratization: Europe and the Americas.* Oxford: Oxford University Press.

2001. "The Emergence of Democracy in Bolivia." In Laurence Whitehead and John Crabtree, eds., *Towards Democratic Viability: The Bolivian Experience*, pp. 21–40. London: Palgrave.

Whitfield, Teresa. 1994. *Paying the Price: Ignacio Ellacuria and the Murdered Jesuits of El Salvador.* Philadelphia: Temple University Press.

Wiarda, Howard J. 1996. *Corporatism and Comparative Politics: The Other Great Ism.* Armonk, NJ: M. E. Sharpe.

Wilde, Alexander. 1982. *Conversaciones de caballeros. La quiebra de la democracia en Colombia.* Bogotá: Ediciones Tercer Mundo.

Williams, Philip J., and Knut Walter. 1997. *Militarization and Demilitarization in El Salvador's Transition to Democracy.* Pittsburgh: University of Pittsburgh Press.

Williams, Robert G. 1994. *States and Social Evolution: Coffee and the Rise of National Governments in Central America.* Chapel Hill: University of North Carolina Press.

Wilson, Richard. 1995. *Mayan Resurgence in Guatemala.* Norman: University of Oklahoma Press.

Wood, Elisabeth Jean. 2000a. *Forging Democracy from Below: Insurgent Transitions in South Africa and El Salvador.* Cambridge: Cambridge University Press.

2000b. "The Transformation of Elite Representation in El Salvador." In Kevin Middlebrook, ed., *Conservative Parties, the Right, and Democracy in Latin America*, pp. 223–54. Baltimore, MD: Johns Hopkins University Press.

2001. "An Insurgent Path to Democracy: Popular Mobilization, Economic Interests, and Regime Transition in South Africa and El Salvador." *Comparative Political Studies* 34 No. 8: 862–88.

2003. *Insurgent Collective Action and Civil War in El Salvador.* Cambridge: Cambridge University Press.

World Bank. 1997. *Guatemala, Investing for Peace: A Public Investment Review. Report No. 16392-GU.* Washington, DC: World Bank.

2000a. *Guatemala: Expenditure Reform in a Post-Conflict Country.* Washington, DC: World Bank.

2000b. *Guatemala: A Preliminary Poverty Diagnostic Based on the 1998/99 ENIGFAM.* Washington, DC: World Bank.

2000c. *World Development Report: 1999/2000.* Washington, DC: Oxford University Press.

2001a. "Estrategia de la reducción de pobreza: Guatemala." Washington, DC: World Bank. Typescript.

2001b. *World Development Indicators* [CD-ROM file]. Washington, DC: The World Bank.

2001c. *World Development Report: 2000/2001.* Washington, DC: Oxford University Press.

2002. *World Development Report 2003.* New York: Oxford University Press.

2003. *World Development Indicators.* Washington, DC: World Bank.

Yashar, Deborah. 1996. "Indigenous Protest and Democracy in Latin America." In Jorge I. Domínguez and Abraham F. Lowenthal, eds., *Constructing Democratic*

Governance: Latin America and the Caribbean in the 1990s, pp. 87–105. Baltimore, MD: Johns Hopkins University Press.

2005. *Indigenous Movements and the State in Latin America*. Cambridge: Cambridge University Press.

Zakaria, Fareed. 1997. "The Rise of Illiberal Democracy." *Foreign Affairs* 76 No. 6: 22–43.

Zamora R., Rubén. 1998. *El Salvador: Heridas que no Cierran. Los Partidos Políticos en el Post-Guerra*. San Salvador: FLACSO.

Zartman, I. William. 1995. *Collapsed States: The Disintegration and Restoration of Legitimate Authority*. Boulder, CO: Lynne Rienner.

Zaverucha, Jorge. 2000. *Frágil Democracia: Collor, Itamar, FHC e os Militares (1990–1998)*. Rio de Janeiro: Civilização Brasileira.

Zuluaga, Jaime. 1999. "Sueños de paz. Realidades de la guerra." In Luis Alberto Restrepo, ed., *Síntesis '99. Anuario Social, Político y Económico de Colombia*, pp. 45–54. Bogotá: IEPRI–Fundación Social–TM Editores.

Index